A MODERN BOOK OF ESTHETICS

A MODERN BOOK OF ESTHETICS

An Anthology

Fifth Edition

Edited with Introduction and Notes by
MELVIN RADER
University of Washington

HOLT, RINEHART AND WINSTON
New York Chicago San Francisco Dallas
Montreal Toronto London Sydney

Senior Acquisitions Editor *David P. Boynton*
Managing Editor *Jeanette Ninas Johnson*
Project Editor *Robin Moses*
Production Manager *Annette Wentz*
Art Director *Robert Kopelman*

Library of Congress Cataloging in Publication Data

Rader, Melvin Miller, 1903– , ed.
A modern book of esthetics.

Bibliography: p. 523
Includes index.
1. Esthetics—Addresses, essays, lectures. I. Title.
BH21.R3 1979 111.8'5 78-16041
ISBN 0-03-019331-1

Printed in the United States of America
2 038 9 8 7 6 5 4

Acknowledgments

Grateful acknowledgment is made to the following persons and publishers who have kindly granted permission to quote from copyrighted works:

George Allen & Unwin Ltd. for British Empire rights to reprint from *Ways of Knowledge and Experience* by Louis Arnaud Reid and from *Introductory Lectures on Psycho-Analysis* by Sigmund Freud, 1922. Revised Second Edition, 1929.

The American Philosophical Quarterly and Maurice Mandelbaum for permission to reprint "Family Resemblances and Generalizations Concerning the Arts" by Maurice Mandelbaum, *The American Philosophical Quarterly,* Vol. 2 (1965).

The American Society for Aesthetics for permission to reprint "Art and the Language of the Emotions" by Curt J. Ducasse, *The Journal of Aesthetics and Art Criticism,* Vol. 22 (1964).

The American Society for Aesthetics and Morris Weitz for permission to reprint "The Role of Theory in Aesthetics" by Morris Weitz, *The Journal of Aesthetics and Art Criticism,* Vol. 15 (1956).

Art Education and *The Journal of Aesthetic Education* for permission to reprint "Education for Aesthetic Vision" by Virgil C. Aldrich and "The Classification of Critical Reasons" by Monroe C. Beardsley in *Art Education,* Vol. 22 (1968) and *The Journal of Aesthetic Education,* Vol. 2 (1968). Also by permission of the authors.

Basic Books, Inc., for permission to reprint from *Collected Papers* by Sigmund Freud, 1925.
Basil Blackwell & Mott Ltd. and G. E. M. Anscombe for permission to reprint from *Philosophical Investigations* by Ludwig Wittgenstein, 1953.
Bell & Hyman Ltd., London, for permission to reprint from *The Philosophy of Fine Art* by G. W. F. Hegel, Vol. IV (1920), translated by F. P. B. Osmaston.
The *British Journal of Psychology* for permission to reprint " 'Psychical Distance' as a Factor in Art and an Aesthetic Principle" by Edward Bullough, *British Journal of Psychology,* Vol. V (1913).
Chatto & Windus, Ltd., and Professor Quentin Bell for British Empire rights to reprint from *Art* by Clive Bell.
The Clarendon Press, Oxford, for permission to reprint from *On the Aesthetic Education of Man in a Series of Letters,* by Friedrich Schiller, translated by Elizabeth M. Wilkinson and L. A. Willoughby, 1967, Letter 27.
Constable & Company, Ltd., for British Empire rights to reprint from *The Sense of Beauty* by George Santayana.
The Cornell University Press for permission to reprint from George Dickie: *Art and the Aesthetic.* Copyright © 1974 by Cornell University. Used by permission of Cornell University Press.
Doubleday & Company, Inc., for permission to reprint from *Design with Nature* by Ian McHarg. Copyright © 1969 by Ian McHarg; and to reprint from "Laughter" by Henri Bergson in *Comedy,* edited by Wylie Sypher. Copyright © 1956 by Doubleday & Company, Inc.
Encyclopaedia Britannica, Inc., for permission to reprint "Aesthetics" by Benedetto Croce in *Encyclopaedia Britannica,* 14th edition, © 1929 by Encyclopaedia Britannica, Inc.
Harcourt Brace Jovanovich, Inc., for permission to reprint from *Technics and Civilization* by Lewis Mumford, copyright 1934, by Harcourt Brace Jovanovich, Inc., renewed 1962, by Lewis Mumford; and for permission to reprint "Benefit of Clergy: Some Notes on Salvador Dali" from *Dickens, Dali and Others* by George Orwell, copyright 1964, 1974, by Sonia Orwell. Reprinted by permission of Harcourt Brace Jovanovich, Inc.
Harper & Row, Publishers, Inc., for permission to reprint from pp. 141-142 in *The Grundrisse* by Karl Marx, edited and translated by David McLellan. Copyright © 1971 by David McLellan. By permission of Harper & Row, Publishers, Inc.
Harvard University Press, Cambridge, for permission to reprint from *The Basis of Criticism in the Arts* by Stephen C. Pepper. Copyright 1945 by the President and Fellows of Harvard College; and from *The Shape of Content* by Ben Shahn, Cambridge, Mass.: Harvard University Press. Copyright © 1957 by the President and Fellows of Harvard College.
A. M. Heath & Company, Ltd., Mrs. Sonia Brownell Orwell, and Martin Secker and Warburg, for permission to reprint George Orwell, "Benefit of Clergy: Some Notes on Salvador Dali" from *Dickens, Dali and Others,* 1964.
The Hogarth Press, Ltd., for British Empire rights to reprint from *Collected Papers* by Sigmund Freud, 1925.
Humanities Press Inc. for permission to reprint from *The Hidden God* by Lucien Goldmann, translated by Philip Thody, copyright 1964.
Lund Humphries Publishers Ltd. and Rudolf Arnheim for permission to reprint "Gestalt Psychology and Artistic Form" by Rudolf Arnheim in *Aspects of Form,* edited by Lancelot Law Whyte. Copyright 1951 by Percy Lund Humphries and Company, Ltd.
International Publishers for permission to reprint from *Illusion and Reality* by Christopher Caudwell, 1947.
Alfred A. Knopf, Inc. for permission to reprint from *The Social History of Art,* Volume II, by Arnold Hauser. Published 1941 by Alfred A. Knopf, Inc. Reprinted by permission of the publisher.
Lawrence & Wishart Ltd. for British Empire rights to reprint from *Illusion and Reality* by Christopher Caudwell, 1947.
Liveright Publishing Company for permission to reprint from *Introductory Lectures on Psycho-Analysis* by Sigmund Freud, 1922. Revised Second Edition, 1929.

McGraw-Hill Book Company for permission to reprint from *Early Writings* by Karl Marx, translated and edited by T. B. Bottomore. © by T. B. Bottomore, 1963.

Macmillan, London, and Basingstoke for permission to reprint from Bernard Bosanquet, *Three Lectures on Aesthetic,* 1915.

Harold Osborne for permission to reprint from his *Aesthetics and Art Theory,* copyright by Harold Osborne, 1968.

Oxford University Press for permission to reprint from *Ways of Knowledge and Experience* by Louis Arnaud Reid, © George Allen & Unwin, Ltd., 1961; and from *What is Art?* by Leo Tolstoy, translated by Aylmer Maude, copyright 1930 by the Oxford University Press.

Pantheon Books for permission to reprint from *Aesthetics and History in the Visual Arts* by Bernard Berenson. Copyright 1948 by Pantheon Books. Reprinted by permission of Pantheon Books, a Division of Random House, Inc.

A. D. Peters & Co., Ltd., for world rights excluding the United States to reprint from *The Grundrisse* by Karl Marx, edited and translated by David McClellan, 1971.

Prentice-Hall, Inc., for permission to reprint from *Art and Human Values* by Melvin Rader and Bertram Jessup, © 1976, pp. 143-146, 286-295, 347-348. Reprinted by permission of Prentice-Hall, Inc., Englewood Cliffs, New Jersey.

Princeton University Press for permission to reprint Chapter II, "Truth and the Stereotype" from *Art and Illusion* by E. H. Gombrich, No. 5 in the A. W. Mellon Lectures in the Fine Arts, Bollingen Series, XXXV. Copyright © 1960, 1961, and 1969 by the Trustees of the National Gallery of Art, Washington, D.C.

G. P. Putnam's Sons for permission to reprint from *Art* by Clive Bell; and from *Art as Experience* by John Dewey. Copyright © 1934, 1962 by John Dewey.

Random House, Inc., for permission to reprint from *The Birth of Tragedy and the Case of Wagner* by Friedrich Nietzsche, translated by Walter Kaufmann. Copyright © 1967 by Random House, Inc.

Routledge & Kegan Paul Ltd. for world rights, excluding the United States, her dependencies and the Phillipines, to reprint from *The Social History of Art,* Vol. II by Arnold Hauser, 1941; for British Empire rights to reprint from *The Hidden God* by Lucien Goldmann, translated by Philip Thody, copyright 1964: from *Problems of Art* by Susanne K. Langer; and from *Technics and Civilization* by Lewis Mumford.

Charles Scribner's Sons for permission to reprint from *Forms and Substances in the Arts* by Étienne Gilson. Copyright © 1966 by Étienne Gilson; from *Problems of Art* by Susanne K. Langer. Copyright © 1957 by Susanne K. Langer; and from *The Sense of Beauty* by George Santayana. Copyright 1896 Charles Scribner's Sons, 1924 George Santayana.

University of California Press for permission to reprint from *Art and Visual Perception* by Rudolf Arnheim, 1954.

University of Chicago Press for permission to reprint "Style" by Meyer Schapiro from *Anthropology Today,* edited by A. L. Kroeber, 1953.

C. A. Watts & Company for British Empire rights to reprint from *Early Writings* by Karl Marx, translated by T. B. Bottomore.

Wesleyan University Press for permission to reprint from *Literature and Knowledge* by Dorothy Walsh. Copyright © by Wesleyan University, 1969.

Cole Weston and Nathan Lyons for permission to reprint "Seeing Photographically" by Edward Weston in *Photographers on Photography,* edited by Nathan Lyons.

Preface

In preparing this fifth edition, I have interpreted "modern" in the title to include writers from Kant to our contemporaries. Some old selections have been omitted or reduced, others have been expanded, substitutions have been made, and much new material has been added, especially from works that have appeared since the last edition.

I have been guided by a number of considerations in my choice of selections: the originality of the author, the importance of his thought, the beauty of the style, the clarity of the expression, the extent to which the selections fit into the plan of the book, and the degree to which each is integral and unmutilated by removal from its original context. Some excellent works have been omitted because they would be suitable only for advanced students. I have in mind a wider audience.

As in previous editions, the selections are varied to avoid one-sidedness and to present supplementary or conflicting points of view. Part I is devoted to the definition of art as a creative process; Part II discusses the work of art, its matter, expressiveness, and form; Part III examines the response of individual spectators, critics, philosophers, and the community. These divisions are not sharp and the divisions overlap and interlock in a great variety of ways. The book is planned to cover, within the necessary limits of space, almost the entire field of esthetics and all the major arts, including music, architecture, painting, sculpture, literature, dance, motion pictures, and industrial design. In my general Introduction and the Introductory Note to each chapter, I try to clarify and interrelate the readings and provide a context for their more adequate interpretation. Finally, there is a comprehensive bibliography.

The variant spellings "esthetics" and "aesthetics" appear in the fourth edition, in contrast to the uniform spelling "esthetics" of the three previous editions. In this fifth edition I have followed the earlier practice, except for retaining the original spelling in the titles of books and articles.

M. R.

Contents

INTRODUCTION
The Meaning of Art

I. Imitation, Form, and Expression

A natural object, such as the song of a meadowlark, has esthetic qualities; and therefore esthetics, which is the theory of esthetic objects and experiences, applies both to natural objects and to works of art. In appreciating the latter, we respond not only to sensuous qualities and forms but also to technical, psychological, and cultural values—to the *human* expressiveness of the works. The writers represented in the present anthology have a great deal to say about natural objects, but their main emphasis is upon art; and it is art that I now wish to discuss.

In tracing the philosophy of art from ancient Greece to modern times, we find three concepts of major importance—*imitation, form,* and *expression*. Each has left its mark on the essays included in this book.

"Mimesis" in Greek, or "imitation" in most translations, has maintained a powerful hold on philosopher and ordinary viewer alike. But very few philosophers, ancient or modern, would defend "imitation" in its *literal* meaning. Neither Plato nor Aristotle, for example, favors imitation in the sense of nonexpressive copying. Plato refers to the painters and poets that he condemns as imitators of superficial appearances; and in many passages, he recognizes the existence of artistic inspiration, which is nonimitative in any literal sense. According to the *Laws, Phaedrus, Symposium,* and *Ion,* the highest art is inspired by a direct vision of the pure eternal forms of Beauty, Truth, Goodness, and the like. Plato distinguishes in the *Timaeus* (#28) between those who fasten their gaze upon the unchanging forms and archetypes and those whose gaze is limited to the changing things of the perceptual world. The former, he says, create artifacts that are beautiful; the latter do not. Plato's conclusion in the *Republic* is that "the real artist, who knew what he was imitating, would be interested in realities and not in imitations."[1] The context of this remark indicates that Plato was thinking mainly of the "art" of statesmanship, which he regarded as the highest of all the arts. He was not referring exclusively to the fine arts, because the Greeks did not distinguish the arts from the crafts; but his remarks are extensible to such arts as painting, sculpture, and poetry. Taking all his dialogues into consideration, we can see that his position is not far removed from that of Plotinus, who said that "the arts do not simply imitate the visible thing but go back to the principles of its nature."[2]

In the *Poetics,* Aristotle maintains that poetry has sprung from the mimetic impulse and the instinct for harmony and rhythm. He thus recognizes form as no less fundamental than imitation—indeed, the importance of unity and design is emphasized throughout his essay. The reality imitated, he indicates, is human life and human nature—acts expressive of spirit. An act viewed merely as an external process is not the true object of esthetic imitation. A work of art imitates its original, not as it is in itself but as it *appears* to the senses and imagination. Accordingly, the poet ought to prefer "probable impossibilities to possible improbabilities"; that is to say, he should aim at convincing semblance. If literal truth is stranger than fiction, then all the worse for truth in the literal sense. Art imitates the *universal*; it expresses the real, rid of irrelevancies and the disturbances of chance; it exhibits the common designs of destiny; it is in this sense more philosophical than history. Tragic characters are "imitated" not as they are but as they "ought to be," displaying a lofty nobility and greatness despite their tragic flaws. In the *Politics* Aristotle contends that music is, in a sense, the *most* imitative of the arts. "Melodies have the power of representing character in themselves," he declares. "There seems to be a sort of kinship of harmonies and rhythms to our souls."[3]

The imitation theory in the cast given to it by Plato, Aristotle, and Plotinus exercised a strong influence in the Middle Ages. In the thought of St. Thomas Aquinas, generally regarded as the foremost medieval philosopher, "imitation" was subordinated to "beauty" and "art." He never wrote a treatise on esthetic theory, but we can piece together his ideas about art and beauty from scattered sources. Following Aristotle's scheme, he classified human activities as follows:

1. *Pure Knowing* (corresponding to Aristotle's theoretical sciences—metaphysics, mathematics, and physics).
2. *Action,* or doing as distinct from knowing.
    - (a) *Practice* (corresponding to Aristotle's practical sciences—politics, ethics, economics).
    - (b) *Making,* or *Art* in the wide sense (corresponding to Aristotle's productive sciences—poetics, rhetoric, technology in general).
        - (1) *Craftsmanship,* or the making of *useful* things—for example, shoemaking, tailoring, carpentry.
        - (2) *Fine Art,* or the making of *beautiful* things—for example, painting, poetry, music.

Neither Aristotle nor St. Thomas distinguished sharply between craft and fine art, but the distinction is implicit in some of their remarks.

"Let that be called beauty," Thomas said, "the very perception of which pleases."[4] This definition contains two ideas. First, beautiful things are pleasant to apprehend. Second, not every pleasant thing is beautiful, but only that which is pleasant in immediate perception. Beauty delights the spectator by the bare fact of being perceived. If it gives pleasure exclusively in some other way, for example, because it is useful or edifying, it is not beautiful. The basis of the enjoyment is not wholly in the object nor wholly in the mind of the beholder, but in a correspondence between the two. The object is fitted, as it were, to be joyfully received by the senses and the intellect: what is intelligible in the object is appreciated by what is intelligent in the subject. Imitation is the means to this delightful apprehension—it is not the end in itself.

According to St. Thomas, the main constituent of beauty is "form," which is not bare abstract design, but a revelation of the specific principle of the thing contemplated (as when the basic meaning of death seems to be revealed in a tragedy). The form may be the essence of a type or species, or of an individual, or of a particular attitude or quality; but in any event it is, in art, a concrete presentment, a vision, appealing simultaneously to the senses and the intelligence. The goal of art is thus delightful meaning that shines out in the unity and design of the sensible constituents. To embody such meaning, the work of art must exhibit clarity, integrity, and right proportion. With its emphasis on order and intelligibility, this theory is akin to Aristotle's doctrine of imitation.

The Renaissance inherited the concept of imitation from Greece and the Middle Ages. Conservatives in the Church indicted secular art as mere imitation of particulars. The humanists defended art as a showing forth, or "imitation," of the Platonic universals of Truth, Goodness, and Beauty. Neoplatonists such as Marsilio Ficino (1433–1499) and Pico della Mirandola (1463–1494) gave to the theory of imitation this idealistic twist.

Although imitation was implicitly accepted down through the eighteenth century as the goal of the fine arts, the concept gradually slipped into disrepute as Neoclassicism waned. In the Romantic period, with its emphasis on spontaneity and self-expression, imitation was felt to be incompatible with the creative role of the artist. "Imitation," as a term, was discarded or subordinated to "originality," and the word "representation" was often substituted. It is now almost universally recognized that art is not in any literal sense imitative. E. H. Gombrich, in the selection included in Chapter 1, formulates a kind of modern analogue of the ancient theory of imitation. He maintains that the artistic imitation of nature cannot be separated from imaginative expression. The more extreme rebellion against the naïve theory of imitation is reflected in the paradoxes of Oscar Wilde.

The idea of "form," like "imitation," received its classic expression in Greece. Plato, again to cite his ideas as illustrative, emphasized form as having a profound affinity to spirit and as thus providing a necessary basis for the expression and cultivation of the human soul. He saw that esthetic experience is shot through with formal characteristics—with rhythm, harmony, design—the collaboration of which constitutes the whole. He believed that esthetic education, especially in the early and most formative years of life, would cultivate the habit of seeing things thus in context, in their unity and inward coherence. Little by little, the mind would develop its power of imaginative sympathy, its intuitive sense of order, until the feeling for likeness and fellowship and harmony would become second nature, almost an instinct. The reason that he wanted to censor art is not that he valued it so little but that he valued it so much. He was wrong, I think, in his desire to censor, but right in his emphasis upon form and his estimate of art and esthetic education. When thoroughly ingrained and integral to the psyche, esthetic culture impresses the sense of interrelatedness upon the deepest levels of the mind. Without such a deep spontaneous appreciation of vivid qualities, in their mutual relevance and interfusion, there could be little feeling for the unity of life or the spiritual integration of a community. The best life and the best society, Plato was convinced, have the same formal structure as the well-wrought work of art.

Aristotle, with less emphasis upon moral implications, applies the concept of form to art as well as to nature. A statue, for example, is a synthesis of matter and form produced by a purposive human being, while a living organism is a synthesis of matter and form produced by nature. The form of the statue can therefore be called "organic" by analogy. In the *Poetics*, Aristotle applied the concept of organic form to tragedy and epic poetry. The subsequent history of "organic unity" as an esthetic concept is traced by Harold Osborne in Chapter 9. I shall not repeat his admirable summary.

In the twentieth century, the organic unity of form and content has been the subject of much discussion. A. C. Bradley, in his famous lecture "Poetry for Poetry's Sake" (1901), uses the term "significant form" to epitomize that unity:

> There is no such thing as mere form in poetry. All form is expression. . . . So that what you apprehend may be called indifferently an expressed meaning or a significant form.[5]

Not long after Bradley's essay appeared, "significant form" became the key term in the esthetics of Clive Bell. In his theory as contrasted with Bradley's, there is less emphasis on content and more on sheer abstract design. Later, Susanne Langer, with the organic analogy in mind, referred to "living form," or with a view to its expressiveness, "symbolic form." Finally, because of the misleading connotations of the word "symbolic," she substituted the term "expressive form." Similarly, many of the other writers who have contributed to this anthology have emphasized form under one rubric or another. Whatever the terminology, the concept of form is basic in modern esthetics.

"Expression," the third of the basic terms that we are considering, emerged clearly in the writings of Herder, Schlegel, Coleridge, and others.[6] Before the nineteenth century was over it was a commonly accepted principle. An expressionist esthetics was formulated by Eugene Véron in the 1870s (see Chapter 2). Walter Pater's celebrated "Essay on Style" (1888) concluded that "all beauty is in the long run only fineness of truth, or what we call expression. . . ." Another characteristic writer of the period, R. L. Nettleship, spoke of the oneness of expression and feeling: "The feeling is not truly felt until it is expressed, and in being expressed it is still felt but in a different way."[7] Nettleship is here anticipating Croce's notion of lyrical expression (see Chapter 3).

There is now a considerable consensus among estheticians that art is, in some sense, expressive. In *An Introduction to Aesthetics* (London, 1949), Professor E. F. Carritt quoted from over forty representative estheticians, ancient and modern, to illustrate the recognition that art, as a creative process, is the expression of mood, feeling, or spirit. There are two parts to this consensus: first, that art is expression, and second, that spirit, feeling, or mood is expressed.

The prevalence of the concept of expression has been remarked by Alan Tormey:

> The history of the philosophy of art could, without excessive distortion, be written as a study of the significance of a handful of concepts. The successive displacement of "imitation" by "representation," and of "representation" by "expression," for example, marks one of the more revealing developments in the literature of esthetics; and it would be only a slight exaggeration to claim that from the close of the eighteenth century to the present "expression" and its cognates have dominated both esthetic theorizing and the critical appraisal of the arts.[8]

Some writers in this anthology use other words, such as "communication" (Tolstoy), "objectification" (Santayana), "embodiment" (Bosanquet and Reid), and "symbolization" (Langer and Arnheim). These are not alternatives to "expression" but are cognate terms.

A considerable number of estheticians point out that "expression" does not mean self-expression. The artist expresses, as Langer has said, "not his own actual feelings, but what he knows about human feelings." Hence, it is not the case, as some critics have supposed, that the expression theory commits us to treating art works as autobiographical revelations. Almost all estheticians distinguish between a mere gushing or venting of emotion, which has nothing to do with art, and artistic expression of the "quality," "mental image," or "epitome" of emotion. Expressing a mood or feeling, Ducasse points out (see Chapter 2), is not the same as *arousing* it in someone's mind. For example, music that expresses sadness need not make the listener feel sad. Without transmitting the actual feeling, the music conveys the impression, or as some would prefer to say, the conception or abstracted pattern, of sadness. As Carroll C. Pratt remarked, "Music sounds the way emotions feel."[9] Expressive qualities in objects do not always imply some correlative *act* of expression. Sophisticated proponents of the expression theory, especially those steeped in Gestalt psychology, recognize that many things have expressive qualities without being *created* with this end in view, or without being created at all. These qualities abound in the world quite apart from art, and this is the reason that artists can so often borrow a motif from actuality. Arnheim, in a selection reproduced in this anthology (see Chapter 8), refers to the soft or threateningly harsh profile of a mountain, the twisted, sad, tired appearance of a blanket thrown over a chair, the weariness of slowly floating tar, or the energetic ringing of a telephone bell. Hence, not all but only some expressiveness is the product of artistic activity.

The skeptic might still contend that art in no way implies expression, and this is true in some meanings of the word. But if by "expression" one means the intentional making of objects with expressive qualities, it is difficult to deny that art is a kind of expression. We would not call a wholly inexpressive object a work of art. Since the concept of expression, as used in esthetic discourse, is open to alternative statements and misunderstandings, it has been subjected to considerable criticism; but these criticisms can be met by more exact explication of its meaning. "Expression" may be used in a limited sense so as to exclude exemplification, representation, or symbolism, but I intend no such restricted usage.

Neither imitation nor form, taken as exclusive, could be considered the defining mark of art, whereas expression comes much closer to the required degree of generality. The expressionist theory, when adequately formulated, incorporates the insights involved in the other two theories, treating the representational and formal elements as the means of expression. Not mere imitation but *expressive* imitation, not mere form but *expressive* form, have artistic point and relevance. The recognition of this fact constitutes the central standpoint of modern esthetics.

Of course, there is some disagreement about what side or aspect of the mind is expressed in art. Santayana emphasizes pleasure; Hegel, ideas; Bergson and Croce, intuition; Nietzsche and Freud, desire and the unconscious; Schiller, the play of imagination; Bosanquet and Dewey, the mind as an organic whole. But it is easy to exaggerate the differences. Freud agrees with Santayana that art is surcharged with pleasure, and with Tolstoy that it expresses emotions and not merely desires. Schiller agrees with Dewey and Bosanquet that art engages and harmonizes the whole mind-body. Hegel meets Croce halfway in recognizing the particularity as well as the universality of art. So, likewise, with other writers in this book—they tend to reach out and embrace the truths represented by different points of view.

We have mentioned that there is considerable consensus among estheticians that art is a mode of expression, and that it expresses the inner life of the psyche, such as mood, feeling, and desire. Although this sort of definition contains a large measure of truth, it puts too much emphasis on the subjective side, to the exclusion of more objective viewpoints. Perhaps a better way to characterize art is to say that it is a joint creation of the object and the observer:

> A balance, an ennobling interchange
> Of action from without and from within;
> The excellence, pure function, and best power
> Both of the object seen, and eye that sees.[10]

This is the position of Louis Arnaud Reid in Chapter 6. In declaring that art is the embodiment of values, he avoids both one-sided subjectivism and one-sided objectivism. He defines value in relational terms as a thing or quality felt and appreciated.

The pivot of this doctrine is the distinction between facts and values. Let us therefore carefully examine this distinction. "X is square" is judged a *fact* if a number of competent observers, upon carefully measuring X, find it to be square. Science is the coordination of facts, and the very meaning of a fact, or of a scientific truth as the accurate description of facts, is that it can meet the test of *social* verification. The distinguishing mark of science is its public character, the result of a process of abstraction, generalization, and collective verification; no belief has scientific validity as long as it remains private, the esoteric object of a single individual's perspective. It must be transmitted and interpreted to others and substantiated by them; it must be verified by stubborn and irreducible data, admitted by all qualified observers. It must be consistent with established laws and theories, which in turn have been verified by scientists, living and dead. Science is therefore appropriately characterized by Charles Peirce and Josiah Royce as a "community of interpretation."

A *value,* on the other hand, is a quality that excites appreciation. Art, as value-expressive, springs from attitudes of appraisal. It does not reflect existence as merely neutral and colorless; it selects, distorts, and intensifies. What Francis Bacon wrote about poetry applies to all art: ". . . It doth raise and erect the Mind, by submitting the shows of things to the desires of the Mind, whereas reason doth buckle and bow the Mind unto the Nature of things."[11] Thus, a natural landscape is valued esthetically because it has certain qualities, but some other of its qualities will be quite indifferent or unsatisfactory. An artist intent upon expressing the positive values of the landscape would select the qualities he appreciates and would express these and not the indifferent features. The only way he can do so is to remodel the landscape by means of imagination.

Values, in contrast to facts, are often merely imaginary. "Possibility," as Emily Dickinson said, "is a fairer house than Prose."[12] Even when values are not possibilities envisaged by the imagination, they are always related to our appreciative attitudes, which *may* be quite private and peculiar. Whereas facts have a uniform character for a community of observers, values have a variable character depending upon the subjective preferences of the individual appreciator. But, as I shall explain in some detail, this variability can be confined within limits; and through art, values attain a kind of social objectivity that is quite different from the objectivity of science.

Values are expressed in the creative activity of the artist whenever he purposefully creates the objective occasions for appreciations. Usually, he communicates attitudes of valuation by supplying an appropriate object—namely, a work of art—to another mind; but the object may be created for the artist himself to contemplate as the adequate ground for his own appreciative attitudes. The problem of the artist is to find the objective forms and qualities that will induce the person who contemplates them to discover in the object the values that he wishes to embody. If he succeeds in doing this, he has "expressed" the values. This does not mean that the values which the artist expresses need be completely in mind before he starts work. As Croce insists (see Chapter 3), both Beethoven in writing a symphony and Michelangelo in decorating the Sistine Chapel must have elaborated an inward vision in the process of objectifying—and it is this vision that is expressed. To this extent, intuition and expression are identical.

The problem of the contemplator is somewhat different. The work of art that he beholds consists of an array of signs which he must interpret. It is for him, himself, to supply the sense of values to which these signs correspond. It will depend upon him whether the work awakens to life in his imagination or remains dead and inexpressive. He must evoke from within himself the appropriate attitudes—and thereby intensify his qualitative appreciation of the object—in which he thus discovers the values that the artist has embodied. If he succeeds in doing all this, he has "expressed" values in contemplation, since his own activity is, like all interpretative art, essentially creative. From the standpoint of the artist and also from that of the contemplator, art is the expression of values—though we should distinguish between the free expression of the artist and the interpretative expression of the contemplator.

Science, it may be argued, deals with the more permanent, public, and universal elements of experience; art, with the more fleeting, private, and particular elements. Now this contrast has some basis, but I believe that it is a mistake to set up such a sharp dichotomy. Gregory Vlastos pointed out that *both* art and science are essentially communal. "In science," he wrote, "one finds truth only insofar as one recasts one's private insight into its most universally sharable form; thus placing it at the disposal of all. Scientific truth is discovered in a community of inquiry in which there is a minimum of hoarding and the maximum of sharing—where each receives the fruit of the labors of others and gives back to the utmost of his ability." Artistic expression is similarly interpersonal: "Beauty is created only in a process of communication wherein the product of individual originality becomes the common possession of mankind. . . . The creator must lose to find himself, lose a subjective intuition to recover it as objective form."[13] Art is man's supreme means of socializing the world of appreciations. By communicating the "incommunicable," art creates a community of appreciation to supplement the community of scientific interpretation. Just as the objectivity of science implies the recognition of a "common world" of describable objects, so the communicability of art implies a "social ego," a common *inner* world of value-appreciation.

II. The Creative Process

We can characterize art in terms of three standpoints; the creative activity of the artists, the work of art, and the reception of art by the public. Each of these is covered by a Part of the present volume. The divisions are not sharp; each Part throws light on all three standpoints. I shall first characterize the creative process.

To illustrate, I cite the following passage from a letter written by Vincent van Gogh to his brother:

> I should like to paint the portrait of an artist friend, a man who dreams great dreams, who works as the nightingale sings, because it is his nature. He'll be a fair man. I want to put into my picture my appreciation, the love that I have for him. So I paint him as he is, as faithfully as I can. But the picture is not finished

> yet. To finish it I am now going to be the arbitrary colorist. I exaggerate the fairness of the hair; I come even to orange tones, chromes, and pale lemon-yellow. Beyond the head, instead of painting the ordinary wall of the mean room, I paint infinity, a plain background of the richest, intensest blue that I can contrive, and by this simple combination of the bright head against the rich blue background I get a mysterious effect, like a star in the depths of an azure sky.[14]

What van Gogh sought to communicate through his painting was not a mere factual description; he wished to paint his "appreciation," his "love," the qualities that excited his preference. He did not literally imitate; faithful reproduction, as he said, is only a point of departure. He imagined the colors and shapes, the contrasts and relationships that would express his sense of values—the mood of appreciation that his friend excited within him.

Yet van Gogh did not merely express his admiration for his friend. He created new values in the very act of expression. Each color or shape that he painted has a worth of its own. The "rich blue," for example, is beautiful in itself, and it is more beautiful in contrast with the orange shades, the chrome, the pale lemon-yellow. The finished painting can be enjoyed as a pattern of colors and shapes even if it were to be turned upside down so that it is no longer regarded as the representation of a human figure. Many modern pictures, as we all know, do not represent or imitate any natural fact, just as a fugue of Bach does not thus represent or imitate. Since the time of Pythagoras, philosophers have recognized the value-expressiveness of harmonies, rhythms, patterns of color, three-dimensional shapes, and other nonrepresentational elements. One of the merits of certain writers in this anthology, such as Susanne Langer and Rudolf Arnheim, is that they help to explain how such expressiveness occurs.

Many works of art are representational; all works of art have form. Like most artists in Western tradition, van Gogh expresses both representational and formal values. A writer such as Clive Bell, who minimized representational values, and a writer such as Leo Tolstoy, who minimized formal values, were both one-sided.

The appreciations expressed by an artist are not separate from their mode of expression. The *what* of art is not separable from the *how*. When James Joyce expresses a shaver's disgust at "the clammy slather of the lather in which the brush was stuck," it is a clammy-slathery disgust that he is expressing. When Picasso expresses serenity with the muted colors and voluminous form of his "Woman in White," it is a color-muted and voluminous serenity that is being expressed. The sadness of music is a peculiarly musical sadness; it is impossible, for instance, to give an adequate verbal phrasing to the majestic sadness of Chopin's Sonata in B Flat Minor. Even in poetry, the values cannot truly be formulated in words other than those of the poem itself. These is a real creative synthesis, a fusion of mood with sensory configuration. As sensation blends with sensation to create a new quality (for instance, when notes combine to form a chord), so feeling or desire blends with sensation to create the esthetic effect.

To depict the artist as he is sometimes depicted—a kind of spiritual Robinson Crusoe forever marooned on the island of his own subjectivity—is to forget that in art the duality of subject and other object disappears. The artist's inner experiences, his appreciative thoughts and moods, are expressed outwardly in the language of sensory qualities. As in dreams, subjective thought and feeling are embodied in sensory images, but in a form communicable to others. The work of art is objective and yet is dyed with emotion and sensibility. It radiates spiritual expressiveness and is thus a link between mind and mind. Art is the only "language" whereby we can *vividly* transmit our values to others. It breaks down the walls between human beings, and is thus a great solvent of conflict and selfishness. "Love consists in this," the poet Rilke has written, "that two solitudes protect and touch and greet each other."[15] By means of art, the solitudes flow together; love and imaginative understanding become possible.

The artist not only discloses his own moods but also transcends his private feelings. He has the singular ability to draw the outer object into his own being—to sense its qualities and to feel at one with it. John Keats was reporting more than a personal idiosyncrasy when he wrote: "If a Sparrow come before my window, I take part in its existence and pick about the gravel."[16] In another letter, Keats described the nature of a poet and cited himself as an example:

> A poet is the most unpoetical of anything in existence, because he has no Identity—he is continually in for [*sic*] and filling some other body. The Sun,—the Moon,—the Sea, and men and women, who are creatures of impulse, are poetical, and have about them an unchangeable attribute, the poet has none, no identity—he is certainly the most unpoetical of all God's creatures. . . . It is a wretched thing to confess; but it is a very fact, that not one word I ever utter can be taken for granted as an opinion growing out of my identical Nature—how can it, when I have no Nature? When I am in a room with people, if I ever am free from speculating on creations of my own brain, then, not myself goes home to myself, but the identity of everyone in the room begins to press upon me, so that I am in a very little time annihilated—not only among men; it would be the same in a nursery of Children."[17]

Keats is here describing, in rather paradoxical language, the sensibility that is preeminently the artist's but which is shared to a degree by everyone. It is thus that we are "in touch" with other people and things. All of the arts—not simply poetry—cultivate this empathic sensitivity. "Empathy," in this broad sense, still retains meaning for art, in characterizing not only the beholder but also the creator of the work of art. The tendency in contemporary esthetics to abandon the theory of Theodor Lipps (see Chapter 10) has gone too far.

In characterizing the creative process, I have not reviewed all the interpretations in Part I. To what extent that process should be described as imitation, expression of emotion, intuition, wish-fulfillment, or enhancement of experience, I leave to the judgment of my readers. I have stated that I find Reid's theory, that art is the embodiment of values, the most adequate.

III. The Work of Art

The work of art conveys the sense of a living presence—it is infused with emotion, instinct with a kind of life. Its beholder reaches out and touches another spirit.

For this reason, idealistic writers such as Croce (see Chapter 3) maintain that the work of art is spiritual rather than physical. A number of recent writers have attacked this position, contending that the work is, at least in many cases, a physical artifact. Both sides of the dispute are calling attention to important facts. Except in the case of mere imagery, which we would hesitate to call a work of art, there is indeed a physical artifact, such as a canvas covered with pigments. But the more idealistic philosophers say that this artifact is only a means to an end, awakening in the mind an imaginative process that creates the real work of art; conversely, the more materialistic philosophers contend that the physical thing is the work of art itself. I think that, as occasions vary, we choose to mean different things by the phrase "work of art," and sometimes our meaning is more akin to the materialist's and at other times is more like the idealist's. A theory such as that sketched by Stephen Pepper (see Chapter 11) in the latter part of his essay on "Contextualistic Criticism" seems more meaningful because it recognizes and gives due credit to both the physical and the mental sides. The insistence of Bernard Bosanquet and Edward Weston (see Chapter 7) on the importance of the physical medium is a corrective to a purely idealistic theory.

The work of art may be defined as an organic unity of value-expressive constituents. The constituents include representations, connotations, and purely sensuous materials, and there is almost no value that cannot be represented, connoted, or sensuously presented. It is therefore impossible to restrict the content of works of art, as Santayana initially and many other writers tried to do, by limiting it to *beauty*. The content, of course, must be *valued* in concrete terms, and hence must be concretely appreciated. The qualities of the object must be apprehended as, for example, gay, sad, horrible, sublime, or demonic; they must be liked or disliked because of some such concrete value-character; and, I believe, the experience of the work must somehow have intrinsic perceptual worth if it is properly to be called *esthetic*. But no other limitation can be put upon the content of works of art. Not all arts, of course, have the same scope, and it takes all in combination to include, even potentially, every kind of value-content.

Some artists and estheticians agree with Tolstoy and Véron that ugliness may be legitimately introduced into the work of art, not merely as a foil to beauty but also for the sake of its own independent expressiveness. Others agree with Croce that artistic beauty is simply success in art, or in other words, that the beautiful in art is the completely expressive and the ugly is the inexpressive. Croce's theory would not be seriously transformed if every mention of beauty and ugliness in his pages were deleted: the concepts of expressiveness and inexpressiveness would suffice. Most contemporary artists seem to agree with either Croce or Véron and Tolstoy. Works of art, in the modern mode, have a vast range:

They embrace whatever is spiritually expressive, even if the expressiveness is achieved by cacophony in poetry, discords in music, harshness in painting, or unsparing realism in literature.

A coherent work of art, whatever its content, is an organic unity—a concrete structure in which the character of the whole influences the *intrinsic* character of the parts. Every chord in a musical composition, every patch of color in a painting, every sound or image in a poem, attains its meaning and value in its *context*: It is infected through and through by its relations to the other elements and to the whole. This implies that the distinction between form and content is relative; the content is the elements in relation, the form is the relation among the elements, and the total work is both in irrefrangible unity. This is the meaning of organic unity as sketched by Harold Osborne (see Chapter 9).

Another characteristic of a work of art, according to Bergson and Croce, is that it is highly individual. Noting that artists shun mere abstractions, they define art as the intuition of particulars rather than the knowing of universals. A particular, they supposed, was a unique quality apprehended by an individual mind. Their emphasis upon the particularity of the work of art makes it difficult to explain the sharability of the esthetic vision. They failed to note, or at least to emphasize, that qualities may be ever so individualized and still be repeated. The high-fidelity recording of a musical masterpiece by a superb orchestra is a very particularized and unique creation, but it may be issued in thousands of identical copies. Even when the record is played, and the music comes to life in the feeling and imagination of the auditor, its qualities may be essentially the same as in the experience of another listener. In Keats' great *Ode*, the song of the nightingale, which symbolizes the work of art, is no abstract universal; yet it remains the same in the most varied times and places:

> Thou wast not born for death, immortal Bird!
> No hungry generations tread thee down;
> The voice I hear this passing night was heard
> In ancient days by emperor and clown:
> Perhaps the self-same song that found a path
> Through the sad heart of Ruth, when, sick for home,
> She stood in tears amid the alien corn;
> The same that oft-times hath
> Charm'd magic casements, opening on the foam
> Of perilous seas, in faery lands forlorn.

The work of art, like the nightingale's song, is vivid and emotionally toned, but it is as communicable as the most abstract scientific description. When two sensitive beholders contemplate the same work of art, their experiences may not be identical, but they are surely quite similar. The contagiousness of art—its capacity to create a community of appreciation—can be explained upon no other assumption. Art thus involves, even in its uniqueness, a social element: The work of art conveys a *repeatable* particularity.

There is another side to art, the generic, that Bergson and Croce tended to deny. The content of the work of art is both specific and general, intuitional and intellectual. Bergson's contention that every tragic protagonist is an individual, never a type, is one-sided. The great tragic characters, such an Antigone and Hamlet, impress us so profoundly because they make our lives less petty; they lift us to a universal plane. As Hegel, Nietzsche, and Freud intimate, these characters wrestle with issues that far transcend the particular time and place. So it is with great works of art in general. What distinguishes them is largely the capacity to express some new concrete variation of an old universal theme. About two-thirds of the poems in the *Oxford Book of English Verse* deal with the timeless themes of love and death, and yet each one is a unique creation.

The artist pours his knowledge into works of art. He *knows*—he does not merely feel—but he knows by sympathetic identification and imaginative insight. He knows as the perspicacious lover knows about the nature of love, by "proving it upon his pulses." He knows by feeling at one with the object, as Keats felt at one with the sparrow. He knows the reality that he suffers when the outer object is drawn into his own being, into the mysterious depths of subjectivity. He knows not bare facts or abstract laws but vivid values—he knows things appreciatively, in their immediacy and concreteness. He knows with the totality of his mind and body: with sense, mood, instinct, and intelligence, both conscious and subconscious. He knows by descending to the roots of being, which no abstract idea can encompass—to the obscure spring of man's creative intuition—the source of dreams and of art alike.

There, in the deep recesses of his mind, he is in touch with the instinctively common part of man's nature—with the values that are not peculiar to him as an artist nor to one man or a few, but are basic in the emotional experiences and secret longings of most human begins. If it were not so, art could not serve as the language of all humanity—a way of communicating across all the barriers of time and place. The cave paintings by men of the reindeer age—the paintings at Lascaux and Altamira—would not speak so eloquently to us today; nor would the art of the whole world be a "museum without walls," where any man can find incomparable treasures. The work of all ages and countries—Gothic counterpoint, Egyptian sculpture, Chinese landscape, Mayan temple, Russian ballet, English drama, and American novel—bear alike the spiritual imprint of humanity. In the realm of art, far more than in morals, politics, or religion, the whole world is kin.

As Dorothy Walsh indicates in Chapter 5, an artist sometimes expresses not what he subjectively likes or dislikes but what he actually finds to be characteristic of the nature of life. (If some of my readers refuse to call this "truth," I shall not quarrel with them. In many works of art there is a kind of value-significance that is faithful to the nature of human existence—call it whatever you will.) A work of art may, in this sense, be as severely subordinated to reality-thinking as a scientific treatise. The tendency of Freud to conceive of art as evasion has only a limited validity. At the same time, the appropriate response to a work of art is *not* belief in abstract factual propositions, but rather a kind of imaginative enactment of value-experience. The imagination must have free play, which ordinary literal belief does not permit. In creating or appreciating art—to again quote Keats—the capacity that we need is the "quality . . . which Shakespeare possessed so enormously—I mean *Negative Capability*, that is, when a man is capable of being in uncertainties, mysteries, doubts without any irritable reaching after fact and reason."[18] Only with this freedom of the imagination can the values expressed in works of art be realized in their immediacy and vividness. Schiller and Langer, in their doctrine of "semblance," agree with Keats.

I have classified the readings in Part II under the headings of matter, expressiveness, and form. Although these divisions are not sharp, each is distinguishable enough so that it can be considered in a separate chapter. My Introductory Note to each chapter is sufficient to orient the reader.

IV. The Response to the Work of Art

If we turn from the work of art to the audience, we can distinguish between a contemplative and a critical aspect in the response. Esthetic contemplation, which is described in the present volume in such terms as "psychical distance," "dehumanization," "empathy," and "prehension," can be more simply characterized as receptivity to the qualities expressed by, or embodied in, the esthetic object. It is, so to speak, a "listening" or "looking" or "tasting" with our capacity for appreciation. The qualities are what are to be "tasted" and rolled on one's appreciative "tongue"; and the attitudes of distance, empathy, prehension, and so forth are the means of tasting and savoring the qualities. "Tasting" is a metaphor, but it suggests the nature of contemplation—the throwing open of oneself to esthetic values as intrinsically interesting, the development of keenness and breadth of appreciation.

A fundamental issue in Part III is to be found in the contrast between the writers who emphasize isolation and *high* distance, and the writers who emphasize context and *low* distance. The cleavage between the isolationists and the contextualists appears also in other Parts of our anthology. Roughly on the side of isolationism are Wilde, with his estheticism; Kant, with his disinterestedness; Ortega y Gasset, with his dehumanization; Bell, with his formalism; and Croce, with his fencing off of art from other activities. Typical of isolationism is Bell's statement that "to create and appreciate the greatest art the most absolute abstraction from the affairs of life is essential."[19] Aligned on the contextualist side are Tolstoy (Chapter 2), Nietzsche (Chapter 4), Goldmann (Chapter 11), and Mumford (Chapter 13). Typical of contextualism is the statement of Dewey:

> I have tried to show . . . that the esthetic is no intruder in experience from without, whether by way of idle luxury or transcendent ideality, but that it is the clarified and intensified development of traits that belong to every normally complete experience.[20]

The isolationist type of theory stresses the uniqueness and immediacy of "pure" esthetic experience. If we concentrate solely upon this component, our senses and concrete imagery *do* fence us off from the world. Insofar as the artist is exclusively absorbed in this phase of art, he concerns himself not with "the why, the whence, or the whither" of things, nor with their discursive import or ulterior connections, but with "the what" as he immediately apprehends them. The experience out of which a work of art springs stirs the mind because of no merely ulterior reason, nor because it is the sign or correlate of something absent, but because it is intrinsically moving. The work of art, as the embodiment of such experience, is likewise exciting in its own right, and therefore the beholding of it involves an absorption in certain values as immediately present to sense and imagination.

Recently, the concept of esthetic distance has been sharply criticized by George Dickie and other estheticians. John Hospers, for example, has remarked that Bullough's discussion is so full of ambiguities as to "render the use of the term 'distance' more confusing than helpful."[21] Although these ambiguities need to be eliminated and "distance" clarified, I should not like to see the concept discarded. As Schiller said:

> As long as man . . . is merely a passive recipient of the world of sense, i.e., does no more than feel, he is still completely One with the world; and just because he is himself nothing but world, there exists for him as yet no world. Only when, at the esthetic stage, he puts it outside himself, or contemplates it, does his personality differentiate itself from it, and a world becomes manifest to him because he has ceased to be One with it.[22]

Clarity of vision requires some distance, and involvement may blind us. Not the original emotion but the "emotion recollected in tranquillity" is expressed by the artist, and a similar measure of detachment is required of the contemplator. There must be a forcing back of the raw material of art, its removal to a distance, so that it no longer impinges too violently on the beholder or tempts him to become practically, rather than contemplatively, involved. In the phrasing of Nietzsche, the Dionysian strain in art needs to be moderated and transfigured by an infusion of the Apollinian.

Although there is an important measure of truth in theories of distance and isolation, we may question whether it is the whole truth. The conception of art as the expression and appreciation of values lends support to the contextualist view that art is broadly human. Life, in its very essence, is the experience of values; and hence art, which alone can express values in all their vividness, is terribly relevant to life, and is limited in its scope and depth only by its autonomous nature and the bounds of human life and human genius. Whether we are speaking of the artist or the contemplator, we should try to reconcile the truth in the contextualist type of theory with the truth in the isolationist type. One of the merits of Bullough's essay is that he seeks a balance between participation and detachment, low and high distance, isolationism and contextualism. As I indicate in the Introductory Note to Chapter 10, there is both an inhibitory and an elaborative side to esthetic experience. Lipps and Aldrich illuminate the elaborative side, Kant sheds light on both sides, and Bullough mediates between the two.

The *critical* aspect of the esthetic response includes judgment of the worth of the esthetic object. Such judgment requires some standard of appraisal, and in Chapter 11 we find various standards proposed: unity, complexity, and intensity (Beardsley), degree of realism (Goldmann), and vividness of quality (Pepper). Tolstoy would add sincerity and communicative efficacy; Kant and Santayana, beauty and sublimity. But the basic criterion of art is the richness and the fineness of the appreciation that it excites in an unbiased and sensitive beholder. I am using "appreciation" not in the superficial sense of amusement or entertainment, but in the deeper sense, so eloquently stated by Dewey and Pepper, of a memorable and satisfying experience. We must remember that the worth of any great work of art is not something that can be grasped in a moment. To appreciate and judge an excellent painting, for example, we must do much more than glance at it in a gallery. Ordinarily, we must *live* with it until its sensuous qualities, meanings, and forms sink deep into our conscious and subconscious mind. If then, day after day, it works its magic upon us—if its appeal is deep and varied enough to be lasting—we can realize its excellence because our lives are being substantially enriched. The expert critic is one who can sense this amplitude and fineness of value more quickly and surely than the ordinary man.

It should not be overlooked that contemplation and criticism, as Dewey points out, are necessary aspects of the artist's activity and not merely of the public's reaction to his works. No artist can create without appreciating the values that he wishes to express; without contemplating the expressive medium, elements, and forms; and without criticizing the work as it takes shape under his hand. The artist himself is a beholder and judge, and the fineness of his art depends largely upon the quality of his appreciation and judgment. The work of art, on the other hand, comes alive only in imagination, and hence the public must share something of the creative capacity of the artist. There is no absolute distinction between creation and contemplation, between artist and beholder.

The whole community as well as the individual experiences and judges art. The public response is often unsympathetic, and the artist or lover of the arts tends to feel estranged. In a predominantly technological and commercial civilization, the mass of people is preoccupied with getting and spending. A "high standard of living"—the goal of almost everybody—has come to mean greater material comfort rather than spiritual enrichment. Even the scientists and technicians, who have so largely created the texture and set the tone of modern life, are much more concerned with their factual and technical problems than with imaginative or spiritual values. The objectives of the artist are in sharp contrast to the main preoccupations of modern man: The artist is bent upon creativeness rather than acquisitiveness; original design rather than standardized and quantitative production; imaginative freedom and human breadth rather than specialization; cultivation of the sensuous and instinctive elements of the personality rather than narrow rationality; the search for a common spiritual center rather than competitive individualism; the principle of form, harmony, and inner coherence rather than the chaotic rush, din, and overstimulation of urban living. Consequently, the works of artists have seemed to have nothing to do with everyday problems. Those artists who put themselves, either as commercial designers or as purveyors of luxury and amusement, at the disposal of organized business are considered good enough to spark sales or wile away leisure hours, but stubbornly independent artists may appear to the practical men of affairs little better than fools or idle dreamers.

In Chapter 13, this "practical" reaction to the arts is challenged. Schiller, Marx, Mumford, McHarg, and Rader and Jessup contend that art is not a delicate, special luxury existing on the margin of life, but a necessity at the very center. They foreshadow that profound transvaluation and reconstruction of life which is now the very mandate of human survival.

V. The Problem of Definition

Let us now turn to the question posed in Chapter 12 of whether art can be defined. The reader in quest of a definition may feel defeated at the outset by the apparent disagreements among estheticians. As he turns the pages of this book, he finds that art is interpreted in many ways. Among the primary concepts employed are play, illusion, imitation, beauty, emotional expression, imagination, intuition, wish-fulfillment, pleasure, technique, sensuous surface, meaning, form, function, empathy, abstraction, and esthetic distance. At first glance, these concepts represent a bewildering diversity of opinion; but careful study will reveal that much of this disagreement is merely nominal. Terms such as "imagination," "form," "meaning," and "distance" indicate different facets of a rich and varied subject rather than mutually exclusive definitions. Some of the terms refer primarily to the creation of art, others to the art object, and still others to the act of appreciation. Many unnecessary disputes, as Morris Weitz has suggested, can be avoided if esthetic labels are not pasted in one piece on the whole body of art, but rather are applied separately to the various constituents of the creative process, the esthetic artifact, and the esthetic experience.[23]

Further confusion can be avoided by Kant's distinction between "pure" and "dependent" art. Pure esthetic art is unmixed with the nonesthetic. An example would be a Bach fugue or a Mondrian painting. Dependent art is a mixture of the esthetic and the nonesthetic, as in a fondly-made pot, a handsome garment, an imposing bridge, or an eloquent philosophical style. Even works that we unhesitatingly call art, such as a representational painting or a dramatic performance, may stir cognitive or practical interests. The strands of human life are too intertwined to permit a neat demarcation between art and nonart. Things may have a touch of art, more or less, without being art through and through.

In the attempt to disentangle art from nonart, we can examine paradigm examples of "pure art." We may note in detail the relevant features of ideally clear instances and study the respects in which they differ from unclear or less clear instances. Thus, we can refine our understanding of pure art, but we cannot hope to find a sharp division between art and other human activities. A strict definition may fit the paradigms but not the borderline cases.

The problem of the esthetician in seeking a definition is analogous to that of a judge in interpreting a law. Judges are frequently puzzled about whether a law does or does not apply in a specific instance. Suppose that there is a law that no "vehicle" is to be used in a public park. The judge can be sure that the law excludes an automobile or even a motorcycle; he may be uncertain about excluding a bicycle, and still more hesitant about a tricycle or roller skates.[24] The problem of borderline instances is not confined to esthetics—it plagues many fields.

Despite puzzlement caused by borderline examples, all the readings in this book maintain that a work of art is not the report of a bare matter of fact, but rather the projection of the artist's inspiration, his emotions, appreciations, or sense of values. Suppose we overlook this consensus and conclude that all extant definitions fail. The reasonable inference would be that *past* attempts to define art have not succeeded, not that every definition in the future *must* fail. Perhaps a more complex definition or, as Mandelbaum thinks, a definition based on nonmanifest characteristics, will ultimately suffice. We should *try* to define what we are concerned with in esthetics—otherwise our ideas will be hazy or chaotic. Rather than accepting the advice of Wittgenstein, "Beware of definition," I prefer the guiding principle, "Seek definition *but distrust it*." This recognizes the virtue of defining while adding the necessary note of caution.

Morris Weitz in Chapter 12 contends that any definitions of art and its subclasses in terms of "necessary and sufficient" criteria must violate their fluid and creative nature. Horace's definition of tragedy in terms of the "three unities" of time, place, and action, for example, does not fit Shakespearean and much post-Shakespearean tragedy. Similarly, a definition of art in terms of "representation" (at least as commonly understood) precludes modern "nonobjective" art. Weitz is convinced that innovation in the arts will continue to invalidate all "closed" definitions. There are no "necessary and sufficient conditions," but only strands of similarities, none of which needs be present. This argument is cogent in warning us against narrow and static definitions, but not so cogent against unrestrictive definitions.

A good example of an unrestrictive definition in another field than esthetics is the definition of a "commodity." Economists agree that a commodity, stated very simply, is something that can be bought and sold (either in barter or money-exchange). Even the most precise definition of a commodity, stating the necessary and sufficient criteria for its application, in no way precludes novelty. When Heraclitus in ancient Greece remarked that "wares are exchanged for gold and gold for wares," he was recognizing the essential characteristics of a commodity. Neither he nor anyone else then alive could anticipate that electronic computers, supersonic aircraft, photocopiers, and the innumerable products of chemical synthesis—not to mention the avant-garde art creations of the twentieth century—would some day be commodities. Similarly, art may be definable without precluding creative innovations. Perhaps unrestrictive definitions are possible in economics and not in esthetics, but no one has demonstrated that this is the case.

Let us grant the point that a work of art is not definable simply by "looking and seeing." The manifest resemblance of a nonart object to a work of art may be accidental. In James Joyce's novel, *Portrait of the Artist as a Young Man,* Stephen asks the question: "If a man hacking in fury at a block of wood makes there an image of a cow, is that image a work of art?" The answer is that the image is not a work of art—it is an accident, albeit an unlikely one. Likewise, something formed by an unconscious natural process, such as the driftwood mentioned by Weitz, is not a work of art however much it may resemble nonobjective sculpture. But if it were removed to an appropriate setting and tastefully mounted and lighted, it would have at least a touch of art. One of the defining characteristics of a work of art is that it is the product in some measure of skill. This is the meaning in common usage, and I see no good reason to reject this usage.

Believing that a definition in terms of nonmanifest characteristics is feasible, George Dickie declares that a work of art is an artifact (*genus*) that has the status of a candidate for appreciation conferred on it by a representative of the artworld (*differentia*). This proposed differentia is an *extrinsic* denomination, and not a statement of the intrinsic nature of art. It does not tell us what something is, but only what some person or institution does to it. More is required of a satisfactory definition. The conferring of "status" would be entirely baseless and capricious if there were nothing intrinsic in the object to justify it. Contrary to what Dickie says, a representative of the artworld cannot make a work of art out of a sow's ear by nominating it as a candidate for appreciation, because the ear is not a work of art, even a bad one.

An artworld, we should bear in mind, could not exist unless there were *already* works of art. As a critic of Dickie has written:

> Works of art are logically (and indeed temporally) prior to the institution of the artworld. The only reason for the development of an artworld is that there are first works of art for the institution to develop around.[25]

Dickie has put the cart before the horse. His theory explains why certain objects are *called* works of art—it does not define the intrinsic nature of art.

Similar criticism can be directed against any "definition" of art in terms of extrinsic characteristics. The fallacy involved is like the "intentional fallacy" described by Wimsatt and Beardsley (see Introductory Note to Chapter 11). The intentional fallacy is to interpret and judge a work of art by the intention of the artist—an extrinsic and hence "irrelevant" factor. But to so judge is not necessarily a fallacy. If the artist's intention is incorporated in and internal to the work, it is a relevant factor. That the intention may be thus embodied is argued by Guy Sircello. Using the example of Poussin's *Rape of the Sabine Women,* he maintains that a spectator knows by simply looking at the painting that Poussin

> has painted the scene in an aloof, detached way. The cold light, the statuesque poses, the painstaking linearity are all visible in the work. . . . Thus one may, without change of meaning, say either . . . that Poussin paints his violent scene in an aloof, detached way or that the Sabine picture is an aloof, detached painting.[26]

We do not have to read a biography of Poussin to know his intention. To interpret the painting in terms of that intention is not a fallacy.

The institutional setting may likewise be internalized. Caudwell, in discussing the novel, and Goldmann, in discussing tragedy, indicate that social dimensions may enter into the very substance of works of art. If such internality can be shown with respect to art in general, an "institutional definition" may be more than extrinsic. So far Dickie has not shown that this is the case, but he may yet overcome the limitations of his definition. He has already performed a useful service in calling attention to the social ramifications of art.

In considering the readings in Chapter 12, the reader may wonder how precise a definition needs to be. During a recent national meeting of the American Society for Aesthetics, Professor Julius Moravsik remarked that we should avoid "the fallacy of misplaced rigor." This fallacy is to seek a greater degree of exactitude than is possible for the given field of inquiry. In certain fields, but not in others, a very exact definition is possible. The precision of a definition in geometry is not possible in ethics or esthetics. As Aristotle said: "Precision is not to be sought for alike in all discussions . . . for it is the mark of an educated man to look for precision in each class of things just as far as the nature of the subject permits."[27] Perhaps an "educated man" has reason to be satisfied with some of the definitions in esthetics.

VI. Conclusion

In the foregoing pages, I have tried to do justice to the diverse standpoints represented in this anthology. It has been one of my contentions that the main diversities and oppositions in esthetic theory find their synthesis in the concept of value-expressive form. There are many important problems that I have not mentioned, but I have suggested some basis for the reconciliation of doctrines that might appear contradictory.

This attempt to resolve conflicts in theory seems to me peculiarly appropriate to esthetics, for art itself is the great reconciler of those opposites in our practical life which ordinarily exclude each other. More than any other form of human experience, art combines such contrasting moments as variety and unity, familiarity and strangeness, repose and stimulation, order and spontaneity, distance and engagement, the Apollinian and Dionysian moods. In great tragedy, the intensification of emotions, far from excluding a sense of repose, produces the dynamic calmness that Aristotle termed "catharsis" and Santayana "the liberation of self." As Freud and Caudwell point out, art involves the harmonious co-working of the conscious and the subconscious: The dream is inserted into the texture of waking life; the "ir-real" and the real are fused. Or as Schiller indicates, art is the reconciliation of law and impulse: The form, the pattern, the "lawfulness" of the experience becomes the expression, not the repression, of impulse. Or, as Lipps observes, the images of esthetic experience are seemingly objective and yet are colored by the emotion and sensibility of the beholder: The duality of subject and object disappears; the work of art is, in a sense, myself, and I am the object, since I am empathically at one with it. Or as Aristotle and Hegel maintain, the universal essence merges into the specific image; the more seamless is the unity, the more perfect is the esthetic moment.

Because art, in combining such opposites, is more inclusive than other modes of experience, Schiller is justified in his contention that it makes man whole and that man is only whole when he engages in such activity. Likewise, John Dewey is right when he declares: "Art is the living and concrete proof that man is capable of restoring consciously, and thus on the plane of meaning, the union of sense, need, impulse, and action characteristic of the live creature."[28]

Art was once at the very center of life's text, but in our scientific and technological age, it tends to be shoved into the periphery. No one questions it as a diversion or amusement, but some of us are not satisfied with this conception. We feel that it has a vital function that should be taken seriously in our schools, from the primary level to the university, and even in our city councils and legislative chambers.

Hegel predicted that art would die out and be superseded by religion and philosophy; but there is no good reason to think that this is the case. For an increasing number of men and women, art is taking over from religion the function of expressing their deepest values. While clinging to traditional faith, others believe that art, religion, philosophy, and science should achieve some kind of working harmony. Armed with such positive convictions, we shall retain our hope for the lasting vitality of art.

Notes

1. *Republic* (translated by Benjamin Jowett), X, #599. Plato used "artists" in a sense wide enough to include the philosopher-king.
2. Plotinus, *Enneads,* V, viii, 1. Quoted by E. F. Carritt, *The Theory of Beauty* (Methuen, London, 1928), p. 46.
3. Translated by E. F. Carritt, *Philosophies of Beauty* (Oxford University Press, New York, 1943), p. 34.
4. *Summa Theologica,* I-a II-ae, q. 27, translated by Wladyslaw Tatarkiewicz, *History of Aesthetics* (Mouton, The Hague, 1970), II, p. 258.
5. A. C. Bradley, *Oxford Lectures on Poetry* (Macmillan, London, 1923), pp. 18–19.
6. See Charles Taylor, *Hegel* (Cambridge University Press, Cambridge, England, 1975), Chapter 1, "Aims of a New Epoch."

7. R. L. Nettleship, *Philosophical Remains* (Macmillan, London, 1888), p. 132.
8. Alan Tormey, *The Concept of Expression* (Princeton University Press, Princeton, N.J., 1971), p. 97.
9. Carroll C. Pratt, "Design of Music," *Journal of Aesthetics and Art Criticism,* Vol. 12 (1954), p. 296.
10. William Wordsworth, *Prelude* (1850) XIII, lines 375–378.
11. *The Proficience and Advancement of Learning* (1605), II, xiii.
12. *The Poems of Emily Dickinson* (Little, Brown, Boston, 1932), p. 289.
13. Gregory Vlastos, "The Religious Foundations of Democracy, Fraternity, and Equality," *Journal of Religion,* Vol. 22 (1942), pp. 152–153.
14. Irving Stone, *Dear Theo: The Autobiography of Vincent van Gogh* (Houghton Mifflin, Boston, 1937), p. 441.
15. Quoted by Walter de la Mare, *Love* (Morrow, New York, 1946), p. 11.
16. Letter to Benjamin Bailey, Nov. 22, 1817.
17. Letter to Richard Woodhouse, Oct. 27, 1818.
18. Letter to George and Thomas Keats, Dec. 21, 1817.
19. *Art* (Frederick A. Stokes Co., Philadelphia, 1914), p. 266.
20. *Art as Experience* (Putnam, New York, 1934), p. 46.
21. John Hospers, "Problems of Aesthetics," in Paul Edwards (ed.), *The Encyclopedia of Philosophy* (Macmillan and Free Press, New York, 1967), Vol. I, p. 38.
22. *On the Aesthetic Education of Man in a Series of Letters,* edited and translated by Elizabeth M. Wilkinson and L. A. Willoughby (Clarendon Press, Oxford, 1967), p. 183.
23. Morris Weitz, *Philosophy of the Arts* (Harvard University Press, Cambridge, Mass., 1950), p. 2.
24. See H. L. A. Hart, "Positivism and the Separation of Law and Morals" in Frederick A. Olafson (ed.), *Society, Law, and Morality* (Prentice-Hall, Englewood Cliffs, N.J., 1961), especially pp. 450–451. Hart's discussion of the "core" and "penumbra" meanings of legal terms is very suggestive for the analysis of similar meanings in esthetics.
25. Bruce N. Morton, review of Dickie, *Aesthetics: An Introduction* (1971) in *Journal of Aesthetics and Art Criticism,* Vol. 32 (1973), p. 117.
26. Guy Sircello, *Mind and Art* (Princeton University Press, Princeton, N.J., 1972), pp. 27–30.
27. Aristotle, *Ethics,* translated by W. D. Ross (Oxford University Press, London, 1942), #1094b.
28. *Art as Experience* (Putnam, New York, 1934), p. 25.

PART I
The Creative Process

CHAPTER 1

Imitation and Imagination

OSCAR WILDE: Nature's Imitation of Art
E. H. GOMBRICH: Truth and the Stereotype

One of the perennial themes of esthetic theory is the relation of art to nature. In the history of Western thought, the two most influential treatments of this theme are the theory of "imitation," enunciated by Plato and Aristotle, and the theory of "imagination," formulated by Coleridge and other romanticists. The theory of imitation emphasizes the cognitive and realistic elements in art; the theory of imagination stresses the emotional and purely imaginative factors. These contrasting points of view are reflected in the interpretations set forth in this chapter.

Because he was a notorious wit and dandy, Oscar Wilde (1854–1900) sometimes diverted attention from his substantial achievements in poetry, the short story, the novel (*The Picture of Dorian Gray*), and the drama (*Salome, Lady Windermere's Fan, The Importance of Being Earnest*). His ideas, often expressed in essays or dialogues, are almost always worth serious consideration.

His attitude toward art and nature is summed up in his dialogue *The Decay of Lying*:

> My own experience is that the more we study Art, the less we care for Nature. What Art really reveals to us is Nature's lack of design, her curious crudities, her extraordinary monotony, her absolutely unfinished condition. Nature has good intentions, of course, but, as Aristotle once said, she cannot carry them out.

With this point of view, Wilde swings to an extreme emphasis upon imagination rather than imitation.

With his flair for paradox, he gave to the theory of imitation an ingenious twist. Instead of maintaining that art imitates nature, he contended that nature imitates art. The art provides a kind of education of the imagination and the senses, so that we see in nature what art has prepared us to see. After the impressionist painters have done their work, for example, we can behold impressionist landscapes in nature that were never seen before. Similarly, human life imitates art, not the other way round. Young ladies imitate the kind of beauty found in paintings of Rossetti and Burne-Jones. Underneath this light-hearted bantering is an attack on representationalism in art and utilitarian moralism in life.

Against the practical man or the moralist, Wilde asserts that "all art is perfectly useless," and in that its excellence lies. He wants life to be pure artifice—the adopting of a role and playing it to perfection. "The first duty of life is to be as artificial as possible. What the second duty is no one has as yet discovered." Moral standards have nothing to do with art: "The fact of a man being a poisoner is nothing against his prose." The following Preface to *The Picture of Dorian Gray* sums up his esthetic creed.

Estheticism is often associated with the 1890s, the period of Aubrey Beardsley and James McNeill Whistler; but the belief in "art for art's sake" has persisted in the twentieth century. An outlook akin to Wilde's, although expressed with less flippancy, was cultivated in the "Bloomsbury Circle," of which Clive Bell (see Chapter 9) was an articulate spokesman. The ideal of Bell, like that of Wilde, is the heightening of esthetic experience as the supreme value. He and Wilde force us to consider the place of art in our scheme of life.

While not sharing Wilde's amoralism or estheticism, Ernst H. Gombrich (1909–   ) rejects the naïve theory of imitation. Formerly professor of fine art at both Oxford and Cambridge and now Director of the Warburg Institute and professor at the University of London, he has written a profound study of the role of representation and illusion in art. The selection from his influential book, *Art and Illusion,* maintains that there is no "innocent eye" which perceives the world in its bare actuality. The cultural tradition, embodied in the artistic style of each historical period, acts as a selective screen that admits only those features which the prevailing mental set is prepared to recognize. Hence, the artist tends "to see what he paints rather than to paint what he sees," and we who behold the picture see what the painter has taught us to see. Imagination and imitation are intertwined; the objectification of spirit and the subjectification of nature are two parts of the same creative process.

OSCAR WILDE

Nature's Imitation of Art

I. Art and Imitation

Vivian: . . . Paradox though it may seem—and paradoxes are always dangerous things—it is nonetheless true that Life imitates Art far more than Art imitates Life. We have all seen in our own day in England how a certain curious and fascinating type of beauty, invented and emphasized by two imaginative painters, has so influenced Life that whenever one goes to a private view or to an artistic salon one sees, here the mystic eyes of Rossetti's dream, the long ivory throat, the strange square-cut jaw, the loosened shadowy hair that he so ardently loved, there the sweet maidenhood of "The Golden Stair," the blossom-like mouth and weary loveliness of the "Laus Amoris," the passion-pale face of Andromeda, the thin hands and lithe beauty of the Vivien in "Merlin's Dream." And it has always been so. A great artist invents a type, and Life tries to copy it, to reproduce it in a popular form, like an enterprising publisher. Neither Holbein nor Vandyck found in England what they have given us. They brought their types with them, and Life with her keen imitative faculty set herself to supply the master with models. The Greeks, with their quick artistic instinct, understood this, and set in the bride's chamber the statue of Hermes or of Apollo, that she might bear children as lovely as the works of art that she looked at in her rapture or her pain. They knew that Life gains from Art not merely spirituality, depth of thought and feeling, soul-turmoil or soul-peace, but that she can form herself on the very lines and colors of art, and can reproduce the dignity of Phidias as well as the grace of Praxiteles. Hence came their objection to realism. They disliked it on purely social grounds. They felt that it inevitably makes people ugly, and they were perfectly right. We try to improve the conditions of the race by means of good air, free sunlight, wholesome water, and hideous bare buildings for the better housing of the lower orders. But these things merely produce health, they do not produce beauty. For this, Art is required, and the true disciples of the great artist are not his studio-imitators, but those who become like his works of art, be they plastic as in Greek days, or pictorial as in modern times; in a word, Life is Art's best, Art's only pupil. . . .

However, I do not wish to dwell any further upon individual instances. Personal experience is a most vicious and limited circle. All that I desire to point out is the general principle that Life imitates Art far more than Art imitates Life, and I feel sure that if you think seriously about it you will find that it is true. Life holds the mirror up to Art, and either reproduces some strange type imagined by painter or sculptor, or realizes in fact what has been dreamed in fiction. Scientifically speaking, the basis of life—the energy of life, as Aristotle would call it—is simply the desire for expression, and Art is always presenting various forms through which this expression can be attained. Life seizes on them and uses them, even if they be to her own hurt. Young men have committed suicide because Rolla did so, have died by their own hand because by his own hand Werther died. Think of what we owe to the imitation of Christ, of what we owe to the imitation of Cæsar.

Cyril. The theory is certainly a very curious one, but to make it complete you must show that Nature, no less than Life, is an imitation of Art. Are you prepared to prove that?

Vivian. My dear fellow, I am prepared to prove anything.

Cyril. Nature follows the landscape painter then, and takes her effects from him?

Vivian. Certainly. Where, if not from the Impressionists, do we get those wonderful brown fogs that come creeping down our streets, blurring the gas-lamps and changing the houses into monstrous shadows? To whom, if not to them and their master, do we owe the lovely silver mists that brood over our river, and turn to faint forms of fading grace curved bridge and swaying barge? The extraordinary change that has taken place in the climate of London during the last ten years is entirely due to this particular school of Art. You smile. Consider the matter from a scientific or a metaphysical point of view, and you will find that I am right. For what is Nature? Nature is no great mother who has borne us. She is our creation. It is in our brain that she quickens to life. Things are because we see them, and what we see, and how we see it, depends on the Arts that have influenced us. To look at a thing is very different from seeing a thing. One does not see anything until one sees its beauty. Then, and then only, does it come into existence. At present, people see fogs, not because there are fogs, but because poets and painters have taught them the mysterious loveliness of such effects. There may have been fogs for centuries in London. I dare say there were. But no one saw them, and so we do not know anything about them. They did not exist till Art had invented them. Now, it must be admitted, fogs are carried to excess. They have become the mere mannerism of a clique, and the exaggerated realism of their method gives dull people bronchitis. Where the cultured catch an effect, the uncultured catch cold. And so, let us be humane, and invite Art to turn her wonderful eyes elsewhere. She has done so already, indeed. That white quivering sunlight that one sees now in France, with its strange blotches of mauve, and its restless violet shadows, is her latest fancy, and, on the whole, Nature reproduces it quite admirably. Where she used to give us Corots and Daubignys, she gives us now exquisite Monets and entrancing Pissarros. Indeed there are moments—rare, it is true, but still to be observed from time to time—when Nature becomes absolutely modern. Of course, she is not always to be relied upon. The fact is that she is in this unfortunate position. Art creates an incomparable and unique effect, and, having done so, passes on to other things. Nature, upon the other hand, forgetting that imitation can be made the sincerest form of insult, keeps on repeating this effect until we all become absolutely wearied of it. Nobody of any real culture, for instance, ever talks nowadays about the beauty of a sunset. Sunsets are quite old-fashioned. They belong to the time when Turner was the last note in art. To admire them is a distinct sign of provincialism of temperament. Upon the other hand they go on. Yesterday evening Mrs. Arundel insisted on my going to the window and looking at the glorious sky, as she called it. Of course I had to look at it. She is one of those absurdly pretty Philistines, to whom one can deny nothing. And what was it? It was simply a very second-rate Turner, a Turner of a bad period, with all the painter's worst faults exaggerated and overemphasized. . . . I wish the Channel, especially at Hastings, did not look quite so often like a Henry Moore [an English painter of seascapes], grey pearl with yellow lights, but then, when Art is more varied, Nature will, no doubt, be more varied also. That she imitates Art, I don't think even her worst enemy would deny now. It is the one thing that keeps her in touch with civilized man. But have I proved my theory to your satisfaction?

Cyril. You have proved it to my dissatisfaction, which is better. But even admitting this strange imitative instinct in Life and Nature, surely you would acknowledge that Art expresses the temper of its age, the spirit of its time, the moral and social conditions that surround it, and under whose influence it is produced.

Vivian. Certainly not! Art never expresses anything but itself. This is the principle of my new esthetics; and it is this, more than that vital connection between form and substance, on which Mr. Pater dwells, that makes music the type of all the arts. Of course, nations and individuals, with that healthy natural vanity which is the secret of existence, are always under the impression that it is of them that the Muses are talking, always trying to find in the calm dignity of imaginative art some mirror of their own turbid passions, always forgetting that the singer of life is not Apollo, but Marsyas. Remote from reality, and with her eyes turned away from the shadows of the cave, Art reveals her own perfection, and the wondering crowd that watches the opening of the marvellous, many-petalled rose fancies that it is its own history that is being told to it, its own spirit that is finding expression in a new form. But it is not so. The highest art rejects the burden of the human spirit, and gains more from a new medium or a fresh material than she does from any enthusiasm for art, or from any lofty passion, or from any great awakening of the human consciousness. She develops purely on her own lines. She is not symbolic of any age. It is the ages that are her symbols.

Even those who hold that Art is representative of time and place and people cannot help admitting that the more imitative an art is, the less it represents to us the spirit of its age. The evil faces of the Roman emperors look out at us from the foul porphyry and spotted jasper in which the realistic artists of the day delighted to work, and we fancy that in those cruel lips and heavy sensual jaws we can find the secret of the ruin of the Empire. But it was not so. The vices of Tiberius could not destroy that supreme civilization, any more than the virtues of the Antonines could save it. It fell for other, for less interesting reasons. The sibyls and prophets of the Sistine may indeed serve to interpret for some that new birth of the emancipated spirit that we call the Renaissance; but what do the drunken boors and brawling peasants of Dutch art tell us about the great soul of Holland? The more abstract, the more ideal an art is, the more it reveals to us the temper of its age. If we wish to understand a nation by means of its art, let us look at its architecture or its music.

Cyril. I quite agree with you there. The spirit of an age may be best expressed in the abstract ideal arts, for the spirit itself is abstract and ideal. Upon the other hand, for the visible aspect of an age, for its look, as the phrase goes, we must of course go to the arts of imitation.

Vivian. I don't think so. After all, what the imitative arts really give us are merely the various styles of particular artists, or of certain schools of artists. Surely you don't imagine that the people of the Middle Ages bore any resemblance at all to the figures on medieval stained glass, or in medieval stone and wood carving, or on medieval metalwork, or tapestries, or illuminated [manuscripts]. They were probably very ordinary-looking people, with nothing grotesque, or remarkable, or fantastic in their appearance. The Middle Ages, as we know them in art, are simply a definite form of style, and there is no reason at all why an artist with this style should not be produced in the nineteenth century. No great artist ever sees things as they really are. If he did, he would cease to be an artist. Take an example from our own day. I know that you are fond of Japanese things. Now, do you really imagine that the Japanese people, as they are presented to us in art, have any existence? If you do, you have never understood Japanese art at all. The Japanese people are the deliberate self-conscious creation of certain individual artists. If you set a picture by Hokusai, or Hokkei, or any of the great native painters, beside a real Japanese gentleman or lady, you will see that there is not the slightest resemblance between them. The actual people who live in Japan are not unlike the general run of English people; that is to say, they are extremely commonplace, and have nothing curious or extraordinary about them. In fact the whole of Japan is a pure invention. There is no such country, there are no such people. One of our most charming painters went recently to the Land of the Chrysanthemum in the foolish hope of seeing the Japanese. All he saw, all he had the chance of painting, were a few lanterns and some fans. He was quite unable to discover the inhabitants, as his delightful exhibition at Messrs. Dowdeswell's Gallery showed only too well. He did not know that the Japanese people are, as I have said, simply a mode of style, an exquisite fancy of art. And so, if you desire to see a Japanese effect, you will not behave like a tourist and go to Tokyo. On the contrary, you will stay at home, and steep yourself in the work of certain Japanese artists, and then, when you have absorbed the spirit of their style, and caught their imaginative manner of vision, you will go some afternoon and sit in the Park or stroll down Piccadilly, and if you cannot see an absolutely Japanese effect there, you will not see it anywhere. Or, to return again to the past, take as another instance the ancient Greeks. Do you think that Greek art ever tells us what the Greek people were like? Do you believe that the Athenian women were like the stately dignified figures of the Parthenon frieze, or like those marvelous goddesses who sat in the triangular pediments of the same building? If you judge from the art, they certainly were so. But read an authority, like Aristophanes, for instance. You will find that the Athenian ladies laced tightly, wore high-heeled shoes, dyed their hair yellow, painted and rouged their faces, and were exactly like any silly fashionable or fallen creature of our own day. The fact is that we look back on the ages entirely through the medium of Art, and Art, very fortunately, has never once told us the truth.

Cyril. But modern portraits by English painters, what of them? Surely they are like the people they pretend to represent?

Vivian. Quite so. They are so like them that a hundred years from now no one will believe in them. The only portraits in which one believes are portraits where there is very little of the sitter, and a very great deal of the artist. Holbein's drawings of the men and women of his time impress us with a sense of their absolute reality. But this is simply because Holbein compelled life to accept his conditions, to restrain itself within his limitations, to reproduce his type, and to appear as he wished it to appear. It is style that makes us believe in a thing—nothing but style. Most of our modern portrait painters are doomed to absolute oblivion. They never paint what they see. They paint what the public sees, and the public never sees anything.

Cyril. . . . [I]n order to avoid making an error I want you to tell me briefly the doctrines of the new esthetics.

Vivian. Briefly, then, they are these. Art never expresses anything but itself. It has an independent life, just as Thought has, and develops purely on its own lines. It is not necessarily realistic in an age of realism, nor spiritual in an age of faith. So far from being the creation of its time, it is usually in direct opposition to it, and the only history that it preserves for us is the history of its own progress. Sometimes it returns upon its footsteps, and revives some antique form, as happened in the archaistic movement of late Greek Art, and in the pre-Raphaelite movement of our own day. At other times it entirely anticipates its age, and produces in one century work that it takes another century to understand, to appreciate, and to enjoy. In no case does it reproduce its age. To pass from the art of a time to the time itself is the great mistake that all historians commit.

The second doctrine is this. All bad art comes from returning to Life and Nature, and elevating them into ideals. Life and Nature may sometimes be used as part of Art's rough material, but before they are of any real service to Art they must be translated into artistic conventions. The moment Art surrenders its imaginative medium it surrenders everything. As a method Realism is a complete failure, and the two things that every artist should avoid are modernity of form and modernity of subject matter. To us, who live in the nineteenth century, any century is a suitable subject for art except our own. The only beautiful things are the things that do not concern us. It is, to have the pleasure of quoting myself, exactly because Hecuba is nothing to us that her sorrows are so suitable a motive for a tragedy. Besides, it is only the modern that ever becomes old-fashioned. M. Zola sits down to give us a picture of the Second Empire. Who cares for the Second Empire now? It is out of date. Life goes faster than Realism, but Romanticism is always in front of Life.

The third doctrine is that Life imitates Art far more than Art imitates Life. This results not merely from Life's imitative instinct, but from the fact that the self-conscious aim of Life is to find expression, and that Art offers it certain beautiful forms through which it may realize that energy. It is a theory that has ever been put forward before, but it is extremely fruitful, and throws an entirely new light upon the history of Art.

It follows, as a corollary from this, that external Nature also imitates Art. The only effects that she can show us are effects that we have already seen through poetry, or in paintings. This is the secret of Nature's charm, as well as the explanation of Nature's weakness.

The final revelation is that Lying, the telling of beautiful untrue things, is the proper aim of Art. But of this I think I have spoken at sufficient length. And now let us go out on the terrace, where "droops the milk-white peacock like a ghost," while the evening star "washes the dusk with silver." At twilight Nature becomes a wonderfully suggestive effect, and is not without loveliness, though perhaps its chief use is to illustrate quotations from the poets. Come! We have talked long enough.

—"The Decay of Lying" in *Intentions and the Soul of Man* (1891)

II. Art for Art's Sake

The artist is the creator of beautiful things.

To reveal art and conceal the artist is art's aim.

The critic is he who can translate into another manner or a new material his impression of beautiful things.

The highest, as the lowest, form of criticism is a mode of autobiography.

Those who find ugly meanings in beautiful things are corrupt without being charming. This is a fault.

Those who find beautiful meanings in beautiful things are the cultivated. For these there is hope.

They are the elect to whom beautiful things mean only Beauty.

There is no such thing as a moral or an immoral book. Books are well written or badly written. That is all.

The nineteenth-century dislike of Realism is the rage of Caliban seeing his own face in a glass.

The nineteenth-century dislike of Romanticism is the rage of Caliban not seeing his own face in a glass.

The moral and immoral life of man forms part of the subject matter of the artist, but the morality of art consists in the perfect use of an imperfect medium.

No artist desires to prove anything. Even things that are true can be proved.

No artist has ethical sympathies. An ethical sympathy in an artist is an unpardonable mannerism of style.

No artist is ever morbid. The artist can express everything.

Thought and language are to the artist instruments of an art.

Vice and virtue are to the artist materials for an art.

From the point of view of form, the type of all the arts is the art of the musician. From the point of view of feeling, the actor's craft is the type.

All art is at once surface and symbol.

Those who go beneath the surface do so at their peril.

Those who read the symbol do so at their peril.

It is the spectator, and not life, that art really mirrors.

Diversity of opinion about a work of art shows that the work is new, complex, and vital.

When critics disagree the artist is in accord with himself.

We can forgive a man for making a useful thing as long as he does not admire it. The only excuse for making a useless thing is that one admires it intensely.

All art is quite useless.

—Preface to *The Picture of Dorian Gray* (1891)

E. H. GOMBRICH

Truth and the Stereotype[1]

The schematism by which our understanding deals with the phenomenal world . . . is a skill so deeply hidden in the human soul that we shall hardly guess the secret trick that Nature here employs.

IMMANUEL KANT, *Kritik der reinen Vernunft*

I

In his charming autobiography, the German illustrator Ludwig Richter relates how he and his friends, all young art students in Rome in the 1820s, visited the famous beauty spot of Tivoli and sat down to draw. They looked with surprise, but hardly with approval, at a group of French artists who approached the place with enormous baggage, carrying large quantities of paint which they applied to the canvas with big, coarse brushes. The Germans, perhaps roused by this self-confident artiness, were determined on the opposite approach. They selected the hardest, best-pointed pencils, which could render the motif firmly and minutely to its finest detail, and each bent down over his small piece of paper, trying to transcribe what he saw with the utmost fidelity. "We fell in love with every blade of grass, every tiny twig, and refused to let anything escape us. Everyone tried to render the motif as objectively as possible."

Nevertheless, when they then compared the fruits of their efforts in the evening, their transcripts differed to a surprising extent. The mood, the color, even the outline of the motif had undergone a subtle transformation in each of them. Richter goes on to describe how these different versions reflected the different dispositions of the four friends, for instance, how the melancholy painter had straightened the exuberant contours and emphasized the blue tinges. We might say he gives an illustration of the famous definition by Emile Zola, who called a work of art "a corner of nature seen through a temperament."

It is precisely because we are interested in this definition that we must probe it a little further. The "temperament" or "personality" of the artist, his selective preferences, may be one of the reasons for the transformation which the motif undergoes under the artist's hands, but there must be others—everything, in fact, which we bundle together into the word "style," the style of the period and the style of the artist. When this transformation is very noticeable we say the motif has been greatly "stylized," and the corollary to this observation is that those who happen to be interested in the motif, for one reason or another, must learn to discount the style. This is part of that natural adjustment, the change in what I call "mental set," which we all perform quite automatically when looking at old illustrations. We can "read" the Bayeux tapestry without reflecting on its countless "deviations from reality." We are not tempted for a moment to think the trees at Hastings in 1066 looked like palmettes and the ground at that time consisted of scrolls. It is an extreme example, but it brings out the all-important fact that the word "stylized" somehow tends to beg the question. It implies there was a special activity by which the artist transformed the trees, much as the Victorian designer was taught to study the forms of flowers before he turned them into patterns. It was a practice which chimed in well with ideas of Victorian architecture, when railways and factories were built first and then adorned with the marks of a style. It was not the practice of earlier times.

The very point of Richter's story, after all, is that style rules even where the artist wishes to reproduce nature faithfully, and trying to analyze these limits to objectivity may help us get nearer to the riddle of style. One of these limits . . . is indicated in Richter's story by the contrast between coarse brush and fine pencil. The artist, clearly, can render only what his tool and his medium are capable of rendering. His technique restricts his freedom of choice. The features and relationships the pencil picks out will differ from those the brush can indicate. Sitting in front of his motif, pencil in hand, the artist will, therefore, look out for those aspects which can be rendered in lines—as we say in a pardonable abbreviation, he will tend to see his motif in terms of lines, while, brush in hand, he sees it in terms of masses.

The question of why style should impose similar limitations is less easily answered, least of all when we do not know whether the artist's intentions were the same as those of Richter and his friends.

Historians of art have explored the regions where Cézanne and van Gogh set up their easels and have photographed their motifs. Such comparisons will always retain their fascination since they almost allow us to look over the artist's shoulder—and who does not wish he had this privilege? But however instructive such confrontations may be when handled with care, we must clearly beware of the fallacy of "stylization." Should we believe the photograph represents the "objective truth" while the painting records the artist's subjective vision—the way he transformed "what he saw"? Can we here compare "the image on the retina" with the "image in the mind"? Such speculations easily lead into a morass of unprovables. Take the image on the artist's retina. It sounds scientific enough, but actually there never was *one* such image which we could single out for comparison with either photograph or painting. What there was was an endless succession of innumerable images as the painter scanned the landscape in front of him, and these images sent a complex pattern of impulses through the optic nerves to his brain. Even the artist knew nothing of these events, and we know even less. How far the picture that formed in his mind corresponded to or deviated from the photograph it is even less profitable to ask. What we do know is that these artists went out into nature to look for material for a picture and their artistic wisdom led them to organize the elements of the landscape into works of art of marvelous complexity that bear as much relationship to a surveyor's record as a poem bears to a police report.

Does this mean, then, that we are altogether on a useless quest? That artistic truth differs so much from prosaic truth that the question of objectivity must never be asked? I do not think so. We must only be a little more circumspect in our formulation of the question.

II

The National Gallery in Washington possesses a landscape painting by a nineteenth-century artist which almost seems made to clarify this issue.

It is an attractive picture by George Inness of "The Lackawanna Valley," which we know from the master's son was commissioned in 1855 as an advertisement for a railroad. At the time there was only one track running into the roundhouse, "but the president insisted on having four or five painted in, easing his conscience by explaining that the road would eventually have them." Inness protested, and we can see that when he finally gave in for the sake of his family, he shamefacedly hid the patch with the nonexistent tracks behind puffs of smoke. To him this patch was a lie, and no esthetic explanation about mental images or higher truth could have disputed this away.

But, strictly speaking, the lie was not in the painting. It was in the advertisement, if it claimed by caption or implication that the painting gave accurate information about the facilities of the railway's roundhouses. In a different context the same picture might have illustrated a true statement—for instance, if the president had taken it to a shareholders' meeting to demonstrate improvements he was anxious to make. Indeed in that case, Inness' rendering of the nonexistent tracks might conceivably have given the engineer some hints about where to lay them. It would have served as a sketch or blueprint.

Logicians tell us—and they are not people to be easily gainsaid—that the terms "true" and "false" can only be applied to statements, propositions. And whatever may be the usage of critical parlance, a picture is never a statement in that sense of the term. It can no more be true or false than a statement can be blue or green. Much confusion has been caused in esthetics by disregarding this simple fact. It is an understandable confusion because in our culture pictures are usually labeled, and labels, or captions, can be understood as abbreviated statements. When it is said "the camera cannot lie," this confusion is apparent. Propaganda in wartime often made use of photographs falsely labeled to accuse or exculpate one of the warring parties. Even in scientific illustrations it is the caption which determines the truth of the picture. In a *cause célèbre* of the last century, the embryo of a pig, labeled as a human embryo to prove a theory of evolution, brought about the downfall of a great reputation. Without much reflection, we can all expand into statements the laconic captions we find in museums and books. When we read the name "Ludwig Richter" under a landscape painting, we know we are thus informed that he painted it and can begin arguing whether this information is true or false. When we read "Tivoli," we infer the picture is to be taken as a view of that spot, and we can again agree or disagree with the label. How and when we agree, in such a case, will largely depend on what we want to know about the object represented. The Bayeux tapestry, for instance, tells us there was a battle at Hastings. It does not tell us what Hastings "looked like."

Now the historian knows that the information pictures were expected to provide differed widely in different periods. Not only were images scarce in the past, but so were the public's opportunities to check their captions.

How many people ever saw their ruler in the flesh at sufficiently close quarters to recognize his likeness? How many traveled widely enough to tell one city from another? It is hardly surprising, therefore, that pictures of people and places changed their captions with sovereign disregard for truth. The print sold on the market as a portrait of a king would be altered to represent his successor or enemy.

There is a famous example of this indifference to truthful captions in one of the most ambitious publishing projects of the early printing press, Hartmann Schedel's so-called "Nuremberg Chronicle" with woodcuts by Dürer's teacher Wolgemut. What an opportunity such a volume should give the historian to see what the world was like at the time of Columbus! But as we turn the pages of this big folio, we find the same woodcut of a medieval city recurring with different captions as Damascus, Ferrara, Milan, and Mantua. Unless we are prepared to believe these cities were as indistinguishable from one another as their suburbs may be today, we must conclude that neither the publisher nor the public minded whether the captions told the truth. All they were expected to do was to bring home to the reader that these names stood for cities.

These varying standards of illustration and documentation are of interest to the historian of representation precisely because he can soberly test the information supplied by picture and caption without becoming entangled too soon in problems of esthetics. Where it is a question of information imparted by the image, the comparison with the correctly labeled photograph should be of obvious value. Three topographical prints representing various approaches to the perfect picture post card should suffice to exemplify the results of such an analysis.

The first shows a view of Rome from a German sixteenth-century newssheet reporting a catastrophic flood when the Tiber burst its banks. Where in Rome could the artist have seen such a timber structure, a castle with black-and-white walls, and a steep roof such as might be found in Nuremberg? Is this also a view of a German town with a misleading caption? Strangely enough, it is not. The artist, whoever he was, must have made some effort to portray the scene, for this curious building turns out to be the Castel Sant' Angelo in Rome, which guards the bridge across the Tiber. A comparison with a photograph shows that it does embody quite a number of features which belong or belonged to the castle: the angel on the roof that gives it its name, the main round bulk, founded on Hadrian's mausoleum, and the outworks with the bastions that we know were there.

I am fond of this coarse woodcut because its very crudeness allows us to study the mechanism of portrayal as in a slow-motion picture. There is no question here of the artist's having deviated from the motif in order to express his mood or his esthetic preferences. It is doubtful, in fact, whether the designer of the woodcut ever saw Rome. He probably adapted a view of the city in order to illustrate the sensational news. He knew the Castel Sant' Angelo to be a castle, and so he selected from the drawer of his mental stereotypes the appropriate cliché for a castle—a German *Burg* with its timber structure and high-pitched roof. But he did not simply repeat his stereotype—he adapted it to its particular function by embodying certain distinctive features which he knew belonged to that particular building in

Rome. He supplies some information over and above the fact that there is a castle by a bridge.

Once we pay attention to this principle of the adapted stereotype, we also find it where we would be less likely to expect it: that is, within the idiom of illustrations, which look much more flexible and therefore plausible.

The example from the seventeenth century, from the views of Paris by that well-known and skillful topographical artist Matthäus Merian, represents Notre Dame and gives, at first, quite a convincing rendering of that famous church. Comparison with the real building, however, demonstrates that Merian has proceeded in exactly the same way as the anonymous German woodcutter. As a child of the seventeenth century, his notion of a church is that of a lofty symmetrical building with large, rounded windows, and that is how he designs Notre Dame. He places the transept in the center with four large, rounded windows on either side, while the actual view shows seven narrow, pointed Gothic windows to the west and six in the choir. Once more portrayal means for Merian the adaptation or adjustment of his formula or scheme for churches to a particular building through the addition of a number of distinctive features—enough to make it recognizable and even acceptable to those who are not in search of architectural information. If this happened to be the only document extant to tell us about the Cathedral of Paris, we would be very much misled.

One last example in this series: a nineteenth-century lithograph of Chartres Cathedral, done in the heyday of English topographical art. Here, surely, we might expect a faithful visual record. By comparison with the previous instances, the artist really gives a good deal of accurate information about that famous building. But he, too, it turns out, cannot escape the limitations which his time and interests impose on him. He is a romantic to whom the French cathedrals are the greatest flowers of the Gothic centuries, the true age of faith. And so he conceives of Chartres as a Gothic structure with pointed arches and fails to record the Romanesque rounded windows of the west façade, which have no place in his universe of form.

I do not want to be misunderstood here. I do not want to prove by these examples that all representation must be inaccurate or that all visual documents before the advent of photography must be misleading. Clearly, if we had pointed out to the artist his mistake, he could have further modified his scheme and rounded the windows. My point is rather that such matching will always be a step-by-step process—how long it takes and how hard it is will depend on the choice of the initial schema to be adapted to the task of serving as a portrait. I believe that in this respect these humble documents do indeed tell us a lot about the procedure of any artist who wants to make a truthful record of an individual form. He begins not with his visual impression but with his idea or concept: the German artist with his concept of a castle that he applies as well as he can to that individual castle, Merian with his idea of a church, and the lithographer with his stereotype of a cathedral. The individual visual information, those distinctive features I have mentioned, are entered, as it were, upon a pre-existing blank or formulary. And, as often happens with blanks, if they have no provisions for certain kinds of information we consider essential, it is just too bad for the information.

The comparison, by the way, between the formularies of administration and the artist's stereotypes is not my invention. In medieval parlance there was one word for both, a *simile*, or pattern, that is applied to individual incidents in law no less than in pictorial art.

And just as the lawyer or the statistician could plead that he could never get hold of the individual case without some sort of framework provided by his forms or blanks, so the artist could argue that it makes no sense to look at a motif unless one has learned how to classify and catch it within the network of a schematic form. This, at least, is the conclusion to which psychologists have come who knew nothing of our historical series but who set out to investigate the procedure anyone adopts when copying what is called a "nonsense figure," an inkblot, let us say, or an irregular patch. By and large, it appears, the procedure is always the same. The draftsman tries first to classify the blot and fit it into some sort of familiar schema—he will say, for instance, that it is triangular or that it looks like a fish. Having selected such a schema to fit the form approximately, he will proceed to adjust it, noticing for instance that the triangle is rounded at the top, or that the fish ends in a pigtail. Copying, we learn from these experiments, proceeds through the rhythms of schema and correction. The schema is not the product of a process of "abstraction," of a tendency to "simplify"; it represents the first approximate, loose category which is gradually tightened to fit the form it is to reproduce.

III

One more important point emerges from these psychological discussions of copying: it is dangerous to confuse the way a figure is drawn with the way it is seen. "Reproducing the simplest figures," writes Professor Zangwill, "constitutes a process itself by no means psychologically simple. This process typically displays an essentially constructive or reconstructive character, and with the subjects employed, reproduction was mediated preeminently through the agency of verbal and geometrical formulae. . . ."

If a figure is flashed on a screen for a short moment, we cannot retain it without some appropriate classification. The label given it will influence the choice of a schema. If we happen to hit on a good description we will succeed best in the task of reconstruction. In a famous investigation by F. C. Bartlett, students had to draw such a "nonsense figure" from memory. Some called it a pickax and consequently drew it with pointed prongs. Others accepted it as an anchor and subsequently exaggerated the size of the ring. There was only one person who reproduced the shape correctly. He was a student who had labeled the shape for himself "a pre-historic battle axe." Maybe he was trained in classifying such objects and was therefore able to portray the figure that happened to correspond to a schema with which he was familiar.

Where such a pre-existing category is lacking, distortion sets in. Its effects become particularly amusing when the psychologist imitates the parlor game of "drawing consequences." Thus F. C. Bartlett had an

Egyptian hieroglyph copied and recopied till it gradually assumed the familiar shape and formula of a pussycat.

To the art historian these experiments are of interest because they help to clarify certain fundamentals. The student of medieval art, for instance, is constantly brought up against the problem of tradition through copy. Thus the copies of classical coins by Celtic and Teutonic tribes have become fashionable of late as witnesses to the barbaric "will-to-form." These tribes, it is implied, rejected classical beauty in favor of the abstract ornament. Maybe they really disapproved of naturalistic shapes, but if they did we would need other evidence. The fact that in being copied and recopied the image became assimilated into the schemata of their own craftsmen demonstrates the same tendency which made the German woodcut transform the Castel Sant' Angelo into a timbered *Burg*. The "will-to-form" is rather a "will-to-make-conform," the assimilation of any new shape to the schemata and patterns an artist has learned to handle.

The Northumbrian scribes were marvelously skilled in the weaving of patterns and the shaping of letters. Confronted with the task of copying the image of a man, the symbol of St. Matthew, from a very different tradition, they were quite satisfied to build it up from those units they could handle so well. The solution in the famous Echternach Gospels is so ingenious as to arouse our admiration. It is creative, not because it differs from the presumed prototype—Bartlett's pussycat also differs from the owl—but because it copes with the challenge of the unfamiliar in a surprising and successful way. The artist handles the letter forms as he handles his medium, with complete assurance in creating from it the symbolic image of a man.

But did the designer of the Bayeux tapestry act very differently? He was obviously trained in the intricate interlace work of eleventh-century ornament and adjusted these forms as far as he thought necessary to signify trees. Within his universe of form this procedure was both ingenious and consistent.

Could he have done otherwise? Could he have inserted naturalistic renderings of beeches or firs if only he had wanted to? The student of art is generally discouraged from asking this question. He is supposed to look for explanations of style in the artist's will rather than in his skill. Moreover, the historian has little use for questions of might-have-been. But is not this reluctance to ask about the degree of freedom that exists for artists to change and modify their idiom one of the reasons why we have made so little progress in the explanation of style?

In the study of art no less than in the study of man, the mysteries of success are frequently best revealed through an investigation of failures. Only a pathology of representation will give us some insight into the mechanisms which enabled the masters to handle this instrument with such assurance.

Not only must we surprise the artist when he is confronted with an unfamiliar task that he cannot easily adjust to his means; we must also know that his aim was in fact portrayal. Given these conditions, we may do without the actual comparison between photograph and representation that was our starting point. For, after all, nature is sufficiently uniform to allow us to judge the information value of a picture even when we have never seen the specimen portrayed. The beginnings of illustrated reportage, therefore, provide another test case where we need have no doubt about the will and can, consequently, concentrate on the skill.

IV

Perhaps the earliest instance of this kind dates back more than three thousand years, to the beginnings of the New Kingdom in Egypt, when the Pharaoh Thutmose included in his picture chronicle of the Syrian campaign a record of plants he had brought back to Egypt. The inscription, though somewhat mutilated, tells us that Pharoah pronounces these pictures to be "the truth." Yet botanists have found it hard to agree on what plants may have been meant by these renderings. The schematic shapes are not sufficiently differentiated to allow secure identification.

An even more famous example comes from the period when medieval art was at its height, from the volume of plans and drawings by the Gothic master builder, Villard de Honnecourt, which tells us so much about the practice and outlook of the men who created the French cathedrals. Among the many architectural, religious, and symbolic drawings of striking skill and beauty to be found in this volume, there is a curiously stiff picture of a lion, seen *en face*. To us, it looks like an ornamental or heraldic image, but Villard's caption tells us that he regarded it in a different light: *"Et sacies bien,"* he says, *"qu'il fu contrefais al vif."* "Know well that it is drawn from life." These words obviously had a very different meaning for Villard than they have for us. He can have meant only that he had drawn his schema in the presence of a real lion. How much of his visual observation he allowed to enter into the formula is a different matter.

Once more the broadsheets of popular art show us to what extent this attitude survived the Renaissance. The letterpress of a German woodcut from the sixteenth century informs us that we here see "the exact counterfeit" of a kind of locust that invaded Europe in menacing swarms. But the zoologist would be rash to infer from this inscription that there existed an entirely different species of creatures that has never been recorded since. The artist had again used a familiar schema, compounded of animals he had learned to portray, and the traditional formula for locusts that he knew from an Apocalypse where the locust plague was illustrated. Perhaps the fact that the German word for a locust is *Heupferd (hay horse)* tempted him to adopt a schema of a horse for the rendering of the insect's prance.

The creation of such a name and the creation of the image have, in fact, much in common. Both proceed by classifying the unfamiliar with the familiar, or more exactly, to remain in the zoological sphere, by creating a subspecies. Since the locust is called a kind of horse it must therefore share some of its distinctive features.

The caption of a Roman print of 1601 is as explicit as that of the German woodcut. It claims the engraving represents a giant whale that had been washed ashore near Ancona the same year and "was drawn accurately from nature." ("*Ritratto qui dal naturale appunto.*") The claim would be more trustworthy if there did not exist an earlier print recording a similar "scoop" from the Dutch coast in 1598. But surely the Dutch artists of the late sixteenth century, those masters of realism, would be able to portray a whale? Not quite, it seems, for the creature looks suspiciously as if it had ears, and whales with ears, I am assured on higher authority, do not exist. The draftsman probably mistook one of the whale's flippers for an ear and therefore placed it far too close to the eye. He, too, was misled by a familiar schema, the schema of the typical head. To draw an unfamiliar sight presents greater difficulties than is usually realized. And this, I suppose, was also the reason why the Italian preferred to copy the whale from another print. We need not doubt the part of the caption that tells the news from Ancona, but to portray it again "from the life" was not worth the trouble.

In this respect, the fate of exotic creatures in the illustrated books of the last few centuries before the advent of photography is as instructive as it is amusing. When Dürer published his famous woodcut of a rhinoceros, he had to rely on secondhand evidence which he filled in from his own imagination, colored, no doubt, by what he had learned of the most famous of exotic beasts, the dragon with its armored body. Yet it has been shown that this half-invented creature served as a model for all renderings of the rhinoceros, even in natural-history books, up to the eighteenth century. When, in 1790, James Bruce published a drawing of the beast in his *Travels to Discover the Source of the Nile*, he proudly showed that he was aware of this fact:

"The animal represented in this drawing is a native of Tcherkin, near Ras el Feel . . . and this is the first drawing of the rhinoceros with a double horn that has ever yet been presented to the public. The first figure of the Asiatic rhinoceros, the species having but one horn, was painted by Albert Dürer, from the life. . . . It was wonderfully ill-executed in all its parts, and was the origin of all the monstrous forms under which that animal has been painted, ever since. . . . Several modern philosophers have made amends for this in our days; Mr. Parsons, Mr. Edwards, and the Count de Buffon, have given good figures of it from life; they have indeed some faults, owing chiefly to preconceived prejudices and inattention. . . . This . . . is the first that has been published with two horns, it is designed from the life, and is an African."

If proof were needed that the difference between the medieval draftsman and his eighteenth-century descendant is only one of degree, it could be found here. For the illustration, presented with such flourishes of trumpets, is surely not free from "preconceived prejudices" and the all-pervading memory of Dürer's woodcut. We do not know exactly what species of rhinoceros the artist saw at Ras el Feel, and the comparison of his picture with a photograph taken in Africa may not, therefore, be quite fair. But I am told that none of the species known to zoologists corresponds to the engraving claimed to be drawn *al vif!*

The story repeats itself whenever a rare specimen is introduced into Europe. Even the elephants that populate the paintings of the sixteenth and seventeenth centuries have been shown to stem from a very few archetypes and to embody all their curious features, despite the fact that information about elephants was not particularly hard to come by.

These examples demonstrate, in somewhat grotesque magnification, a tendency which the student of art has learned to reckon with. The familiar will always remain the likely starting point for the rendering of the unfamiliar; an existing representation will always exert its spell over the artist even while he strives to record the truth. Thus it was remarked by ancient critics that several famous artists of antiquity had made a strange mistake in the portrayal of horses: they had represented them with eyelashes on the lower lid, a feature which belongs to the human eye but not to that of the horse. A German ophthalmologist who studied the eyes of Dürer's portraits, which to the layman appear to be such triumphs of painstaking accuracy, reports somewhat similar mistakes. Apparently not even Dürer knew what eyes "really look like."

This should not give us cause for surprise, for the greatest of all the visual explorers, Leonardo himself, has been shown to have made mistakes in his anatomical drawings. Apparently he drew features of the human heart which Galen made him expect but which he cannot have seen.

The study of pathology is meant to increase our understanding of health. The sway of schemata did not prevent the emergence of an art of scientific illustration that sometimes succeeds in packing more correct visual information into the image than even a photograph contains. But the diagrammatic maps of muscles in our illustrated anatomies are not "transcripts" of things seen but the work of trained observers who build up the picture of a specimen that has been revealed to them in years of patient study.

Now in this sphere of scientific illustration it obviously makes sense to say that Thutmose's artists or Villard himself could not have done what the modern illustrator can do. They lacked the relevant schemata, their starting point was too far removed from their motif, and their style was too rigid to allow a sufficiently supple adjustment. For so much certainly emerges from a study of portrayal in art: you cannot create a faithful image out of nothing. You must have learned the trick if only from other pictures you have seen.

V

In our culture, where pictures exist in such profusion, it is difficult to demonstrate this basic fact. There are freshmen in art schools who have facility in the objective rendering of motifs that would appear to belie this assumption. But those who have given art classes in other cultural settings tell a different story. James Cheng, who taught painting to a group of Chinese trained in different conventions, once told me of a sketching expedition he made with his students to a famous beauty spot, one of Peking's old city gates. The task baffled them. In the end, one of the students asked to be given at least a picture post card of the building so that they would have something to copy. It is stories such as these, stories of breakdowns, that explain why art has a history and artists need a style adapted to a task.

I cannot illustrate this revealing incident. But luck allows us to study the next stage, as it were—the adjustment of the traditional vocabulary of Chinese art to the unfamiliar task of topographical portrayal in the Western sense. For some decades Chiang Yee, a Chinese writer and painter of great gifts and charm, has delighted us with contemplative records of the Silent Traveller, books in which he tells of his encounters with scenes and people of the English and Irish countryside and elsewhere. I take an illustration from the volume on the English Lakeland.

It is a view of Derwentwater. Here we have crossed the line that separates documentation from art. Mr. Chiang Yee certainly enjoys the adaptation of the Chinese idiom to a new purpose; he wants us to see the English scenery for once "through Chinese eyes." But it is precisely for this reason that it is so instructive to compare his view with a typical "picturesque" rendering from the Romantic period. We see how the relatively rigid vocabulary of the Chinese tradition acts as a selective screen which admits only the features for which schemata exist. The artist will be attracted by motifs which can be rendered in his idiom. As he scans the landscape, the sights which can be matched successfully with the schemata he has learned to handle will leap forward as centers of attention. The style, like the medium, creates a mental set which makes the artist look for certain aspects in the scene around him that he can render. Painting is an activity, and the artist will therefore tend to see what he paints rather than to paint what he sees.

It is this interaction between style and preference which Nietzsche summed up in his mordant comment on the claims of realism:

> "All Nature faithfully"—But by what feint
> Can Nature be subdued to art's constraint?
> Her smallest fragment is still infinite!
> And so he paints but what he likes in it.
> What does he like? He likes, what he can paint!

There is more in this observation than just a cool reminder of the limitations of artistic means. We catch a glimpse of the reasons why these limitations will never obtrude themselves within the domain of art itself. Art presupposes mastery, and the greater the artist the more surely will he instinctively avoid a task where his mastery would fail to serve him. The layman may wonder whether Giotto could have painted a view of Fiesole in sunshine, but the historian will suspect that, lacking the means, he would not have wanted to, or rather that he could not have wanted to. We like to assume, somehow, that where there is a will there is also a way, but in matters of art the maxim should read that only where there is a way is there also a will. The individual can enrich the ways and means that his culture offers him; he can hardly wish for something that he has never known is possible.

The fact that artists tend to look for motifs for which their style and training equip them explains why the problem of representational skill looks different to the historian of art and to the historian of visual information. The one is concerned with success, the other must also observe the failures. But these failures suggest that we sometimes assume a little rashly that the ability of art to portray the visible world developed, as it were, along a uniform front. We know of specialists in art—of Claude Lorrain, the master of landscape whose figure paintings were poor, of Frans Hals who concentrated almost exclusively on portraits. May not skill as much as will have dictated this type of preference? Is not all naturalism in the art of the past selective?

A somewhat Philistine experiment would suggest that it is. Take the next magazine containing snapshots of crowds and street scenes and walk with it through any art gallery to see how many gestures and types that occur in life can be matched from old paintings. Even Dutch genre paintings that appear to mirror life in all its bustle and variety will turn out to be created from a limited number of types and gestures, much as the apparent realism of the picaresque novel or of Restoration comedy still applies and modifies stock figures which can be traced back for centuries. There is no neutral naturalism. The artist, no less than the writer, needs a vocabulary before he can embark on a "copy" of reality.

VI

Everything points to the conclusion that the phrase the "language of art" is more than a loose metaphor, that even to describe the visible world in images we need a developed system of schemata. This conclusion rather clashes with the traditional distinction, often discussed in the eighteenth century, between spoken words which are conventional signs and painting which uses "natural" signs to "imitate" reality. It is a plausible distinction, but it has led to certain difficulties. If we assume, with this tradition, that natural signs can simply be copied from nature, the history of art represents a complete puzzle. It has become increasingly clear since the late nineteenth century that primitive art and child art use a language of symbols rather than "natural signs." To account for this fact it was postulated that there must be a special kind of art grounded not on seeing but rather on knowledge, an art which operates with "conceptual images." The child—it is argued—does not look at trees; he is satisfied with the "conceptual" schema of a tree that fails to correspond to any reality since it does not embody the characteristics of, say, birch or beech, let alone those of individual trees. This reliance on construction rather than on imitation was attributed to the peculiar mentality of children and primitives who live in a world of their own.

But we have come to realize that this distinction is unreal. Gustaf Britsch and Rudolf Arnheim have stressed that there is no opposition between the crude map of the world made by a child and the richer map presented in naturalistic images. All art originates in the human mind, in our reactions to the world rather than in the visible world itself, and it is precisely because all art is "conceptual" that all representations are recognizable by their style.

Without some starting point, some initial schema, we could never get hold of the flux of experience. Without categories, we could not sort our impressions. Paradoxically, it has turned out that it matters relatively little what these first categories are. We can always adjust them according to need. Indeed, if the schema remains loose and flexible, such initial vagueness may prove not a hindrance but a help. An entirely fluid system would no longer serve its purpose; it could not register facts because it would lack pigeonholes. But how we arrange the first filing system is not very relevant.

The progress of learning, of adjustment through trial and error, can be compared to the game of "Twenty Questions," where we identify an object through inclusion or exclusion along any network of classes. The traditional initial scheme of "animal, vegetable, or mineral" is certainly neither scientific nor very suitable, but it usually serves us well enough to narrow down our concepts by submitting them to the corrective test of "yes" or "no." The example of this parlor game has become popular of late as an illustration of that process of articulation through which we learn to adjust ourselves to the infinite complexity of this world. It indicates, however crudely, the way in which not only organisms but even machines may be said to "learn" by trial and error. Engineers at their thrilling work on what they call "servo mechanisms," that is, self-adjusting machines, have recognized the importance of some kind of "initiative" on the part of the machine. The first move such a machine may make will be, and indeed must be, a random movement, a shot in the dark. Provided a report of success or failure, hit or miss, can be fed back into the machine, it will increasingly avoid the wrong moves and repeat the correct ones. One of the pioneers in this field has recently described this machine rhythm of schema and correction in a striking verbal formula: he calls all learning "an arboriform stratification of guesses about the world." Arboriform, we may take it, here describes the progressive creation of classes and subclasses such as might be described in a diagrammatic account of "Twenty Questions."

We seem to have drifted far from the discussion of portrayal. But it is certainly possible to look at a portrait as a schema of a head modified by the distinctive features about which we wish to convey information. The American police sometimes employ draftsmen to aid witnesses in the identification of criminals. They may draw any vague face, a random schema, and let witnesses guide their modifications of selected features simply by saying "yes" or "no" to various suggested standard alterations until the face is sufficiently individualized for a search in the files to be profitable. This account of portrait drawing by remote control may well be over-tidy, but as a parable it may serve its purpose. It reminds us that the starting point of a visual record is not knowledge but a guess conditioned by habit and tradition.

Need we infer from this fact that there is no such thing as an objective likeness? That it makes no sense to ask, for instance, whether Chiang Yee's view of Derwentwater is more or less correct than the nineteenth-century lithograph in which the formulas of classical landscapes were applied to the same task? It is a tempting conclusion and one which recommends itself to the teacher of art appreciation because it brings home to the layman how much of what we call "seeing" is conditioned by habits and expectations. It is all the more important to clarify how far this relativism will take us. I believe it rests on the confusion between pictures, words, and statements which we saw arising the moment truth was ascribed to paintings rather than to captions.

If all art is conceptual, the issue is rather simple. For concepts, like pictures, cannot be true or false. They can only be more or less useful for the formation of descriptions. The words of a language, like pictorial formulas, pick out from the flux of events a few signposts which allow us to give direction to our fellow speakers in that game of "Twenty Questions" in which we are engaged. Where the needs of users are similar, the signposts will tend to correspond. We can mostly find equivalent terms in English, French, German, and Latin, and hence the idea has taken root that concepts exist independently of language as the constituents of "reality." But the English language erects a signpost on the roadfork between "clock" and "watch" where the German has only *"Uhr."* The sentence from the German primer, *"Meine Tante hat eine Uhr,"* leaves us in doubt whether the aunt has a clock or a watch. Either of the two translations may be wrong as a description of a fact. In Swedish, by the way, there is an additional roadfork to distinguish between aunts who are "father's sisters," those who are "mother's sisters," and those who are just ordinary aunts. If we were to play our game in Swedish we would need additional questions to get at the truth about the timepiece.

This simple example brings out the fact, recently emphasized by Benjamin Lee Whorf, that language does not give name to pre-existing things or concepts so much as it articulates the world of our experience. The images of art, we suspect, do the same. But this difference in styles or languages need not stand in the way of correct answers and descriptions. The world may be approached from a different angle and the information given may yet be the same.

From the point of view of information there is surely no difficulty in discussing portrayal. To say of a drawing that it is a correct view of Tivoli does not mean, of course, that Tivoli is bounded by wiry lines. It means that those who understand the notation will derive *no false information* from the drawing—whether it gives the contour in a few lines or picks out "every blade of grass" as Richter's friends wanted to do. The complete portrayal might be the one which gives as much correct information about the spot as we would obtain if we looked at it from the very spot where the artist stood.

Styles, like languages, differ in the sequence of articulation and in the number of questions they allow the artist to ask; and so complex is the information that reaches us from the visible world that no picture will ever embody it all. This is not due to the subjectivity of vision but to its richness. Where the artist has to copy a human product he can, of course, produce a facsimile which is indistinguishable from the original. The forger of banknotes succeeds only too well in effacing his personality and the limitations of a period style.

But what matters to us is that the correct portrait, like the useful map, is an end product on a long road through schema and correction. It is not a faithful record of a visual experience but the fruitful construction of a relational model.

Neither the subjectivity of vision nor the sway of conventions need lead us to deny that such a model can be constructed to any required degree of accuracy. What is decisive here is clearly the word "required." The form of representation cannot be divorced from its purpose and the requirements of the society in which the given visual language gains currency.

—*Art and Illusion* (1960; second edition revised, 1961)

Note

1. Footnotes that appear in the original have been omitted.

CHAPTER 2
Emotion

EUGENE VÉRON: Art as the Expression of Emotion
LEO TOLSTOY: The Communication of Emotion
CURT J. DUCASSE: Art and the Language of the Emotions

One of the consequences of the Romantic movement was the shift in emphasis from imitation theories of art to expression and communication theories. The Romantic exaltation of the artist-genius in conjunction with the stress on originality led naturally to theories of this latter type. "Who touches this touches a man," wrote Walt Whitman of his poetry. The assumption was that the subject of the work of art is the artist, especially his inner life of feeling and imagination, and that through the art work the beholder comes into sympathetic communion with a master spirit. With the passing of the Romantic movement, expression theories have persisted in a more sober and analytical form. Theorists of this type contend that the great function of art is to express the whole gamut of human emotions, even the sad and the terrible, and that ugliness may be created for its own expressiveness, not merely as a foil to beauty.

This point of view was formulated by Eugene Véron (1825–1889) in *L'Esthetique* (1878). Véron defines art as the expression of emotion. "The merit of a work of art," he declares, "can be finally measured by the power with which it manifests or interprets the emotion that was its determining cause, and that, for a like reason, must constitute its innermost and supreme unity." Some art, he recognizes, is simply decorative: Its aim is to create beauty. But other art is broadly expressive: Its aim is to express emotions that may be quite unconnected with beauty. We should approach expressive art not with the criterion of beauty or pleasure but with the criterion of expressiveness or significance. The question is not, Does this please me? but, Out of how deep a life does this spring? Great art, to paraphrase Longinus, is the echo of a great soul. But it is the emotional, or subjective, side of the human personality that is expressed; and art is distinguished from science by the predominance of subjectivity over objectivity. Whereas the scientist is one "whose imagination has no modifying influence over the results of his direct observation," the artist is "one whose imagination, impressionability

—in a word, whose personality, is so lively and excitable that it spontaneously transforms everything, dyeing them in its own colors, and unconsciously exaggerating them in accordance with its own preferences."

The main contentions of Véron reappear with altered emphasis in the influential pages of Leo Tolstoy (1828–1910). In certain respects they disagree. Tolstoy thinks *communication* is indispensable to art: Véron defines art simply as the *expression* of emotion. Also, Tolstoy formulates a more antihedonistic and moral interpretation of art. But both maintain that art is the "language" of emotions.

Defining art as the *deliberate* communication of emotions (thus excluding spontaneous yawning, swearing, laughing, or weeping), Tolstoy distinguishes between the *technical adequacy* of the work as a vehicle of emotional communication, and the value and character of the emotions expressed. He thus recognizes that there are two questions to be asked in evaluating a work of art: First, are the emotions of the artist put into effective communicable form? Second, are the emotions worthwhile?

It makes a great difference, he believes, whether the emotions are beneficial or injurious; for art is the great molder of human attitudes —coequal in importance with science. The only emotions, he thinks, that art should transmit are simple and universal feelings that all men can appreciate, and Christian feelings, particularly of love and human brotherhood. He condemns most of the sophisticated art of Western culture, even such masterpieces as those of Shakespeare and Beethoven and his own *Anna Karenina* and *War and Peace*.

Tolstoy took the extreme stand he did partly because he appreciated so vividly the power of art to mold human character. His book is the most impressive statement in modern esthetics of the view that the value of art lies in its immense social usefulness. The noble ideal to which he wished to dedicate art, the universal brotherhood of man, is the more moving because, in his own life, he tried with such intense conviction to abide by it. There have been others, such as the Marxists, who have insisted upon the social utility of art, but never with a greater compassion or sincerity.

Curt John Ducasse (1881–1969), Professor of Philosophy at the University of Washington and later at Brown University, was the foremost American champion of a theory of art akin to that of Véron and Tolstoy. His analytical and empiricist method eliminated most of the ambiguities found in the emotionalist theories of his predecessors. It should be noted that he sides with Véron and against Tolstoy in declaring that expression, not communication, of emotion is the essence of art, and that when artistic communication does occur, it is not the raw emotion but its abstracted "image" or "quality" that is transmitted, so that the work of art has, for example, the capacity to make its beholder "taste, or sample, sadness without actually making him sad." Ducasse calls this "tasting" of the emotional import "ecpathy" or "ecpathizing," which he defines as "an extracting from [the object] of the feeling it embodies."[1]

NOTE

1. Cf. Curt John Ducasse, *The Philosophy of Art* (Dover Publications, New York, 1966), pp. 173–178.

EUGENE VÉRON

Art as the Expression of Emotion

I. GENERAL DEFINITION OF ART

Art, far from being the blossom and fruit of civilization, is rather its germ. It began to give evidence of its existence as soon as man became self-conscious, and is to be found clearly defined in his very earliest works.

By its psychologic origin it is bound up with the constituent principles of humanity. The salient and essential characteristic of man is his incessant cerebral activity, which is propagated and developed by countless acts and works of varied kind. The aim and rule of this activity is the search after *the best*; that is to say, the more and more complete satisfaction of physical and moral wants. This instinct, common to all animals, is seconded in man by an exceptionally well-developed faculty to adapt the means to the end.

The effort to satisfy physical wants has given birth to all industries that defend, preserve, and smooth the path of life; the effort to satisfy the moral wants—of which one of the most important is the gratification of our cerebral activity itself—has created the arts, long before it could give them power sufficient for the conscious elaboration of ideas. The life of sentiment preceded the manifestations of intellectual life by many centuries.

The gratification, *in esse* or *in posse*, of either real or imaginary wants, is the cause of happiness, joy, pleasure, and of all the feelings connected with them; the contrary is marked by grief, sadness, fear, etc.: but in both cases there is emotion to give more or less lively evidence of its existence by means of exterior signs. When expressed by gesture and rhythmic movement, such emotion produces the dance; when by rhythmic notes, music; when by rhythmic words, poetry.

As in another aspect man is essentially sympathetic and his joy or pain is often caused as much by the good or evil fortunes of others as by his own; as, besides, he possesses in a very high degree the faculty of combining series of fictitious facts, and of representing them in colors even more lively than those of reality: it results that the domain of art is of infinite extent for him. For the causes of emotion are multiplied for every man—not only by the number of similar beings who live around him and are attached to him by the more or less closely knit bonds of affection, alliance, similitude of situation or community of ideas and interests; but also, by the never-ending multitude of beings and events that are able to originate or direct the imaginings of poets.

To these elements of emotion and moral enjoyment must be added the combinations of lines, of forms and of colors, the dispositions and opposition of light and shade, etc. The instinctive search after this kind of emotion or pleasure, the special organ of which is the eye, has given birth to what are called the arts of design—sculpture, painting and architecture.

We may say then, by way of general definition, that art is the manifestation of emotion, obtaining external interpretation, now by expressive arrangements of line, form or color, now by a series of gestures, sounds, or words governed by particular rhythmical cadence.

If our definition is exact, we must conclude, from it, that the merit of a work of art, whatever it may be, can be finally measured by the power with which it manifests or interprets the emotion that was its determining cause, and that, for a like reason, must constitute its innermost and supreme unity. . . .

II. What We Admire in a Work of Art Is the Genius of the Artist. Definition of Esthetics

Imitation is no more the aim of art than a mere collection of letters and syllables is the aim of a writer who wishes to express his thoughts and feelings by the aid of the words which they form. The poet arranging his verses, the musician composing his airs and harmonies, are well aware that their real object lies beyond words and notes. This distinction, as we have here explained it, is perhaps less clear in matters of painting and sculpture. Some artists, and these not the least capable, are quite convinced that when they have a model before them, their one duty is to imitate it. And indeed they do nothing else; and, by virtue of such imitation, they succeed in producing works of incontestable artistic value.

Here we have simply a misunderstanding. If an artist were really able to reduce himself to the condition of a copying machine; if he could so far efface and suppress himself as to confine his work to the servile reproduction of all the features and details of an object or event passing before his eyes: the only value his work would possess would be that of a more or less exact *procès verbal,* and it would perforce remain inferior to reality. Where is the artist who would attempt to depict sunlight without taking refuge in some legerdemain, calling to his aid devices which the true sun would despise? But enough of this. Just because he is endowed with sensibility and imaginative power, the artist, in presence of the facts of nature or the events of history, finds himself, whether he will or not, in a peculiar situation. However thorough a realist he may think himself, he does not leave himself to chance. Now, choice of subject alone is enough to prove that, from the very beginning, some preference has existed, the result of a more or less predeterminate impression, and of a more or less unconscious agreement between the character of the object and that of the artist. This impression and agreement he sets to work to embody in outward form; it is the real aim of his work, and its possession gives him claim to the name of artist. Without wishing or even knowing it, he molds the features of nature to his dominant impression and to the idea that caused him to take pencil in hand. His work has an accidental stamp, in addition to that of the permanent genius which constitutes his individuality. Poet, musician, sculptor and architect, all pay more or less strict obedience to the same law. To it, point all those rules of artistic composition which pedantic academicism has subtly multiplied until they contradict each other.

The more of this personal character that a work possesses; the more harmonious its details and their combined expression; the more clearly each part communicates the impression of the artist, whether of grandeur, of melancholy or of joy; in fine, the more that expression of human sensation and will predominates over mere imitation, the better will be its chance of obtaining sooner or later the admiration of the world—always supposing that the sentiment expressed be a generous one, and that the execution be not of such a kind as to repel or baffle connoisseurs. It is not of course impossible that an artist endowed with an ill-regulated or morbid imagination may place himself outside all normal conditions and condemn himself to the eternal misapprehension of the public. Impressions that are too particular, eccentric feelings, fantastic execution or processes, which do nothing to raise the intrinsic value or power of inspiration of a work, may give it so strange and ultra-individual a character that it may become impossible for us to arrive at its real merit. The best qualities, when exaggerated, become faults; and that very personality or individuality which, when added to imitative power, results in a work of art, produces when pushed to extravagance nothing but an enigma.

We see, then, if we have succeeded in making ourselves understood, that the beautiful in art springs mainly from the intervention of the genius of man when more or less excited by special emotion.

A work is beautiful when it bears strong marks of the individuality of its author, of the permanent personality of the artist, and of the more or less accidental impression produced upon him by the sight of the object or event rendered.

In a word, it is from the worth of the artist that that of his work is derived. It is the manifestation of the faculties and qualities he possesses which attracts and fascinates us. The more sympathetic power and individuality that these faculties and qualities display, the easier is it for them to obtain our love and admiration. On the other hand, we, for a similar reason, reject and contemn bold and vulgar works that by their shortcomings demonstrate the moral and intellectual mediocrity of their authors, and prove the latter to have mistaken their vocation.

Consequently, then, beauty in art is a purely human creation. Imitation may be its means, as in sculpture and painting; or, on the other hand, it may have nothing to do with it, as in poetry and music. This beauty is of so peculiar a nature that it may exist even in ugliness itself; inasmuch as the exact reproduction of an ugly model may be a beautiful work of art, by the ensemble of qualities which the composition of it may prove are possessed by its author.

The very theory of imitation is but the incomplete and superficial statement of the ideas which we are here advocating. What is it that we admire in imitation? The resemblance? We have that much better in the object itself. But how is it that the similitude of an ugly object can be beautiful? It is obvious that between the object and its counterfeit some new element intervenes. This element is the personality, or, at least, the skill of the artist. This latter, indeed, is what they admire who will have it that beauty consists in imitation. What these applaud, in fact, is the talent of the artist. If we look below the surface and analyze their admiration we shall find that it is so; whether they mean it or not, what they praise in a work is the worker.

This was the opinion of Bürger, who, in his *Salon* of 1863, says: "In works which interest us the authors in a way substitute themselves for nature. However common or vulgar the latter may be, they have some rare and peculiar way of looking at it. It is Chardin himself whom we admire in his representation of a glass of water. We admire the genius of Rembrandt in the profound and individual character which he imparted to every head that posed before him. Thus did they seem to him, and this explains everything simple or fantastic in his expression and execution."

After all this, we need not stop to refute the theory which would found artistic beauty upon the imitation of "beautiful nature." In spite of the brilliant reputation that its triumph in three academies has given to M. Ch. Sevêyne's book upon the science of beauty, it does not seem to us to be founded upon arguments worthy of respect; it has not shown us where "beautiful nature" *(la belle nature)* is to be found in *Le Pouilleux,* in the *Raft of the Medusa,* in the *Battlefield of Eylau,* in the character of *Tartuffe,* or of *La Marneffe.*

The only beauty in a work of art is that placed there by the artist. It is both the result of his efforts and the foundation of his success. As often as he is struck by any vivid impression—whether moral, intellectual, or physical—and expresses that impression by some outward process—by poetry, music, sculpture, painting or architecture—in such a way as to cause its communication with the soul of spectator or auditor; so often does he produce a work of art the beauty of which will be in exact proportion to the intelligence and depth of the sentiment displayed, and the power shown in giving it outward form.

The union of all these conditions constitutes artistic beauty in its most complete expression.

With a few reservations, then, we may preserve the definition of esthetics which usage has sanctified—*The Science of Beauty.* For the sake of clearness, however, and to prevent confusion, we prefer to call it the *Science of Beauty in Art.* Had not the tyranny of formulae by custom become too strong, we would willingly refrain from using the word "beauty" at all, for it has the drawback of being too exclusively connected with the sense of seeing, and of calling up too much the idea of visible form. The employment of this word became general when *the* art *par excellence* was sculpture. To make it apply to the other arts, it was necessary to foist upon it a series of extensions which deprived it of all accuracy. Language possesses no word more vague or less precise. This absence of precision has perhaps contributed more than might at first be supposed to that confusion of ideas which can alone explain the multiplicity and absurdity of current esthetic theories.

All these inconveniences and obscurities may be avoided by simply putting it thus:

Esthetics is the science whose object is the study and elucidation of the manifestations of artistic genius. . . .

III. Decorative and Expressive Art

There are two distinct kinds of art. The one, decorative art, we understand to be that whose main object is the gratification of the eye and ear, and whose chief means to perfection of form are harmony and grace of contour, diction, or sound. Such art rests upon the desire for beauty, and has nothing in view beyond the peculiar delight caused by the sight of beautiful objects. It has produced admirable works in the past, and may produce them again now or in the future, on condition that its inspiration be sought in actual and existing life, and not in the imitation of works sanctified by time. We must recognize, however, that modern art has no tendency in this latter direction. Beauty no longer suffices for us. Indeed, for the last two thousand years something more has been required; for even among the *chefs d'œuvre* of the Greeks not a few owe their creation to a different sentiment. Some of the great artists of antiquity were certainly occupied with the interpretation of the moral life; and had not time destroyed their painted works, we should, at the present moment, probably be able to show absolute proofs of this tendency. But we may readily dispense with the confirmation which they would have afforded to our arguments; for we find more than sufficient evidence in the avowed character of the music of the Greeks, in many of the most important works of their sculptors, and in most of their great poems.

The chief characteristic of modern art—of art, that is, left to follow its own inspiration free from academic patronage—is power of expression. Through form this, the second kind of art, traces the moral life, and endeavors to occupy man, body and soul, but with no thought of sacrificing the one to the other. It is ever becoming more imbued with the quite modern idea that the whole being is *one,* metaphysicians notwithstanding, and that its aim can only be complete by refusing to separate the organ from its function. The moral life is but the general result of the conditions of the physical. The one is bound to the other by necessary connections which cannot be broken without destroying both. The first care of the artist should be to seek out and grasp the methods of manifestation so as to comprehend and master their unity.

Art, thus understood, demands from its votary an ensemble of intellectual faculties higher and more robust than if founded solely upon an ideal of beauty. Art founded upon the latter notion would be sufficiently served by one possessing an acute sense of the beautiful—the degree of his sensibility being indicated by the plastic perfection of his work. But expressive art demands a capability of being moved by many varying sentiments, demands the power to penetrate beneath outward appearances and to seize a hidden thought, the power to grasp either the permanent characteristic or the particular and momentary emotion; in a word, it demands that complete eloquence of representation which art might have dispensed with while it confined itself to the investigation or delineation of a single expression, but which became absolutely indispensable from the moment that the interpretation of the entire man became its avowed object.

We may say, too, that modern art is doubly expressive; because, while the artist is indicating by form and sound the sentiments and ideas of the personages whom he introduces, he is also by the power and manner of such manifestation giving an unerring measure of his own sensibility, imagination, and intelligence.

Expressive art is in no way hostile to beauty; it makes use of it as one element in the subjects which require it, but its domain is not enclosed within the narrow bounds of such a conception. It is by no means indifferent to the pleasures of sight and hearing, but it sees something beyond them. Its worth must not be measured only by perfection of form, but also and chiefly, by the double power of expression which we have pointed out, and, as we must not omit to add, by the value of the sentiments and ideas expressed. This latter point is too often and wrongly ignored by artists.

Between two works which give evidence of equal talent—that is to say, of equal facility to grasp the true accents and characteristics of nature, and equal power to bring out both the inner meaning of things and the personality of the artist—we, for our part, would not hesitate to accord the preference to that of which the *Conception* showed the more vigorous intelligence and elevated feeling. The art critics seem to have made it one of their principles to take no account of choice of subject, but only to look at the technical result. Such a principle is plausible rather than true. The individuality of the author can never be excluded from a work, and choice of subject is frequently one of the points by which this individuality is most clearly indicated.

It is true, of course, that elevation of sentiment can never take the place of art talent. On this point we cannot too strongly condemn the practice of academic juries who, on the one hand, reward mere mechanical labor simply because it has been exercised upon what are called classic subjects; and, on the other, persecute more independent artists to punish their obstinacy in deserting the beaten track. Nothing, then, can be further from our thoughts than to require critics to substitute, in every case, consideration of the subject for that of the work itself; or to condemn *a priori* all artists who remain faithful to the traditions, ideas, and sentiments of the past. In these, indeed, some find their only inspiration. We only wish to affirm our conviction that choice of subject is not so indifferent a matter as some say it is, and that it must be taken into account as of considerable weight in determining an opinion of a work of art.

The necessity for this is one consequence of the distinction which we have established between decorative and expressive art. The former, solely devoted to the gratification of eye and ear, affords no measure of its success beyond the pleasure which it gives. The latter, whose chief object is to express the feelings and ideas, and, through them, to manifest the power of conception and expression possessed by the artist, must obviously be estimated, partly at least, by the moral or other value of the ideas and sentiments in question. And, as the value of a work depends directly upon the capability of its author, and as many artists have been about equal in their technical ability, we must be ready to acknowledge that moral and intellectual superiority is a real superiority, and is naturally marked by the possession of an instinctive and spontaneous power of sympathy.

IV. Style and Personality

Style is the man, says Buffon; and he is right. Get some one who *can* read, to read a page of Demosthenes *and* of Cicero, of Bossuet and of Massillon, of Corneille and of Racine, of Lamartine and of Victor Hugo. However slight may be your literary perceptions, you will at once notice that no two of them sound the same. Apart altogether from the subjects or ideas, which may be identical, each one has an air, an accent, which can never either be confounded or replaced. In some of them we find elegance, finesse, grace, the most seductive and soothing harmony; in others, a force and *élan* like the sound of a trumpet, enough to awaken the Seven Sleepers.

Style only exists by virtue of what Bürger calls *the law of separation.* "A being only exists in consequence of his separation from other beings. . . . This law of successive detachment—which alone renders progress possible—may be proved to influence the course of religion, of politics, of literature, and of art. What was the renaissance but a break in the continuity of the middle ages?" It is by style, by the manner of comprehension, of feeling and interpretation, that epochs, races, schools and individuals are separated and distinguished one from the other. In all the arts, analogous differences are to be found; plainly marked, in proportion as a more or less extensive field is offered for the development of artistic personality. Michelangelo and Raphael, Leonardo and Veronese, Titian and Correggio, Rubens and Rembrandt, resembled each other no more and no less than Beethoven resembled Rossini; Weber, Mozart; or Wagner resembles Verdi. Each has his own style, his peculiar mode of thinking and feeling, and of expressing those feelings and thoughts.

Why have mediocre artists no style? For the same reasons that they are mediocrities. The particular characteristic of mediocrity is commonness or vulgarity of thought and feeling. At each moment in the evolution of a social system, there is a general level which marks, for that moment, the average value of the human soul and intellect. Such works as rise above this general level imply an amount of talent or genius in exact proportion to the amount of superior elevation and spontaneity which they display. Mediocrity comes up to the general level, but does not pass it; thus the mediocre artist thinks and feels like the ordinary run of mankind, and has nothing to "separate" him from the crowd. He may have a manner, an ensemble of habits of working peculiar to himself; but he can have no style in the accurate sense of the word. Facility is not style; for the latter is really a product, a reverberation, if we may use the word, from the soul itself, and can no more be artificially acquired than can the sonorousness of bronze or silver be acquired by lead. . . .

Style, which is a simple reflection of the artist's personality, is naturally found in the work of every artist who possesses any personality. The indescribable quality, the *je ne sais quoi* of which Fromentin speaks, is precisely the assemblage of qualities, the condition of being and temperament which caused Rubens to see things differently from Rembrandt. The two extracted from one and the same object or subject emotions widely different though congenial to their respective natures; just as a tightened string in a concert room will vibrate in response to the note which it would itself produce if struck. The one thing needful is the power to vibrate, which is too often wanting.

The question of style has considerable importance. We might even say that it includes the whole of esthetics, which is in fact the question of personality in art. . . .

Truth and personality: these are the alpha and omega of art formulas; *truth* as to facts, and the *personality* of the artist. But, if we look more closely, we shall see that these two terms are in reality but one. Truth as to fact, so far as art is concerned, is above all the truth of our own sensations, of our own sentiments. It is truth as we see it, as it appears modified by our own temperaments, preferences, and physical organs. It is, in fact, our personality itself. Reality, as given by the photographer, reality taken from a point of view without connection with us or our impressions, is the very negation of art. When this kind of truth predominates in a work of art, we cry, "There is realism for you!" Now, realism partakes of the nature of art, only because the most downright of realists must, whether he will or not, put something of his own individuality into his work. When, on the other hand, the dominant quality is what we call human or personal truth, then we at once exclaim, "Here is an artist!"

And the latter is the right meaning of the word. Art consists essentially in the predominance of subjectivity over objectivity; it is the chief distinction between it and science. The man intended for science is he whose imagination has no modifying influence over the results of his direct observation. The artist, on the other hand, is one whose imagination, impressionability—in a word, whose personality is so lively and excitable that it spontaneously transforms everything, dyeing them in its own colors, and unconsciously exaggerating them in accordance with its own preferences.

We think ourselves justified, then, in calling art the direct and spontaneous manifestation of human personality. But we must not omit also to remember the fact that personality—individual and particular as it is from some points of view—is nevertheless exposed to many successive and temporary modifications caused by the various kinds of civilization through which it has had to pass.

—*Æsthetics* (1878; translated 1879 by W. H. Armstrong)

LEO TOLSTOY

The Communication of Emotion

There is no objective definition of beauty. The existing definitions . . . amount only to one and the same subjective definition, which is (strange as it seems to say so), that art is that which makes beauty manifest, and beauty is that which pleases (without exciting desire). Many estheticians have felt the insufficiency and instability of such a definition, and in order to give it a firm basis have asked themselves why a thing pleases. And they have converted the discussion on beauty into a question of taste, as did Hutcheson, Voltaire, Diderot, and others. But all attempts to define what taste is must lead to nothing, as the reader may see both from the history of esthetics and experimentally. There is and can be no explanation of why one thing pleases one man and displeases another, or *vice versa*; so that the whole existing science of esthetics fails to do what we might expect from it as a mental activity calling itself a science, namely, it does not define the qualities and laws of art, or of the beautiful (if that be the content of art), or the nature of taste (if taste decides the question of art and its merit), and then on the basis of such definitions acknowledge as art those productions which correspond to these laws and reject those which do not come under them. But this science of esthetics consists in first acknowledging a certain set of productions to be art (because they please us), and then framing such a theory of art as all these productions which please a certain circle of people can be fitted into. There exists an art-canon according to which certain productions favored by our circle are acknowledged as being art,—the works of Phidias, Sophocles, Homer, Titian, Raphael, Bach, Beethoven, Dante, Shakespeare, Goethe, and others,—and the esthetic laws must be such as to embrace all these productions. In esthetic literature you will constantly meet with opinions on the merit and importance of art, founded not on any certain laws by which this or that is held to be good or bad, but merely on consideration as to whether this art tallies with the art-canon we have drawn up. . . .

So that the theory of art founded on beauty, expounded by esthetics and in dim outline professed by the public, is nothing but the setting up as good of that which has pleased and pleases us, that is, pleases a certain class of people.

In order to define any human activity, it is necessary to understand its sense and importance; and in order to do this it is primarily necessary to examine that activity in itself, in its dependence on its causes and in connection with its effects, and not merely in relation to the pleasure we can get from it.

If we say that the aim of any activity is merely our pleasure and define it solely by that pleasure, our definition will evidently be a false one. But this is precisely what has occurred in the efforts to define art. . . .

What is art if we put aside the conception of beauty, which confuses the whole matter? The latest and most comprehensible definitions of art, apart from the conception of beauty, are the following:—(1) *a*, Art is an activity arising even in the animal kingdom, and springing from sexual desire and the propensity to play (Schiller, Darwin, Spencer), and *b*, accompanied by a pleasurable excitement of the nervous system (Grant Allen). This is the physiological-evolutionary definition. (2) Art is the external manifestation, by means of lines, colors, movements, sounds, or words, of emotions felt by man (Véron). This is the experimental definition. According to the very latest definition (Sully), (3) Art is "the production of some permanent object or passing action which is fitted not only to supply an active enjoyment to the producer, but to convey a pleasurable impression to a number of spectators or listeners, quite apart from any personal advantage to be derived from it."

Notwithstanding the superiority of these definitions to the metaphysical definitions which depended on the conception of beauty, they are yet far from exact. The first, the physiological-evolutionary definition (1), *a*, is inexact, because instead of speaking about the artistic activity itself, which is the real matter in hand, it treats of the derivation of art. The modification of it, *b*, based on the physiological effects on the human organism, is inexact because within the limits of such definition many other human activities can be included, as has occurred in the neo-esthetic theories which reckon as art the preparation of handsome clothes, pleasant scents, and even of victuals.

The experimental definition, (2), which makes art consist in the expression of emotions, is inexact because a man may express his emotions by means of lines, colors, sounds, or words and yet may not act on others by such expression—and then the manifestation of his emotions is not art.

The third definition (that of Sully) is inexact because in the production of objects or actions affording pleasure to the producer and a pleasant emotion to the spectators or hearers apart from personal advantage, may be included the showing of conjuring tricks or gymnastic exercises, and other activities which are not art. And further, many things the production of which does not afford pleasure to the producer and the sensation received from which is unpleasant, such as gloomy, heart-rending scenes in a poetic description or a play, may nevertheless be undoubted works of art.

The inaccuracy of all these definitions arises from the fact that in them all (as also in the metaphysical definitions) the object considered is the pleasure art may give, and not the purpose it may serve in the life of man and of humanity.

In order to define art correctly it is necessary first of all to cease to consider it as a means to pleasure, and to consider it as one of the conditions of human life. Viewing it in this way we cannot fail to observe that art is one of the means of intercourse between man and man.

Every work of art causes the receiver to enter into a certain kind of relationship both with him who produced or is producing the art, and with all those who, simultaneously, previously, or subsequently, receive the same artistic impression.

Speech transmitting the thoughts and experiences of men serves as a means of union among them, and art serves a similar purpose. The peculiarity of this latter means of intercourse, distinguishing it from intercourse by means of words, consists in this, that whereas by words a man transmits his thoughts to another, by art he transmits his feelings.

The activity of art is based on the fact that a man receiving through his sense of hearing or sight another man's expression of feeling, is capable of experiencing the emotion which moved the man who expressed it. To take the simplest example: one man laughs, and another who hears becomes merry, or a man weeps, and another who hears feels sorrow. A man is excited or irritated, and another man seeing him is brought to a similar state of mind. By his movements or by the sounds of his voice a man expresses courage and determination or sadness and calmness, and this state of mind passes on to others. A man suffers, manifesting his suffering by groans and spasms, and this suffering transmits itself to other people; a man expresses his feelings of admiration, devotion, fear, respect, or love, to certain objects, persons, or phenomena, and others are infected by the same feelings of admiration, devotion, fear, respect, or love, to the same objects, persons, or phenomena.

And it is on this capacity of man to receive another man's expression of feeling and to experience those feelings himself, that the activity of art is based.

If a man infects another or others directly, immediately, by his appearance or by the sounds he gives vent to at the very time he experiences the feeling; if he causes another man to yawn when he himself cannot help yawning, or to laugh or cry when he himself is obliged to laugh or cry, or to suffer when he himself is suffering—that does not amount to art.

Art begins when one person with the object of joining another or others to himself in one and the same feeling, expresses that feeling by certain external indications. To take the simplest example: a boy having experienced, let us say, fear on encountering a wolf, relates that encounter, and in order to evoke in others the feeling he has experienced, describes himself, his condition before the encounter, the surroundings, the wood, his own lightheartedness, and then the wolf's appearance, its movements, the distance between himself and the wolf, and so forth. All this, if only the boy when telling the story again experiences the feelings he had lived through, and infects the hearers and compels them to feel what he had experienced—is art. Even if the boy had not seen a wolf but had frequently been afraid of one, and if wishing to evoke in others the fear he had felt, he invented an encounter with a wolf and recounted it so as to make his hearers share the feelings he experienced when he feared the wolf, that also would be art. And just in the same way it is art if a man, having experienced either the fear of suffering or the attraction of enjoyment (whether in reality or in imagination), expresses these feelings on canvas or in marble so that others are infected by them. And it is also art if a man feels, or imagines to himself, feelings of delight, gladness, sorrow, despair, courage, or despondency, and the transition from one to another of these feelings, and expresses them by sounds so that the hearers are infected by them and experience them as they were experienced by the composer.

The feelings with which the artist infects others may be most various—very strong or very weak, very important or very insignificant, very bad or very good: feelings of love of one's country, self-devotion and submission to fate or to God expressed in a drama, raptures of lovers described in a novel, feelings of voluptuousness expressed in a picture, courage expressed in a triumphal march, merriment evoked by a dance, humor evoked by a funny story, the feeling of quietness transmitted by an evening landscape or by a lullaby, or the feeling of admiration evoked by a beautiful arabesque—it is all art.

If only the spectators or auditors are infected by the feelings which the author has felt, it is art.

To evoke in oneself a feeling one has once experienced and having evoked it in oneself then by means of movements, lines, colors, sounds, or forms expressed in words, so to transmit that feeling that others experience the same feeling—this is the activity of art.

Art is a human activity consisting in this, that one man consciously by means of certain external signs, hands on to others feelings he has lived through, and that others are infected by these feelings and also experience them.

Art is not, as the metaphysicians say, the manifestation of some mysterious Idea of beauty or God; it is not, as the esthetic physiologists say, a game in which man lets off his excess of stored-up energy; it is not the expression of man's emotions by external signs; it is not the production of pleasing objects; and, above all, it is not pleasure; but it is a means of union among men joining them together in the same feelings, and indispensable for the life and progress towards well-being of individuals and of humanity.

As every man, thanks to man's capacity to express thoughts by words, may know all that has been done for him in the realms of thought by all humanity before this day, and can in the present, thanks to this capacity to understand the thoughts of others, become a sharer in their activity and also himself hand on to his contemporaries and descendants the thoughts he has assimilated from others as well as those that have arisen in himself; so, thanks to man's capacity to be infected with the feelings of others by means of art, all that is being lived through by his contemporaries is accessible to him, as well as the feelings experienced by men thousands of years ago, and he has also the possibility of transmitting his own feelings to others.

If people lacked the capacity to receive the thoughts conceived by men who preceded them and to pass on to others their own thoughts, men would be like wild beasts, or like Kasper Hauser.[1]

And if men lacked this other capacity of being infected by art, people might be almost more savage still, and above all more separated from, and more hostile to, one another.

And therefore the activity of art is a most important one, as important as the activity of speech itself and as generally diffused.

As speech does not act on us only in sermons, orations, or books, but in all those remarks by which we interchange thoughts and experiences with one another, so also art in the wide sense of the word permeates our whole life, but it is only to some of its manifestations that we apply the term in the limited sense of the word.

We are accustomed to understand art to be only what we hear and see in theaters, concerts, and exhibitions; together with buildings, statues, poems, and novels. . . . But all this is but the smallest part of the art by which we communicate with one another in life. All human life is filled with works of art of every kind—from cradle-song, jest, mimicry, the ornamentation of houses, dress, and utensils, to church services, buildings, monuments, and triumphal processions. It is all artistic activity. So that by art, in the limited sense of the word, we do not mean all human activity transmitting feelings but only that part which we for some reason select from it and to which we attach special importance. . . .

There is one indubitable sign distinguishing real art from its counterfeit —namely, the infectiousness of art. If a man without exercising effort and without altering his standpoint, on reading, hearing, or seeing another man's work experiences a mental condition which unites him with that man and with others who are also affected by that work, then the object evoking that condition is a work of art. And however poetic, realistic, striking, or interesting, a work may be, it is not a work of art if it does not evoke that feeling (quite distinct from all other feelings) of joy and of spiritual union with another (the author) and with others (those who are also infected by it).

It is true that this indication is an *internal* one and that there are people who, having forgotten what the action of real art is, expect something else from art (in our society the great majority are in this state), and that therefore such people may mistake for this esthetic feeling the feeling of diversion and a certain excitement which they receive from counterfeits of art. But though it is impossible to undeceive these people, just as it may be impossible to convince a man suffering from color-blindness that green is not red, yet for all that, this indication remains perfectly definite to those whose feeling for art is neither perverted nor atrophied, and it clearly distinguishes the feeling produced by art from all other feelings.

The chief peculiarity of this feeling is that the recipient of a truly artistic impression is so united to the artist that he feels as if the work were his own and not some one else's—as if what it expresses were just what he had long been wishing to express. A real work of art destroys in the consciousness of the recipient the separation between himself and the artist, and not that alone, but also between himself and all whose minds receive this work of art. In this freeing of our personality from its separation and isolation, in this uniting of it with others, lies the chief characteristic and the great attractive force of art.

If a man is infected by the author's condition of soul, if he feels this emotion and this union with others, then the object which has effected this is art; but if there be no such infection, if there be not this union with the author and with others who are moved by the same work—then it is not art. And not only is infection a sure sign of art, but the degree of infectiousness is also the sole measure of excellence in art.

The stronger the infection the better is the art, as art, speaking of it now apart from its subject-matter—that is, not considering the value of the feelings it transmits.

And the degree of the infectiousness of art depends on three conditions:

(1) On the greater or lesser individuality of the feeling transmitted; (2) on the greater or lesser clearness with which the feeling is transmitted; (3) on the sincerity of the artist, that is, on the greater or lesser force with which the artist himself feels the emotion he transmits.

The more individual the feeling transmitted the more strongly does it act on the recipient; the more individual the state of soul into which he is transferred the more pleasure does the recipient obtain and therefore the more readily and strongly does he join in it.

Clearness of expression assists infection because the recipient who mingles in consciousness with the author is the better satisfied the more clearly that feeling is transmitted which, as it seems to him, he has long known and felt and for which he has only now found expression.

But most of all is the degree of infectiousness of art increased by the degree of sincerity in the artist. As soon as the spectator, hearer, or reader, feels that the artist is infected by his own production and writes, sings, or plays, for himself, and not merely to act on others, this mental condition of the artist infects the recipient; and, on the contrary, as soon as the spectator, reader, or hearer, feels that the author is not writing, singing, or playing, for his own satisfaction—does not himself feel what he wishes to express, but is doing it for him, the recipient—resistance immediately springs up, and the most individual and the newest feelings and the cleverest technique not only fail to produce any infection but actually repel.

I have mentioned three conditions of contagion in art, but they may all be summed up into one, the last, sincerity; that is, that the artist should be impelled by an inner need to express his feeling. That condition includes the first; for if the artist is sincere he will express the feeling as he experienced it. And as each man is different from everyone else, his feeling will be individual for everyone else; and the more individual it is—the more the artist has drawn it from the depths of his nature—the more sympathetic and sincere will it be. And this same sincerity will impel the artist to find clear expression for the feeling which he wishes to transmit.

Therefore this third condition—sincerity—is the most important of the three. It is always complied with in peasant art, and this explains why such art always acts so powerfully; but it is a condition almost entirely absent from our upper-class art, which is continually produced by artists actuated by personal aims of covetousness or vanity.

Such are the three conditions which divide art from its counterfeits, and which also decide the quality of every work of art considered apart from its subject matter.

The absence of any one of these conditions excludes a work from the category of art and relegates it to that of art's counterfeits. If the work does not transmit the artist's peculiarity of feeling and is therefore not individual, if it is unintelligibly expressed, or if it has not proceeded from the author's inner need for expression—it is not a work of art. If all these conditions are present even in the smallest degree, then the work even if a weak one is yet a work of art.

The presence in various degrees of these three conditions: individuality, clearness, and sincerity, decides the merit of a work of art as art, apart from subject matter. All works of art take order of merit according to the degree in which they fulfil the first, the second, and the third, of these conditions. In one the individuality of the feeling transmitted may predominate; in another, clearness of expression; in a third, sincerity; while a fourth may have sincerity and individuality but be deficient in clearness; a fifth, individuality and clearness, but less sincerity; and so forth, in all possible degrees and combinations.

Thus is art divided from what is not art, and thus is the quality of art, as art, decided, independently of its subject matter, that is to say, apart from whether the feelings it transmits are good or bad. . . .

How in the subject matter of art are we to decide what is good and what is bad?

Art like speech is a means of communication and therefore of progress, that is, of the movement of humanity forward towards perfection. Speech renders accessible to men of the latest generation all the knowledge discovered by the experience and reflection both of preceding generations and of the best and foremost men of their own times; art renders accessible to men of the latest generations all the feelings experienced by their predecessors and also those felt by their best and foremost contemporaries. And as the evolution of knowledge proceeds by truer and more necessary knowledge dislodging and replacing what was mistaken and unnecessary, so the evolution of feeling proceeds by means of art—feelings less kind and less necessary for the well-being of mankind being replaced by others kinder and more needful for that end. That is the purpose of art. And speaking now of the feelings which are its subject matter, the more art fulfils that purpose the better the art, and the less it fulfils it the worse the art.

The appraisement of feelings (that is, the recognition of one or other set of feelings as more or less good, more or less necessary for the well-being of mankind) is effected by the religious perception of the age.

In every period of history and in every human society there exists an understanding of the meaning of life, which represents the highest level to which men of that society have attained—an understanding indicating the highest good at which that society aims. This understanding is the religious perception of the given time and society. And this religious perception is always clearly expressed by a few advanced men and more or less vividly perceived by members of the society generally. Such a religious perception and its corresponding expression always exists in every society. If it appears to us that there is no religious perception in our society, this is not because there really is none, but only because we do not wish to see it. And we often wish not to see it because it exposes the fact that our life is inconsistent with that religious perception.

Religious perception in a society is like the direction of a flowing river. If the river flows at all it must have a direction. If a society lives, there must be a religious perception indicating the direction in which, more or less consciously, all its members tend.

And so there always has been, and is, a religious perception in every society. And it is by the standard of this religious perception that the feelings transmitted by art have always been appraised. It has always been only on the basis of this religious perception of their age, that men have chosen from amid the endlessly varied spheres of art that art which transmitted feelings making religious perception operative in actual life. And such art has always been highly valued and encouraged, while art transmitting feelings already outlived, flowing from the antiquated religious perceptions of a former age, has always been condemned and despised. All the rest of art transmitting those most diverse feelings by means of which people commune with one another was not condemned and was tolerated if only it did not transmit feelings contrary to religious perception. Thus for instance among the Greeks, art transmitting feelings of beauty, strength, and courage (Hesiod, Homer, Phidias) was chosen, approved, and encouraged, while art transmitting feelings of rude sensuality, despondency, and effeminacy, was condemned and despised. Among the Jews, art transmitting feelings of devotion and submission to the God of the Hebrews and to His will (the epic of Genesis, the prophets, the Psalms) was chosen and encouraged, while art transmitting feelings of idolatry (the Golden Calf) was condemned and despised. All the rest of art—stories, songs, dances, ornamentation of houses, of utensils, and of clothes—which was not contrary to religious perception, was neither distinguished nor discussed. Thus as regards its subject matter has art always and everywhere been appraised and thus it should be appraised, for this attitude towards art proceeds from the fundamental characteristics of human nature, and those characteristics do not change.

I know that according to an opinion current in our times religion is a superstition humanity has outgrown, and it is therefore assumed that no such thing exists as a religious perception common to us all by which art in our time can be appraised. I know that this is the opinion current in the pseudo-cultured circles of today. People who do not acknowledge Christianity in its true meaning because it undermines their social privileges, and who therefore invent all kinds of philosophic and esthetic theories to hide from themselves the meaninglessness and wrongfulness of their lives, cannot think otherwise. These people intentionally, or sometimes unintentionally, confuse the notion of a religious cult with the notion of religious perception, and think that by denying the cult they get rid of the perception. But even the very attacks on religion and the attempts to establish an idea of life contrary to the religious perception of our times, most clearly demonstrate the existence of a religious perception condemning the lives that are not in harmony with it.

If humanity progresses, that is, moves forward, there must inevitably be a guide to the direction of that movement. And religions have always furnished that guide. All history shows that the progress of humanity is accomplished no otherwise than under the guidance of religion. But if the race cannot progress without the guidance of religion—and progress is always going on, and consequently goes on also in our own times—then there must be a religion of our times. So that whether it pleases or displeases the so-called cultured people of today, they must admit the existence of religion—not of a religious cult, Catholic, Protestant, or another, but of religious perception—which even in our times is the guide always present where there is any progress. And if a religious perception exists amongst us, then the feelings dealt with by our art should be appraised on the basis of that religious perception; and as has been the case always and everywhere, art transmitting feelings flowing from the religious perception of our time should be chosen from amid all the indifferent art, should be acknowledged, highly valued, and encouraged, while art running counter to that perception should be condemned and despised, and all the remaining, indifferent, art should neither be distinguished nor encouraged.

The religious perception of our time in its widest and most practical application is the consciousness that our well-being, both material and spiritual, individual and collective, temporal and eternal, lies in the growth of brotherhood among men—in their loving harmony with one another. This perception is not only expressed by Christ and all the best men of past ages, it is not only repeated in most varied forms and from most diverse sides by the best men of our times, but it already serves as a clue to all the complex labor of humanity, consisting as this labor does on the one hand in the destruction of physical and moral obstacles to the union of men, and on the other hand in establishing the principles common to all men which can and should unite them in one universal brotherhood. And it is on the basis of this perception that we should appraise all the phenomena of our life and among the rest our art also: choosing from all its realms and highly prizing and encouraging whatever transmits feelings flowing from this religious perception, rejecting whatever is contrary to it, and not attributing to the rest of art an importance that does not properly belong to it. . . .

Whatever the work may be and however it may have been extolled, we have first to ask whether this work is one of real art, or a counterfeit. Having acknowledged, on the basis of the indication of its infectiousness even to a small class of people, that a certain production belongs to the realm of art, it is necessary on this basis to decide the next question, Does this work belong to the category of bad exclusive art opposed to religious perception, or of Christian art uniting people? And having acknowledged a work to belong to real Christian art, we must then, according to whether it transmits feelings flowing from love of God and man, or merely the simple feelings uniting all men, assign it a place in the ranks of religious art, or in those of universal art.

Only on the basis of such verification shall we find it possible to select from the whole mass of what in our society claims to be art, those works which form real, important, necessary, spiritual food, and to separate them from all the harmful and useless art and from the counterfeits of art which surround us. Only on the basis of such verification shall we be able to rid ourselves of the pernicious results of harmful art and avail ourselves of that beneficent action which is the purpose of true and good art, and which is indispensable for the spiritual life of man and of humanity.

—*What Is Art?* (1896; translated 1905 by Aylmer Maude)

Note

1. "The foundling of Nuremberg," found in the marketplace of that town on 23rd May 1828, apparently some sixteen years old. He spoke little and was almost totally ignorant even of common objects. He subsequently explained that he had been brought up in confinement underground and visited by only one man, whom he saw but seldom.

C. J. DUCASSE

Art and the Language of the Emotions

That art is the language of the emotions has been widely held since Eugène Véron in 1878 declared that art is "the emotional expression of human personality," and Tolstoy in 1898 that "art is a human activity consisting in this, that one man consciously, by means of certain external signs, hands on to others feelings he has lived through, and that other people are infected by these feelings, and also experience them."

1. *Expression? or expression and transmission?* Whether transmission of the emotions expressed occurs or not, however, is largely accidental; for a given work of art may happen never to come to the attention of persons other than the artist himself; and yet it remains a work of art. Moreover, the individual psychological constitution of persons other than the artist who may contemplate his work is one of the variables that determine whether the feelings those persons then experience are or are not the same as the feelings the artist intended the object he has created to express. Evidently the activity of the artist *as artist* terminates with his creation of the work of art. What the word *language* signifies in the phrase *language of the emotions* is therefore essentially *medium of expression,* and only adventitiously means of transmission.

But even after this has been realized, the term *language of the emotions* still remains ambiguous in several respects. The present paper attempts to eliminate its ambiguities and thereby to make clear in precisely what sense the statement that art is the language of the emotions must be taken if it is to constitute a true answer to the two questions, What is art? and What is a work of art?

2. *The arts, and the fine arts.* The first of the facts to which attention must be called is that the word *art* in its generic sense means *skill;* and that the purposes in pursuit of which one employs skill may be more specifically pragmatic, or epistemic, or esthetic.

Let it therefore be understood that, in what follows, only *esthetic* art, i.e., what is commonly called *fine art,* will be in view. Indeed, because of the limited space here available, only the visual and the auditory arts, but not the literary arts, will be directly referred to. What will be said about the former arts, however, would in essentials apply also to the latter.

3. *The two central questions.* So much being clear, the two questions mentioned above may now be stated more fully as follows:

a. Just what does the *creative operation* termed *expression of emotion* consist in, which *the artist* is performing at the time he is creating a work of art? b. Just what is meant by saying that *the work of art,* once it has come into existence, then itself "expresses emotions"?

4. *The feelings, and the emotions.* Before the attempt is made to answer these two questions, it is necessary to point out that a fairer statement of what is really contended when art is said to be the language of the emotions would be that art is the language *of the feelings.* For the term *the emotions* ordinarily designates the relatively few feelings—anger, love, fear,

joy, anxiety, jealousy, sadness, etc.—for which names were needed because their typical spontaneous manifestations, and the typical situations that arouse those particular feelings, present themselves again and again in human life. And if, when art is said to be the language of the emotions, "the emotions" were taken to designate only the few dozen varieties of feelings that have names, then that conception of art would apply to only a small proportion of the things that are admittedly works of art. The fact is that human beings experience, and that works of art and indeed works of nature too express, many feelings besides the few ordinarily thought of when the term *the emotions* is used. These other feelings are too rare, or too fleeting, or too unmanifested, or their nuances too subtle, to have pragmatic importance and therefore to have needed names.

5. *Being sad vs. imagining sadness.* Taking it as granted, then, that the emotions of which art is said to be the language include these many nameless feelings as well as the emotions, moods, sentiments, and attitudes that have names, the next important distinction is between *having* a feeling—for instance, *being* sad—and only *imagining* the feeling called sadness; that is, imagining it not in the sense of supposing oneself to be sad, but in the sense of entertaining a *mental image* of sadness.

The essential distinction here as regards feelings, and in the instance as regards the feeling-quality called *sadness* is the same as the distinction in the case of a color, or a tone, or a taste, etc., between actually *sensing* it, and only *imagining* it; for example, between *seeing* some particular shade of red, and only *imagining* that shade, i.e., calling up a mental image of it as one does when perhaps remembering the red one saw the day before.

6. *Venting vs. objectifying sadness.* Next two possible senses of the statement that *a person* is expressing sadness must be clearly distinguished.

If a person who *is* sad manifests the fact at all in his behavior, the behavior that manifests it consists of such things as groans, or sighs, or a dejected posture or countenance; and these behaviors express his sadness in the sense of *venting* it, i.e., of being *effusions* of it. They are not intentional; and the interest of other persons in them is normally not aesthetic interest, but *diagnostic*—diagnostic of the nature of his emotional state; and possibly also *pragmatic* in that these evidences of his sadness may move other persons to try to cheer him up.

Unlike such venting or effusion, however, which is automatic, the *composing* of sad music—or, comprehensively, the creating of a work of any of the arts—is *a critically controlled purposively creative operation.* If the composer manages to accomplish it, *he* then has expressed sadness. In order to do it, however, he need not at all—and preferably should not—himself *be* sad at the time but rather, and essentially, *intent* and striving to achieve his intent. This is, to compose music that will be sad not in the sense of itself experiencing sadness, since music does not experience feelings, but in the sense of *objectifying* sadness.

And that a particular musical composition objectifies sadness means that it has the *capacity*—the power—to cause an *image* of sadness to arise in the consciousness of a person who attends to the music with aesthetic interest; or, as we might put it, the capacity to make him taste, or sample, sadness without actually making him sad. It is sad in the sense in which quinine is bitter even at times when it is not being tasted; for bitter, as predicated of *quinine,* is the name of the *capacity or power* of quinine, when put on the tongue, to cause experience of bitter taste; whereas bitter, as predicated *of a taste,* is the name not of a capacity or power of that taste, but *of that taste quality itself.*

7. *Aesthetic contemplation.* A listener who is attending to the music with interest in its emotional import is engaged in aesthetic contemplation of the music. He is doing what the present writer has elsewhere proposed to call *ecpathizing* the music—ecpathizing being the analogue in the language of feeling of what reading is in the language of concepts. Reading *acquaints* the reader with, for instance, the opinion which a given sentence formulates but does not necessarily cause him to adopt it himself. Similarly, listening with aesthetic interest to sad music *acquaints* the listener with the taste of sadness, but does not ordinarily make him sad.

8. *The process of objectification of feeling.* The psychological process in the artist, from which a work of art eventually results, is ordinarily gradual. Except in very simple works of art, the artist very seldom imagines precisely from the start either the finished elaborate work he is about to record or the rich complex of feelings it will objectify in the sense stated above. Normally, the creative process has many steps, each of them of the trial and error type. In the case of music, the process may get started by some sounds the composer hears, or more likely by some sound-images that emerge spontaneously out of his subconsciousness and inspire him. That they inspire him means that they move him to add to them some others in some particular temporal pattern. Having done so, he then contemplates aesthetically the bit of music he has just invented and perhaps actually played; and, if need be, he then alters it until its emotional import satisfies the inspiration that generated it. Next, contemplation in turn of the created and now satisfactory musical fragment generates spontaneously some addition to it, the emotional import of which in the temporal context of the previously created fragment is then in its turn contemplated, judged, and either approved or altered until found satisfactory. Each such complex step both inspires a particular next step, and rules out particular others which a different composer might have preferred.

This process—of inspiration-creation-contemplation-judgment and correction or approval—is repeated again and again until the musical composition, or as the case may be the painting, or statue, or work of one of the other arts, is finished; each image that is found satisfactory being ordinarily recorded in musical notation, or in paint on canvas, etc., rather than trusted to memory.

9. *The sources of the emotional import of an object.* The feelings, of which images are caused to arise in a person when he contemplates with aesthetic interest a given work of art, or indeed any object, have several possible sources.

One of them is the *form* of the object; that is, the particular *arrangement of its parts in space, or in time, or both.* Taking as simplest example a tone expressive of sadness, its form would consist of its *loudness-shape,* e.g., diminuendo from moderately loud to nothing.

A second source of feeling would be what might be called the *material* of the tone; that is, its *quality* as made up of its fundamental pitch, of such overtones as may be present, and of the mere noise it may also contain.

And still another source of feeling would be the emotional import of what the presented tone may *represent* whether consciously or subconsciously to a particular hearer; that is, the emotional import which the tone may be *borrowing* from past experiences of his to which it was intrinsic, that happened to be closely associated with experience of that same tone at some time in the history of the person now hearing it again. For instance the tone, although itself rather mournful, might happen to have been the signal of quitting time at the factory where he worked at a tedious job. This would have made the tone *represent* something cheerful—would have given the tone a cheerful *meaning*; the cheerfulness of which henceforth automatically mingles with, or perhaps masks for him, the otherwise mournful feeling-import of the tone's presented quality and loudness shape. This third possible source of the emotional import of an aesthetically contemplated object may be termed the object's *connotation*; so that in the example just used the tone has mournfulness of quality and form, but cheerfulness of *connotation*. . . .

10. *"The language of the emotions" defined.* The effect of the several distinctions, to the indispensability of which attention has been called in what precedes, is, the writer believes, to make it possible now to state precisely the sense in which it is true that art is the language of the emotions. This sense is as follows.

Art is the critically controlled purposive activity which aims to create an object having the capacity to reflect to its creator, when he contemplates it with interest in its emotional import, the feeling-images that had dictated the specific form and content he gave the object; the created object being capable also of generating, in other persons who contemplate it aesthetically, feeling-images similar or dissimilar to those which dictated the specific features given the object by the artist, according as the psychological constitution of these other persons resembles or differs from that of the artist who created the particular work of art.

—*The Journal of Aesthetics and Art Criticism,* Vol. 22 (1964)

CHAPTER 3
Intuition-Expression

HENRI BERGSON: The Individual and the Type
BENEDETTO CROCE: Intuition and Expression

The philosophers represented in this chapter are like Tolstoy, Véron, and Ducasse in maintaining that art is wider in scope than the creation of beauty, and like Gombrich in contending that art combines imagination and knowledge. Unlike Aristotle and Hegel, they believe that the objects known through art are particulars, not universals; unique qualities, not general characteristics.

The great French philosopher, Henri Bergson (1859–1941), contrasts intellect and intuition, and identifies art with the latter. Ordinary experience, he thinks, is more intellectual than intuitive. The average person's senses give him a greatly conceptualized version of reality. Since he seldom has a clear grasp of the individuality of things, his description of objects will be in general terms. He may say that a certain table is brown, for example, but he is not saying anything that indicates the individuality of the table—there are thousands of things that are brown. Every word that he chooses to describe the table will have this defect—it will not reveal the unique essence of the table, but only, let us say, its rectangularity or smoothness, features that are not at all peculiar to this particular table. This generalized description and awareness of the object is sufficient for practical purposes. If the individuality of the thing eludes him, he nevertheless has distinguished the features that make the object an instrument for his use. Since man's primary need is not knowledge but action, intellect has been slowly developed throughout the course of evolution to deal with things in this way. The concepts employed by the intellect are a kind of mental shorthand to economize effort and expedite action.

To know reality truly, in its uniqueness and novelty, we need to relax the tension of practical effort and teach our minds a new docility to nature. We will then penetrate, by a kind of sympathy, to the real nature of the object, thus discovering for the first time the strangeness and multiplicity of its qualities. Turning our gaze inward, we will discern the continuity and freshness of our inner life. Intuition is this sympathy or direct vision, and the artist is unusually gifted with it. Most works of art are the records of intuition, which alone penetrates to the nature of reality—an ever-changing flux of unique qualities.

One type of art is an exception. In the art of comedy the intellect predominates—what we find laughable is not the individual but the type, not the fresh and creative but the stereotyped and inflexible. This rigidity is comic, and laughter is its corrective. Comedy does not belong to the esthetic sphere alone, since it pursues a utilitarian aim of general improvement and uses the intellect as an instrument of criticism. Incidentally, Bergson's brief remarks about tragedy stand in interesting contrast to Aristotle's and Hegel's emphasis upon the universality of tragic characterization and plot.

Benedetto Croce (1866–1952), the most famous Italian philosopher of this century, has been a very influential proponent of the intuitional interpretation of art. Clinging to idealism, the view that reality consists of minds and their activities, he is intent upon analyzing the stages of mental activity. Apart from sensation, which is relatively passive, these stages may be schematized as follows:

1. *Knowing,* or theoretic activity.
   - (a) *Art,* the knowing of particulars, or intuition.
     Its value is the *beautiful*; its disvalue the *ugly*.[1]
   - (b) *Pure Science and Philosophy,* the knowing of universals, or conception.
     Value: the *true*; disvalue: the *false*.
2. *Doing,* or practical activity.
   - (a) *Economic and Prudential Activity,* the pursuit of individual ends.
     Value: the *useful*; disvalue, the *harmful*.
   - (b) *Morality,* the pursuit of universal ends.
     Value: the *morally good*; disvalue, the *morally evil*.

These divisions are not sharp. "The forms of the spirit," declares Croce, "are distinct and not separate, and when the spirit is found in one of its forms, or is *explicit* in it, the other forms are also in it, but *implicit*."[2] For example, thinking involves doing, and vice versa. Also intuition is accompanied by conception and by the two forms of practical activity. But each stage is marked by its fundamental emphasis, whereby it is defined. Esthetic philosophy, for Croce, consists in explaining the nature of art as intuition, and in contrasting art with sensation and the other stages of human activity.

Sensation is passive; art is active. Art is not mere passive perception or daydreaming; it is inner vision formulated in images. Halfway between the passivity of sensation and the activity of art is fancy. It is art only in the making because it lacks the unity of genuine intuition. Fancy is too passive; it allows images and sensations to float lazily through the mind, or combines them arbitrarily. Art is complete only when the spirit works upon the relatively formless materials of experience, converting them into expressive and harmonious images.

What gives unity to this imaginative vision is a *lyrical content,* the pervasive expression of "feeling." "Feeling" does not mean merely *emotion,* but rather any subjective mood, including volitional attitudes. "We do not ask the artist for a philosophical system nor for a relation of facts," Croce declares, "but for a dream of his own, for nothing but the expression of a world desired or abhorred, or partly desired and partly abhorred. If he makes us live again in this dream the rapture of joy or the incubus of terror, in solemnity or in humility, in tragedy or in laughter, that suffices."[3] In thus including both emotion and desire, Croce in effect synthesizes the voluntaristic theory of Schopenhauer, Nietzsche, and Freud and the emotionalist theory of Véron and Tolstoy.

As an imaginative grasp of the unique, art is not concerned with the true and false, real and unreal, useful or harmful, good or bad. Nothing counts in art but the perfection of the imaginative vision in itself, and by its own standard of "expressiveness," which was for Croce another word for "beauty."

Intuition, so interpreted, is equivalent to expression. Croce doubts the existence of "mute inglorious Miltons," burdened with inspiration but lacking the gift of expression. If a man truly has Miltonic intuitions, he has no difficulty expressing himself. Indeed, he does not know what he wants to express until he has expressed it, imaginatively, if not overtly.

My selection from Croce is taken from the article on esthetics in the fourteenth edition of the *Encyclopedia Britannica* as translated by R. G. Collingwood (1889–1943), professor at Oxford University. Because space is limited and Croce is the more original thinker, I have omitted a selection from Collingwood, but I recommend his *Principles of Art* to anyone who wishes to understand the Croce–Collingwood theory of intuition-expression.

Notes

1. For Croce, value is tendency-fulfillment. Value results when the activity unfolds freely; disvalue, when the activity is hindered, impeded.
2. Benedetto Croce, *The Philosophy of the Practical* (Macmillan, London, 1913), pp. 33–34.
3. Ibid., p. 268.

HENRI BERGSON

The Individual and the Type

What is the object of art? Could reality come into direct contact with sense and consciousness, could we enter into immediate communion with things and with ourselves, probably art would be useless, or rather we should all be artists, for then our soul would continually vibrate in perfect accord with nature. Our eyes, aided by memory, would carve out in space and fix in time the most inimitable of pictures. Hewn in the living marble of the human form, fragments of statues, beautiful as the relics of antique statuary, would strike the passing glance. Deep in our souls we should hear the strains of our inner life's unbroken melody—a music that is ofttimes gay, but more frequently plaintive and always original. All this is around and within us, and yet no whit of it do we distinctly perceive. Between nature and ourselves, nay, between ourselves and our own consciousness a veil is interposed: a veil that is dense and opaque for the common herd—thin, almost transparent, for the artist and the poet. What fairy wove that veil? Was it done in malice or in friendliness? We have to live, and life demands that we grasp things in their relations to our own needs. Life is action. Life implies the acceptance only of the *utilitarian* side of things in order to respond to them by appropriate reactions: all other impressions must be dimmed or else reach us vague and blurred. I look and I think I see, I listen and I think I hear, I examine myself and I think I am reading the very depths of my heart. But what I see and hear of the outer world is purely and simply a selection made by my senses to serve as a light to my conduct; what I know of myself is what comes to the surface, what participates in my actions. My senses and my consciousness, therefore, give me no more than a practical simplification of reality. In the vision they furnish me of myself and of things, the differences that are useless to man are obliterated, the resemblances that are useful to him are emphasized; ways are traced out for me in advance, along which my activity is to travel. These ways are the ways which all mankind has trod before me. Things have been classified with a view to the use I can derive from them. And it is this classification I perceive, far more clearly than the color and the shape of things. Doubtless man is vastly superior to the lower animals in this respect. It is not very likely that the eye of a wolf makes any distinction between a kid and a lamb; both appear to the wolf as the same identical quarry, alike easy to pounce upon, alike good to devour. We, for our part, make a distinction between a goat and sheep; but can we tell one goat from another, one sheep from another? The *individuality* of things or of beings escapes us, unless it is materially to our advantage to perceive it. Even when we do take note of it—as when we distinguish one man from another—it is not the individuality itself that the eye grasps, that is, an entirely original harmony of forms and colors, but only one or two features that will make practical recognition easier.

In short, we do not see the actual things themselves; in most cases we confine ourselves to reading the labels affixed to them. This tendency, the result of need, has become even more pronounced under the influence of speech; for words—with the exception of proper nouns—all denote genera. The word, which only takes note of the most ordinary function and commonplace aspect of the thing, intervenes between it and ourselves, and would conceal its form from our eyes, were that form not already masked beneath the necessities that brought the world into existence. Not only external objects, but even our own mental states, are screened from us in their inmost, their personal aspect, in the original life they possess. When we feel love or hatred, when we are gay or sad, is it really the feeling itself that reaches our consciousness with those innumerable fleeting shades of meaning and deep resounding echoes that make it something altogether our own? We should all, were it so, be novelists or poets or musicians. Mostly, however, we perceive nothing but the outward display of our mental state. We catch only the impersonal aspect of our feelings, that aspect which speech has set down once for all because it is almost the same, in the same conditions, for all men. Thus, even in our own individual, individuality escapes our ken. We move amidst generalities and symbols, as within a tilt-yard in which our force is effectively pitted against other forces; and fascinated by action, tempted by it, for our own good, on to the field it has selected, we live in a zone midway between things and ourselves, externally to things, externally also to ourselves. From time to time, however, in a fit of absentmindedness, nature raises up souls that are more detached from life. Not with that intentional, logical, systematical detachment—the result of reflection and philosophy—but rather with a natural detachment, one innate in the structure of sense or consciousness, which at once reveals itself by a virginal manner, so to speak, of seeing, hearing or thinking. Were this detachment complete, did the soul no longer cleave to action by any of its perceptions, it would be the soul of an artist such as the world has never yet seen. It would excel alike in every art at the same time; or rather, it would fuse them all into one. It would perceive all things in their native purity: the forms, colors, sounds of the physical world as well as the subtlest movements of the inner life. But this is asking too much of nature. Even for such of us as she has made artists, it is by accident, and on one side only, that she has lifted the veil. In one direction only has she forgotten to rivet the perception to the need. And since each direction corresponds to what we call a *sense*—through one of his senses, and through that sense alone, is the artist usually wedded to art. Hence, originally, the diversity of arts. Hence also the speciality of predispositions. This one applies himself to colors and forms, and since he loves color for color and form for form, since he perceives them for their sake and not for his own, it is the inner life of things that he sees appearing through their forms and colors. Little by little he insinuates it into our own perception, baffled though we may be at the outset. For a few moments at least, he diverts us from the prejudices of form and color that come between ourselves and reality. And thus he realizes the loftiest ambition of art, which here consists in revealing to us nature. Others, again, retire within themselves. Beneath the thousand rudimentary actions which are the outward and visible signs of an emotion, behind the commonplace, conventional expression that both reveals and conceals an individual mental state, it is the emotion, the original mood, to which they attain in its undefiled essence. And then, to induce us to make the same effort ourselves, they contrive to make us see something of what they have seen: by rhythmical arrangement of words, which thus become organized and animated with a life of their own, they tell us—or rather suggest—things that speech was not calculated to express. Others delve yet deeper still. Beneath these joys and sorrows which can, at a pinch, be translated into language, they grasp something that has nothing in common with language, certain rhythms of life and breath that are closer to man than his inmost feelings, being the living law—varying with each individual—of his enthusiasm and despair, his hopes and regrets. By setting free and emphasizing this music, they force it upon our attention; they compel us, willy-nilly, to fall in with it, like passers-by who join in a dance. And thus they impel us to set in motion, in the depths of our being, some secret chord which was only waiting to thrill. So art, whether it be painting or sculpture, poetry or music, has no other object than to brush aside the utilitarian symbols, the conventional and socially accepted generalities, in short, everything that veils reality from us, in order to bring us face to face with reality itself. It is from a misunderstanding on this point that the dispute between realism and idealism in art has arisen. Art is certainly only a more direct vision of reality. But this purity of perception implies a break with utilitarian convention, an innate and specially localized disinterestedness of sense or consciousness, in short, a certain immateriality of life, which is what has always been called idealism. So we might say, without in any way playing upon the meaning of the words, that realism is in the work when idealism is in the soul, and that it is only through ideality that we can resume contact with reality.

Dramatic art forms no exception to this law. What drama goes forth to discover and brings to light, is a deep-seated reality that is veiled from us, often in our own interests, by the necessities of life. What is this reality? What are these necessities? Poetry always expresses inward states. But amongst these states some arise mainly from contact with our fellowmen. They are the most intense as well as the most violent. As contrary electricities attract each other and accumulate between the two plates of the condenser from which the spark will presently flash, so, by simply bringing people together, strong attractions and repulsions take place, followed by an utter loss of balance, in a word, by that electrification of the soul known as passion. Were man to give way to the impulse of his natural feelings, were there neither social nor moral law, these outbursts of violent feeling would be the ordinary rule in life. But utility demands that these outbursts should be foreseen and averted. Man must live in society, and consequently submit to rules. And what interest advises, reason commands: duty calls, and we have to obey the summons. Under this dual influence has perforce been formed an outward layer of feelings and ideas which make for permanence, aim at becoming common to all men, and cover, when they are not strong enough to extinguish it, the inner fire of individual passions. The slow progress of mankind in the direction of an increasingly peaceful social life has gradually consolidated this layer, just as the life of our planet itself has been one long effort to cover over with a cool and solid crust the fiery mass of seething metals. But volcanic eruptions occur. And if the earth were a living being, as mythology has feigned, most likely when in repose it would take delight in dreaming of these sudden explosions, whereby it suddenly resumes possession of its innermost nature. Such is just the kind of pleasure that is provided for us by drama. Beneath the quiet humdrum life that reason and society have fashioned for us, it stirs something within us which luckily does not explode, but which it makes us feel in its inner tension. It offers nature her revenge upon society. Sometimes it makes straight for the goal, summoning up to the surface, from the depths below, passions that produce a general upheaval. Sometimes it effects a flank movement, as is often the case in contemporary drama; with a skill that is frequently sophistical, it shows up the inconsistencies of society; it exaggerates the shams and shibboleths of the social law; and so indirectly, by merely dissolving or corroding the outer crust, it again brings us back to the inner core. But, in both cases, whether it weakens society or strengthens nature, it has the same end in view: that of laying bare a secret portion of ourselves —what might be called the tragic element in our character. This is indeed the impression we get after seeing a stirring drama. What has just interested us is not so much what we have been told about others as the glimpse we have caught of ourselves—a whole host of ghostly feelings, emotions and events that would fain have come into real existence, but, fortunately for us, did not. It also seems as if an appeal had been made within us to certain ancestral memories belonging to a far-away past—memories so deep-seated and so foreign to our present life that this latter, for a moment, seems something unreal and conventional, for which we shall have to serve a fresh apprenticeship. So it is indeed a deeper reality that drama draws up from beneath our superficial and utilitarian attainments, and this art has the same end in view as all the others.

Hence it follows that art always aims at what is *individual.* What the artist fixes on his canvas is something he has seen at a certain spot, on a certain day, at a certain hour, with a coloring that will never be seen again. What the poet sings of is a certain mood which was his, and his alone, and which will never return. What the dramatist unfolds before us is the life-history of a soul, a living tissue of feelings and events—something, in short, which has once happened and can never be repeated. We may, indeed, give general names to these feelings, but they cannot be the same thing in another soul. They are *individualized.* Thereby, and thereby only, do they belong to art; for generalities, symbols or even types, form the current coin of our daily perception. How, then, does a misunderstanding on this point arise?

The reason lies in the fact that two very different things have been mistaken for each other: the generality of things and that of the opinions we come to regarding them. Because a feeling is generally recognized as true, it does not follow that it is a general feeling. Nothing could be more unique than the character of Hamlet. Though he may resemble other men in some respects, it is clearly not on that account that he interests us most. But he is universally accepted and regarded as a living character. In this sense only is he universally true. The same holds good of all the other products of art. Each of them is unique, and yet, if it bear the stamp of genius, it will come to be accepted by everybody. Why will it be accepted? And if it is unique of its kind, by what sign do we know it to be genuine? Evidently, by the very effort it forces us to make against our predispositions in order to see sincerely. Sincerity is contagious. What the artist has seen we shall probably never see again, or at least never see in exactly the same way; but if he has actually seen it, the attempt he has made to lift the veil compels our imitation. His work is an example which we take as a lesson. And the efficacy of the lesson is the exact standard of the genuineness of the work. Consequently, truth bears within itself a power of conviction, nay, of conversion, which is the sign that enables us to recognize it. The greater the work and the more profound the dimly apprehended truth, the longer may the effect be in coming, but, on the other hand, the more universal will that effect tend to become. So the universality here lies in the effect produced, and not in the cause.

Altogether different is the object of comedy. Here it is in the work itself that the generality lies. Comedy depicts characters we have already come across and shall meet with again. It takes note of similarities. It aims at placing types before our eyes. It even creates new types, if necessary. In this respect it forms a contrast to all the other arts.

The very titles of certain classical comedies are significant in themselves. Le Misanthrope, l'Avare, le Joueur, le Distrait, and so on, are names of whole classes of people; and even when a character comedy has a proper noun as its title, this proper noun is speedily swept away, by the very weight of its contents, into the stream of common nouns. We say "a Tartuffe," but we should never say "a Phèdre" or "a Polyeucte."

Above all, a tragic poet will never think of grouping around the chief character in his play secondary characters to serve as simplified copies, so to speak, of the former. The hero of a tragedy represents an individuality unique of its kind. It may be possible to imitate him, but then we shall be passing, whether consciously or not, from the tragic to the comic. No one is like him, because he is like no one. But a remarkable instinct, on the contrary, impels the comic poet, once he has elaborated his central character, to cause other characters, displaying the same general traits, to revolve as satellites round him. Many comedies have either a plural noun or some collective term as their title. "*Les* Femmes savantes," "*Les* Précieuses ridicules," "*Le Monde* où l'on s'ennuie," and so forth, represent so many rallying points on the stage adopted by different groups of characters, all belonging to one identical type. It would be interesting to analyze this tendency in comedy. Maybe dramatists have caught a glimpse of a fact recently brought forward by mental pathology, namely that cranks of the same kind are drawn, by a secret attraction, to seek each others' company. Without precisely coming within the province of medicine, the comic individual, as we have shown, is in some way absentminded, and the transition from absentmindedness to crankiness is continuous. But there is also another reason. If the comic poet's object is to offer us types, that is to say, characters capable of self-repetition, how can he set about it better than by showing us, in each instance, several different copies of the same model? That is just what the naturalist does in order to define a species. He enumerates and describes its main varieties.

The essential difference between tragedy and comedy, the former being concerned with individuals and the latter with classes, is revealed in yet another way. It appears in the first draft of the work. From the outset it is manifested by two radically different methods of observation.

Though the assertion may seem paradoxical, a study of other men is probably not necessary to the tragic poet. We find some of the great poets have lived a retiring, homely sort of life, without having a chance of witnessing around them an outburst of the passions they have so faithfully depicted. But, supposing even they had witnessed such a spectacle, it is doubtful whether they would have found it of much use. For what interests us in the work of the poet is the glimpse we get of certain profound moods or inner struggles. Now, this glimpse cannot be obtained from without. Our souls are impenetrable to one another. Certain signs of passion are all that we ever apperceive externally. These we interpret—though always, by the way, defectively—only by analogy with what we have ourselves experienced. So what we experience is the main point, and we cannot become thoroughly acquainted with anything but our own heart—supposing we ever get so far. Does this mean that the poet has experienced what he depicts, that he has gone through the various situations he makes his characters traverse, and lived the whole of their inner life? Here, too, the biographies of poets would contradict such a supposition. How, indeed, could the same man have been Macbeth, Hamlet, Othello, King Lear, and many others? But then a distinction should perhaps here be made between the personality *we have* and all those we might have had. Our character is the result of a choice that is continually being renewed. There are points—at all events there seem to be—all along the way, where we may branch off, and we perceive many possible directions though we are unable to take more than one. To retrace one's steps, and follow to the end the faintly distinguishable directions, appears to be the essential element in poetic imagination. Of course, Shakespeare was neither Macbeth, nor Hamlet, nor Othello; still, he *might have been* these several characters if the circumstances of the case on the one hand, and the consent of his will on the other, had caused to break out into explosive action what was nothing more than an inner prompting. We are strangely mistaken as to the part played by poetic imagination, if we think it pieces together its heroes out of fragments filched from right and left, as though it were patching together a harlequin's motley. Nothing living would result from that. Life cannot be recomposed; it can only be looked at and reproduced. Poetic imagination is but a fuller view of reality. If the characters created by a poet give us the impression of life, it is only because they are the poet himself—a multiplication or division of the poet—the poet plumbing the depths of his own nature in so powerful an effort of inner observation that he lays hold of the potential in the real, and takes up what nature has left as a mere outline or sketch in his soul in order to make of it a finished work of art.

Altogether different is the kind of observation from which comedy springs. It is directed outwards. However interested a dramatist may be in the comic features of human nature, he will hardly go, I imagine, to the extent of trying to discover his own. Besides, he would not find them, for we are never ridiculous except in some point that remains hidden from our own consciousness. It is on others, then, that such observation must perforce be practiced. But it will, for this very reason, assume a character of generality that it cannot have when we apply it to ourselves. Settling on the surface, it will not be more than skin-deep, dealing with persons at the point at which they come into contact and become capable of resembling one another. It will go no further. Even if it could, it would not desire to do so, for it would have nothing to gain in the process. To penetrate too far into the personality, to couple the outer effect with causes that are too deep-seated, would mean to endanger and in the end to sacrifice all that was laughable in the effect. In order that we may be tempted to laugh at it, we must localize its cause in some intermediate region of the soul. Consequently, the effect must appear to us as an average effect, as expressing an average of mankind. And, like all averages, this one is obtained by bringing together scattered data, by comparing analogous cases and extracting their essence, in short by a process of abstraction and generalization similar to that which the physicist brings to bear upon facts with the object of grouping them under laws. In a word, method and object arc here of the same nature as in the inductive sciences, in that observation is always external and the result always general.

And so we come back, by a roundabout way, to the double conclusion we reached in the course of our investigations. On the one hand, a person is never ridiculous except through some mental attribute resembling absent-mindedness, through something that lives upon him without forming part of his organism, after the fashion of a parasite; that is the reason this state of mind is observable from without and capable of being corrected. But, on the other hand, just because laughter aims at correcting, it is expedient that the correction should reach as great a number of persons as possible. This is the reason comic observation instinctively proceeds to what is general. It chooses such peculiarities as admit of being reproduced and consequently are not indissolubly bound up with the individuality of a single person—a possibly common sort of uncommonness, so to say—pecularities that are held in common. By transferring them to the stage, it creates works which doubtless belong to art in that their only visible aim is to please, but which will be found to contrast with other works of art by reason of their generality and also of their scarcely confessed or scarcely conscious intention to correct and instruct. So we were probably right in saying that comedy lies midway between art and life. It is not disinterested, as genuine art is. By organizing laughter, comedy accepts social life as a natural environment, it even obeys an impulse of social life. And in this respect it turns its back upon art, which is a breaking away from society and a return to pure nature.

—*Laughter* (1909; translated by Cloudesley Brereton and Fred Rothwell, 1913)

BENEDETTO CROCE

Intuition and Expression

Poetry as Intuition

If we examine a poem in order to determine what it is that makes us feel it to be a poem, we at once find two constant and necessary elements: a complex of *images,* and a *feeling* that animates them. Let us, for instance, recall a passage learnt at school: Virgil's lines (*Aeneid,* iii, 294, *sqq.*), in which Aeneas described how on hearing that in the country to whose shores he had come the Trojan Helenus was reigning, with Andromache, now his wife, he was overcome with amazement and a great desire to see this surviving son of Priam and to hear of his strange adventures. Andromache, whom he meets outside the walls of the city, by the waters of a river renamed Simois, celebrating funeral rites before a cenotaph of green turf and two altars to Hector and Astyanax; her astonishment on seeing him, her hesitation, the halting words in which she questions him, uncertain whether he is a man or a ghost; Aeneas's no less agitated replies and interrogations, and the pain and confusion with which she recalls the past —how she lived through scenes of blood and shame, how she was assigned by lot as slave and concubine to Pyrrhus, abandoned by him and united to Helenus, another of his slaves, how Pyrrhus fell by the hand of Orestes and Helenus became a free man and a king; the entry of Aeneas and his men into the city, and their reception by the son of Priam in this little Troy, this mimic Pergamon with its new Xanthus, and its Scaean Gate whose threshold Aeneas greets with a kiss—all these details, and others here omitted, are images of persons, things, attitudes, gestures, sayings, joy and sorrow; mere images, not history or historical criticism, for which they are neither given nor taken. But through them all there runs a feeling, a feeling which is our own no less than the poet's, a human feeling of bitter memories, of shuddering horror, of melancholy, of homesickness, of tenderness, of a kind of childish *pietas* that could prompt this vain revival of things perished, these playthings, fashioned by a religious devotion. . . . something inexpressible in logical terms, which only poetry can express in full. Moreover, these two elements may appear as two in a first abstract analysis, but they cannot be regarded as two distinct threads, however intertwined; for in effect, the feeling is altogether converted into images, into this complex of images, and is thus a feeling that is contemplated and therefore resolved and transcended. Hence poetry must be called neither feeling, nor image, nor yet the sum of the two, but "contemplation of feeling" or "lyrical intuition" or (which is the same thing) "pure intuition" —pure, that is, of all historical and critical reference to the reality or unreality of the images of which it is woven, and apprehending the pure throb of life in its ideality. Doubtless, other things may be found in poetry besides these two elements or moments and the synthesis of the two; but these other things are either present as extraneous elements in a compound (reflections, exhortations, polemics, allegories, etc.), or else they are just these image-feelings themselves taken in abstraction from their context as so much material, restored to the condition in which it was before the act of poetic creation. In the former case, they are nonpoetic elements merely interpolated into or attached to the poem; in the latter, they are divested of poetry, rendered unpoetical by a reader either unpoetical or not at the moment poetical, who has dispelled the poetry, either because he cannot live in its ideal realm, or for the legitimate ends of historical enquiry or other practical purposes which involve the degradation—or rather, the conversion—of the poem into a document or an instrument.

Artistic Qualities

What has been said of "poetry" applies to all the other "arts" commonly enumerated; painting, sculpture, architecture, music. Whenever the artistic quality of any product of the mind is discussed, the dilemma must be faced, that either it is a lyrical intuition, or it is something else, something just as respectable, but not art. If painting (as some theorists have maintained) were the imitation or reproduction of a given object, it would be, not art, but something mechanical and practical; if the task of the painter (as other theorists have held were to combine lines and lights and colors with ingenious novelty of invention and effect, he would be, not an artist, but an inventor. . . . Thus the critics of these arts advise the artist to exclude, or at least not to rely upon, what they call the "literary" elements in painting, sculpture and music, just as the critic of poetry advises the writer to look for "poetry" and not be led astray by mere literature. The reader who understands poetry goes straight to this poetic heart and feels its beat upon his own; where this beat is silent, he denies that poetry is present, whatever and however many other things may take its place, united in the work, and however valuable they may be for skill and wisdom, nobility of intellect, quickness of wit and pleasantness of effect. The reader who does not understand poetry loses his way in pursuit of these other things. He is wrong not because he admires them, but because he thinks he is admiring poetry.

Other Forms of Activity As Distinct from Art

By defining art as lyrical or pure intuition we have implicitly distingushed it from all other forms of mental production. If such distinctions are made explicit, we obtain the following negations:

1. *Art is not philosophy,* because philosophy is the logical thinking of the universal categories of being, and art is the unreflective intuition of being. Hence, while philosophy transcends the image and uses it for its own purposes, art lives in it as in a kingdom. It is said that art cannot behave in an irrational manner and cannot ignore logic; and certainly it is neither irrational nor illogical; but its own rationality, its own logic, is a quite different thing from the dialectical logic of the concept, and it was in order to indicate this peculiar and unique character that the name "logic of sense" or "esthetic" was invented. The not uncommon assertion that art has a logical character, involves either an equivocation between conceptual logic and esthetic logic, or a symbolic expression of the latter in terms of the former.

2. *Art is not history,* because history implies the critical distinction between reality and unreality; the reality of the fact and the reality of a fancied world; the reality of action and the reality of desire. For art, these distinctions are as yet unmade; it lives, as we have said, upon pure images. The historical existence of Helenus, Andromache, and Aeneas makes no difference to the poetical quality of Virgil's poem. Here, too, an objection has been raised: namely, that art is not wholly indifferent to historical criteria, because it obeys the laws of "verisimilitude"; but, here again, "verisimilitude" is only a rather clumsy metaphor for the mutual coherence of images, which without this internal coherence would fail to produce their effect as images. . . .

3. *Art is not natural science,* because natural science is historical fact classified and so made abstract; nor is it *mathematical science,* because

mathematics performs operations with abstractions and does not contemplate. The analogy sometimes drawn between mathematical and poetical creation is based on merely external and generic resemblances; and the alleged necessity of a mathematical or geometrical basis for the arts is only another metaphor, a symbolic expression of the constructive, cohesive and unifying force of the poetic mind building itself a body of images.

4. *Art is not the play of fancy,* because the play of fancy passes from image to image, in search of variety, rest or diversion, seeking to amuse itself with the likenesses of things that give pleasure or have an emotional and pathetic interest; whereas in art the fancy is so dominated by the single problem of converting chaotic feeling into clear intuition, that we recognize the propriety of ceasing to call it fancy and calling it imagination, poetic imagination or creative imagination. Fancy as such is as far removed from poetry as are the works of Mrs. Radcliffe or Dumas *père.*

5. *Art is not feeling in its immediacy. . . .* [T]he poet does not lose his wits or grow stiff as he gazes; he does not totter or weep or cry; he expresses himself in harmonious verses, having made these various perturbations the object of which he sings. Feelings in their immediacy are "expressed" for if they are not, if they were not also sensible and bodily facts ("psycho-physical phenomena," as the positivists used to call them) they would not be concrete things, and so they would be nothing at all. Andromache expressed herself in the way described above. But "expression" in this sense, even when accompanied by consciousness, is a mere metaphor from "mental" or "esthetic expression" which alone really expresses, that is, gives to feeling a theoretical form and converts it into words, song and outward shape. This distinction between contemplated feeling, or poetry, and feeling enacted or endured, is the source of the power, ascribed to art, of "liberating us from the passions" and "calming" us (the power *of catharsis*), and of the consequent condemnation, from an esthetic point of view, of works of art, or parts of them, in which immediate feeling has a place or finds a vent. Hence, too, arises another characteristic of poetic expression—really synonymous with the last—namely its "infinity" as opposed to the "finitude" of immediate feeling or passion; or, as it is also called, the "universal" or "cosmic" character of poetry. Feeling, not crushed but contemplated by the work of poetry, is seen to diffuse itself in widening circles over all the realm of the soul, which is the realm of the universe, echoing and reechoing endlessly: joy and sorrow, pleasure and pain, energy and lassitude, earnestness and frivolity, and so forth, are linked to each other and lead to each other through infinite shades and gradations; so that the feeling, while preserving its individual physiognomy and its original dominating motive, is not exhausted by or restricted to this original character. A comic image, if it is poetically comic, carries with it something that is not comic, as in the case of Don Quixote or Falstaff; and the image of something terrible is never, in poetry, without an atoning element of loftiness, goodness and love.

6. *Art is not instruction or oratory:* it is not circumscribed and limited by service to any practical purpose whatever, whether this be the inculcation of a particular philosophical, historical or scientific truth, or the advocacy of a particular way of feeling and the action corresponding to it. Oratory

at once robs expression of its "infinity" and independence, and, by making it the means to an end, dissolves it in this end. Hence arises what Schiller called the "nondetermining" character of art, as opposed to the "determining" character of oratory; and hence the justifiable suspicion of "political poetry"—political poetry being, proverbially, bad poetry.

7. As art is not to be confused with the form of practical action most akin to it, namely instruction and oratory, so *a fortiori,* it must not be confused with other forms directed to the production of certain effects, whether these consist in pleasure, enjoyment, and utility, or in goodness and righteousness. We must exclude from art not only meretricious works, but also those inspired by a desire for goodness, as equally, though differently, inartistic and repugnant to lovers of poetry. . . .

Art in Its Relations

The "negations" here made explicit are obviously, from another point of view, "relations"; for the various distinct forms of mental activity cannot be conceived as separate each from the rest and acting in self-supporting isolation. This is not the place to set forth a complete system of the forms or categories of the mind in their order and their dialectic; confining ourselves to art, we must be content to say that the category of art, like every other category, mutually presupposes and is presupposed by all the rest: It is conditioned by them all and conditions them all. How could the esthetic synthesis, which is poetry, arise, were it not preceded by a state of mental commotion? . . . And what is this state of mind which we have called feeling, but the whole mind, with its past thoughts, volitions, and actions, now thinking and desiring and suffering and rejoicing, travailing within itself? Poetry is like a ray of sunlight shining upon this darkness, lending it its own light and making visible the hidden forms of things. Hence it cannot be produced by an empty and dull mind; hence those artists who embrace the creed of pure art or art for art's sake, and close their hearts to the troubles of life and the cares of thought, are found to be wholly unproductive, or at most rise to the imitation of others or to an impressionism devoid of concentration. Hence the basis of all poetry is human personality, and, since human personality finds its completion in morality, the basis of all poetry is the moral consciousness. Of course this does not mean that the artist must be a profound thinker or an acute critic; nor that he must be a pattern of virtue or a hero; but he must have a share in the world of thought and action which will enable him, either in his own person or by sympathy with others, to live the whole drama of human life. He may sin, lose the purity of his heart, and expose himself, as a practical agent, to blame; but he must have a keen sense of purity and impurity, righteousness and sin, good and evil. He may not be endowed with great practical courage; he may even betray signs of timidity and cowardice; but he must feel the dignity of courage. Many artistic inspirations are due, not to what the artist, as a man, is in practice, but to what he is not, and feels that he ought to be, admiring and enjoying the qualities he lacks when he sees them in others. Many, perhaps the finest, pages of heroic and warlike poetry are by men who never had the nerve or the skill to handle a weapon. On the other hand, we are not maintaining that the possession of a moral personality is enough to make a poet or an artist. . . . The *sine qua non* of poetry is poetry, that form of theoretical synthesis which we have defined above; the spark of poetical genius without which all the rest is mere fuel, not burning because no fire is at hand to light it. But the figure of the pure poet, the pure artist, the votary of pure Beauty, aloof from contact with humanity, is no real figure but a caricature.

That poetry not only presupposes the other forms of human mental activity but is presupposed by them, is proved by the fact that without the poetic imagination which gives contemplative form to the workings of feeling, intuitive expression to obscure impressions, and thus becomes representations and words, whether spoken or sung or painted or otherwise uttered, logical thought could not arise. Logical thought is not language, but it never exists without language, and it uses the language which poetry has created; by means of concepts, it discerns and dominates the representations of poetry, and it could not dominate them unless they, its future subjects, had first an existence of their own. Further, without the discerning and criticizing activity of thought, action would be impossible; and if action, then good action, the moral consciousness, duty. Every man, however much he may seem to be all logical thinker, critic, scientist, or all absorbed in practical interests or devoted to duty, cherishes at the bottom of his heart his own private store of imagination and poetry; even Faust's pedantic *famulus,* Wagner, confessed that he often had his "grillenhafte Stunden." Had this element been altogether denied him, he would not have been a man, and therefore not even a thinking or acting being. This extreme case is an absurdity; in proportion as this private store is scanty, we find a certain superficiality and aridity in thought, and a certain coldness of action.

Intuition and Expression

One of the first problems to arise, when the work of art is defined as "lyrical image," concerns the relation of "intuition" to "expression" and the manner of the transition from one to the other. At bottom this is the same problem which arises in other parts of philosophy: the problem of inner and outer, of mind and matter, of soul and body, and, in ethics, of intention and will, will and action, and so forth. Thus stated, the problem is insoluble; for once we have divided the inner from the outer, body from mind, will from action, or intuition from expression, there is no way of passing from one to the other or of reuniting them, unless we appeal for their reunion to a third term, variously represented as God or the Unknowable. Dualism leads necessarily either to transcendence or to agnosticism. But when a problem is found to be insoluble in the terms in which it is stated the only course open is to criticize these terms themselves, to inquire how they have been arrived at, and whether their genesis was logically sound. In this case, such inquiry leads to the conclusion that the terms depend not upon a philosophical principle, but upon an empirical and naturalistic classification, which has created two groups of facts called internal and external respectively (as if internal facts were not also external, and as if an external fact could exist without being also internal), or souls and bodies, or images and expressions; and everyone knows that it is hopeless to try to find a dialectical unity between terms that have been distinguished not philosophically or formally but only empirically and materially. The soul is only a soul in so far as it is a body; the will is only a will in so far as it moves arms and legs, or is action; intuition is only intuition in so far as it is, in that very act, expression. An image that does not express, that is not speech, song, drawing, painting, sculpture or architecture—speech at least murmured to oneself, song at least echoing within one's own breast, line and color seen in imagination and coloring with its own tint the whole soul and organism—is an image that does not exist. We may assert its existence, but we cannot support our assertion; for the only thing we could adduce in support of it would be the fact that the image was embodied or expressed. This profound philosophical doctrine, the *identity of intuition and expression* is, moreover, a principle of ordinary common sense, which laughs at people who claim to have thoughts they cannot express or to have imagined a great picture which they cannot paint. . . . This identity, which applies to every sphere of the mind, has in the sphere of art a clearness and self-evidence lacking, perhaps, elsewhere. In the creation of a work of poetry, we are present, as it were, at the mystery of the creation of the world; hence the value of the contribution made by esthetics to philosophy as a whole, or the conception of the One that is All. Esthetics, by denying in the life of art an abstract spiritualism and the resulting dualism, prepares the way and leads the mind towards idealism or absolute spiritualism.

Expression and Communication

Objections to the identity of intuition and expression generally arise from psychological illusions which lead us to believe that we possess at any given moment a profusion of concrete and lively images, when in fact we only possess signs and names for them; or else from faulty analysis of cases like that of the artist who is believed to express mere fragments of a world of images that exists in his mind in its entirety, whereas he really has in his mind only these fragments, together with—not the supposed complete world, but at most an aspiration or obscure working towards it, towards a greater and richer image which may take shape or may not. But these objections also arise from a confusion between *expression* and *communication,* the latter being really distinct from the image and its expression. Communication is the fixation of the intuition-expression upon an object metaphorically called material or physical; in reality, even here we are concerned not with material or physical things but with a mental process. The proof that the so-called physical object is unreal, and its resolution into terms of mind, is primarily of interest for our general philosophical conceptions, and only indirectly for the elucidation of esthetic questions; hence for brevity's sake we may let the metaphor or symbol stand and speak of matter or nature. It is clear that the poem is complete as soon as the poet has expressed it in words which he repeats to himself. When he comes to repeat them aloud, for others to hear, or looks for someone to learn them by heart and repeat them to others . . . or sets them down in writing or in printing, he has entered upon a new stage, not esthetic but practical, whose social and cultural importance need not, of course, be insisted upon. So with the painter; he paints on his panel or canvas, but he could not paint unless at every stage in his work, from the original blur or sketch to the finishing touches, the intuited image, the line and color painted in his imagination, preceded the brush-stroke. Indeed, when the brush-stroke outruns the image, it is cancelled and replaced by the artist's correction of his own work. The exact line that divides expression from communication is difficult to draw in the concrete case, for in the concrete case the two processes generally alternate rapidly and appear to mingle, but it is clear in idea, and it must be firmly grasped. Through overlooking it, or blurring it through insufficient attention, arise the confusions between *art* and *technique*. Technique is not an intrinsic element of art but has to do precisely with the concept of communication. In general it is a cognition or complex of cognitions disposed and directed to the furtherance of practical action; and, in the case of art, of the practical action which makes objects and instruments for the recording and communicating of works of art; e.g., cognitions concerning the preparation of panels, canvases or walls to be painted, pigments, varnishes, ways of obtaining good pronunciation and declamation and so forth. Technical treatises are not esthetic treatises, nor yet parts or chapters of them. Provided, that is, that the ideas are rigorously conceived and the words used accurately in relation to them it would not be worth while to pick a quarrel over the use of the word "technique" as a synonym for the artistic work itself, regarded as "inner technique" or the formation of intuition-expressions. The confusion between art and technique is especially beloved by impotent artists, who hope to obtain from practical things and practical devices and inventions the help which their strength does not enable them to give themselves.

—"Aesthetics," in *Encyclopaedia Britannica*, 14th edition (1944; translated by R. G. Collingwood)

CHAPTER 4

Imaginative Satisfaction of Desire

FRIEDRICH NIETZSCHE: Apollinian and Dionysian Art
SIGMUND FREUD: Wish-Fulfillment and the Unconscious
CHRISTOPHER CAUDWELL: Poetry's Dream-Work

The intuitionists Bergson and Croce define art as a kind of lyrical and disinterested vision. Most of the other writers in this volume similarly emphasize the nonpractical character of art. Friedrich Nietzsche (1844–1900), like his great contemporary Leo Tolstoy, challenged this nonutilitarian interpretation. "What does all art do?" he asks. "Does it not praise? Does it not glorify? Does it not select? Does it not bring things into prominence? In all this it *strengthens* or *weakens* certain valuations."[1] Art is thus fundamental to the whole enterprise of living. It is sublimely utilitarian.

Paradoxically combining pessimism and optimism, Nietzsche believes that the world, if untransformed by the will and imagination, is a thoroughly nasty place; but that, by means of art and a masterful morality, existence can be made profoundly satisfactory. There are two artistic ways of transforming the values of life—the Apollinian and the Dionysian. Apollinian art is similar to a dream (Apollo is the god of dreams). Man creates in his waking dreams a world of tranquillity and formal beauty, embodied especially in sculpture, architecture, painting, and the more chaste types of literature. The other type of art, symbolized by Dionysus, the god of wine and fertility, is similar to the state of love or intoxication, either of which impels us ecstatically to embrace experience. To explore by means of Dionysian art the depths and agonies of life, and imaginatively to cry "Yea," is the supreme triumph of the will to mastery. This type of art is represented above all by music (which for Nietzsche is the most intense of all the arts), but subordinately by dancing, lyric poetry, and tragedy. Nietzsche exhibits a keen insight into the subconscious depths of art, its relation to desire, and its alliance with dreams and love.

The esthetic theory of Sigmund Freud (1856–1939) is a continuation of such voluntaristic esthetics, but deepened and clarified by the knowledge derived from his general theory of psychoanalysis. Like Schopenhauer and Nietzsche, he believed that volition is the most fundamental and dynamic element in the mind. It shows itself in unrest and seeking, leading finally to action that brings the unrest to a close. We might define it broadly as an "impulse toward a goal." If the impulse succeeds, the result is a state of satisfaction. The question arises, Is it possible to separate volition from pleasure and unpleasure? The answer of Freud is *no*. The unrest of desire necessarily involves pain or unpleasure, and the appeasement of desire involves pleasure; these are, in a sense, phases of volition. His theory might be called hedonistic voluntarism.

In his essay, "The Relation of the Poet to Daydreaming," Freud reveals his indebtedness to the play theory of Schiller (see Chapter 13). Both play and art are described as imaginative expressions and fulfillments of wish. When a person grows up, he must put aside childish play, but he substitutes phantasy, in the form either of day or night dreams, and art. But with profound insight and originality, Freud goes far beyond the play theory in interpreting both dreams and art as the disguised expression of wishes—repressed but powerfully operative in "the unconscious." The "libido," the deep instinctive force of life, manifests itself in a continual striving for expression. When it is actively repressed by the more critical faculties, it assumes a multitude of disguises in order to circumvent the repressive forces. Chief among these disguises are the imagery of dreams and phantasies, and the symptoms of neurotic disorders. But the artist has an additional resource. By means of what Freud called "sublimation," he can deflect his psychic energy into channels of creative endeavor. He then learns to control his phantasies, and thus to sublimate his ambition and his sexual impulse in creative art. The dream is consciously inserted into the texture of waking life, and the repressed wishes, which might otherwise lead to neurosis, are fulfilled in imagination.

The shock and disillusionment of the First World War caused Freud to revise his ideas. He thereafter put less emphasis upon "Eros"—the impulse of love—and greater emphasis upon "Thanatos"—the impulse of death and destruction. In addition, he worked out the theory of a threefold structure of human personality. First, there is the *Id* (Latin for "it")—so-called because we tend to regard its manifestations as foreign to ourselves, as when we say, "That was not what I meant." It is governed by "the pleasure principle," and is the bearer of the primal energies of our deepest instinctive nature. Second, there is the *Ego*. It is our wide-awake "social self," governed by "the reality principle," and concerned with the perception of the environment and the self's adjustment to it. Third, there is the *Super-Ego*. It is the seat of our ideals and moral standards, largely unconscious, and built up in the individual in early childhood. The mind as "Censor" acts frequently at the behest of the Super-Ego, whose demands are more archaic and severe than those of the conscious Ego.

As Herbert Read, the English poet and critic, wrote, the work of art derives from all three regions of the mind: "It derives its energy, its irrationality and its mysterious power from the id, which is to be regarded as the source of what we usually call inspiration. It is given formal synthesis and unity by the ego; and finally it may be assimilated to those ideologies or spiritual aspirations which are the peculiar creation of the super-ego."[2] Unfortunately, Freud himself never wrote a sustained exposition of his more mature esthetic theories.

Toward the end of his essay, "The Relation of the Poet to Day-dreaming," he remarks that the poet may draw upon the "creations of racial psychology" as expressed in myths, legends, and fairy tales; and in our selection from *The Interpretation of Dreams,* he recognizes universal tragic themes that appear in such literary works as *Oedipus Rex* and *Hamlet*. A number of writers, such as Maud Bodkin and Joseph Campbell, explored this lead. They showed that similar symbols, however superficially various, are to be found in the dreams, myths, and imaginative creations of human beings everywhere. This contention has been supported by much data gathered by James Frazer and other anthropologists and by the Swiss psychiatrist, Carl Gustav Jung, who, with Freud and Adler, was one of the chief founders of psychoanalysis.

A similar interpretation of art is propounded by Christopher St. John Sprigg, who wrote under the pen name of Christopher Caudwell (1907–1937). He attained maturity in the period when fascism and economic crisis were threatening the very existence of civilization; and like many other minds—André Gide, Pablo Picasso, Stephen Spender, and Ignazio Silone, to mention only a few—he was greatly attracted by the ideas and program of Marxism. Moved to the quick by the Spanish Civil War, he joined the International Brigade, and was killed in action on February 12, 1937. In his brief life, he produced a number of outstanding books: *Illusion and Reality, Studies in a Dying Culture* (two volumes), *Poems, The Crisis in Physics,* and other works, all published posthumously.

His esthetic doctrines represent primarily a highly original synthesis of Freudian and Marxian ideas, although he also drew upon his wide knowledge of physical science to define the difference between science and art. He believed that Freud had thought too exclusively in terms of individual psychology, and that the Marxian social emphasis is needed to correct his one-sidedness. The dreams and illusions of the neurotic, he maintained, are just peculiar or aberrant in a personal way; the creations of the artist are more social and general—growing out of the funded experiences and traditions of mankind. The artist draws more fully upon the subconscious than does the ordinary normal person; but he differs from the neurotic in being more social, free, and normal. The artist *uses* his subconscious mind, masters it; the neurotic is *used by* it, enslaved to it. The artist plumbs man's universal instinctive nature (which Caudwell terms "the genotype"), but he socializes the visions that arise from these subconscious depths. With profound insight, Caudwell compares poetry with dreams, contrasts it with prose fiction, and defines the nature and function of art in contradistinction to science.

He declares that the purpose of art is to give external reality an affective organization drawn from the inner heart of life. He thus suggests that not merely the content but the form of the work of art is a sublimation, or imaginative fulfillment, of desire. In Chapter 8, "Form," the selection from DeWitt H. Parker is an elaboration of this theme, and it may be read as a supplement to the present chapter.

NOTES

1. Friedrich Nietzsche, *The Twilight of the Idols* (Macmillan; New York, 1924), p. 79.

2. Herbert Read, *Art and Society* (Pantheon Books, New York, 1945), p. 92.

FRIEDRICH NIETZSCHE

Apollinian and Dionysian Art

I. THE BIRTH OF TRAGEDY

1

We shall have gained much for the science of esthetics, once we perceive not merely by logical inference, but with the immediate certainty of vision, that the continuous development of art is bound up with the *Apollinian* and *Dionysian* duality—just as procreation depends on the duality of the sexes, involving perpetual strife with only periodically intervening reconciliations. The terms Dionysian and Apollinian we borrow from the Greeks, who disclose to the discerning mind the profound mysteries of their view of art, not, to be sure, in concepts, but in the intensely clear figures of their gods. Through Apollo and Dionysus, the two art deities of the Greeks, we come to recognize that in the Greek world there existed a tremendous opposition, in origin and aims,[1] between the Apollinian art of sculpture, and the nonimagistic, Dionysian art of music. These two different tendencies run parallel to each other, for the most part openly at variance; and they continually incite each other to new and more powerful births, which perpetuate an antagonism. Only superficially reconciled by the common term "art"; till eventually,[2] by a metaphysical miracle of the Hellenic "will," they appear coupled with each other, and through this coupling ultimately generate an equally Dionysian and Apollinian form of art—Attic tragedy.

In order to grasp these two tendencies, let us first conceive of them as the separate art worlds of dreams and intoxication. These physiological phenomena present a contrast analogous to that existing between the Apollinian and the Dionysian. It was in dreams, says Lucretius, that the glorious divine figures first appeared to the souls of men; in dreams the great shaper beheld the splendid bodies of superhuman beings; and the Hellenic poet, if questioned about the mysteries of poetic inspiration, would likewise have suggested dreams and he might have given an explanation like that of Hans Sachs in the *Meistersinger:*

The poet's tasks is this, my friend,
to read his dreams and comprehend.
The truest human fancy seems
to be revealed to us in dreams:
all poems and versification
are but true dreams' interpretation.[3]

The beautiful illusion[4] of the dream worlds, in the creation of which every man is truly an artist, is the prerequisite of all plastic art, and, as we shall see, of an important part of poetry also. In our dreams we delight in the immediate understanding of figures; all forms speak to us; there is nothing unimportant or superfluous. But even when this dream reality is most intense, we still have, glimmering through it, the sensation that it is *mere appearance*: at least this is my experience, and for its frequency—indeed, normality—I could adduce many proofs, including the sayings of the poets.

Philosophical men even have a presentiment that the reality in which we live and have our being is also mere appearance and that another, quite different reality lies beneath it. Schopenhauer actually indicates as the criterion of philosophical ability the occasional ability to view men and things as mere phantoms of dream images. Thus the esthetically sensitive man stands in the same relation to the reality of dreams as the philosopher does to the reality of existence; he is a close and willing observer, for these images afford him an interpretation of life, and by reflecting on these processes he trains himself for life.

It is not only the agreeable and friendly images that he experiences as something universally intelligible: the serious, the troubled, the sad, the gloomy, the sudden restraints, the tricks of accident, anxious expectations, in short, the whole divine comedy of life, including the inferno, also pass before him, not like mere shadows on a wall—for he lives and suffers with these scenes—and yet not without that fleeting sensation of illusion. And perhaps many will, like myself, recall how amid the dangers and terrors of dreams they have occasionally said to themselves in self-encouragement, and not without success: "It is a dream! I will dream on!" I have likewise heard of people who were able to continue one and the same dream for three and even more successive nights—facts which indicate clearly how our innermost being, our common ground, experiences dreams with profound delight and a joyous necessity.

This joyous necessity of the dream experience has been embodied by the Greeks in their Apollo: Apollo, the god of all plastic energies, is at the same time the soothsaying god. He, who (as the etymology of the name indicates) is the "shining one,"[5] the deity of light, is also ruler over the beautiful illusion of the inner world of fantasy. The higher truth, the perfection of these states in contrast to the incompletely intelligible everyday world, this deep consciousness of nature, healing and helping in sleep and dreams, is at the same time the symbolical analogue of the soothsaying faculty and of the arts generally, which make life possible and worth living. But we must also include in our image of Apollo that delicate boundary which the dream image must not overstep lest it have a pathological effect (in which case mere appearance would deceive us as if it were crude reality). We must keep in mind that measured restraint, that freedom from the wilder emotions, that calm of the sculptor god. His eye must be "sunlike," as befits his origin; even when it is angry and distempered it is still hallowed by beautiful illusion. And so, in one sense, we might apply to Apollo the words of Schopenhauer when he speaks of the man wrapped in the veil of *maya*[6] (*Welt als Wille und Vorstellung*, I, p. 416[7]): "Just as in a stormy sea that, unbounded in all directions, raises and drops mountainous waves, howling, a sailor sits in a boat and trusts in his frail bark: so in the midst of a world of torments the individual human being sits quietly, supported by and trusting in the *principium individuationis*."[8] In fact, we might say of Apollo that in him the unshaken faith in this *principium* and the calm repose of the man wrapped up in it receive their most sublime expression; and we might call Apollo himself the glorious divine image of the *principium individuationis*, through whose gestures and eyes all the joy and wisdom of "illusion," together with its beauty, speak to us.

In the same work Schopenhauer has depicted for us the tremendous *terror* which seizes man when he is suddenly dumfounded by the cognitive form of phenomena because the principle of sufficient reason, in some one of its manifestations, seems to suffer an exception. If we add to this terror the blissful ecstasy that wells from the innermost depths of man, indeed of nature, at this collapse of the *principium individuationis*, we steal a glimpse into the nature of the *Dionysian* which is brought home to us most intimately by the analogy of intoxication.

Either under the influence of the narcotic draught, of which the songs of all primitive men and peoples speak, or with the potent coming of spring that penetrates all nature with joy, these Dionysian emotions awake, and as they grow in intensity everything subjective vanishes into complete self-forgetfulness. In the German Middle Ages, too, singing and dancing crowds, ever increasing in number, whirled themselves from place to place under this same Dionysian impulse. In these dancers of St. John and St. Vitus, we rediscover the Bacchic choruses of the Greeks, with their prehistory in Asia Minor, as far back as Babylon and the orgiastic Sacaea.[9] There are some who, from obtuseness or lack of experience, turn away from such phenomena as from "folk-disease," with contempt or pity born of the consciousness of their own "healthy-mindedness." But of course such poor wretches have no idea how corpselike and ghostly their so-called "healthy-mindedness" looks when the glowing life of the Dionysian revelers roars past them.

Under the charm of the Dionysian not only is the union between man and man reaffirmed, but nature which has become alienated, hostile, or subjugated, celebrates once more her reconciliation with her lost son,[10] man. Freely, earth proffers her gifts, and peacefully the beasts of prey of the rocks and desert approach. The chariot of Dionysus is covered with flowers and garlands; panthers and tigers walk under its yoke. Transform Beethoven's "Hymn to Joy" into a painting; let your imagination conceive the multitudes bowing to the dust, awestruck—then you will approach the Dionysian. Now the slave is a free man; now all the rigid, hostile barriers that necessity, caprice, or "impudent convention"[11] have fixed between man and man are broken. Now, with the gospel of universal harmony, each one feels himself not only united, reconciled and fused with his neighbor, but as one with him, as if the veil of *maya* had been torn aside and were now merely fluttering in tatters before the mysterious primordial unity.

In song and in dance man expresses himself as a member of a higher community; he has forgotten how to walk and speak and is on the way toward flying into the air, dancing. His very gestures express enchantment. Just as the animals now talk, and the earth yields milk and honey, supernatural sounds emanate from him, too: he feels himself a god, he himself now walks about enchanted, in ecstasy, like the gods he saw walking in his dreams. He is no longer an artist, he has become a work of art: in these paroxysms of intoxication the artistic power of all nature reveals itself to the highest gratification of the primordial unity. The noblest clay, the most costly marble, man, is here kneaded and cut, and to the sound of the chisel strokes of the Dionysian world-artist rings out the cry of the Eleusinian mysteries: "Do you prostrate yourselves, millions? Do you sense your Maker, world?"[12]

2

Thus far we have considered the Apollinian and its opposite, the Dionysian, as artistic energies which burst forth from nature herself, *without the mediation of the human artist*—energies in which nature's art impulses are satisfied in the most immediate and direct way—first in the image world of dreams, whose completeness is not dependent upon the intellectual attitude or the artistic culture of any single being; and then as intoxicated reality, which likewise does not heed the single unit, but even seeks to destroy the individual and redeem him by a mystic feeling of oneness. With reference to these immediate art-states of nature, every artist is an "imitator," that is to say, either an Apollinian artist in dreams or a Dionysian artist in ecstasies, or finally—as for example in Greek tragedy—at once artist in both dreams and ecstasies; so we may perhaps picture him sinking down in his Dionysian intoxication and mystical self-abnegation, alone and apart from the singing revelers, and we may imagine how, through Apollinian dream-inspiration, his own state, i.e., his oneness with the inmost ground of the world, is revealed to him in a *symbolical dream image*.

So much for these general premises and contrasts. Let us now approach the *Greeks* in order to learn how highly these *art impulses of nature* were developed in them. Thus we shall be in a position to understand and appreciate more deeply that relation of the Greek artist to his archetypes which is, according to the Aristotelian expression, "the imitation of nature." In spite of all the dream literature and the numerous dream anecdotes of the Greeks, we can speak of their *dreams* only conjecturally, though with reasonable assurance. If we consider the incredibly precise and unerring plastic power of their eyes, together with their vivid, frank delight in colors, we can hardly refrain from assuming even for their dreams (to the shame of all those born later) a certain logic of line and contour, colors and groups, a certain pictorial sequence reminding us of their finest bas-reliefs whose perfection would certainly justify us, if a comparison were possible, in designating the dreaming Greeks as Homers and Homer as a dreaming Greek—in a deeper sense than that in which modern man, speaking of his dreams, ventures to compare himself with Shakespeare.

On the other hand, we need not conjecture regarding the immense gap which separates the *Dionysian Greek* from the Dionysian barbarian. From all quarters of the ancient world—to say nothing here of the modern—from Rome to Babylon, we can point to the existence of Dionysian festivals, types which bear, at best, the same relation to the Greek festivals which the bearded satyr, who borrowed his name and attributes from the goat, bears to Dionysus himself. In nearly every case these festivals centered in extravagant sexual licentiousness, whose waves overwhelmed all family life and its venerable traditions; the most savage natural instincts were unleashed, including even that horrible mixture of sensuality and cruelty which has always seemed to me to be the real "witches' brew." For some time, however, the Greeks were apparently perfectly insulated and guarded against the feverish excitements of these festivals, though knowledge of them must have come to Greece on all the routes of land and sea; for the figure of Apollo, rising full of pride, held out the Gorgon's head to this grotesquely uncouth Dionysian power—and really could not have countered any more dangerous force. It is in Doric art that this majestically rejecting attitude of Apollo is immortalized.

The opposition between Apollo and Dionysus became more hazardous and even impossible, when similar impulses finally burst forth from the deepest roots of the Hellenic nature and made a path for themselves: the Delphic god, by a seasonably effected reconciliation, now contented himself with taking the destructive weapons from the hands of his powerful antagonist. This reconciliation is the most important moment in the history of the Greek cult: wherever we turn we note the revolutions resulting from this event. The two antagonists were reconciled; the boundary lines to be observed henceforth by each were sharply defined, and there was to be a periodical exchange of gifts of esteem. At bottom, however, the chasm was not bridged over. But if we observe how, under the pressure of this treaty of peace, the Dionysian power revealed itself, we shall now recognize in the Dionysian orgies of the Greeks, as compared with the Babylonian Sacaea with their reversion of man to the tiger and the ape, the significance of festivals of world redemption and days of tranfiguration. It is with them that nature for the first time attains her artistic jubilee; it is with them that the destruction of the *principium individuationis* for the first time becomes an artistic phenomenon.

The horrible "witches' brew" of sensuality and cruelty becomes ineffective; only the curious blending and duality in the emotions of the Dionysian revelers remind us—as medicines remind us of deadly poisons—of the phenomenon that pain begets joy, that ecstasy may wring sounds of agony from us. At the very climax of joy there sounds a cry of horror or a yearning lamentation for an irretrievable loss. In these Greek festivals, nature seems to reveal a sentimental[13] trait; it is as if she were heaving a sigh at her dismemberment into individuals. The song and pantomime of such dually-minded revelers was something new and unheard-of in the Homeric-Greek world; and the Dionysian *music* in particular excited awe and terror. If music, as it would seem, had been known previously as an Apollinian art, it was so, strictly speaking, only as the wave beat of rhythm whose formative power was developed for the representation of Apollinian states. The music of Apollo was Doric architectonics in tones, but in tones that were merely suggestive, such as those of the cithara. The very element which forms the essence of Dionysian music (and hence of music in general) is carefully excluded as un-Apollinian—namely, the emotional power of the tone, the uniform flow of the melody, and the utterly incomparable world of harmony. In the Dionysian dithyramb man is incited to the greatest exaltation of all his symbolic faculties; something never before experienced struggles for utterance—the annihilation of the veil of *maya*, oneness as the soul of the race and of nature itself. The essence of nature is now to be expressed symbolically; we need a new world of symbols; and the entire symbolism of the body is called into play, not the mere symbolism of the lips, face, and speech but the whole pantomime of dancing, forcing every member into rhythmic movement. Then the other symbolic powers suddenly press forward, particularly those of music, in rhythmics, dynamics, and harmony. To grasp this collective release of all the symbolic powers, man must have already attained that height of self-abnegation which seeks to express itself symbolically through all these powers—and so the dithyrambic votary of Dionysus is understood only by his peers. With what astonishment must the Apollinian Greek have beheld him! With an astonishment that was all the greater the more it was mingled with the shuddering suspicion that all this was actually not so very alien to him after all, in fact, that it was only his Apollinian consciousness which, like a veil, hid this Dionysian world from his vision.

3

To understand this, it becomes necessary to level the artistic structure of the *Apollinian culture*, as it were, stone by stone, till the foundations on which it rests become visible. First of all we see the glorious *Olympian* figures of the gods, standing on the gables of this structure. Their deeds, pictured in brilliant reliefs, adorn its friezes. We must not be misled by the fact that Apollo stands side by side with the others as an individual deity, without any claim to priority of rank. For the same impulse that embodied itself in Apollo gave birth to this entire Olympian world, and in this sense Apollo is its father. What terrific need was it that could produce such an illustrious company of Olympian beings?

Whoever approaches these Olympians with another religion in his heart, searching among them for moral elevation, even for sanctity, for disincarnate spirituality, for charity and benevolence, will soon be forced to turn his back on them, discouraged and disappointed. For there is nothing here that suggests asceticism, spirituality, or duty. We hear nothing but the accents of an exuberant, triumphant life in which all things, whether good or evil, are deified.[14] And so the spectator may stand quite bewildered before this fantastic excess of life, asking himself by virtue of what magic potion these high-spirited men could have found life so enjoyable that, wherever they turned, their eyes beheld the smile of Helen, the ideal picture of their own existence, "floating in sweet sensuality." But to this spectator, who has already turned his back, we must say: "Do not go away, but stay and hear what Greek folk wisdom has to say of this very life, which with such inexplicable gaiety unfolds itself before your eyes.

"There is an ancient story that King Midas hunted in the forest a long time for the wise Silenus, the companion of Dionysus, without capturing him. When Silenus at last fell into his hands, the king asked what was the best and most desirable of all things for man. Fixed and immovable, the demigod said not a word, till at last, urged by the king, he gave a shrill laugh and broke out into these words: 'Oh, wretched ephemeral race, children of chance and misery, why do you compel me to tell you what it would be most expedient for you not to hear? What is best of all is utterly beyond your reach: not to be born, not to *be,* to be *nothing.* But the second best for you is—to die soon.' "[15]

How is the world of the Olympian gods related to this folk wisdom? Even as the rapturous vision of the tortured martyr to his suffering.

Now it is as if the Olympian magic mountain[16] had opened before us and revealed its roots to us. The Greek knew and felt the terror and horror of existence. That he might endure this terror at all, he had to interpose between himself and life the radiant dream-birth of the Olympians. That overwhelming dismay in the face of the titanic powers of nature, the Moira[17] enthroned inexorably over all knowledge, the vulture of the great lover of mankind, Prometheus, the terrible fate of the wise Oedipus, the family curse of the Atridae which drove Orestes to matricide: in short, that entire philosophy of the sylvan god, with its mythical exemplars, which caused the downfall of the melancholy Etruscans—all this was again and again overcome by the Greeks with the aid of the Olympian *middle world* of art; or at any rate it was veiled and withdrawn from sight. It was in order to be able to live that the Greeks had to create these gods from a most profound need. Perhaps we may picture the process to ourselves somewhat as follows: out of the original Titanic divine order of terror, the Olympian divine order of joy gradually evolved through the Apollinian impulse toward beauty, just as roses burst from thorny bushes. How else could this people, so sensitive, so vehement in its desires, so singularly capable of *suffering,* have endured existence, if it had not been revealed to them in their gods, surrounded with a higher glory?

The same impulse which calls art into being, as the complement and consummation of existence, seducing one to a continuation of life, was also the cause of the Olympian world which the Hellenic "will" made use of as a transfiguring mirror. Thus do the gods justify the life of man: they themselves live it—the only satisfactory theodicy! Existence under the bright sunshine of such gods is regarded as desirable in itself, and the real pain of Homeric men is caused by parting from it, especially by early parting: so that now, reversing the wisdom of Silenus, we might say of the Greeks that "to die soon is worst of all for them, the next worst—to die at all." Once heard, it will ring out again; do not forget the lament of the short-lived Achilles, mourning the leaflike change and vicissitudes of the race of men and the decline of the heroic age. It is not unworthy of the greatest hero to long for a continuation of life, even though he live as a day laborer.[18] At the Apollinian stage of development, the 'will' longs so vehemently for this existence, the Homeric man feels himself so completely at one with it, that lamentation itself becomes a song of praise.

Here we should note that this harmony which is contemplated with such longing by modern man, in fact, this oneness of man with nature (for which Schiller introduced the technical term "naïve"), is by no means a simple condition that comes into being naturally and as if inevitably. It is not a condition that, like a terrestrial paradise, *must* necessarily be found at the gate of every culture. Only a romantic age could believe this, an age which conceived of the artist in terms of Rousseau's *Emile* and imagined that in Homer it had found such an artist Emile, reared at the bosom of nature. Where we encounter the "naïve" in art, we should recognize the highest effect of Apollinian culture—which always must first overthrow an empire of Titans and slay monsters, and which must have triumphed over an abysmal and terrifying view of the world and the keenest susceptibility to suffering through recourse to the most forceful and pleasurable illusions. But how rarely is the naïve attained—that consummate immersion in the beauty of mere appearance! How unutterably sublime is *Homer* therefore, who, as an individual being, bears the same relation to this Apollinian folk culture as the individual dream artist does to the dream faculty of the people and of nature in general.

The Homeric "naïveté" can be understood only as the complete victory of Apollinian illusion: this is one of those illusions which nature so frequently employs to achieve her own ends. The true goal is veiled by a phantasm: and while we stretch out our hands for the latter, nature attains the former by means of our illusion. In the Greeks the "will" wished to contemplate itself in the transfiguration of genius and the world of art; in order to glorify themselves, its creatures had to feel themselves worthy of glory; they had to behold themselves again in a higher sphere, without this perfect world of contemplation acting as a command or a reproach. This is the sphere of beauty, in which they saw their mirror images, the Olympians. With this mirroring of beauty the Hellenic will combated its artistically correlative talent for suffering and for the wisdom of suffering—and, as a monument of its victory, we have Homer, the naïve artist.

4

Now the dream analogy may throw some light on the naïve artist. Let us imagine the dreamer: in the midst of the illusion of the dream world and without disturbing it, he calls out to himself: "It is a dream, I will dream on." What must we infer? That he experiences a deep inner joy in dream contemplation; on the other hand, to be at all able to dream with this inner joy in contemplation, he must have completely lost sight of the waking reality and its ominous obtrusiveness. Guided by the dream-reading Apollo, we may interpret all these phenomena in roughly this way.

Though it is certain that of the two halves of our existence, the waking and the dreaming states, the former appeals to us as infinitely preferable, more important, excellent, and worthy of being lived, indeed, as that which alone is lived—yet in relation to that mysterious ground of our being of which we are the phenomena, I should, paradoxical as it may seem, maintain the very opposite estimate of the value of dreams. For the more clearly I perceive in nature those omnipotent art impulses, and in them an ardent longing for illusion, for redemption through illusion, the more I feel myself impelled to the metaphysical assumption that the truly existent primal unity, eternally suffering and contradictory, also needs the rapturous vision, the pleasurable illusion, for its continuous redemption. And we, completely wrapped up in this illusion and composed of it, are compelled to consider this illusion as the truly nonexistent—i.e., as a perpetual becoming in time, space, and causality—in other words, as empirical reality. If, for the moment, we do not consider the question of our own "reality," if we conceive of our empirical existence, and of that of the world in general, as a continuously manifested representation of the primal unity, we shall then have to look upon the dream as a *mere appearance of mere appearance,* hence as a still higher appeasement of the primordial desire for mere appearance. And that is why the innermost heart of nature feels that ineffable joy in the naïve artist and the naïve work of art, which is likewise only "mere appearance of mere appearance."

In a symbolic painting, *Raphael,* himself one of these immortal "naïve" ones, has represented for us this demotion of appearance to the level of mere appearance, the primitive process of the naïve artist and of Apollinian culture. In his *Transfiguration,* the lower half of the picture, with the possessed boy, the despairing bearers, the bewildered, terrified disciples, shows us the reflection of suffering, primal and eternal, the sole ground of the world: the "mere appearance" here is the reflection of eternal contradiction, the father of things. From this mere appearance arises, like ambrosial vapor, a new visionary world of mere appearances, invisible to those wrapped in the first appearance—a radiant floating in purest bliss, a serene contemplation beaming from wide-open eyes. Here we have presented, in the most sublime artistic symbolism, that Apollinian world of beauty and its substratum, the terrible wisdom of Silenus; and intuitively we comprehend their necessary interdependence. Apollo, however, again appears to us as the apotheosis of the *principium individuationis,* in which alone is consummated the perpetually attained goal of the primal unity, its redemption through mere appearance. With his sublime gestures, he shows us how necessary is the entire world of suffering, that by means of it the individual may be impelled to realize the redeeming vision, and then, sunk in contemplation of it, sit quietly in his tossing bark, amid the waves.

If we conceive of it at all as imperative and mandatory, this apotheosis of individuation knows but one law—the individual, i.e., the delimiting of the boundaries of the individual, *measure* in the Hellenic sense. Apollo, as ethical deity, exacts measure of his disciples, and, to be able to maintain it, he requires self-knowledge. And so, side by side with the esthetic necessity for beauty, there occur the demands "know thyself" and "nothing in excess"; consequently overweening pride and excess are regarded as the truly hostile demons of the non-Apollinian sphere, hence as characteristics of the pre-Apollinian age—that of the Titans; and of the extra-Apollinian world—that of the barbarians. Because of his titanic love for man, Prometheus must be torn to pieces by vultures; because of his excessive wisdom, which could solve the riddle of the Sphinx, Oedipus must be plunged into a bewildering vortex of crime. Thus did the Delphic god interpret the Greek past.

The effects wrought by the *Dionysian* also seemed "titanic" and "barbaric" to the Apollinian Greek; while at the same time he could not conceal from himself that he, too, was inwardly related to these overthrown Titans and heroes. Indeed, he had to recognize even more than this: despite all its beauty and moderation, his entire existence rested on a hidden substratum of suffering and of knowledge, revealed to him by the Dionysian. And behold: Apollo could not live without Dionysus! The "titanic" and the "barbaric" were in the last analysis as necessary as the Apollinian.

And now let us imagine how into this world, built on mere appearance and moderation and artificially dammed up, there penetrated, in tones ever more bewitching and alluring, the ecstatic sound of the Dionysian festival; how in these strains all of nature's *excess* in pleasure, grief, and knowledge became audible, even in piercing shrieks; and let us ask ourselves what the psalmodizing artist of Apollo, with his phantom harp-sound, could mean in the face of this demonic folk-song! The muses of the arts of "illusion" paled before an art that, in its intoxication, spoke the truth. The wisdom of Silenus cried "Woe! woe!" to the serene Olympians. The individual, with all his restraint and proportion, succumbed to the self-oblivion of the Dionysian states, forgetting the precepts of Apollo. *Excess* revealed itself as truth. Contradiction, the bliss born of pain, spoke out from the very heart of nature. And so, wherever the Dionysian prevailed, the Apollinian was checked and destroyed. But, on the other hand, it is equally certain that, wherever the first Dionysian onslaught was successfully withstood, the authority and majesty of the Delphic god exhibited itself as more rigid and menacing than ever. For to me the *Doric* state[19] and Doric art are explicable only as a permanent military encampment of the Apollinian. Only incessant resistance to the titanic-barbaric nature of the Dionysian could account for the long survival of an art so defiantly prim and so encompassed with bulwarks, a training so warlike and rigorous, and a political structure so cruel and relentless.

Up to this point we have simply enlarged upon the observation made at the beginning of this essay: that the Dionysian and the Apollinian, in new births ever following and mutually augmenting one another, controlled the Hellenic genius; that out of the age of "bronze," with its wars of the Titans and its rigorous folk philosophy, the Homeric world developed under the sway of the Apollinian impulse to beauty; that this "naïve" splendor was again overwhelmed by the influx of the Dionysian; and that against this new power the Apollinian rose to the austere majesty of Doric art and the Doric view of the world. If amid the strife of these two hostile principles, the older Hellenic history thus falls into four great periods of art, we are now impelled to inquire after the final goal of these developments and processes, lest perchance we should regard the last-attained period, the period of Doric art, as the climax and aim of these artistic impulses. And here the sublime and celebrated art of *Attic tragedy* and the dramatic dithyramb presents itself as the common goal of both these tendencies whose mysterious union, after many and long precursory struggles, found glorious consummation in this child—at once Antigone and Cassandra.[20]

—*The Birth of Tragedy* (1872; translated by Walter Kaufmann, 1967)

Notes

1. In the first edition: ". . . an opposition of style: two different tendencies run parallel in it, for the most part in conflict; and they . . ." Most of the changes in the revision of 1874 are as slight as this (compare the next footnote) and therefore not indicated in the following pages. This translation, like the standard German editions, follows Nietzsche's revision.

2. First edition: "till eventually, at the moment of the flowering of the Hellenic 'will,' they appear fused to generate together the art form of Attic tragedy."

3. Wagner's original text reads:

> Mein Freund, das grad' ist Dichters Werk,
> dass er sein Träumen deut' und merk'.
> Glaubt mir, des Menschen wahrster Wahn
> wird ihm im Traume aufgethan:
> all' Dichtkunst und Poëterei
> ist nichts als Wahrtraum-Deuterei.

4. *Schein* has been rendered in these pages sometimes as "illusion" and sometimes as "mere appearance."

5. *Der "Scheinende."* The German words for illusion and appearance are *Schein* and *Erscheinung.*

6. A Sanskrit word usually translated as illusion. For detailed discussions see, e.g., *A Source Book of Indian Philosophy,* ed. S. Radhakrishnan and Charles Moore (Princeton, N.J., Princeton University Press, 1957); Heinrich Zimmer, *Philosophies of India,* ed. Joseph Campbell (New York, Meridian Books, 1956); and Helmuth von Glasenapp, *Die Philosophie der Inder* (Stuttgart, Kröner, 1949), consulting the indices.

7. This reference, like subsequent references to the same work, is Nietzsche's own and refers to the edition of 1873 edited by Julius Frauenstädt—still one of the standard editions of Schopenhauer's works.

8. Principle of individuation.

9. A Babylonian festival that lasted five days and was marked by general license. During this time slaves are said to have ruled their masters, and a criminal was given all royal rights before he was put to death at the end of the festival. For references, see e.g., *The Oxford Classical Dictionary.*

10. In German, "the prodigal son" is *der verlorene Sohn* (the lost son).

11. An illusion to Friedrich Schiller's hymn *An die Freud* (to joy), used by Beethoven in the final movement of his Ninth Symphony.

12. Quotation from Schiller's hymn.

13. *Sentimentalisch* (not *sentimental*): an illusion to Schiller's influential contrast of *naïve* (Goethean) poetry with his own *sentimentalische Dichtung.*

14. This presage of the later coinage "beyond good and evil" is lost when *base* is mistranslated as "bad" instead of "evil."

15. Cf. Sophocles, *Oedipus at Colonus*, lines 1224ff.
16. *Zauberberg*, as in the title of Thomas Mann's novel.
17. Fate.
18. An allusion to Homer's *Odyssey*, XI, lines 489ff.
19. Sparta.
20. In footnote 32 of his first polemic (1872) Wilamowitz said: "Whoever explains these last words, to which Mephistopheles' remark about the witch's arithmetic [Goethe's *Faust*, lines 2565–66] applies, receives a suitable reward from me." It would seem that Sophocles' Antigone is here seen as representative of the Apollinian, while Aeschylus' Cassandra (in *Agamemnon*) is associated with the Dionysian.

II. The Will to Power in Art

1

Apollinian, Dionysian

There are two conditions in which art manifests itself in man even as a force of nature, and disposes of him whether he consent or not: it may be as a constraint to visionary states, or it may be an orgiastic impulse. Both conditions are to be seen in normal life, but they are then somewhat weaker: in dreams and in moments of elation or intoxication.

But the same contrast exists between the dream state and the state of intoxication: both of these states let loose all manner of artistic powers within us, but each unfetters powers of a different kind. Dreamland gives us the power of vision, of association, of poetry: intoxication gives us the power of grand attitudes, of passion, of song, and of dance.

2

The word "*Dionysian*" expresses a constraint to unity, a soaring above personality, the commonplace, society, reality, and above the abyss of the *ephemeral;* the passionately painful sensation of superabundance, in darker, fuller, and more fluctuating conditions; an ecstatic saying of yea to the collective character of existence, as that which remains the same, and equally mighty and blissful throughout all change; the great pantheistic sympathy with pleasure and pain, which declares even the most terrible and most questionable qualities of existence good, and sanctifies them; the eternal will to procreation, to fruitfulness, and to recurrence; the feeling of unity in regard to the necessity of creating and annihilating.

The word "*Apollinian*" expresses the constraint to be absolutely isolated, to the typical "individual," to everything that simplifies, distinguishes, and makes strong, salient, definite, and typical: to freedom within the law.

The further development of art is just as necessarily bound up with the antagonism of these two natural art-forces, as the further development of mankind is bound up with the antagonism of the sexes. The plenitude of power and restraint, the highest form of self-affirmation in a cool, noble, and reserved kind of beauty; the Apollinianism of the Hellenic will.

This antagonism of the Dionysian and of the Apollinian in the Greek soul, is one of the great riddles which made me feel drawn to the essence of Hellenism. At bottom, I troubled about nothing save the solution of the question, why precisely Greek Apollinianism should have been forced to grow out of a Dionysian soil: the Dionysian Greek had need of being Apollinian; that is to say in order to break his will to the titanic, to the complex, to the uncertain, to the horrible by a will to measure, to simplicity, and to submission to rule and concept. Extravagance, wildness, and Asiatic tendencies lie at the root of the Greeks. Their courage consists in their struggle with their Asiatic nature: they were not given beauty, any more than they were given logic and moral naturalness: in them these things are victories, they are willed and fought for—they constitute the *triumph* of the Greeks.

3

"Beauty" is, to the artist, something which is above all order of rank, because in beauty contrasts are overcome, the highest sign of power thus manifesting itself in the conquest of opposites; and achieved without a feeling of tension: violence being no longer necessary, everything submitting and obeying so easily, and doing so with good grace; this is what delights the powerful will of the artist.

4

If one should require the most astonishing proof of how far the power of transfiguring, which comes of intoxication, goes, this proof is at hand in the phenomenon of love; or what is called love in all the languages and silences of the world. Intoxication works to such a degree upon reality in this passion that in the consciousness of the lover the cause of his love is quite suppressed, and something else seems to take its place—a vibration and a glitter of all the charm-mirrors of Circe. . . . In this respect to be man or an animal makes no difference: and still less does spirit, goodness, or honesty. If one is astute, one is befooled astutely; if one is thick-headed, one is befooled in a thick-headed way. But love, even the love of God, saintly love, "the love that saves the soul," are at bottom all one; they are nothing but a fever which has reasons to transfigure itself—a state of intoxication which does well to lie about itself. . . . And, at any rate, when a man loves, he is a good liar about himself and to himself: he seems to himself transfigured, stronger, richer, more perfect; he *is* more perfect. . . . *Art* here acts as an organic function: we find it present in the most angelic instinct "love"; we find it as the greatest stimulus of life—thus art is sublimely utilitarian, even in the fact that it lies. . . . But we should be wrong to halt at its power to lie: it does more than merely imagine; it actually transposes values. And it not only transposes the *feeling* for values: the lover actually *has* a greater value; he is stronger. In animals this condition gives rise to new weapons, colors, pigments, and forms, and above all to new movements, new rhythms, new love-calls and seductions. In man it is just the same. His whole economy is richer, mightier, and *more complete* when he is in love than when he is not. The lover becomes a spendthrift; he is rich enough for it. He now dares; he becomes an adventurer, and even a donkey in magnanimity and innocence; his belief in God and in virtue revives, because he believes in love. Moreover, such idiots of happiness acquire wings and new capacities, and even the door to art is opened to them.

If we cancel the suggestion of this intestinal fever from the lyric of tones and words, what is left to poetry and music? . . . *L'art pour l'art* perhaps; the professional cant of frogs shivering outside in the cold, and dying of despair in their swamp. . . . Everything else was created by love.

5

Pessimism in Art?

The artist gradually learns to like for their own sake, those means which bring about the condition of esthetic elation; extreme delicacy and glory of color, definite delineation, quality of tone; distinctness where in normal conditions distinctness is absent. All distinct things, all nuances, in so far as they recall degrees of power which give rise to intoxication, kindle this feeling of intoxication by association; the effect of works of art is the excitation of the state which creates art, of esthetic intoxication.

The essential feature in art is its power of perfecting existence, its production of perfection and plenitude; art is essentially the affirmation, the blessing, and the deification of existence. . . . What does a pessimistic art signify? Is it not a *contradictio*? Yes. Schopenhauer is in error when he makes certain works of art serve the purpose of pessimism. Tragedy does not teach "resignation." . . . To represent terrible and questionable things is, in itself, the sign of an instinct of power and magnificence in the artist; he doesn't fear them. . . . There is no such thing as a pessimistic art. . . . Art affirms. Job affirms. But Zola? and the Goncourts?—the things they show us are ugly; their reason, however, for showing them to us is their love of ugliness. . . . I don't care what you say! You simply deceive yourselves if you think otherwise. What a relief Dostoevsky is!

6

Romanticism and its opposite. In regard to all esthetic values I now avail myself of this fundamental distinction: in every individual case I ask myself, has hunger or has superabundance been creative here? At first another distinction might perhaps seem preferable—it is far more obvious—for example, the distinction which decides whether a desire for stability, for eternity, for Being, or whether a desire for destruction, for change, for Becoming, has been the cause of creation. But both kinds of desire, when examined more closely, prove to be ambiguous, and really susceptible of interpretation only according to that scheme already mentioned and which I think is rightly preferred.

The desire for destruction, for change, for Becoming, may be the expression of an overflowing power pregnant with promises for the future (my term for this, as is well known, is Dionysian); it may, however, also be the hate of the ill-constituted, of the needy and of the physiologically botched, that destroys, and must destroy, because such creatures are indignant at, and annoyed by everything lasting and stable.

The act of immortalizing can, on the other hand, be the outcome of gratitude and love: an art which has this origin is always an apotheosis art;

dithyrambic, as perhaps with Rubens; happy, as perhaps with Hafiz; bright and gracious, and shedding a ray of glory over all things, as in Goethe. But it may also, however, be the outcome of the tyrannical will of the great sufferer who would make the most personal, individual, and narrow trait about him, the actual idiosyncrasy of his pain—in fact, into a binding law and imposition, and who thus wreaks his revenge upon all things by stamping, branding, and violating them with the image of his torment. The latter case is romantic pessimism in its highest form, whether this be Schopenhauerian voluntarism or Wagnerian music.

7

What is tragic? Again and again I have pointed to the great misunderstanding of Aristotle in maintaining that the tragic emotions were the two depressing emotions—fear and pity. Had he been right, tragedy would be an art unfriendly to life: it would have been necessary to caution people against it as against something generally harmful and suspicious. Art, otherwise the great stimulus of life, the great intoxicant of life, the great will to life, here became a tool of decadence, the handmaiden of pessimism and ill-health (for to suppose, as Aristotle supposed, that by exciting these emotions we thereby purged people of them, is simply an error). Something which habitually excites fear or pity, disorganizes, weakens, and discourages: and supposing Schopenhauer were right in thinking that tragedy taught resignation (that is, a meek renunciation of happiness, hope, and of the will to live), this would presuppose an art in which art itself was denied. Tragedy would then constitute a process of dissolution; the instinct of life would destroy itself in the instinct of art. Christianity, nihilism, tragic art, physiological decadence; these things would then be linked, they would then preponderate together and assist each other onwards—downwards. . . . Tragedy would thus be a symptom of decline.

This theory may be refuted in the most cold-blooded way, namely, by measuring the effect of a tragic emotion by means of a dynamometer. The result would be a fact which only the bottomless falsity of a doctrinaire could misunderstand: that tragedy is a tonic. If Schopenhauer refuses to see the truth here, if he regards general depression as a tragic condition, if he would have informed the Greeks (who to his disgust were not "resigned") that they did not firmly possess the highest principles of life, it is only owing to his *parti pris*, to the need of consistency in his system, to the dishonesty of the doctrinaire—that dreadful dishonesty which step for step corrupted the whole psychology of Schopenhauer (he who had arbitrarily and almost violently misunderstood genius, art itself, morality, pagan religion, beauty, knowledge, and almost everything).

8

The Tragic Artist

Whether, and in regard to what, the judgment "beautiful" is established is a question of an individual's or of a people's strength. The feeling of plenitude, of overflowing strength (which gayly and courageously meets many an obstacle before which the weakling shudders)—the feeling of power utters the judgment "beautiful" concerning things and conditions which the instinct of impotence can only value as hateful and ugly. The *flair* which enables us to decide whether the objects we encounter are dangerous, problematic, or alluring, likewise determines our esthetic Yea. ("This is beautiful" is an affirmation.)

From this we see that, generally speaking, a preference for questionable and terrible things is a symptom of strength; whereas the taste for pretty and charming trifles is characteristic of the weak and the delicate. The love of tragedy is typical of strong ages and characters: its *non plus ultra* is perhaps the Divina Commedia. It is the heroic spirits which in tragic cruelty say Yea unto themselves: they are hard enough to feel pain as a pleasure.

On the other hand, supposing weaklings desire to get a pleasure from an art which was not designed for them, what interpretation must we suppose they would like to give tragedy in order to make it suit their taste? They would interpret their own feelings of value into it: for example, the "triumph of the moral order of things," or the teaching of the "uselessness of existence," or the excitement to "resignation" (or also half-medicinal and half-moral outpourings, *à la* Aristotle). Finally, the art of terrible natures, insofar as it may excite the nerves, may be regarded by the weak and exhausted as a stimulus: this is now taking place, for instance, in the case of the admiration meted out to Wagner's art. A test of man's well-being and consciousness of power is the extent to which he can acknowledge the terrible and questionable character of things, and whether he is in need of a faith at the end.

This kind of artistic pessimism is precisely the reverse of that religio-moral pessimism which suffers from the corruption of man and the enigmatic character of existence: the latter insists upon deliverance, or at least upon the hope of deliverance. Those who suffer, doubt, and distrust themselves—the sick, in other words—have in all ages required the transporting influence of visions in order to be able to exist at all (the notion "blessedness" arose in this way). A similar case would be that of the artists of decadence, who at bottom maintain a Nihilistic attitude to life, and take refuge in the beauty of form—in those select cases in which Nature is perfect, in which she is indifferently great and indifferently beautiful. (The "love of the beautiful" may thus be something very different from the ability to see or create the beautiful: it may be the expression of impotence in this respect.) The most convincing artists are those who make harmony ring out of every discord, and who benefit all things by the gift of their power and inner harmony: in every work of art they merely reveal the symbol of their innermost experiences—their creation is gratitude for their life.

The depth of the tragic artist consists in the fact that his esthetic instinct surveys the more remote results, that he does not halt shortsightedly at the thing that is nearest, that he says Yea to the whole cosmic economy, which justifies the terrible, the evil, and the questionable; which more than justifies it.

9
Art in the Birth of Tragedy

A. The conception of the work which lies right in the background of this book is extraordinarily gloomy and unpleasant: among all the types of pessimism which have ever been known hitherto, none seems to have attained to this degree of malice. The contrast of a true and of an apparent world is entirely absent here: there is but one world, and it is false, cruel, contradictory, seductive, and without sense. . . . A world thus constituted is the true world. We are in need of lies in order to rise superior to this reality, to this truth—that is to say, in order to live. . . . That lies should be necessary to life is part and parcel of the terrible and questionable character of existence.

Metaphysics, morality, religion, science—in this book, all these things are regarded merely as different forms of falsehood: by means of them we are led to believe in life. "Life must inspire confidence": the task which this imposes upon us is enormous. In order to solve this problem man must already be a liar in his heart, but he must above all else be an artist. And he is that. Metaphysics, religion, morality, science—all these things are but the offshoot of his will to art, to falsehood, to a flight from "truth," to a denial of "truth." This ability, this artistic capacity par excellence of man—thanks to which he overcomes reality with lies—is a quality which he has in common with all other forms of existence. He himself is indeed a piece of reality, of truth, of nature: how could he help being also a piece of genius in prevarication?

The fact that the character of existence is misunderstood is the profoundest and the highest secret motive behind everything relating to virtue, science, piety, and art. To be blind to many things, to see many things falsely, to fancy many things: Oh, how clever man has been in those circumstances in which he believed he was anything but clever! Love, enthusiasm, "God" are but subtle forms of ultimate self-deception; they are but seductions to life and to the belief in life! In those moments when man was deceived, when he had befooled himself and when he believed in life: Oh, how his spirit swelled within him! Oh, what ecstasies he had! What power he felt! And what artistic triumphs in the feeling of power! . . . Man had once more become master of "matter"—master of truth! . . . And whenever man rejoices it is always in the same way: he rejoices as an artist, his power is his joy, he enjoys falsehood as his power. . . .

B. Art and nothing else! Art is the great means of making life possible, the great seducer to life, the great stimulus of life.

Art is the only superior counteragent to all will to the denial of life; it is par excellence the anti-Christian, the anti-Buddhistic, the antinihilistic force.

Art is the alleviation of the seeker after knowledge—of him who recognizes the terrible and questionable character of existence, and who *will* recognize it—of the tragic seeker after knowledge.

Art is the alleviation of the man of action—of him who not only sees the terrible and questionable character of existence, but also lives it, will live it—of the tragic and warlike man, the hero.

Art is the alleviation of the sufferer—as the way to states in which pain is willed, is transfigured, is deified, where suffering is a form of great ecstasy.

C. It is clear that in this book pessimism, or, better still, nihilism, stands for "truth." But truth is not postulated as the highest measure of value, and still less as the highest power. The will to appearance, to illusion, to deception, to becoming, and to change (to objective deception), is here regarded as more profound, as more primeval, as more metaphysical than the will to truth, to reality, to appearance: the latter is merely a form of the will to illusion. Happiness is likewise conceived as more primeval than pain: and pain is considered as conditioned, as a consequence of the will to happiness (of the will to Becoming, to growth, to forming, that is, to creating; in creating, however, destruction is included). The highest state of Yea-saying to existence is conceived as one from which the greatest pain may not be excluded: the tragico-Dionysian state.

D. In this way this book is even antipessimistic, namely, in the sense that it teaches something which is stronger than pessimism and which is more "divine" than truth: art. Nobody, it would seem, would be more ready seriously to utter a radical denial of life, an actual denial of action even more than a denial of life, than the author of this book. Except that he knows—for he has experienced it, and perhaps experienced little else!—that art is of more value than truth.

Even in the preface, in which Richard Wagner is, as it were, invited to join with him in conversation, the author expresses this article of faith, this gospel for artists: "Art is the only task of life, art is the metaphysical activity of life. . . ."

—*The Will to Power* (1896; translated 1910 by Anthony M. Ludovici)

SIGMUND FREUD

Wish-Fulfillment and the Unconscious

I. Phantasy-making and Art

. . . Consider . . . the origin and meaning of that mental activity called "phantasy-making." In general, as you know, it enjoys high esteem, although its place in mental life has not been clearly understood. I can tell you as much as this about it. You know that the ego in man is gradually trained by the influence of external necessity to appreciate reality and to pursue the reality-principle, and that in so doing it must renounce temporarily or permanently various of the objects and aims—not only sexual—of its desire for pleasure. But renunciation of pleasure has always been very hard for man; he cannot accomplish it without some kind of compensation. Accordingly he has evolved for himself a mental activity in which all these relinquished sources of pleasure and abandoned paths of gratification are permitted to continue their existence, a form of existence in which they are free from the demands of reality and from what we call the exercise of "testing reality." Every longing is soon transformed into the idea of its fulfillment; there is no doubt that dwelling upon a wish-fulfillment in phantasy brings satisfaction, although the knowledge that it is not reality remains thereby unobscured. In phantasy, therefore, man can continue to enjoy a freedom from the grip of the external world, one which he has long relinquished in actuality. He has contrived to be alternately a pleasure-seeking animal and a reasonable being; for the meager satisfaction that he can extract from reality leaves him starving. "There is no doing without accessory constructions," said Fontane. The creation of the mental domain of phantasy has a complete counterpart in the establishment of "reservations" and "nature-parks" in places where the inroads of agriculture, traffic, or industry threaten to change the original face of the earth rapidly into something unrecognizable. The "reservation" is to maintain the old condition of things which has been regretfully sacrificed to necessity everywhere else; there everything may grow and spread as it pleases, including what is useless and even what is harmful. The mental realm of phantasy is also such a reservation reclaimed from the encroachments of the reality-principle.

The best-known productions of phantasy have already been met by us; they are called daydreams, and are imaginary gratifications of ambitious, grandiose, erotic wishes, dilating the more extravagantly the more reality admonishes humility and patience. In them is shown unmistakably the essence of imaginary happiness, the return of gratification to a condition in which it is independent of reality's sanction. We know that these daydreams are the kernels and models of night dreams; fundamentally the night dream is nothing but a daydream distorted by the nocturnal form of mental activity and made possible by the nocturnal freedom of instinctual excitations. We are already familiar with the idea that a daydream is not necessarily conscious, that unconscious daydreams also exist[1]; such unconscious daydreams are therefore just as much the source of night dreams as of neurotic symptoms. . . .

The return of the libido[2] . . . to phantasy is an intermediate step on the way to symptom-formation which well deserves a special designation. C. G. Jung has coined for it the very appropriate name of *Introversion,* but inappropriately he uses it also to describe other things. We will adhere to the position that *introversion* describes the deflection of the libido away from the possibilities of real satisfaction and its excessive accumulation upon phantasies previously tolerated as harmless. An introverted person is not yet neurotic, but he is in an unstable condition; the next disturbance of the shifting forces will cause symptoms to develop, unless he can yet find other outlets for his pent-up libido. The unreal character of neurotic satisfaction and the disregard of the difference between phantasy and reality are already determined by the arrest at this stage of introversion. . . .

Before you leave today I should like to direct your attention for a moment to a side of phantasy-life of very general interest. There is, in fact, a path from phantasy back again to reality, and that is—art. The artist has also an introverted disposition and has not far to go to become neurotic. He is one who is urged on by instinctual needs which are too clamorous; he longs to attain to honor, power, riches, fame, and the love of women;

but he lacks the means of achieving these gratifications. So, like any other with an unsatisfied longing, he turns away from reality and transfers all his interest, and all his libido too, on to the creation of his wishes in the life of phantasy, from which the way might readily lead to neurosis. There must be many factors in combination to prevent this becoming the whole outcome of his development; it is well known how often artists in particular suffer from partial inhibition of their capacities through neurosis. Probably their constitution is endowed with a powerful capacity for sublimation and with a certain flexibility in the repressions determining the conflict. But the way back to reality is found by the artist thus: He is not the only one who has a life of phantasy; the intermediate world of phantasy is sanctioned by general human consent, and every hungry soul looks to it for comfort and consolation. But to those who are not artists the gratification that can be drawn from the springs of phantasy is very limited; their inexorable repressions prevent the enjoyment of all but the meager daydreams which can become conscious. A true artist has more at his disposal. First of all he understands how to elaborate his daydreams, so that they lose that personal note which grates upon strange ears and become enjoyable to others; he knows too how to modify them sufficiently so that their origin in prohibited sources is not easily detected. Further, he possesses the mysterious ability to mold his particular material until it expresses the ideas of his phantasy faithfully; and then he knows how to attach to this reflection of his phantasy-life so strong a stream of pleasure that, for a time at least, the repressions are outbalanced and dispelled by it. When he can do all this, he opens out to others the way back to the comfort and consolation of their own unconscious sources of pleasure, and so reaps their gratitude and admiration; then he has won—through his phantasy—what before he could only win in phantasy: honor, power, and the love of women.

—*Introductory Lectures on Psychoanalysis* (Lectures delivered 1915–17; translated 1922 by Joan Riviere)

Notes

1. As Freud earlier explains, a latent dream, the realization of a wish-phantasy, is frequently built up in the unconsciousness. The act of repression creates in the unconscious sphere hidden ideas and impulses isolated from the rest of the personality (Editor's note).

2. For the meaning of "libido," and an explanation of its artistic sublimation, see the editor's introductory note to this chapter.

II. The Relation of the Poet to Daydreaming

We laymen have always wondered greatly—like the cardinal who put the question to Ariosto—how that strange being, the poet, comes by his material. What makes him able to carry us with him in such a way and to arouse emotions in us of which we thought ourselves perhaps not even capable? Our interest in the problem is only stimulated by the circumstance that if we ask poets themselves they give us no explanation of the matter, or at least no satisfactory explanation. The knowledge that not even the clearest insight into the factors conditioning the choice of imaginative material, or into the nature of the ability to fashion that material, will ever make writers of us does not in any way detract from our interest.

If we could only find some activity in ourselves, or in people like ourselves, which was in any way akin to the writing of imaginative works! If we could do so, then examination of it would give us a hope of obtaining some insight into the creative powers of imaginative writers. And indeed, there is some prospect of achieving this—writers themselves always try to lessen the distance between their kind and ordinary human beings; they so often assure us that every man is at heart a poet, and that the last poet will not die until the last human being does.

We ought surely to look in the child for the first traces of imaginative activity. The child's best-loved and most absorbing occupation is play. Perhaps we may say that every child at play behaves like an imaginative writer, in that he creates a world of his own or, more truly, he rearranges the things of his world and orders it in a new way that pleases him better. It would be incorrect to think that he does not take this world seriously; on the contrary, he takes his play very seriously and expends a great deal of emotion on it. The opposite of play is not serious occupation but—reality. Notwithstanding the large affective cathexis[1] of his play-world, the child distinguishes it perfectly from reality; only he likes to borrow the objects and circumstances that he imagines from the tangible and visible things of the real world. It is only this linking of it to reality that still distinguishes a child's "play" from "daydreaming."

Now the writer does the same as the child at play; he creates a world of phantasy which he takes very seriously; that is, he invests it with a great deal of affect, while separating it sharply from reality. Language has preserved this relationship between children's play and poetic creation. It designates certain kinds of imaginative creation, concerned with tangible objects and capable of representation, as "plays"; the people who present them are called "players." The unreality of this poetical world of imagination, however, has very important consequences for literary technique; for many things which if they happened in real life could produce no pleasure can nevertheless give enjoyment in a play—many emotions which are essentially painful may become a source of enjoyment to the spectators and hearers of a poet's work.

There is another consideration relating to the contrast between reality and play on which we will dwell for a moment. Long after a child has grown up and stopped playing, after he has for decades attempted to grasp the realities of life with all seriousness, he may one day come to a state of mind in which the contrast between play and reality is again abrogated. The adult can remember with what intense seriousness he carried on his childish play; then by comparing his would-be serious occupations with his childhood's play, he manages to throw off the heavy burden of life and obtain the great pleasure of humor.

As they grow up, people cease to play, and appear to give up the pleasure they derived from play. But anyone who knows anything of the mental life of human beings is aware that hardly anything is more difficult to them than to give up a pleasure they have once tasted. Really we never can relinquish anything; we only exchange one thing for something else. When we appear to give something up, all we really do is to adopt a substitute. So when the human being grows up and ceases to play he only gives up the connection with real objects; instead of playing he then begins to create phantasy. He builds castles in the air and creates what are called daydreams. I believe that the greater number of human beings create phantasies at times as long as they live. This is a fact which has been overlooked for a long time, and its importance has therefore not been properly appreciated.

The phantasies of human beings are less easy to observe than the play of children. Children do, it is true, play alone, or form with other children a closed world in their minds for the purposes of play; but a child does not conceal his play from adults, even though his playing is quite unconcerned with them. The adult, on the other hand, is ashamed of his daydreams and conceals them from other people; he cherishes them as his most intimate possessions and as a rule he would rather confess all his misdeeds than tell his daydreams. For this reason he may believe that he is the only person who makes up such phantasies, without having any idea that everybody else tells themselves stories of the same kind. Daydreaming is a continuation of play, nevertheless, and the motives which lie behind these two activities contain a very good reason for this different behavior in the child at play and in the daydreaming adult.

The play of children is determined by their wishes—really by the child's *one* wish, which is to be grown-up, the wish that helps to "bring him up." He always plays at being grown-up; in play he imitates what is known to him of the lives of adults. Now he has no reason to conceal this wish. With the adult it is otherwise; on the one hand, he knows that he is expected not to play any longer or to daydream, but to be making his way in a real world. On the other hand, some of the wishes from which his phantasies spring are such as to have to be entirely hidden; therefore he is ashamed of his phantasies as being childish and as something prohibited.

If they are concealed with so much secretiveness, you will ask, how do we know so much about the human propensity to create phantasies? Now there is a certain class of human beings upon whom not a god, indeed, but a stern goddess—Necessity—has laid the task of giving an account of what they suffer and what they enjoy. These people are the neurotics; among other things they have to confess their phantasies to the physician to whom they go in the hope of recovering through mental treatment. This is our best source of knowledge, and we have later found good reason to suppose that our patients tell us about themselves nothing that we could not also hear from healthy people.

Let us try to learn some of the characteristics of daydreaming. We can begin by saying that happy people never make phantasies, only unsatisfied ones. Unsatisfied wishes are the driving power behind phantasies; every separate phantasy contains the fulfillment of a wish, and improves on unsatisfactory reality. The impelling wishes vary according to the sex, character, and circumstances of the creator; they may be easily divided, however, into two principal groups. Either they are ambitious wishes, serving to exalt the person creating them, or they are erotic. In young women erotic wishes dominate the phantasies almost exclusively, for their ambition is generally comprised in their erotic longings; in young men egoistic and ambitious wishes assert themselves plainly enough alongside their erotic desires. But we will not lay stress on the distinction between these two trends; we prefer to emphasize the fact that they are often united. In many altarpieces the portrait of the donor is to be found in one corner of the picture; and in the greater number of ambitious daydreams, too, we can discover a woman in some corner, for whom the dreamer performs all his heroic deeds and at whose feet all his triumphs are to be laid. Here you see we have strong enough motives for concealment; a well-brought-up woman is, indeed, credited with only a minimum of erotic desire, while a young man has to learn to suppress the overweening self-regard he acquires in the indulgent atmosphere surrounding his childhood, so that he may find his proper place in a society that is full of other persons making similar claims.

We must not imagine that the various products of this impulse towards phantasy, castles in the air or daydreams, are stereotyped or unchangeable. On the contrary, they fit themselves into the changing impressions of life, alter with the vicissitudes of life; every deep new impression gives them what might be called a "date stamp." The relation of phantasies to time is altogether of great importance. One may say that a phantasy at one and the same moment hovers between three periods of time—the three periods of our ideation. The activity of phantasy in the mind is linked up with some current impression, occasioned by some event in the present, which had the power to rouse an intense desire. From there it wanders back to the memory of an early experience, generally belonging to infancy, in which this wish was fulfilled. Then it creates for itself a situation which is to emerge in the future, representing the fulfillment of the wish—this is the daydream or phantasy, which now carries in it traces both of the occasion which engendered it and of some past memory. So past, present, and future are threaded, as it were, on the string of the wish that runs through them all.

A very ordinary example may serve to make my statement clear. Take the case of a poor orphan lad, to whom you have given the address of some employer where he may perhaps get work. On the way there he falls into a daydream suitable to the situation from which it springs. The content of the phantasy will be somewhat as follows: He is taken on and pleases his new employer, makes himself indispensable in the business, is taken into the family of the employer, and marries the charming daughter of the house. Then he comes to conduct the business, first as a partner, and then as successor to his father-in-law. In this way the dreamer regains what he had in his happy childhood, the protecting house, his loving parents and the first objects of his affection. You will see from such an example how the wish employs some event in the present to plan a future on the pattern of the past.

Much more could be said about phantasies, but I will only allude as briefly as possible to certain points. If phantasies become over-luxuriant and over-powerful, the necessary conditions for an outbreak of neurosis or psychosis are constituted; phantasies are also the first preliminary stage in the mind of the symptoms of illness of which our patients complain. A broad bypath here branches off into pathology.

I cannot pass over the relation of phantasies to dreams. Our nocturnal dreams are nothing but such phantasies, as we can make clear by interpreting them.[2] Language, in its unrivaled wisdom, long ago decided the question of the essential nature of dreams by giving the name of "day-dreams" to the airy creations of fantasy. If the meaning of our dreams usually remains obscure in spite of this clue, it is because of the circumstance that at night wishes of which we are ashamed also become active in us, wishes which we have to hide from ourselves, which were consequently repressed and pushed back into the unconscious. Such repressed wishes and their derivatives can therefore achieve expression only when almost completely disguised. When scientific work had succeeded in elucidating the distortion in dreams, it was no longer difficult to recognize that nocturnal dreams are fulfillments of desires in exactly the same way as day-dreams are—those phantasies with which we are all so familiar.

So much for daydreaming; now for the poet! Shall we dare really to compare an imaginative writer with "one who dreams in broad daylight," and his creations with daydreams? Here, surely, a first distinction is forced upon us; we must distinguish between poets who, like the bygone creators of epics and tragedies, take over their material ready-made, and those who seem to create their material spontaneously. Let us keep to the latter, and let us also not choose for our comparison those writers who are most highly esteemed by critics. We will choose the less pretentious writers of romances, novels, and stories, who are read all the same by the widest circles of men and women. There is one very marked characteristic in the productions of these writers which must strike us all: they all have a hero who is the center of interest, for whom the author tries to win our sympathy by every possible means, and whom he places under the protection of a special providence. If at the end of one chapter the hero is left unconscious and bleeding from severe wounds, I am sure to find him at the beginning of the next being carefully tended and on the way to recovery; if the first volume ends in the hero being shipwrecked in a storm at sea, I am certain to hear at the beginning of the next of his hair-breadth escape—otherwise, indeed, the story could not continue. The feeling of security with which I follow the hero through his dangerous adventures is the same as that with which a real hero throws himself into the water to save a drowning man, or exposes himself to the fire of the enemy while storming a battery. It is this very feeling of being a hero which one of our best authors has well expressed in the famous phrase, "*Es kann mir nix g'schehen!*"[3] It seems to me, however, that this significant mark of invulnerability very clearly betrays—His Majesty the Ego, the hero of all day-dreams and all novels.

The same relationship is hinted at in yet other characteristics of these egocentric stories. When all the women in a novel invariably fall in love with the hero, this can hardly be looked upon as a description of reality, but it is easily understood as an essential constituent of a daydream. The same thing holds good when the other people in the story are sharply divided into good and bad, with complete disregard of the manifold variety in the traits of real human beings; the "good" ones are those who help the ego in its character of hero, while the "bad" are his enemies and rivals.

We do not in any way fail to recognize that many imaginative productions have traveled far from the original naïve daydream, but I cannot suppress the surmise that even the most extreme variations could be brought into relationship with this model by an uninterrupted series of transitions. It has struck me in many so-called psychological novels, too, that only one person—once again the hero—is described from within; the author dwells in his soul and looks upon the other people from outside. The psychological novel in general probably owes its peculiarities to the tendency of modern writers to split up their ego by self-observation into many component-egos, and in this way to personify the conflicting trends in their own mental life in many heroes. There are certain novels, which might be called "eccentric," that seem to stand in marked contradiction to the typical daydream; in these the person introduced as the hero plays the least active part of anyone, and seems instead to let the actions and sufferings of other people pass him by like a spectator. Many of the later novels of Zola belong to this class. But I must say that the psychological analysis of people who are not writers, and who deviate in many things from the so-called norm, has shown us analogous variations in their daydreams in which the ego contents itself with the role of spectator.

If our comparison of the imaginative writer with the daydreamer, and of poetic production with the daydream, is to be of any value, it must show itself fruitful in some way or other. Let us try, for instance, to examine the works of writers in reference to the idea propounded above, the relation of the phantasy to the wish that runs through it and to the three periods of time; and with its help let us study the connection between the life of the writer and his productions. Hitherto it has not been known what preliminary ideas would constitute an approach to this problem; very often this relation has been regarded as much simpler than it is; but the insight gained from phantasies leads us to expect the following state of things. Some actual experience which made a strong impression on the writer had stirred up a memory of an earlier experience, generally belonging to childhood, which then arouses a wish that finds a fulfillment in the work in question, and in which elements of the recent event and the old memory should be discernible.

Do not be alarmed at the complexity of this formula; I myself expect that in reality it will prove itself to be too schematic, but that possibly it may contain a first means of approach to the true state of affairs. From some attempts I have made I think that this way of approaching works of the imagination might not be unfruitful. You will not forget that the stress laid on the writer's memories of his childhood, which perhaps seems so strange, is ultimately derived from the hypothesis that imaginative creation, like daydreaming, is a continuation of and substitute for the play of childhood.

We will not neglect to refer also to that class of imaginative work which must be recognized not as spontaneous production, but as a refashioning of ready-made material. Here, too, the writer retains a certain amount of independence, which can express itself in the choice of material and in changes in the material chosen, which are often considerable. As far as it goes, this material is derived from the racial treasure-house of myths, legends, and fairy tales. The study of these creations of racial psychology is in no way complete, but it seems extremely probable that myths, for example, are distorted vestiges of the wish-phantasies of whole nations—the age-long dreams of young humanity.

You will say that, although writers came first in the title of this paper, I have told you far less about them than about phantasy. I am aware of that, and will try to excuse myself by pointing to the present state of our knowledge. I could only throw out suggestions and bring up interesting points which arise from the study of phantasies, and which pass beyond them to the problem of the choice of literary material. We have not touched on the other problem at all, that is, what are the means which writers use to achieve those emotional reactions in us that are roused by their productions. But I would at least point out to you the path which leads from our discussion of daydreams to the problems of the effect produced on us by imaginative works.

You will remember that we said the daydreamer hid his phantasies carefully from other people because he had reason to be ashamed of them. I may now add that even if he were to communicate them to us, he would give us no pleasure by his disclosures. When we hear such phantasies they repel us, or at least leave us cold. But when a man of literary talent presents his plays, or relates what we take to be his personal daydreams, we experience great pleasure arising probably from many sources. How the writer accomplishes this is his innermost secret; the essential *ars poetica* lies in the technique by which our feeling of repulsion is overcome, and this has certainly to do with those barriers erected between every individual being and all others. We can guess at two methods used in this technique. The writer softens the egotistical character of the daydream by changes and disguises, and he bribes us by the offer of a purely formal, that is esthetic, pleasure in the presentation of his phantasies. The increment of pleasure which is offered us in order to release yet greater pleasure arising from deeper sources in the mind is called an "incitement premium" or technically, "fore-pleasure." I am of the opinion that all the esthetic pleasure we gain from the works of imaginative writers is of the same type as this "fore-pleasure," and that the true enjoyment of literature proceeds from the release of tensions in our minds. Perhaps much that brings about this result consists in the writer's putting us into a position in which we can enjoy our own daydreams without reproach or shame. Here we reach a path leading into novel, interesting, and complicated researches, but we also, at least for the present, arrive at the end of the present discussion.

—*New Revue,* Volume I (1908); translation first published in *Collected Papers,* Volume IV (1925) by I. F. Grant Duff

Notes

1. From a Greek word, *Kathexo,* to occupy. "Cathexis" is used here to signify a state of being charged or invested with emotional energy. (Editor's note.)
2. *Cf.* Freud, *Die Traumdeutung (The Interpretation of Dreams).*
3. Anzengruber. [The phrase means "Nothing can happen to *me!*"—Translator.]

III. Tragic Themes

According to my already extensive experience, parents play a leading part in the infantile psychology of all persons who subsequently become psychoneurotics. Falling in love with one parent and hating the other forms part of the permanent stock of the psychic impulses which arise in early childhood, and are of such importance as the material of the subsequent neurosis. But I do not believe that psychoneurotics are to be sharply distinguished in this respect from other persons who remain normal—that is, I do not believe that they are capable of creating something absolutely new and peculiar to themselves. It is far more probable—and this is confirmed by incidental observations of normal children—that in their amorous or hostile attitude toward their parents, psychoneurotics do no more than reveal to us, by magnification, something that occurs less markedly and intensively in the minds of the majority of children. Antiquity has furnished us with legendary matter which corroborates this belief, and the profound and universal validity of the old legends is explicable only by an equally universal validity of the above-mentioned hypothesis of infantile psychology.

I am referring to the legend of King Oedipus and the *Oedipus Rex* of Sophocles. Oedipus, the son of Laius, king of Thebes, and Jocasta, is exposed as a suckling, because an oracle had informed the father that his son, who was still unborn, would be his murderer. He is rescued, and grows up as a king's son at a foreign court, until, being uncertain of his origin, he, too, consults the oracle, and is warned to avoid his native place, for he is destined to become the murderer of his father and the husband of his mother. On the road leading away from his supposed home he meets King Laius, and in a sudden quarrel strikes him dead. He comes to Thebes, where he solves the riddle of the Sphinx, who is barring the way to the city, whereupon he is elected king by the grateful Thebans, and is rewarded with the hand of Jocasta. He reigns for many years in peace and honor, and begets two sons and two daughters upon his unknown mother, until at last a plague breaks out—which causes the Thebans to consult the oracle anew. Here Sophocles' tragedy begins. The messengers bring the reply that the plague will stop as soon as the murderer of Laius is driven from the country. But where is he?

> "Where shall be found,
> Faint, and hard to be known, the trace of the ancient guilt?"

The action of the play consists simply in the disclosure, approached step by step and artistically delayed (and comparable to the work of a psychoanalysis) that Oedipus himself is the murderer of Laius, and that he is the son of the murdered man and Jocasta. Shocked by the abominable crime which he has unwittingly committed, Oedipus blinds himself, and departs from his native city. The prophecy of the oracle has been fulfilled.

The *Oedipus Rex* is a tragedy of fate; its tragic effect depends on the conflict between the all-powerful will of the gods and the vain efforts of human beings threatened with disaster; resignation to the divine will, and the perception of one's own impotence is the lesson which the deeply moved spectator is supposed to learn from the tragedy. Modern authors have therefore sought to achieve a similar tragic effect by expressing the same conflict in stories of their own invention. But the playgoers have looked on unmoved at the unavailing efforts of guiltless men to avert the fulfillment of curse or oracle; the modern tragedies of destiny have failed of their effect.

If the *Oedipus Rex* is capable of moving a modern reader or playgoer no less powerfully than it moved the contemporary Greeks, the only possible explanation is that the effect of the Greek tragedy does not depend upon the conflict between fate and human will, but upon the peculiar nature of the material by which this conflict is revealed. There must be a voice within us which is prepared to acknowledge the compelling power of fate in the *Oedipus,* while we are able to condemn the situations occurring in *Die Ahnfrau* or other tragedies of fate as arbitrary inventions. And there actually is a motive in the story of King Oedipus which explains the verdict of this inner voice. His fate moves us only because it might have been our own, because the oracle laid upon us before our birth the very curse which rested upon him. It may be that we were all destined to direct our first sexual impulses toward our mothers, and our first impulses of hatred and violence toward our fathers; our dreams convince us that we were. King Oedipus, who slew his father Laius and wedded his mother Jocasta, is nothing more or less than a wish-fulfillment—the fulfillment of the wish of our childhood. But we, more fortunate than he, in so far as we have not become psychoneurotics, have since our childhood succeeded in withdrawing our sexual impulses from our mothers, and in forgetting our jealousy of our fathers. We recoil from the person for whom this primitive wish of our childhood has been fulfilled with all the force of the repression which these wishes have undergone in our minds since childhood. As the poet brings the guilt of Oedipus to light by his investigation, he forces us to become aware of our own inner selves, in which the same impulses are still extant, even though they are suppressed. The antithesis with which the chorus departs:—

> ". . . Behold, this is Oedipus,
> Who unravelled the great riddle, and was first in power,
> Whose fortune all the townsmen praised and envied;
> See in what dread adversity he sank!"

—this admonition touches us and our own pride, us who since the years of our childhood have grown so wise and so powerful in our own estimation. Like Oedipus, we live in ignorance of the desires that offend morality, the desires that nature has forced upon us and after their unveiling we may well prefer to avert our gaze from the scenes of our childhood.

In the very text of Sophocles' tragedy there is an unmistakable reference to the fact that the Oedipus legend had its source in dream-material of immemorial antiquity, the content of which was the painful disturbance of the child's relations to its parents caused by the first impulses of sexuality. Jocasta comforts Oedipus—who is not yet enlightened, but is troubled by the recollection of the oracle—by an allusion to a dream which is often dreamed, though it cannot, in her opinion, mean anything:—

> "For many a man hath seen himself in dreams
> His mother's mate, but he who gives no heed
> To suchlike matters bears the easier life."

The dream of having sexual intercourse with one's mother was as common then as it is today with many people, who tell it with indignation and astonishment. As may well be imagined, it is the key to the tragedy and the complement to the dream of the death of the father. The Oedipus fable is the reaction of phantasy to these two typical dreams, and just as such a dream, when occurring to an adult, is experienced with feelings of aversion, so the content of the fable must include terror and self-chastisement. The form which it subsequently assumed was the result of an uncomprehending secondary elaboration of the material, which sought to make it serve a theological intention. The attempt to reconcile divine omnipotence with human responsibility must, of course, fail with this material as with any other.

Another of the great poetic tragedies, Shakespeare's *Hamlet,* is rooted in the same soil as *Oedipus Rex*. But the whole difference in the psychic life of the two widely separated periods of civilization, and the progress, during the course of time, of repression in the emotional life of humanity, is manifested in the differing treatment of the same material. In *Oedipus Rex* the basic wish-phantasy of the child is brought to light and realized as it is in dreams; in *Hamlet* it remains repressed, and we learn of its existence—as we discover the relevant facts in a neurosis—only through the inhibitory effects which proceed from it. In the more modern drama, the curious fact that it is possible to remain in complete uncertainty as to the character of the hero has proved to be quite consistent with the overpowering effect of the tragedy. The play is based upon Hamlet's hesitation in accomplishing the task of revenge assigned to him; the text does not give the cause or the motive of this hesitation, nor have the manifold attempts at interpretation succeeded in doing so. According to the still prevailing conception, a conception for which Goethe was first responsible, Hamlet represents the type of man whose active energy is paralyzed by excessive intellectual activity: "Sicklied o'er with the pale cast of thought." According to another conception, the poet has endeavored to portray a morbid, irresolute character, on the verge of neurasthenia. The plot of the drama, however, shows us that Hamlet is by no means intended to appear as a character wholly incapable of action. On two separate occasions we see him assert himself: once in a sudden outburst of rage, when he stabs the eavesdropper behind the arras, and on the other occasion when he deliberately, and even craftily, with the complete unscrupulousness of a prince of the Renaissance, sends the two courtiers to the death which was intended for himself. What is it, then, that inhibits him in accomplishing the task which his father's ghost has laid upon him? Here the explanation offers itself that it is the peculiar nature of this task. Hamlet is able to do anything but take vengeance upon the man who did away with his father and has taken his father's place with his mother—the man who shows him in realization the repressed desires of his own childhood. The loathing which should have driven him to revenge is thus replaced by self-reproach, by conscientious scruples, which tell him that he himself is no better than the murderer whom he is required to punish. I have here translated into consciousness what had to remain unconscious in the mind of the hero; if anyone wishes to call Hamlet an hysterical subject I cannot but admit that this is the deduction to be drawn from my interpretation. The sexual aversion which Hamlet expresses in conversation with Ophelia is perfectly consistent with this deduction—the same sexual aversion which during the next fews years was increasingly to take possession of the poet's soul, until it found its supreme utterance in *Timon of Athens*. It can, of course, be only the poet's own psychology with which we are confronted in *Hamlet*; and in a work on Shakespeare by Georg Brandes (1896) I find the statement that the drama was composed immediately after the death of Shakespeare's father (1601)—that is to say, when he was still mourning his loss, and during a revival, as we may fairly assume, of his own childish feelings in respect of his father. It is known, too, that Shakespeare's son, who died in childhood, bore the name of Hamnet (identical with Hamlet). Just as *Hamlet* treats of the relation of the son to his parents, so *Macbeth*, which was written about the same period, is based upon the theme of childlessness. Just as all neurotic symptoms, like dreams themselves, are capable of hyper-interpretation, and even require such hyper-interpretation before they become perfectly intelligible, so every genuine poetical creation must have proceeded from more than one motive, more than one impulse in the mind of the poet, and must admit of more than one interpretation. I have here attempted to interpret only the deepest stratum of impulses in the mind of the creative poet.

—*The Interpretation of Dreams* (1900; translated 1913 by A. A. Brill)

CHRISTOPHER CAUDWELL

Poetry's Dream-Work

1

Dream is neither directed thinking nor directed feeling, but free—that is non-social—association. Hence the associations of dream are personal and can only be understood by reference to the dreamer's personal life. The secret law of dream's structure is the "dream-work."

Poetic irrationality bears this resemblance to dream, that its flow of images is explained by affective laws; but it is not "free" association as in dream. Poetic feeling is directed feeling—feeling controlled by the social ego. Poetic associations are social.

As the dreamer lives entirely in the images of his dream, without reference to another reality, so the reader of poetry lives in the words of the poetry, without reference to the external world. The poet's world is *his* world. As he reads the poem he feels the emotions of the poet. Just as the pythoness or bacchante speaks for the god in the first person, so the reader under the influence of poetic illusion feels for the poet in the first person.

The images of dream, like the ideas of poetry, are concrete. In each dream, and in each poem, the memory-image and the word play a different part, and therefore have different meanings. Dreams and poems are inconsistent among themselves. Each dream and each poem is a world of its own.

Poetry is rhythmical. Rhythm secures the heightening of physiological consciousness so as to shut out sensory perception of the environment. In the rhythm of dance, music or song we become *self*-conscious instead of conscious. The rhythm of heart-beat and breathing and physiological periodicity negates the physical rhythm of the environment. In this sense sleep too is rhythmical. The dreamer retires into the citadel of the body and closes the doors.

Why is "physiological" introversion more necessary in poetry than in story, so that the poet accepts the difficulties of meter and rhyme? The answer is that introversion must be stronger in poetry. By introversion is not meant merely a turning-away from immediate environment—that could be secured by sitting in a quiet study, without disturbance. Such introversion is equally desirable for all kinds of thought, for scientific thinking and novel-reading as well as poetry, and it is not secured by the order of the words but by an effort of concentration. Some people can "concentrate" on a difficult scientific book or a book of poetry in conditions where others cannot. This kind of introversion does not therefore depend upon the order of the words. No one has suggested facilitating scientific writing by making it metrical.

But there is another aspect of introversion. In introversion for scientific phantasy it is true that we turn away from immediate environment, yet none the less we turn towards those parts of external reality of which the words are symbols. Ordinarily we see, hovering behind language, the world of external reality it describes. But in poetry the thoughts are to be directed on to the feeling-tone of the words themselves. Attention must sink below the pieces of external reality symbolized by the poetry, down into the emotional underworld adhering to those pieces. In poetry we must penetrate behind the dome of many-colored glass into the white radiance of the self. Hence the need for a physiological introversion, which is a turning-away not from the immediate environment of the reader *but from the environment (or external reality) depicted in the poem.* Hence poetry in its use of language continually distorts and denies the structure of reality to exalt the structure of the self. By means of rhyme, assonance or alliteration it couples together words which have no rational connection, that is, no nexus through the world of external reality. It breaks the words up into lines of arbitrary length, cutting across their logical construction. It breaks down their associations, derived from the world of external reality, by means of inversion and every variety of artificial stressing and counterpoint.

Thus the world of external reality recedes, and the world of instinct, the affective emotional linkage behind the words, rises to the view and becomes the world of reality. The subject emerges from the object: the social ego from the social world. Wordsworth said correctly: "The tendency of meter is to divest language, in a certain degree, of its reality, and thus to throw a sort of half-consciousness of unsubstantial existence over the whole composition." In the same way Coleridge reached out after a like conception to ours: "Meter is simply a stimulant of attention"—not of any attention but a special kind of attention—attention to the affective associations of the words themselves.

We have here a distinction between poetry and the novel which it is vital to grasp. In the novel too the subjective elements are valued for themselves and rise to view, but in a different way. The novel blots out external reality by substituting a more or less consistent mock reality which has sufficient "stuff" to stand between reader and reality. This means that in the novel the emotional associations attach not to the words but to the moving current of mock reality symbolized by the words. That is why rhythm, "preciousness," and style are alien to the novel; why the novel translates so well; why novels are not composed of words. They are composed of scenes, actions, *stuff*, people, just as plays are. A "jeweled" style is a disadvantage to the novel because it distracts the eye from the things and people to the words—not as words, as black outlines, but as symbols to which a variety of feeling-tone is directly attached. For example when someone exclaims "Brute!" we do not think of animals and then of brutish qualities, but have a powerful subjective reaction suggesting cruelty and clumsiness. This is a poetic reaction to a word; the other is a story reaction.

Because words are few they are what Freud called "over-determined." One word has many affective associations because it has many "meanings" (for example, the word "brute" can mean a foolish person, a cruel person, the order of animals, etc.). In novel-writing the words are arranged so that all other pieces of reality are excluded except the piece required, and the emotional association is to the resulting structure. Poetic writing is concerned with making the emotional associations either exclude or reinforce each other, without a prior reference to a coherent piece of reality; for example, in novel-writing, in the phrase "the Indian Ocean" the word "ocean" has been restricted to a specific geographical ocean, which *then* has emotional associations for the reader. In poetry "the Indian sea" has a different meaning, for the emotional associations are, not to a particular sea but to the word "Indian" and the word "sea," which affect each other and blend to produce a glowing cloudy "feeling" quite different from the novel-writer's phrase.

Of course there may be stretches of poetic writing in a novel (for example in Proust, Malraux, Lawrence, and Melville) or of novel-writing in poetry (the purely explanatory patches in Shakespeare's plays), but this does not affect the general characteristics. The difference is so marked that it explains the strange insensitivity to poetry displayed by so many great novelists, and a similar fondness for bad novels on the part of so many great poets. This difference between the technique of poetry and the novel determines the difference between the spheres of the two arts.

2

What is the basis of literary art? What is the inner contradiction which produces its onward movement? Evidently it can only be a special form of the contradiction which produces the whole movement of society, the contradiction between the instincts and the environment, the endless struggle between man and Nature which is life.

I, the artist, have a certain consciousness, molded by my social world. As artist I am concerned with my artistic consciousness, represented by the direct and indirect effect on me of all the art I have felt, and all the emotional organization which has produced in me a conscious subject. This consciousness is contradicted by my experience—that is, I have a *new* personal experience, something not given in the social world of poetry. Therefore I desire what is called self-expression but is really self-socialization, the casting of my private experience in such a form that it will be incorporated in the social world of art and appear as an art-work. The art-work represents the negation of the negation—the synthesis between the existing world of art (existing consciousness of theory) and my experience (life or practice).[1]

Therefore at the finish the world of art will be changed by the incursion of my art-work. That is the revolutionary aspect of my role as artist. But also my consciousness will be changed because I have, through the medium of the art world, forced my life experience, new, dumb, and unformulated, to become conscious, to enter my conscious sphere. That is the adaptative aspect of my role as artist. In the same way with the appreciator of art, his consciousness will be revolutionized by the incursion into it of a new art-work; but his appreciation of it will only be possible to the extent that he had had some similar experience in life. The former process will be revolutionary; the latter adaptative.

Rather than use the word revolutionary, however, it would be better to use the word evolutionary, restricting the other to cases where the new content of experience is so opposed to the existing consciousness that it requires a wholesale change, a complete revision of existing categories (conventions, traditions, artistic standards) for its inclusion, a revision which is only possible because concrete life itself has undergone a similar change in the period. The Elizabethan age was one of such periods. We are at the beginning of another such now.

It is plain that it is the emotional consciousness—that consciousness which springs directly from the instincts—with which the artist is concerned. Yet exactly the same relation holds between the scientist and his hypothesis (equivalent of the art-work) and the rational consciousness, that consciousness which springs directly from the perception.

Since the mediating factor in art processes is the social ego in its relation to the experience of individuals, it is plain that the integration performed by the art-work can only be achieved on condition that the item of private experience which is integrated *(a) is important,* concerned with deep emotional drives, with the unchanging instincts which, because they remain the same beneath the changing adaptations of culture, act as the skeleton, the main organizing force in the social ego which ages of art have built up; *(b)* is *general,* is not a contradictory item of experience peculiar to the artist or one of two men, but is encountered in a dumb unconscious way in the experiences of most men—otherwise how could the art-work be meaningful to them, how could it integrate and give expression to their hitherto anarchic experience as it gave expression to the artist's?

Condition (*a*) secures that great art—art which performs a wide and deep feat of integration—has something universal, something timeless and enduring from age to age. This timelessness we now see to be the timelessness of the instincts, the unchanging secret face of the genotype which persists beneath all the rich superstructure of civilization. Condition (*b*) explains why contemporary art has a special and striking meaning for us, why we find in even minor contemporary poets something vital and immediate not to be found in Homer, Dante, or Shakespeare. They live in the same world and meet the same bodiless forces whose power they experience.

This also explains why it is correct to have a materialist approach to art, to look in the art-works of any age for a reflection of the social relations of that age. For the experience of men in general is determined in general by the social relations of that age or, to be more accurate, the social relations of that age are simply man's individual experiences averaged out, just as a species is a group of animals' physical peculiarities averaged out. Since art lives in the social world, and can only be of value in integrating experiences general to men, it is plain that the art of any age can only express the general experiences of men in that age. So far from the artist's being a lone wolf, he is the normal man of that age—insofar as he is an artist. Of course normality in consciousness is as rare as normality in vision, and, unlike the latter, it is not a fixed physical standard but one which varies from year to year. Moreover his normality is, so to speak, the norm of abnormal experiences. It is the norm of the queerness and newness and accident in contemporary men's lives: all the incursions of the unexpected which shake their inherited consciousness. Hence the apparent abnormality of the artist.

This, finally, explains why in a class society art is class art. For a class, in the Marxian sense, is simply a group of men whose life-experiences are substantially similar, that is, with less internal differences on the average than they have external differences from the life-experiences of men in other classes. This difference of course has an economic basis, a material cause arising from the inevitable conditions of economic production. Therefore the artist will necessarily integrate the new experience and voice the consciousness of that group whose experience in general resembles his own—his own class. This will be the class which practices art—

the class at whose pole gathers the freedom and consciousness of society, in all ages the ruling class.

This is the most general movement of literary art, reflecting the most general law of society. Because of the different techniques of poetry and the novel—already explained—this movement is expressed in different ways in poetry and in the novel.

Poetry concentrates on the immediate affective associations of the word, instead of going first to the object or entity symbolized by the word and then drawing the affective association from that. Since words are fewer than the objects they symbolize, the affects of poetry are correspondingly condensed, but poetry itself is correspondingly cloudy and ambiguous. This ambiguity, which Empson takes to be the essence of poetry, is in fact a by-product.[2] Now this concentration upon the affective tones of words, instead of going first to the symbolized reality and then to the feeling-tone of that reality, is—because of the nature of language—a concentration on the more dumb and instinctive part of man's consciousness. It is an approach to the more instinctively common part of man's consciousness. It is an approach to the secret unchanging core of the genotype in adapted man. Hence the importance of physiological introversion in poetry.

This genotype is undifferentiated because it is relatively unchanging. Hence the timelessness of poetry as compared to the importance of time sequence in the novel. Poetry speaks timelessly for one common "I" round which all experience is orientated. In poetry all the emotional experiences of men are arranged round the instincts, round the "I." Poetry is a bundle of instinctive perspectives of reality taken from one spot. Precisely because it is cloudly and ambiguous, its view is far-reaching; its horizon seems to open and expand and stretch out to dim infinity. Because it is instinctive, it is enduring. In it the instincts give one loud cry, a cry which expresses what is common in the general relation of every man to contemporary life as a whole.

But the novel goes out first to reality to draw its subjective associations from it. Hence we do not seem to feel the novel "in us," we do not identify our feelings with the feeling-tones of the novel. We stand inside the mock world of the novel and survey it; at the most we identify ourselves with the hero and look round with him at the "otherness" of his environment. The novel does not express the general tension between the instincts and the surroundings, but the changes of tension which take place as a result of change in the surroundings (life-experience). This incursion of the time element (reality as a process) so necessary in a differentiated society where men's time-experiences differ markedly among themselves, means that the novel must particularize and have characters whose actions and feelings are surveyed from without. Poetry is internal—a bundle of "I" perspectives of the world taken from one point, the poet. The story is external—a bundle of perspectives of one "I" (the character) taken from different parts of the world.

Obviously the novel can only evolve in a society where men's experiences do differ so markedly among themselves as to make this objective approach necessary, and this difference of experience is itself the result of rapid change in society, of an increased differentiation of functions, of an increased realization of life as process, as dialectic. Poetry is the product of a tribe, where life flows on without much change between youth and age; the novel belongs to a restless age where things are always happening to people and people therefore are always altering.

3

Yet all art is subjective. All art is emotional and therefore concerned with the instincts whose adaptation to social life produces emotional consciousness. Hence art cannot escape its close relation with the genotype whose secret desires link in one endless series all human culture.

Now this genotype can be considered from two aspects: the timeless and the timeful, the changeless and changeful, the general and the particular.

(*a*) Timeless, changeless, general in that on the whole the genotype is substantially constant in all societies and all men. There is a substratum of likeness. Man does not change from Athenian to Ancient Briton and then to Londoner by innate differences stamped in by natural selection, but by acquired changes derived from social evolution. Poetry expresses this constant instinctive factor.

(*b*) Yet beneath this likeness the genotypes, because they are bundles of genes, reveal individual differences. These genes are perpetually shuffled to reveal new personalities. Because men differ in this way among themselves they cannot be satisfied with the simple tribal life of collective civilization. They demand "luxuries," freedom, special products which cannot be satisfied within the ambit of such a primitive economy. This leads to an economic differentiation of society which . . . is not the means of suppressing individuality but of realizing it. Hence these individual genetic differences produce change in time and also the realization of *characters*, of man's deviation from the social "norm." Thus the very technique of the novel makes it interested in the way characters strive to realize in existing society their individual differences.

Poetry expresses the freedom which inheres in man's general timeless unity in society; it is interested in society as the sum and guardian of common instinctive tendencies; it speaks of death, love, hope, sorrow, and despair as all men experience them. The novel is the expression of that freedom which men seek, not in their unity in society but in their differences, of their search for freedom in the pores of society, and therefore of their repulsions from, clashes with, and concrete motions against *other* individuals different from themselves.

The novel was bound to develop therefore under capitalism, whose increase in the productive forces brought about by the division of labor not only vastly increased the differentiation of society but also, by continually revolutionizing its own basis, produced an endless flux and change in life. Equally, as capitalism decayed, the novel was bound to voice the experience of men that economic differentiation had changed from a means of freedom to a rubber-stamp crushing individuality (the ossification of classes), and that the productive forces, by being held back from developing further, had choked the free movement of life (the general economic crisis). Necessarily therefore in such a period the decay of the novel occurs together with a general revolutionary turmoil.

Thus we see in the technical differences of poetry and the novel the difference between changelessness and change, space and time, and it is clear that these are not mutually exclusive opposites but are opposites which interpenetrate, and, as they fly apart, continually generate an enrichening reality.

This was the same kind of difference as that between the evolutionary and classificatory sciences.[3] And just as the technique of poetry demands an immediate concentration on the word, so the classificatory sciences, such as geometry and mathematics, demand an immediate concentration on the symbol. The novel demands that we pass from the symbol to reality, and only then to the affective organization; biology demands that we go first to the concrete objects, and only then to their rational organization. Poetry passes straight from the word to the affective organization, careless of the reality whose relation it accepts as already given in the word. Mathematics passes straight from the symbol to the perceptual organization, careless of the concrete object, whose important qualities (to it) are already accepted as crystallized in the symbol. Hence the vital importance of precise speech—of the absolutely correct word or correct symbol—both to poet and mathematician, contrasted with the looser speech permitted to the biologist or novelist.

We have seen that music is an extreme kind of poetry, that just as mathematics escapes almost altogether from the subjective qualities of matter, so music (unlike poetry) escapes almost altogether from the objective references of sounds. Therefore the musician is even preciser in his language than the poet, and the affective laws of music's symbols are as careful and minute as are the perceptual laws of mathematical symbols.

We can now understand more clearly why poetry resembles dream in its technique. The characteristic of dreams is that the dreamer always plays the leading part in it. He is always present in it, sometimes (as analysis shows) in many disguises. The same egocentricity is characteristic of poetry. Quite naïvely the poet records directly all his impressions, experiences, thought, images. Hence the apparent egoism of poetry, for everything is seen and experienced directly. Poetry is a relationship of memory-images mediated by only two words—"I" and "like."

But this is not the egoism of dream; it is a social egoism. The particular emotional organization of the poet is condensed into words, and the words are read, and the psyche of the reader experiences the same emotional reorganization. The reader puts himself, for the duration of the poem, in the place of the poet, and sees with his eyes. He *is* the poet.

In a poem by Shelley, we are Shelley. As we read Shakespeare, we see with his profound shimmering vision. Hence the unexpected individuality of the poet. Though it is the common human creature, the genotype, and not the "character" who looks out in poetry on the common contemporary scene, she looks at it through the eyes of one man, through the windows of the poet's psyche.

How is this done? That is the peculiar secret of poetic technique. Just as poetry can be equated with dream, poetic technique is similar to dream technique. The nature of dream technique has been explored by analysts under the general name of "the dream-work."

A dream consists of two layers. Obvious is the *manifest* content. We are walking by the seaside, a ship comes alongside, we step on it, we land in France, certain adventures befall us, and so on. This is the manifest content of the dream as we tell it at breakfast next morning to our bored family, who cannot understand our interest in it. But our interest in it was due to the fact that the illusion was perfect. While they lasted, these things really seemed to be happening to us. And this vividness must spring from some affective cause. But we felt little real emotion in the dream, however surprising the adventures that befell us. If we felt emotion, it was out of all real proportion to our adventures. Surprising things happened and we were not surprised. Trifling things happened and we were appalled. The affects were displaced in relation to reality. If we are asked to give our associations to these various component images just as they spring to our mind, a whole undergrowth of displaced affective life is revealed. Each symbol is associated with memories in our life, not by association of ideas but by affective associations.

The characteristic of "dream-work" is that every dream-symbol is overdetermined and has a multitude of different emotional significances. This we also saw was the characteristic of poetic words, and springs from the same cause, that dream-symbols are valued directly for their affective content and not as symbols of a consistent mock world in which we first orientate ourselves. Hence the inconsequence of dream matches the "illogical" rhythm and assonance of poetry.

The organization of the psyche is such that in sleep all the conscious wishes, hopes, fears and love of the instinctive are replaced by apparently arbitrary memory-images, but which really are associated by the affective ties of simple unconscious wishes. They are organized by the appetitive activity of the instinctive and therefore unsleeping part of the psyche which, because it is archaic phylogenetically, is unmodified and therefore anti-social, or rather non-social. This affective substratum does not normally appear in dream. It is "repressed." Only the arbitrary symbols, apparently unconnected, appear in the consciousness. But this affective basis is the "reasoning" of the dream, and directs its course. It is the latent content. . . . Dreams, then, contain a manifest and a latent content. The manifest content is imagic phantasy, the latent content is affective reality. . . .

4

. . . Poetry, like dream, contains *manifest* and *latent* contents. The manifest content can be roughly arrived at by paraphrasing the poem. It is the imagery or the "ideas." In a paraphrase the latent content, that is, the emotional content, has almost entirely vanished. It was contained, then, not in the external reality symbolized by the words (for this has been preserved) but in the words themselves. The manifest content is the poetry interpreted "rationally." It is the external reality in the poem. It can be expressed in other ways and other languages. But the latent content of poetry is in that particular form of wording, and in no other.

How is the latent content contained in the original words and not contained in the *sense* of the words—that is, in the portions of external reality which the words symbolize? The emotions are not associated affectively with the portion of external reality symbolized by the manifest content, for another language can be made to symbolize the same portion of external reality, and still it is not the poem. How then did the original words contain the emotional content "in themselves" and not in the things they symbolized? Dream analysis gives us the answer, by *affective* association of ideas. In any association of ideas two images are tied to each other by something different, like sticks by a cord. In poetry they are tied by affects.

If a word is abstracted from its surroundings and concentrated on in the same way as an analyst asked his patient to concentrate on any particular image of a dream, a number of associations will rise vaguely to the mind. In a simple word like "spring" there are hundreds of them; of greenness, of youth, of fountains, of jumping; every word drags behind it a vast bag and baggage of emotional associations, picked up in the thousands of different circumstances in which the word was used. It is these associations that provided the latent content of affect which is the poem. Not the ideas of "greenness," "youth," but the affective cord linking the ideas of "greenness" and "youth" to the word "spring," constitutes the raw material of poetry.

Of course the *thing* "spring" (the season) denoted by the word "spring" also has many affective associations. These are used by the novel. Poetry is concerned with the more general, subtle and instinctive affects which are immediately associated with the word "spring" and therefore include such almost punning associations as those connected with spring (a fountain) and spring (to jump). Hence the tendency of poetry to play with words, to pun openly or secretly, to delight in the texture of words. This is part of the technique of poetry which treats words anti-grammatically to realize their immediate and even contradictory affective tones. The novel uses words grammatically so as sharply to exclude all meanings and therefore all affective tones, except one clear piece of reality, and then derives the emotional content from this piece of reality and its active relation with the other pieces of reality in the story as part of a perceptual life-experience.

When we read a line of poetry these other ideas to which the affects are associated do not rise to the mind. We get the leaping and gushiness of "spring" in poetry's use of it as a word for the idea "season," but we do not get the fountain or the jump except in an open poetic pun. They remain unconscious. *Poetry is a kind of inverted dream.* Whereas in dream the real affects are partly suppressed and the blended images rise into the conscious, in poetry the associated images are partly suppressed and it is the blended affects that are present in the consciousness, in the form of affective organization.

Why is there a manifest content at all? Why are not all images suppressed? Why is not great poetry like the poetry of the extreme symbolists, a mere collection of words, meaning nothing, but words themselves full of affective association? Why should poetry state, explain, narrate, obey grammar, have syntax, be capable of paraphrase, since if paraphrased it loses its affective value?

The answer is, because poetry is an adaptation to external reality. It is an emotional attitude towards the world. It is made of language and language was created to signify otherness, to indicate portions of objective reality shared socially. It lives in the same language as scientific thought. The manifest content represents a statement of external reality. The manifest content is symbolic of a certain *piece* of external reality—be it scene, problem, thought, event. And the emotional content is *attached* to this statement of reality, not in actual experience but in the poem. The emotional content sweats out of the piece of external reality. In life this piece of external reality is devoid of emotional tone, but described in those particular words, and no others, it suddenly and magically shimmers with affective coloring. That affective coloring represents an emotional organization similar to that which the poet himself felt when faced (in phantasy or actuality) with that piece of external reality. When the poet says,

> Sleep, that knits up the ravelled sleave of care,

he is making a manifest statement. The paraphrase

> Slumber, that unties worry, which is like a piece of tangled knitting,

carries over most of the manifest content, but the affective tones which lurked in the associations of the words used have vanished. It is like a conjuring trick. The poet holds up a piece of the world and we see it glowing with a strange emotional fire. If we analyze it "rationally," we find no fire. Yet none the less, for ever afterwards, that piece of reality still keeps an after glow about it, is still fragrant with emotional life. So poetry enriches external reality for us.

The affective associations used by poetry are of many forms. Sometimes they are sound associations, and then we call the line "musical"—not that the language is specially harmonious; to a foreigner it would probably have no particular verbal melody:

> Thick as autumnal leaves that strow the brooks
> In Vallambrosa

is not musical to someone who knows no English. But to an English ear the emotive associations wakened are aroused through sound rather than sense linkages, and hence we call the line musical. So, too, with Verlaine's line, musical only to ears attuned to the emotive associations of French nasals:

> *Et O—ces voix d'enfants chantant dans la coupole,*

or the old fairy-tale title, "La Belle aux bois dormant."

It is impossible to have affects in poetry without their adherence to symbols of external reality, for poetry's affects (insofar as they are poetic) are social, and it is impossible for different subjects to be linked except by a common object (by "matter"). The logical conclusion of symbolism is not poetry but music. And here it may be objected—music consists of sounds which refer to no external reality and yet music is an art and has a social content. Exactly—because in music the symbols have ceased to "refer" to external reality and have become portions of external reality themselves and, in doing so, have necessarily generated a formal structure (the scale, "rules" of harmony, etc.) which gives them the rigidity and social status of external reality. The notes of music themselves are the manifest content of music, and they therefore obey not grammatical (subjective) but pseudo-mathematical (objective) laws: of course they are necessarily distorted or organized within the compass of those rules. In the same way architecture becomes external reality and is distorted or organized within the compass of the rules of use-function.

The technique of the poet consists in this, that not all the affects associated with any particular words rise up into the consciousness, but only those that are required. This is done by the arrangement of the words in such a way that their clusters of associations, impinging on each other heighten some affective associations and inhibit the others, and so form an organized mass of emotion. The affective coloring of one word takes reflected shadow and light from the colors of the other words. It does this partly through their contiguity, particularly in synthetic languages (Latin and Greek), and partly through their grammatical connection, particularly in analytic languages (English, Chinese); but chiefly through the "meaning" as a whole. The manifest content, the literal meaning, the paraphrasable sense, is a kind of bridge, or electrical conductor which puts all the affective currents of each word into contact. It is like a switchboard; some of the affective associations fade away directly they enter it, others run down into other words and alter their color; others blend together and heighten a particular word. The whole forms the specific fused glow which is that poem's affective organization or emotional attitude to its meaning. Hence the same word has a different affective coloration in one poem from what it has in another, and it is for this reason that a poem is concrete. It is affectively concrete; each word has a special affective significance in that poem different from what it has in another. In this way the emotional content does not float about fluidly in the mind; it is firmly attached, by a hundred interweaving strands, to the manifest content—a piece of external reality. A poem's content is not just emotion, it is *organized* emotion, an organized emotional attitude to a piece of external reality. Hence its value—and difficulty—as compared with other emotions, however strong, but unorganized—a sudden inexplicable fit of sorrow, a gust of blind rage, a blank despair. Such emotions are unesthetic because unorganized. They are unorganized socially because they are not organized in relation to a socially accepted external reality. They are unconscious of outer necessity. The emotions of poetry are *part* of the manifest content. They seem to be in the external reality as it appears in the poem. We do not appear to take up an emotional attitude to a piece of reality; it is there, given in the reality: that is the way of emotional cognition. In poetic cognition, objects are presented already stamped with feeling-judgments. Hence the adaptive value of poetry. It is like a real emotional experience.

It is plain that poetry may be judged in different ways; either by the importance of the manifest content, or by the vividness of the affective coloring. To a poet who brings a new portion of external reality into the ambit of poetry, we feel more gratitude than to one who brings the old stale manifest contents. But the first poet may be poor in the affective coloring with which he soaks his piece of reality. It may be the old stale coloring, whereas our other poet, in spite of his conventional piece of reality, may achieve a new affective tone. Old poets we shall judge almost entirely by their affective tone; their manifest contents have long belonged to our world of thought. Hence the apparent triteness of old poetry which yet is a *great* triteness. From new poets we demand new manifest contents and new affective coloring, for it is their function to give us new emotional attitudes to a new social environment. A poet who provides both to a high degree will be a good poet. A poet who brings into his net a vast amount of new reality to which he attaches a wide-ranging affective coloring we shall call a *great* poet, giving Shakespeare as an instance. Hence great poems are always long poems, just because of the quantity of reality they must include as manifest content. But the manifest content, whatever it is, is not the *purpose* of the poem. The purpose is the specific emotional organization directed towards the manifest content and provided by the released affects. The affects are not "latent," as in dream; it is the associated ideas which are suppressed to form the latent content. Just as the key to dream is a series of instinctive attitudes which provide the mechanism of dream-work, so the key to poetry is a cluster of suppressed pieces of external reality—a vague unconscious world of life-experience.

Poetry colors the world of reality with affective tones. These affective colors are not "pretty-pretty," for it is still the real world of necessity, and great poetry will not disguise the nakedness of outer necessity, only cause it to shine with the glow of interest. Poetry soaks external reality—nature and society—with emotional significance. This significance, because it gives the organism an appetitive interest in external reality, enables the organism to deal with it more resolutely, whether in the world of reality or of phantasy. The primitive who would lose interest in the exhausting labor necessary to plow an arid abstract collection of soil, will find heart when the earth is charged with the affective coloring of "Mother Nature," for now, by the magic of poetry, it glows with the appetitive tints of sexuality or filial love. These affective colors are not unreal because they are not scientific, for they are the coloring of the genotype's own instincts, and these instincts are as real as the earth is real. The significant expression projected by poetry on to the face of external reality is simply this, a prophecy of the endless attempt of the genotype to mold necessity to its own likeness, in which it obtains a continually increasing success. "Matter, surrounded by a sensuous poetic glamour, seems to attract man's whole entity by winning smiles." So said Marx and Engels of materialism before it became one-sided mechanical materialism, when it was still bathed in the artistic splendor of the Renaissance. That sensuous glamour is given by poetry; and materialism became one-sided when, afraid of feeling the self, it became aridly scientific, and matter vanishes in a logical but empty wave-system. Poetry restores life and value to matter and puts back the genotype into the world from which it was banished. . . .

5

If we are asked the purpose of art, we can make an answer—the precise nature of it depending on what we mean by *purpose*. Art has "survived"; cultures containing art have outlived and replaced those that have not, because art adapts the psyche to the environment, and is therefore one of the conditions of the development of society. But we get another answer if we ask *how* art performs its task, for it does this by taking a piece of environment and distorting it, giving it a non-likeness to external reality which is also a likeness to the genotype. It remolds external reality nearer to the likeness of the genotype's instincts, but since the instinctive genotype is nothing but an unconscious and dynamic desire it remolds external reality nearer to the heart's desire. Art becomes more socially and biologically valuable and greater art the more that remolding is comprehensive and true to the nature of reality, using as its material the sadness, the catastrophes, the blind necessities, as well as the delights and pleasures of life. An organism which thinks life is all "for the best in the best possible of worlds" will have little survival value. Great art can thus be great tragedy, for here, reality at its bitterest—death, despair, eternal failure—is yet given an organization, a shape, an affective arrangement which expresses a deeper and more social view of fate. By giving external reality an affective organization drawn from its heart, the genotype makes all reality, even death, more interesting because more true. The world glows with interest; our hearts go out to it with appetite to encounter it, to live in it, to get to grips with it. A great novel is how we should like our own lives to be, not petty or dull, but full of great issues, turning even death to a noble sound:

Notre vie est noble et tragique
Comme le masque d'un tyran
Nul drame hazardeux et magique
Aucun détail indifférent
Ne rend notre amour pathetique.[4]

A great picture is how we should like the world to look to us—brighter, full of affective color. Great music is how we should like our emotions to run on, full of strenuous purpose and deep aims. And because, for a moment, we saw how it might be, were given the remade object into our hands, forever after we tend to make our lives less petty, tend to look around us with a more-seeing eye, tend to feel richly and strenuously.

If we ask why art, by making the environment wear the expression of the genotype, comes to us with the nearness and significance it does, we must say still more about art's essence. In making external reality glow with our expression, art tells us about ourselves. No man can look directly at himself, but art makes of the Universe a mirror in which we catch glimpses of ourselves, not as we are, but as we are in active potentiality of becoming in relation to reality through society. The genotype we see is the genotype stamped with all the possibilities and grandeur of mankind—an elaboration which in its turn is extracted by society from the rest of reality. Art gives us so many glimpses of the inner heart of life; and that is its significance, different from and yet arising out of its purpose. It is like a magic lantern which projects our real selves on the Universe and promises us that we, as we desire, can alter the Universe, alter it to the measure of our needs. But to do so, we must know more deeply our real needs, must make ourselves yet more conscious of ourselves. The more we grip external reality, the more our art develops and grows increasingly subtle, the more the magic lantern show takes on new subtleties and fresh richnesses. Art tells us what science cannot tell us, and what religion only feigns to tell us—what we are and why we are, why we hope and suffer and love and die. It does not tell us this in the language of science, as theology and dogma attempt to do, but in the only language that can express these truths, the language of inner reality itself, the language of affect and emotion. And its message is generated by our attempt to realize its essence in an active struggle with Nature, the struggle called life.

—*Illusion and Reality* (1937)

Notes

1. According to Hegel and Marx, development generally takes the form of a threefold movement: first, an active force or tendency (the thesis); second, a counterforce or conflicting tendency (the antithesis, or *negation*); and third, a reconciliation of the conflicting forces or tendencies in a new synthesis (the synthesis, or *negation of the negation*). Caudwell is here maintaining that the art-work represents a creative synthesis which reconciles the *personal* consciousness and self-expression of the artist with the *social* traditions and demands of art. (Editor's note.)

2. *Cf.* William Empson's discussion of poetic ambiguity in his *Seven Types of Ambiguity* (Chatto and Windus, London, 1930). (Editor's note.)

3. Caudwell refers to this distinction in an earlier passage (pp. 184–5): "The classificatory sciences, of which mathematics is the queen and physics an important sphere, deal with space-like orderings which are independent of time. . . . The evolutionary sciences . . . are historical in their approach. They deal with reality as a process, as the emergence of new qualities. Sociology, biology, geology, psychology, astronomy, and physiology are all sciences which are interested in time. . . . The same division in the field of art gives rise to a similar distinction. In literary art the novel is evolutionary and the poem is classificatory." Music, architecture, and the static plastic arts are "classificatory" like poetry; prose drama, film, and ballet are "evolutionary" like the novel. (Editor's note.)

4. Apollinaire.

CHAPTER 5

Enhancement of Experience

JOHN DEWEY: Having an Experience
DOROTHY WALSH: Virtual Experience

Siding with writers such as Nietzsche and Caudwell in opposing an isolationist interpretation of art, the great American pragmatist, John Dewey (1859–1952), reacts strongly against the idea that esthetic and practical activity are quite separate. Instead of emphasizing the difference between art and nature or between art and actual experience, he maintains that the function of art is to organize experience more meaningfully, more coherently, more vividly, than ordinary life permits. Art is experience in its most articulate and adequate form: "the union of sense, mood, impulse, and action characteristic of the live creature." It is not differentiated by the predominance of any one mental faculty, such as emotion or imagination, but by a greater inclusiveness of psychological factors. It has no highly restricted subject matter: anything vividly and imaginatively realized, indeed, may be the source of "an experience that is *an* experience"—the kind of experience that is art.

Underlying this doctrine of the oneness of art and life is the conviction that means and ends should not be sharply separated. Experience is most satisfactory when means and ends interpenetrate, and art is experience when it reaches this peak. For art is not a mere anodyne, an escape, an isolated pastime, nor is it a grim discipline undertaken simply for the sake of its consequences. It is full of enjoyed meanings, and yet it is instrumental to new satisfying events. The frequent tendency to separate means and ends leads to some of the worst evils of our civilization. As Irwin Edman, a follower of Dewey, says, "It produces, on the one hand, a practical civilization in which there is no interest in sensuous charm or imaginative grace, the Land of Smoke-Over celebrated in the legends of L. P. Jacks. It produces, on the other hand, the soft luxuriance of the esthete whose dainty creations and enjoyments have no connection with the rest of life."[1] Against such dualism, Dewey's philosophy is a powerful protest.

We must not exaggerate this insistence on the continuity of art and life. The esthetician Andrew Paul Ushenko expressed to Dewey his opinion that the emphasis on this continuity "does not do justice to the fact that an esthetic experience is disinterested, that is, indifferent to matters of practical concern." Dewey answered that conception of "an esthetic experience, as defined in *Arts as Experience*, is intended to recognize both the basic continuity between life and art and the distinctive quality of being completed in itself, which makes a work of art stand apart from the field of practical transaction."[2] A careful reading of the following selection will confirm Dewey's answer.

Among the many estheticians who have been influenced by Dewey is Dorothy Walsh (1901–), Professor Emeritus of philosophy at Smith College. While developing her own divergent interpretations, she is indebted to Dewey's distinction between ordinary experience and experience of outstanding quality, and to Susanne Langer's distinction between actual experience and "virtual experience." "Life experience, as actual experience, is idiosyncratic, fragmentary, and fleeting; only virtual experience, structured and articulated, lifted out of the temporal flux of ongoing happening, provides something that can be fully realized and shared."[3] By creating a kind of virtual experience, literary art provides knowledge by imaginative acquaintance rather than knowledge by abstract reference.

Professor Walsh thus answers one of the lively questions in esthetics: whether art contributes to knowledge and thereby justifies belief. If by "truth" one means abstract description, the positivists are right in maintaining that it falls within the realm of science and not of art. But if by "truth" one means imaginative insight into the felt qualities of life, such truth has a poignancy, a warmth, a vividness, a specificity that withers in a scientific description. It is "*an* experience" in Dewey's sense enhanced and communicated as "virtual experience." When the virtual experience strikes us as authentic, we call it truth; when it deepens our understanding of life, we call it knowledge.

Another American philosopher deeply influenced by Dewey is Stephen Pepper. His discussion of "contextualistic criticism" in Chapter 12 may be read as a further elucidation and extension of Dewey's theory.

Notes

1. Irwin Edman, *The World, The Arts, and the Artist* (Norton, New York, 1928), pp. 34–35.
2. Andrew Paul Ushenko, *Dynamics of Art* (Indiana University Press, Bloomington, 1953), pp. 11–12.
3. Dorothy Walsh, *Literature and Knowledge* (Wesleyan University Press, Middletown, Conn., 1969), p. 139.

JOHN DEWEY

Having an Experience

Experience occurs continuously, because the interaction of live creature and environing conditions is involved in the very process of living. Under conditions of resistance and conflict, aspects and elements of the self and the world that are implicated in this interaction qualify experience with emotions and ideas so that conscious intent emerges. Oftentimes, however, the experience had is inchoate. Things are experienced but not in such a way that they are composed into *an* experience. There is distraction and dispersion; what we observe and what we think, what we desire and what we get, are at odds with each other. We put our hands to the plow and turn back; we start and then we stop, not because the experience has reached the end for the sake of which it was initiated but because of extraneous interruptions or of inner lethargy.

In contrast with such experience, we have *an* experience when the material experienced runs its course to fulfillment. Then and then only is it integrated within and demarcated in the general stream of experience from other experiences. A piece of work is finished in a way that is satisfactory; a problem receives its solution; a game is played through; a situation, whether that of eating a meal, playing a game of chess, carrying on a conversation, writing a book, or taking part in a political campaign, is so rounded out that its close is a consummation and not a cessation. Such an experience is a whole and carries with it its own individualizing quality and self-sufficiency. It is *an* experience.

Philosophers, even empirical philosophers, have spoken for the most part of experience at large. Idiomatic speech, however, refers to experiences each of which is singular, having its own beginning and end. For life is no uniform uninterrupted march or flow. It is a thing of histories, each with its own plot, its own inception and movement toward its close, each having its own particular rhythmic movement; each with its own unrepeated quality pervading it throughout. A flight of stairs, mechanical as it is, proceeds by individualized steps, not by undifferentiated progression, and an inclined plane is at least marked off from other things by abrupt discreteness.

Experience in this vital sense is defined by those situations and episodes that we spontaneously refer to as being "real experiences"; those things of which we say in reading them, "that *was* an experience." It may have been something of tremendous importance—a quarrel with one who was once an intimate, a catastrophe finally averted by a hair's breadth. Or it may have been something that in comparison was slight—and which perhaps because of its very slightness illustrates all the better what it is to be an experience. There is that meal in a Paris restaurant of which one says "that *was* an experience." It stands out as an enduring memorial of what food may be. Then there is that storm one went through in crossing the Atlantic—the storm that seemed in its fury, as it was experienced, to sum up in itself all that a storm can be, complete in itself, standing out because marked out from what went before and what came after.

In such experiences, every successive part flows freely, without seam and without unfilled blanks, into what ensues. At the same time there is no sacrifice of the self-identity of the parts. A river, as distinct from a pond, flows. But its flow gives a definiteness and interest to its successive portions greater than exist in the homogenous portions of a pond. In an experience, flow is from something to something. As one part leads into another and as one part carries on what went before, each gains distinctness in itself. The enduring whole is diversified by successive phases that are emphases of its varied colors.

Because of continuous merging, there are no holes, mechanical junctions, and dead centers when we have *an* experience. There are pauses, places of rest, but they punctuate and define the quality of movement. They sum up what has been undergone and prevent its dissipation and idle evaporation. Continued acceleration is breathless and prevents parts from gaining distinction. In a work of art, different acts, episodes, occurrences melt and fuse into unity, and yet do not disappear and lose their own character as they do so—just as in a genial conversation there is a continuous interchange and blending, and yet each speaker not only retains his own character but manifests it more clearly than is his wont.

An experience has a unity that gives it its name, that meal, that storm, that rupture of friendship. The existence of this unity is constituted by a single *quality* that pervades the entire experience in spite of the variation of its constituent parts. This unity is neither emotional, practical, nor intellectual, for these terms name distinctions that reflection can make within it. In discourse *about* an experience, we must make use of these adjectives of interpretation. In going over an experience in mind *after* its occurrence, we may find that one property rather than another was sufficiently dominant so that it characterizes the experience as a whole. There are absorbing inquiries and speculations which a scientific man and philosopher will recall as "experiences" in the emphatic sense. In final import they are intellectual. But in their actual occurrence they were emotional as well; they were purposive and volitional. Yet the experience was not a sum of these different characters; they were lost in it as distinctive traits. No thinker can ply his occupation save as he is lured and rewarded by total integral experiences that are intrinsically worthwhile. Without them he would never know what it is really to think and would be completely at a loss in distinguishing real thought from the spurious article. Thinking goes on in trains of ideas, but the ideas form a train only because they are much more than what an analytic psychology calls ideas. They are phases, emotionally and practically distinguished, of a developing underlying quality; they are its moving variations, not separate and independent like Locke's and Hume's so-called ideas and impressions, but are subtle shadings of a pervading and developing hue.

We say of an experience of thinking that we reach or draw a conclusion. Theoretical formulation of the process is often made in such terms as to conceal effectually the similarity of "conclusion" to the consummating phase of every developing integral experience. These formulations apparently take their cue from the separate propositions that are premises and the proposition that is the conclusion as they appear on the printed page. The impression is derived that there are first two independent and ready-made entities that are then manipulated so as to give rise to a third. In fact, in an experience of thinking, premises emerge only as a conclusion becomes manifest. The experience, like that of watching a storm reach its height and gradually subside, is one of continuous movement of subject-matters. Like the ocean in the storm, there are a series of waves; suggestions reaching out and being broken in a clash, or being carried onwards by a cooperative wave. If a conclusion is reached, it is that of a movement of anticipation and cumulation, one that finally comes to completion. A "conclusion" is no separate and independent thing; it is the consummation of a movement.

Hence *an* experience of thinking has its own esthetic quality. It differs from those experiences that are acknowledged to be esthetic, but only in its materials. The material of the fine arts consists of qualities; that of experience having intellectual conclusion are signs or symbols having no intrinsic quality of their own, but standing for things that may in another experience be qualitatively experienced. The difference is enormous. It is one reason why the strictly intellectual art will never be popular as music is popular. Nevertheless, the experience itself has a satisfying emotional quality because it possesses internal integration and fulfillment reached through ordered and organized movement. This artistic structure may be immediately felt. Insofar, it is esthetic. What is even more important is that not only is this quality a significant motive in undertaking intellectual inquiry and in keeping it honest, but that no intellectual activity is an integral event (is *an* experience), unless it is rounded out with this quality. Without it, thinking is inconclusive. In short, esthetic cannot be sharply marked off from intellectual experience since the latter must bear an esthetic stamp to be itself complete.

The same statement holds good of a course of action that is dominantly practical, that is, one that consists of overt doings. It is possible to be efficient in action and yet not have a conscious experience. The activity is too automatic to permit of a sense of what it is about and where it is going. It comes to an end but not to a close or consummation in consciousness. Obstacles are overcome by shrewd skill, but they do not feed experience. There are also those who are wavering in action, uncertain, and inconclusive like the shades in classic literature. Between the poles of aimlessness and mechanical efficiency, there lie those courses of action in which through successive deeds there runs a sense of growing meaning conserved and accumulating toward an end that is felt as accomplishment of a process. Successful politicians and generals who turn statesmen like Caesar and Napoleon have something of the showman about them. This of itself is not art, but it is, I think, a sign that interest is not exclusively, perhaps not mainly, held by the result taken by itself (as it is in the case of mere efficiency), but by it as the outcome of a process. There is interest in completing an experience. The experience may be one that is harmful to the world and its consummation undesirable. But it has esthetic quality.

The Greek identification of good conduct with conduct having proportion, grace, and harmony, the *kalon-agathon,* is a more obvious example of distinctive esthetic quality in moral action. One great defect in what passes as morality is its anesthetic quality. Instead of exemplifying wholehearted action, it takes the form of grudging piecemeal concessions to the demands of duty. But illustrations may only obscure the fact that any practical activity will, provided that it is integrated and moves by its own urge to fulfillment, have esthetic quality.

A generalized illustration may be had if we imagine a stone, which is rolling downhill, to have an experience. The activity is surely sufficiently "practical." The stone starts from somewhere, and moves, as consistently as conditions permit, toward a place and state where it will be at rest—toward an end. Let us add, by imagination, to these external facts, the ideas that it looks forward with desire to the final outcome; that it is interested in the things it meets on its way, conditions that accelerate and retard its movement with respect to their bearing on the end; that it acts and feels toward them according to the hindering or helping function it attributes to them; and that the final coming to rest is related to all that went before as the culmination of a continuous movement. Then the stone would have an experience, and one with esthetic quality.

If we turn from this imaginary case to our own experience we shall find much of it is nearer to what happens to the actual stone than it is to anything that fulfills the conditions fancy just laid down. For in much of our experience we are not concerned with the connection of one incident with what went before and what comes after. There is no interest that controls attentive rejection or selection of what shall be organized into the developing experience. Things happen, but they are neither definitely included nor decisively excluded; we drift. We yield according to external pressure, or evade and compromise. There are beginnings and cessations, but no genuine initiations and concludings. One thing replaces another, but does not absorb it and carry it on. There is experience, but so slack and discursive that it is not *an* experience. Needless to say, such experiences are anesthetic.

Thus the non-esthetic lies within two limits. At one pole is the loose succession that does not begin at any particular place and that ends—in the sense of ceasing—at no particular place. At the other pole is arrest, constriction, proceeding from parts having only a mechanical connection with one another. There exists so much of one and the other of these two kinds of experience that unconsciously they come to be taken as norms of all experience. Then, when the esthetic appears, it so sharply contrasts with the picture that has been formed of experience, that it is impossible to combine its special qualities with the features of the picture and the esthetic is given an outside place and status. The account that has been given of experience dominantly intellectual and practical is intended to show that there is no such contrast involved in having an experience; that, on the contrary, no experience of whatever sort is a unity unless it has esthetic quality.

The enemies of the esthetic are neither the practical nor the intellectual. They are the humdrum; slackness of loose ends; submission to convention in practice and intellectual procedure. Rigid abstinence, coerced submission, tightness on one side and dissipation, incoherence and aimless indulgence on the other, are deviations in opposite directions from the unity of an experience. . . .

I have spoken of the esthetic quality that rounds out an experience into completeness and unity as emotional. The reference may cause difficulty. We are given to thinking of emotions as things as simple and compact as are the words by which we name them. Joy, sorrow, hope, fear, anger, curiosity, are treated as if each in itself were a sort of entity that enters full-made upon the scene, an entity that may last a long time or a short time, but whose duration, whose growth and career, is irrelevant to its nature. In fact emotions are qualities, when they are significant, of a complex experience that moves and changes. I say, when they are *significant,* for otherwise they are but the outbreaks and eruptions of a disturbed infant. All emotions are qualifications of a drama and they change as the drama develops. Persons are sometimes said to fall in love at first sight. But what they fall into is not a thing of that instant. What would love be were it compressed into a moment in which there is no room for cherishing and for solicitude? The intimate nature of emotion is manifested in the experience of one watching a play on the stage or reading a novel. It attends the development of a plot; and a plot requires a stage, a space, wherein to develop and time in which to unfold. Experience is emotional but there are no separate things called emotions in it.

By the same token, emotions are attached to events and objects in their movement. They are not, save in pathological instances, private. And even an "objectless" emotion demands something beyond itself to which to attach itself, and thus it soon generates a delusion in lack of something real. Emotion belongs of a certainty to the self. But it belongs to the self that is concerned in the movement of events toward an issue that is desired or disliked. We jump instantaneously when we are scared, as we blush on the instant when we are ashamed. But fright and shamed modesty are not in this case emotional states. Of themselves they are but automatic reflexes. In order to become emotional they must become parts of an inclusive and enduring situation that involves concern for objects and their issues. The jump of fright becomes emotional fear when there is found or thought to exist a threatening object that must be dealt with or escaped from. The blush becomes the emotion of shame when a person connects, in thought, an action he has performed with an unfavorable reaction to himself of some other person.

Physical things from far ends of the earth are physically transported and physically caused to act and react upon one another in the construction of a new object. The miracle of mind is that something similar takes place in experience without physical transport and assembling. Emotion is the moving and cementing force. It selects what is congruous and dyes what is selected with its color, thereby giving qualitative unity to materials externally disparate and dissimilar. It thus provides unity in and through the varied parts of an experience. When the unity is of the sort already described, the experience has esthetic character even though it is not, dominantly, an esthetic experience.

Two men meet; one is the applicant for a position, while the other has the disposition of the matter in his hands. The interview may be mechanical, consisting of set questions, the replies to which perfunctorily settle the matter. There is no experience in which the two men meet, nothing that is not a repetition, by way of acceptance or dismissal, of something which has happened a score of times. The situation is disposed of as if it were an exercise in bookkeeping. But an interplay may take place in which a new experience develops. Where should we look for an account of such an experience? Not to ledger-entries nor yet to a treatise on economics or sociology or personnel-psychology, but to drama or fiction. Its nature and import can be expressed only by art, because there is a unity of experience that can be expressed only as an experience. The *experience* is of material fraught with suspense and moving toward its own consummation through a connected series of varied incidents. The primary emotions on the part of the applicant may be at the beginning hope or despair, and elation or disappointment at the close. These emotions qualify the experience as a unity. But as the interview proceeds, secondary emotions are evolved as variations of the primary underlying one. It is even possible for each attitude and gesture, each sentence, almost every word, to produce more than a fluctuation in the intensity of the basic emotion; to produce, that is, a change of shade and tint in its quality. The employer sees by means of his own emotional reactions the character of the one applying. He projects him imaginatively into the work to be done and judges his fitness by the way in which the elements of the scene assemble and either clash or fit together. The presence and behavior of the applicant either harmonize with his own attitudes and desires or they conflict and jar. Such factors as these, inherently esthetic in quality, are the forces that carry the varied elements of the interview to a decisive issue. They enter into the settlement of every situation, whatever its dominant nature, in which there are uncertainty and suspense.

There are, therefore, common patterns in various experiences, no matter how unlike they are to one another in the details of their subject matter. There are conditions to be met without which an experience cannot come to be. The outline of the common pattern is set by the fact that every experience is the result of interaction between a live creature and some aspect of the world in which he lives. A man does something; he lifts, let us say, a stone. In consequence he undergoes, suffers, something: the weight, strain, texture of the surface of the thing lifted. The properties thus undergone determine further doing. The stone is too heavy or too angular, not solid enough; or else the properties undergone show it is fit for the use for which it is intended. The process continues until a mutual adaptation of the self and the object emerges and that particular experience comes to a close. What is true of this simple instance is true, as to form, of every experience. The creature operating may be a thinker in his study and the environment with which he interacts may consist of ideas instead of a stone. But interaction of the two constitutes the total experience that is had, and the close which completes it is the institution of a felt harmony.

An experience has pattern and structure, because it is not just doing and undergoing in alternation, but consists of them in relationship. To put one's hand in the fire that consumes it is not necessarily to have an experience. The action and its consequence must be joined in perception. This relationship is what gives meaning; to grasp it is the objective of all intelligence. The scope and content of the relations measure the significant content of an experience. A child's experience may be intense, but, because of lack of background from past experience, relations between undergoing and doing are slightly grasped, and the experience does not have great depth or breadth. . . .

Experience is limited by all the causes which interfere with perception of the relations between undergoing and doing. There may be interference because of excess on the side of doing or of excess on the side of receptivity, of undergoing. Unbalance on either side blurs the perception of relations and leaves the experience partial and distorted, with scant or false meaning. Zeal for doing, lust for action, leaves many a person, especially in this hurried and impatient human environment in which we live, with experience of an almost incredible paucity, all on the surface. No one experience has a chance to complete itself because something else is entered upon so speedily. What is called experience becomes so dispersed and miscellaneous as hardly to deserve the name. Resistance is treated as an obstruction to be beaten down, not as an invitation to reflection. An individual comes to seek, unconsciously even more than by deliberate choice, situations in which he can do the most things in the shortest time.

Experiences are also cut short from maturing by excess of receptivity. What is prized is then the mere undergoing of this and that, irrespective of perception of any meaning. The crowding together of as many impressions as possible is thought to be "life," even though no one of them is more than a flitting and a sipping. The sentimentalist and the daydreamer may have more fancies and impressions pass through their consciousness than has the man who is animated by lust for action. But his experience is equally distorted, because nothing takes root in mind when there is no balance between doing and receiving. Some decisive action is needed in order to establish contact with the realities of the world and in order that impressions may be so related to facts that their value is tested and organized.

Because perception of relationship between what is done and what is undergone constitutes the work of intelligence, and because the artist is controlled in the process of his work by his grasp of the connection between what he has already done and what he is to do next, the idea that the artist does not think as intently and penetratingly as a scientific inquirer is absurd. A painter must consciously undergo the effect of his every brush stroke or he will not be aware of what he is doing and where his work is going. Moreover, he has to see each particular connection of doing and undergoing in relation to the whole that he desires to produce. To apprehend such relations is to think, and is one of the most exacting modes of thought. The difference between the pictures of different painters is due quite as much to differences of capacity to carry on this thought as it is to differences of sensitivity to bare color and to differences in dexterity of execution. As respects the basic quality of pictures, difference depends, indeed, more upon the quality of intelligence brought to bear upon perception of relations than upon anything else—though of course intelligence cannot be separated from direct sensitivity and is connected, though in a more external manner, with skill.

Any idea that ignores the necessary role of intelligence in production of works of art is based upon identification of thinking with use of one special kind of material, verbal signs and words. To think effectively in terms of relations of qualities is as severe a demand upon thought as to think in terms of symbols, verbal and mathematical. Indeed, since words are easily manipulated in mechanical ways, the production of a work of genuine art probably demands more intelligence than does most of the so-called thinking that goes on among those who pride themselves on being "intellectuals."

I have tried to show . . . that the esthetic is no intruder in experience from without, whether by way of idle luxury or transcendent ideality, but that it is the clarified and intensified development of traits that belong to every normally complete experience. This fact I take to be the only secure basis upon which esthetic theory can build. It remains to suggest some of the implications of the underlying fact.

We have no word in the English language that unambiguously includes what is signified by the two words "artistic" and "esthetic." Since "artistic" refers primarily to the act of production and "esthetic" to that of perception and enjoyment, the absence of a term designating the two processes taken together is unfortunate. Sometimes, the effect is to separate the two from each other, to regard art as something superimposed upon esthetic material, or, upon the other side, to an assumption that, since art is a process of creation, perception and enjoyment of it have nothing in common with the creative act. In any case, there is a certain verbal awkwardness in that we are compelled sometimes to use the term "esthetic" to cover the entire field and sometimes to limit it to the receiving perceptual aspect of the whole operation. I refer to these obvious facts as preliminary to an attempt to show how the conception of conscious experience as a perceived relation between doing and undergoing enables us to understand the connection that art as production and perception and appreciation as enjoyment sustain to each other.

Art denotes a process of doing or making. This is as true of fine as of technological art. Art involves molding of clay, chipping of marble, casting of bronze, laying on of pigments, construction of buildings, singing of songs, playing of instruments, enacting roles on the stage, going through rhythmic movements in the dance. Every art does something with some physical material, the body or something outside the body, with or without the use of intervening tools, and with a view to production of something visible, audible, or tangible. So marked is the active or "doing" phase of art, that the dictionaries usually define it in terms of skilled action, ability in execution. The Oxford Dictionary illustrates by a quotation from John Stuart Mill: "Art is an endeavor after perfection in execution" while Matthew Arnold calls it "pure and flawless workmanship."

The word "esthetic" refers, as we have already noted, to experience as appreciative, perceiving, and enjoying. It denotes the consumer's rather than the producer's standpoint. It is Gusto, taste; and, as with cooking, overt skillful action is on the side of the cook who prepares, while taste is on the side of the consumer, as in gardening there is a distinction between the gardener who plants and tills and the householder who enjoys the finished product.

These very illustrations, however, as well as the relation that exists in having an experience between doing and undergoing, indicate that the distinction between esthetic and artistic cannot be pressed so far as to become a separation. Perfection in execution cannot be measured or defined in terms of execution; it implies those who perceive and enjoy the product that is executed. The cook prepares food for the consumer and the measure of the value of what is prepared is found in consumption. Mere perfection in execution, judged in its own terms in isolation, can probably be attained better by a machine than by human art. By itself, it is at most technique, and there are great artists who are not in the first ranks as technicians (witness Cézanne), just as there are great performers on the piano who are not great esthetically, and as Sargent is not a great painter.

Craftsmanship to be artistic in the final sense must be "loving"; it must care deeply for the subject matter upon which skill is exercised. A sculptor comes to mind whose busts are marvelously exact. It might be difficult to tell in the presence of a photograph of one of them and of a photograph of the original which was of the person himself. For virtuosity they are remarkable. But one doubts whether the maker of the busts had an experience of his own that he was concerned to have those share who look at his products. To be truly artistic, a work must also be esthetic—that is, framed for enjoyed receptive perception. Constant observation is, of course, necessary for the maker while he is producing. But if his perception is not also esthetic in nature, it is a colorless and cold recognition of what has been done, used as a stimulus to the next step in a process that is essentially mechanical.

In short, art, in its form, unites the very same relation of doing and undergoing, outgoing and incoming energy, that makes an experience to be an experience. Because of elimination of all that does not contribute to mutual organization of the factors of both action and reception into one another, and because of selection of just the aspects and traits that contribute to their interpenetration of each other, the product is a work of esthetic art. Man whittles, carves, sings, dances, gestures, molds, draws and paints. The doing or making is artistic when the perceived result is of such a nature that *its* qualities *as perceived* have controlled the question of production. The act of producing that is directed by intent to produce something that is enjoyed in the immediate experience of perceiving has qualities that a spontaneous or uncontrolled activity does not have. The artist embodies in himself the attitude of the perceiver while he works.

Suppose, for the sake of illustration, that a finely wrought object, one whose texture and proportions are highly pleasing in perception, has been believed to be a product of some primitive people. Then there is discovered evidence that proves it to be an accidental natural product. As an external thing, it is now precisely what it was before. Yet at once it ceases to be a work of art and becomes a natural "curiosity." It now belongs in a museum of natural history, not in a museum of art. And the extraordinary thing is that the difference that is thus made is not one of just intellectual classification. A difference is made in appreciative perception and in a direct way. The esthetic experience—in its limited sense—is thus seen to be inherently connected with the experience of making.

The sensory satisfaction of eye and ear, when esthetic, is so because it does not stand by itself but is linked to the activity of which it is the consequence. Even the pleasures of the palate are different in quality to an epicure than in one who merely "likes" his food as he eats it. The difference is not of mere intensity. The epicure is conscious of much more than the taste of the food. Rather, there enter into the taste, as directly experienced, qualities that depend upon reference to its source and its manner of production in connection with criteria of excellence. As production must absorb into itself qualities of the product as perceived and be regulated by them, so, on the other side, seeing, hearing, tasting, become esthetic when relation to a distinct manner of activity qualifies what is perceived.

There is an element of passion in all esthetic perception. Yet when we are overwhelmed by passion, as in extreme rage, fear, jealousy, the experience is definitely non-esthetic. There is no relationship felt to the qualities of the activity that has generated the passion. Consequently, the material of the experience lacks elements of balance and proportion. For these can be present only when, as in the conduct that has grace or dignity, the act is controlled by an exquisite sense of the relations which the act sustains—its fitness to the occasion and to the situation.

life

The process of art in production is related to the esthetic in perception organically—as the Lord God in creation surveyed his work and found it good. Until the artist is satisfied in perception with what he is doing, he continues shaping and reshaping. The making comes to an end when its result is experienced as good—and that experience comes not by mere intellectual and outside judgment but in direct perception. An artist, in comparison with his fellows, is one who is not only especially gifted in powers of execution but in unusual sensitivity to the qualities of things. This sensitivity also directs his doings and makings.

As we manipulate, we touch and feel, as we look, we see; as we listen, we hear. The hand moves with etching needle or with brush. The eye attends and reports the consequence of what is done. Because of this intimate connection, subsequent doing is cumulative and not a matter of caprice nor yet of routine. In an emphatic artistic-esthetic experience, the relation is so close that it controls simultaneously both the doing and the perception. Such vital intimacy of connection cannot be had if only hand and eye are engaged. When they do not, both of them, act as organs of the whole being, there is but a mechanical sequence of sense and movement, as in walking that is automatic. Hand and eye, when the experience is esthetic, are but instruments through which the entire live creature, moved and active throughout, operates. Hence the expression is emotional and guided by purpose.

Because of the relation between what is done and what is undergone, there is an immediate sense of things in perception as belonging together or as jarring; as reinforcing or as interfering. The consequences of the act of making as reported in sense show whether what is done carries forward the idea being executed or marks a deviation and break. In as far as the development of an experience is *controlled* through reference to these immediately felt relations of order and fulfillment, that experience becomes dominantly esthetic in nature. The urge to action becomes an urge to that kind of action which will result in an object satisfying in direct perception. The potter shapes his clay to make a bowl useful for holding grain; but he makes it in a way so regulated by the series of perceptions that sum up the serial acts of making, that the bowl is marked by enduring grace and charm. The general situation remains the same in painting a picture or molding a bust. Moreover, at each stage there is anticipation of what is to come. This anticipation is the connecting link between the next doing and its outcome for sense. What is done and what is undergone are thus reciprocally, cumulatively, and continuously instrumental to each other.

The doing may be energetic, and the undergoing may be acute and intense. But unless they are related to each other to form a whole in perception, the thing done is not fully esthetic. The making, for example, may be a display of technical virtuosity, and the undergoing a gush of sentiment or a revery. If the artist does not perfect a new vision in his process of doing, he acts mechanically and repeats some old model fixed like a blueprint in his mind. An incredible amount of observation and of the kind of intelligence that is exercised in perception of qualitative relations characterizes creative work in art. The relations must be noted not only with respect to one another, two by two, but in connection with the whole under construction; they are exercised in imagination as well as in observation. Irrelevancies arise that are tempting distractions; digressions suggest themselves in the guise of enrichments. There are occasions when the grasp of the dominant idea grows faint, and then the artist is moved unconsciously to fill in until his thought grows strong again. The real work of an artist is to build up an experience that is coherent in perception while moving with constant change in its development.

When an author puts on paper ideas that are already clearly conceived and consistently ordered, the real work has been previously done. Or, he may depend upon the greater perceptibility induced by the activity and its sensible report to direct his completion of the work. The mere act of transcription is esthetically irrelevant save as it enters integrally into the formation of an experience moving to completeness. Even the composition conceived in the head and, therefore, physically private, is public in its significant content, since it is conceived with reference to execution in a product that is perceptible and hence belongs to the common world. Otherwise it would be an aberration or a passing dream. The urge to express through painting the perceived qualities of a landscape is continuous with demand for pencil or brush. Without external embodiment, an experience remains incomplete; physiologically and functionally, sense organs are motor organs and are connected, by means of distribution of energies in the human body and not merely anatomically, with other motor organs. It is no linguistic accident that "building," "construction," "work," designate both a process and its finished product. Without the meaning of the verb that of the noun remains blank.

Writer, composer of music, sculptor, or painter can retrace, during the process of production, what they have previously done. When it is not satisfactory in the undergoing or perceptual phase of experience, they can to some degree start afresh. This retracing is not readily accomplished in the case of architecture—which is perhaps one reason why there are so many ugly buildings. Architects are obliged to complete their idea before its translation into a complete object of perception takes place. Inability to build up simultaneously the idea and its objective embodiment imposes a handicap. Nevertheless, they too are obliged to think out their ideas in terms of the medium of embodiment and the object of ultimate perception unless they work mechanically and by rote. Probably the esthetic quality of medieval cathedrals is due in some measure to the fact that their constructions were not so much controlled by plans and specifications made in advance as is now the case. Plans grew as the building grew. But even a Minerva-like product, if it is artistic, presupposes a prior period of gestation in which doings and perceptions projected in imagination interact and mutually modify one another. Every work of art follows the plan of, and pattern of, a complete experience, rendering it more intensely and concentratedly felt.

It is not so easy in the case of the perceiver and appreciator to understand the intimate union of doing and undergoing as it is in the case of the maker. We are given to supposing that the former merely takes in what is there in finished form, instead of realizing that this taking in involves activities that are comparable to those of the creator. But receptivity is not passivity. It, too, is a process consisting of a series of responsive acts that accumulate toward objective fulfillment. Otherwise, there is not perception but recognition. The difference between the two is immense. Recognition is perception arrested before it has a chance to develop freely. In recognition there is a beginning of an act of perception. But this beginning is not allowed to serve the development of a full perception of the thing recognized. It is arrested at the point where it will serve some *other* purpose, as we recognize a man on the street in order to greet or to avoid him, not so as to see him for the sake of seeing what is there.

In recognition we fall back, as upon a stereotype, upon some previously formed scheme. Some detail or arrangement of details serves as cue for bare identification. It suffices in recognition to apply this bare outline as a stencil to the present object. Sometimes in contact with a human being we are struck with traits, perhaps of only physical characteristics, of which we were not previously aware. We realize that we never knew the person before; we had not seen him in any pregnant sense. We now begin to study and to "take in." Perception replaces bare recognition. There is an act of reconstructive doing, and consciousness becomes fresh and alive. *This* act of seeing involves the cooperation of motor elements even though they remain implicit and do not become overt, as well as cooperation of all funded ideas that may serve to complete the new picture that is forming. Recognition is too easy to arouse vivid consciousness. There is not enough resistance between new and old to secure consciousness of the experience that is had. Even a dog that barks and wags his tail joyously on seeing his master return is more fully alive in his reception of his friend than is a human being who is content with mere recognition. . . .

For to perceive, a beholder must *create* his own experience. And his creation must include relations comparable to those which the original producer underwent. They are not the same in any literal sense. But with the perceiver, as with the artist, there must be an ordering of the elements of the whole that is in form, although not in details, the same as the process of organization the creator of the work consciously experienced. Without an act of re-creation the object is not perceived as a work of art. The artist selected, simplified, clarified, abridged and condensed according to his interest. The beholder must go through these operations according to his point of view and interest. In both, an act of abstraction, that is of extraction of what is significant, takes place. In both there is comprehension in its literal signification—that is, a gathering together of details and particulars physically scattered into an experienced whole. There is work done on the part of the percipient as there is on the part of the artist. The one who is too lazy, idle, or indurated in convention to perform his work will not see or hear. His "appreciation" will be a mixture of scraps of learning with conformity to norms of conventional admiration and with a confused, even if genuine, emotional excitation.

The considerations that have been presented imply both the community and the unlikeness, because of specific emphasis, of *an* experience, in its pregnant sense, and esthetic experience. The former has esthetic quality; otherwise its materials would not be rounded out into a single coherent experience. It is not possible to divide in a vital experience the practical, emotional, and intellectual from one another and to set the properties of one over against the characteristics of the others. The emotional phase binds parts together into a single whole; "intellectual" simply names the fact that the experience has meaning; "practical" indicates that the organism is interacting with events and objects which surround it. The most elaborate philosophic or scientific inquiry and the most ambitious industrial or political enterprise has, when its different ingredients constitute an integral experience, esthetic quality. For then its varied parts are linked to one another, and do not merely succeed one another. And the parts through their experienced linkage move toward a consummation and close, not merely to cessation in time. This consummation, moreover, does not wait in consciousness for the whole undertaking to be finished. It is anticipated throughout and is recurrently savored with special intensity.

Nevertheless, the experiences in question are dominantly intellectual or practical, rather than *distinctly* esthetic, because of the interest and purpose that initiate and control them. In an intellectual experience, the conclusion has value on its own account. It can be extracted as a formula or as a "truth," and can be used in its independent entirety as factor and guide in other inquiries. In a work of art there is not such single self-sufficient deposit. The end, the terminus, is significant not by itself but as the integration of the parts. It has no other existence. A drama or novel is not the final sentence, even if the characters are disposed of as living happily ever after. In a distinctly esthetic experience, characteristics that are subdued in other experiences are dominant; those that are subordinate are controlling—namely, the characteristics in virtue of which the experience is an integrated complete experience on its own account.

In every integral experience there is form because there is dynamic organization. I call the organization dynamic because it takes time to complete it, because it is a growth. There are inception, development, fulfillment. Material is ingested and digested through interaction with that vital organization of the results of prior experience that constitutes the mind of the worker. Incubation goes on until what is conceived is brought forth and is rendered perceptible as part of the common world. An esthetic experience can be crowded into a moment only in the sense that a climax of prior long enduring processes may arrive in an outstanding movement which so sweeps everything else into it that all else is forgotten. That which distinguishes an experience as esthetic is conversion of resistance and tensions, of excitations that in themselves are temptations to diversion, into a movement toward an inclusive and fulfilling close.

Experiencing like breathing is a rhythm of intakings and outgivings. Their succession is punctuated and made a rhythm by the existence of intervals, periods in which one phase is ceasing and the other is inchoat and preparing. William James aptly compared the course of a conscious experience to the alternate flights and perchings of a bird. The flights and perchings are intimately connected with one another; they are not so many unrelated lightings succeeded by a number of equally unrelated hoppings. Each resting place in experience is an undergoing in which is absorbed and taken home the consequences of prior doing, and, unless the doing is that of utter caprice or sheer routine, each doing carries in itself meaning that has been extracted and conserved. As with the advance of an army, all gains from what has been already effected are periodically consolidated, and always with a view to what is to be done next. If we move too rapidly, we get away from the base of supplies—of accrued meanings—and the experience is flustered, thin, and confused. If we dawdle too long after having extracted a net value, experience perishes of inanition.

The *form* of the whole is therefore present in every member. Fulfilling, consummating, are continuous functions, not mere ends, located at one place only. An engraver, painter, or writer is in process of completing at every stage of his work. He must at each point retain and sum up what has gone before as a whole and with reference to a whole to come. Otherwise there is no consistency and no security in his successive acts. The series of doings in the rhythm of experience give variety and movement; they save the work from monotony and useless repetitions. The undergoings are the corresponding elements in the rhythm, and they supply unity; they save the work from the aimlessness of a mere succession of excitations. An object is peculiarly and dominantly esthetic, yielding the enjoyment characteristic of esthetic perception, when the factors that determine anything which can be called *an* experience are lifted high above the threshold of perception and are made manifest for their own sake.

—*Art as Experience* (1934)

DOROTHY WALSH

Virtual Experience

John Dewey in . . . *Art as Experience* remarked that although philosophers talk a lot about experience they usually fail to take account of the notion of *an* experience. When someone says that he has had *an* experience he does not merely mean that he has had experience, for experience is something we have every conscious moment. *An* experience, by contrast to mere experience, "stands out" from the general flow of conscious awareness and presents itself as having some kind of unity. The reference to "when someone says" is intended to refer to ordinary talk, not technical discourse. If we take account of technical discourse we quickly recognize that we cannot rely on grammar to bring out the kind of singularity that Dewey wishes to emphasize. There are contexts in which the phrase "an experience" functions for classification, for example, "a visual experience," "an emotional experience." We can readily see that this is not all that is involved in the context of conversation when someone reports that he has had an experience. What then is "an experience" as understood in this context? The answer Dewey offers to this question seems to me to be unsatisfactory as a general account, however much it may be relevant to certain special cases.

It is certainly obvious that *an* experience must stand out from the general flow of experience. Now since any experience, as actual life experience, is something that occurs and that takes time, it seemed to Dewey that the way *an* experience could stand out and be individualized was by means of a temporal pattern. Accordingly, he specifies as the distinguishing trait of *an* experience a temporal pattern of "inception, development, and consummation." Well, certainly an experience might present itself as having such a pattern, but it seems not plausible to suppose that such a pattern is an invariable feature of everything that might be referred to as *an* experience. When someone says: "Yesterday I had a strange (or interesting or delightful) experience," we certainly take him to be referring to something that occurred during a time, but we do not take it for granted that his experience necessarily had the kind of sequential structure specified by Dewey. What *takes time* to be experienced is not necessarily experienced as temporal in the sense that what is most evident and arresting about it is a pattern of "inception, development, and consummation." For example, an experience might be a case of what we call "sudden illumination." "While I was watering the flowers, putting on my coat . . . I suddenly got the idea of how to solve such-and-such a problem." Then, again, an experience may be one that seems nontemporal. The esthetic appreciation of some visual effect in nature—the diffusion of moonlight through mist, the panoramic expanse, is not usually, certainly not necessarily, remembered as *an* experience because of a clearly marked pattern of inception, development, and consummation. This is not to deny the possibility of such a pattern. We would not be surprised if a person's account of an experience was presented with emphasis on sequential happening, for, after all, an experience can be something in the nature of an adventure, something that plays itself out as drama. Since *an* experience does indeed stand out from the general flow of experience, we may be tempted to say that it is in some way "dramatic," but if we do we must remember that "dramatic" as it functions in ordinary conversation does not always mean "playing itself out as drama"; it sometimes means no more than "startling" or "arresting" or "unusual" as, for example, the experience of visual or auditory hallucination.

It is indeed the case that when an experience is life experience it has some temporal reference. Someone may speak of *the* experience of first seeing the sea or the high mountains; he may emphasize as *an* experience the occasion when he first realized something. Anything long heard about and *then* experienced, such as nightingale's song or religious awe, will be remembered as tied to a specific temporal "then"—the occasion when the experience was had. But this does not mean that the experience *itself* is marked by temporal pattern. Moreover, we often speak of an experience, in the singular sense, without even this reference to the episodic. An experience of grief occasioned by the death of someone can be endured as a kind of haunting oppressive presence that characterizes or colors some protracted period of our existence, however much the surface play of life may provide this or that incidental pleasure or delight.

In discussing the nature of *an* experience, Dewey is intent on emphasizing the fact that *an* experience may be said to have "esthetic quality." Certainly when and if an experience has a marked formal pattern of inception, development, and consummation, the claim that it has esthetic quality is plausible enough, for it is easy to recognize the esthetic appeal of such a pattern. We can, of course, take Dewey's account as having reference exclusively to certain particular cases, but if we do, we shall have to find some other account that will do justice to the wider range of reference to "an experience" that seems to characterize ordinary talk. "I had an experience of intense frustration on the occasion when . . ." is not a remark that seems odd to us, but this is certainly not a case of *an* experience in Dewey's celebrative sense.

Dewey is certainly right in his claim that *an* experience, in the singular sense, is something different from mere experience, but wrong, I would say, in assuming that what individuates experience is some clearly marked temporal pattern. I would suggest that what individuates an experience, what makes it stand out from the general flow of experience, is the duality of self-reflexive awareness. *An* experience, as life experience, is self-consciously recognized by the experiencer as *his*. An experience is not just awareness; it is awareness of awareness. Animals, no doubt, can be said to have experiences but only a being capable of self-consciousness can be said to have "an experience."

It is important to notice that awareness of awareness is not to be identified with every case of heightened awareness. The close and concentrated focusing of attention on something—the exact color of the sodium flame, the exact rhythm of the patient's heartbeat—provides a heightened awareness of what is scrutinized, but if no evident sense of *being* aware is here included, no self-reference, then this is not awareness of awareness and therefore not a case of an experience in the singular sense. Of course there is an object of attention in cases of awareness of awareness and it need not be thought that the object here is some pure psychic occurrence, some pure mental act. It may be doubted whether we can catch such a thing, and, in any case, the self involved in "an experience" is not some mysterious pure ego but a particular person. An awareness of awareness is *both* an awareness of something given in experience, *and also* an awareness of a mode or manner of experiencing it; in short, it is a "me-experiencing-this." How much emphasis there may be on "me" and how much on "this" will vary from occasion to occasion.

Every kind of awareness of awareness involves a duality of the self—the self who is aware and the self who is aware of being aware—but how sharply these selves are distinguished will depend on the nature of the experience and the circumstances of its occurrence. An experience can be such as to involve only a minimal distinction in the form of awareness of response. There is something experienced with a response of delight, or distress, or surprise. There must, of course, be a self who is aware of the responding "me," but this self may not show forth as sharply distinguished on every occasion. I can be aware of how I am "taking," of how I am responding to, or undergoing, some presented something without a pronounced sense of separation between the responding "me" and the apprehending "I." But this duality of the "me" and the "I" which is implicitly operative can show forth as sharply marked. These are the occasions when the responding "me" is observed as from a distance, that is, apprehended as a phenomenal self who plays a role in a situation. The responding self and the observing self can be so separated that the observing self watches with wonder, or pleased surprise, or helpless distress, the role enacted by the phenomenal self. This sense of separation, of duality of the self, is most clearly marked when the response of the observing self is a response to the response of the observed self and any such state of affairs necessarily presupposes a still further self who is aware of the response of the observing self. If this talk of a self behind the self behind the self sounds queer, I can only plead that the queerness, after all, resides in us.

Every form of self-conscious awareness, every case of awareness of awareness involves the assumption of an elusive, "ungetatable," observing self. If we try to observe this observing self, questioning, for example, whether its observation is biased or impartial, we can do this only by retreating to a further self. It is useless to be exasperated or tantalized by this state of affairs and it is unnecessary to construe it as a situation that makes knowledge impossible. Knowledge always involves some distinction between the knower and what is known; to be unhappy with this distinction and to hanker for some sort of transcendent identity is no doubt to hanker for something but something necessarily noncognitive. There is, indeed, a difference between "knowing remotely" and "knowing intimately," but we delude ourselves if we suppose that the advantages that accrue to intimate knowing can be carried further and further until we find a consummation in identification. The elimination of all duality is the elimination of knowledge. This is because *to know* is one thing and *to be* is another.

No person exists who has not had "an experience"; indeed, we have all had many such, but a little reflection is sufficient to suggest that persons may differ considerably in the interest they take in this state of affairs. Broadly and generally speaking, what degree of understanding we have with regard to anything depends only partly on native intelligence; it depends mostly on interest. Subtlety of perception, delicacy of discernment, are largely a matter of cultivation, and cultivation is dependent on interest. It is, then, to be expected that persons will differ in the degree to which they take account of the distinctive character of their experience, and this is to say that awareness of awareness can vary from little more than simple recognition to relatively full realization.

It will be important, in this connection, to consider the meaning of the word "realize." There is a perfectly intelligible meaning of "realize" which is synonymous with "recognize" as used in such queries as: "Do you realize the causal connection between X and Y?" "Do you realize the practical advantage of going about the task this way?" In all such cases "recognize" can be substituted for "realize" without any distortion of meaning. But there are cases when "realize" is differently used, cases where we concede recognition but look for or require something more. It could happen that when someone says that he realizes the difficulty of my situation, I might think to myself: "He doesn't realize a thing! He doesn't realize it at all! He merely recognizes that it is the kind of situation that might be called difficult." When we hear the note of urgent requirement in such imperatives as: "Realize how he must feel!" "Realize how the situation must appear to him!" we are aware of being called upon to do something more than merely recognize the existence of some state of affairs. This difference is not quite adequately understood if we interpret it as the difference between thought and feeling, intellect and emotion, for though we may be asked to realize a feeling or emotional state, we can, with equal propriety, be asked to realize a conviction or belief. The essential thing, in either case, is to apprehend it *as* a form or mode of human experience. To realize our own experience is to attend to the qualitative character of our mode of having or undergoing it; to realize another person's experience is to engage in an act of imaginative participation. So much for actual life experience. Let us now consider literary experience.

What is it that we experience when we read a poem or other work of literary art? It seems that what we experience is itself experience. The experience expressed, articulated, formalized, or, one might say, incarnated, in the poem, is the object of our apprehension when we read the poem and our experience of the poem is an experience of this experience.

Thus the phrase "literary experience" is ambiguous, since experience may be qualified as literary because it is experience raised to the level of literary expression, or because it is experience derived from literature, as distinguished from that derived from life. Literary experience, in the latter sense, is actual experience, for it is always someone's experience, but literary experience in the former sense is not actual experience. Caught out of the flux of nature, it is not evanescent, not a perishing occurrence; it is permanent and stable. Accordingly, "realization" as the enterprise of the literary artist is not identical with "realization" as the task of the reader; the former is creative articulation, the latter is imaginative apprehension. But insofar as a reader succeeds with a work of literature with which the artist has succeeded, what the reader apprehends can properly be said to be a realization of a realization.

We take it for granted that a good reader will, in initial encounter, expose himself with a completely open, free, and unguarded receptivity to the deliverance of the poem. Critical analysis and all that goes with it is a perfectly appropriate activity, but it is appropriate only as an activity subsequent to the hospitality of an unguarded reception. It will be characteristic of any such initial reception, if it moves unimpeded and is not forced into self-consciousness by the distress of noncomprehension, that what we experience will seem to be the very experience that is the poem. It is after the event that we remember what we know, namely, that there can be a difference between the experience presented in the poem and our experience of it, since, with respect to that to which we respond, our experience can be in many ways incomplete or incorrect. It is the recognition of this that leads to analysis and deliberate intellectual scrutiny. All such analysis is, of course, based on the belief that postanalytical apprehension can be superior to preanalytical encounter. Yet this belief is not incompatible with a concern for the innocence of initial reception which derives from the recognition that feeling can be prior to formulation and that we can sense such a thing as power and presence before we can say, much less explain, wherein it lies. I am here distinguishing between ignorance and innocence. Ignorance is a fact of nature; innocence is a spiritual discipline achieved by intent, and this discipline is for the nonignorant, the reader who has a wide knowledge of other works of literature. In the end, of course, the understanding of any work of literature must depend heavily on the appropriate use of just this knowledge; the discipline of innocence in initial reception is a matter of courage and confidence, comparable to the noble gesture ascribed to the Bedouin Arab who first extends hospitality to the stranger and only afterwards inquires about his identity and business.

As I have already noted, the experience of the reader can in one sense be called "literary" in that it is an experience derived from literature. We may wish to distinguish such experience from "ordinary" experience, the experience that accrues when we put down the book and take up the tasks and adventures of life, and we sometimes make the distinction by referring to literary experience as contemplative or imaginative. But it is to be observed that contemplating or imagining, however little it may show as gross overt behavior is, none the less, activity. It uses up time, it uses up energy, and it can be engaged in with various degrees of concentration and proficiency. Consequently, this, whatever its peculiarity, is actually experience. But the experience incarnated in the poem, the experience that is the very substance of the poem, is not actual experience. It cannot be said to be the poet's experience, since the poet is a person and any experience of a person is a perishing occurrence. It is not fully satisfactory to speak of it as a record of the poet's experience because any such way of talk is likely to introduce the question: How accurate? How reliable? and we are not concerned with this. It is perhaps best to adopt the phrase suggested by Susanne Langer in *Feeling and Form* and speak of it as "virtual experience."

We need not suppose that every work of literary art is "a monument of unaging intellect" or that even the best are absolutely immune from the tooth of time; nevertheless, the contrast between the passing and perishing character of actual experience and the enduring fixity of nonoccurrent virtual experience is sufficiently impressive. The virtual experience presented in literary art is far more available for realization than actual life experience. It is not simply that it will "stand still to be examined," that it can be reapprehended by the reader. As something "made," rather than merely "found," it can be not only shaped and formed by the literary artist, but elaborated and developed in point of subtlety and in point of complexity. It is therefore hardly a matter for wonder that we should look to literary art for a disclosure of the possibilities of experience, for an understanding of what things might come to *as* forms or modes of human experience. Yet the understanding of literature and the appreciation of its superior luminosity would not be possible if life experience provided no occasion for realization. If I am correct in my account of "an experience" as somebody's life experience, "having an experience" involves at least some degree of realization, a realization not only of something given or occurrent but of "what it is like" to apprehend this given, to undergo this happening. The chief, though by no means the only, difference between realizations achieved in life and realizations provided by literary art is that the latter can be superior in point of elaboration and in point of intelligibility.

It may be helpful, at this stage, to gather up some conclusions. There certainly is a difference between experience, considered as just any kind or form of conscious awareness, and what, in ordinary conversation, would be referred to as "an experience." An experience, in the singular sense, might happen to have the temporal pattern of "inception, development, consummation" emphasized by Dewey, but this is not an invariable feature of everything that might be referred to as "an experience." What *is* an invariable feature is the presence of some kind of duality; there is something experienced together with some awareness of *how* what is experienced *is* experienced. This is why "an experience" is not just awareness but awareness of awareness. Although every case of "an experience" as life experience involves this duality, and therefore involves some degree of what we can call "realization," the extent of such realization can vary from person to person, and from occasion to occasion.

Experience, as embodied in literary art, is not actual experience. It may be derived from actual experience, but it is not itself actual experience; it is more properly referred to as virtual experience. This virtual experience, embodied, objectified, expressed, in the literary presentation has a kind of "public presence" and a kind of "permanent presence" not possible in any case of actual experience. Because it has a public presence it is potentially sharable, and because it has a permanent presence it is more available for full realization than actual experience can be. For these reasons, it may not seem surprising that we should look to literary art for the better understanding of the possibilities of experience.

It will now, I hope, be possible to sum up. This essay does not attempt to offer a comprehensive theory of literature. It has been concerned with a single question: What kind of knowledge, if any, does literary art afford? The answer I propose is that literary art, when functioning successfully as literary art, provides knowledge in the form of realization: the realization of what anything might come to as a form of lived experience. The kind of knowledge, as well as the manner of knowing, is something familiar to us on the basis of life experience, and it receives acknowledgement in the common remark: "You don't really know what it is unless and until you've experienced it." This is knowing by living through, and it is something distinguishably different from knowing about.

All knowing involves duality; there is no good reason for calling mere awareness knowledge. Nevertheless, it is a mistake to suppose that the only passage from mere awareness to knowledge is by the path of inference, so that anything properly describable as knowledge must be inferential knowledge about something. I have sought to argue, as cogently as I can, that the essential difference between what is just experience and what is *an* experience is that *an* experience involves duality. *An* experience, as actual experience, is self-consciously recognized by the experiencer as his. This involves a duality of the self: the I–me duality. Thus *an* experience involves the apprehension of what is experienced, together with the apprehension of the manner in which what is experienced is experienced. The importance of literary art, from the strictly cognitive point of view, is that it provides an enormous extension and elaboration of this kind of knowledge. Successful literary art is so much more ambitious and luminous than anything life affords that we may be tempted to overlook its humble analogue in common events. This overlooking is somewhat similar to the way in which, dazzled by the intellectual achievements of developed scientific knowledge, we overlook its humble analogue in simple commonsense knowledge about natural phenomena.

Everything describable as knowledge is shaped and structured in some fashion, and the more ambitious the cognitive enterprise, the more elaborate the structuring is likely to be. We can be impatient with this, and there is much in the record of intellectual history that testifies to such impatience. The philosopher who tells us that propositions are pictures of facts, or that bedrock knowledge consists in the direct awareness of sense data; the historian who proposes the program of eschewing all interpretation in favor of direct report on how things actually occurred; the mystic who brushes aside all theology as necessarily misleading, exhibit a common, and quite understandable, wish for immediacy. However, nothing can be known except as distanced, and nothing can be distanced except as structured in some way.

There is, it might be said, a paradox about literary art, but this is a paradox in the sense of something which, though it may seem puzzling and odd on initial encounter, is understandable on the basis of reflection. The kind of knowledge and the mode of knowing afforded by successful literary art seems to have an intimacy and an immediacy not characteristic of knowledge as knowledge about this or that. Yet this very intimacy, this very immediacy, is a product not simply of distancing but of double distancing.

We can know *about* a work of literature as we can know about anything else, but this knowing about has utility as a preparation for a further and different kind of knowing: knowing through imaginative participation. In so far as this imaginative participation is controlled by the literary presentation, it is a vicarious experience of a virtual experience. How can anything so remote as this, so twice removed, so doubly distanced seem to have about it such an air of intimacy, of immediacy? That answer, I think, is that what literary art presents is designed to elicit a full response, sensuous, intellectual, and emotional, not separated but interfused. It is this fullness of presentation and fullness of response that accounts for the sense of immediacy. Knowing by living through is distinguishably different from knowing through the process of inference, and the sense of its being lived experience is associated with this, for, however much any particular realization may involve an emphasis on the sensuous, or the intellectual, or the emotional, this is only a matter of emphasis. Otherwise expressed, a totality of presentation and response is a totality regardless of how this totality is formed. But though life provides occasions for such realizations, it is to literature that we must look for the development of the implicit potentialities of this kind of knowledge. Life experience, as actual experience, is idiosyncratic, fragmentary, and fleeting; only virtual experience, structured and articulated, lifted out of the temporal flux of ongoing happening, provides something that can be fully realized and shared. Anyone who prefers communal participation in spontaneous "Happenings" to the experience of ordered art is, of course, perfectly entitled to his preference. All the same, this preference is the product of impatience. The lonely soul craves some quick alleviation of its situation, and it can, no doubt, achieve this alleviation through immersion in the Happening. Nothing is wrong with this simply as such, but it is useless to look to it for insight, illumination, revelation.

Man can be understood in many ways. Natural science will deal with him as one phenomenon among others in a natural world. History, anthropology, social and political theory, can deal with him in an intelligible and useful manner. The importance of all of this is so obvious and so universally recognized, that no one need lift his voice to point out that there *is* such a thing as inferential knowledge about man and that we stand in need of it. But literary art, as revelatory disclosure, calls for something in the nature of explanation and defense. This is not because readers and lovers of literature are likely to be startled by the claim that literary art can be revelatory. Most readers are, I think, inclined to assume that this is so, and for the very good reason that they seem to derive such revelatory insights in their commerce with works of literature. Insofar as I am correct on this matter, I might be said to be preaching to the converted, but there can, after all, be a point in such preaching, since some, at least, of the converted may wish to consider a reasoned defense of the faith that is in them. In an argumentative, critical, and skeptical age a reasoned defense, if cogent, can be useful. Furthermore, I candidly confess to a certain missionary zeal in this matter. The kind of knowledge and the mode of knowing that literary art can provide seems to me so important for the quality of our human life that anything that will signal it out, emphasize it, draw attention to it, surely seems worthwhile. Literary art is humanistic not simply in the sense that it relates to man; it is, one might say, man's distinctive presentation of himself to himself. "Speak to me that I may see you." *This* particular speaking is the voice of literary art, and the visibility it provides is the visibility of man as total person.

—*Literature and Knowledge* (1969)

CHAPTER 6

Embodiment of Values

GEORGE SANTAYANA: The Nature of Beauty
LOUIS ARNAUD REID: Values, Feeling and Embodiment

In turning from Dewey and Walsh to Santayana and Reid there is no sharp contrast. Dewey more often uses the term "quality" than the term "value," but his "enhancement of experience" is synonymous with "embodiment of values." Basically, he agrees with the contention of Alfred North Whitehead, his friend and admirer, that "the habit of art is the habit of enjoying vivid values."[1] His concept of value is broader than Santayana's hedonism but similar to Reid's "subjective–objective idea" of value. Also Walsh's remarks about "knowledge" are strikingly similar to Reid's.

Traditionally, it has been thought that the value embodied in the work of art is beauty—the third of the classical trilogy of the Good, the True, and the Beautiful. Art, it is said, is the incarnation of beauty in human artifacts. There was no more eloquent representative of this doctrine than George Santayana (1863–1952). Born in Madrid of Spanish parents, but educated largely in America, he was steeped in the Greek and Catholic tradition. Nevertheless, he was a naturalist by conviction and drew his inspiration from diverse sources. While a young professor of philosophy at Harvard, he wrote his first book, *The Sense of Beauty* (1896), in which he defines beauty in terms of pleasure and conceives art as the making of beautiful things.

In his penetrating analysis, he delimits beauty by a series of exclusions. Since beauty is a value and there is no value apart from conscious preference, the beautiful cannot be the unconscious or the merely indifferent. The purely rational must also be excluded, since value in general and beauty in particular involve feeling rather than reason or knowledge. Moral values, which are mainly negative and extrinsic, must also be distinguished from esthetic values, which are positive and intrinsic. Next, Santayana contrasts esthetic and physical pleasures: The former give us the illusion of being relatively free of our bodies; the latter do not. He finally defines beauty as *objectified pleasure.*

By "objectification" he means the process of imputing some subjective quality to an object, as when we speak of a *nasty* snow storm or a *lonely* place. Nothing is more natural and primitive than thus to project our mental states into phenomenal objects. Pleasure is transformed into beauty whenever the value is unconsciously imputed to the object contemplated and not to the body or mind of the person contemplating.

Santayana recognizes three kinds of beauty: the sensuous beauty of the physical stuff; the formal beauty of the design; and the expressive beauty of the meaning and connotations ultimately derived from past experience. This is a narrower meaning of "expression" than in the writings of most estheticians, and I have included an excerpt to elucidate its meaning.

To the division of expressive beauty belongs the effect of sublimity. The "Stoic sublime" consists of a lofty feeling of self-integrity and detachment. This reaction arises especially in the contemplation of evil, as in tragedy. We purge the self of pity and fear by eliminating from consciousness all the elements that are personal and self-regarding.

> . . . to envisage circumstance, all calm,
> That is the top of sovereignty.

Santayana points out that there is another kind of sublimity—"the Epicurean sublime." Just as Epicurus, the Greek philosopher, recoiled from the immensity of the material universe into the equipoise of the detached spirit, so the beholder of stellar spaces, or of any other object immeasurably great, may achieve an exalted feeling of detachment by inwardly bracing himself against so overwhelming a prospect. This reaction is not the opposite of the beautiful, in the wide sense of that term, but it is rather "the supremely, the intoxicatingly beautiful," so intense "that it begins to lose its objectivity, and to declare itself, what it always fundamentally was, an inward passion of the soul." This theory is similar to Kant's doctrine of sublimity (see Chapter 11). One aspect of sublimity that Santayana discusses but Kant does not is its relation to tragic "catharsis." Although his "liberation of the self" may be different from Aristotle's "purgation through pity and fear," it is a significant doctrine in its own right.

In his late writings, Santayana expounds a materialism strangely blended with Platonic ideas and expressed with gentle irony. Beauty is characterized as "a vital harmony felt and fused into an image under the form of eternity." It is regarded as an "essence"; that is to say, it is contemplated merely for its intrinsic qualities and belief or disbelief does not arise. An essence thus intuited is felt to be independent of the act of apprehension: "It visits time, but belongs to eternity."

In the twentieth century, the concept of beauty has lost its primacy as a single most important idea in esthetics. The pluralistic interpretation that now prevails has been characterized by W. P. Montague: "Beauty is objectified joy, and as such the highest and loveliest of esthetic values. But Beauty is not all—she is a queen, a constitutional sovereign, but not a dictator."[2] The wider conception of esthetic value is accepted by Louis Arnaud Reid (1895–), Professor Emeritus of philosophy at the University of London.

Value, as he conceives it, is a relational property, the quality of an object related to a human interest. Far from being a mere subjective phantom, or at the other extreme, a thing-in-itself sundered from human attitudes, a value is always something felt and appreciated. The stuff of art is the felt qualities of things—"not the things alone, nor the feelings alone, but the things-as-experienced-with-feeling." In art, value is concrete and individualized—not detached and free-floating but intrinsic to the work. From this point of view, art is in its very nature the embodiment of values. In using the term "embodiment," Reid is emphasizing that values in art are inseparable from qualities in the object, as mere feelings are not. Esthetic value unites feeling and quality in a subject–object configuration.

Notes

1. Alfred North Whitehead, *Science and the Modern World* (Macmillan, New York, 1925), p. 287.
2. W. P. Montague, *The Ways of Things* (Prentice-Hall, Englewood Cliffs, N.J., 1940). See also Jerome Stolnitz, "Beauty," in *The Encyclopedia of Philosophy*, edited by Paul Edwards (Macmillan and Free Press, New York, 1967), pp. 263–266.

GEORGE SANTAYANA

The Nature of Beauty

I. Beauty Defined

The Philosophy of Beauty Is a Theory of Values

It would be easy to find a definition of beauty that should give in a few words a telling paraphrase of the word. We know on excellent authority that beauty is truth, that it is the expression of the ideal, the symbol of divine perfection, and the sensible manifestation of the good. A litany of these titles of honor might easily be compiled, and repeated in praise of our divinity. Such phrases stimulate thought and give us a momentary pleasure, but they hardly bring any permanent enlightenment. A definition that should really define must be nothing less than the exposition of the origin, place, and elements of beauty as an object of human experience. We must learn from it, as far as possible, why, when, and how beauty appears, what conditions an object must fulfill to be beautiful, what elements of our nature make us sensible of beauty, and what the relation is between the constitution of the object and the excitement of our susceptibility. Nothing less will really define beauty or make us understand what esthetic appreciation is. The definition of beauty in this sense will be the task of this whole book, a task that can be only very imperfectly accomplished within its limits.

The historical titles of our subject may give us a hint towards the beginning of such a definition. Many writers of the last century called the philosophy of beauty *Criticism,* and the word is still retained as the title for the reasoned appreciation of works of art. We could hardly speak, however, of delight in nature as criticism. A sunset is not criticized; it is felt and enjoyed. The word "criticism," used on such an occasion, would emphasize too much the element of deliberate judgment and of comparison with standards. Beauty, although often so described, is seldom so perceived, and all the greatest excellences of nature and art are so far from being approved of by a rule that they themselves furnish the standard and ideal by which critics measure inferior effects.

This age of science and of nomenclature has accordingly adopted a more learned word, *Esthetics,* that is, the theory of perception or of susceptibility. If criticism is too narrow a word, pointing exclusively to our more artificial judgments, esthetics seems to be too broad and to include within its sphere all pleasures and pains, if not all perceptions whatsoever. Kant used it, as we know, for his theory of time and space as forms of all perception; and it has at times been narrowed into an equivalent for the philosophy of art.

If we combine, however, the etymological meaning of criticism with that of esthetics, we shall unite two essential qualities of the theory of beauty. Criticism implies judgment, and esthetics perception. To get the common ground, that of perceptions which are critical, or judgments which are perceptions, we must widen our notion of deliberate criticism so as to include those judgments of value which are instinctive and immediate, that is, to include pleasures and pains; and at the same time we must narrow our notion of esthetics so as to exclude all perceptions which are not appreciations, which do not find a value in their objects. We thus reach the sphere of critical or appreciative perception, which is, roughly speaking, what we mean to deal with. And retaining the word "esthetics," which is now current, we may therefore say that esthetics is concerned with the perception of values. The meaning and conditions of value are, then, what we must first consider.

Since the days of Descartes it has been a conception familiar to philosophers that every visible event in nature might be explained by previous visible events, and that all the motions, for instance, of the tongue in speech, or of the hand in painting, might have merely physical causes. If consciousness is thus accessory to life and not essential to it, the race of man might have existed upon the earth and acquired all the arts necessary for its subsistence without possessing a single sensation, idea, or emotion.

Natural selection might have secured the survival of those automata which made useful reactions upon their environment. An instinct of self-preservation would have been developed, dangers would have been shunned without being feared, and injuries revenged without being felt.

In such a world there might have come to be the most perfect organization. There would have been what we should call the expression of the deepest interests and the apparent pursuit of conceived goods. For there would have been spontaneous and ingrained tendencies to avoid certain contingencies and to produce others; all the dumb show and evidence of thinking would have been patent to the observer. Yet there would surely have been no thinking, no expectation, and no conscious achievement in the whole process.

The onlooker might have feigned ends and objects of forethought, as we do in the case of the water that seeks its own level, or in that of the vacuum which nature abhors. But the particles of matter would have remained unconscious of their collocation, and all nature would have been insensible of their changing arrangement. We only, the possible spectators of that process, by virtue of our own interests and habits, could see any progress or culmination in it. We should see culmination where the result attained satisfied our practical or esthetic demands, and progress wherever such a satisfaction was approached. But apart from ourselves, and our human bias, we can see in such a mechanical world no element of value whatever. In removing consciousness, we have removed the possibility of worth.

But it is not only in the absence of all consciousness that value would be removed from the world; by a less violent abstraction from the totality of human experience, we might conceive beings of a purely intellectual cast, minds in which the transformations of nature were mirrored without any emotion. Every event would then be noted, its relations would be observed, its recurrence might even be expected; but all this would happen without a shadow of desire, of pleasure, or of regret. No event would be repulsive, no situation terrible. We might, in a word, have a world of idea without a world of will. In this case, as completely as if consciousness were absent altogether, all value and excellence would be gone. So that for the existence of good in any form it is not merely consciousness but emotional consciousness that is needed. Observation will not do, appreciation is required.

Preference Is Ultimately Irrational

We may therefore at once assert this axiom, important for all moral philosophy and fatal to certain stubborn incoherences of thought, that there is no value apart from some appreciation of it, and no good apart from some preference of it before its absence or its opposite. In appreciation, in preference, lie the root and essence of all excellence. Or, as Spinoza clearly expresses it, we desire nothing because it is good, but it is good only because we desire it.

It is true that in the absence of an instinctive reaction we can still apply these epithets by an appeal to usage. We may agree that an action is bad or a building good, because we recognize in them a character which we have learned to designate by that adjective; but unless there is in us some trace of passionate reprobation or of sensible delight, there is no moral or esthetic judgment. It is all a question of propriety of speech, and of the empty titles of things. The verbal and mechanical proposition, that passes for judgment of worth, is the great cloak of ineptitude in these matters. Insensibility is very quick in the conventional use of words. If we appealed more often to actual feelings, our judgments would be more diverse, but they would be more legitimate and instructive. Verbal judgments are often useful instruments of thought, but it is not by them that worth can ultimately be determined.

Values spring from the immediate and inexplicable reaction of vital impulse, and from the irrational part of our nature. The rational part is by its essence relative; it leads us from data to conclusions, or from parts to wholes; it never furnishes the data with which it works. If any preference or precept were declared to be ultimate and primitive, it would thereby be declared to be irrational, since mediation, inference, and synthesis are the essence of rationality. The idea of rationality is itself as arbitrary, as much dependent on the needs of a finite organization, as any other ideal. Only as ultimately securing tranquillity of mind, which the philosopher instinctively pursues, has it for him any necessity. In spite of the verbal propriety of saying that reason demands rationality, what really demands rationality, what makes it a good and indispensable thing and gives it all its authority, is not its own nature, but our need of it both in safe and economical action and in the pleasures of comprehension.

It is evident that beauty is a species of value, and what we have said of value in general applies to this particular kind. A first approach to a definition of beauty has therefore been made by the exclusion of all intellectual judgments, all judgments of matter of fact or of relation. To substitute judgments of fact for judgments of value, is a sign of a pedantic and borrowed criticism. If we approach a work of art or nature scientifically, for the sake of its historical connections or proper classification, we do not approach it esthetically. The discovery of its date or of its author may be otherwise interesting; it only remotely affects our esthetic appreciation by adding to the direct effect certain associations. If the direct effect were absent, and the object in itself uninteresting, the circumstances would be immaterial. Molière's *Misanthrope* says to the court poet who commends his sonnet as written in a quarter of an hour,

Voyons, monsieur, le temps ne fait rien à l'affaire,

and so we might say to the critic that sinks into the archaeologist, show us the work, and let the date alone.

In an opposite direction the same substitution of facts for values makes its appearance, whenever the reproduction of fact is made the sole standard of artistic excellence. Many half-trained observers condemn the work of some naïve or fanciful masters with a sneer, because, as they truly say, it is out of drawing. The implication is that to be correctly copied from a model is the prerequisite of all beauty. Correctness is, indeed, an element of effect and one which, in respect to familiar objects, is almost indispensable, because its absence would casue a disappointment and dissatisfaction incompatible with enjoyment. We learn to value truth more and more as our love and knowledge of nature increase. But fidelity is a merit only because it is in this way a factor in our pleasure. It stands on a level with all other ingredients of effect. When a man raises it to a solitary pre-eminence and becomes incapable of appreciating anything else, he betrays the decay of esthetic capacity. The scientific habit in him inhibits the artistic.

That facts have a value of their own, at once complicates and explains this question. We are naturally pleased by every perception, and recognition and surprise are particularly acute sensations. When we see a striking truth in any imitation we are therefore delighted, and this kind of pleasure is very legitimate, and enters into the best effects of all the representative arts. Truth and realism are therefore esthetically good, but they are not all-sufficient, since the representation of everything is not equally pleasing and effective. The fact that resemblance is a source of satisfaction justifies the critic in demanding it, while the esthetic insufficiency of such veracity shows the different value of truth in science and in art. Science is the response to the demand for information, and in it we ask for the whole truth and nothing but the truth. Art is the response to the demand for entertainment, for the stimulation of our senses and imagination, and truth enters into it only as it subserves these ends.

Even the scientific value of truth is not, however, ultimate or absolute. It rests partly on practical, partly on esthetic interests. As our ideas are gradually brought into conformity with the facts by the painful process of selection—for intuition runs equally into truth and into error, and can settle nothing if not controlled by experience—we gain vastly in our command over our environment. This is the fundamental value of natural science, and the fruit it is yielding in our day. We have no better vision of nature and life than some of our predecessors, but we have greater material resources. To know the truth about the composition and history of things is good for this reason. It is also good because of the enlarged horizon it gives us, because the spectacle of nature is a marvelous and fascinating one, full of a serious sadness and large peace, which gives us back our birthright as children of the planet and naturalizes us upon the earth. This is the poetic value of the scientific *Weltanschauung*. From these two benefits, the practical and the imaginative, all the value of truth is derived.

Esthetic and moral judgments are accordingly to be classed together in contrast to judgments intellectual; they are both judgments of value, while intellectual judgments are judgments of fact. If the latter have any value, it is only derivative, and our whole intellectual life has its only justification in its connection with our pleasures and pains.

Contrast between Moral and Esthetic Values

The relation between esthetic and moral judgments, between the spheres of the beautiful and the good, is close, but the distinction between them is important. One factor of this distinction is that while esthetic judgments are mainly positive, that is, perceptions of good, moral judgments are mainly and fundamentally negative, or perceptions of evil. Another factor of the distinction is that whereas, in the perception of beauty, our judgment is necessarily intrinsic and based on the character of the immediate experience, and never consciously on the idea of an eventual utility in the object, judgments about moral worth, on the contrary, are always based, when they are positive, upon the consciousness of benefits probably involved. Both these distinctions need some elucidations.

Hedonistic ethics have always had to struggle against the moral sense of mankind. Earnest minds, that feel the weight and dignity of life, rebel against the assertion that the aim of right conduct is enjoyment. Pleasure usually appears to them as a temptation, and they sometimes go so far as to make avoidance of it a virtue. The truth is that morality is not mainly concerned with the attainment of pleasure; it is rather concerned, in all its deeper and more authoritative maxims, with the prevention of suffering. There is something artificial in the deliberate pursuit of pleasure; there is something absurd in the obligation to enjoy oneself. We feel no duty in that direction; we take to enjoyment naturally enough after the work of life is done, and the freedom and spontaneity of our pleasures are what is most essential to them.

The sad business of life is rather to escape certain dreadful evils to which our nature exposes us—death, hunger, disease, weariness, isolation, and contempt. By the awful authority of these things which stand like specters behind every moral injunction, conscience in reality speaks, and a mind which they have duly impressed cannot but feel, by contrast, the hopeless triviality of the search for pleasure. It cannot but feel that a life abandoned to amusement and to changing impulses must run unawares into fatal dangers. The moment, however, that society emerges from the early pressure of the environment and is tolerably secure against primary evils, morality grows lax. The forms that life will further assume are not to be imposed by moral authority, but are determined by the genius of the race, the opportunities of the moment, and the tastes and resources of individual minds. The reign of duty gives place to the reign of freedom, and the law and the covenant to the dispensation of grace.

The appreciation of beauty and its embodiment in the arts are activities which belong to our holiday life, when we are redeemed for the moment from the shadow of evil and the slavery to fear, and are following the bent of our nature where it chooses to lead us. The values, then, with which we here deal are positive; they were negative in the sphere of morality. The ugly is hardly an exception, because it is not the cause of any real pain. In itself it is rather a source of amusement. If its suggestions are vitally repulsive, its presence becomes a real evil towards which we assume a practical and moral attitude. And, correspondingly, the pleasant is never, as we have seen, the object of a truly moral injunction.

Work and Play

We have here, then, an important element of the distinction between esthetic and moral values. It is the same that has been pointed to in the famous contrast between work and play. These terms may be used in different senses and their importance in moral classification differs with the meaning attached to them. We may call everything play which is useless activity, exercise that springs from the physiological impulse to discharge the energy which the exigencies of life have not called out. Work will then be all action that is necessary or useful for life. Evidently if work and play are thus objectively distinguished as useful and useless action, work is a eulogistic term and play a disparaging one. It would be better for us that all our energy should be turned to account, that none of it should be wasted in aimless motion. Play, in this sense, is a sign of imperfect adaptation. It is proper to childhood, when the body and mind are not yet fit to cope with the environment, but it is unseemly in manhood and pitiable in old age, because it marks an atrophy of human nature, and a failure to take hold of the opportunities of life.

Play is thus essentially frivolous. Some persons, understanding the term in this sense, have felt an aversion, which every liberal mind will share, to classifying social pleasures, art, and religion under the head of play, and by that epithet condemning them, as a certain school seems to do, to gradual extinction as the race approaches maturity. But if all the useless ornaments of our life are to be cut off in the process of adaptation, evolution would impoverish instead of enriching our nature. Perhaps that is the tendency of evolution, and our barbarous ancestors amid their toils and wars, with their flaming passions and mythologies, lived better lives than are reserved to our well-adapted descendants.

We may be allowed to hope, however, that some imagination may survive parasitically even in the most serviceable brain. Whatever course history may take—and we are not here concerned with prophecy—the question of what is desirable is not affected. To condemn spontaneous and delightful occupations because they are useless for self-preservation shows an uncritical prizing of life irrespective of its content. For such a system the worthiest function of the universe should be to establish perpetual motion. Uselessness is a fatal accusation to bring against any act which is done for its presumed utility, but those which are done for their own sake are their own justification.

At the same time there is an undeniable propriety in calling all the liberal and imaginative activities of man play, because they are spontaneous, and not carried on under pressure of external necessity or danger. Their utility for self-preservation may be very indirect and accidental, but they are not worthless for that reason. On the contrary, we may measure the degree of happiness and civilization which any race has attained by the proportion of its energy which is devoted to free and generous pursuits, to the adornment of life and the culture of the imagination. For it is in the spontaneous play of his faculties that man finds himself and his happiness. Slavery is the most degrading condition of which he is capable, and he is as often a slave to the niggardliness of the earth and the inclemency of heaven, as to a master or an institution. He is a slave when all his energy is spent in avoiding suffering and death, when all his action is imposed from without, and no breath or strength is left him for free enjoyment.

Work and play here take on a different meaning, and become equivalent to servitude and freedom. The change consists in the subjective point of view from which the distinction is now made. We no longer mean by work all that is done usefully, but only what is done unwillingly and by the spur of necessity. By play we are designating, no longer what is done fruitlessly, but whatever is done spontaneously and for its own sake, whether it have or not an ulterior utility. Play, in this sense, may be our most useful occupation. So far would a gradual adaptation to the environment be from making this play obsolete, that it would tend to abolish work, and to make play universal. For with the elimination of all the conflicts and errors of instinct, the race would do spontaneously whatever conduced to its welfare and we should live safely and prosperously without external stimulus or restraint. . . .

In this second and subjective sense, then, work is the disparaging term and play the eulogistic one. All who feel the dignity and importance of the things of the imagination, need not hesitate to adopt the classification which designates them as play. We point out thereby, not that they have no value, but that their value is intrinsic, that in them is one of the sources of all wotth. Evidently all values must be ultimately intrinsic. The useful is good because of the excellence of its consequences; but these must somewhere cease to be merely useful in their turn, or only excellent as means; somewhere we must reach the good that is good in itself and for its own sake, else the whole process is futile, and the utility of our first object illusory. We here reach the second factor in our distinction, between esthetic and moral values, which regards their immediacy. . . .

Esthetic and Physical Pleasure

We have now separated with some care intellectual and moral judgments from the sphere of our subject, and found that we are to deal only with perceptions of value, and with these only when they are positive and immediate. But even with these distinctions the most remarkable characteristic of the sense of beauty remains undefined. All pleasures are intrinsic and positive values, but all pleasures are not perceptions of beauty. Pleasure is indeed the essence of that perception, but there is evidently in this particular pleasure a complication which is not present in others and which is the basis of the distinction made by consciousness and language between it and the rest. It will be instructive to notice the degrees of this difference.

The bodily pleasures are those least resembling perceptions of beauty. By bodily pleasures we mean, of course, more than pleasures with a bodily seat; for that class would include them all, as well as all forms and elements of consciousness. Esthetic pleasures have physical conditions, they depend on the activity of the eye and the ear, of the memory and the other ideational functions of the brain. But we do not connect those pleasures with their seats except in physiological studies; the ideas with which esthetic pleasures are associated are not the ideas of their bodily causes. The pleasures we call physical, and regard as low, on the contrary, are those which call our attention to some part of our own body, and which make no object so conspicuous to us as the organ in which they arise.

There is here, then, a very marked distinction between physical and esthetic pleasure; the organs of the latter must be transparent, they must not intercept our attention, but carry it directly to some external object. The greater dignity and range of esthetic pleasure is thus made very intelligible The soul is glad, as it were, to forget its connection with the body and to fancy that it can travel over the world with the liberty with which it changes the objects of its thought. The mind passes from China to Peru without any conscious change in the local tensions of the body. This illusion of disembodiment is very exhilarating, while immersion in the flesh and confinement to some organ gives a tone of grossness and selfishness to our consciousness. The generally meaner associations of physical pleasures also help to explain their comparative crudity. . . .

The Differentia of Esthetic Pleasure: Its Objectification

There is, however, something more in the claim to universality in esthetic judgments than the desire to generalize our own opinions. There is the expression of a curious but well-known psychological phenomenon, namely, the transformation of an element of sensation into the quality of a thing. If we say that other men should see the beauties we see, it is because we think those beauties *are in the object,* like its color, proportion, or size. Our judgment appears to us merely the perception and discovery of an external existence, of the real excellence that is without. But this notion is radically absurd and contradictory. Beauty, as we have seen, is a value; it cannot be conceived as an independent existence which affects our senses and which we consequently perceive. It exists in perception, and cannot exist otherwise. A beauty not perceived is a pleasure not felt, and a contradiction. But modern philosophy has taught us to say the same thing of every element of the perceived world; all are sensations; and their grouping into objects imagined to be permanent and external is the work of certain habits of our intelligence. We should be incapable of surveying or retaining the diffused experiences of life, unless we organize and classified them, and out of the chaos of impressions framed the world of conventional and recognizable objects.

How this is done is explained by the current theories of perception. External objects usually affect various senses at once, the impressions of which are thereby associated. Repeated experiences of one object are also associated on account of their similarity; hence a double tendency to merge and unify into a single percept, to which a name is attached, the group of those memories and reactions which in fact had one external thing for their cause. But this percept, once formed, is clearly different from those particular experiences out of which it grew. It is permanent, they are variable. They are but partial views and glimpses of it. The constituted notion therefore comes to be the reality, and the materials of it merely the appearance. The distinction between substance and quality, reality and appearance, matter and mind, has no other origin.

The objects thus conceived and distinguished from our ideas of them, are at first compacted of all the impressions, feelings, and memories, which offer themselves for association and fall within the vortex of the amalgamating imagination. Every sensation we get from a thing is originally treated as one of its qualities. Experiment, however, and the practical need of a simpler conception of the structure of objects lead us gradually to reduce the qualities of the object to a minimum, and to regard most perceptions as an effect of those few qualities upon us. These few primary qualities, like extension which we persist in treating as independently real and as the quality of a substance, are those which suffice to explain the order of our experiences. All the rest, like color, are relegated to the subjective sphere, as merely effects upon our minds, and apparent or secondary qualities of the object.

But this distinction has only a practical justification. Convenience and economy of thought alone determine what combination of our sensations we shall continue to objectify and treat as the cause of the rest. The right and tendency to be objective is equal in all, since they are all prior to the artifice of thought by which we separate the concept from its materials, the thing from our experiences.

The qualities which we now conceive to belong to real objects are for the most part images of sight and touch. One of the first classes of effects to be treated as secondary were naturally pleasures and pains, since it could commonly conduce very little to intelligent and successful action to conceive our pleasures and pains as resident in objects. But emotions are essentially capable of objectification, as well as impressions of sense; and one may well believe that a primitive and inexperienced consciousness would rather people the world with ghosts of its own terrors and passions than with projections of those luminous and mathematical concepts which as yet it could hardly have formed.

This animistic and mythological habit of thought still holds its own at the confines of knowledge, where mechanical explanations are not found. In ourselves, where nearness makes observation difficult, in the intricate chaos of animal and human life, we still appeal to the efficacy of will and ideas, as also in the remote night of cosmic and religious problems. But in all the intermediate realm of vulgar day, where mechanical science has made progress, the inclusion of emotional or passionate elements in the concept of the reality would be now an extravagance. Here our idea of things is composed exclusively of perceptual elements, of the ideas of form and of motion.

The beauty of objects, however, forms an exception to this rule. Beauty is an emotional element, a pleasure of ours, which nevertheless we regard as a quality of things. But we are now prepared to understand the nature of this exception. It is the survival of a tendency originally universal to make every effect of a thing upon us a constituent of its conceived nature. The scientific idea of a thing is a great abstraction from the mass of perceptions and reactions which that thing produces; the esthetic idea is less abstract, since it retains the emotional reaction, the pleasure of the perception, as an integral part of the conceived thing.

Nor is it hard to find the ground of this survival in the sense of beauty of an objectification of feeling elsewhere extinct. Most of the pleasures which objects cause are easily distinguished and separated from the perception of the object: the object has to be applied to a particular organ, like the palate, or swallowed like wine, or used and operated upon in some way before the pleasure arises. The cohesion is therefore slight between the pleasure and the other associated elements of sense; the pleasure is separated in time from the perception, or it is localized in a different organ, and consequently is at once recognized as an effect and not as a quality of the object. But when the process of perception itself is pleasant, as it may easily be, when the intellectual operation, by which the elements of sense are associated and projected, and the concept of the form and substance of the thing produced, is naturally delightful, then we have a pleasure intimately bound up in the thing, inseparable from its character and constitution, the seat of which in us is the same as the seat of the perception. We naturally fail, under these circumstances, to separate the pleasure from the other objectified feelings. It becomes, like them, a quality of the object, which we distinguish from pleasures not so incorporated in the perception of things, by giving it the name of beauty.

The Definition of Beauty

We have now reached our definition of beauty, which, in the terms of our successive analysis and narrowing of the conception, is value positive, intrinsic, and objectified. Or, in less technical language, Beauty is pleasure regarded as the quality of a thing.

This definition is intended to sum up a variety of distinctions and identifications which should perhaps be here more explicitly set down. Beauty is a value, that is, it is not a perception of a matter of fact or of a relation: it is an emotion, an affection of our volitional and appreciative nature. An object cannot be beautiful if it can give pleasure to nobody: a beauty to which all men were forever indifferent is a contradiction in terms.

In the second place, this value is positive, it is the sense of the presence of something good, or (in the case of ugliness) of its absence. It is never the perception of a positive evil, it is never a negative value. That we are endowed with the sense of beauty is a pure gain which brings no evil with it. When the ugly ceases to be amusing or merely uninteresting and becomes disgusting, it becomes indeed a positive evil: but a moral and practical, not an esthetic, one. In esthetics that saying is true—often so disingenuous in ethics—that evil is nothing but the absence of good: for even the tedium and vulgarity of an existence without beauty is not itself ugly so much as lamentable and degrading. The absence of esthetic goods is a moral evil: the esthetic evil is merely relative, and means less of esthetic good than was expected at the place and time. No form in itself gives pain, although some forms give pain by causing a shock of surprise even when they are really beautiful: as if a mother found a fine bull pup in her child's cradle, when her pain would not be esthetic in its nature.

Further, this pleasure must not be in the consequence of the utility of the object or event, but in its immediate perception; in other words, beauty is an ultimate good, something that gives satisfaction to a natural function, to some fundamental need or capacity of our minds. Beauty is therefore a positive value that is intrinsic; it is a pleasure. These two circumstances sufficiently separate the sphere of esthetics from that of ethics. Moral values are generally negative, and always remote. Morality has to do with the avoidance of evil and the pursuit of good: esthetics only with enjoyment.

Finally, the pleasures of sense are distinguished from the perception of beauty, as sensation in general is distinguished from perception; by the objectification of the elements and their appearance as qualities rather of things than of consciousness. The passage from sensation to perception is gradual, and the path may be sometimes retraced: so it is with beauty and the pleasures of sensation. There is no sharp line between them, but it depends upon the degree of objectivity my feeling has attained at the moment whether I say "It pleases me," or "It is beautiful." If I am self-conscious and critical, I shall probably use one phrase; if I am impulsive and susceptible, the other. The more remote, interwoven, and inextricable the pleasure is, the more objective it will appear; and the union of two pleasures often makes one beauty. In Shakespeare's LIVth sonnet are these words:

> O how much more doth beauty beauteous seem
> By that sweet ornament which truth doth give!
> The rose looks fair, but fairer we it deem
> For that sweet odor which doth in it live.
> The canker-blooms have full as deep a dye
> As the perfumèd tincture of the roses,
> Hang on such thorns, and play as wantonly
> When summer's breath their maskèd buds discloses.
> But, for their beauty only is their show,
> They live unwooed and unrespected fade;
> Die to themselves. Sweet roses do not so:
> Of their sweet deaths are sweetest odors made.

One added ornament, we see, turns the deep dye, which was but show and mere sensation before, into an element of beauty and reality; and as truth is here the cooperation of perceptions, so beauty is the cooperation of pleasures. If color, form, and motion are hardly beautiful without the sweetness of the odor, how much more necessary would they be for the sweetness itself to become a beauty! If we had the perfume in a flask, no one would think of calling it beautiful: it would give us too detached and controllable a sensation. There would be no object in which it could be easily incorporated. But let it float from the garden, and it will add another sensuous charm to objects simultaneously recognized, and help to make them beautiful. Thus beauty is constituted by the objectification of pleasure. It is pleasure objectified.

II. Beauty as Expression

Expression Defined

We have found in the beauty of material and form the objectification of certain pleasures connected with the process of direct perception, with the formation, in the one case of a sensation, or quality, in the other of a synthesis of sensations or qualities. But the human consciousness is not a perfectly clear mirror, with distinct boundaries and clear-cut images, determinate in number and exhaustively perceived. Our ideas half emerge for a moment from the dim continuum of vital feeling and diffused sense, and are hardly fixed before they are changed and transformed, by the shifting of attention and the perception of new relations, into ideas of really different objects. This fluidity of the mind would make reflection impossible, did we not fix in words and other symbols certain abstract contents; we thus become capable of recognizing in one perception the repetition of another, and of recognizing in certain recurrences of impressions a persistent object. This discrimination and classification of the contents of consciousness is the work of perception and understanding, and the pleasures that accompany these activities make the beauty of the sensible world.

But our hold upon our thoughts extends even further. We not only construct visible unities and recognizable types, but remain aware of their affinities to what is not at the time perceived; that is, we find in them a certain tendency and quality, not original to them, a meaning and a tone, which upon investigation we shall see to have been the proper characteristics of other objects and feelings, associated with them once in our experience. The hushed reverberations of these associated feelings continue in the brain, and by modifying our present reaction, color the image upon which our attention is fixed. The quality thus acquired by objects through association is what we call their expression. Whereas in form or material there is one object with its emotional effect, in expression there are two, and the emotional effect belongs to the character of the second or suggested one. Expression may thus make beautiful by suggestion things in themselves indifferent, or it may come to heighten the beauty which they already possess.

Expression is not always distinguishable in consciousness from the value of material or form, because we do not always have a distinguishable memory of the related idea which the expressiveness implies. When we have such a memory, as at the sight of some once frequented garden, we clearly and spontaneously attribute our emotion to the memory and not to the present fact which it beautifies. The revival of a pleasure and its embodiment in a present object which in itself might have been indifferent, is here patent and acknowledged.

The distinctness of the analysis may indeed be so great as to prevent the synthesis; we may so entirely pass to the suggested object, that our pleasure will be embodied in the memory of that, while the suggestive sensation will be overlooked, and the expressiveness of the present object will fail to make it beautiful. Thus the mementos of a lost friend do not become beautiful by virtue of the sentimental associations which may make them precious. The value is confined to the images of the memory; they are too clear to let any of that value escape and diffuse itself over the rest of our consciousness, and beautify the objects which we actually behold. We say explicitly: I value this trifle for its associations. And so long as this division continues, the worth of the thing is not for us esthetic.

But a little dimming of our memory will often make it so. Let the images of the past fade, let them remain simply as a halo and suggestion of happiness hanging about a scene; then this scene, however empty and uninteresting in itself, will have a deep and intimate charm; we shall be pleased by its very vulgarity. We shall not confess so readily that we value the place for its associations; we shall rather say: I am fond of this landscape; it has for me an ineffable attraction. The treasures of the memory have been melted and dissolved, and are now gilding the object that supplants them; they are giving this object expression. . . .

In all expression we may thus distinguish two terms: the first is the object actually presented, the word, the image, the expressive thing; the second is the object suggested, the further thought, emotion, or image evoked, the thing expressed.

These lie together in the mind, and their union constitutes expression. If the value lies wholly in the first term, we have no beauty of expression. The decorative inscriptions in Saracenic monuments can have no beauty of expression for one who does not read Arabic; their charm is wholly one of material and form. Or if they have any expression, it is by virtue of such thoughts as they might suggest, as, for instance, of the piety and oriental sententiousness of the builders and of the aloofness from us of all their world. And even these suggestions, being a wandering of our fancy rather than a study of the object, would fail to arouse a pleasure which would be incorporated in the present image. The scroll would remain without expression, although its presence might have suggested to us interesting visions of other things. The two terms would be too independent, and the intrinsic values of each would remain distinct from that of the other. There would be no visible expressiveness, although there might have been discursive suggestions.

Indeed, if expression were constituted by the external relation of object with object, everything would be expressive equally, indeterminately, and universally. The flower in the crannied wall would express the same thing as the bust of Cæsar or the *Critique of Pure Reason.* What constitutes the individual expressiveness of these things is the circle of thoughts allied to each in a given mind; my words, for instance, express the thoughts which they actually arouse in the reader; they may express more to one man than to another, and to me they may have expressed more or less than to you. My thoughts remain unexpressed, if my words do not arouse them in you, and very likely your greater wisdom will find in what I say the manifestation of a thousand principles of which I never dreamed. Expression depends upon the union of two terms, one of which must be furnished by the imagination; and a mind cannot furnish what it does not possess. The expressiveness of everything accordingly increases with the intelligence of the observer.

But for expression to be an element of beauty, it must, of course, fulfil another condition. I may see the relations of an object, I may understand it perfectly, and may nevertheless regard it with entire indifference. If the pleasure fails, the very substance and protoplasm of beauty is wanting. Nor, as we have seen, is even the pleasure enough; for I may receive a letter full of the most joyous news, but neither the paper, nor the writing, nor the style, need seem beautiful to me. Not until I confound the impressions, and suffuse the symbols themselves with the emotions they arouse, and find joy and sweetness in the very words I hear, will the expressiveness constitute a beauty; as when they sing, *Gloria in excelsis Deo.*

The value of the second term must be incorporated in the first; for the beauty of expression is as inherent in the object as that of material or form, only it accrues to that object not from the bare act of perception, but from the association with it of further processes, due to the existence of former impressions. We may conveniently use the word "expressiveness" to mean all the capacity of suggestion possessed by a thing, and the word "expression" for the esthetic modification which that expressiveness may cause in it. Expressiveness is thus the power given by experience to any image to call up others in the mind; and this expressiveness becomes an esthetic value, that is, becomes expression, when the value involved in the associations thus awakened are incorporated in the present object. . . .

Esthetic Value in the Second Term

That the noble associations of any object should embellish that object is very comprehensible. Homer furnishes us with a good illustration of the constant employment of this effect. The first term, one need hardly say, leaves with him little to be desired. The verse is beautiful. Sounds, images, and composition conspire to stimulate and delight. This immediate beauty is sometimes used to clothe things terrible and sad; there is no dearth of the tragic in Homer. But the tendency of his poetry is nevertheless to fill the outskirts of our consciousness with the trooping images of things no less fair and noble than the verse itself. The heroes are virtuous. There is none of importance who is not admirable in his way. The palaces, the arms, the horses, the sacrifices, are always excellent. The women are always stately and beautiful. The ancestry and the history of every one are honorable and good. The whole Homeric world is clean, clear, beautiful, and providential, and no small part of the perennial charm of the poet is that he thus immerses us in an atmosphere of beauty; a beauty not concentrated and reserved for some extraordinary sentiment, action, or person, but permeating the whole and coloring the common world of soldiers and sailors, war and craft, with a marvellous freshness and inward glow. There is nothing in the associations of life in this world or in another to contradict or disturb our delight. All is beautiful, and beautiful through and through.

Something of this quality meets us in all simple and idyllic compositions. There is, for instance, a popular demand that stories and comedies should "end well." The hero and heroine must be young and handsome; unless they die,—which is another matter,—they must not in the end be poor. The landscape in the play must be beautiful; the dresses pretty; the plot without serious mishap. A pervasive presentation of pleasure must give warmth and ideality to the whole. In the proprieties of social life we find the same principle; we study to make our surroundings, manner, and conversation suggest nothing but what is pleasing. We hide the ugly and disagreeable portion of our lives, and do not allow the least hint of it to come to light upon festive and public occasions. Whenever, in a word, a thoroughly pleasing effect is found, it is found by the expression, as well as presentation, of what is in itself pleasing—and when this effect is to be produced artificially, we attain it by the suppression of all expression that is not suggestive of something good.

If our consciousness were exclusively esthetic, this kind of expression would be the only one allowed in art or prized in nature. We should avoid as a shock or an insipidity, the suggestion of anything not intrinsically beautiful. As there would be no values not esthetic, our pleasure could never be heightened by any other kind of interest. But as contemplation is actually a luxury in our lives, and things interest us chiefly on passionate and practical grounds, the accumulation of values too exclusively esthetic produces in our minds an effect of closeness and artificiality. So selective a diet cloys, and our palate, accustomed to much daily vinegar and salt, is surfeited by such unmixed sweet.

Instead we prefer to see through the medium of art—through the beautiful first term of our expression—the miscellaneous world which is so well known to us—perhaps so dear, and at any rate so inevitable, an object. We are more thankful for this presentation of the unlovely truth in a lovely form, than for the like presentation of an abstract beauty; what is lost in the purity of the pleasure is gained in the stimulation of our attention, and in the relief of viewing with esthetic detachment the same things that in practical life hold tyrannous dominion over our souls. The beauty that is associated only with other beauty is therefore a sort of esthetic dainty; it leads the fancy through a fairyland of lovely forms, where we must forget the common objects of our interest. The charm of such an idealization is undeniable; but the other important elements of our memory and will cannot long be banished. Thoughts of labor, ambition, lust, anger, confusion, sorrow, and death must needs mix with our contemplation and lend their various expressions to the objects with which in experience they are so closely allied. Hence the incorporation in the beautiful of values of other sorts, and the comparative rareness in nature or art of expressions the second term of which has only esthetic value. . . .

The Liberation of Self

The esthetic effect of objects is always due to the total emotional value of the consciousness in which they exist. We merely attribute this value to the object by a projection which is the ground of the apparent objectivity of beauty. Sometimes this value may be inherent in the process by which the object itself is perceived; then we have sensuous and formal beauty; sometimes the value may be due to the incipient formation of other ideas, which the perception of this object evokes; then we have beauty of expression. But among the ideas with which every object has relation there is one vaguest, most comprehensive, and most powerful one, namely, the idea of self. The impulses, memories, principles, and energies which we designate by that word baffle enumeration; indeed, they constantly fade and change into one another; and whether the self is anything, everything, or nothing depends on the aspect of it which we momentarily fix, and especially on the definite object with which we contrast it.

Now, it is the essential privilege of beauty so to synthesize and bring to a focus the various impulses of the self, so to suspend them to a single image, that a great peace falls upon that perturbed kingdom. In the experience of these momentary harmonies we have the basis of the enjoyment of beauty, and of all its mystical meanings. But there are always two methods of securing harmony: one is to unify all the given elements, and another is to reject and expunge all the elements that refuse to be unified. Unity by inclusion gives us the beautiful; unity by exclusion, opposition, and isolation gives us the sublime. Both are pleasures: but the pleasure of the one is warm, passive, pervasive; that of the other, cold, imperious, and keen. The one identifies us with the world, the other raises us above it.

There can be no difficulty in understanding how the expression of evil in the object may be the occasion of this heroic reaction of the soul. In the first place, the evil may be felt; but at the same time the sense that, great as it may be in itself, it cannot touch us, may stimulate extraordinarily the consciousness of our own wholeness. This is the sublimity which Lucretius calls "sweet" in the famous lines in which he so justly analyzes it. We are not pleased because another suffers an evil, but because, seeing it is an evil, we see at the same time our own immunity from it. We might soften the picture a little, and perhaps make the principle even clearer by so doing. The shipwreck observed from the shore does not leave us wholly unmoved; we suffer, also, and if possible, would help. So, too, the spectacle of the erring world must sadden the philosopher even in the Acropolis of his wisdom; he would, if it might be, descend from his meditation and teach. But those movements of sympathy are quickly inhibited by despair of success; impossibility of action is a great condition of the sublime. If we could count the stars, we should not weep before them. While we think we can change the drama of history, and of our own lives, we are not awed by our destiny. But when the evil is irreparable, when our life is lived, a strong spirit has the sublime resource of standing at bay and of surveying almost from the other world the vicissitudes of this.

The more intimate to himself the tragedy he is able to look back upon with calmness, the more sublime that calmness is, and the more divine the ecstasy in which he achieves it. For the more of the accidental vesture of life we are able to strip ourselves of, the more naked and simple is the surviving spirit; the more complete its superiority and unity, and, consequently, the more unqualified its joy. There remains little in us, then, but that intellectual essence, which several great philosophers have called eternal and identified with the Divinity.

A single illustration may help to fix these principles in the mind. When Othello has discovered his fatal error, and is resolved to take his own life, he stops his groaning, and addresses the ambassadors of Venice thus:

> Speak of me as I am: nothing extenuate,
> Nor set down aught in malice: then, must you speak
> Of one that loved, not wisely, but too well;
> Of one not easily jealous, but, being wrought,
> Perplexed in the extreme; of one whose hand,
> Like the base Indian, threw a pearl away
> Richer than all his tribe; of one whose subdued eyes,
> Albeit unusèd to the melting mood,
> Drop tears as fast as the Arabian trees
> Their medicinal gum. Set you down this:

> And say, besides, that in Aleppo once
> When a malignant and a turbaned Turk
> Beat a Venetian, and traduced the state,
> I took by the throat the circumcisèd dog,
> And smote him, thus.

There is a kind of criticism that would see in all these allusions, figures of speech, and wandering reflections, an unnatural rendering of suicide. The man, we might be told, should have muttered a few broken phrases, and killed himself without this pomp of declamation, like the jealous husbands in the daily papers. But the conventions of the tragic stage are more favorable to psychological truth than the conventions of real life. If we may trust the imagination (and in imagination lies, as we have seen, the test of propriety), this is what Othello would have felt. If he had not expressed it, his dumbness would have been due to external hindrances, not to the failure in his mind of just such complex and rhetorical thoughts as the poet has put into his mouth. The height of passion is naturally complex and rhetorical. Love makes us poets, and the approach of death should make us philosophers. When a man knows that his life is over, he can look back upon it from a universal standpoint. He has nothing more to live for, but if the energy of his mind remains unimpaired, he will still wish to live, and, being cut off from his personal ambitions, he will impute to himself a kind of vicarious immortality by identifying himself with what is eternal. He speaks of himself as he is, or rather as he was. He sums himself up, and points to his achievement. This I have been, says he, this I have done.

This comprehensive and impartial view, this synthesis and objectification of experience, constitutes the liberation of the soul and the essence of sublimity. That the hero attains it at the end consoles us, as it consoles him, for his hideous misfortunes. Our pity and terror are indeed purged; we go away knowing that, however tangled the net may be in which we feel ourselves caught, there is liberation beyond, and an ultimate peace.

The Sublime Independent of the Expression of Evil

So natural is the relation between the vivid conception of great evils, and that self-assertion of the soul which gives the emotion of the sublime, that the sublime is often thought to depend upon the terror which these conceived evils inspire. To be sure, that terror would have to be inhibited and subdued, otherwise we should have a passion too acute to be incorporated in any object; the sublime would not appear as an esthetic quality in things, but remain merely an emotional state in the subject. But this subdued and objectified terror is what is commonly regarded as the essence of the sublime, and so great an authority as Aristotle would seem to countenance some such definition. The usual cause of the sublime is here confused, however, with the sublime itself. The suggestion of terror makes us withdraw into ourselves: there with the supervening consciousness of safety or indifference comes a rebound, and we have that emotion of detachment and liberation in which the sublime really consists.

Thoughts and actions are properly sublime, and visible things only by analogy and suggestion when they induce a certain moral emotion;

whereas beauty belongs properly to sensible things, and can be predicated of moral facts only by a figure of rhetoric. What we objectify in beauty is a sensation. What we objectify in the sublime is an act. This act is necessarily pleasant, for if it were not the sublime would be a bad quality and one we should rather never encounter in the world. The glorious joy of self-assertion in the face of an uncontrollable world is indeed so deep and entire, that it furnishes just that transcendent element of worth for which we were looking when we tried to understand how the expression of pain could sometimes please. It can please, not in itself, but because it is balanced and annulled by positive pleasures, especially by this final and victorious one of detachment. If the expression of evil seems necessary to the sublime, it is so only as a condition of this moral reaction.

We are commonly too much engrossed in objects and too little centered in ourselves and our inalienable will, to see the sublimity of a pleasing prospect. We are then enticed and flattered, and won over to a commerce with these external goods, and the consummation of our happiness would lie in the perfect comprehension and enjoyment of their nature. This is the office of art and of love; and its partial fulfilment is seen in every perception of beauty. But when we are checked in this sympathetic endeavor after unity and comprehension; when we come upon a great evil or an irreconcilable power, we are driven to seek our happiness by the shorter and heroic road; then we recognize the hopeless foreignness of what lies before us, and stiffen ourselves against it. We thus for the first time reach the sense of our possible separation from our world, and of our abstract stability; and with this comes the sublime.

But although experience of evil is the commonest approach to this attitude of mind, and we commonly become philosophers only after despairing of instinctive happiness, yet there is nothing impossible in the attainment of detachment by other channels. The immense is sublime as well as the terrible; and mere infinity of the object, like its hostile nature, can have the effect of making the mind recoil upon itself. Infinity, like hostility, removes us from things, and makes us conscious of our independence. The simultaneous view of many things, innumerable attractions felt together, produce equilibrium and indifference, as effectually as the exclusion of all. If we may call the liberation of the self by the consciousness of evil in the world, the Stoic sublime, we may assert that there is also an Epicurean sublime, which consists in liberation by equipoise. Any wide survey is sublime in that fashion. Each detail may be beautiful. We may even be ready with a passionate response to its appeal. We may think we covet every sort of pleasure, and lean to every kind of vigorous, impulsive life. But let an infinite panorama be suddenly unfolded; the will is instantly paralyzed, and the heart choked. It is impossible to desire everything at once, and when all is offered and approved, it is impossible to choose everything. In this suspense, the mind soars into a kind of heaven, benevolent but unmoved. . . .

The sense of the sublime is essentially mystical: it is the transcending of distinct perception in favor of a feeling of unity and volume. So in the moral sphere, we have the mutual cancelling of the passions in the breast that includes them all, and their final subsidence beneath the glance that comprehends them. This is the Epicurean approach to detachment and perfection; it leads by systematic acceptance of instinct to the same goal which the stoic and the ascetic reach by systematic rejection of instinct. It is thus possible to be moved to that self-enfranchisement which constitutes the sublime, even when the object contains no expression of evil.

This conclusion supports that part of our definition of beauty which declares that the values beauty contains are all positive; a definition which we should have had to change if we had found that the sublime depended upon the suggestion of evil for its effect. But the sublime is not the ugly, as some descriptions of it might lead us to suppose; it is the supremely, the intoxicatingly beautiful. It is the pleasure of contemplation reaching such an intensity that it begins to lose its objectivity, and to declare itself, what it always fundamentally was, an inward passion of the soul. For while in the beautiful we find the perfection of life by sinking into the object, in the sublime we find a purer and more inalienable perfection by defying the object altogether. The surprised enlargement of the vision, the sudden escape from our ordinary interests and the identification of ourselves with something permanent and superhuman, something much more abstract and inalienable than our changing personality, all this carries us away from the blurred objects before us, and raises us into a sort of ecstasy.

In the trite examples of the sublime, where we speak of the vast mass, strength, and durability of objects, or of their sinister aspect, as if we were moved by them on account of our own danger, we seem to miss the point. For the suggestion of our own danger would produce a touch of fear; it would be a practical passion, or if it could by chance be objectified enough to become esthetic, it would merely make the object hateful and repulsive, like a mangled corpse. The object is sublime when we forget our danger, when we escape from ourselves altogether, and live as it were in the object itself, energizing in imitation of its movement, and saying, "Be thou me, impetuous one!" This passage into the object, to live its life, is indeed a characteristic of all perfect contemplation. But when in thus translating ourselves we rise and play a higher personage, feeling the exhilaration of a life freer and wilder than our own, then the experience is one of sublimity. The emotion comes not from the situation we observe, but from the powers we conceive; we fail to sympathize with the struggling sailors because we sympathize too much with the wind and waves. And this mystical cruelty can extend even to ourselves; we can so feel the fascination of the cosmic forces that engulf us as to take a fierce joy in the thought of our own destruction. We can identify ourselves with the abstractest essence of reality, and, raised to that height, despise the human accidents of our own nature. Lord, we say, though thou slay me, yet will I trust in thee. The sense of suffering disappears in the sense of life and the imagination overwhelms the understanding.

—*The Sense of Beauty* (1896)

LOUIS ARNAUD REID

Values, Feeling and Embodiment

1. The Embodiment of Values

In the light of all that has been said, the question "What does art embody?" must be put carefully and the answer must be a complex one. There are on the one hand the sources of art in life-experiences. On the other, there are meanings which arise directly out of the use of the various materials of the arts, with their symbolic import. These latter meanings are also related to ordinary life, are attached to it by a sort of umbilical cord. Sounds, shapes, colours, the sounds of words . . . and their significances, are all part of our sensitive ordinary experiences.

Esthetic meaning may be found, upon analytic examination, to be *derived* in part from sources in life outside art. Viewed from *inside* the experience of art, it may well seem that the question "What does art embody?" is the wrong question. Looked at from within, the short answer is that what art embodies, what it means, cannot be stated in words at all. Even if the art is an art of words, as poetry is, a paraphrase will not do; the meaning of the poem is what the poem as read, says. Likewise, the "meaning" of a picture or a piece of music cannot be put into words; if it could, the art would be superfluous. Experience-knowledge of esthetic meaning is a unique way of knowing, is *sui generis*. On the other hand, if we think not of the meaning as actually known in esthetic experience, of the history, of the genesis of the work, of what "inspired" it, we can often, though not always, discover some relation of meaning in art to life-experiences. This is more often true of "representative" arts like literature, drama, and a good deal of painting. (It is much less apparent in music.) And further, there is a quite *general* sense in which we can ask the question, "What is embodied?" It is the sense in which we may be asking, not about the particular origins of what is embodied here and now in this individual work, but about the *kind* of thing which is embodied, and its ontological status. Is it, for instance, matter of *fact* which is embodied? Is it *emotion*? Is it "*values*"? I will speak first of this last question, returning to the others.

Thinking for the time being of the partial derivation of art meanings from life-experiences (always a one-sided kind of thinking)—from what *sort* of life-experiences are they derived? Crudely put, What is it that is trying to get "expressed"?[1] Is it "facts" apprehended—the facts of the structure of a landscape or a face or the details of a person's character, acts, life? Is it "ideas" about love, or duty, or suffering, or mortality, or God . . . freedom, immortality? Or can it be "feelings" or "emotions"?

None of these answers seem to me to be adequate, though all of them may enter as elements into the true answer. The true answer, I venture to think, is that it is not facts or ideas as such, nor feelings nor emotions as such that try "to get expressed," but feelings-about-things, or things (facts, ideas, anything)—as-felt. Things-we-are-interested in, things-experienced-as-interesting, exciting, as in some very broad sense of the term, good, evil, attractive, repulsive, etc. The life-resources of art are events or facts or concepts or images as experienced, and as experienced with feeling. They are not the things alone, nor the feelings alone, but the things-as-experienced-with feeling.

Another way, and a short way of saying the same thing is to affirm that what "tries to get expressed" are *values*. Professor R. B. Perry once defined "value" as "object of interest."[2] Without necessarily accepting this as a final definition of value, I take it to be a fair account of what we ordinarily mean. The much used word "value" is also much abused; it is a dangerous world because it is a substantive, and it is all too easy to think of "values" as vaguely floating about somewhere. But taken as standing for a relationship between things and our interested selves ("interest" involving some degree of "feeling") it is a useful word, particularly in esthetics, because it avoids a one-sided emphasis on object, or on subject. To avoid one-sided emphasis I have used hyphens above. It is, then, "values" which "try to get expressed," or things-as-felt (or experienced, with interest and feeling), feelings-about-things. . . .

It is not bare facts (or "knowledge that") which "get expressed." When Tennyson wrote, "Into the valley of death rode the six hundred," he was not merely affirming the fact, but was concerned with it as an event moving the feelings. If a painter paints trees or cows, he is not, *qua* artist, depicting the bare literal facts; he attends to what interests and excites him. He is moved by colours and shapes and dynamic relationships in such a way that the form of a painted tree may reveal, perhaps, as ordinary matter-of-fact seeing will not do, the fascinating way it springs up, spreads its branches and leaves, and supports its weight. If, again, we think of art as partially arising from the "unconscious," it is no exception to the statement that events . . . experienced as exciting are the causes or subject-matter of some arts. Art may express unconscious wishes or fantasies, and some—perhaps all—art is "symbolic" in one or more of the several psychoanalytic senses. And these contents of course are very highly charged with "value"; the artist must have felt strongly about them or they would not have been repressed or expressed.

An example of the fallacy that it is facts which "get expressed" is a confused belief among architects and writers on architecture, that architecture should "express function or structure." "Express" is not defined. It may mean little more than "show up." A modern building ought, some think to "show up" its engineering structure unashamedly (though much engineering structure is too complex to be shown up in a building and for various reasons must be hidden). Why? Because architecture is nothing but engineering? But if engineering, why "ought" it to show its structure? There must be esthetic premises somewhat concealed. The concealed premises are that architecture is not only engineering but art and ought to show structure because structure is beautiful. Structure and function, however, as independent facts and in themselves, are neither beautiful nor ugly. To a percipient who sees them as embodying the "values" of function and structure, they may appear as beautiful (though it is a doubtful assumption that *any* structure may be so perceived). Sheer structure often delights and may be esthetically perceived (with the inward selectiveness which esthetic perception always involves) and in some cases it may be enough for an architect to let the structure show. But this is a *deliberate* and esthetic choice. Often, however, the architect shows up the esthetic quality by selective treatment, emphasis, simplification, elaboration. This takes many different forms. There is the freedom and variety of the essential Gothic structure, with esthetic treatment of vaulting or buttress, or the modern deliberate emphasis of the glass-and-steel structural grid, or the use in various ways of organic or geometrical *motifs*. In all cases architecture as art is more than engineering, and more than the mere factual presentation of structure and function to the eye. It is a deliberate creation of something new, arising out of delight in the *value* of these things.

Nor is it bare *ideas* which "get expressed." If by "ideas" we mean concepts, then philosophy or science are the proper media for the expression of concepts and their relations. Concepts are abstractions, they are structures or forms which can best be expressed in language which is quite cold and impersonal. Such language is simply a means to clearer conception, and a means to the communication of ideas. If scientists and philosophers are talking about mathematical propositions, or electrons, or duty, freedom, the status of secondary qualities . . . they rightly use this "cold" impersonal abstract language in the endeavour to clarify, express and convey the truths they are claiming. The language is a means to this end, and there are often equally good alternative ways of saying exactly the same thing—as in art there are not. (Two philosophers may entirely agree on a point, but they seldom use *exactly* the same language.) And the ideas of philosophy and science can be adequately translated into, or re-expressed in, various languages.

Of course scientists and philosophers sometimes get excited about their ideas and about the clarity of thought. If a philosopher is moved to enthusiasm by these, and happens also to be a master of prose and an artist, his feeling may "get into" his writing and make art of it. As well as clear and efficient exposition (which can also be inelegantly expressed[3]) one gets in his style the sense of the *joy* of ideas, the joy of clarity, which may show itself in choice and placing of words, rhythms, emphasis, balance, even in punctuation. A philosopher may be a prose artist in his writing of philosophy. English and French philosophy are fortunately plentiful in examples of clear joyous philosophical writing elegantly done. But the *first*, and the *essential*, aim of philosophical (and scientific) language is efficiency in conveying, not feeling of ideas, but ideas themselves. "Well said" in philosophy primarily means conveying an abstract idea clearly. "Well said" in art means more than this.

Consider now a poem "about" ideas. Suppose a poet is writing—like Shelley, for example—about "scientific" or "philosophical" ideas. He is not a philosopher (or a scientist); his first loyalty is not to ideas as such. He is a poet, and it is his excitement-in-ideas which moves him to write. He has a freedom in the selection and manipulation of his subject-matter (in exactly the same way as the painter freely selects from the features of a landscape) to which the philosopher has no right. It is ideas-as-he-feels-them (ideas as "values"), that "get into" the poem. As with the painter, his emphasis, his style, is affected by the rhythm and pulsings of his feeling.

Whereas in the writing of philosophy and science the quality of style is primarily subordinate to the clarity of ideas, now it embodies the *values* of ideas.

2. Value, Feeling and Emotion

What of the place of feeling and emotion? After the Romantic Revival it became an almost unexamined assumption that the artist "expresses" in art his feelings or emotions. Temporarily letting the term "expression" pass, can it be feeling or emotion which is expressed in works of art? Mrs Susanne Langer, who herself strongly inclines to the view that in some sense feelings inhere in art objects, points out the difficulties of this language. She refers to Otto Baensch who believes that we can objectify and hold and handle feelings by "creating objects wherein the feelings we seek to hold are so definitely embodied that any subject confronted with these objects, and emphatically disposed towards them, cannot but experience a non-sensuous apperception of the feelings in question. Such objects are called 'Works of Art.' "[4] About this Mrs Langer remarks[5] that "feeling that is not subjective presents a . . . paradox," and (p. 22) "the status of the unfelt feelings that inhere in art objects is ontologically obscure. . . ." Mrs Langer's distinguished book, *Feeling and Form,* is in a way a systematic attempt to make sense of this idea of objectified feelings embodied in a work of art. Here I can only observe that it seems to me that she gets into difficulties about feeling which she would not have encountered had she, alternatively, conceived of art as embodying *values.* Feeling, and sometimes emotion, is very intimately bound up with the creation, the enjoyment, and the interpretation of works of art. But, since the terms "feeling" and "emotion" are so irreducibly associated with subjective states and processes, it does not seem possible to conceive of feelings or emotions as being sufficiently "objectified" to inhere in perceived works of art.

"Value," on the other hand, is a subjective-objective idea. Feeling by itself belongs to the subjective side. But our feelings-about-an-event, a fact, an idea, can be expressed by the way, the manner, the mode in which the event, fact, idea is represented. Tennyson felt about the event of the charge of the Light Brigade. He "expressed" not his own strictly incommunicable private subjective feelings, but the idea of the Charge-of-the-Light-Brigade-as-he-felt-it, and he did it by representing the Charge in a particular rhythmical *form.* The painter, excited by the springing tree, does not "objectify" sheer subjective excitement. (He cannot.) He paints the *tree* he sees in a certain way, so that when he, and we, see the painting, our experience in part derives from his delight in the springing tree. "Value," since it is a two-sided notion, objective as well as subjective, can be "expressed" objectively in art. Feeling alone cannot. The mistakes of theories which stress only the objective side ("Mirror to Nature theories"), which say that art represents facts or ideas only, is that they can condone dull uninspired-literalism which is not art but poor photography. The mistakes of traditional theories which say "the function of art is to 'express' the artist's feeling or emotion" are that they are describing the esthetically impossible, and that the stress on feelings and emotions leads to unbalance, sentimentality and emotionalism and too much emphasis upon what goes on inside the artist's "personality."

We have been discussing for the last few pages what *kind* of thing it is which is embodied in the work of art, and have, simply for convenience sake, considered life-sources for art—facts, ideas, emotions—which may "try to get expressed." The phrase, however, "try to get expressed" was deliberately crude, and it needs now to be corrected.

3. Art, "Expression" and Embodiment

The view that art is "expression" is capable of many different interpretations. Some of them are, I have urged, inadmissible, as that the artist has an experience, "expresses" this experience in a work, so that others can in turn have the same experience. There are various subtler versions of the expression view—in Croce, Carritt, Collingwood, Langer. And "expression" may be used as a synonym for "embodiment", in the sense in which I have expounded it here.[6] (But "embodiment" in my sense stresses the importance of the actual *material* medium in a way these thinkers do not consistently do.[7])

It is not necessary to say much more about "expression" as expression of life-experience, or of facts, ideas, feelings, in art. The process of making a work of art may certainly include "expression" in various senses. It may relieve the tension of gestation: to put something "into" words or action or paint ("express" it) is easing. To discover meaning through embodiment is satisfying; satisfaction follows the restless and often vague desire to discover through doing one hardly knows what; this can be called a satisfaction of "expression." But the "expression" which is relief need not be aesthetic. It may mean only the relief which John Dewey calls vulgarly "spewing forth".[8] Any action may "express" a pent-up emotion even if it is stamping with rage or jumping for joy. Further, such actions may "express" in the sense of *exhibiting* to others. These "expressions" *exhibit* the kind of feeling it was: stamping or jumping are crudely appropriate to the feeling. There is, too, the partially valid sense in which one can say that a life-experience, idea, value . . . is *represented* in a poem or a play or a picture. "The artist is expressing the idea that. . . ." And there is what is called, vaguely, "self-expression" or "expression of one's personality." Perhaps other kinds of "expression" may enter, in complex and overlapping ways, into the making and completion of works of art. They are in their own way interesting and important, sometimes psychologically and educationally very important indeed. The practice of art can be cathartic, therapeutic, or nourishing to the growth of personality. It can bring a person out of himself into the external world and the world of other people, establishing communication with them. Although its educational potency is often considerably overdrawn, artistic "expression" can be a kind of conversion and a beginning of new life.

All this can be said confidently, and without implying that the nature of art *is* expression of "life" outside art. Artistic activity, when it comes to its fruition, is never just expression in art of anything that existed completely before it, but is (to repeat) discovery of new embodied meaning, of meaning in embodiment. If, therefore, we say, as we have been saying, that it is *values* which art "embodies," and if we have taken "life"-values as examples, this crude picture must now be corrected by asserting all over again that the values which art embodies are the values to be discovered *in* the art, and never, completely, anywhere else. All esthetic expression is consummated and transformed in the new creation of embodiment.

Not all arts have their source or genesis—at least in any obvious sense—in life-experiences. Pure music may start with musical ideas and with experiment in musical material. However that be, once the work of art is made, its meaning and its embodiment, its "content" or "matter," and its "form," are of a single piece, one spirit and one body. Collingwood writes:[9] "When the poem is written, there is nothing in it of which we can say 'this is a matter which might have taken a different form' or 'this is a form which might have been realized in a different matter.'" Or as Mrs Langer has it;[10] "in a 'presentational symbol [e.g. art] the symbolic import permeates the whole structure, because every articulation of that structure is an articulation of the idea it conveys; the meaning . . . is the content of the symbolic form, given with it, as it were, to perception." Again, criticizing the distinction between form and content, she says (p. 520), "An artistic symbol is a much more intricate thing than what we usually think of as a 'form,' because it involves *all* the relationships of its elements to one another, all similarities and differences of quality, not only geometric or other familiar relations. That is why qualities enter directly into the form itself, not as its contents, but as constitutive elements in it. . . . A work of art is a structure whose interrelated elements are often qualities, or properties of qualities such as their degrees of intensity; qualities enter into the form and in this way are as much one with it as the relations which they, and they only, have; and to speak of them as 'content,' from which the form could be abstracted logically, is nonsense."

The same kind of thing "goes" for all the other "life" subject-matters of art. Psychoanalysis, no doubt, can throw light upon the genesis of at least some art. But it is impossible to discover embodied meaning directly by psychoanalysis. Unconscious events may be the genesis of artistic creation; the embodied meaning can only be found in the full and living appreciation of the completed work of art itself.

—*Ways of Knowledge and Experience* (1961)

Notes

1. For a brief criticism of "expression," see below, pp. 70–2. In the meantime I deliberately use an awkward phrase to indicate that the idea, provisionally used, *is* an awkward one.
2. R. B. Perry, *The General Theory of Value* (New York, Longmans).
3. This is debatable. I incline to believe that the philosopher who writes clearly with economic elegance is the better thinker for it.
4. Otto Baensch: 'Kunst unt Gefuhl', *Logos,* Vol. II, p. 14.
5. *Feeling and Form* (Routledge & Kegan Paul, 1953), p. 18.

6. Mr. H. Osborne (*Aesthetics and Criticism,* Routledge & Kegan Paul, pp. 142–3) accuses me, along with Carritt, Collingwood and Stace, of having come under the "spell" of Croce. I do not think that was ever true. And, though I formerly used the word "expressive" a good deal, perhaps sometimes loosely, it was intended very much as an equivalent for embodiment in the present sense. The main thesis of my *A Study in Aesthetics* was a *protest* against the idea that art is a translation of life-experience into the medium of art. See *A Study in Aesthetics* (Allen & Unwin), e.g., pp. 196–201.

7. For a fuller treatment, see my *Aesthetics and Education* (Bretton Hall, Wakefield).

8. Quoted by John Hospers, "Expression," *Proceedings of the Aristotelian Society,* Vol. LV. See this paper for a good discussion of expression.

9. R. G. Collingwood, *The Principles of Art* (Oxford: Oxford University Press, 1938), p. 24.

10. Susanne K. Langer, "The Principles of Creation in Art," *Hudson Review,* Vol. 2 (1949–1950), p. 521.

PART II The Work of Art

CHAPTER 7
The Matter of the Arts

BERNARD BOSANQUET: The Esthetic Attitude in Its Embodiments
BERNARD BERENSON: Materials and Techniques
EDWARD WESTON: Seeing Photographically
ARNOLD HAUSER: The Film Age
ÉTIENNE GILSON: The Dance

Part II is devoted to the work of art—its materials, form, and expressiveness. According to the idealistic interpretation, the work of art is not physical but spiritual. For example, Croce maintained that the physical objects—the statue, the building, the printed poem, and so forth—are not to be confused with art. They are simply "memoranda," physical stimulants for imaginative activity. The work of art, which is an apparition, lives in the imagination and there alone. Croce quite agrees with Walt Whitman:

> All architecture is what you do to it when you look upon it.
> (Did you think it was in the white or gray stone? or the lines of the arches and cornices?)
> All music is what awakens from you when you are reminded by the instruments,
> It is not the violins and the cornets, it is not the oboe nor the beating drums, nor the score of the baritone singing his sweet romanza, nor that of the men's chorus, nor that of the women's chorus,
> It is nearer and farther than they.

The physical object is esthetically important only because it stimulates imagination, and the object in nature is important for the same reason. This point of view is implied by Croce in his identification of intuition and expression, and it has been explicitly developed by R. G. Collingwood in *The Principles of Art* and by Jean-Paul Sartre in *The Psychology of Imagination*.

A less idealistic interpretation of the work of art is contained in Stephen C. Pepper's "Contextualistic Criticism" (see Chapter 11). Pepper distinguishes between the physical work of art—for example, the stone or bronze of a statue—and the esthetic work of art, "which rolls up all that is relevant in the line of preceding perceptions and intuits the whole potentiality of the physical work of art in a total vivid seizure." The physical work of art acts as a continuous substratum and control object, but apart from the spectator, the esthetic qualities of the perceived work would not be actualized.

The present chapter serves as a transition between Part I and Part II. Concerned with the technique of embodiment, it contributes to the theory of artistic creation (Part I); but it is equally concerned with the matter or substance of the work of art, and thus contributes to Part II.

An interpretation of the nature of the work of art similar to Pepper's interpretation is advanced by Bernard Bosanquet (1848–1923), a distinguished British philosopher. Art, he maintains, evokes an integrated response of the whole "body-and-mind." He calls this response "feeling," and the feeling, he says, is always embodied in an object. "It is a *relevant* feeling," he explains. "I mean it is attached, annexed, to the quality of some object—to all its detail. . . . My feeling in its special quality is evoked by the special quality of which it is the feeling, and in fact is one with it."[1] Thus emphasizing the *embodiment* of feeling, he opposes the tendency of Benedetto Croce to minimize the esthetic importance of the sensuous medium and the physical objects of nature. Although Bosanquet was an idealist, he believed that Croce's was a "false idealism" because it neglected the yearning of the creative imagination toward externalization and the influence of the external medium upon the imagination. As he says elsewhere, "To reject the function of the body—our own and nature's—is not to honor but to bereave the spirit."[2]

His emphasis upon the importance of the medium is no new principle. It is at least as old as Aristotle and received its classic expression in Lessing's *Laocoön*. But in a sense, it has been rediscovered by modern artists and estheticians, and it has had an extraordinary cleansing and renovating effect upon the arts. For example, the work of an architect such as Frank Lloyd Wright, of a designer such as Moholy-Nagy, of a sculptor such as Henry Moore, or of a painter such as Henri Matisse, has been profoundly influenced by this principle. "Respect your medium" has been a principal imperative of modern art.

The American art-historian and connoisseur, Bernard Berenson (1865–1959), warns us against exaggerating this imperative. He cites the practice of artists in many locales and periods in covering over or transcending the raw material. Art would shrink intolerably if it were limited to the characteristic use of the medium. "When an artist becomes master of a material or technique to the degree that it can no longer oppose any resistance," remarks Berenson, "it ceases to inspire him."

Whereas the medium is the *particular* natural stuff out of which the work of art is made, the more *general* sensuous qualities—such as line, shape, and color in the visual arts, or pitch, timbre, and degree of loudness in the auditory arts—may be considered apart from the particular medium (color, for example, is common to many media and various arts). The "matter" of art includes this wide repertoire of qualities both particular and general. The imperative in artistic creation is less to keep the medium pure than to combine *all* the constituents in an expressive and unified whole.

Berenson puts greater stress than most estheticians on "ideated" tactile and kinesthetic sensations. His famous books on the paintings of the Italian Renaissance point to features that arouse in the spectator vivid imagined sensations of smoothness, roughness, softness, hardness, thrust or counterthrust, muscular contraction and relaxation. When combined with representational details, these features communicate not only ideated sensations but "life-enhancing" feelings and ideas.[3]

That the medium is nevertheless important is illustrated in the discussion of camera art by Edward Weston (1886–1958), one of America's great photographers. He denounces the folly of using a camera to imitate the work of the painter, and emphasizes the importance of "learning to *see* photographically." One must develop a keen sense of the capacities of photographic tools and processes, such as the color filter, the camera angle, the length of exposure, and the method of developing. Directed by an understanding of his medium, the photographer learns to see things in terms of their potentialities for photographic treatment. He can then use the camera eye "to produce a heightened sense of reality—a kind of superrealism that reveals the vital essences of things."[4] Not only the photographer but also the beholder of his work needs to "see photographically," since his enjoyment depends in part on an appreciation of what the camera can do best.

Allied to photography as an art made possible by modern technology is the motion picture. Arnold Hauser (1892–), Hungarian-born and naturalized British author of *The Social History of Art*, concludes his history with a chapter on "The Film Age." He analyzes the media and forms of expression in recent art, and finds a striking similarity in contemporary film, drama, painting, and fiction. In substance he agrees with Lewis Mumford:

> The moving picture, with its close-ups and synoptic views, with its shifting events and its ever-present camera eye, with its spatial forms always shown through time, with its capacity for representing objects that interpenetrate, and for placing distant environments in immediate juxtaposition—as happens in instantaneous communication—with its ability, finally, to represent subjective elements, distortions, hallucinations, it is today the only art that can represent with any degree of concreteness the emergent world-view that differentiates our culture from every preceding one.[5]

The great significance of the film as an art genre lies in its capacity to represent modern civilization in its full range and complexity. These potentialities are seldom realized because the many individuals involved in film-making—"producers, directors, script-writers, camera men, art-directors and technicians of all kinds"—find it difficult to cooperate to the degree required for the production of masterpieces. In this respect, the making of a film epitomizes the problem of our modern technical society: how to achieve harmony and integration of individual endeavors in an age of extreme specialization.

The dance differs from the arts that we have been discussing in that its primary medium is not some external material such as stone or oil-pigment or film, but the body of the performing artist in motion or rest. Étienne Gilson (1884–), a very distinguished French philosopher, discusses with keen insight the medium of the dance. He points out that "the choice of a body with aptitude for dancing plays the same role and has the same importance as that of any material in any art." Although dancing may be combined with music, pantomime, scenery, and costuming, the true source of its dignity "is to remain faithful to its proper essence, regardless of the multiple alliances into which it may be obliged to enter."

The dance as a spectacle requires of the performer "a particular kind of plastic imagination which enables the individual to see in his mind the exterior aspect of his body in each of its movements and each of its possible attitudes.'" The dancer is aware of tensions and relaxations and other kinesthetic sensations within the body but cannot inspect the outer movements; the spectator is aware of the *outer* appearance of the body but does not experience the inner sensations. Unless the dancer's body-images correspond to objective appearances there will be a painful discrepancy. Hence, the performer must bear in mind the structural similarity of correlated processes in different domains of sense ("isomorphism") so that the experienced kinesthetic sensations may correspond appropriately with the imagined outer show. This isomorphism between different fields of experience is recognized by Susanne Langer and Rudolf Arnheim in their interpretations of expressiveness (see Chapter 8). It is especially relevant to the dance.

The reader can gain greater insight into the varied substance of the arts by studying other selections in this book. Highly illuminating are Gombrich and Shahn on painting, Caudwell on poetry and fiction, Nietzsche and Hegel on tragedy, Greenough on architecture, Mumford on industrial arts, Sessions on music, McHarg on landscape design —not to mention other contributors who discuss particular arts.

In surveying the matter of the arts, we should recognize that the basis of artistic form is already present in the matter. Relations as well as the qualities related are internal and native to the materials. The pitch, timbre, and intensity (degree of loudness) of sound; the hue, saturation, and "brightness" (lightness or darkness) of color; the geometrical properties of lines, surfaces, and masses; and the spatial or temporal extension common to various arts, all afford a natural basis for formal composition or order. The order, in each case, is intrinsic to the elements as such; and one reason that odors, tastes, and tactile qualities are artistically less important than tones and colors is that they lack any intrinsic principle of order, such as pitch or hue.[6]

Notes

1. Bernard Bosanquet, *Three Lecturers on Aesthetic* (Macmillan, London, 1915), pp. 3, 5.

2. Bernard Bosanquet, "Croce's Aesthetic," *Proceedings of the British Academy,* Vol. 9 (1919–1920), p. 272.
3. See, for example, Berenson's analysis of the paintings of Giotto in *The Florentine Painters of the Renaissance* (Putnam, New York, 1896).
4. Edward Weston, "What is Photographic Beauty?" *Camera Craft,* Vol. 46 (1939), p. 254.
5. Lewis Mumford, *Technics and Civilization* (Harcourt, New York, 1934), p. 342.
6. For an excellent discussion of the material basis of form, see David W. Prall, *Aesthetic Analysis* (Crowell, New York, 1936) and Jerome Stolnitz, *Aesthetics and Philosophy of Art Criticism* (Houghton Mifflin, Boston, 1960), Chapter 9: "Matter and Form."

BERNARD BOSANQUET

The Esthetic Attitude in Its Embodiments

Why are there different arts? The simple answer to this question takes us, I believe, to the precise root and source of the whole principle of esthetic expressiveness. . . .

We should begin, I am convinced, from the very simplest facts. Why do artists make different patterns, or treat the same pattern differently, in wood-carving, say, and clay-modeling, and wrought-iron work? If you can answer this question thoroughly, then, I am convinced, you have the secret of the classification of the arts and of the passage of feeling[1] into its esthetic embodiment; that is, in a word, the secret of beauty.

Why, then, in general does a worker in clay make different decorative patterns from a worker in wrought-iron? I wish I could go into this question with illustrations and details, but I will admit at once that I am not really competent to do so, though I have taken very great interest in the problem. But in general there can surely be no doubt of the answer. You cannot make the same things in clay as you can in wrought-iron, except by a *tour de force*. The feeling of the work is, I suppose, altogether different. The metal challenges you, coaxes you, as William Morris said of the molten glass, to do a particular kind of thing with it, where its tenacity and ductility make themselves felt. The clay, again, is delightful, I take it, to handle, to those who have a talent for it; but it is delightful of course in quite different manipulations from those of the wrought-iron. I suppose its facility of surface, how it lends itself to modeling or to throwing on the wheel, must be its great charm. Now the decorative patterns which are carried out in one way or the other may, of course, be suggested *ab extra* by a draughtsman, and have all sorts of properties and interests in themselves as mere lines on paper. But when you come to carry them out in the medium, then, if they are appropriate, or if you succeed in adapting them, they become each a special phase of the embodiment of your whole delight and interest of "body-and-mind" in handling the clay or metal or wood or molten glass. It is alive in your hands, and its life grows or rather magically springs into shapes which it, and you in it, seem to desire and feel inevitable. The feeling for the medium, the sense of what can rightly be done in it only or better than in anything else, and the charm and fascination of doing it so—these, I take it, are the real clue to the fundamental question of esthetics, which is "how feeling and its body are created adequate to one another." It is parallel to the question in general philosophy, "Why the soul has a body." It is the same sort of thing as the theory of the rising mountain,[2] but it is much less open to caprice, being absolute fact all through, and it explains not merely the interpretation of lines and shapes, but the whole range and working of the esthetic imagination in the province of fine art, which is its special province.

To this doctrine belongs the very fruitful modern topic of the relation of beautiful handicraft with the workman's life, as the outcome and expression of his body-and-mind, and amid all the disparagement which the most recent views of art are apt to throw upon Ruskin, we must remember that it was first and foremost to his inspired advocacy that this point of view owes its recognition today, and William Morris, for instance, recognized him, in this respect at least, as his master.

The differences of the great arts then are simply such differences as those between clay-modeling, wood-carving, and wrought-iron work, developed on an enormous scale, and with their inevitable consequences for whole provinces of esthetic imagination.

For this is a fact of the highest importance. Every craftsman, we saw, feels the peculiar delight and enjoys the peculiar capacity of his own medium. This delight and sense of capacity are of course not confined to the moments when he is actually manipulating his work. His fascinated imagination lives in the powers of his medium; he thinks and feels in terms of it; it is the peculiar body of which *his* esthetic imagination and no other is the peculiar soul.

Thus there grow up the distinct traditions, the whole distinctive worlds of imaginative thought and feeling, in which the great imaginative arts have their life and being. . . .

The ideal of every art must be revealed, I take it, in terms of the art itself; and it must be what underlies the whole series of efforts which the artist's imagination has made and is making, to create, in his own medium, an embodied feeling in which he can rest satisfied. It is the world as he has access to it through his art. It may seem to him more than any of his works; but it only has existence in them and in the effort which they imply when taken all together. The danger is to try and make a picture of this effort, apart from any of its achievements, which is really nothing. Then you get the enfeebled ideal, which means the omission of all character and individuality.

Now let us take a particular case. If our view of the distinction and connection of the arts is right, and it is simply a question of the medium adopted by each, and the capacities of that medium as proved by experience, what is to be said of the distinctive character of *poetry?* It seems in a sense to have almost no material element, to work directly with significant ideas in which the objects of the imagination are conveyed. Language is so transparent, that it disappears, so to speak, into its own meaning, and we are left with no characteristic medium at all.

I do not think there can be any doubt about the true attitude here. Poetry, like the other arts, has a physical or at least a sensuous medium, and this medium is sound. It is, however, significant sound, uniting inseparably in itself the factors of formal expression through an immediate pattern, and of representation through the meanings of language, exactly as sculpture and painting deal at once and in the same vision both with formal patterns and with significant shapes. That language is a physical fact with its own properties and qualities is easily seen by comparing different tongues, and noting the form which different patterns, such as sapphic or hexameter verse, necessarily receive in different languages, such as Greek and Latin. To make poetry in different languages, for example, in French and German, is as different a task as to make decorative work in clay and iron. The sound, meter, and meaning are the same inseparable product in a poem as much as the color, form, and embodied feeling in a picture. And it is only an illusion to suppose that because you have significant sentences in poetry, therefore you are dealing with meanings which remain the same outside the poem, any more than a tree or a person whom you think you recognize in a picture, is, as you know them at home so to speak, *the* tree or *the* person *of* the picture. Poetry no more keeps its meaning when turned into corresponding prose, than a picture or a sonata keeps its meaning in the little analyses they print in the catalogues or programs.

Shelley, according to Professor Bradley, had a feeling of the kind referred to. Poetry seemed to him to deal with a perfectly apt and transparent medium, with no qualities of its own, and therefore approaching to being no medium at all, but created out of nothing by the imagination for the use of the imagination. While the media employed by the other arts, being gross and physical and having independent qualities of their own, seemed to him rather obstacles in the way of expression than apt instruments of it. The answer to such a view is what we have just given.

It is the qualities of the media which give them the capacity to serve as embodiments of feeling; and sonorous language, the medium of poetry, has its peculiarities and definite capacities precisely like the others.

Here, I cannot but think, we are obliged to part company, with some regret, from Benedetto Croce. He is possessed, as so often is the case with him, by a fundamental truth, so intensely that he seems incapable of apprehending what more is absolutely necessary to its realization. Beauty, he sees, is for the mind and in the mind. A physical thing, supposed unperceived and unfelt, cannot be said in the full sense to possess beauty. But he forgets throughout, I must think, that though feeling is necessary to its embodiment, yet also the embodiment is necessary to feeling. To say that because beauty implies a mind, therefore it is an internal state, and its physical embodiment is something secondary and incidental, and merely brought into being for the sake of permanence and communication

—this seems to me a profound error of principle, a false idealism. It meets us, however, throughout Croce's system, according to which "intuition"—the inward vision of the artist—is the only true expression. External media, he holds, are, strictly speaking, superfluous, so that there is no meaning in distinguishing between one mode of expression and another (as between paint and musical sound and language). Therefore there can be no classification of the arts, and no fruitful discussion of what can better be done by one art than by another. And esthetic—the philosophy of expression—is set down as all one with linguistic—the philosophy of speech. For there is no meaning in distinguishing between language in the sense of speech, and other modes of expression. Of course, if he had said that speech is not the only form of language, but that every art speaks to us in a language of its own, that would have had much to be said for it. But I do not gather that that is his intention.

His notion is not a new one among theorists. It really is deeply rooted in a philosophical blunder. No doubt it seems obvious, when once pointed out, that things are not all there, not complete in all qualities, except when they are appreciated in a mind. And then, having rightly observed that this is so, we are apt to go on and say that you have them complete, and have all you want of them, if you have them before your mind and have not the things in bodily presence at all. But the blunder is, to think that you can have them completely before your mind without having their bodily presence at all. And because of this blunder, it seems fine and "ideal" to say that the artist operates in the bodiless medium of pure thought or fancy, and that the things of the bodily world are merely physical causes of sensation, which do not themselves enter into the effects he uses. It is rather a natural thing to say about poetry, because we discount the physical side of language. We glance at its words and do not sound them. And Shelley, as we saw, says something very like that.

But at the very beginning of all this notion, as we said, there is a blunder. Things, it is true, are not complete without minds, but minds, again, are not complete without things; not any more, we might say, than minds are complete without bodies. Our resources in the way of sensation, and our experiences in the way of satisfactory and unsatisfactory feeling, are all of them won out of our intercourse with things, and are thought and imagined by us as qualities and properties of the things. Especially we see this in music. Here we have an art entirely made up of a material—musical tone—which one may say does not exist at all in the natural world, and is altogether originated by our inventive and imaginative manipulation of physical things, pressing on in the line of creative discovery which something very like accident must at first have opened up to us.[3] Apart from this imaginative operation upon physical things, our fancy in the realm of music could have done as good as nothing.

And in principle it is the same with all the arts. All the material and the physical process which the artist uses—take our English language as used in poetry for an example—has been elaborated and refined, and, so to speak, consecrated by ages of adaptation and application in which it has been fused and blended with feeling—and it carries the life-blood of all this endeavor in its veins; and that is how, as we have said over and over again, feelings get their embodiment, and embodiments get their feeling. If you try to cut the thought and fancy loose from the body of the stuff in which it molds its pictures and poetic ideas and musical constructions, you impoverish your fancy, and arrest its growth, and reduce it to a bloodless shade. When I pronounce even a phrase so commonplace in itself as "rule, Britannia!" the actual vibrations of the sound, the bodily experience I am aware of in saying it, is alive with the history of England which passed into the words in the usage and formation of the language. Up to a certain point, language is poetry ready-made for us.

And I suppose that a great painter, in his actual handling of his brush, has present with him a sense of meaning and fitness which is one with the joy of execution, both of which the experience of a lifetime has engrained in the co-operation of his hand and eye. I take it, there is a pleasure in the brush stroke, which *is also* a sense of success in the use of the medium, and of meaning in hitting the exact effect which he wants to get. We common people have something analogous to all this, when we enjoy the too-rare sensation of having found the right word. In such "finding" there is a creative element. A word is, quite strictly speaking, not used twice in the same sense.

Croce says, indeed, that the artist has every stroke of the brush in his mind as complete before he executes it as after. The suggestion is that using the brush adds nothing to his inward or mental work of art. I think that this is false idealism. The bodily thing adds immensely to the mere idea and fancy, in wealth of qualities and connections. If we try to cut out the bodily side of our world, we shall find that we have reduced the mental side to a mere nothing.

And so, when we said that you can carry away the soul of a thing and leave its body behind, we always added that you must in doing so confer its soul upon a new and spiritualized body.[4] Your imagination must be an imagination of something, and if you refuse to give that something a definate structure, you pass from the esthetic semblance to the region of abstract thought. I have spoken of sound as physical; if this is a difficulty it is enough to call it sensuous, and sensuous in immediate connection with other physical properties and experiences. This applies both to music and to language.

All this later argument of ours, starting from the importance of medium and technique, has aimed at exhibiting in detail the double process of creation and contemplation which is implied in the esthetic attitude, and the impossibility of separating one factor of it from another. And it is the same question as that stated in other words, how a feeling can be got into an object. This is the central problem of the esthetic attitude; and, as we have seen, the best material for solving it for us who are not great artists comes from any minor experience we may have at command in which we have been aware of the outgoing of feeling into expression. We must think not merely of the picture in the gallery or the statue in the museum, but of the song and the dance, the dramatic reading, the entering into music, or the feel of the material in the minor arts, or simply, of the creative discovery of the right word.

The festal or social view of art will help us here. Suppose a tribe or a nation has won a great victory; "they are feeling big, and they want to make something big," as I have heard an expert say. That, I take it, is the rough account of the beginning of the esthetic attitude. And according to their capacity and their stage of culture, they may make a pile of their enemies' skulls, or they may build the Parthenon. The point of the esthetic attitude lies in the adequate fusion of body and soul, where the soul is a feeling, and the body its expression, without residue on either side.

—*Three Lectures on Æsthetic* (1915)

Notes

1. What Bosanquet means by "feeling" and by "body-and-mind," terms which appear several times in the pages here reproduced, is made clear by the following quotation from the Preface to his book: "I must appear unfortunate in having laid so much stress on 'feeling,' just when high authorities are expressing a doubt whether the word has any meaning at all. . . . I can only say here that the first and main thing which the word suggests to me is the concernment of the whole 'body-and-mind,' as Plato puts it in building up his account of psychical unity on the single sentence, 'The man has a pain in his finger' [*Republic*, 462 D]. It is the whole man, the 'body-and-mind,' who has the pain, and in it is one, though it is referred to the finger and localized there. When a 'body-and-mind' is, as a whole, in any experience, that is the chief feature, I believe, of what we mean by feeling. Think of him as he sings, or loves, or fights. When he is one, I believe it is always through feeling, whatever distinctions may supervene upon it. That unity, at all events, is the main thing the word conveys to me."

2. See the account of empathy by Vernon Lee in *The Beautiful* (1913). (Editor.)

3. This applies even to the development of song, so far as that involves a musical system.

4. This sentence refers back to an idea developed in a preceding part of Bosanquet's lecture, namely, that "the real sting of even the crudest glorification of copying is this wonder that you can carry off with you a thing's soul, and leave its body behind." (Editor.)

BERNARD BERENSON

Materials and Techniques

A little later than the Romantic revolt against cold-storage classicism, a movement was started to deduce standards from materials and techniques, as for example wood, stone, clay, gold, bronze, and textiles; or pigments and varnishes—in short, the raw materials and the technical devices that served in the production of the artifact or work of art.

Instead of considering the materials as we consider the rest of matter, as lifeless and inert until moved and given life by mind, the following doctrine, that still has its adherents, was preached: not that the artist must make the best possible use of materials in order to pursue his end, but that the end itself was inspired and directed by and not merely fashioned out of the materials. All the artist had to do, we were given to understand, was to let himself be guided by the nature as well as the caprices of the materials, to the exclusion of other interests. The means, that is to say the materials, not only justified the end; but by their own volition, as it were, by their own potential, created the end.

Thus in textiles, the degree of flexibility or slipperiness or brittleness of the fibers; in wood the grain, the knots, the pliableness, the splinteriness; in ivory and bone the same nearly; in metals their ductility, their malleability; in minerals and stones of all kinds, the crystallization, the density, the hardness, the resistance to fire and frost, to the hammer, to the chisel, to the saw, were qualities that decided the value of a work of art done in these materials. If art obeyed the exigencies of the same material, submitted to its resistances and caprices, the result was perfect; and if not, it was a failure.

In a negative sense this is so. It is obvious that material will not yield its best to the artificer who does it violence, or ignores its caprices. He must not work against the grain of the wood or ivory or fail to take account of the knots. He will on the contrary take advantage of them and turn them to profit as Chinese and Japanese and Gothic carvers have done, as the Maoris with their canoes and their oars, and the Tlinkits with their grease dishes. If he insists on giving the same edge to porphyry or granite as he gets out of limestone or marble, he fritters away the specific qualities of concentrated density, hardness, and impenetrability that we enjoy in Egyptian statuary and late antique sculpture, with its fat contours and sagging shapes, or in the porphyry sarcophagi in the Vatican and in Constantinople.

Yet, except in unrepresentative *objets d'art*, the material has counted for so little that until the Renaissance and its discovery of an antiquity, whether in ruins of architecture or in fragments of statuary, that had been discolored by time and weather, buildings were coated with paint; and sculpture was tinted when not fully colored. When Praxiteles was asked which of his own marbles he preferred, he answered: "Those that Nicias colored." As late as the fifteenth century, painters as distinguished as Jean Malouel were employed to polychrome Sluter's calvary, now known as "Puits de Moïse" in the Chartreuse near Dijon. And let me quote Huizinga in the *Waning of the Middle Ages* (p. 235) on these same sculptures: "The pedestals were green, the mantles of the prophets were gilt, their tunics red and azure with golden stars. Isaiah wore a dress of gold cloth. The open spaces were filled with golden suns and initials. The pride of blazonry displayed itself not only round the columns below the figures, but on the cross itself, which was entirely gilt. . . . As a crowning *bizarrerie* a pair of spectacles of gilded brass . . . were placed on Jeremiah's nose." On the surviving figures no trace of all this colored splendor remains.

Statues never exposed to the air nor painted by hand, like those of the twelfth century at Étampes, look raw as if wanting a skin. The same may be said of the architectural carvings lately dug up at Sarsina, inland from Cesena, which were overwhelmed by landslide some two thousand years ago before stucco and color covered up the edginess of the raw stone.

Ivory and bone even of the finest grain were likewise painted. As for bronzes in the Greek world, they were burnished like brass, or gilded over, or so thickly varnished that their real substance was unrecognizable.[1] In all probability the Parthenon columns were polychromed with ultramarine and vermilion, as in later times were Romanesque and Gothic porches. These various procedures made it impossible for the specific material to count in the effect. Moreover, in no visual representation do we perceive that design, shape, or even form is modified by difference of material more than is strictly required by their nature. A figure or group in Egyptian or Greek, Romanesque, Gothic, or Renaissance art changes but slightly in obedience to the material in which it is produced, whether wood or ivory, bronze, marble, or baked clay, and does not change at all as it should if the materials decided the shapes and their grouping.

Or take the Greek vase of about 480 B.C. I can detect no connection between the humble clay out of which it is formed and its "Attic shape," adorned with figures of more functional line, of more subtle contour than later draughtmanship ever achieved.

In central Asia and the Far East it is the same; although the so-called "animal style" has even less regard for actual shapes than the most surrealist painters of to-day. The Kozlev expedition of 1924 in Northern Mongolia unearthed objects in wood, in bone, in metals, and in wool as well. In all of them the same patterns, the same distortions prevail, regardless of the material.

Not only in the figure arts and the "fine arts," but in architecture itself, few Italian Renaissance churches or palaces depend for their quality on materials. Many a Florentine building, courtyard, cloister, and hall is stuccoed without, whitewashed within, with no more precious material showing than the grey stone of the columns and stone of finer grain for the capitals and jambs of doors and window frames. All else is a matter of space, of proportions, that is to say of tact, of taste—of trained mind, in short.

Material counts most where its nature is least liable to disguise and concealment. This could occur only in mosaic, in jewelry, in enamels, in glazed ceramics, in glass, and in small *objets d'art* of various kinds and climes. Even the tiniest fragments of Alexandrian glass afford feasts of translucent color that nothing can surpass, not even Christian mosaics, let alone Hellenistic, Sassanian, and Persian textiles. The fascination of an *objet d'art* like the small round dish in dark hard stone, inlaid with little fishes in gold, from the treasury of St. Denis, now in the Louvre, cannot be described. It is as if in the palm of the hand you held night with its constellations. In the same Salle d'Apollon where this small dish is exhibited may be seen an equally small, or even smaller, thirteenth-century Limoges enamel, the material beauty of which would be far more appreciated if the treatment of the subject did not absorb one's attention. Not even Giotto himself or any other artist painting the same subject, St. Francis preaching to the birds, has treated it more poetically.

And who shall say what was the effect of that paradoxically colossal *objet d'art*, the Great Pyramid! Even twenty-five hundred years after it was built, when Herodotus described its coating of highly polished monoliths each at least thirty feet long, daintily joined, with its tip of dazzling electrium, it must have shone under the Egyptian firmament like a mirror reflecting sunrises, sunsets, and rare clouds.

Abundance of a given material and the want of others may inspire artists to get the utmost effect out of its use. Thus, Armenian architects surpassed their Byzantine models because they had at hand plentiful supplies of suitable stone, as did the designers of the gem-like yet noble palaces of the Grand Masters of Malta, or the charmingly tasteful villas leading to the Ombla near Ragusa and those at Risan on the way to Cattaro. On the other hand, Lecce offers a sad example of the misuse of a too-yielding material.

The wood carving of the Northmen, first on their ships and later on their church porches, is easily accounted for by the quality of the wood from forest trees appreciated and exploited by gifted artisans. This no doubt was the case also with the Maoris, who, however, must have valued their wood all the more since, unlike the Northmen's ships and porches, their carvings do not seem to have been completed by painting.

In picture painting there is much talk of materials, of resins and oils, of emulsions, and varnishes, and above all of tempera.

Van Eyck, Antonello, Titian, Rubens, Velásquez, Rembrandt all had an adequate technique. Masaccio was as great as any of them; but who talks of his technique? Antonello's technique was masterly, but what did he do with it before 1475? Little till that date. Then, under the influence of Giovanni Bellini, he became the artist who, in the three or four years of life left him, painted not only his arresting and convincing portraits but the sublime "Pietà" of the Correr Museum, and the nobly magnificent Dresden "St. Sebastian." As for Giovanni Bellini's technique, it consists of uniform little brush-strokes that solicit no attention.

I am not insensitive to the beauty of a well-preserved tempera or oil surface. In the company of two of the most passionate technicians that ever came my way, with the persuasive Roger Fry and the far more subtle, penetrating, and serious Denman Ross, I have been thrilled by the quality of a tempera like the Sassettesque panel in Berlin representing the youthful St. Francis hearing mass, or of an oil like Vermeer's "Painter and Model," of the Czernin collection in Vienna. Unfortunately, few paintings preserve their original color and surface long enough to be enjoyable in themselves or to give a correct idea of what they were like when they left the artist's hand. Not only is painted color apt to undergo deterioration, notoriously so in the blues used by Italian masters, but the surface gets covered over with repeated varnishings that rot and darken—not to speak of deliberate repainting. By now, pictures that are centuries old seldom retain much likeness to their original state. Witness Tintoretto canvases at S. Rocco, most later Rembrandts, many Sir Joshuas, and paintings as recent as

Sargent's, besides nearly all Dutch landscapes whose original vivid greens are now horn-colored. Far from enjoying the material of a picture, the spectator gets only as it were a rouged and repainted skin concealing the corruption beneath. When attempts are made to get rid of this dirt and varnish and repaint, the amateur is outraged, and as in the recent case of a well-cleaned portrait in the Louvre, there rose an outcry of "*on l'a ruiné, mon Rembrandt*"; and no less indignation was expressed a little while ago over the restoration to its original character of a Velásquez in the London National Gallery. We have got as much inured to discolored pictures as to colorless sculptures, and for the same reason, namely, that we almost never see a work in either art that still looks as it did when it was fresh. When, by a miracle, a painting has retained its freshness, as is the case with a Catena "Annunciation" at Capri, it offends our present taste; and under the Tintoretto "Crucifixion" at S. Rocco there is a piece of canvas folded back and never exposed to the light, which is much closer to a Renoir than to any sixteenth-century Venetian in its present state.

Material and technique—I often wonder what they are. Sculpture is carving a solid, we are told, and painting the application of a design to a surface. It follows from these definitions that Ghiberti's "Gates of Paradise" and Filarete's bronze doors of St. Peter's are sculpture. To my eye they are as much painting as any done by their Quattrocento contemporaries. Nor are Donatello's Santo reliefs in Padua sculptural in the sense that the Olympian metopes, the Parthenon marbles, and the Attic tomb-reliefs are sculptural. As for his last works, I cannot believe that their being in clay or bronze makes them so different from the last Rembrandts done with pigments. The Dutch "painter" has ever so much more in common with the Florentine "'sculptor," of whose existence he may have never heard, than with any predecessor in his own craft, whether in the Netherlands or in Italy.

Or take the figures nielloed with silver on the bronze doors of San Michele al Gargano. They are drawn as sinuously, as functionally as an Antonio Pollaiuolo. Must we call them sculpture? And the contemporary eleventh-century enamels, the emperors and empresses, court ladies and gentlemen arrayed in their robes of splendor, fabricated with jewelled purity or color by the craftsmen of Constantinople—what are they but pictures in miniature exactly like those in illuminated manuscripts of the same date and place, but done in materials and with a technique surpassing every possibility of gem-like refulgence that painting with pigments could produce?

Writing at the end of one of the most fruitful periods of art creation our world has known, Vasari, the Herodotus of art history, calls his book the story of the arts of design. By this he did not understand, as we do, design only in the sense of composition or pattern, but, as the Italian language permits, of drawing as well. To the Renaissance artist, draughtsmanship was the basis of all the visual arts, and it was a matter of circumstance, command, or compulsion that led him to practise one art and not the other, as was notably the case with Verrocchio, Pollaiuolo, and Michelangelo.

At times I go further and ask whether the artist's materials do not consist of mind rather than matter. I mean mind in the sense of ideas and problems. The artist lives on these. The rest is a question of ways and means, whether it be as material or technique. The creator is he who, like Masaccio, starts a problem and speeds it towards a solution, or he who, like Michelangelo, finds a solution. Masaccio's technique, as I have already observed, excites no interest, nor does Michelangelo's. Although the latter confessed to having no practice in fresco, no achievements in this technique have equalled the ceiling of the Sistine Chapel. Have any approached it? Perhaps not even Giotto, not even Masaccio. Michelangelo's hand is so indifferent to material and technique, that his chisel-stroke has the same calligraphy—as it were—as his pen-stroke, or whatever other medium he used in drawing. I contemplate, therefore, a less obvious and more significant classification of the arts than can be derived from the materials and techniques employed, a more psychological, more metaphysical, and less materialistic one. Let me in this connection add a note jotted down in March 1907, which reads as follows: "The material of each art is not its medium, but the life-enhancing ideated sensations of which it is compounded."

Earlier in this discussion it was allowed as something obvious, and indisputable, that the artist must never go against the nature of his materials or his technique, but on the contrary must take advantage of their idiosyncrasies and resistances. These present themselves as problems to be solved and thereby serve as a stimulus. As a matter of history, when the artist becomes master of a material or a technique to the degree that it can no longer oppose any resistance, it ceases to inspire him. He is left without a problem and does not know what to turn to, as has been the case again and again in the course of history, and as seems to be the case now. For want of problems he yawns and gesticulates and boasts, but does not create.

In other words, technique is an auxiliary stimulus, but never a creator of art. Art can use a certain technique when the problem of form requires it. Until then, art will ignore it as the centuries preceding the Van Eycks ignored oils, although well acquainted with them. On the other hand, when the problem is urgent, it invents the necessary technique.

Materials, technique, and colors also count more and more as creative genius disappears, as draughtsmanship is neglected and the figure arts decline. The men of mere craft survive to adorn temples and habitations that depend for their effect on the color and semiprecious stones and mosaics. These constructions are reduced to *objets d'art* enjoyed for the intrinsic beauty of the materials and for what the artificer is allowed to extract from the materials with the least mental effort. Other mere artificers fabricate jewelry consisting of childish settings of triangles and lozenges inlaid with coral, with turquoises, with garnets, pastes, and colored glass. The preference for the last was destined to conquer our world from Cádiz to Calcutta and to survive in the Near East till our own day, in the shape particularly of windows and doors filled with panes of screaming blue and ruby and yellow glass.

Thus, neither materials nor techniques offer standards for the application and evaluation of the figure arts, much as they may interest students of crafts that never rise above being minor arts, and easily decline to the products of gipsy coppersmiths.

It is deplorable that we no longer make a sharp division between the fine arts and the minor arts. That is a distinction resting solely on the illustrative elements and on those elements chiefly which deal with the human figure. Indeed, the fine arts may be best described as those whose principal concern is the human figure.

If you would understand what it is for materials and instruments to count, listen to music. There the sounds elicited by wood, or brass, or string tell in every note. In comparison, the effect produced in the visual arts by even the most favorable and undisguisable material is small indeed.

The enjoyment of materials and also the enjoyment of color is perhaps more in the nature of actual than of ideated sensations. This may be the reason why indulgence in the virtues of materials leads to an indifference first to form and then to representation, ending with a preference for artifacts, while those finally are cherished most which sacrifice most to displaying the character of the material.

Hence, no doubt, the present cult of Byzantine coins and enamels as well of barbarian jewelry, and of certain early Christian artifacts—a cult I cannot help practicing myself, although with a bad conscience.

—*Aesthetics and History in the Visual Arts* (1948)

Note

1. And now in 1946, while the "Gates of Paradise" and the other bronze doors of the Florentine Baptistry are being cleaned, it turns out that they were massively gilded. Ghiberti in his memoirs does not mention this, which proves that it was still common practice.

EDWARD WESTON

Seeing Photographically

Each medium of expression imposes its own limitations on the artist—limitations inherent in the tools, materials, or processes he employs. In the older art forms these natural confines are so well established they are taken for granted. We select music or dancing, sculpture or writing because we feel that within the *frame* of that particular medium we can best express whatever it is we have to say.

The Photo-Painting Standard

Photography, although it has passed its hundredth birthday, has yet to attain such familiarization. In order to understand why this is so, we must examine briefly the historical background of this youngest of the graphic arts. Because the early photographers who sought to produce creative work had no tradition to guide them, they soon began to borrow a ready-made one from the painters. The conviction grew that photography was just a new kind of painting, and its exponents attempted by every means possible to make the camera produce painter-like results. This misconception was responsible for a great many horrors perpetrated in the name of art, from allegorical costume pieces to dizzying out of focus blurs.

But these alone would not have sufficed to set back the photographic clock. The real harm lay in the fact that the false standard became firmly established, so that the goal of artistic endeavor became photo-painting rather than photography. The approach adopted was so at variance with the real nature of the medium employed that each basic improvement in the process became just one more obstacle for the photo-painters to overcome. Thus the influence of the painters' tradition delayed recognition of the real creative field photography had provided. Those who should have been most concerned with discovering and exploiting the new pictorial resources were ignoring them entirely, and in their preoccupation with producing pseudo-paintings, departing more and more radically from all photographic values.

As a consequence, when we attempt to assemble the best work of the past, we most often choose examples from the work of those who were not primarily concerned with esthetics. It is in commercial portraits from the daguerreotype era, records of the Civil War, documents of the American frontier, the work of amateurs and professionals who practiced photography for its own sake without troubling over whether or not it was art, that we find photographs that will still stand with the best of contemporary work.

But in spite of such evidence that can now be appraised with a calm, historical eye, the approach to creative work in photography today is frequently just as muddled as it was eighty years ago, and the painters' tradition still persists, as witness the use of texture screens, handwork on negatives, and ready-made rules of composition. People who wouldn't think of taking a sieve to the well to draw water fail to see the folly in taking a camera to make a painting.

Behind the photo-painter's approach lay the fixed idea that a straight photograph was purely the product of a machine and therefore not art. He developed special techniques to combat the mechanical nature of his process. In his system the negative was taken as a point of departure—a first rough impression to be "improved" by hand until the last traces of its unartistic origin had disappeared.

Perhaps if singers banded together in sufficient numbers, they could convince musicians that the sounds they produced through *their machines* could not be art because of the essentially mechanical nature of their instruments. Then the musician, profiting by the example of the photo-painter, would have his playing recorded on special discs so that he could unscramble and rescramble the sounds until he had transformed the product of a good musical instrument into a poor imitation of the human voice!

To understand why such an approach is incompatible with the logic of the medium, we must recognize the two basic factors in the photographic process that set it apart from the other graphic arts: the nature of the recording process and the nature of the image.

Nature of the Recording Process

Among all the arts photography is unique by reason of its instantaneous recording process. The sculptor, the architect, the composer all have the possibility of making changes in, or additions to, their original plans while their work is in the process of execution. A composer may build up a symphony over a long period of time; a painter may spend a lifetime working on one picture and still not consider it finished. But the photographer's recording process cannot be drawn out. Within its brief duration, no stopping or changing or reconsidering is possible. When he uncovers his lens every detail within its field of vision is registered in far less time than it takes for his own eyes to transmit a similar copy of the scene to his brain.

Nature of the Image

The image that is thus swiftly recorded possesses certain qualities that at once distinguish it as photographic. First there is the amazing precision of definition, especially in the recording of fine detail; and second, there is the unbroken sequence of infinitely subtle gradations from black to white. These two characteristics constitute the trade-mark of the photograph; they pertain to the mechanics of the process and cannot be duplicated by any work of the human hand.

The photographic image partakes more of the nature of a mosaic than of a drawing or painting. It contains no *lines* in the painter's sense, but is entirely made up of tiny particles. The extreme fineness of these particles gives a special tension to the image, and when that tension is destroyed—by the intrusion of handwork, by too great enlargement, by printing on a rough surface, etc.—the integrity of the photograph is destroyed.

Finally, the image is characterized by lucidity and brilliance of tone, qualities which cannot be retained if prints are made on dull-surface papers. Only a smooth, light-giving surface can reproduce satisfactorily the brilliant clarity of the photographic image.

Recording the Image

It is these two properties that determine the basic procedure in the photographer's approach. Since the recording process is instantaneous, and the nature of the image such that it cannot survive corrective handwork, it is obvious that *the finished print must be created in full before the film is exposed.* Until the photographer has learned to visualize his final result in advance, and to predetermine the procedures necessary to carry out that visualization, his finished work (if it be photography at all) will represent a series of lucky—or unlucky—mechanical accidents.

Hence the photographer's most important and likewise most difficult task is not learning to manage his camera, or to develop, or to print. It is learning to *see photographically*—that is, learning to see his subject matter in terms of the capacities of his tools and processes, so that he can instantaneously translate the elements and values in a scene before him into the photograph he wants to make. The photo-painters used to contend that photography could never be an art because there was in the process no means for controlling the result. Actually, the problem of learning to see photographically would be simplified if there were fewer means of control than there are.

By varying the position of his camera, his camera angle, or the focal length of his lens, the photographer can achieve an infinite number of varied compositions with a single, stationary subject. By changing the light on the subject, or by using a color filter, any or all of the values in the subject can be altered. By varying the length of exposure, the kind of emulsion, the method of developing, the photographer can vary the registering of relative values in the negative. And the relative values as registered in the negative can be further modified by allowing more or less light to affect certain parts of the image in printing. Thus, within the limits of his medium, without resorting to any method of control that is not photographic (i.e., of an optical or chemical nature), the photographer can depart from literal recording to whatever extent he chooses.

This very richness of control facilities often acts as a barrier to creative work. The fact is that relatively few photographers ever master their medium. Instead they allow the medium to master them and go on an endless squirrel cage chase from new lengths to new paper to new developer to new gadget, never staying with one piece of equipment long enough to learn its full capacities, becoming lost in a maze of technical information that is of little or no use since they don't know what to do with it.

Only long experience will enable the photographer to subordinate technical considerations to pictorial aims, but the task can be made immeasurably easier by selecting the simplest possible equipment and procedures and staying with them. Learning to see in terms of the field of one lens, the scale of one film and one paper, will accomplish a good deal more than gathering a smattering of knowledge about several different sets of tools.

The photographer must learn from the outset to regard his process as a whole. He should not be concerned with the "right exposure," the "perfect negative," etc. Such notions are mere products of advertising mythology. Rather he must learn the kind of negative necessary to produce a given kind of print, and then the kind of exposure and development necessary to produce that negative. When he knows how these needs are fulfilled for one kind of print, he must learn how to vary the process to produce other kinds of prints. Further he must learn to translate colors into their monochrome values, and learn to judge the strength and quality of light. With practice this kind of knowledge becomes intuitive; the photographer learns to see a scene or object in terms of his finished print without having to give conscious thought to the steps that will be necessary to carry it out.

Subject Matter and Composition

So far we have been considering the mechanics of photographic seeing. Now let us see how this camera-vision applies to the fields of subject matter and composition. No sharp line can be drawn between the subject matter appropriate to photography and that more suitable to the other graphic arts. However, it is possible, on the basis of an examination of past work and our knowledge of the special properties of the medium, to suggest certain fields of endeavor that will most reward the photographer, and to indicate others that he will do well to avoid.

Even if produced with the finest photographic technique, the work of the photo-painters referred to could not have been successful. Photography is basically too honest a medium for recording superficial aspects of a subject. It searches out the actor behind the make-up and exposes the contrived, the trivial, the artificial, for what they really are. But the camera's innate honesty can hardly be considered a limitation of the medium, since it bars only that kind of subject matter that properly belongs to the painter. On the other hand it provides the photographer with a means of looking deeply into the nature of things, and presenting his subjects in terms of their basic reality. It enables him to reveal the essence of what lies before his lens with such clear insight that the beholder may find the recreated image more real and comprehensible than the actual object.

It is unfortunate, to say the least, that the tremendous capacity photography has for revealing new things in new ways should be overlooked or ignored by the majority of its exponents—but such is the case. Today the waning influence of the painter's tradition, has been replaced by what we may call *Salon Psychology*, a force that is exercising the same restraint over photographic progress by establishing false standards and discouraging any symptoms of original creative vision.

Today's photographer need not necessarily make his picture resemble a wash drawing in order to have it admitted as art, but he must abide by "the rules of composition." That is the contemporary nostrum. Now to consult rules of composition before making a picture is a little like consulting the law of gravitation before going for a walk. Such rules and laws are deduced from the accomplished fact; they are the products of reflection and after-examination, and are in no way a part of the creative impetus. When subject matter is forced to fit into preconceived patterns, there can be no freshness of vision. Following rules of composition can only lead to a tedious repetition of pictorial clichés.

Good composition is only the strongest way of seeing the subject. It cannot be taught because, like all creative effort, it is a matter of personal growth. In common with other artists the photographer wants his finished print to convey to others his own response to his subject. In the fulfillment of this aim, his greatest asset is the directness of the process he employs.

But this advantage can only be retained if he simplifies his equipment and technique to the minimum necessary, and keeps his approach free from all formula, art-dogma, rules, and taboos. Only then can he be free to put his photographic sight to use in discovering and revealing the nature of the world he lives in.

—*The Complete Photographer*, Vol. 9 (1943)

ARNOLD HAUSER

The Film Age

The crisis of the psychological novel is perhaps the most striking phenomenon in the new literature. The works of Kafka and Joyce are no longer psychological novels in the sense that the great novels of the nineteenth century were. In Kafka, psychology is replaced by a kind of mythology, and in Joyce, although the psychological analyses are perfectly accurate, just as the details in a surrealistic picture are absolutely true to nature, there are not only no heroes, in the sense of a psychological center, but also no particular psychological sphere in the totality of being. The depsychologization of the novel already begins with Proust, who, as the greatest master of the analysis of feelings and thoughts, marks the summit of the psychological novel, but also represents the incipient displacement of the soul in the balance of reality. For, since the whole of existence has become merely the content of the consciousness, and things acquire their significance purely and simply through a spiritual medium by which they are experienced, there can no longer be any question here of psychology as understood by Stendhal, Balzac, Flaubert, George Eliot, Tolstoy, or Dostoevsky. In the novel of the nineteenth century, the soul and character of man are seen as the opposite pole to the world of physical reality, and psychology as the conflict between the subject and object, the self and the nonself, the human spirit and the external world. This psychology ceases to be predominant in Proust. He is not concerned so much with the characterization of the individual personality, although he is an ardent portraitist and caricaturist, as with the analysis of the spiritual mechanism as an ontological phenomenon. His work is a "Summa" not merely in the familiar sense of containing a total picture of modern society, but also because it describes the whole spiritual apparatus of modern man with all his inclinations, instincts, talents, automatisms, rationalisms, and irrationalisms. Joyce's *Ulysses* is therefore the direct continuation of the Proustian novel; we are here confronted literally with an encyclopedia of modern civilization, as reflected in the tissue of the motifs which make up the content of a day in the life of a great city. This day is the protagonist of the novel. The flight from the plot is followed by the flight from the hero. Instead of a flood of events, Joyce describes a flood of ideas and associations, instead of an individual hero, a stream of consciousness, and an unending, uninterrupted inner monologue. The emphasis lies everywhere on the uninterruptedness of the movement, the "heterogeneous continuum," the kaleidoscopic picture of a disintegrated world. The Bergsonian concept of time undergoes a new interpretation, an intensification, and a deflection. The accent is now on the simultaneity of the contents of consciousness, the immanence of the past in the present, the constant flowing together of the different periods of time, the amorphous fluidity of inner experience, the boundlessness of the stream of time by which the soul is borne along, the relativity of space and time—that is to say, the impossibility of differentiating and defining the media in which the mind moves. In this new conception of time, almost all the strands of the texture which form the stuff of modern art converge: the abandonment of the plot, the elimination of the hero, the relinquishing of psychology, the "automatic method of writing" and, above all, the montage technique and the intermingling of temporal and spatial forms of the film. The new concept of time, whose basic element is simultaneity and whose nature consists in the spatialization of the temporal element, is expressed in no other genre so impressively as in this youngest art, which dates from the same period as Bergson's philosophy of time. The agreement between the technical methods of the film and the characteristics of the new concept of time is so complete that one has the feeling that the time categories of modern art altogether must have arisen from the spirit of cinematic form, and one is inclined to consider the film itself as the stylistically most representative, though qualitatively perhaps not the most fertile, genre of contemporary art.

The theatre is in many respects the artistic medium most similar to the film; particularly in view of its combination of spatial and temporal forms, it represents the only real analogy to the film. But what happens on the stage is partly spatial, partly temporal; as a rule spatial and temporal, but never a mixture of the spatial and the temporal, as are the happenings in a film. The most fundamental difference between the film and the other arts is that, in its world-picture, the boundaries of space and time are fluid—space has a quasi-temporal, time, to some extent, a spatial character. In the plastic arts, as also on the stage, space remains static, motionless, unchanging, without a goal and without a direction; we move about quite freely in it, because it is homogeneous in all its parts and because none of the parts presupposes the other temporally. The phases of the movement are not stages, not steps in a gradual development; their sequence is subject to no constraint. Time in literature—above all, in the drama—on the other hand, has a definite direction, a trend of development, an objective goal, independent of the spectator's experience of time; it is no mere reservoir, but an ordered succession. Now, these dramaturgical categories of space and time have their character and functions completely altered in the film. Space loses its static quality, its serene passivity, and now becomes dynamic; it comes into being as it were before our eyes. It is fluid, unlimited, unfinished, an element with its own history, its own scheme and process of development. Homogeneous physical space here assumes the characteristics of heterogeneously composed historical time. In this medium the individual stages are no longer of the same kind, the individual parts of space no longer of equal value; it contains specially qualified positions, some with a certain priority in the development and others signifying the culmination of the spatial experience. The use of the close-ups, for example, not only has spatial criteria, it also represents a phase to be reached or to be surpassed in the temporal development of the film. In a good film the close-ups are not distributed arbitrarily and capriciously. They are not cut in independently of the inner development of the scene, not at any time and anywhere, but only where their potential energy can and should make itself felt. For a close-up is not a cut-out picture with a frame; it is always merely part of a picture, like, for instance, the repoussoir figures in baroque painting which introduce a dynamic quality into the picture similar to that created by the close-ups in the spatial structure of a film.

But as if space and time in the film were interrelated by being interchangeable, the temporal relationships acquire an almost spatial character, just as space acquires a topical interest and takes on temporal characteristics; in other words, a certain element of freedom is introduced into the succession of their moments. In the temporal medium of a film we move in a way that is otherwise peculiar to space, completely free to choose our direction, proceeding from one phase of time into another, just as one goes from one room to another, disconnecting the individual stages in the development of events and grouping them, generally speaking, according to the principles of spatial order. In brief, time here loses, on the one hand, its uninterrupted continuity, on the other, its irreversible direction. It can be brought to a standstill, in close-ups; reversed, in flash-backs; repeated, in recollections; and skipped across, in visions of the future. Concurrent, simultaneous events can be shown successively, and temporally distinct events simultaneously—by double-exposure and alternation; the earlier can appear later, the later before its time. This cinematic conception of time has a thoroughly subjective and apparently irregular character compared with the empirical and the dramatic conception of the same medium. The time of empirical reality is a uniformly progressive, uninterruptedly continuous, absolutely irreversible order, in which events follow one another as if "on a conveyor belt." It is true that dramatic time is by no means identical with empirical time—the embarrassment caused by a clock showing the correct time on the stage comes from this discrepancy—and the unity of time prescribed by classicistic dramaturgy can even be interpreted as the fundamental elimination of ordinary time, and yet the temporal relationships in the drama have more points of contact with the chronological order of ordinary experience than the order of time in a film. Thus in the drama, or at least in one and the same act of drama, the temporal continuity of empirical reality is preserved intact. Here too, as in real life, events follow each other according to the law of a progression which permits neither interruptions and jumps, nor repetitions and inversions, and conforms to a standard of time which is absolutely constant—that is, undergoes no acceleration, retardation or stoppages of any kind within the several sections (acts or scenes). In the film, on the other hand, not only the speed of successive events, but also the chronometric standard itself is often different from shot to shot, according as to whether slow or fast motion, short or long cutting, many or few close-ups, are used.

The dramatist is prohibited by the logic of scenic arrangement from repeating moments and phases of time, an expedient that is often the source of the most intensive esthetic effects in the film. It is true that a part of the story is often treated retrospectively in the drama, and the antecedents followed backwards in time, but they are usually represented indirectly—either in the form of a coherent narrative or of one limited to scattered hints. The technique of the drama does not permit the playwright to go back to past stages in the course of a progressively developing plot and to insert them *directly* into the sequence of events, into the dramatic present—that is, it is only recently that it has begun to permit it, perhaps under the immediate influence of the film, or under the influence of the new conception of time, familiar also from the modern novel. The technical possibility of interrupting any shot without further ado suggests the possibilities of a discontinuous treatment of time from the very outset and provides the film with the means of heightening the tension of a scene either by interpolating heterogeneous incidents or assigning the individual phases of the scene to different sections of the work. In this way the film often produces the effect of someone playing on a keyboard and striking the keys ad libitum, up and down, to right and left. In a film we often see the hero first at the beginning of his career as a young man, later, going back to the past, as a child; we then see him, in the further course of the plot, as a mature man and, having followed his career for a time, we, finally, may see him still living after his death, in the memory of one of his relations or friends. As a result of the discontinuity of time, the retrospective development of the plot is combined with the progressive in complete freedom, with no kind of chronological tie, and through the repeated twists and turns in the time-continuum, mobility, which is the very essence of the cinematic experience, is pushed to the uttermost limits. The real spatialization of time in the film does not take place, however, until the simultaneity of parallel plots is portrayed. It is the experience of the simultaneity of different, spatially separated happenings that puts the audience into that condition of suspense, which moves between space and time and claims the categories of both orders for itself. It is the simultaneous nearness and remoteness of things—their nearness to one another in time and their distance from one another in space—that constitutes the spatio-temporal element, that two-dimensionality of time, which is the real medium of the film and the basic category of its world-picture.

It was discovered in a comparatively early stage in the history of the film that the representation of two simultaneous sequences of events is part of the original stock of cinematic forms. First, this simultaneity was simply recorded and brought to the notice of the audience by clocks showing the same time or by similar direct indications; the artistic technique of the intermittent treatment of a double plot and the alternating montage of the single phases of such a plot only developed step by step. But later on we come across examples of this technique at every turn. And whether we stand between two rival parties, two competitors, or two doubles, the structure of the film is dominated in any case by the crossing and intersecting of the two different lines, by the bilateral character of the development and the simultaneity of the opposing actions. The famous finish of the early, already classical Griffith films, in which the upshot of an exciting plot is made to depend on whether a train or a car, the intriguer or the "king's messenger on horseback," the murderer or the rescuer, reaches the goal first, using the then revolutionary technique of continuously changing pictures, flashing and vanishing like lightning, became the pattern of the dénouement since followed by most films in similar situations.

The time experience of the present age consists above all in an awareness of the moment in which we find ourselves: in an awareness of the present. Everything topical, contemporary, bound together in the present moment is of special significance and value to the man of today, and, filled with this idea, the mere fact of simultaneity acquires new meaning in his eyes. His intellectual world is imbued with the atmosphere of the immediate present, just as that of the Middle Ages was characterized by an other-worldly atmosphere and that of the Enlightenment by a mood of forward-looking expectancy. He experiences the greatness of his cities, the miracles of his technics, the wealth of his ideas, the hidden depths of his psychology in the contiguity, the interconnections and dovetailing of things and processes. The fascination of "simultaneity"—the discovery that, on the one hand, the same man experiences so many different, unconnected, and irreconcilable things in one and the same moment, and that, on the other, different men in different places often experience the same things, that the same things are happening at the same time in places completely isolated from each other—this universalism, of which modern technics have made contemporary man conscious, is perhaps the real source of the new conception of time and of the whole abruptness with which modern art describes life. This rhapsodic quality, which distinguishes the modern novel most sharply from the older novel, is at the same time the characteristic accountable for its most cinematic effects. The discontinuity of the plot and the scenic development, the sudden emersion of the thoughts and moods, the relativity and the inconsistency of the time-standards, are what remind us in the works of Proust and Joyce, Dos Passos and Virginia Woolf of the cuttings, dissolves and interpolations of the film, and it is simply film magic when Proust brings two incidents, which may lie thirty years apart, as closely together as if there were only two hours between them. The way in which, in Proust, past and present, dreams and speculation join hands across the intervals of space and time, the sensibility, always on the scent of new tracks, roams about in space and time, and the boundaries of space and time vanish in this endless and boundless stream of interrelations—all this corresponds exactly to that mixture of space and time in which the film moves. Proust never mentions dates and ages; we never know exactly how old the hero of his novel is, and even the chronological relationships of the events often remain rather vague. The experiences and happenings do not cohere by reason of their proximity in time, and the attempt to demarcate and arrange them chronologically would be all the more nonsensical from his point of view as, in his opinion, every man has his typical experiences which recur periodically. The boy, the youth, and the man always experience fundamentally the same things; the meaning of an incident often does not dawn on him until years after he has experienced and endured it; but he can hardly ever distinguish the deposit of the years that are past from the experience of the present hour in which he is living. Is one not in every moment of one's life the same child or the same invalid or the same lonely stranger with the same wakeful, sensitive, unappeased nerves? Is one not in every situation of life the person capable of experiencing this and that, who possesses, in the recurring features of his experience, the one protection against the passage of time? Do not all our experiences take place as it were at the same time? And is this simultaneity not really the negation of time? And this negation, is it not a struggle for the recovery of that inwardness of which physical space and time deprive us?

Joyce fights for the same inwardness, the same directness of experience, when he, like Proust, breaks up and merges well-articulated, chronologically organized time. In his work, too, it is the interchangeability of the contents of consciousness which triumphs over the chronological arrangement of the experiences, for him, too, time is a road without direction, on which man moves to and fro. But he pushes the spatialization of time even further than Proust, and shows the inner happenings not only in longitudinal but also in cross-sections. The images, ideas, brainwaves, and memories stand side by side with sudden and absolute abruptness; hardly any consideration is paid to their origins, all the emphasis is on their contiguity, their simultaneity. The spatialization of time goes so far in Joyce, that one can begin the reading of *Ulysses* where one likes, with only a rough knowledge of the context—not necessarily only after a first reading, as has been said, and almost in any sequence one cares to choose. The medium in which the reader finds himself is in fact wholly spatial, for the novel describes not only the picture of a great city, but also adopts its structure to some extent—the network of its streets and squares, in which people stroll about, walking in and out and stopping when and where they like. It is supremely characteristic of the cinematic quality of this technique that Joyce wrote his novel not in the final succession of the chapters, but—as is the custom in the production of films—made himself independent of the sequence of the plot and worked at several chapters at the same time.

We meet the Bergsonian conception of time, as used in the film and the modern novel—though not always so unmistakably as here—in all the genres and trends of contemporary art. The "simultanéité des états d'âmes" is, above all, the basic experience connecting the various tendencies of modern painting, the futurism of the Italians with the expressionism of Chagall, and the cubism of Picasso with the surrealism of Giorgio de Chirico or Salvador Dali. Bergson discovered the counterpoint of spiritual processes and the musical structure of their interrelationships. Just as, when we listen properly to a piece of music, we have in our ears the mutual connection of each new note with all those that have already sounded, so we always possess in our deepest and most vital experiences everything that we have ever experienced and made our own in life. If we understand ourselves, we read our own souls as a musical score, we resolve the chaos of the entangled sounds and transform them into a polyphony of different parts. All art is a game with and a fight against chaos; it is always advancing more and more dangerously towards chaos and rescuing more and more extensive provinces of the spirit from its clutch. If there is any progress in the history of art, then it consists in the constant growth of these provinces wrested from chaos. With its analysis of time, the film stands in the direct line of this development: it has made it possible to represent visually experiences that have previously been expressed only in musical forms. The artist capable of filling this new possibility, this still empty form, with real life has not yet arrived, however.

The crisis of the film, which seems to be developing into a chronic illness, is due above all to the fact that the film is not finding its writers or, to put it more accurately, the writers are not finding their way to the film. Accustomed to doing as they like within their own four walls, they are now required to take into account producers, directors, scriptwriters, cameramen, art directors and technicians of all kinds, although they do not acknowledge the authority of this spirit of cooperation, or indeed the idea of artistic cooperation at all. Their feelings revolt against the idea of the production of works of art being surrendered to a collective, to a "concern," and they feel that it is a disparagement of art that an extraneous dictate, or at best a majority, should have the last word in decisions of the motives of which they are often unable to account for themselves. From the point of view of the nineteenth century, the situation with which the writer is asked to come to terms is quite unusual and unnatural. The atomized and uncontrolled artistic endeavours of the present now meet for the first time with a principle opposed to their anarchy. For the mere fact of an artistic enterprise based on cooperation is evidence of an integrating tendency of which —if one disregards the theatre, where it is in any case more a matter of the reproduction than the production of works of art—there had really been no perfect example since the Middle Ages, and, in particular, since the mason's lodge. How far removed film production still is, however, from the generally accepted principle of an artistic cooperative group, is shown not only by the inability of most writers to establish a connection with the film, but also by such a phenomenon as Chaplin, who believes that he must do as much as possible in his films on his own: the acting of the main part, the direction, the script, the music. But even if it is only the beginning of a new method of organized art production, the, for the present, still empty framework of a new integration, nevertheless, here too, as in the whole economic, social, and political life of the present age, what is being striven for is the comprehensive planning without which both our cultural and material world threaten to go to pieces. We are confronted here with the same tension as we find throughout our social life: democracy and dictatorship, specialization and integration, rationalism and irrationalism, colliding with each other. But if even in the field of economics and politics planning cannot always be solved by imposing rules of conduct, it is all the less possible in art, where all violation of spontaneity, all forcible leveling down of taste, all institutional regulation of personal initiative, are involved in great though certainly not such mortal dangers as is often imagined.

But how, in an age of the most extreme specialization and the most sophisticated individualism, are harmony and an integration of individual endeavors to be brought about? How, to speak on a practical level, is the situation to be brought to an end in which the most poverty-stricken literary inventions sometimes underlie the technically most successful films? It is not a question of competent directors against incompetent writers, but of two phenomena belonging to different periods of time—the lonely, isolated writer dependent on his own resources and the problems of the film which can only be solved collectively. The cooperative film unit anticipates a social technique to which we are not yet equal, just as the newly invented camera anticipated an artistic technique of which no one at the time really knew the range and power. The reunion of the divided functions—first of all, the personal union of the director and the author, which has been suggested as a way to surmount the crisis—would be more an evasion of the problem than its solution, for it would prevent but not abolish the specialization that has to be overcome, would not bring about but merely avoid the necessity of the planning which is needed. Incidentally, the monistic-individual principle in the discharge of the various functions, in place of a collectively organized division of labor, corresponds not merely externally and technically to an amateurish method of working, but it also involves a lack of inner tension which is reminiscent of the simplicity of the amateur film. Or may the whole effort to achieve a production of art based on planning only have been a temporary disturbance, a mere episode, which is now being swept away again by the torrent of individualism? May the film be perhaps not the beginning of a new artistic era, but merely the somewhat hesitant continuation of the old individualistic culture, still full of vitality, to which we owe the whole of postmedieval art? Only if this were so would it be possible to solve the film crisis by the personal union of certain functions—that is, by partly surrendering the principle of collective labor.

—*The Social History of Art,* translated in collaboration with the author by Stanley Godman (1952)

ÉTIENNE GILSON

The Dance

It is easy but futile to speculate about the origins of the art of dancing. As with the other arts, all we know about the dance is what it has become, particularly in the West where its technique has been enriched with all the perfection that the creative genius of generations of dancers and dancing masters have bequeathed to it. The latter deserve special mention, for teaching and the schools play a decisive role in the creation and the preservation of the art of the dance. This teaching also explains the local, national, or continental character of the forms of this art. Western dance is a natural subject for the considerations of a philosopher living in the West, but in no way does it exhaust the possibilities of the dance. The

European dancer, or the dancer of European tradition, dances mainly with his legs; the dancers of Asia instead dance primarily with their arms, hands, and fingers; but everywhere dancers tend toward a complete art which would be a dance involving the whole body.

Since the body is the dancer's instrument, the choice of a body with an aptitude for dancing plays the same role and has the same importance as that of any material in any art. The sculptor carefully chooses his stone, his marble, his wood with the work to be wrought in view; so a dance is not executed with a body chosen at random, and dances that are different in style will be obtained from different bodies. Here, as elsewhere, the material of art exists with the form in view and in turn determines the latter.

It is useful to recall that the art of the dance requires an ensemble of exceptional physical qualities: strength, speed, suppleness, and endurance, which will enable the dancer to exert the efforts demanded by this art in which the spectator sees only facility, grace, ease of movements, and absolute mastery over a body free to move at its pleasure. The Radio City Music Hall Rockettes, famous for their perfect precision, are never on stage more than twenty minutes which in effect represents a considerable physical strain, especially on the part of a group in which no individual failing is permitted. A doctor's advice is required in connection with a choice of a future dancer, male or female, and his advice and at times his intercessions will all too often be necessary in the course of a career in which accidents are to be expected. It is not enough to want to be a dancer in order to be able to become one. Here the body has the first and final word.

Different bodies make possible different dances. To avoid going into detail, which would be interminable since it involves individual differences, we shall at least note the primary difference which sex introduces between the art of the male dancer and that of his female counterpart. Some men have an almost feminine suppleness and grace and some women, especially by dint of hard work and training, can equal or surpass some men in strength, but the general rule is that the male dancer excels in efforts that require power, vigor, and solidity in terms of balance. If he moves, he will excel in the leap, or *ballon*, and most often will be what is called an "elevation" dancer. All this can be briefly described by noting that the role of "porteur," so frequently assigned to the male dancer, has no equivalent among female dancers. As a general rule there is no "porteuse," and manly strength is always used to show womanly grace, not inversely. Despite all the reservations that we may make, it must be recognized in the end that the physical differentiation of bodies entails a corresponding differentiation in dances.

The same observation applies to individuals. Although natural beauty is a useful asset to the dancer, it is not indispensable; certain defects can even be advantageous provided they facilitate the effort and movement proper to the dance. A feminine dancer with a fairly small head on a fairly long neck, with legs and arms that are longer than the average can achieve effects that would be otherwise impossible. But we also see male and female dancers with small builds who turn the particularities of their physique to good account. We should especially bear in mind that here bodily movement outweighs bodily structure. The most beautiful Apollo must also be beautiful in motion if he wants to be a dancer. The history of the great artists of the dance could provide us with numberless examples of a fact which everybody has been able to observe, no matter how slight his interest in the art may be.

When we say that the body in motion is the material of the dance, we must not forget that a human body is in question. Intelligence therefore is another requisite of the would-be dancer, and the gifts of the body must be complemented by the gifts of the mind. In the first rank of these gifts must be placed a particular kind of plastic imagination which enables the individual to see in his mind the exterior aspect of his body in each of its movements and each of its possible attitudes. This gift must be common to the body as well as the mind in order to ensure its effectiveness, the body being capable of patterning itself according to the wishes of the mind, as the latter is of picturing to itself the attitudes and movements that it wills to obtain from the body. But language is too analytical to make a faithful translation of reality. The dance is preeminently the domain of the union of body and mind, or as traditional philosophy—ever so close to reality—expressed it: their "substantial union." The born dancer thinks with his body the way he dances with his mind. No other art is so completely and integrally an art of man, understanding thereby the human being in the organic unity of all his constitutive material and spiritual elements. This is the reason indeed why there is no human activity which the dance cannot honor with its contribution. David dancing before the ark is man offering himself in homage to God. To any degree that he possesses this gift of imagining his body in space, and even that of inventing in his mind new plastic forms and new movements possible from it, the born dancer, *homo saltator*, is in the highest degree that soul which "makes use of a body" mentioned by Plato, or that body which moves like a soul thinks, as Aristotle put it, because all is mind in an intelligent being. Like any other art, the dance can be prostituted, but in the eyes of the philosopher nothing can strip it of what its essential nobility confers upon it. It is preeminently the art of the human structure as such, or to express it more simply, the art of the whole man.

Every dancer is a distinct human being and his art will necessarily bear the imprint of his personality, his body as well as his soul or his mind. By electing to dedicate himself to the art of the dance, and in consequence to a life of arduous training and increasing effort—not without its rewards, to be sure—the artist nevertheless cannot even imagine to himself that he will ever dance as he would like to, but only as he will be able to. His physical and intellectual predetermination can go just so far, and he is wise to see it beforehand as a genuine fate. The traditional classifications of dancers into "noble," "character," "semicharacter," "burlesques" and other distinctions of the same kind are reminders that, at least to a certain degree, the dancer's physique will inevitably control the development of his career. Among dancers endowed with eminently superior gifts, the imprint of personality affects the art of the dancer so deeply that it becomes well-nigh impossible to bring two topflight artists together in the same recital. Neither the artist nor a public could endure the absolute dance executed simultaneously in two different manners, in which both styles bring each other into question through their very perfection. The history of the dance provides frequent examples of one of these brilliant dancers driving out the other by his mere presence with the help, if necessary, of a generally keen tactical sense.

Assuming all these gifts are combined in one person, which in fact can never be known beforehand, the would-be dancer must still learn how to make good use of them. The desire to be a dancer does not excuse one from learning to dance any more than the desire to paint, to sculpt, or to write excuses one from learning the techniques of these arts. This is the moment when the phenomenon, well-known in the apprenticeship of all the arts, occurs: the apparent loss of the natural gifts upon which the hope of a vocation is based. Nothing can be done without these gifts, but they will bear no fruit if they are left to themselves. In order to obtain art from them, a passage must be opened to a genre of beauty different from that of nature and which cannot be achieved without effort and sacrifice. The person who runs, spins around, or jumps for his own pleasure does not perform movements that enable him to obtain from his body those positions, attitudes, and movements necessary to the ends of the dance. The passage from nature to art requires a technique transmitted through teaching. It was therefore necessary to create the elements of an art of human movement which would enable the prospective dancer to obtain from his body the desired attitudes, positions, and actions with the minimum of fatigue and the maximum of precision. Hence this sort of grammar of motion, progressively invented and codified by artists and teachers, which the would-be dancer must learn because it contains the constitutive elements of the dance. These movements themselves vary according to different national schools and traditions (Balinese, Hindu, Spanish, Russian dances, and so on) and the grammars of motion which teach its elements vary within them. Borrowing between schools and traditions occurs but less frequently than we might imagine. Each part of the speech in motion, which is what a dance is, bears the mark of a definite style which is that of this speech itself; introduced into a different speech, it tends to break its style and substitute that of the school of dance from which it derives. The constitutive motor elements of a style of any dance share in the formal unity of the style and do not easily lend themselves to dissociation.

The example closest to us is the style of dance common today to the countries of Western Europe. It can be said that it is the joint creation of Italy, France, Spain, European Russia and that, more or less, all the peoples of European civilization have contributed to it. The grammar of this speech is represented by five elementary positions of the feet to which as many elementary positions of the hands were later added. They are far from being the positions easiest and most natural to man, but experience and study have shown that those positions, now become traditional, are the most favorable starting points for the execution of movements whose sequence, combination, and concatenation constitute the very substance of the dance. A description of them can be found in the treatises dealing with the techniques of the dance as it is practiced in the West. Some examples are the battu, the jeté, the jeté battu, the entrechat, the pirouette, without forgetting the pointes, i.e. supporting the foot on the toes, this least natural of all ways to carry oneself or to walk, and which partly for this reason is most manifestly dedicated to art. These willed restraints are to the dance what the rules of versification are to poetry. Whatever the school in which the would-be dancer may be trained, a private course, a troupe which adopts him or the quasi-official school of a great opera house, he will progressively have to master this gymnastic training and learn this syntax of motion. This will require years of effort, beginning sometimes in early childhood and extending from the age of five or six to twenty and beyond. As with all the arts worthy of this name, the apprenticeship of the dance never in fact ends except at that age when the strength of the body fails the dancer. This time comes tragically all too soon. The violinist's instrument improves as it ages, whereas the dancer's tends to grow heavy and stiffen after a period of perfection which is coeval with its successes. Every art of which man himself is the instrument is born, grows, ages, and dies with him.

Whoever says art means technique, and since the means necessary to create beauty must be first acquired as though they themselves were the end of art, they tend to replace it everywhere. It is then that the virtuoso appears, excellent in himself and necessary because virtuosity is the freedom to create beauty. Left to itself, it ends up by substituting the perfection of the means of execution to that of the work. In this case the virtuoso puts the resources of a technique, rightly qualified as "transcendent," at the service of futility because it enables him to cope with any difficulty of execution, however general it may be. The artist proper does not delude himself on this score. Scudo counselled his contemporaries to go listen to Chopin rather than Liszt if they wanted to hear real music being played; although they differed in matters of painting, Ingres and Delacroix were both ill at ease when listening to Paganini; on the other hand, those who knew César Franck assure us that he was not a particularly brilliant organist, and today we are amused by certain extraordinary fingerings which he used in order to get by. But he was a musician.

The dance also has its virtuosi and the dancer is naturally tempted to show off what he can do. Therefore he does so not because the arabesque designed by his body will be beautiful to behold but because the effort necessary to achieve it will be crowned with success. Hence the highest possible leaps, the interminably repeated pirouettes and other exploits of the same kind. They remind us of the unpleasant impression singers produce when they manage to hold on to a high note at the highest range of their voice or hold it for as long as they can hold their breath. What a relief when the former become silent and the latter breathe again! The male dancer is more exposed to this kind of danger than the female dancer. His normally greater strength tends to bring itself to bear by itself. In that case his virtuosity takes the particular form of acrobatics. The latter is also an art of the body in motion which has a beauty of its own, but it is not one of the fine arts because its principal end is not to create beauty but to give proof of skill, strength, suppleness and courage pushed, if necessary, to the point of rashness. The beauty of acrobatics, like that which accompanies the exercise of gymnastics and sports, belongs to the order of natural beauty. The acrobatic dance, in which powerfully muscled men of Herculean strength throw female dancers of average weight back and forth between them like a ball, has no relation at all with the art of the *porteur* whose object is not to display his personal strength but rather to show, if only through a simple effect of contrast, the grace of a female dancer whom he can set into motion merely by lending her the support of a finger. Acrobatics has its place in the music hall or the circus—only fools would disdain its merits; but it is one of the fatal illnesses of the dance, which should be the art of creating beautiful forms in motion in time and space by means of the human body. We would not dream of forbidding those who love acrobatics not to take delight in them; we are merely inviting them not to mistake as dance this legitimate object of their taste.

At the other extreme of the art the dance is beset by the temptation that threatens all the plastic arts: expression. In a time like ours in which architecture itself lays claim to the expression of feelings, how could the dance avoid being gnawed by the same ambition? This desire necessarily leads it to imitation. To imitate for the sake of expression can become the principal object of the dance, but in that case it ceases to be itself and is metamorphosed into another art. Mimicry, according to Littré, is the art of expressing thoughts through gestures, and he adds: "mimicry is a language all its own." Some mimes have other ambitions. They want merely to show the beauty of natural movements through the perfection with which they execute them and, if necessary, by disclosing their structure through a sort of motor analysis of the elements that make up such movements. There is in that case a return to natural beauty which, as we have already said, often is undeniably superior to that of art which, we repeat here, is something else entirely. Through its most ancient origins mimicry, as the very meaning of the word indicates, has always been an imitative art which belongs to that of the theatre. What results from it in that case is pantomime, to which the silent film in the recent past gave an unexpected development. A Charlie Chaplin, for example, has demonstrated how creatively inventive the language of a great mime can be. The fact remains, however, that being a mime is not the same as being a dancer.

The evidence of the facts seems to favor the opposite thesis but it is only because the arts and the philosophy of art do not have the same end. The latter analyzes, defines, and distinguishes in order not to confuse, whereas artists making use of a sovereign freedom—at their risk and peril, to be sure—join, combine, and arrange the resources of the most disparate arts with no other consideration save that of pleasing themselves and pleasing the public. The dance is not mimicry, but insofar as a dancer is master of his attitudes, gestures, and, up to a certain point, even of his expressions, he can also be a mime. The dance can be utilized as a kind of mimicry. The dancer in that case becomes an actor; he can be entrusted with the representation of a dramatic action in dance form, whereupon the dance becomes ballet. We are familiar with the extraordinary development that has been attained in our day by this charming genre—of which there are engaging hybrid types—which with the so-called "Russian" ballet ended up by forming a medley of all the genres, of which it can be said that it is the form of dance preferred by those who have no real love for the dance.

Strictly speaking, one male or female dancer suffices for a ballet. Indeed, the modern development of this art tends to make of it one to be executed by soloist virtuosi. On the other hand, tradition here favored performances conceived as a group composition. There was no ballet without a "corps de ballet." Today this collective body of dancers, where it still manages to survive despite the prohibitive costs of its upkeep, has been reduced to the role of a theatrical element whose patterned movements and ranks of ballerinas with their reappearance on stage in different costumes give the public a pleasure akin to that which it gets from the circus. This is the "ballet" billed as a grand spectacle which is a commercial, indeed almost an industrial, enterprise requiring a formidable outlay of funds, bankers, committees of wealthy patrons, and sometimes the State for its support. This composite art pleases and this fact alone is its justification. There is always an element of the dance in ballet but it includes other arts in variable proportions. A ballet is a theatrical representation in dance form; it requires a play acted by dancers and mimes (*Coppélia, Gisèle*); further, it requires the art of painting for the decor and the costumes; at times, as in the opera-ballet, it also requires poetry and spoken or declaimed language; and, finally, music always. The dance proper, as a distinct art having its proper end, somehow gets a little lost in the process, but this is no reason for disparaging this somewhat mixed genre. This development of the modern dance is bound up with its history: it has provided great artists with a public which would probably have been discouraged by the pure dance; the scenario or the play let the dance get by, so to speak, and it is impossible to imagine how artists such as Grisi, Taglioni, Perrot, Nijinsky and so many others, now legendary, would have been possible without the existence of ballets. It is simply a question of not mistaking for the dance in its pure form these spectacles which can be reproached only for being overgenerous in welcoming all genres—extending their hospitality even to the cinema.

Thanks to its hybrid character, however, the ballet renders the philosopher the service of shedding light on certain problems connected with the nature of the dance.

When we are young there are times when we feel a desire to dance, and as we grow older we long for moments of this kind. We are thus aware of the fact that the dance can be a personal pleasure: we can dance for ourselves, and alone. The dancer who yields to this natural impulse freely improvises the steps of his dance. Many professional or semiprofessional dancers do the same thing, as happens still in many Spanish fondas, not, moreover, without leaning on solidly established traditions which they are content merely to interpret and vary freely. Finally, there is no completely formed dancer and master of the resources of his art who is not capable of improvising to any kind of music, provided only that the rhythm is regular and the cadences foreseeable. In all cases of this kind the dancer is at once the author and interpreter of his art, like the musician who improvises. He is still both if, like the musician who executes one of his own works, the dancer has foreseen and regulated the sequence of his movements in advance. The dance in this case is one of the arts in which the artist is at once author and executant. He conceives the idea of the work and brings it into being.

The opposite necessarily occurs as soon as the dance changes from an individual to a collective execution. Such is the case when the "executant" is a group like a corps de ballet. The executant in this case is subjected to the directives of personages new to him, namely the choreographer and the ballet master. The choreographer is a composer of the dance, similar in his art to the composer of music. His is a work of creative imagination in that he foresees the sequences of the plastic forms unfolding in the dance which upon being joined will constitute the ballet. His directions can run the gamut of extreme vagueness to minute specification according to the nature of the imagined spectacle and the personality of the dancers who are to carry out his project. The modern development of ballet has progressively led to the fusion of different systems of notations which make it possible to compose a dance almost as one composes a piece of music. The positions of the body and the movement of transition do not have the precision of a tone scale nor the exactness of musical duration, they cannot be "written" with the strictness achieved by musical scores. Nor has an agreement yet been reached on a system of notation common to all choreographers. We can, however, already reconstitute with sufficient exactness certain choreographies which in some way bear the name of their creator, such as Petipa, Fokine, Massine, and several others. Thus we can also "revive" a ballet in the choreography of this or that author. This development perhaps heralds a time in which the plastic forms of the dance will furnish the material of definite works, stabilized through the resources of an appropriate score and as easily transmittable as are musical compositions today. In relation to the age when this choreographic repertoire will have been constituted, as regards the dance, the present epoch will be what the music of ancient Greece is for us: only names will be known, but not a single work which could be put together as an organic whole.

The ballet master seems to play a more modest role but one that is no less necessary. Anyway, it is a different role. He ensures the execution and the technical pinpointing of the dance scores invented by the choreographers. He can be both ballet master and choreographer but not necessarily, and he does not always have the qualities required to perform these two tasks successfully. If the choreographer can be compared to the composer of music, the ballet master is comparable to the orchestra conductor. He must have an exact knowledge of the technical resources placed at his disposal by the particular troupe that he is to direct, and the intelligence and plastic imagination necessary to foresee what the forms desired by the choreographer will be once they are realized. Often, moreover, he will need sufficient personal inventiveness to make these forms realizable, the talent for assigning the right role to the performers along with the tact necessary to have them accept them, and finally, exceptional pedagogical gifts so that each performer, and the troupe itself, thoroughly understands what is expected of each and every one of them. These are the many qualities that a choreographer does not necessarily possess, even if he is a genius, but which the ballet master must unquestionably possess so that the work may come into being. Without him it would remain simply a potentiality.

Among all the arts with which the dance can be associated, only one is its constant companion, music. This is not necessary, however. Dance without music is possible. Indeed, an adventurous attempt has been made, not without success, to create a silent ballet (Jerome Robbins, *Moves*, 1961). Moreover, it is not necessary to have seen a spectacle of this kind for us to imagine its possibility. The spectacle of a machine in operation whose movements are accomplished silently with impeccable measure and rhythm, at times so fascinating to observe, is enough to convince us that a dance can be performed without music and without loss of its characteristic beauty. The kinship of the two arts explains the frequency of their association. Just as music is made of sonorous forms succeeding each other in time, so is the dance made up of human forms in motion in space also succeeding each other in time. We have already noted that the division and structuration of time through sounds is easier to achieve and more precise than that which is achieved with the aid of forms such as bodily movements. It is therefore natural for the dancer to demand from sound the temporal structure within which his dance will be inscribed. It seems to the spectator in this case that the dancer's movements participate in the strictness of the measure and of the rhythm defined by the sounds. In fact, Spanish castanets, rattles, and even the clapping of hands with which the spectators spontaneously accompany the dancers attest to the common feeling of this formal convenience. But when we see a dancer work in silence, we know that it is an art which is sufficient unto itself and can create its proper beauty by itself.

No general rule can be cited for the propriety of this association. First of all, it can be considered from the point of view of the dance or of music. The dance profits from music to the degree in which the latter has been conceived with the former in view. This is the case with real dance music from the primitive tam-tam to jazz and to the orchestras of opera houses. The musician in that case conceives his musical forms according to the model of the plastic forms of a certain type of dance, or, if a ballet is in question, with an eye to accompanying the execution of classic and classified dance forms. Listening to a music thus conceived, the choreographer, and even the solo dancer, know which patterned bodily movements it is inviting them to execute, which step it is calling forth from them. In such cases, music profits from the dance as much as the dance profits from music. Since all that is being demanded of it are measures and rhythms, music is simply being invited to be itself and to display its own resources by putting them at the service of another art. The proof of this is that a great number of musical forms were dance forms at first: the branle, bourrée, passacaglia, gavotte, minuet, polonaise, waltz, and so many others, including the round and the gallopade. These have become for the musicians as many rhythmic frameworks capable of receiving and sustaining the most varied sonorous forms. There is nothing that we cannot expect from a *tempo di minuetto*, indeed almost anything rather than a minuet!

This is not at all so when the dance, becoming theatre, acrobatics, or mimicry, strays from its proper essence and by so doing assigns music tasks that are alien to rhythm, tasks for which it was never made. Only special cases exist in this respect, too. The only concern of the old comedy-ballets was to find pretexts for their dancers to dance. In them the dance had no other reason for being save itself, and since the spectators often came to the spectacle only to see the dance, it was enough for them. Campra has defined the ballet as a dramatic action which is represented through the dance with the aid of music; but in fact the steps of the dance were always the same and therefore represented practically nothing. The terms of the problem changed when the dramatic action, losing sight of the exigencies proper to music, burdened the dance with tasks beyond its means. There was no harm in trying this, and, besides, the judgments regarding its results exhibit the infinite variety characteristic of all esthetic judgments. It seems reasonable, nevertheless, to assert that it is not a priori certain that any sonorous form can be translated in visual space into a corresponding plastic form. The arabesques performable by the human body do not correspond to sonorous arabesques either in suppleness, rapidity, or in the number of possible variations. It is to be feared, therefore, that by wanting to dance to any music one may end up by spelling the melomane's pleasure in listening to the Sixth Symphony, for example, at the same time that one obliges the dancer to create plastic inventions whose meaning is not in the dance itself but outside it.

The complexity of the problem shows up when it involves music expressly written for a ballet whose subject is frankly mimed theatre. We have seen musicians in various times bend their art to the requirements of representing a dramatic action. We can understand why they agree to do so. In order to justify writing so many operas Camille Saint-Saëns pointed out that a musician has to earn a living! The ballet has provisionally replaced the opera as a recipient of benefices; it likewise involves commissions from wealthy patrons, sometimes rich ladies tormented by the desire to dance themselves, or to mime, which seems less difficult to them. In collaborations of this kind the dance loses all that music gains. The less the composer is a slave to this kind of dance, the more the music he writes for it can be beautiful: to risk a personal impression, Ravel's *Daphnis and Chloë* gains in being heard rather than being seen. On the other hand, the more the musician forces himself to model his music on different episodes of a theatrical representation, the less does he preserve his internal creative compulsions and that "golden thread" which Schumann called one of the surest signs of genius. Some music-lovers feel that Stravinsky's *Petrouchka,* captivating and rich as it is in musical substance, loses as much in not being seen as would an opera in which the singers' parts would be suppressed. For this very reason, perhaps, it is the perfect modern ballet—that is to say, a charming hybrid of a dance that is no longer altogether dance, and of a music that is no longer purely music. This genre has a beauty of its own which is its justification for being, but it is good to know what we are admiring. Concertgoers who are fully satisfied with scores of this kind at bottom do not truly love either music or the dance. But pure forms are not easily accessible, and no pleasure that we take in art is proscribed.

The central problem posed by the arts therefore remains the same. By dint of trying all manners of possible combinations, each of the arts spontaneously comes to prefer those which favor imitation and expression to the detriment of the formal elements which are its very substance. Present Gounod with the first prelude of the *Well-Tempered Clavichord* and he will cap it with an *Ave Maria*; give the same prelude to Fokine and he will find some way of creating a choreography for it; only the real musician will find the musical response to Bach's prelude, which is to write another from it, and we will have the intellectual *Doctor Gradus ad Parnassum*.[1] Thus for the dance it cannot be a question either of interpreting a musical work, which is content to signify itself, or of imparting to it the physical consistence which some may think it lacks in comparison to the plastic arts whose material can be seen, touched and weighed. Thanks to the dance, music in this way shares in the facilities that the arts of space offer to the imagination. It is difficult to approve these ingenious observations except in the way they make music endurable to those who do not like to listen to it. But we cannot see what the dance gains thereby. Its proper nature is not to give a physical content to music which finds that of sounds sufficient. It is no mediocre dignity to be an art of the forms of the eminently human body in motion. The true source of the dignity of the dance is to remain faithful to its proper essence, regardless of the multiple alliances into which it may be obliged to enter.

—*Forms and Substances in the Arts,* translated by Salvator Attanasio (1966)

Note

1. The first piece in Debussy's *Children's Corner* suite for piano. It is a musical portrait of a child bored with practicing who lets his mind wander from the exercise. (With this single exception, footnotes in the original have been omitted. —M.R.)

CHAPTER 8

Expressiveness

GEORG WILHELM FRIEDRICH HEGEL: Tragedy
SUSANNE K. LANGER: Expressiveness and Symbolism
ROGER SESSIONS: The Composer and His Message
RUDOLF ARNHEIM: The Expressiveness of Visual Forms

During the second and third decades of this century, estheticians were especially preoccupied with the problem of form. This was the period when such "formalists" as Clive Bell and Roger Fry exercised their greatest influence. They challenged the esthetic relevance of sentimental associations and directed attention to the great importance of plastic organization. It was a movement toward purification in esthetic theory and was paralleled by "abstract" or "nonobjective" trends in the arts (for example, in the works of Kandinsky, Mondrian, and Brancusi). But, as the century wore on, the interest in meaning and symbolism became ever more pronounced. A brilliant generation of thinkers—Whitehead, Russell, Wittgenstein, Freud, Cassirer, Carnap, to name the more prominent—established the new "keynote" of philosophical thought. Esthetics has reflected this trend. The writers represented in the present chapter are typical of the interest in expressiveness[1] that has characterized esthetics in the past several decades.

The interest in expressiveness is no new feature of esthetic theory. Among the great philosophers, Georg Wilhelm Friedrich Hegel (1770–1831) emphasizes the spiritual expressiveness of works of art. He maintained that art is a way of knowing—it is intellectual and not simply sensuous or emotional. He was an "idealist" in holding that "spirit" and "ideas" are basic to all existence. Ideas, in their dialectical unfoldment, are the acting out, the making explicit, of a latent rationality that pervades all things. Every facet of reality is part of an infinite web of interdependent entities, which arise, evolve, and clash with their opposites in a logical and necessary progression. Everything comes to fruition, comes to grief, and enters transmuted into a "higher truth." No idea, no movement, no reality, is wholly lost in this dialectical progression through conflict to reconciliation and synthesis.

In poetry and, above all, in tragedy, the dialectical nature of reality is most fully revealed. The foundation of Hegel's theory of both comedy and tragedy is summed up by Jacob Loewenberg:

> Life, as Hegel conceives it, is an incessant strife of partisan views. They are partisan because they are particular. . . . Whatever is particular—a particular art, a particular religion, a particular philosophy—is self-absorbed and self-centered and hence never free from bias. The truth is that every particular point of view ineluctably suffers from a warped perspective. The unavoidable tendency of everything particular to emphasize its own particularity Hegel discerns to be the source of all the fatal collisions that render human life so everlastingly unstable.[2]

When we laugh at the inordinate particularity we have comedy; when we pity the victim of a warped perspective, we have tragedy. In comedy, the one-sidedness is ridiculous and not too serious; in tragedy, it is catastrophic.

Tragedy involves conflict between forces which are each, in a limited way, justifiable. That which is destroyed in the catastrophe is not the just cause, but merely its false and one-sided particularity. As A. C. Bradley has written:

> The essentially tragic fact . . . is not so much the war of good with evil as the war of good with good. . . . The end of the tragic conflict is the denial of both the exclusive claims.

In the *Antigone* of Sophocles, for example, "neither the right of the family nor that of the state is denied; what is denied is the absoluteness of the claim of each."[3] (Note the contrast with the more starkly pessimistic theory of Nietzsche in Chapter 4.) Despite the notorious difficulty of the Hegelian language, this interpretation of tragedy rivals in influence and profundity the interpretations of Aristotle and Nietzsche. It is worth the considerable effort required to understand it.

Among recent theorists of expressiveness, Susanne Knauth Langer (1895–), Professor Emeritus of philosophy at Connecticut College, began her philosophical career by exploring logic and the whole field of signs, symbols, languages, and meanings. In her most popular book, *Philosophy in a New Key* (1942), she expounded the fundamental notion of symbolization as the connective link between fields as disparate as music, science, and religion (here following the lead of Ernst Cassirer in his monumental *Philosophy of Symbolic Forms*). Then in *Feeling and Form* (1953) she generalized the theory of music to cover all the arts, and in her *Problems of Art* (1957), *Philosophical Sketches* (1962), and *Mind*, Vol.I, (1967), she responded to her critics by reformulating some of her basic ideas.

Her theory is based upon a distinction between two types of "symbolism," the *discursive*, which we find in pure science, and the *presentational*, which confronts us in art. Discursive symbolism is language in its literal use. It employs conventional meaningful units (the "dictionary" meanings) according to rules of grammar and syntax. Each word has relatively fixed meaning, and the total meaning of the discourse is built up stepwise by using the words successively. The import can be paraphrased by using synonyms and logically equivalent sentences, and it refers to the neutral aspects of our world of observation and thought—the ideas and facts that are *least* tinged by subjective feeling. Presentational symbolism, in contrast, employs no fixed constituents to be combined according to rules; it therefore cannot be broken up into units with independent and conventional meanings; its meaning inheres in the total form, and cannot be paraphrased; it expresses, in its total range, the whole subjective side of existence that discourse is incapable of expressing—our moods, emotions, desires, and sense of movement, growth, felt tensions and resolutions, even sensations and thoughts in their characteristic passage. It does this not by a gushing forth of emotion but by an articulation of the "logical forms" of subjectivity.

This articulation is made possible by a congruence between the patterns of art and the patterns of sentience. At this point Professor Langer invokes a well-known theory of Gestalt psychology—that there may be a similarity of form between different fields of experience. It will be helpful to cite a concrete example from an essay by Carroll C. Pratt: "In the space below are two meaningless forms. The reader will be able to decide without any trouble which of the meaningless sounds, *uloomu* and *takete,* applies to each form. The demonstration shows that impressions

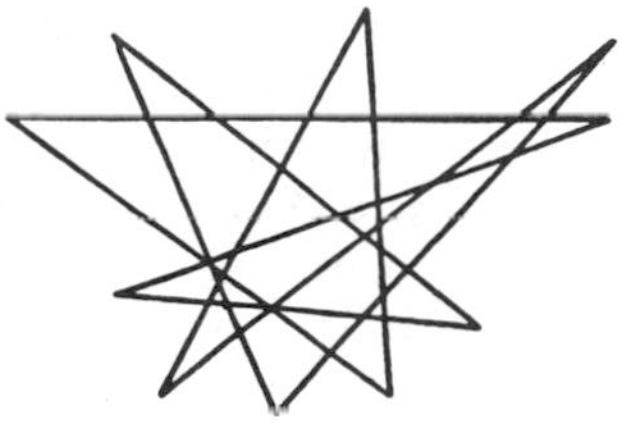

from different sense departments may be very similar with respect to form. Each of the sounds, *takete* and *uloomu,* fits perfectly one of the visual designs, but not the other. The impressions are different in content —one is visual and the other auditory—but similar in form."[4] Dr. Langer points out that such congruence of form holds not only between one sense department and another but between a pattern of sense and a pattern of feeling. "The tonal structures we call 'music,' " for example, "bear a close logical similarity to the forms of human feeling—forms of growth and of attenuation, flowing and stowing, conflict and resolution, speed, arrest, terrific excitement, calm, or subtle activation and dreamy lapses."[5] Thus subjective experience has a structure that can be abstracted and articulated by the congruent form of a work of art. But resemblance is not reference, and in the moment of esthetic vision, any sense of reference is superseded by the immediate reality of the esthetic apparition. Since the word "symbol" is almost always used to denote reference, the work of art is a "symbol" in a somewhat unusual meaning of the word. Symbols, in the ordinary sense, may occur within the work of art, but they function at a different level from the work that contains them.

In explaining the nature of musical expressiveness, Langer cites[6] the "remarkably discerning" essay by Roger Sessions (1896–), of which the Sessions selection in the present chapter is an excerpt. Both Langer and Sessions find a correspondence between the dynamics of musical form and the deep organic rhythms of life and breath.

Educated at Harvard and Yale, Sessions was later a student and assistant under Ernest Bloch, one of the great modern composers, at the Cleveland Institute of Music. It was during this period that he began to compose music of his own, but not until after several years of study in Europe did he become one of America's foremost composers in a variety of musical modes, such as the string quartet, the symphony, and the opera. He has also won fame as a lecturer in musical theory at Princeton University and as a writer of lucid essays and books about music.

Sessions points out that *time* is the principal basis of musical expressiveness. He thinks there is a profound correspondence between the dynamic structure of musical time and the instinctive dynamism of the human organism, such as the beating of the heart, the movements of breathing, the involuntary tensions and relaxations of our nervous system. He recognizes a connotative element in musical expressiveness, for example, the similarity between an agitated musical movement and a storm; but he thinks that music goes deeper than to arouse such associations in the mind—it stirs up and sets pulsating the primal energies of our psychic life. The expressiveness of music, of course, is immeasurably heightened by its formal aspects—the infinite possibilities in harmonic combinations of sounds, and the use of premonition, recognition, progression, and contrast in the elaboration of musical motifs. "Form in music," he concludes, "is identical with content."

Although Sessions never refers by name to Gestalt psychology, his recognition of the similarity between tonal structures and psychological patterns is akin to the insights of the Gestalt psychologists. A more explicit appeal to Gestalt principles occurs in the writings of Rudolf Arnheim (1904–), Professor Emeritus at Harvard University and author of important books and articles on the psychology of art. In the Preface to his *Art and Visual Perception,* he states: "As long as I can remember I have concerned myself with art, studied its nature and history, tried my eyes and hands at it, and sought the company of artists, art theorists, art educators. This interest has been enhanced by my psychological studies." His initial studies were made in Germany, the land of his birth, where he became familiar with the writings of Von Ehrenfels, Max Wertheimer, Wolfgang Köhler, Kurt Koffka, and other Gestalt theorists. The combination of this theoretical background with intensive experience of the arts has lent solidity and concreteness to Arnheim's esthetics.

In the selection included in this chapter, he takes issue with the traditional theory of the relation of sensory perception to expression. According to this theory, you perceive pure sense-data and then associate feelings and ideas with these original data. The expressiveness is due to this association. For example, what you perceive when you watch the flames in a fireplace would simply be bright reddish shapes in rapid movement. But you know from past experience "that fire hurts and destroys. It may remind you of violence. Perhaps you associate red with blood, which will reinforce the element of violence. The flames may seem to be moving like snakes. Also, your cultural environment has accustomed you to thinking of red as a color of passion. In consequence of all this, you not only see colors and shapes in motion, but are also struck by the expression of something frightening, violent, passionate."[7] In other words, you *perceive* only sensory data such as color, shape, sound; and expression is a superadded and secondary response due to the association of ideas. Arnheim opposes this theory of expression, which is represented in the present volume by Santayana's account, and he similarly opposes the view of Lipps and Lee that expressiveness is largely the result of empathic projection (see Chapter 10).

As Arnheim explains in this chapter, expression is original and primary. In the case of the fire, one sees "the graceful play of aggressive tongues, flexible striving, lively color." The expressiveness appears in the visible pattern itself and strikes our attention immediately. An expressive whole is not attained by adding up isolated parts, thus combining associated ideas and feelings with sensory data. The expressiveness is intrinsic to the integrated structure of the whole, and this is cognized en bloc. The important consequences of this Gestalt theory for art and esthetic education are discussed by Arnheim.

Notes

1. The word "expression," in contrast to "expressiveness," has a dual meaning. It may refer to either the *act* of expressing or the *content* expressed. Because it is the latter meaning that I intend in the present chapter, I have used the word "expressiveness" in my title to the chapter and in my Introductory Note.

2. J. Loewenberg, *Hegel Selections* (Scribner, New York, 1929), p. xix.

3. A. C. Bradley, "Hegel's Theory of Tragedy," *Oxford Lectures on Poetry* (Macmillan, London, 1950), pp. 71, 74.

4. Carroll C. Pratt, *Music as the Language of Emotion* (Library of Congress, Washington, D.C., 1952), p. 18.

5. Susanne K. Langer, *Feeling and Form* (Scribner, New York, 1953), p. 27.

6. Ibid., p. 67.

7. Rudolf Arnheim, "The Priority of Expression," *Journal of Aesthetics and Art Criticism*, Vol. 7 (1949), p. 106.

GEORG WILHELM FRIEDRICH HEGEL

Tragedy

. . . The . . . fundamental feature of dramatic composition is that of the *individuals* who act in *conflict* with each other. In Greek tragedy it is not at all bad will, crime, worthlessness, or mere misfortune, stupidity, and the like, which act as an incentive to such collisions, but, rather, as I have frequently urged, the ethical right to a definite course of action. Abstract evil neither possesses truth in itself, nor does it arouse interest. At the same time, when we attribute ethical traits of characterization to the individuals of the action, these ought not to appear merely as a matter of opinion. It is rather implied in their right or claim that they are actually there as essential on their own account. The hazards of crime, such as are present in modern drama, the useless, or quite as much the so-called noble criminal, with his empty talk about fate, we meet with in the tragedy of ancient literature, rarely, if at all, and for the good reason that the decision and deed depends on the wholly personal aspect of interest and character, upon lust for power, love, honor, or other similar passions, whose justification has its roots exclusively in the particular inclination and individuality. A resolve of this character, whose claim is based upon the content of its object, which it carries into execution in one restricted direction of particularization, violates, under certain circumstances, which are already essentially implied in the actual possibility of conflicts, a further and equally ethical sphere of human volition, which the character thus confronted adheres to, and, by his thus stimulated action, enforces, so that in this way the collision of powers and individuals equally entitled to the ethical claim is completely set up in its movement.

The sphere of this content, although capable of great variety of detail, is not in its essential features very extensive. The principal source of opposition, which Sophocles in particular, in this respect following the lead of Aeschylus, has accepted and worked out in the finest way, is that of the *body politic,* the opposition, that is, between ethical life in its social universality and the family as the natural ground of moral relations. These are the purest forces of tragic representation. It is, in short, the harmony of these spheres and the concordant action within the bounds of their realized content, which constitute the perfected reality of the moral life. In this respect I need only recall the "Seven before Thebes" of Aeschylus and, as a yet stronger illustration, the "Antigone" of Sophocles. Antigone reverences the ties of blood-relationship, the gods of the nether world. Creon alone recognizes Zeus, the paramount Power of public life and the commonwealth. We come across a similar conflict in the "Iphigenia in Aulis," as also in the "Agamemnon," the "Choephorae," and "Eumenides" of Aeschylus, and in the "Electra" of Sophocles. Agamemnon, as king and leader of his army, sacrifices his daughter in the interest of the Greek folk and the Trojan expedition. He shatters thereby the bond of love as between himself and his daughter and wife, which Clytemnestra retains in the depths of a mother's heart, and in revenge prepares an ignominious death for her husband on his return. Orestes, their son, respects his mother, but is bound to represent the right of his father, the king, and strikes dead the mother who bore him.

A content of this type retains its force through all times, and its presentation, despite all difference of nationality, vitally arrests our human and artistic sympathies.

Of a more formal type is that second kind of essential collision, an illustration of which in the tragic story of Oedipus the Greek tragedians especially favored. Of this Sophocles has left us the most complete example in his "Oedipus Rex," and "Oedipus at Colonus." The problem here is concerned with the claim of alertness in our intelligence, with the nature of the obligation implied in that which a man carries out with a volition fully aware of its acts as contrasted with that which he has done in fact, but unconscious of and with no intention of doing what he has done under the directing providence of the gods. Oedipus slays his father, marries his mother, begets children in this incestuous alliance, and nevertheless is involved in these most terrible of crimes without active participation either in will or knowledge. The point of view of our profounder modern consciousness of right and wrong would be to recognize that crimes of this description, inasmuch as they were neither referable to a personal knowledge or volition, were not deeds for which the true personality of the perpetrator was responsible. The plastic nature of the Greek on the contrary adheres to the bare fact which an individual has achieved, and refuses to face the division implied by the purely ideal attitude of the soul in the self-conscious life on the one hand and the objective significance of the fact accomplished on the other.

For ourselves, to conclude this survey, other collisions, which either in general are related to the universally accepted association of personal action to the Greek conception of Destiny, or in some measure to more exceptional conditions, are comparatively speaking less important.

In all these tragic conflicts, however, we must above all place on one side the false notion of *guilt* or *innocence*. The heroes of tragedy are quite as much under one category as the other. If we accept the idea as valid that a man is guilty only in the case that a choice lay open to him, and he deliberately decided on the course of action which he carried out, then these plastic figures of ancient drama are guiltless. They act in accordance with a specific character, a specific pathos, for the simple reason that they are this character, this pathos. In such a case there is no lack of decision and no choice. The strength of great characters consists precisely in this that they do not choose, but are entirely and absolutely just that which they will and achieve. They are simply themselves, and never anything else, and their greatness consists in that fact. Weakness in action, in other words, wholly consists in the division of the personal self as such from its content, so that character, volition and final purpose do not appear as absolutely one unified growth; and inasmuch as no assured end lives in the soul as the very substance of the particular personality, as the pathos and might of the individual's entire will, he is still able to turn with indecision from this course to that, and his final decision is that of caprice.

A wavering attitude of this description is alien to these plastic creations. The bond between the psychological state of mind and the content of the will is for them indissoluble. That which stirs them to action is this very pathos which implies an ethical justification and which, even in the pathetic aspects of the dialogue, is not enforced in and through the merely personal rhetoric of the heart and the sophistry of passion, but in the equally masculine and cultivated objective presence, in the profound possibilities, the harmony and vitally plastic beauty of which Sophocles was to a superlative degree master. At the same time, however, such a pathos, with its potential resources of collision, brings them to deeds that are both injurious and wrongful. They have no desire to avoid the blame that results therefrom. On the contrary, it is their fame to have done what they have done. One can in fact urge nothing more intolerable against a hero of this type than by saying that he has acted innocently. It is a point of honor with such great characters that they are guilty. They have no desire to excite pity or our sensibilities. For it is not the substantive, but rather the wholly personal deepening of the personality which stirs our individual pain. His securely strong character, however, coalesces entirely with his essential pathos, and this indivisible accord inspires wonder, not compassion. The drama of Euripides marks the transition to that.

The final result, then, of the development of tragedy conducts us to this issue and only this—namely, that the twofold vindication of the mutually conflicting aspects is no doubt retained, but the *one-sided* mode is cancelled, and the undisturbed ideal harmony brings back again that condition of the chorus, which attributes without reserve equal honor to all the gods. The true course of dramatic development consists in the annulment of *contradictions* viewed as such, in the reconciliation of the forces of human action, which alternately strive to negate each other in the conflict. Only so far is misfortune and suffering not the final issue, but rather the satisfaction of spirit, as for the first time, in virtue of such a conclusion, the necessity of all that particular individuals experience, is able to appear in complete accord with reason, and our emotional attitude is tranquilized on a true ethical basis; rudely shaken by the calamitous result to the heroes, but reconciled in the substantial facts. And it is only in so far as we retain such a view securely that we shall be in a position to understand ancient tragedy. We have to guard ourselves therefore from concluding that a *dénouement* of this type is merely a moral issue conformably to which evil is punished and virtue rewarded, as indicated by the proverb that "when crime turns to vomit, virtue sits down at table." We have nothing to do here with this wholly personal aspect of a self-reflecting personality and its conception of good and evil, but are concerned with the appearance of the affirmative reconciliation and the equal validity of both powers engaged in conflict, if the collision is complete. To as little extent is the necessity of the issue a blind destiny, or, in other words, a purely irrational, unintelligible fate, identified with the classical world by many; rather it is the rationality of destiny, albeit it does not as yet appear as self-conscious Providence, the divine final end of which in conjunction with the world and individuals appears on its own account and for others, depending as it does on just this fact that the highest Power paramount over particular gods and mankind cannot suffer this—namely, that the forces, which affirm their self-subsistence in modes that are abstract or incomplete, and thereby overstep the boundary of their warrant, no less than the conflicts which result from them, should retain their self-stability. Fate drives personality back upon its limits, and shatters it, when it has grown overweening. An irrational compulsion, however, an innocence of suffering would rather only excite indignation in the soul of the spectator than ethical tranquility. From a further point of view, therefore, the reconciliation of *tragedy* is equally distinct from that of the *Epos*. If we look at either Achilles or Odysseus in this respect we observe that both attain their object, and it is right that they do so; but it is not a continuous happiness with which they are favored; they have, on the contrary, to taste in its bitterness the feeling of finite condition, and are forced to fight wearily through difficulties, losses, and sacrifices. It is in fact a universal demand of truth that in the course of life and all that takes place in the objective world the nugatory character of finite conditions should compel attention. So no doubt the anger of Achilles is reconciled; he obtains from Agamemnon that in respect of which he had suffered the sense of insult; he is revenged upon Hector; the funeral rites of Patroclus are consummated, and the character of Achilles is acknowledged in all its glory. But his wrath and its reconciliation have for all that cost him his dearest friend, the noble Patroclus; and, in order to avenge himself upon Hector for this loss, he finds himself compelled to disengage himself from his anger, to enter once more the battle against the Trojans, and in the very moment when his glory is acknowledged, receives the prevision of his early death. In a similar way Odysseus reaches Ithaca at last, the goal of his desire; but he does so alone and in his sleep, having lost all his companions, all the war-booty from Ilium, after long years of endurance and fatigue. In this way both heroes have paid their toll to finite conditions and the claim of nemesis is evidenced in the destruction of Troy and the misfortunes of the Greek heroes. But this nemesis is simply justice as conceived of old, which merely humiliates what is everywhere too exalted, in order to establish once more the abstract balance of fortune by the instrumentality of misfortune, and which merely touches and affects finite existence without further ethical signification. And this is the justice of the Epic in the field of objective fact, the universal reconciliation of simple accommodation. The higher conception of reconciliation in tragedy is on the contrary related to the resolution of specific ethical and substantive facts from their contradiction into their true harmony. The way in which such an accord is established is asserted under very different modes; I propose therefore merely to direct attention to the fundamental features of the actual process herein involved.

First, we have particularly to emphasize the fact, that if it is the one-sidedness of the pathos which constitutes the real basis of collisions this merely amounts to the statement that it is asserted in the action of life, and therewith has become the unique pathos of a particular individual. If this one-sidedness is to be abrogated then it is this individual which, to the extent that his action is exclusively identified with this isolated pathos, must perforce be stripped and sacrificed. For the individual here is merely this single life, and, if this unity is not secured in its stability on its own account, the individual is shattered.

The most complete form of this development is possible when the individuals engaged in conflict relatively to their concrete or objective life appear in each case essentially involved in one whole, so that they stand fundamentally under the power of that against which they battle, and consequently infringe that, which, conformably to their own essential life, they ought to respect. Antigone, for example, lives under the political authority of Creon; she is herself the daughter of a king and the affianced of Haemon, so that her obedience to the royal prerogative is an obligation. But Creon also, who is on his part father and husband, is under obligation to respect the sacred ties of relationship, and only by breach of this can give an order that is in conflict with such a sense. In consequence of this we find immanent in the life of both that which each respectively combats, and they are seized and broken by that very bond which is rooted in the compass of their own social existence. Antigone is put to death before she can enjoy what she looks forward to as bride, and Creon too is punished in the fatal end of his son and wife, who commit suicide, the former on account of Antigone's death, and the latter owing to Haemon's. Among all the fine creations of the ancient and the modern world—and I am acquainted with pretty nearly everything in such a class, and one ought to know it, and it is quite possible—the "Antigone" of Sophocles is from this point of view in my judgment the most excellent and satisfying work of art.

The tragic issue does not, however, require in every case, as a means of removing both over-emphasized aspects and the equal honor which they respectively claim, the downfall of the contestant parties. The "Eumenides" ends, as we all know, not with the death of Orestes, or the destruction of the Eumenides, these avenging spirits of matricide and filial affection, as opposed to Apollo, who seeks to protect unimpaired the worth of and reverence for the family chief and king, who prompted Orestes to slay Clytemnestra, but with Orestes released from the punishment and honor bestowed on both divinities. At the same time we cannot fail to see in this adjusted conclusion the nature of the authority which the Greeks attached to their gods when they presented them as mere individuals contending with each other. They appear, in short, to the Athenian of everyday life merely as definite aspects of ethical experience which the principles of morality viewed in their complete and harmonious coherence bind together. The votes of the Areopagus are equal on either side. It is Athene, the goddess, the life of Athens, that is, imagined in its essential unity, who adds the white pebble, who frees Orestes, and at the same time promises altars and a cult to the Eumenides no less than Apollo. As a contrast to this type of objective reconciliation the settlement may be, *secondly*, of a more personal character. In other words, the individual concerned in the action may in the last instance surrender his one-sided point of view. In this betrayal by personality of its essential pathos, however, it cannot fail to appear destitute of character; and this contradicts the masculine integrity of such plastic figures. The individual, therefore, can only submit to a higher Power and its counsel or command, to the effect that while on his own account he adheres to such a pathos, the will is nevertheless broken in its bare obstinacy by a god's authority. In such a case the knot is not loosened, but, as in the case of Philoctetes, it is severed by a deus ex machina.

But as a *further* and final class, and more beautiful than the above rather external mode of resolution, we have the reconciliation more properly of the soul itself, in which respect there is, in virtue of the personal significance, a real approach to our modern point of view. The most perfect example of this in ancient drama is to be found in the ever admirable "Oedipus at Colonos" of Sophocles. The protagonist here has unwittingly slain his father, secured the sceptre of Thebes, and the bridal bed of his own mother. He is not rendered unhappy by these unwitting crimes; but the power of divination he has of old possessed makes him realize, despite himself, the darkness of the experience that confronts him, and he becomes fearfully, if indistinctly, aware of what his position is. In this resolution of the riddle in himself he resembles Adam, losing his happiness when he obtains the knowledge of good and evil. What he then does, the seer, is to blind himself, then abdicate the throne and depart from Thebes, very much as Adam and Eve are driven from Paradise. From henceforth he wanders about, a helpless old man. Finally, a god calls the terribly afflicted man to himself—the man, that is, who, refusing the request of his sons that he should return to Thebes, prefers to associate with the Erinyes; the man, in short, who extinguishes all the disruption in himself and who purifies himself in his own soul. His blind eyes are made clear and bright, his limbs are healed, and become a treasure of the city which received him as a free guest. And this illumination in death is for ourselves no less than for him the more truly visible reconciliation which is worked out both in and for himself as individual man, in and through, that is, his essential character. Critics have endeavoured to discover here the temper of the Christian life; we are told we have here the picture of a sinner, whom God receives into His grace; and the fateful misfortunes which expire in their finite condition are made good with the seal of blessedness in death. The reconciliation of the Christian religion, however, is an illumination of the soul, which, bathed in the everlasting waters of salvation, is raised above mortal life and its deeds. Here it is the heart itself, for in such a view the spiritual life can effect this, which buries that life and its deed in the grave of the heart itself, counting recriminations of earthly guilt as part and parcel of its own earthly individuality; and which, in the full assuredness of the eternally pure and spiritual condition of blessedness, holds itself in itself calm and steadfast against such impeachment. The illumination of Oedipus, on the contrary, remains throughout, in consonance with ancient ideas, the restoration of conscious life from the strife of ethical powers and violations to the renewed and harmonious unity of this *ethical content itself*.

—*The Philosophy of Fine Art* (1820–1826; translated 1920 by F. P. B. Osmaston)

SUSANNE K. LANGER

Expressiveness and Symbolism

I. Expressiveness

When we talk about "Art" with a capital "A"—that is, about any or all of the arts: painting, sculpture, architecture, the potter's and goldsmith's and other designers' arts, music, dance, poetry, and prose fiction, drama and film—it is a constant temptation to say things about "Art" in this general sense that are true only in one special domain, or to assume that what holds for one art must hold for another. For instance, the fact that music is made for performance, for presentation to the ear, and is simply not the same thing when it is given only to the tonal imagination of a reader silently perusing the score, has made some estheticians pass straight to the conclusion that literature, too, must be physically heard to be fully experienced, because words are originally spoken, not written; an obvious parallel, but a careless and, I think, invalid one. It is dangerous to set up principles by analogy, and generalize from a single consideration.

But it is natural, and safe enough, to ask analogous questions: "What is the function of sound in music? What is the function of sound in poetry? What is the function of sound in prose composition? What is the function of sound in drama?" The answers may be quite heterogeneous; and that is itself an important fact, a guide to something more than a simple and sweeping theory. Such findings guide us to exact relations and abstract, variously exemplified basic principles.

At present, however, we are dealing with principles that have proven to be the same in all the arts, when each kind of art—plastic, musical, balletic, poetic, and each major mode, such as literary and dramatic writing, or painting, sculpturing, building plastic shapes—has been studied in its own terms. Such candid study is more rewarding than the usual passionate declaration that all the arts are alike, only their materials differ, their principles are all the same, their techniques all analogous, etc. That is not only unsafe, but untrue. It is in pursuing the differences among them that one arrives, finally, at a point where no more differences appear; then one has found, not postulated, their unity. At that deep level there is only one concept exemplified in all the different arts, and that is the concept of Art.

The principles that obtain wholly and fundamentally in every kind of art are few, but decisive; they determine what is art, and what is not. Expressiveness, in one definite and appropriate sense, is the same in all art works of any kind. What is created is not the same in any two distinct arts —this is, in fact, what makes them distinct—but the principle of creation is the same. And "living form" means the same in all of them.

A work of art is an expressive form created for our perception through sense or imagination, and what it expresses is human feeling. The word "feeling" must be taken here in its broadest sense, meaning *everything that can be felt,* from physical sensation, pain and comfort, excitement and repose, to the most complex emotions, intellectual tensions, or the steady feeling-tones of a conscious human life. In stating what a work of art is, I have just used the words "form," "expressive," and "created"; these are key words. One at a time, they will keep us engaged.

Let us consider first what is meant, in this context, by a *form*. The word has many meanings, all equally legitimate for various purposes; even in connection with art it has several. It may, for instance—and often does—denote the familiar, characteristic structures known as the sonnet form, the sestina, or the ballad form in poetry, the sonata form, the madrigal, or the symphony in music, the contredance or the classical ballet in choreography, and so on. This is not what I mean; or rather, it is only a very small part of what I mean. There is another sense in which artists speak of "form" when they say, for instance, "form follows function," or declare that the one quality shared by all good works of art is "significant form," or entitle a book *The Problem of Form in Painting and Sculpture*, or *The Life of Forms in Art*, or *Search for Form*. They are using "form" in a wider sense, which on the one hand is close to the commonest, popular meaning, namely just the *shape* of a thing, and on the other hand to the quite unpopular meaning it has in science and philosophy, where it designates something more abstract; "form" in its most abstract sense means structure, articulation, a whole resulting from the relation of mutually dependent factors, or more precisely, the way that whole is put together.

The abstract sense, which is sometimes called "logical form," is involved in the notion of expression, at least the kind of expression that characterizes art. That is why artists, when they speak of achieving "form," use the word with something of an abstract connotation, even when they are talking about a visible and tangible art object in which that form is embodied.

The more recondite concept of form is derived, of course, from the naive one, that is, material shape. Perhaps the easiest way to grasp the idea of "logical form" is to trace its derivation.

Let us consider the most obvious sort of form, the shape of an object, say a lampshade. In any department store you will find a wide choice of lampshades, mostly monstrosities, and what is monstrous is usually their shape. You select the least offensive one, maybe even a good one, but realize that the color, say violet, will not fit into your room; so you look about for another shade of the same shape but a different color, perhaps green. In recognizing this same shape in another object, possibly of another material as well as another color, you have quite naturally and easily abstracted the concept of this shape from your actual impression of the first lampshade. Presently it may occur to you that this shade is too big for your lamp; you ask whether they have *this same shade* (meaning another one of this shape) in a smaller size. The clerk understands you.

But what is *the same* in the big violet shade and the little green one? Nothing but the interrelations among their respective various dimensions. They are not "the same" even in their spatial properties, for none of their actual measures are alike; but their shapes are congruent. Their respective spatial factors are put together in the same way, so they exemplify the same form.

It is really astounding what complicated abstractions we make in our ordinary dealing with forms—that is to say, through what twists and transformations we recognize the same logical form. Consider the similarity of your two hands. Put one on the table, palm down, superimpose the other, palm down, as you may have superimposed cut-out geometric shapes in school—they are not alike at all. But their shapes are *exact opposites.* Their respective shapes fit the same description, provided that the description is modified by a principle of application whereby the measures are read one way for one hand and the other way for the other—like a timetable in which the list of stations is marked: "Eastbound, read down; Westbound, read up."

As the two hands exemplify the same form with a principle of reversal understood, so the list of stations describes two ways of moving, indicated by the advice to "read down" for one and "read up" for the other. We can all abstract the common element in these two respective trips, which is called the *route.* With a return ticket we may return only by the same route. The same principle relates a mold to the form of the thing that is cast in it, and establishes their formal correspondence, or common logical form.

So far we have considered only objects—lampshades, hands, or regions of the earth—as having forms. These have fixed shapes; their parts remain in fairly stable relations to each other. But there are also substances that have no definite shapes, such as gases, mists, and water, which take the shape of any bounded space that contains them. The interesting thing about such amorphous fluids is that when they are put into violent motion they do exhibit visible forms, not bounded by any container. Think of the momentary efflorescence of a bursting rocket, the mushroom cloud of an atomic bomb, the funnel of water or dust screwing upward in a whirlwind. The instant the motion stops, or even slows beyond a certain degree, those shapes collapse and the apparent "thing" disappears. They are not shapes of things at all, but forms of motions, or dynamic forms.

Some dynamic forms, however, have more permanent manifestations, because the stuff that moves and makes them visible is constantly replenished. A waterfall seems to hang from the cliff, waving streamers of foam. Actually, of course, nothing stays there in mid-air; the water is always passing; but there is more and more water taking the same paths, so we have a lasting shape made and maintained by its passage—permanent dynamic form. A quiet river, too, has dynamic form; if it stopped flowing it would either go dry or become a lake. Some twenty-five hundred years ago, Heracleitos was struck by the fact that you cannot step twice into the same river at the same place—at least, if the river means the water, not its dynamic form, the flow.

When a river ceases to flow because the water is deflected or dried up, there remains the river bed, sometimes cut deeply in solid stone. That bed is shaped by the flow, and records as graven lines the currents that have ceased to exist. Its shape is static, but it *expresses* the dynamic form of the river. Again, we have two congruent forms, like a cast and its mold, but this time the congruence is more remarkable because it holds between a dynamic form and a static one. That relation is important; we shall be dealing with it again when we come to consider the meaning of "living form" in art.

The congruence of two given perceptible forms is not always evident upon simple inspection. The common *logical* form they both exhibit may become apparent only when you know the principle whereby to relate them, as you compare the shapes of your hands not by direct correspondence, but by correspondence of opposite parts. Where the two exemplifications of the single logical form are unlike in most other respects one needs a rule for matching up the relevant factors of one with the relevant factors of the other; that is to say, a *rule of translation,* whereby one instance of the logical form is shown to correspond formally to the other.

The logical form itself is not another thing, but an abstract concept, or better an *abstractable* concept. We usually don't abstract it deliberately, but only use it, as we use our vocal cords in speech without first learning all about their operation and then applying our knowledge. Most people perceive intuitively the similarity of their two hands without thinking of them as conversely related; they can guess at the shape of the hollow inside a wooden shoe from the shape of a human foot, without any abstract study of topology. But the first time they see a map in the Mercator projection—with parallel lines of longitude, not meeting at the poles—they find it hard to believe that this corresponds logically to the circular map they used in school, where the meridians bulged apart toward the equator and met at both poles. The visible shapes of the continents are different on the two maps, and it takes abstract thinking to match up the two representations of the same earth. If, however, they have grown up with both maps, they will probably see the geographical relationships either way with equal ease, because these relationships are not *copied* by either map, but *expressed,* and expressed equally well by both; for the two maps are different *projections* of the same logical form, which the spherical earth exhibits in still another—that is, a spherical—projection.

An expressive form is any perceptible or imaginable whole that exhibits relationships of parts, or points, or even qualities or aspects within the whole, so that it may be taken to represent some other whole whose elements have analogous relations. The reason for using such a form as a symbol is usually that the thing it represents is not perceivable or readily imaginable. We cannot see the earth as an object. We let a map or a little globe express the relationships of places on the earth, and think about the earth by means of it. The understanding of one thing through another seems to be a deeply intuitive process in the human brain; it is so natural that we often have difficulty in distinguishing the symbolic expressive form from what it conveys. The symbol seems to be the thing itself, or contain it, or be contained in it. A child interested in a globe will not say, "This means the earth," but "Look, this is the earth." A similar identification of symbol and meaning underlies the widespread conception of holy names, of the physical efficacy of rites, and many other primitive but culturally persistent phenomena. It has a bearing on our perception of artistic import; that is why I mention it here.

The most astounding and developed symbolic device humanity has evolved is language. By means of language we can conceive the intangible, incorporeal things we call our *ideas*, and the equally inostensible elements of our perceptual world that we call *facts*. It is by virtue of language that we can think, remember, imagine, and finally conceive a universe of facts. We can describe things and represent their relations, express rules of their interactions, speculate and predict and carry on a long symbolizing process known as reasoning. And above all, we can communicate, by producing a serried array of audible or visible words, in a pattern commonly known, and readily understood to reflect our multifarious concepts and percepts and their interconnections. This use of language is *discourse*; and the pattern of discourse is known as *discursive form*. It is a highly versatile, amazingly powerful pattern. It has impressed itself on our tacit thinking, so that we call all systematic reflection "discursive thought." It has made, far more than most people know, the very frame of our sensory experience —the frame of objective facts in which we carry on the practical business of life.

Yet even the discursive pattern has its limits of usefulness. An expressive form can express any complex of conceptions that, via some rule of projection, appears congruent with it, that is, appears to be of that form. Whatever there is in experience that will not take the impress—directly or indirectly—of discursive form, is not discursively communicable or, in the strictest sense, logically thinkable. It is unspeakable, ineffable; according to practically all serious philosophical theories today, it is unknowable.

Yet there is a great deal of experience that is knowable, not only as immediate, formless, meaningless impact, but as one aspect of the intricate web of life, yet defies discursive formulation, and therefore verbal expression: that is what we sometimes call the *subjective aspect* of experience, the direct feeling of it—what it is like to be waking and moving, to be drowsy, slowing down, or to be sociable, or to feel self-sufficient but alone; what it feels like to pursue an elusive thought or to have a big idea. All such directly felt experiences usually have no names—they are named, if at all, for the outward conditions that normally accompany their occurrence. Only the most striking ones have names like "anger," "hate," "love," "fear," and are collectively called "emotion." But we feel many things that never develop into any designable emotion. The ways we are moved are as various as the lights in a forest; and they may intersect, sometimes without cancelling each other, take shape and dissolve, conflict, explode into passion, or be transfigured. All these inseparable elements of subjective reality compose what we call the "inward life" of human beings. The usual factoring of that life-stream into mental, emotional, and sensory units is an arbitrary scheme of simplification that makes scientific treatment possible to a considerable extent; but we may already be close to the limit of its usefulness, that is, close to the point where its simplicity becomes an obstacle to further questioning and discovery instead of the revealing, ever-suitable logical projection it was expected to be.

Whatever resists projection into the discursive form of language is, indeed, hard to hold in conception, and perhaps impossible to communicate, in the proper and strict sense of the word "communicate." But fortunately our logical intuition, or form-perception, is really much more powerful than we commonly believe, and our knowledge—genuine knowledge, understanding—is considerably wider than our discourse. Even in the use of language, if we want to name something that is too new to have a name (for example, a newly invented gadget or a newly discovered creature), or want to express a relationship for which there is no verb or other connective word, we resort to metaphor; we mention it or describe it as something else, something analogous. The principle of metaphor is simply the principle of saying one thing and meaning another, and expecting to be understood to mean the other. A metaphor is not language, it is an idea expressed by language, an idea that in its turn functions as a symbol to express something. It is not discursive and therefore does not really make a statement of the idea it conveys; but it formulates a new conception for our direct imaginative grasp.

Sometimes our comprehension of a total experience is mediated by a metaphorical symbol because the experience is new, and language has words and phrases only for familiar notions. Then an extension of language will gradually follow the wordless insight, and discursive expression will supersede the non-discursive pristine symbol. This is, I think, the normal advance of human thought and language in that whole realm of knowledge where discourse is possible at all.

But the symbolic presentation of subjective reality for contemplation is not only tentatively beyond the reach of language—that is, not merely beyond the words we have; it is impossible in the essential frame of language. That is why those semanticists who recognize only discourse as a symbolic form must regard the whole life of feeling as formless, chaotic, capable only of symptomatic expression, typified in exclamations like "Ah!" "Ouch!" "My sainted aunt!" They usually do believe that art is an expression of feeling, but that "expression" in art is of this sort, indicating that the speaker has an emotion, a pain, or other personal experience, perhaps also giving us a clue to the general kind of experience it is—pleasant or unpleasant, violent or mild—but not setting that piece of inward life objectively before us so we may understand its intricacy, its rhythms and shifts of total appearance. The differences in feeling-tones or other elements of subjective experience are regarded as differences in quality, which must be felt to be appreciated. Furthermore, since we have no intellectual access to pure subjectivity, the only way to study it is to study the symptoms of the person who is having subjective experiences. This leads to physiological psychology—a very important and interesting field. But it tells us nothing about the phenomena of subjective life, and sometimes simplifies the problem by saying they don't exist.

Now, I believe the expression of feeling in a work of art—the function that makes the work an expressive form—is not symptomatic at all. An artist working on a tragedy need not be in personal despair or violent upheaval; nobody, indeed, could work in such a state of mind. His mind would be occupied with the causes of his emotional upset. Self-expression does not require composition and lucidity; a screaming baby gives his feeling far more release than any musician, but we don't go into a concert hall to hear a baby scream; in fact, if that baby is brought in we are likely to go out. We don't want self-expression.

A work of art presents feeling (in the broad sense I mentioned before, as everything that can be felt) for our contemplation, making it visible or audible or in some way perceivable through a symbol, not inferable from a symptom. Artistic form is congruent with the dynamic forms of our direct sensuous, mental, and emotional life; works of art are projections of "felt life," as Henry James called it, into spatial, temporal, and poetic structures. They are images of feeling, that formulate it for our cognition. What is artistically good is whatever articulates and presents feeling to our understanding.

Artistic forms are more complex than any other symbolic forms we know. They are, indeed, not abstractable from the works that exhibit them. We may abstract a shape from an object that has this shape, by disregarding color, weight and texture, even size; but to the total effect that is an artistic form, the color matters, the thickness of lines matters, and the appearance of texture and weight. A given triangle is the same in any position, but to an artistic form its location, balance, and surroundings are not indifferent. Form, in the sense in which we artists speak of "significant form" or "expressive form," is not an abstracted structure, but an apparition; and the vital processes of sense and emotion that a good work of art expresses seem to the beholder to be directly contained in it, not symbolized but really presented. The congruence is so striking that symbol and meaning appear as one reality. Actually, as one psychologist who is also a musician has written, "Music sounds as feelings feel." And likewise, in good painting, sculpture, or building, balanced shapes and colors, lines and masses look as emotions, vital tensions and their resolutions feel.

An artist, then, expresses feeling, but not in the way a politician blows off steam or a baby laughs and cries. He formulates that elusive aspect of reality that is commonly taken to be amorphous and chaotic; that is, he objectifies the subjective realm. What he expresses is, therefore, not his own actual feelings, but what he knows about human feeling. Once he is in possession of a rich symbolism, that knowledge may actually exceed his entire personal experience. A work of art expresses a conception of life, emotion, inward reality. But it is neither a confessional nor a frozen tantrum; it is a developed metaphor, a non-discursive symbol that articulates what is verbally ineffable—the logic of consciousness itself.

II. The Art Symbol and the Symbol in Art[1]

The problems of semantics and logic seem to fit into one frame, those of feeling into another. But somewhere, of course, mentality has arisen from more primitive vital processes. Somehow they belong into one and the same scientific frame. I am scouting the possibility that *rationality arises as an elaboration of feeling.*

Such a hypothesis leads one, of course, to the possible forms of feeling, and raises the problem of how they can be conceived and abstractly handled. Every theoretical construction requires a model. Especially if you want to get into elaborate structures you have to have a model—not an instance, but a symbolic form that can be manipulated, to convey, or perhaps to hold, your conceptions.

Language is the symbolic form of rational thought. It is more than that, but at least it can be fairly well pared down to abstract the elements of such thought and cognition. The structure of discourse expresses the forms of rational cogitation; that is why we call such thinking "discursive."

But discursive symbols offer no apt model of primitive forms of feeling. There has been a radical change—a special organization—in the making of rationality, perhaps under the influence of very specialized perception, perhaps under some other controlling condition. To express the forms of what might be called "unlogicized" mental life (a term we owe to Professor Henry M. Sheffer of Harvard), or what is usually called the "life of feeling," requires a different symbolic form.

This form, I think, is characteristic of art and is, indeed, the essence and measure of art. If this be so, then a work of art is a symbolic form in another way than the one (or ones) usually conceded to it. We commonly think of a work of art as representing something, and of its symbolic function, therefore, as representation. But this is not what I mean; not even secret or disguised representation. Many works represent nothing whatever. A building, a pot, a tune is usually beautiful without intentionally representing anything; and its unintentional representation may be found in bad and ugly pieces too. But if it is beautiful it is expressive; what it expresses is not an idea of some other thing, but an idea of a feeling. Representational works, if they are good art, are so for the same reason as non-representational ones. They have more than one symbolic function —representation, perhaps after two kinds, and also artistic expression, which is presentation of ideas of feeling.

There are many difficulties connected with the thesis that a work of art is primarily an expression of feeling—an "expression" in the logical sense, presenting the fabric of sensibility, emotion, and the strains of more concerted cerebration, for our impersonal cognition—that is, *in abstracto.* This sort of symbolization is the prime office of works of art, by virtue of which I call a work of art an *expressive form.*

In *Feeling and Form* I called it "the art symbol." This aroused a flood of criticism from two kinds of critics—those who misunderstood the alleged symbolic function and assimilated everything I wrote about it to some previous, familiar theory, either treating art as a genuine language or *symbolism,* or else confusing the art symbol with *the symbol of art* as known to iconologists or to modern psychologists; and, secondly, those critics who understood what I said but resented the use of the word "symbol" that differed from accepted usage in current semantical writings. Naturally the critics who understood what I said were the more influential ones; and their objections brought home the nature and extent of the difference between the function of a genuine symbol and a work of art. The difference is greater than I had realized before. Yet the function of what I called "the art symbol"—which is, in every case, the work of art as a whole, and purely as such—is more *like* a symbolic function than like anything else. A work of art is expressive in the way a proposition is expressive—as the formulation of an idea for conception. An idea may be well expressed or badly expressed. Similarly, in a work of art, feeling is well expressed or badly, and the work accordingly is good, or poor, or even bad—note that in the last case an artist would condemn it as *false.* The "significance" of a work, by virtue of which some early twentieth-century writers called it "significant form," is what is expressed. Since, however, *signification* is not its semantic function—it is quite particularly *not* a signal—I prefer Professor Melvin Rader's phrase, which he proposed in a review of *Feeling and Form*: "expressive form." This, he said, would be a better term than "the art symbol." I have used it ever since. Similarly, Professor Ernest Nagel objected to calling that which it expresses its "meaning," since it is not "meaning" in any of the precise senses known to semanticists; since then I have spoken of the *import* of an expressive form. This is the more convenient as the work may have *meanings* besides.

As a work of art is an expressive form somewhat like a symbol, and has import which is something like meaning, so it makes a logical abstraction, but not in the familiar way of genuine symbols—perhaps, indeed, a pseudo-abstraction. The best way to understand all these pseudo-semantics is to consider what a work of art is and does, and then compare it with language, and its doings with what language (or any genuine symbolism) does.

The expressive form, or art symbol, is, as I said before, the work of art itself, as it meets the eye (let us, for simplicity's sake, stay in the realm of pictorial art). It is the visible form, the apparition created out of paint deployed on a ground. The paint and the ground themselves disappear. One does not see a picture as a piece of spotted canvas, any more than one sees a screen with shadows on it in a movie. Whether there be things and persons in the picture or not, it presents volumes in a purely created space. These volumes define and organize the pictorial space which they are, in fact, creating; the purely visual space seems to be alive with their balanced or strained interactions. The lines that divide them (which may be physically drawn, or implied) create a rhythmic unity, for what they divide they also relate, to the point of complete integration. If a picture is successful it presents us with something quite properly, even though metaphorically, called "living form."

The word "form" connotes to many people the idea of a dead, empty shell, a senseless formality, lip-service, and sometimes an imposed rule to which actions, speeches, and works must *conform.* Many people think of form as a set of prescriptions when they speak of art forms, such as the sonata form or the rondo in music, the French ballade in poetry, etc. In all these uses the word "form" denotes something general, an abstracted concept that may be exemplified in various instances. This is a legitimate and widespread meaning of "form." But it is not the meaning Bell and Fry had in mind, and which I propose here. When they spoke of "significant form" (or, as now I would say, "expressive form") they meant a visible, individual form produced by the interaction of colors, lines, surfaces, lights and shadows, or whatever entered into a specific work. They used the word in the sense of something *formed,* as sometimes wonderful figures of soft color and melting contours are formed by clouds, or a spiral like a coiled spring is formed by the growth of a fern shoot; as a pot is formed out of clay, and a landscape out of paint spots. It may be a solid material form like the pot, or an illusory object like Hamlet's cloudy weasel. But it is a form for perception.

A work of art is such an individual form given directly to perception. But it is a special kind of form, since it seems to be more than a visual phenomenon—seems, indeed, to have a sort of life, or be imbued with feeling, or somehow, without being a genuine practical object, yet present the beholder with more than an arrangement of sense data. It carries with it something that people have sometimes called a quality (Clive Bell called "significant form" a quality), sometimes an emotional content, or the emotional tone of the work, or simply its life. This is what I mean by *artistic import*. It is not one of the qualities to be distinguished in the work, though our perception of it has the immediacy of qualitative experience; artistic import is *expressed*, somewhat as meaning is expressed in a genuine symbol, yet not exactly so. The analogy is strong enough to make it legitimate, even though easily misleading, to call the work of art the art symbol.

The difference, however, between an art symbol and a genuine symbol are of great interest and importance, for they illuminate the relations that obtain between many kinds of symbols, or things that have been so called, and show up the many levels on which symbolic and pseudo-symbolic functions may lie. I think a study of artistic expressiveness shows up a need of a more adaptable, that is to say more general, definition of "symbol" than the one accepted in current semantics and analytical philosophy. But we had better defer this problem to a later point. Let us, for the time being, call a *genuine symbol* whatever meets the strictest definition. Here is a definition offered by Ernest Nagel, in an article called "Symbolism and Science": "By a symbol I understand any occurrence (or type of occurrence), usually linguistic in status, which is taken to signify something else by way of tacit or explicit conventions or rules of language."

A word, say a familiar common noun, is a symbol of this sort. I would say that it conveys a concept, and refers to, or denotes, whatever exemplifies that concept. The word "man" conveys what we call the concept of "man," and denotes any being that exemplifies the concept—i.e., any man.

Now, words—our most familiar and useful symbols—are habitually used not in isolation, but in complex concepts of states of affairs, rather than isolated things, and refer to facts or possibilities or even impossibilities: those bigger units are descriptions and statements and other forms of *discourse*.

In discourse, another function of symbols comes into play, that is present but not very evident in the use of words simply to name things. This further function is the expression of ideas *about* things. A thing cannot be asserted by a name, only mentioned. As soon as you make an assertion you are symbolizing some sort of relation between concepts of things, or maybe things and properties, such as: "The grapes are sour." "All men are born equal." "I hate logic." Assertions, of course, need not be true—that is, they need not refer us to facts.

That brings us to the second great office of symbols, which is not to refer to things and communicate facts, but to express ideas; and this, in turn, involves a deeper psychological process, the formulation of ideas, or conception itself. Conception—giving form and connection, clarity and proportion to our impressions, memories, and objects of judgment—is the beginning of all rationality. Conception itself contains the elementary principles of knowledge: that an object of thought keeps its identity (as Aristotle put it, "A = A"), that it may stand in many relations to other things, that alternative possibilities exclude each other, and one decision entails another. Conception is the first requirement for thought.

This basic intellectual process of conceiving things in connection belongs, I think, to the same deep level of the mind as symbolization itself. That is the level where imagination is born. Animal intelligence or response to signs, of course, goes further back than that. The process of symbolic presentation is the beginning of human mentality, "mind" in a strict sense. Perhaps that beginning occurs at the stage of neural development where speech originates, and with speech the supreme talent of *envisagement.*

Response to stimuli, adaptation to conditions may occur without any envisagement of anything. Thought arises only where ideas have taken shape, and actual or possible conditions imagined. The word "imagined" contains the key to a new world: the image. I think the popular notion of an image as a replica of a sense impression has made epistemologists generally miss the most important character of images, which is that they are symbolic. That is why, in point of sensuous character, they may be almost indescribably vague, fleeting, fragmentary, or distorted; they may be sensuously altogether unlike what they represent. We think of mathematical relations in images that are just arbitrarily posited symbols; but these symbols are our mathematical images. They may be visual or auditory or what not, but functionally they are images, that articulate the logical relations we contemplate by means of them.

The great importance of reference and communication by means of symbols has led semanticists to regard these uses as the defining properties of symbols—that is, to think of a symbol as essentially a sign which stands for something else and is used to represent that thing in discourse. This preoccupation has led them to neglect, or even miss entirely, the more primitive function of symbols, which is to formulate experience as something imaginable in the first place—to fix entities, and formulate facts and the fact-like elements of thought called "fantasies." This function is *articulation.* Symbols articulate ideas. Even such arbitrarily assigned symbols as mere names serve this purpose, for whatever is named becomes an entity in thought. Its unitary symbol automatically carves it out as a unit in the world pattern.

Now let us return to the Art Symbol. I said before that it is a symbol in a somewhat special sense, because it performs some symbolic functions, but not all; especially, it does not stand for something else, nor refer to anything that exists apart from it. According to the usual definition of "symbol," a work of art should not be classed as a symbol at all. But that usual definition overlooks the greatest intellectual value and, I think, the prime office of symbols—their power of formulating experience, and presenting it objectively for contemplation, logical intuition, recognition, understanding.

That is articulation, or logical expression. And this function every good work of art does perform. It formulates the appearance of feeling, of subjective experience, the character of so-called "inner life," which discourse—the normal use of words—is peculiarly unable to articulate, and which therefore we can only refer to in a general and quite superficial way. The actual felt process of life, the tensions interwoven and shifting from moment to moment, the flowing and slowing, the drive and directedness of desires, and above all the rhythmic continuity of our selfhood, defies the expressive power of discursive symbolism. The myriad forms of subjectivity, the infinitely complex sense of life, cannot be rendered linguistically, that is, stated. But they are precisely what comes to light in a good work of art (not necessarily a "masterpiece"; there are thousands of works that are good art without being exalted achievements). A work of art is an expressive form, and vitality, in all its manifestations from sheer sensibility to the most elaborate phases of awareness and emotion, is what it may express.

But what is meant by saying it does not connote a concept or denote its instances? What I mean is that a genuine symbol, such as a word, is only a sign; in appreciating its meaning our interest reaches beyond it to the concept. The word is just an instrument. Its meaning lies elsewhere, and once we have grasped its connotation or identified something as its denotation we do not need the word any more. But a work of art does not point us to a meaning beyond its own presence. What is expressed cannot be grasped apart from the sensuous or poetic form that expresses it. In a work of art we have the direct presentation of a feeling, not a sign that points to it. That is why "significant form" is a misleading and confusing term: an Art Symbol does not signify, but only articulate and present its emotive content; hence the peculiar impression one always gets that feeling is in a beautiful and integral form. The work seems to be imbued with the emotion or mood or other vital experience that it expresses. That is why I call it an "expressive form," and call that which it formulates for us not its meaning, but its *import*. The import of art is perceived as something in the work, articulated by it but not further abstracted; as the import of a myth or a true metaphor does not exist apart from its imaginative expression.

The work as a whole is the image of feeling, which may be called the Art Symbol. It is a single organic composition, which means that its elements are not independent constituents, expressive, in their own right, of various emotional ingredients, as words are constituents of discourse, and have meanings in their own right, which go to compose the total meaning of the discourse. Language is a *symbolism,* a system of symbols with definable though fairly elastic meanings, and rules of combination whereby larger units—phrases, sentences, whole speeches—may be compounded, expressing similarly built-up ideas; Art, contrariwise, is not a symbolism. The elements in a work are always newly created with the total image, and although it is possible to . . . analyze what they contribute to the image, it is not possible to assign them any of its import apart from the whole. That is characteristic of organic form. The import of a work of art is its "life," which, like actual life, is an indivisible phenomenon. Who could say how much of a natural organism's life is in the lungs, how much in the legs, or how much more life would be added to us if we were given a lively tail to wave? The Art Symbol is a single symbol, and its import is not compounded of partial symbolic values. It is, I think, what Cecil Day Lewis means by "the poetic image," and what some painters, valiantly battling against popular misconceptions, call "the absolute image." It is the objective form of life-feeling in terms of space, or musical passage, or other fictive and plastic medium.

At last we come to the issue proposed in the title of this lecture. If the Art Symbol is a single, indivisible symbol, and its import is never compounded of contributive cargoes of import, what shall we make of the fact that many artists incorporate symbols in their works? Is it a mistake to interpret certain elements in poems or pictures, novels or dances, as symbols? Are the symbolists, imagists, surrealists, and the countless religious painters and poets before them all mistaken—everybody out of step except Johnnie?

Symbols certainly do occur in art, and in many, if not most, cases contribute notably to the work that incorporates them. Some artists work with a veritable riot of symbols; from the familiar halo of sacrosanct personages to the terrible figures of the *Guernica,* from the obvious rose of womanhood or the lily of chastity to the personal symbols of T. S. Eliot, sometimes concentric as a nest of tables, painters and poets have used symbols. Iconography is a fertile field of research; and where no influence-hunting historian has found any symbols, the literary critics find Bloom as a symbol of Moses, and the more psychological critics find Moses a symbol of birth.

They may all be right. One age revels in the use of symbolism in pictures, drama, and dance, another all but dispenses with it; but the fact that symbols and even whole systems of symbols (like the gesture-symbolism in Hindu dances) may occur in works of art is certainly patent.

All such elements, however, are genuine symbols; they have meanings, and the meanings may be stated. Symbols in art connote holiness, or sin, or rebirth, womanhood, love, tyranny, and so forth. These meanings enter into the work of art as elements, creating and articulating its organic form, just as its subject-matter—fruit in a platter, horses on a beach, a slaughtered ox, or a weeping Magdalen—enter into its construction. Symbols used in art lie on a different semantic level from the work that contains them. Their meanings are not part of its import, but elements in the form that has import, the expressive form. The meanings of incorporated symbols may lend richness, intensity, repetition or reflection or a transcendent unrealism, perhaps an entirely new balance to the work itself. But they function in the normal manner of symbols: they mean something beyond what they present in themselves. It makes sense to ask what a Hound of Heaven or brown sea-girls or Yeat's Byzantium may stand for, though in a poem where symbols are perfectly used it is usually unnecessary. Whether the interpretation has to be carried out or is skipped in reception of the total poetic image depends largely on the reader. The important point for us is that there is a literal meaning (sometimes more than one) connoted by the symbol that occurs in art.

The use of symbols in art is, in fine, a principle of construction—a device, in the most general sense of that word, "device." But there is a difference, often missed by theorists, between principles of construction and principles of art. The principles of art are few: the creation of what might be termed "an apparition" (this term would bear much discussion, but we have no time for it, and I think any one conversant with the arts knows what I mean), the achievement of organic unity or "livingness," the articulation of feeling. These principles of art are wholly exemplified in every work that merits the name of "art" at all, even though it be not great or in the current sense "original" (the anonymous works of ancient potters, for instance, were rarely original designs). Principles of construction, on the other hand, are very many; the most important have furnished our basic devices, and given rise to the Great Traditions of art. Representation in painting, diatonic harmony in music, metrical versification in poetry are examples of such major devices of composition. They are exemplified in thousands of works; yet they are not indispensable. Painting can eschew representation, music can be atonal, poetry can be poetry without any metrical scaffold.

The excited recognition and exploitation of a new constructive device—usually in protest against the traditional devices that have been used to a point of exhaustion, or even the point of corruption—is an artistic revolution. Art in our own day is full of revolutionary principles. Symbols, crowding metaphorical images, indirect subject-matter, dream elements instead of sights or events of waking life, often the one presented through the other, have furnished us lately with a new treasure-trove of motifs that command their own treatments, and the result is a new dawning day in art. The whole old way of seeing and hearing and word-thinking is sloughed off as the possibilities inherent in the modern devices of creation and expression unfold. In that excitement it is natural for the young—the young spirits, I mean, who are not necessarily the people of military or marriageable age—to feel that they are the generation that has discovered, at last, the principles of art, and that heretofore art labored under an incubus, the false principles they repudiate, so there never really was a pure and perfectable art before. They are mistaken, of course; but what of it? So were their predecessors—the Italian Camerata, the English Lake Poets, the early Renaissance painters—who discovered new principles of artistic organization and thought they had discovered how to paint, or how to make real music, or genuine poetry, for the first time. It is we, who philosophize about art and seek to understand its mission, that must keep distinctions clear.

In summary, then, it may be said that the difference between the Art Symbol and the symbol used in art is a difference not only of function but of kind. Symbols occurring in art are symbols in the usual sense, though of all degrees of complexity, from simplest directness to extreme indirectness, from singleness to deep interpenetration, from perfect lucidity to the densest over-determination. They have meanings, in the full sense that any semanticist would accept. And those meanings, as well as the images that convey them, enter into the work of art as elements in its composition. They serve to create the work, the expressive form.

The art symbol, on the other hand, *is* the expressive form. It is not a symbol in the full familiar sense, for it does not convey something beyond itself. Therefore it cannot strictly be said to have a meaning; what it does have is import. It is a symbol in a special and derivative sense, because it does not fulfill all the functions of a true symbol: it formulates and objectifies experience for direct intellectual perception, or intuition, but it does not abstract a concept for discursive thought. Its import is seen in it; not, like the meaning of a genuine symbol, by means of it but separable from the sign. The symbol in art is a metaphor, an image with overt or covert literal signification; the art symbol is the absolute image—the image of what otherwise would be irrational, as it is literally ineffable: direct awareness, emotion, vitality, personal identity—life lived and felt, the matrix of mentality.

—*Problems of Art* (1957)

ROGER SESSIONS

The Composer and His Message

It seems to me that the essential medium of music, the basis of its expressive powers and the element which gives it its unique quality among the arts, is *time*, made living for us through its expressive essence, *movement*.

Music is apprehended through the ear; the visual arts, painting, sculpture, and architecture through the eye. Is there not, more than a difference in function, a genuine and essential contrast in content, between what the eye sees and what the ear hears? I am speaking, of course, not in terms of science, but of ordinary experience. The visual arts govern a world of space, and it seems to me that perhaps the profoundest sensation which we derive from space is not so much that of extension as of permanence. On the most primitive level we feel space to be something permanent, fundamentally unchangeable; when movement is apprehended through the eye it takes place, so to speak, within a static framework, and the psychological impact of this framework is much more powerful than that of the vibrations which occur within its limits. For our experience the visual arts are undifferentiated in time. When we cease to look at a painting or a statue, it nevertheless continues to exist; it undergoes no perceptible change while we are looking at it, and we find it unchanged when we return to it after absence. We may contemplate it as long as we like, and though continued or repeated contemplation will make us familiar with more and more of its details or characteristics, these features have been present from the start, even to our eyes; it is our consciousness, following its own laws and not those of the object itself, which has developed. And when through these or other visual arts movement is suggested, it is through energy implied but not expressed.

Literature, to be sure, takes place in time, and in poetry and the drama time is, in a sense, not wholly unlike music, controlled. But even in poetry time is only a part, and a relatively small part, of the total expression; to a far greater extent than in music it is variable according to the will of the interpreter; its subtle rhythms, moreover, are subject to the laws of speech and of concrete literary sense. The real medium of literature is language, as shaped by the literary imagination. One of the expressive elements of language is rhythm, which is employed by the poet as an active, controlled medium in order to heighten its effect. I venture to say, however, that only in rare and fleeting instances does movement assume the whole or even the principal expressive burden.

In speaking of musical movement, on the other hand, we do not refer to rhythm alone, but rather to music as a complete and essentially indivisible whole. In this connection it is relevant to compare our ordinary experience of sound, the medium of musical movement, with the experience of space as I have described it above. If our visual experience is primarily of the permanent and static, sound, as we are ordinarily aware of it, is essentially of limited duration, fleeting and elusive—and the very essence of our adjustment to it is closely bound up with this fact. We cannot escape from it without fleeing its presence; and if it assumes anything like unchanging permanence this is such an exceptional occurrence that either we become quickly unaware of it, or it becomes intolerable. Sound for us, in other words, is naturally and inextricably associated with our sensation of time.

Time becomes real to us primarily through movement, which I have called its expressive essence; and it is easy to trace our primary musical responses to the most primitive movement of our being—to those movements which are indeed at the very basis of animate existence. The feeling for tempo, so often derived from the dance, has in reality a much more primitive basis in the involuntary movements of the nervous system and the body in the beating of the heart, and more consciously in breathing, later in walking. Accelerated movement is, from these very obvious causes, inevitably associated with excitement, retarded movement with a lessening of dynamic tension. The experience of meter has the most obvious and essential of its origins in the movements of breathing, with its alternation of upward and downward movements. The sense of effort, preparation, suspense, which is the psychological equivalent of the up-beat, finds its prototype in the act of inhalation, and the sense of weight, release, and finality produced by the down-beat corresponds most intimately to the act of exhalation. "In the beginning was rhythm," remarked Hans von Bülow; another distinguished musician remarked later that life begins, according to this above analogy, with an up-beat, the first breath of the new born child corresponding to the preparatory anacrusis of a musical statement, and ends, like the most natural and satisfying rhythm, with a down-beat.

The other primary elements of music—melody and rhythm—derive from more complicated but only slightly less essential muscular movements, which, it has been fairly well demonstrated, are reproduced in miniature by the human nervous system in response to musical impressions. If we instinctively respond to a rising melodic pitch by a feeling of increased tension and hence of heightened expression, or a falling pitch by the opposite sensation; if an increase in intensity of sound intensifies our dynamic response to the music, and vice versa, it is because we have already in our vocal experiences—the earliest and most primitive as well as later and more complicated ones—lived intimately through exactly the same effects. A raising of pitch or an increase in volume is the result of an intensification of effort, energy, and emotional power in the crying child just as truly as in the highly-evolved artistry of a Chaliapin or an Anderson.

Similarly, our feeling for rhythm, in the stricter sense, derives from the subtle and more expressive nervous and muscular movements, such as occur in speech, song, gesture, and the dance. A melodic phrase, for instance, is analogous psychologically to a vocal phrase, even though, because of its range, its length, or its specific technical demands, it may be realizable only on instruments; it must be thought, by the interpreter as well as the listener, "in one breath"—that is to say, with a psychological energy and control, precisely analogous to that with which the singer or orator husbands his vocal resources and controls his breathing, according to the expressive curve of melody or rhetorical declamation. The association between music and dancing is probably even older than that between music and words, and needs no further illustration here; the point I wish to make is that the basic elements of our musical sense, of musical expression, hence of music itself, have their sources in the most primitive regions of our being. In this sense music is the oldest, just as in a quite other sense it is the youngest, of the arts; the primary sensations on which it is based antedate in human experience those of visual perception and, to a greater extent, those of language.

On a still less primitive level than melody or rhythm as such, we meet with the one basic element of music which is not derived directly from movement. This element, harmony, has its origins in the nature of musical sound itself rather than in the impulses of the human organism. Already in speaking of *musical* sound we have moved far from the primitive elements to which I have drawn attention; we have in fact taken note of a stage in the process of their *organization*. When the ear has learned to discriminate between musical "tone" and undifferentiated sound, it has already achieved a high degree of refinement and begun to shape its raw materials into something approaching a controlled medium of expression. The musical tone, however, is not a simple sound but a complex of sounds. It is this fact which, apprehended by the musical ear at an advanced stage in its development, leads to the elaboration of an always more complex set of relationships between sounds, and thereby opens up still further and more decisive possibilities of organization. Speaking for the moment in historical terms, it was only about 1600 that the harmonic sense reached maturity: it was at approximately the same period that music loosed itself from exclusive association with words and gesture, and achieved complete autonomy. From the purely technical standpoint, it was the development of the harmonic sense which made this possible. For this enriched the composer's vocabulary by revealing to him new possibilities in the combination of sounds; through these possibilities, derived from the physical nature of the tone itself, it provided him with a point of departure which enables the ear to find its way through the intricacies of a much vaster tonal design than had ever been dreamed of before. In other words, it added incalculable resources to musical expression, by making possible an infinitely more complex, more supple, and more finely differentiated musical movement.

Harmony, then, more than any other musical element, brings to music the possibility of extension, of larger design, by reason of the well-nigh inexhaustible wealth and variety of tonal relationships which it embraces —and these relationships, as I have said before, have their origin in the unity of the tone itself. I have no intention of entering at this point on a detailed discussion of what musicians call "tonality." It is one of the most intricate and elusive of technical questions, and today so problematical that the term itself must needs be exactly and carefully defined before any fruitful or illuminating discussion could take place. What is not problematical is the psychological need which the principle of tonality, or key, fulfills; the necessity for a unifying organization in the sphere of sound, just as tempo and meter constitute a unifying principle in that of rhythm. Movement becomes expressive only if its directions are clear. To this end points of reference are necessary; suffice it to say that each new development in music has created, on a convincing psychological basis, its own points of reference. Without them, music would hardly be possible. One of the most vivid and effective means by which this is accomplished in music is harmony, with all that this implies.

If the above be true, it will be seen that harmony brings into music its only inherently static element. I have stated that it rests in principle on relationships implicit in the nature of a single tone. The extension and elaboration of these relationships gives musical movement an endless variety and nuance. The unity from which they are derived, however, and their constant implicit reference to that unity, gives them a psychologically compulsive power, an inherent sense of direction which is one of the most compelling expressive means at the composer's disposal. The tensions which it creates in the minds of the hearer are of the very essence of musical expression, and serve admirably to illustrate the real psychological character of what I have called "movement" in music.

Let me take as an illustration the opening bars of the Tristan Prelude—an admirable illustration, because the composer has told us so clearly what the music intends to convey—hopeless, unsatisfied longing. Please observe these points: First, the expression is attained by raising the tensions of which I have spoken to the highest degree of vividness and force. Secondly, the tension is achieved not by purely harmonic means, but rather by the interplay of several other musical means, of which I have mentioned only the most essential. Finally, in their entirety, they constitute a coherent musical design, achieved through the cumulative growth of a harmonic impression, and through the association of musical ideas in the repetition of a musical pattern. . . .

I have brought forward this illustration in order to show certain aspects of what I have called "movement" in music, and in doing so, I have touched upon the question of musical expression. What is it, actually, that music expresses?

Let us consider for a moment the music to which I have just referred. It is associated in Wagner's drama with a definite situation, with definite characters—hence we are accustomed to say it "expresses" the tragic love of Tristan and Isolde. Is it, however, the music that tells us this? Does it tell us anything, in any definite and inevitable sense, of love and tragedy? How much of what is implied in this definition of its content is there by virtue of its association with the drama? Is this association an inevitable one, or is it in the last analysis arbitrary?

The music certainly tells us nothing specifically about Tristan and Isolde, as concrete individuals; in no sense does it identify them or enlighten us regarding the concrete situation in which they find themselves. Does it tell us, then, specifically, anything about love and tragedy which we could identify as such without the aid of the dramatic and poetic images with which Wagner so richly supplies us?

It seems to me that the answer in each case is, inevitably, a negative one. There is, in any specific sense, neither love nor tragedy in the music.

I have attempted a description of . . . music in terms of movement. I have tried to point out how intimately our musical impulses are connected with those primitive movements which are among the very conditions of our existence. I have tried to show, too, how vivid is our response to the primitive elements of musical movement.

Is not this the key both to the content of music and to its extraordinary power? These bars from the Prelude to Tristan do not express for us love or frustration or even longing: but they reproduce for us, both qualitatively and dynamically, certain gestures of the spirit which are to be sure less specifically definable than any of these emotions, but which energize them and make them vital to us.

So it seems to me that this is the essence of musical expression. "Emotion" is specific, individual and conscious; music goes deeper than this, to the energies which animate our psychic life, and out of these creates a pattern which has an existence, laws, and human significance of its own. It reproduces for us the most intimate essence, the tempo and the energy, of our spiritual being; our tranquility and our restlessness, our animation and our discouragement, our vitality and our weakness—all, in fact, of the fine shades of dynamic variation of our inner life. It reproduces these far more directly and more specifically than is possible through any other medium of human communication.

In saying this I do not wish to deny that there is also an associative element in musical expression, or that this has its very definite place in certain types of music. It must be remembered that the emergence of music as an entirely separate art has been, as I have pointed out, of very recent origin; that until the last three hundred years it was always connected with more concrete symbols, whether of the word or the dance. It is but natural, therefore, that this associative element should form a part of the composer's medium. It is, however, I believe, not an essential part, especially since it consists so largely in associations which have their basis in movement. Quiet, lightly contrasted movement, for instance, may be associated with outer as well as inner tranquility—the light rustling of leaves in the wind, or the movement of a tranquil sea—just as agitated movement may be employed to suggest the storms in nature, as well as the perturbations of the spirit. On the other hand, we meet with associations of a far less essential nature—the tone of the trumpet, for instance, suggesting martial ideas, or certain localisms—folk songs, exotic scales, bizarre instrumental combinations, etc., which are used for the purposes of specific and literal coloring. But one would hardly attach more than a very superficial musical significance to associations of this type. They belong definitely in the sphere of applied art, and when they occur in works of serious import they serve, in conformity with an expressed intention of the composer, in a decidedly subordinate capacity, to direct the listener to more concrete associations than the music, in its essential content, can convey.

The above considerations indicate why a certain type of literary rhapsody seems to the musician quite amateurish and beside the point, in spite of the fact that musicians themselves—even great ones—have occasionally indulged in it. At best it is a literary production, bearing no real relationship to the music and throwing no real light on its content, but expressing the literary impulses of the author with more or less significance, according to his personality. Thus it is that of three distinguished commentators on Beethoven's Seventh Symphony—all three of them composers, and two of them composers of genius—one finds it a second Eroica, another a second Pastorale, and the third "the apotheosis of the dance." It must not be forgotten that, for the composer, notes, chords, melodic intervals—all the musical materials—are far more real, far more expressive, than words; that, let us say, a "leading tone" or a chord of the subdominant are for him not only notes, but sensations, full of meaning and capable of infinite nuances of modification; and that when he speaks or thinks in terms of them he is using words which, however obscure and dry they may sound to the uninitiated, are for him fraught with dynamic sense.

So, in trying to understand the work of the composer, one must first think of him as living in a world of sounds, which in response to his creative impulse become animated with movement. The first stage in his work is that of what is generally known by the somewhat shopworn and certainly unscientific term "inspiration." The composer, to use popular language again, "has an idea"—an idea, let me make clear, consisting of definite musical notes and rhythms, which will engender for him the momentum with which his musical thought proceeds. The inspiration may come in a flash, or as sometimes happens, it may grow and develop gradually. I have in my possession photostatic copies of several pages of Beethoven's sketches for the last movement of his "Hammerklavier Sonata"; the sketches show him carefully modelling, then testing in systematic and apparently cold-blooded fashion, the theme of the fugue. Where, one might ask, is the inspiration here? Yet if the word has any meaning at all, it is certainly appropriate to this movement, with its irresistible and titanic energy of expression, already present in the theme. The inspiration takes the form, however, not of a sudden flash of music, but a clearly-envisaged impulse toward a certain goal for which the composer was obliged to strive. When this perfect realization was attained, however, there could have been no hesitation—rather a flash of recognition that this was exactly what he wanted.

Inspiration, then, is the impulse which sets creation in movement: it is also the energy which keeps it going. The composer's principal problem is that of recapturing it in every phase of his work; of bringing, in other words, the requisite amount of energy to bear on every detail, as well as, constantly, on his vision of the whole.

This vision of the whole I should call the conception. For the musician this too takes the form of concrete musical materials—perceived, however, not in detail but in foreshortened form. The experience, I believe, is quite different for the mature and experienced composer from what it is for the young beginner. As he grows in practice and imagination it assumes an ever more preponderant rôle, and appears more and more to be the essential act of creation. It differs from what I have described as "inspiration" only in works of large dimensions which cannot be realized in a short space of time. It arises out of the original inspiration, and is, so to speak, an extension of its logic.

What I have described as inspiration, embodies itself in what is the only true sense of the word "style"; conception, in the only true sense of the word "form." Neither style nor form, in their essence, are derived from convention; they always must be, and are, created anew, and establish and follow their own laws. It is undeniable that certain periods—and the most fortunate ones—have established clearly defined patterns or standards which give the artist a basis on which to create freely. Our own is not one of these; today the individual is obliged to discover his own language before he has completed the mastery of it. Where such standards exist, however, they retain their vitality only as long as they are in the process of development. After this process has stopped, they wither and die, and can be re-created only by a conscious and essentially artificial effort, since they are produced by a unique and unrecoverable impulse, and are suited only to the content which has grown with them.

After inspiration and conception comes execution. The process of execution is first of all that of listening inwardly to the music as it shapes itself; of allowing the music to grow; of following both inspiration and conception wherever they may lead. A phrase, a motif, a rhythm, even a chord, may contain within itself, in the composer's imagination, the energy which produces movement. It will lead the composer on, through the force of its own momentum or tension, to other phrases, other motifs, other chords.

The principles underlying what is generally called musical structure are not briefly or easily formulated. We may, however, easily observe certain general characteristics which are always present in music and which seem inseparable from its nature as an art of movement.

Primary among these is the principle of *association.* I use the term here in a purely musical sense; certain features of the music must recur, and they gain their significance through the fact of their recurrence. The famous first four notes of Beethoven's Fifth Symphony, in spite of the various literary interpretations attached to them, have no possible significance by themselves. To be sure they remind us, who are familiar with musical literature, inevitably of Beethoven—but in the absence of all association they would have no meaning whatever. Musically, they begin to have significance only when they are followed by four other notes, similar in tempo, accent, and interval, but differing slightly in pitch and by this fact becoming, so to speak, the vehicle of movement. The accented E flat, in the second measure, is carried through this associative means downward to the D in the fourth measure. The sense of this motion is the direct result of the association of measures three and four with a parallel passage in the first two measures.

Obviously, such an example is rudimentary in the extreme and serves only to illustrate the principle in its simplest form; to show in some slight measure how association brings to music significance and coherence, and how, through its means, musical movement may be organized on a vaster basis than is possible within the limits of a single phrase. It would be possible of course to proceed with an analysis of the whole first movement of the Symphony and to show how, later, certain variations or transformations of the motif play an important and fateful rôle in introducing contrasts or in intensifying the dynamic outlines.

It is necessary, I feel, to draw a careful distinction between the *psychological* principles of association and the purely material one of repetition, even though the former so often takes shape as the latter in its most literal sense. The classic composers had the finest of instincts in this respect and their art is incredibly rich in resource and variety of associative means. Some of their successors, unfortunately, are more literal minded, often substituting a materialistic principle of repetition for the creative principle of association, and later music finds itself in this respect as in others frequently caught in the toils of a sterile academicism. Artistic form has vitality and coherence only as long as its vitalizing principle is the imagination and impulse of the composer; it withers and dies as soon as the "materials" of music assume an independent existence—a condition which is possible only when the genuine creative impulse is weak.

Closely allied to the principle of association is that of *progression.* This is so obvious, in an art which has its basis in time, as scarcely to need mention. To say that in such an art each individual moment must be, generally speaking, of greater intensity and significance than the one which precedes it, is perhaps a truism. Less obvious and more difficult to describe are the infinitely various means through which progression is achieved. The two examples already given, however, the Tristan Prelude and the opening bars of the Fifth Symphony—each illustrate the principle as clearly as possible; and, indeed, the analysis of each, even from quite different points of view, was largely concerned precisely with the gradual and progressive movement towards a clearly envisaged goal, and, especially in the case of the Tristan Prelude, the steady intensification of effect until this goal is reached.

In music of large design, the various elements group themselves into larger patterns. In the passage from the Tristan Prelude, . . . four short phrases contribute to the unfolding of a sort of superphrase, as clear and expressive in its highly organized outline as the simple primitive vocalization which is the origin and the basis of music. Such organization is, of course, indispensable to music of large dimensions.

I will mention, finally, a third principle, that of *contrast.* In the sense in which I use the word it denotes something quite other than what I have called progression. The latter term applies, obviously, to the development of a single impulse and is the process by which the impulse takes extended shape. When the impulse is complete, however, other necessities appear, and the need for contrast arises. What form the contrast shall take—whether the same materials shall be presented under different aspects, or whether a quite new departure is needed—such questions and the infinite degrees of difference which they include, depend upon the conception, the context, and the scope of the work in question. The large contrasts contained in a work of music, however, reveal its essential outlines and give it its largest rhythm, through the alternation of musical ideas with their contrasting movement, emphasis, and dynamic intensity.

From these remarks it may be inferred quite clearly that conception and execution are inseparable and in the last analysis identical. "Form" in music is identical with "content," regardless of whether the latter be significant or the former coherent. The actual process of composition remains mysterious—the composer is following, as best he can and with all the means at his disposal, the demands of his conception, listening for the sounds and rhythms which embody it, and giving them the shape which his creative vision prescribes.

—*The Intent of the Artist,* edited by Augusto Centeno (1941)

RUDOLF ARNHEIM

The Expressiveness of Visual Forms

1. Expression

Every work of art must express something. This means, first of all, that the content of the work must go beyond the presentation of the individual objects of which it consists. But such a definition is too large for our purpose. It broadens the notion of "expression" to include any kind of communication. True, we commonly say, for example, that a man "expresses his opinion." Yet artistic expression seems to be something more specific. It requires that the communication of the data produce an "experience," the active presence of the forces that make up the perceived pattern. How is such an experience achieved?

Inside Linked to Outside

In a limited sense of the term, expression refers to features of a person's external appearance and behavior that permit us to find out what the person is feeling, thinking, striving for. Such information may be gathered from a man's face and gestures, the way he talks, dresses, keeps his room, handles a pen or a brush, as well as from the opinions he holds, the interpretation he gives to events. This is less and also more than what I mean here by expression: less, because expression must be considered even when no reference is made to a mind manifesting itself in appearance;

more, because much importance cannot be attributed to what is merely inferred intellectually and indirectly from external clues. Nevertheless this more familiar meaning of the term must be discussed briefly here.

We look at a friend's face, and two things may happen: we understand what his mind is up to; and we find in ourselves a duplicate of his experiences. The traditional explanation of this accomplishment may be gathered from a playful review of Lavater's *Physiognomic Fragments for the Advancement of the Knowledge and Love of Our Fellow Man* written by the poet Matthias Claudius around 1775. "Physiognomics is a science of faces. Faces are *concreta* for they are related *generaliter* to natural reality and *specialiter* are firmly attached to people. Therefore the question arises whether the famous trick of the 'abstractio' and the 'methodus analytica' should not be applied here, in the sense of watching out whether the letter *i*, whenever it appears, is furnished with a dot and whether the dot is never found on top of another letter; in which case we should be sure that the dot and the letter are twin brothers so that when we run into Castor we can expect Pollux not to be far away. For an example we posit that there be one hundred gentlemen, all of whom are very quick on their feet, and they had given sample and proof of this, and all of these hundred gentlemen had a wart on their noses. I am not saying that gentlemen with a wart on their noses are cowards but am merely assuming it for the sake of the example. . . . Now *ponamus* there comes to my house a fellow who calls me a wretched scribbler and spits me into the face. Suppose I am reluctant to get into a fist fight and also cannot tell what the outcome would be, and I am standing there and considering the issue. At that moment I discover a wart on his nose, and now I cannot refrain myself any longer, I go after him courageously and, without any doubt, get away unbeaten. This procedure would represent, as it were, the royal road in this field. The progress might be slow but just as safe as that on other royal roads."

In a more serious vein, the theory was stated early in the eighteenth century by the philosopher Berkeley. In his essay on vision he speaks about the way in which the observer sees shame or anger in the looks of a man. "Those passions are themselves invisible: they are nevertheless let in by the eye along with colors and alterations of countenance, which are the immediate object of vision, and which signify them for no other reason than barely because they have been observed to accompany them: without which experience, we should no more have taken blushing for a sign of shame than gladness." Charles Darwin, in his book on the expression of emotions, devoted a few pages to the same problem. He believed that external manifestations and their physical counterparts are connected by the observer either on the basis of an inborn instinct or of learning. "Moreover, when a child cries or laughs, he knows in a general manner what he is doing and what he feels; so that a very small exertion of reason would tell him what crying or laughing meant in others. But the question is, do our children acquire their knowledge of expression solely by experience through the power of association and reason? As most of the movements of expression must have been gradually acquired, afterwards becoming instinctive, there seems to be some degree of *a priori* probability that their recognition would likewise have become instinctive."

Recently a new version of the traditional theory has developed from a curious tendency on the part of many social scientists to assume that when people agree on some fact it is probably based on an unfounded convention. According to this view, judgments of expression rely on "stereotypes," which individuals adopt ready-made from their social group. For example, we have been told that aquiline noses indicate courage and that protruding lips betray sensuality. The promoters of the theory generally imply that such judgments are wrong, as though information not drawn from the individual's firsthand experience could never be trusted. The real danger does not lie in the social origin of the information, but rather in the fact that people have a tendency to acquire simply structured concepts on the basis of insufficient evidence, which may have been gathered firsthand or secondhand, and to preserve these concepts unchanged in the face of contrary experience. Whereas this may make for many one-sided or entirely wrong evaluations of individuals and groups of people, the existence of stereotypes does not explain the origin of physiognomic judgments. If these judgments stem from tradition, what is the tradition's source? Are they right or wrong? Even though often misapplied, traditional interpretations of physique and behavior may still be based on sound observation. In fact, perhaps they are so hardy because they are so true.

Within the framework of associationist thinking, a step forward was made by Lipps, who pointed out that the perception of expression involves the activity of forces. His theory of "empathy" was designed to explain why we find expression even in inanimate objects, such as the columns of a temple. The reasoning was as follows. When I look at the columns, I know from past experience the kind of mechanical pressure and counterpressure that occurs in them. Equally from past experience, I know how I should feel myself if I were in the place of the columns and if those physical forces acted upon and within my own body. I project my own kinesthetic feelings into the columns. Furthermore, the pressures and pulls called up from the stores of memory by the sight tend to provoke responses also in other areas of the mind. "When I project my strivings and forces into nature I do so also as to the way my strivings and forces make me feel, that is, I project my pride, my courage, my stubbornness, my lightness, my playful assuredness, my tranquil complacence. Only thus my empathy with regard to nature becomes truly esthetic empathy."

The characteristic feature of traditional theorizing in all its varieties is the belief that the expression of an object is not inherent in the visual pattern itself. What we see provides only clues for whatever knowledge and feelings we may mobilize from memory and project upon the object. The visual pattern has as little to do with the expression we confer upon it as words have to do with the content they transmit. The letters "pain" mean "suffering" in English and "bread" in French. Nothing in them suggests the one rather than the other meaning. They transmit a message only because of what we have learned about them.

Expression Embedded in Structure

William James was not so sure that body and mind have nothing intrinsically in common. "I cannot help remarking that the disparity between motions and feelings, on which these authors lay so much stress, is somewhat less absolute than at first sight it seems. Not only temporal succession, but such attributes as intensity, volume, simplicity or complication, smooth or impeded change, rest or agitation, are habitually predicated of both physical facts and mental facts." Evidently James reasoned that although body and mind are different media—the one being material, the other not—they might still resemble each other in certain structural properties.

This point was greatly stressed by *gestalt* psychologists. Particularly Wertheimer asserted that the perception of expression is much too immediate and compelling to be explainable merely as a product of learning. When we watch a dancer, the sadness or happiness of the mood seems to be directly inherent in the movements themselves. Wertheimer concluded that this was true because formal factors of the dance reproduced identical factors of the mood. The meaning of this theory may be illustrated by reference to an experiment by Binney in which members of a college dance group were asked individually to give improvisations of such subjects as sadness, strength, or night. The performances of the dancers showed much agreement. For example, in the representation of sadness the movement was slow and confined to a narrow range. It was mostly curved in shape and showed little tension. The direction was indefinite, changing, wavering, and the body seemed to yield passively to the force of gravitation rather than being propelled by its own initiative. It will be admitted that the physical mood of sadness has a similar pattern. In a depressed person the mental processes are slow and rarely go beyond matters closely related to immediate experiences and interests of the moment. In all his thinking and striving are softness and a lack of energy. There is little determination, and activity is often controlled by outside forces.

Naturally there is a traditional way of representing sadness in a dance, and the performances of the students may have been influenced by it. What counts, however, is that the movements, whether spontaneously invented or copied from other dancers, exhibited a formal structure so strikingly similar to that of the intended mood. And since such visual qualities as speed, shape, or direction are immediately accessible to the eye, it seems legitimate to assume that they are the carriers of an expression directly comprehensible to the eye.

If we examine the facts more closely, we find that expression is conveyed not so much by the "geometric-technical" properties of the percept as such, but by the forces they can be assumed to arouse in the nervous system of the observer. Regardless of whether the object moves (dancer, actor) or is immobile (painting, sculpture), it is the kind of directed tension or "movement"—its strength, place, and distribution—transmitted by the visible patterns that is perceived as expression. . . .

The Priority of Expression

The impact of the forces transmitted by a visual pattern is an intrinsic part of the percept, just as shape or color. In fact, expression can be described as the primary content of vision. We have been trained to think of perception as the recording of shapes, distances, hues, motions. The awareness of these measurable characteristics is really a fairly late accomplishment of the human mind. Even in the Western man of the twentieth century it presupposes special conditions. It is the attitude of the scientist and the engineer or of the salesman who estimates the size of a customer's waist, the shade of a lipstick, the weight of a suitcase. But if I sit in front of a fireplace and watch the flames, I do not normally register certain shades of red, various degrees of brightness, geometrically defined shapes moving at such and such a speed. I see the graceful play of aggressive tongues, flexible striving, lively color. The face of a person is more readily perceived and remembered as being alert, tense, concentrated rather than as being triangularly shaped, having slanted eyebrows, straight lips, and so on. This priority of expression, although somewhat modified in adults by a scientifically oriented education, is striking in children and primitives, as has been shown by Werner and Köhler. The profile of a mountain is soft or threateningly harsh; a blanket thrown over a chair is twisted, sad, tired.

The priority of physiognomic properties should not come as a surprise. Our senses are not self-contained recording devices operating for their own sake. They have been developed by the organism as an aid in properly reacting to the environment. The organism is primarily interested in the forces that are active around it—their place, strength, direction. Hostility and friendliness are attributes of forces. And the perceived impact of forces makes for what we call expression.

If expression is the primary content of vision in daily life, the same should be all the more true for the way the artist looks at the world. The expressive qualities are his means of communication. They capture his attention, through them he understands and interprets his experiences, and they determine the form patterns he creates. Therefore the training of art students should be expected to consist basically in sharpening their sense of these qualities and in teaching them to look to expression as the guiding criteria for every stroke of the pencil, brush, or chisel. In fact many good art teachers do precisely this. But there are also plenty of times when the spontaneous sensitivity of the student to expression not only is not developed further, but is even disturbed and suppressed. There is, for example, an old-fashioned but not extinct way of teaching students to draw from the model by asking them to establish the exact length and direction of contour lines, the relative position of points, the shape of masses. In other words, students are to concentrate on the geometric-technical qualities of what they see. In its modern version this method consists in urging the young artist to think of the model or of a freely invented design as a configuration of masses, planes, directions. Again interest is focussed on geometric-technical qualities.

This method of teaching follows the principles of scientific definition rather than those of spontaneous vision. There are, however, other teachers who will proceed differently. With a model sitting on the floor in a hunched-up position, they will not begin by making the students notice that the whole figure can be inscribed in a triangle. Instead they will ask about the expression of the figure; they may be told, for example, that the person on the floor looks tense, tied together, full of potential energy. They will suggest, then, that the student try to render this quality. In doing so the student will watch proportions and directions, but not as geometric properties in themselves. These formal properties will be perceived as being functionally dependent upon the primarily observed expression, and the correctness and incorrectness of each stroke will be judged on the basis of whether or not it captures the dynamic "mood" of the subject. Equally, in a lesson of design, it will be made clear that to the artist, just as to any unspoiled human being, a circle is not a line of constant curvature, whose points are all equally distant from a center, but first of all a compact, hard, restful thing. Once the student has understood that roundness is not identical with circularity, he may try for a design whose structural logic will be controlled by the primary concept of something to be expressed. For whereas the artificial concentration on formal qualities will leave the student at a loss as to which pattern to select among innumerable and equally acceptable ones, an expressive theme will serve as a natural guide to forms that fit the purpose.

It will be evident that what is advocated here is not the so-called "self-expression." The method of self-expression plays down, or even annihilates, the function of the theme to be represented. It recommends a passive, "projective" pouring-out of what is felt inside. On the contrary, the method discussed here requires active, disciplined concentration of all organizing powers upon the expression that is localized in the object of representation.

It might be argued that an artist must practice the purely formal technique before he may hope to render expression successfully. But that is exactly the notion that reverses the natural order of the artistic process. In fact all good practicing is highly expressive. This first occurred to me many years ago when I watched the dancer Gret Palucca perform one of her most popular pieces, which she called "Technical Improvisations." This number was nothing but the systematic exercise that the dancer practiced every day in her studio in order to loosen up the joints of her body. She would start out by doing turns of her head, then move her neck, then shrug her shoulders, until she ended up wriggling her toes. This purely technical practice was a success with the audience because it was thoroughly expressive. Forcefully precise and rhythmical movements presented, quite naturally, the entire catalogue of human pantomime. They passed through all the moods from lazy happiness to impertinent satire.

In order to achieve technically precise movements, a capable dance teacher may not ask students to perform "geometrically" defined positions, but to strive for the muscular experience of uplift, or attack, or yielding, that will be created by correctly executed movements. (Comparable methods are nowadays applied therapeutically in physical rehabilitation work. For example, the patient is not asked to concentrate on the meaningless, purely formal exercise of flexing and stretching his arm, but on a game or piece of work that involves suitable motions of the limbs as a means to a sensible end.)

The Physiognomics of Nature

The perception of expression does not therefore necessarily—and not even primarily—serve to determine the state of mind of another person by way of externally observable manifestations. Köhler has pointed out that people normally deal with and react to expressive physical behavior in itself rather than being conscious of the psychical experiences reflected by such behavior. We perceive the slow, listless, "droopy" movements of one person as contrasted to the brisk, straight, vigorous movements of another, but do not necessarily go beyond the meaning of such appearance by thinking explicitly of the physical weariness or alertness behind it. Weariness and alertness are already contained in the physical behavior itself; they are not distinguished in any essential way from the weariness of slowly floating tar or the energetic ringing of the telephone bell. It is true, of course, that during a business conversation one person may be greatly concerned with trying to read the other's thoughts and feelings through what can be seen in his face and gestures. "What is he up to? How is he taking it?" But in such circumstances we clearly go beyond what is apparent in the perception of expression itself, and secondarily apply what we have seen to the mental processes that may be hidden "behind" the outer image.

Particularly the content of the work of art does not consist in states of mind that the dancer may pretend to be experiencing in himself or that our imagination may bestow on a painted Mary Magdalen or Sebastian. The substance of the work consists in what appears in the visible pattern itself. Evidently, then, expression is not limited to living organisms that we assume to possess consciousness. A steep rock, a willow tree, the colors of a sunset, the cracks in a wall, a tumbling leaf, a flowing fountain, and in fact a mere line or color or the dance of an abstract shape on the movie screen have as much expression as the human body, and serve the artist equally well. In some ways they serve him even better, for the human body is a particularly complex pattern, not easily reduced to the simplicity of shape and motion that transmits compelling expression. Also it is overloaded with nonvisual associations. The human figure is not the easiest, but the most difficult, vehicle of artistic expression.

The fact that nonhuman objects have genuine physiognomic properties has been concealed by the popular assumption that they are merely dressed up with human expression by an illusory "pathetic fallacy," by empathy, anthropomorphism, primitive animism. But if expression is an inherent characteristic of perceptual patterns, its manifestations in the human figure are but a special case of a more general phenomenon. The comparison of an object's expression with a human state of mind is a secondary process. A weeping willow does not look sad because it looks like a sad person. It is more adequate to say that since the shape, direction, and flexibility of willow branches convey the expression of passive hanging, a comparison with the structurally similar state of mind and body that we call sadness imposes itself secondarily. The columns of a temple do not strive upward and carry the weight of the roof so dramatically because we put ourselves in their place, but because their location, proportion, and shape are carefully chosen in such a way that their image contains the desired expression. Only because and when this is so, are we enabled to "sympathize" with the columns, if we so desire. An inappropriately designed temple resists all empathy.

To define visual expression as a reflection of human feelings would seem to be misleading on two counts: first, because it makes us ignore the fact that expression has its origin in the perceived pattern and in the reaction of the brain field of vision to this pattern; second, because such a description unduly limits the range of what is being expressed. We found as the basis of expression a configuration of forces. Such a configuration interests us because it is significant not only for the object in whose image it appears, but for the physical and mental world in general. Motifs like rising and falling, dominance and submission, weakness and strength, harmony and discord, struggle and conformance, underlie all existence. We find them within our own mind and in our relations to other people, in the human community and in the events of nature. Perception of expression fulfills its spiritual mission only if we experience in it more than the resonance of our own feelings. It permits us to realize that the forces stirring in ourselves are only individual examples of the same forces acting throughout the universe. We are thus enabled to sense our place in the whole and in the inner unity of that whole.

Some objects and events resemble each other with regard to the underlying patterns of forces; others do not. Therefore, on the basis of their expressive appearance, our eye spontaneously creates a kind of Linnean classification of all things existing. This perceptual classification cuts across the order suggested by other kinds of categories. Particularly in our modern Western civilization we are accustomed to distinguishing between animate and inanimate things, human and nonhuman creatures, the mental and the physical. But in terms of expressive qualities, the character of a given person may resemble that of a particular tree more closely than that of another person. The state of affairs in a human society may be similar to the tension in the skies just before the outbreak of a thunderstorm. Further, our kind of scientific and economic thinking makes us define things by measurements rather than by the dynamics of their appearance. Our criteria for what is useful or useless, friendly or hostile, have tended to sever the connections with outer expression, which they possess in the minds of children or primitives. If a house or a chair suits our practical purposes, we may not stop to find out whether its appearance expresses our style of living. In business relations we define a man by his census data, his income, age, position, nationality, or race—that is, by categories that ignore the inner nature of the man as it is manifest in his outer expression.

Primitive languages give us an idea of the kind of world that derives from a classification based on perception. Instead of restricting itself to the verb "to walk," which rather abstractly refers to locomotion, the language of the African Ewe takes care to specify in every kind of walking the particular expressive qualities of the movement. There are expressions for "the gait of a little man whose limbs shake very much, to walk with a dragging step like a feeble person, the gait of a long-legged man who throws his legs forward, of a corpulent man who walks heavily, to walk in a dazed fashion without looking ahead, an energetic and firm step," and many others. These distinctions are not made out of sheer esthetic sensitivity, but because the expressive properties of the gait are believed to reveal important practical information on what kind of man is walking and what is his intent at the moment.

Although primitive languages often surprise us by their wealth of subdivisions for which we see no need, they also reveal generalizations that to us may seem unimportant or absurd. For example, the language of the Klamath Indians has prefixes for words referring to objects of similar shape or movement. Such a prefix may describe "the outside of a round or spheroidal, cylindrical, discoid or bulbed object, or a ring; also voluminous; or again, an act accomplished with an object which bears such a form; or a circular or semi-circular or waving movement of the body, arms, hands, or other parts. Therefore this prefix is to be found connected with clouds, celestial bodies, rounded slopes on the earth's surface, fruits rounded or bulbed in shape, stones and dwellings (these last being usually circular in form.) It is employed too, for a crowd of animals, for enclosures, social gatherings (since an assembly usually adopts the form of a circle), and so forth."

Such a classification groups things together that to our way of thinking belong in very different categories and have little or nothing in common. At the same time, these features of primitive language remind us that the poetical habit of uniting practically disparate objects by metaphor is not a sophisticated invention of artists, but derives from and relies on the universal and spontaneous way of approaching the world of experience.

George Braque advises the artist to seek the common in the dissimilar. "Thus the poet can say, The swallow knifes the sky, and thereby makes a knife out of a swallow." It is the function of the metaphor to make the reader penetrate the concrete shell of the world of things by combinations of objects that have little in common but the underlying pattern. Such a device, however, would not work unless the reader of poetry was still alive, in his own daily experience, to the symbolic or metaphoric connotation of all appearance and activity. For example, hitting or breaking things normally evokes, if ever so slightly, the overtone of attack and destruction. There is a tinge of conquest and achievement to all rising—even the climbing of a staircase. If the shades are pulled in the morning and the room is flooded with light, more is experienced than a simple change of illumination. One aspect of the wisdom that belongs to a genuine culture is the constant awareness of the symbolic meaning expressed in concrete happening, the sensing of the universal in the particular. This gives significance and dignity to all daily pursuits, and prepares the ground on which the arts can grow. In its pathological extreme this spontaneous symbolism manifests itself in what is known to the psychiatrist as the "organ speech" of psychosomatic and other neurotic symptoms. There are people who cannot swallow because there is something in their lives they "cannot swallow" or whom an unconscious sense of guilt compels to spend hours every day on washing and cleaning. . . .

All Art is Symbolic

If art could do nothing better than reproduce the things of nature, either directly or by analogy, or to delight the senses, there would be little justification for the honorable place reserved to it in every known society. Art's reputation must be due to the fact that it helps man to understand the world and himself, and presents to his eyes what he has understood and believes to be true. Now everything in this world is a unique individual; no two things can be equal. But anything can be understood only because it is made up of ingredients not reserved to itself but common to many or all other things. In science, greatest knowledge is achieved when all existing phenomena are reduced to a common law. This is true for art also. The mature work of art succeeds in subjecting everything to a dominant law of structure. In doing so, it does not distort the variety of existing things into uniformity. On the contrary, it clarifies their differences by making them all comparable. Braque has said, "By putting a lemon next to an orange they cease to be a lemon and an orange and become fruit. The mathematicians follow this law. So do we." He fails to remember that the virtue of such correlation is two-fold. It shows the way in which things are similar and, by doing so, defines their individuality. By establishing a common "style" for all objects, the artist creates a whole, in which the place and function of every one of them are lucidly defined. Goethe said: "The beautiful is a manifestation of secret laws of nature, which would have remained hidden to us forever without its appearance."

Every element of a work of art is indispensable for the one purpose of pointing out the theme, which embodies the nature of existence for the artist. In this sense we find symbolism even in works that, at first sight, seem to be little more than arrangements of fairly neutral objects. We need only glance at the bare outlines of the two still lifes sketched in Figures *a* and *b* to experience two different conceptions of reality. Cézanne's picture (*a*) is dominated by the stable framework of verticals and horizontals in the background, the table, and the axes of bottles and glass. This skeleton is strong enough to give support even to the sweeping folds of the fabric. A simple order is conveyed by the upright symmetry of each bottle and that of the glass. There is abundance in the swelling volumes and emphasis on roundness and softness even in the inorganic matter. Compare this

a

b

image of prosperous peace with the catastrophic turmoil in Picasso's work (*b*). Here we find little stability. The vertical and horizontal orientations are avoided. The room is slanted, the right angles of the table, which is turned over, are either hidden by oblique position or distorted. The four legs do not run parallel, the bottle topples, the desperately sprawling corpse of the bird is about to fall off the table. The contours tend to be hard, sharp, lifeless, even in the body of the animal.

Since the basic perceptual pattern carries the theme, we must not be surprised to find that art continues to fulfill its function even when it ceases to represent objects of nature. "Abstract" art does in its own way what art has always done. It is not better than representational art, which also does not hide but reveals the meaningful skeleton of forces. It is no less good, for it contains the essentials. It is not "pure form," because even the simplest line expresses visible meaning and is therefore symbolic. It does not offer intellectual abstractions, because there is nothing more concrete than color, shape, and motion. It does not limit itself to the inner life of man, or to the unconscious, because for art the distinctions between the outer and the inner world and the conscious and the unconscious mind are artificial. The human mind receives, shapes, and interprets its image of the outer world with all its conscious and unconscious powers, and the realm of the unconscious could never enter our experience without the reflection of perceivable things. There is no way of presenting the one without the other. But the nature of the outer and the inner world can be reduced to a play of forces, and this "musical" approach is attempted by the misnamed abstract artists.

We do not know what the art of the future will look like. But we know that "abstraction" is not art's final climax. No style will ever be that. It is one valid way of looking at the world, one view of the holy mountain, which offers a different image from every place but can be seen as the same everywhere.

—*Art and Visual Perception* (1954)

2. Gestalt Psychology and Artistic Form

The French speak of Gestalt psychology as *la psychologie de la forme.* This translation is meant to indicate that the Gestalt principle is only indirectly concerned with the "subject-matter" of natural things. To call a football team or a painting or an electric circuit a Gestalt is to describe a property of their organisation. Gestalten function as wholes, which determine their parts. Four musicians who form a string quartet will create a unified style of performance. This style is a delicate crystallisation of affinities and conflicts of temper. It is the balance of convergent and divergent social forces and, in turn, modifies the behaviour of each player. Change the arm of the left boy in the Laocoon group, and the entire piece of sculpture assumes a different composition. Such internal play of influences obeys rules that are largely independent of the particular medium in which they are observed. In a sense, they refer to "formal" properties.

If, however, we mean by "form" the outer appearance of things—as we do when speaking of the arts—it is necessary to see that the Gestalt theory deals with form only as the manifestation of forces, which are the true object of its interest. Physical and psychical forces can be studied only by their perceivable effects. Thus the overall direction of energy in a given system may appear as a visible axis in the observed pattern. The degree of balance in the distribution of forces may be reflected in the degree of observable symmetry. The direction and strength of water power shows in the "form" of the flow. In the star shape of a flower we recognise the even spread of undisturbed growth. The flaws of a crippled tree or a hunched back tell of interferences with lawful development. Anxiety may express itself in the muscle tension of the body or the broken curve of a gesture.

In all these cases, form is strongly determined by forces inherent in the object itself. This is not always so. It is hardly true at all for the work of art. In the visual arts, except for the effect of such inherent qualities of the medium as the weight of stone, the grain of wood, or the viscosity of oil paint, form is imposed on matter by external force. Neither can a work of art be grown, nor does the artist often use highly organised materials such as crystals or plants. Dancers and actors, who use their own bodies, and to some extent photography, which uses the direct registration of physical objects, are the outstanding exceptions; but it is precisely for this reason that they are suspected of being hybrids of art and nature. The artist prefers the submissiveness of amorphous matter.

Physically, then, the work of art is a "weak Gestalt," an object of low organisation. It makes little difference to the marble of the Laocoon group that an arm is broken off, nor does the paint of a landscape revolt when a busy restorer adds a glaring blue to its faded sky. But, as Benedetto Croce would point out to us, we are now not speaking of art at all. Art cannot be a physical fact because "physical facts have no reality, whereas art, to which so many devote their entire lives and which fills everybody with divine joy, is eminently real". This means that art exists only as a psychological experience; and the forces which generate such experience are the proper object of our attention.

The work of art defined as an experience turns out to be a Gestalt of the highest degree. In fact, from the beginning, Gestalt theorists looked to art for the most convincing examples of sensitively organised wholes. Christian von Ehrenfels, whose essay "Ueber Gestaltqualitäten" gave the theory its name, speaks of a melody as being different from the sum of the tones which constitute it. And we discover with delight such testimony as Cézanne's answer to Vollard, who had pointed out to him two tiny spots of uncovered canvas in his portrait: "You understand, Monsieur Vollard, if I should put there something haphazard, I should be compelled to do my whole picture over, starting from that place!"

The psychological forces that determine artistic form operate essentially in the perceptual process of vision and in the area of motivation and "personality". For the purpose of analysis these factors can be discussed separately. Actually, they interact all the time. Also a more complete presentation would require consideration of further psychological levels, notably thinking and memory.

Vision cannot be explained merely by the properties of the observed object but is dependent on what goes on in the brain. Think of a red triangle in the centre of a rectangular grey ground. "Objectively" we have nothing but two areas of different colour, situated in the same plane, independent of each other, and at perfect rest. If we scrutinise the observer's experience and consider at the same time what is going on in the neural mechanism of vision, we realise first of all that we are dealing with a highly dynamic process. The triangle has broken up the unity of the grey constantly defending itself against the tendency of the plane to regain its homogeneity and to expel the invader. This is successful to the extent that the triangle appears suspended in front of the grey plane thus permitting the ground to continue "behind" the triangle and to maintain its wholeness. The triangle also is far from static. It is dense, compared with the looser texture of the ground. Its pointed corners stab outward in directed, centrifugal movement. Also the red, being a more active colour than grey, shows the property of long wave-length hues to appear closer to the observer. It attacks him. Were it blue, it would withdraw from him. Red is warm and irradiates across the ground. Were it blue, it would be cold and contract toward its centre. Furthermore, the triangle is held in balance by its central location. If it were placed eccentrically, we could actually experience the pushes and pulls that would tend to displace it—for instance, by drawing it toward the centre of the ground. Even in its central position our triangle is no more "at rest" than a rope that does not move because two men of equal strength are pulling it in opposite directions. The antagonistic forces happen to balance each other. Nevertheless, their power remains perceivable to the sensitive eye.

This is not all. Shape and size of the two units constantly define each other. The smallness of the triangle determines the largeness of the ground. The stable verticals and horizontals of the rectangle are enhanced and challenged by the obliqueness of the triangle, and vice versa. The brightness and colour values also interact. The lightness of the ground darkens the triangle. The red evokes in the grey the complementary green.

A simple example has been analysed with some detail in order to show that any description of form in the static terms of sheer geometry, quantity, or location will fatally impoverish the facts. Only if one realises that all visual form is constantly endowed with striving and yielding, contraction and expansion, contrast and adaptation, attack and retreat, can one understand the elementary impact of a painting, statue, or building and its capacity to symbolise the action of life by means of physically motionless objects.

Since visual dynamics is not inherent in the physical object—where are the forces which constitute it? Gestalt psychologists refuse to describe them as an effect of empathy, that is, as a mere projection of previously acquired knowledge upon the percept. They assume that the sensations of push and pull are the conscious counterpart of the physiological processes which organise the percept in the neural field of the optical sector, that is, the cerebral cortex, the optic nerve, and possibly the retinæ of the eyes. According to this theory, visual dynamics is not a secondary attachment of the stimulus, due to accidental, subjective associations, but rather precedes the "geometric" pattern of shape and colour in that this pattern is the result of the organising forces, of whose activity the observer is partially aware. The theory would seem to explain why in actual experience the dynamic, or expressive, qualities are the most powerful and immediate qualities of the percept. In comparison, the static attributes of shape, size, line, or location, on which scientists have concentrated their attention, would seem to be relatively indirect and late products of vision. The detached, measuring gaze of the investigator in the laboratory preserves little of the spontaneous excitement which the child, the primitive, the artist find in the world of sight.

Once this point is strongly made, one may turn to the principles of articulation, to which Gestalt psychologists have devoted most of their investigations of visual form. What makes the visual field split up into segregated objects—trees, houses, cars, people? What makes the "abstract" painter confident that all observers will see roughly the same units of form in his composition? Experiments have shown that articulation is controlled essentially by the nature of the stimulus configuration itself. Thirty years ago, Max Wertheimer established some "rules of visual grouping." It seems now probable that these rules can be reduced to one, namely, the principle of similarity. The relative degree of similarity in a given perceptual pattern makes for a corresponding degree of connection or fusion. Units which resemble each other in shape, size, direction, colour, brightness, or location will be seen together. [See Fig. 1.]

The principle of similarity organises stimulus elements in time as well as in space. The form pattern of a painting, which impinges upon the observer's mind, is not his first visual experience. It is the most recent phase of a prolonged process, within which memory traces interact according to the principle of similarity. The relative strength of the factors which make up the temporal and the spatial contexts will determine what the observer sees at any given moment. Due to its high degree of unity and precision, good artistic form is capable of imposing its own articulation upon different observers in spite of the different "visual history" which each individual brings to the present experience.

It is possible and necessary to interpret the principle of similarity as a special case of a more general law, according to which the forces which

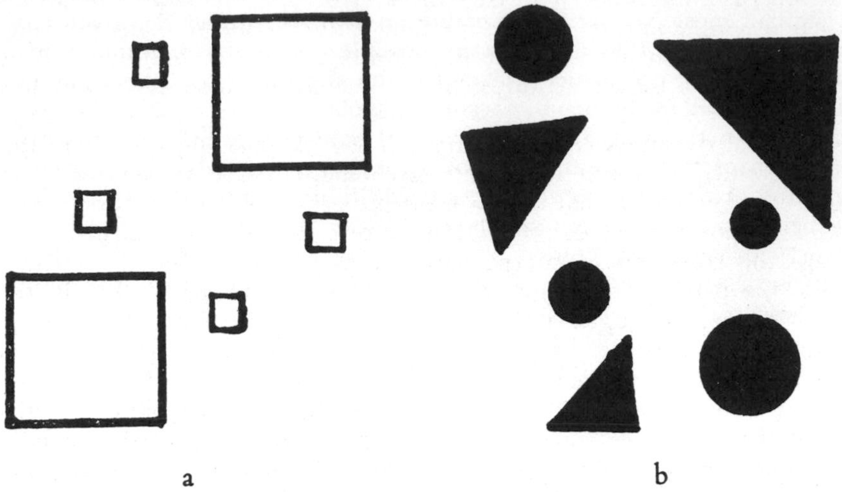

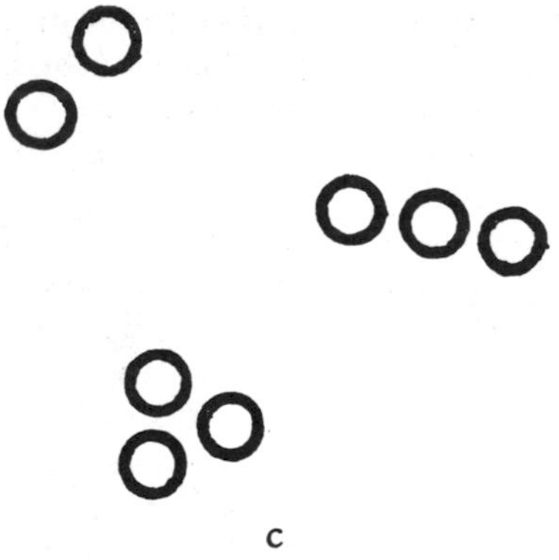

FIG. 1 Visual grouping results from similarity of a. size
b. shape
c. location
d. direction
e. brightness and color

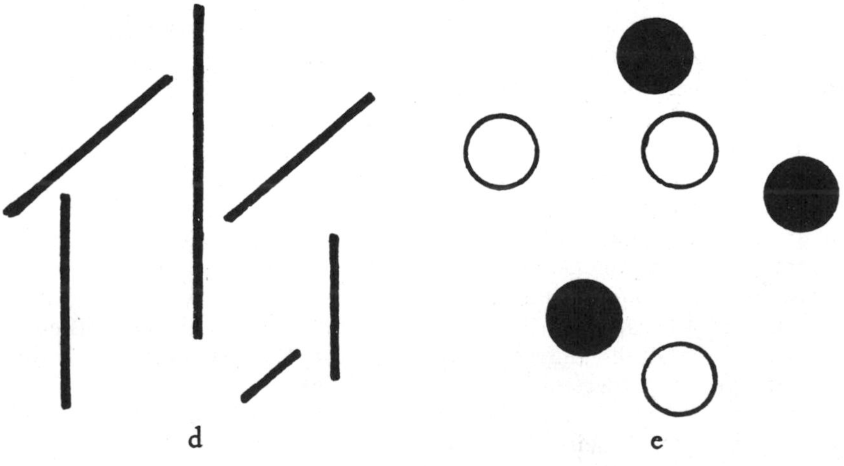

constitute a psychological or physiological field tend toward the simplest, most regular, most symmetrical distribution available under the given conditions. This means that of the many possible groupings of elements in a visual pattern the one which makes for the simplest organisation of the whole context will spontaneously occur to the observer.

Described in this way, the organisational processes, which take place in the creation of visual form, are shown to obey a law which governs the functioning of the mind as a whole. In addition, we thus discover a similarity between the behaviour of psychological and physical processes. In fact, in 1920, Wolfgang Köhler in his book on "Die physischen Gestalten" pointed to the second law of thermodynamics as a manifestation of the basic Gestalt principle. Physicists assume that the world tends to pass from less probable to more probable configurations or states. There is no reason why the physiological forces in the nervous system should make an exception to this rule. In other words, the mental processes which create visual form can be understood as a reflection of the tendency to simplest structure assumed to exist in the corresponding brain field. [See Fig. 2.]

Psychologists and physicists have arrived at similar conclusions independently of each other. As a curiosity it may be mentioned that while Gestalt theorists recognise a tendency to "good form" or "well organised structure," the physicists see a development from order to disorder. Presumably the contradiction is partly terminological; but the necessary unification of these views is likely to lead to considerations that will be of interest for both parties.

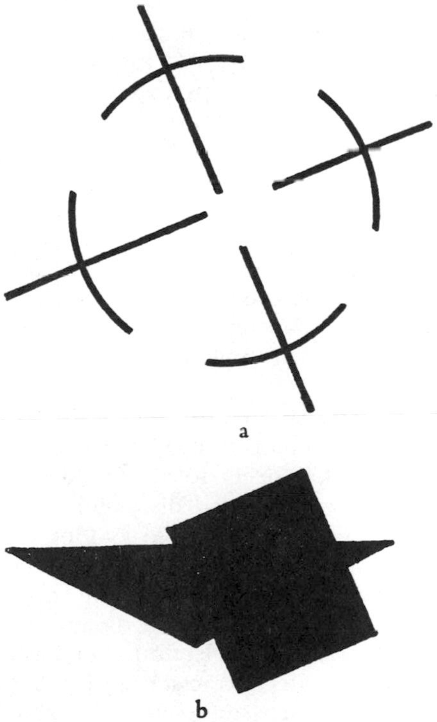

FIG. 2. The principle of simple form.
a. Circle and cross are seen instead of four independent patterns.
b. Complex figure breaks up into triangle and rectangle.

If the human mind in general and the mechanism of vision in particular are governed by a tendency to simplest structure, we may ask why we see any objects at all. Obviously, the simplest possible field of sight would be totally homogeneous like a whitewashed wall—inarticulate, plain, motionless, a foretaste of the dismal state in which, according to the physicists, the chilled universe will find itself at the end of time. Our eyes are saved from such boredom by the fact that the organism is not a "closed system." The influx of external energy constantly upsets and delays the striving toward final rest. In vision, the disturber of the peace is light energy, which, through the action of the eye-lenses, comes to us in the form of information about objects. Now information, according to Norbert Wiener, is negative entropy; that is, it imports order or form. For our purposes, "objects" can be defined as processes that have been temporarily arrested on their way to final equilibrium. The images of all objects show the partial success of that process, namely, some regularity, some symmetry, some simplicity of form. But they also show the marks of striving and growing, of segregation and independence. Thus the form of objects allows us symbolically to envisage the nature of life in its restless striving towards rest.

Far from being a passive mechanism of registration like the photographic camera, our visual apparatus copes with the incoming images in active struggle. It is upset by the intrusion and animated by the stimulation. It seizes upon the regularities of form, which allow comprehension, and tries to subject the bewilderingly accidental agglomeration of objects in space to whatever order is obtainable. Every-day vision initiates and anticipates the duel of the artist with the image.

So far we have "bracketed out" the activity of the eye, as though it were a self-contained organism, minding its own business and forming pictures for the pictures' sake. This makes for a short-sighted psychology of perception. If applied to esthetics, it leads to a narrow conception of art as a purely formal manipulation of images. But vision, in daily life as well as in art, functions as a part of the total mind. As such it is an instrument of observation at the service of vital needs. It also reflects symbolically the entire state of mental affairs which constitute "personality." Consequently, pictorial form can be expected to be determined essentially by four factors: (1) the structure of the images of external objects projected on the eyes; (2) the formative powers of the visual apparatus; (3) the need of the organism for observing, selecting, and understanding; (4) attitudes, mood, temperament, tensions, inner conflicts, etc.

The first factor would bear on the realistic truthfulness of pictorial representation. The second accounts for the exploration of shape, for "composition" as a pleasing arrangement of balanced form, for decorative ornament. The third and fourth require more detailed discussion.

The function of artistic form remains incomprehensible as long as one fails to remember that vision does not primarily serve to satisfy detached curiosity and enjoyment. By means of the eyes the organism scans the environment beyond the limits of its own body in order to discover useful or dangerous things. Needs make for perceptual selection. For instance, any movement in the environment automatically attracts attention because movement means a change of conditions, which may call for a reaction.

Uninteresting things cast their images on the retina, but as a rule are not perceived.

This selective factor manifests itself in pictorial representation. It determines subject matter and form. It tells what the artist—or his patron—considers important or safe. The psychologist notices that some historical periods or individual artists concentrate on the human figure, others on objects connected with utility and consumption, others again on nature. He finds that under certain conditions art withdraws from subject matter altogether. Form is influenced by concern with, or neglect of, detail. Needs and mores make for distortion. Pictures of the human figure may show large breasts but no genitals. In children's drawings much more space may be devoted to the face than to the body. Arms or clothes may be left out entirely. The dependence of form factors such as size, proportion, location, shape, shading, direction, on the inner needs of the draftsman, are being studied in a recently developed psychological test, which requires patients to draw the picture of a man and a woman. In a more passive way, an observer's interpretation of the perceptual qualities of inkblots (whole vs. part, shape vs. colour, shading, movement, etc.) is found to be significant in the Rorschach test. With certain precautions, it may be possible to apply these findings fruitfully to the analysis of artistic form.

Visual form must also be considered as a basic means of understanding the environment. Man's notions of what things are, how they act, and how they are related to each other, rely greatly on appearance. Particularly the young mind of children and primitives derives most of its judgments from the direct interpretation of perceptual form. Thus a latch-key may look lazy or aggressive, or magic power may be attributed to an object of disturbing shape. In a more general sense the child by gradually conquering the basic geometric forms and applying them to trees, houses, people, or animals grasps something of the nature of these objects. The towering size of a father, the generous spreading of a tree, the flimsiness of smoke are captured by means of comprehensible form and thus acquired for the child's conception of the world.

The child conquers form by observing the objects around him, but also by freely exploring the products of his pencil and crayon on paper. There is no reason to assume that the early drawings and paintings of children are all representations of the environment and that the basic geometric forms evolve from copying the shape of objects. A Gestalt psychologist would expect that the tendency to simple structure would increasingly direct the child's first scribbles. The clear, balanced, comprehensible shape of a circle, a straight line, or a rectangular relationship will be a source of great pleasure. In fact, unless parental pressure hampers free development, non-representational forms—which look like "abstractions" to an art critic but are eminently concrete to the child—will be created for their own sake. Increasingly often, they will also be related to objects of the environment. There is constant interplay between the growing complexity of the forms that can be mastered and the subtler observation of reality, to which richer forms can do better justice.

The clarification of visual forms and their organization in integrated patterns as well as the attribution of such forms to suitable objects is one of the most effective training grounds of the young mind. Educators and psychologists are beginning to see that intelligence does not only operate in verbal abstractions. Visual thinking manifests and develops general intelligence, and the stepwise progress of visual order reflects the development of the person as a whole.

Visual order as a tool of insight has been stressed by the late Gustaf Britsch and his disciples, Kornmann and Schaefer-Simmern. Their findings in the field of art education are in striking agreement with Gestalt principles. It is true that these educators have concentrated on the "formal" aspects of art, but they have also stressed the fact that mechanical copying or imitation leads to the neglect of visual organisation, that is, to ugliness. An image can only be valid if it transmits the artist's conception of his subject by means of the spontaneous symbolism of orderly form. Beauty can be defined as the correspondence of meaning and perceptual symbolism. In the true work of art, the deepest meaning is conveyed by the elementary properties of size, shape, distance, location, or colour. The power of this visual language lies in its spontaneous evidence, its almost childlike simplicity. Darkness means darkness, things that belong together are shown together, and what is great and high appears in large size in high location.

Beauty is lost when meaning and form are split asunder. This results, on the one hand, in playing with formal relationships or pure "composition," which carries no message or contradicts meaning. On the other hand, it leads to the misnamed "literary" approach, which limits meaning to what the observer knows about the subject-matter and therefore offers chaotic, visually incomprehensible form. The tragic consequence of this split in our time has been that so many people have become blind to the meaning of form and that they believe they "see" when they absorb meaning without form.

Point Four of our programme remains to be considered. The symbolism of form is not only a means of interpreting the environment visually, it also reflects the person of its creator. A human body means one thing to Lucas Cranach and another thing to Giorgione, because two different people are looking. Systematic attempts to understand pictorial representations as "projections" of the human personality are being made by therapeutically oriented psychologists. They deal with visual symbolism in two ways.

One of them is used by the psycho-analysts. Whereas Freud himself had cautioned his students that for a correct analysis of symbols one must rely on the comments of the individual who produced them; other analysts, in their discussions of art, do not hesitate to use easy standard interpretations of the dream-book type. This makes for an embarrassingly shallow approach to art. Visual form becomes a code language used by the artist to refer, with monotonous insistence, to the basic physiology of sex. The suspicion that most analyses of this kind are arbitrary is not only based on their disappointing results but also on their method. They use what we may term metaphoric symbolism. One concrete thing is said to stand for another concrete thing, a mandolin for a woman, a man for the artist's father, a bird or a cave for the male or the female genitals. Now interpretations of this kind are safe when metaphors have become institutionalised, that is, when they have been consciously established by cultural convention. For instance, in Christian art the dove stands for the holy ghost and the lily for virginity. But it is in the nature of the psycho-analytic symbols that much of the time their meaning is not permitted to reach consciousness. Only the avowed practice of some surrealists, who have institutionalised Freud, permits us to be sure that they do what the analyst says they are doing. In other cases no such proof exists, unless a reliable depth analysis of the particular artist is available.

Art can also be interpreted psychologically by means of what may be called isomorphic symbolism. This method does not depend on alleged associations of one object with another object but on perceptual qualities inherent in visual form itself. As an example the investigation of Rose H. Alschuler and La Berta Weiss Hattwick, "Painting and Personality," may be cited. These authors analysed a large number of "designs" done by nursery school children and compared them statistically with what was known about the children themselves. They assert, for example, that children who prefer warm colours show "warmer" relationships to other people while cold colours go with more controlled behaviour. The practice of overlaying one colour with another is found in highly "repressed" children. Children who use heavy strokes and squares, rectangles, or verticals are more assertive than the self-centred children, who like circles in their pictures.

In order to interpret these results one must assume that structural characteristics of visual form are spontaneously related to similar characteristics in human behaviour. We have called this type of symbolism "isomorphic" because this is the term used by gestalt psychologists to describe identity of structure in different media. For instance, a person's mood may be structurally identical with the bodily behaviour which accompanies that mood. This isomorphic correspondence has been used to explain the fact that the "expression" of physical behaviour seems to be directly comprehensible to the onlooker. The gesture of a dancer, but also the motions of a towel on the clothes-line or the shape of a cloud, contain structural features whose kinship with similarly structured mental features is immediately felt. If it is true that structural similarities transcend the difference between body and mind and make for unified total behaviour and experience, then we should expect the child to choose, for the pictures he makes, forms that match his own attitudes. Thus here again the findings of Gestalt theory and work in the arts seem to confirm each other.

The four determinants of visual form which we have discussed have been variously considered in the theory and practice of the arts, often in a one-sided way. There are those who hold that art is merely a faithful recording of whatever percept, memory, image, or phantasy besets the artist's mind. Others, on the contrary, concentrate on the organising powers of the eye without considering that all creation of form involves a coping with the world of experience. Again, the gradual progress of visual order is studied with little reference to the manifestations of the total personality in every stroke or shape. Or the picture is viewed as nothing but a kind of clinical map without sufficient awareness of the developmental steps in visual and motor organisation.

If we wish to understand the relationship between visual form and the total organism, we must consider the complex interaction of the many forces that make up a person.

—*Aspects of Form*, edited by Lancelot Law Whyte (1951)

CHAPTER 9

Form

CLIVE BELL: Significant Form
BEN SHAHN: The Shape of Content
HAROLD OSBORNE: Organic Unity
HORATIO GREENOUGH: Structure and Organization
MEYER SCHAPIRO: Style

The work of art is an organized complex of sensuous and expressive elements, and its organization is its form. Recent art and esthetics have tended to emphasize formal values, but estheticians have disagreed as to the meaning of form. A number of writers have interpreted form as sheer abstract design, minimizing or excluding connotations and representations. A similar interpretation, with particular reference to the visual arts, was formulated by the famous English critics Roger Fry (1886–1934) and Clive Bell (1881–1964).

Their ideas were greatly influenced by "the Bloomsbury circle," a group of intimate friends, including the philosopher G. E. Moore, the economist John Maynard Keynes, and the novelist Virginia Woolf. A close study will reveal the indebtedness of Fry and Bell to the ideas of Moore, especially to the remarks about esthetic emotion and formal beauty in his *Principia Ethica* (1903) and the contention that goodness or beauty is a unique and "nonnatural" quality (refer to Moore's remarks in *Principia Ethica* about the "naturalistic fallacy"). It is not surprising that Bell and Fry, thus linked together, came to much the same conclusions. Although Fry had the more subtle and complex theory of art, Bell was the more uncompromising in his espousal of formalism. I shall quote the latter as the more challenging of the two.

Bell agrees with Véron and Tolstoy that art is emotional, but he thinks that there is a peculiarly esthetic emotion, quite different from the emotions of ordinary life, that is directed to "significant form."' By significant form he means a unique quality resulting from certain combinations of lines, colors, and spatial elements. The representation of space is necessary to achieve certain kinds of visual form, but any other kind of representation is esthetically irrelevant. Like Hanslick and Gurney in musical esthetics, Bell insists upon the "isolated" character of esthetic experience and works of art.

What, then, does he mean by the word "significant"? The significance in question, it would appear, consists of the expression of the artist's emotion, but the only emotion that Bell considers legitimate in art—the peculiarly "esthetic" emotion—is aroused by the vision of significant form. He suggests, however, a possible escape from the circularity of this definition. Art may be a revelation, he says, of the universal "rhythm of reality." But since he insists that the significance of art "is unrelated to the significance of life," this so-called "metaphysical hypothesis" remains extremely vague. Perhaps we may interpret it as meaning that the artist emulates, without definitely imitating, the structural harmonies of his natural environment, such as the pattern of a sea shell or the floret of a sunflower.

The question naturally arises whether Bell extended his formalist theory to the nonvisual arts. He indicates that his doctrine is applicable to nonprogrammatic music, and indeed he finds in pure music the very ideal of art. But in a later essay he declares that literature is an exception.

> I can see no formal beauty worth speaking of in Balzac or Dickens. . . . Now a picture is quite valueless without formal beauty, . . . and he who has no sense of this sort of beauty will get nothing worth having from visual art. The fact is, subject and the overtones emanating from it, wit, pathos, drama, criticism, didacticism even—qualities which in painting count for little or nothing—do seem to be the essence of literature. . . . A reasonable explanation seems to be that literature is one thing, painting and music another.[1]

This statement was not Bell's final word. In a little book on *Proust* (1928), he declared that "the supreme masterpieces" of literature "derive their splendor, their supernatural power, not from flashes of insight, nor yet from characterization, nor from an understanding of the human heart even, but from *form*—I use the word in its richest sense, I mean the thing that artists create, their expression. Whether you call it 'significant form' or something else, the supreme quality in art is formal; it has to do with order, sequence, movement and shape."[2]

Ben Shahn (1898–1969) represents the antithesis of Bell's formalism. Born in Lithuania, he and his family migrated in 1906 to the United States, where he eventually achieved fame by combining realist and expressionist techniques in painting. The Sacco and Vanzetti case (when two immigrant anarchists were falsely convicted of murder and executed) led to a series of biting comments, both drawings and paintings (1931–1932). He was strongly influenced by the French painter Georges Roualt and the Mexican painter Diego Rivera, collaborating with the latter on the Radio City murals in 1933.

In *The Shape of Content* he states his esthetic creed. While intent on socially significant content, he rejects the antithesis between content and form. In a well-composed work of art, they are not two separate things, but a unified whole regarded from two points of view. "Form is the very shape of content." In his examination of "nonobjective painting"—the works of such artists as Pollock, Rothko, Malevitch, de Kooning, Baziotes, and Mathieu—he finds differences of content even in this most extreme wing of "noncontent painting." He by no means rejects modernism, finding much to admire in "great imaginers" such as Picasso and Calder; but he also expresses intense sympathy for the works of such older masters as Thomas Eakins and Winslow Homer—so "full of content, full of story." For these masters, too, "form is the right and only possible shape of a certain content." Implicit in Shahn's whole orientation is his insistence on "organic" rather than "mechanic" form. As Coleridge said:

> The form is mechanic when on any given material we impress a predetermined form, not necessarily arising out of the properties of the material, as when to a mass of wet clay we give whatever shape we wish it to retain when hardened. The organic form, on the other hand, is innate; it shapes as it develops itself from within, and the fullness of its development is one and the same with the perfection of its outer form.[3]

The principle that Coleridge enunciates is commonly called "organic unity." All other principles of form—theme, thematic variation, balance, rhythm, emphasis and subordination, and growth or evolution—serve this one master principle.[4] Thus organic unity is not independent of either content or other formal principles, but is the perfectly natural and inevitable development of expression.

As in the case of all analogies, there is both resemblance and difference between the things being compared. A well-composed work of art resembles a healthy organism with respect to adequacy, economy, and coherence. In a real organism, however, there is a *life* of the whole which is the end of the parts. While the coherence is analogous to the work of art, life in any literal sense is not. No one is tempted literally to attribute life to a statue, as in the myth of Pygmalion or Daedalus. But the unity in variey of a work of art is so akin to living form that the concept of "organic unity" has had a lasting influence.

Harold Osborne (1905–), formerly editor of *The British Journal of Aesthetics* and a fine esthetician, has traced the historical development of this concept from the time of Plato and Aristotle to Ehrenfels and other Gestalt psychologists. Especially illuminating is his discussion of the atomistic interpretation of Hume, influenced by British associationist psychology, and the organic interpretation of Baumgarten, influenced by the Leibnizian tradition. Osborne's remarks throw light on the difference between scientific analysis and artistic perception. Even Francis Hutcheson, although he recognized the principle of organic unity to a greater extent than Hume, accepted the "passive" notion of perception common to the "scientific" psychology of his time.

Osborne recognizes the difficulty in identifying the organic feature "which successful works of art and other things of beauty possess and which nonesthetic configurational wholes do not possess." "It is not certain," he concludes, "whether this feature applies generally to all art objects, and much work remains still to be done on the elucidation of the concept of organic unity in relation to esthetic objects."

In architecture and industrial crafts, form has been closely linked to function. The idea that form must be harmonized with function is no recent discovery; it was enunciated by Vitruvius in ancient Rome and it was practiced by primitive man long before any esthetic theory was formulated. But it has often been violated or forgotten; and it has been, in a sense, rediscovered by such modern architects and designers as Le Corbusier (1887–1965), and Moholy-Nagy (1895–1946).

The great prophet in this revival of functionalism was Horatio Greenough (1805–1852)—a worthy contemporary of Emerson and Thoreau. Leaving the United States before he received his Harvard diploma, Greenough set up a studio in Florence and practiced the art of sculpture for the next twenty-two years. Then he returned and surprised the people of Boston by praising the clipper ship as a work of art. "*There* is something," he exclaimed, "I should not be ashamed to show Phidias!" In shipbuilding the form is determined by the function: The adaptation to wind and wave results in harmony and grace. So should it be in architecture. The rule must be "to plant a building firmly on the ground," that is, to adapt its design to the site; then, "instead of forcing the functions of every sort of building into one general form, without reference to the inner distribution, let us begin from the heart of a nucleus, and *work outward,*" achieving "the *external expression* of the *inward functions* of the building." All meaningless, inorganic decoration should be stripped away: There must be "the entire and immediate banishment of all makeshift and make-believe."

To his countrymen, Greenough, a lover of Greek architecture, gives this advice:

> The fundamental laws of building found at the basis of every style of architecture must be the basis of ours. The adaptation of the forms and magnitude of structures to the climate they are exposed to, and the offices for which they are intended, teaches us to study our own varied wants in these respects. The harmony of their ornaments with the nature that they embellished, and the institutions from which they sprang, calls on us to do the like justice to our country, our government, and our faith. . . . So the American builder by a truly philosophic investigation of ancient art will learn of the Greeks to be American. . . . I contend for Greek principles, not Greek things. . . . The men who have reduced locomotion to its simplest elements, in the trotting wagon and the yacht *America,* are nearer to Athens at this moment than they who would bend the Greek temple to every use.

In other words, we should respect the eternal laws of building but plagiarize nothing from the past.

Greenough breaks down any sharp distinction between the applied and the fine arts, and insists that a machine should be a thing of beauty: "If we compare the form of a newly invented machine with the perfected type of the same instrument, we observe, as we trace it through the phases of improvement, how weight is shaken off where strength is less needed, how functions are made to approach without impeding each other, how straight becomes curved, and the curve is straightened, till the straggling and cumbersome machine becomes the compact, effective, and beautiful engine." Thus the fundamental principle of sound design, according to Greenough, whether it be in architecture or in the industrial arts, is a stripping down to essentials and an adaptation of form to function.

The concept of style applies to all the arts, functionalist and nonfunctionalist alike, and is the historical adaptation of the idea of form, marking off periods and phases in the development of the arts. Hence, it is of particular concern to the art historian. The meaning of style is elucidated in the following selection from Meyer Schapiro (1904–), professor of fine arts and archeology at Columbia University and author of such important works as *Van Gogh* (1950) and *Cézanne* (1952). Style, as a persistent form and manner of expression, may be exhibited by an individual, group, civilization, or historical period. Although such an inclusive term suffers from vagueness, Schapiro's discussion is admirably clear and precise. I have produced less than half of his essay; the remaining part is devoted to an erudite interpretation of the causes and morphology of style, reviewing the theories of Wöllflin, Riegl, and others. I know of no better introduction to the subject of style.

Notes

1. "The 'Difference' of Literature," *New Republic*, Vol. 33 (Nov. 29, 1922), pp. 18–19.
2. *Proust* (Hogarth, London, 1928), p. 67.
3. Coleridge, *Shakespearean Criticism*, edited by T. M. Rayson (Harvard University Press, Cambridge, Mass., 1930), Vol. 1, p. 224.
4. For an excellent discussion of these subordinate principles of form and their relation to organic unity, see DeWitt H. Parker, *The Analysis of Art* (Yale University Press, New Haven, Conn., 1926), Chapter II.

CLIVE BELL

Significant Form

I The Esthetic Hypothesis

The starting-point for all systems of esthetics must be the personal experience of a peculiar emotion. The objects that provoke this emotion we call works of art. All sensitive people agree that there is a peculiar emotion provoked by works of art. I do not mean, of course, that all works provoke the same emotion. On the contrary, every work produces a different emotion. But all these emotions are recognizably the same in kind; so far, at any rate, the best opinion is on my side. That there is a particular kind of emotion provoked by works of visual art, and that this emotion is provoked by every kind of visual art, by pictures, sculptures, buildings, pots, carvings, textiles, etc., is not disputed, I think, by any one capable of feeling it. This emotion is called the esthetic emotion; and if we can discover some quality common and peculiar to all the objects that provoke it, we shall have solved what I take to be the central problem of esthetics. We shall have discovered the essential quality in a work of art, the quality that distinguishes works of art from all other classes of objects.

For either all works of visual art have some common quality, or when we speak of "works of art" we gibber. Every one speaks of "art," making a mental classification by which he distinguishes the class "works of art" from all other classes. What is the justification of this classification? What is the quality common and peculiar to all members of this class? Whatever it be, no doubt it is often found in company with other qualities; but they are adventitious—it is essential. There must be some one quality without which a work of art cannot exist; possessing which, in the least degree, no work is altogether worthless. What is this quality? What quality is shared by all objects that provoke our esthetic emotions? What quality is common to Sta. Sophia and the windows at Chartres, Mexican sculpture, a Persian bowl, Chinese carpets, Giotto's frescoes at Padua, and the masterpieces of Poussin, Piero della Francesca, and Cézanne? Only one answer seems possible—significant form. In each, lines and colors combined in a particular way, certain forms and relations of forms, stir our esthetic emotions. These relations and combinations of lines and colors, these esthetically moving forms, I call "Significant Form"; and "Significant Form" is the one quality common to all works of visual art.

At this point it may be objected that I am making esthetics a purely subjective business, since my only data are personal experiences of a particular emotion. It will be said that the objects that provoke this emotion vary with each individual, and that therefore a system of esthetics can have no objective validity. It must be replied that any system of esthetics which pretends to be based on some objective truth is so palpably ridiculous as not to be worth discussing. We have no other means of recognizing a work of art than our feeling for it. The objects that provoke esthetic emotion vary with each individual. Esthetic judgments are, as the saying goes, matters of taste; and about tastes, as every one is proud to admit, there is no disputing. A good critic may be able to make me see in a picture that had left me cold things that I had overlooked, till at last, receiving the esthetic emotion, I recognize it as a work of art. To be continually pointing out those parts, the sum, or rather the combination, of which unite to produce significant form, is the function of criticism. But it is useless for a critic to tell me that something is a work of art; he must make me feel it for myself. This he can do only by making me see; he must get at my emotions through my eyes. Unless he can make me see something that moves me, he cannot force my emotions. I have no right to consider anything a work of art to which I cannot react emotionally; and I have no right to look for the essential quality in anything that I have not *felt* to be a work of art. The critic can affect my esthetic theories only by affecting my esthetic experience. All systems of esthetics must be based on personal experience—that is to say, they must be subjective.

Yet, though all esthetic theories must be based on esthetic judgments, and ultimately all esthetic judgments must be matters of personal taste, it would be rash to assert that no theory of esthetics can have general validity. For, though A, B, C, D are the works that move me, and A, D, E, F the works that move you, it may well be that *x* is the only quality believed by either of us to be common to all the works in his list. We may all agree about esthetics, and yet differ about particular works of art. We may differ as to the presence or absence of the quality *x*. My immediate object will be to show that significant form is the only quality common and peculiar to all the works of visual art that move me; and I will ask those whose esthetic experience does not tally with mine to see whether this quality is not also, in their judgment, common to all works that move them, and whether they can discover any other quality of which the same can be said. . . .

"Are you forgetting about color?" some one inquires. Certainly not; my term "significant form" included combinations of lines and of colors. The distinction between form and color is an unreal one; you cannot conceive a colorless line or a colorless space; neither can you conceive a formless relation of colors. In a black and white drawing the spaces are all white and all are bounded by black lines; in most oil paintings the spaces are multi-colored and so are the boundaries; you cannot imagine a boundary line without any content, or a content without a boundary line. Therefore, when I speak of significant form, I mean a combination of lines and colors (counting white and black as colors) that moves me esthetically.

Some people may be surprised at my not having called this "beauty." Of course, to those who define beauty as "combinations of lines and colors that provoke esthetic emotion," I willingly concede the right of substituting their word for mine. But most of us, however strict we may be, are apt to apply the epithet "beautiful" to objects that do not provoke that peculiar emotion produced by works of art. Every one, I suspect, has called a butterfly or a flower beautiful. Does any one feel the same kind of emotion for a butterfly or a flower that he feels for a cathedral or a picture? Surely, it is not what I call an esthetic emotion that most of us feel, generally, for natural beauty. I shall suggest, later, that some people may, occasionally, see in nature what we see in art, and feel for her an esthetic emotion; but I am satisfied that, as a rule, most people feel a very different kind of emotion for birds and flowers and the wings of butterflies from that which they feel for pictures, pots, temples, and statues. Why these beautiful things do not move us as works of art move is another, and not an esthetic, question. For our immediate purpose we have to discover only what quality is common to objects that do move us as works of art. In the last part of this chapter, when I try to answer the question—"Why are we so profoundly moved by some combinations of lines and colors?" I shall hope to offer an acceptable explanation of why we are less profoundly moved by others.

Since we call a quality that does not raise the characteristic esthetic emotion "Beauty," it would be misleading to call by the same name the quality that does. To make "beauty" the object of the esthetic emotion, we must give to the word an over-strict and unfamiliar definition. Every one sometimes uses "beauty" in an unesthetic sense; most people habitually do so. To every one, except perhaps here and there an occasional esthete, the commonest sense of the word is unesthetic. Of its grosser abuse, patent in our chatter about "beautiful huntin' " and "beautiful shootin'," I need not take account; it would be open to the precious to reply that they never do so abuse it. Besides, here there is no danger of confusion between the esthetic and the non-esthetic use; but when we speak of a beautiful woman there is. When a ordinary man speaks of a beautiful woman he certainly does not mean only that she moves him esthetically; but when an artist calls a withered old hag beautiful he may sometimes mean what he means when he calls a battered torso beautiful. The ordinary man, if he be also a man of taste, will call the battered torso beautiful, but he will not call a withered hag beautiful because, in the matter of women, it is not to the esthetic quality that the hag may possess, but to some other quality that he assigns the epithet. Indeed, most of us never dream of going for esthetic emotions to human beings, from whom we ask something very different. This "something," when we find it in a young woman, we are apt to call "beauty." We live in a nice age. With the man-in-the-street "beautiful" is more often than not synonymous with "desirable"; the word does not necessarily connote any esthetic reaction whatever, and I am tempted to believe that in the minds of many the sexual flavor of the word is stronger than the esthetic. I have noticed a consistency in those to whom the most beautiful thing in the world is a beautiful woman, and the next most beautiful thing a picture of one. The confusion between esthetic and sensual beauty is not in their case so great as might be supposed. Perhaps there is none; for perhaps they have never had an esthetic emotion to confuse with their other emotions. The art that they call "beautiful" is generally closely related to the women. A beautiful picture is a photograph of a pretty girl; beautiful music, the music that provokes emotions similar to those provoked by young ladies in musical farces; and beautiful poetry, the poetry that recalls the same emotions felt, twenty years earlier, for the rector's daughter. Clearly the word "beauty" is used to connote the objects of quite distinguishable emotions, and that is a reason for not employing a term which would land me inevitably in confusions and misunderstandings with my readers.

On the other hand, with those who judge it more exact to call these combinations and arrangements of form that provoke our esthetic emotions, not "significant form," but "significant relations of form," and then try to make the best of two worlds, the esthetic and the metaphysical, by calling these relations "rhythm," I have no quarrel whatever. Having made it clear that by "significant form" I mean arrangements and combinations that move us in a particular way, I willingly join hands with those who prefer to give a different name to the same thing.

The hypothesis that significant form is the essential quality in a work of art has at least one merit denied to many more famous and more striking—it does help to explain things. We are all familiar with pictures that interest us and excite our admiration, but do not move us as works of art. To this class belongs what I call "Descriptive Painting"—that is, painting in which forms are used not as objects of emotion, but as means of suggesting emotion or conveying information. Portraits of psychological and historical value, topographical works, pictures that tell stories and suggest situations, illustrations of all sorts, belong to this class. That we all recognize the distinction is clear, for who has not said that such and such a drawing was excellent as illustration, but as a work of art worthless? Of course many descriptive pictures possess, amongst other qualities, formal significance, and are therefore works of art: but many more do not. They interest us; they may move us too in a hundred different ways, but they do not move us esthetically. According to my hypothesis they are not works of art. They leave untouched our esthetic emotions because it is not their forms but the ideas or information suggested or conveyed by their forms that affect us. . . .

Let no one imagine that representation is bad in itself; a realistic form may be as significant, in its place as part of the design, as an abstract. But if a representative form has value, it is as form, not as representation. The representative element in a work of art may or may not be harmful; always it is irrelevant. For, to appreciate a work of art we need bring with us nothing from life, no knowledge of its ideas and affairs, no familiarity with its emotions. Art transports us from the world of man's activity to a world of esthetic exaltation. For a moment we are shut off from human interests; our anticipations and memories are arrested; we are lifted above the stream of life. The pure mathematician rapt in his studies knows a state of mind which I take to be similar, if not identical. He feels an emotion for his speculations which arises from no perceived relation between them and the lives of men, but springs, inhuman or super-human, from the heart of an abstract science. I wonder, sometimes, whether the appreciators of art and of mathematical solutions are not even more closely allied. Before we feel an esthetic emotion for a combination of forms, do we not perceive intellectually the rightness and necessity of the combination? If we do, it would explain the fact that passing rapidly through a room we recognize a picture to be good, although we cannot say that it has provoked much emotion. We seem to have recognized intellectually the rightness of its forms without staying to fix our attention, and collect, as it were, their emotional significance. If this were so, it would be permissible to inquire whether it was the forms themselves or our perception of their rightness and necessity that caused esthetic emotion. But I do not think I need linger to discuss the matter here. I have been inquiring why certain combinations of forms move us; I should not have traveled by other roads had I enquired, instead, why certain combinations are perceived to be right and necessary, and why our perception of their rightness and necessity is moving. What I have to say is this: the rapt philosopher, and he who contemplates a work of art, inhabit a world with an intense and peculiar significance of its own; that significance is unrelated to the significance of life. In this world the emotions of life find no place. It is a world with emotions of its own.

To appreciate a work of art we need bring with us nothing but a sense of form and color and a knowledge of three-dimensional space. That bit of knowledge, I admit, is essential to the appreciation of many great works, since many of the most moving forms ever created are in three dimensions.

To see a cube or a rhomboid as a flat pattern is to lower its significance, and a sense of three-dimensional space is essential to the full appreciation of most architectural forms. Pictures which would be insignificant if we saw them as flat patterns are profoundly moving because, in fact, we see them as related planes. If the representation of three-dimensional space is to be called "representation," then I agree that there is one kind of representation which is not irrelevant. Also, I agree that along with our feeling for line and color we must bring with us our knowledge of space if we are to make the most of every kind of form. Nevertheless, there are mangificent designs to an appreciation of which this knowledge is not necessary: so, though it is not irrelevant to the appreciation of some works of art it is not essential to the appreciation of all. What we must say is that the representation of three-dimensional space is neither irrelevant nor essential to all art, and that every other sort of representation is irrelevant.

That there is an irrelevant representative or descriptive element in many great works of art is not in the least surprising. Why it is not surprising I shall try to show elsewhere. Representation is not of necessity baneful, and highly realistic forms may be extremely significant. Very often, however, representation is a sign of weakness in an artist. A painter too feeble to create forms that provoke more than a little esthetic emotion will try to eke that little out by suggesting the emotions of life. To evoke the emotions of life he must use representation. Thus a man will paint an execution, and, fearing to miss with his first barrel of significant form, will try to hit with his second by raising an emotion of fear or pity. But if in the artist an inclination to play upon the emotions of life is often the sign of a flickering inspiration, in the spectator a tendency to seek, behind form, the emotions of life is a sign of defective sensibility always. It means that his esthetic emotions are weak or, at any rate, imperfect. Before a work of art people who feel little or no emotion for pure form find themselves at a loss. They are deaf men at a concert. They know that they are in the presence of something great, but they lack the power of apprehending it. They know that they ought to feel for it a tremendous emotion, but it happens that the particular kind of emotion it can raise is one that they can feel hardly or not at all. And so they read into the forms of the work those facts and ideas for which they are capable of feeling emotion, and feel for them the emotions that they can feel—the ordinary emotions of life. When confronted by a picture, instinctively they refer back its forms to the world from which they came. They treat created form as though it were imitated form, a picture as though it were a photograph. Instead of going out on the stream of art into a new world of esthetic experience, they turn a sharp corner and come straight home to the world of human interests. For them the significance of a work of art depends on what they bring to it; no new thing is added to their lives, only the old material is stirred. A good work of visual art carries a person who is capable of appreciating it out of life into ecstasy: to use art as a means to the emotions of life is to use a telescope for reading the news. You will notice that people who cannot feel pure esthetic emotions remember pictures by their subjects; whereas people who can, as often as not, have no idea what the subject of a picture is. They have never noticed the representative element, and so when they discuss pictures they talk about the shapes of forms and the relations and quantities of colors. Often they can tell by the quality of a single line whether or no a man is a good artist. They are concerned only with lines and colors, their relations and quantities and qualities; but from these they win an emotion more profound and far more sublime than any that can be given by the description of facts and ideas.

This last sentence has a very confident ring—over-confident, some may think. Perhaps I shall be able to justify it, and make my meaning clearer too, if I give an account of my own feelings about music. I am not really musical. I do not understand music well. I find musical form exceedingly difficult to apprehend, and I am sure that the profounder subtleties of harmony and rhythm more often than not escape me. The form of a musical composition must be simple indeed if I am to grasp it honestly. My opinion about music is not worth having. Yet, sometimes, at a concert, though my appreciation of the music is limited and humble, it is pure. Sometimes, though I have a poor understanding, I have a clean palate. Consequently, when I am feeling bright and clear and intent, at the beginning of a concert for instance, when something that I can grasp is being played, I get from music that pure esthetic emotion that I get from visual art. It is less intense, and the rapture is evanescent; I understand music too ill for music to transport me far into the world of pure esthetic ecstasy. But at moments I do appreciate music as pure musical form, as sounds combined according to the laws of a mysterious necessity, as pure art with a tremendous significance of its own and no relation whatever to the significance of life; and in those moments I lose myself in that infinitely sublime state of mind to which pure visual form transports me. How inferior is my normal state of mind at a concert. Tired or perplexed, I let slip my sense of form, my esthetic emotion collapses, and I begin weaving into the harmonies, that I cannot grasp, the ideas of life. Incapable of feeling the austere emotions of art, I begin to read into the musical forms human emotions of terror and mystery, love and hate, and spend the minutes, pleasantly enough, in a world of turbid and inferior feeling. At such times, were the grossest pieces of onomatopoeic representation—the song of a bird, the galloping of horses, the cries of children, or the laughing of demons—to be introduced into the symphony, I should not be offended. Very likely I should be pleased; they would afford new points of departure for new trains of romantic feeling or heroic thought. I know very well what has happened. I have been using art as a means to the emotions of life and reading into it the ideas of life. I have been cutting blocks with a razor. I have tumbled from the superb peaks of esthetic exaltation to the snug foothills of warm humanity. It is a jolly country. No one need be ashamed of enjoying himself there. Only no one who has ever been on the heights can help feeling a little crestfallen in the cozy valleys. And let no one imagine, because he has made merry in the warm tilth and quaint nooks of romance, that he can even guess at the austere and thrilling raptures of those who have climbed the cold, white peaks of art.

About music most people are as willing to be humble as I am. If they cannot grasp musical form and win from it a pure esthetic emotion, they confess that they understand music imperfectly or not at all. They recognize quite clearly that there is a difference between the feeling of the musician for pure music and that of the cheerful concert-goer for what music suggests.

The latter enjoys his own emotions, as he has every right to do, and recognizes their inferiority. Unfortunately, people are apt to be less modest about their powers of appreciating visual art. Every one is inclined to believe that out of pictures, at any rate, he can get all that there is to be got; every one is ready to cry "humbug" and "impostor" at those who say that more can be had. The good faith of people who feel pure esthetic emotions is called in question by those who have never felt anything of the sort. It is the prevalence of the representative element, I suppose, that makes the man in the street so sure that he knows a good picture when he sees one. For I have noticed that in matters of architecture, pottery, textiles, etc., ignorance and ineptitude are more willing to defer to the opinions of those who have been blest with peculiar sensibility. It is a pity that cultivated and intelligent men and women cannot be induced to believe that a great gift of esthetic appreciation is at least as rare in visual as in musical art. A comparison of my own experience in both has enabled me to discriminate very clearly between pure and impure appreciation. Is it too much to ask that others should be as honest about their feelings for pictures as I have been about mine for music? For I am certain that most of those who visit galleries do feel very much what I feel at concerts. They have their moments of pure ecstasy; but the moments are short and unsure. Soon they fall back into the world of human interests and feel emotions, good no doubt, but inferior. I do not dream of saying that what they get from art is bad or nugatory; I say that they do not get the best that art can give. I do not say that they cannot understand art; rather I say that they cannot understand the state of mind of those who understand it best. I do not say that art means nothing or little to them; I say they miss its full significance. I do not suggest for one moment that their appreciation of art is a thing to be ashamed of; the majority of the charming and intelligent people with whom I am acquainted appreciate visual art impurely; and, by the way, the appreciation of almost all great writers has been impure. But provided that there be some fraction of pure esthetic emotion, even a mixed and minor appreciation of art is, I am sure, one of the most valuable things in the world—so valuable, indeed, that in my giddier moments I have been tempted to believe that art might prove the world's salvation.

Yet, though the echoes and shadows of art enrich the life of the plains, her spirit dwells on the mountains. To him who woos, but woos impurely, she returns enriched what is brought. Like the sun, she warms the good seed in good soil and causes it to bring forth good fruit. But only to the perfect lover does she give a new strange gift—a gift beyond all price. Imperfect lovers bring to art and take away the ideas and emotions of their own age and civilization. In twelfth-century Europe a man might have been greatly moved by a Romanesque church and found nothing in a T'ang picture. To a man of later age, Greek sculpture meant much and Mexican nothing, for only to the former could he bring a crowd of associated ideas to be the objects of familiar emotions. But the perfect lover, he who can feel the profound significance of form, is raised above the accidents of time and place. To him the problems of archaeology, history, and hagiography are impertinent. If the forms of a work are significant its provenance is irrelevant. Before the grandeur of those Sumerian figures in the Louvre he is carried on the same flood of emotion to the same esthetic ecstasy as, more than four thousand years ago, the Chaldean lover was carried. It is the mark of great art that its appeal is universal and eternal.[1] Significant form stands charged with the power to provoke esthetic emotion in any one capable of feeling it. The ideas of men go buzz and die like gnats; men change their institutions and their customs as they change their coats; the intellectual triumphs of one age are the follies of another; only great art remains stable and unobscure. Great art remains stable and unobscure because the feelings that it awakens are independent of time and place, because its kingdom is not of this world. To those who have and hold a sense of the significance of form what does it matter whether the forms that move them were created in Paris the day before yesterday or in Babylon fifty centuries ago? The forms of art are inexhaustible; but all lead by the same road of esthetic emotion to the same world of esthetic ecstasy.

II The Metaphysical Hypothesis

It seems to me possible, though by no means certain, that created form moves us so profoundly because it expresses the emotion of its creator. . . . If this be so, it will explain that curious but undeniable fact, to which I have already referred, that what I call material beauty (*e.g.*, the wing of a butterfly) does not move most of us in at all the same way as a work of art moves us. It is beautiful form, but it is not significant form. It moves us, but it does not move us esthetically. It is tempting to explain the difference between "significant form" and "beauty"—that is to say, the difference between form that provokes our esthetic emotions and form that does not—by saying that significant form conveys to us an emotion felt by its creator and that beauty conveys nothing.

For what, then, does the artist feel the emotion that he is supposed to express? Sometimes it certainly comes to him through material beauty. The contemplation of natural objects is often the immediate cause of the artist's emotion. Are we to suppose, then, that the artist feels, or sometimes feels, for material beauty what we feel for a work of art? Can it be that sometimes for the artist material beauty is somehow significant—that is, capable of provoking esthetic emotion? And if the form that provokes esthetic emotion be form that expresses something, can it be that material beauty is to him expressive? Does he feel something behind it as we imagine that we feel something behind the forms of a work of art? . . .

The emotion that the artist felt in his moment of inspiration he did not feel for objects seen as means, but for objects seen as pure forms—that is, as ends in themselves. He did not feel emotion for a chair as a means to physical well-being, nor as an object associated with the intimate life of a family, nor as the place where some one sat saying things unforgettable, nor yet as a thing bound to the lives of hundreds of men and women, dead or alive, by a hundred subtle ties; doubtless an artist does often feel emotions such as these for the things that he sees, but in the moment of esthetic vision he sees objects, not as means shrouded in associations, but as pure forms. It is for, or at any rate through, pure form that he feels his inspired emotion.

Now to see objects as pure forms is to see them as ends in themselves. For though, of course, forms are related to each other as parts of a whole, they are related on terms of equality; they are not a means to anything except emotion. But for objects seen as ends in themselves, do we not feel a profounder and a more thrilling emotion than ever we felt for them as means? All of us, I imagine, do, from time to time, get a vision of material objects as pure forms. We see things as ends in themselves, that is to say; and at such moments is seems possible, and even probable, that we see them with the eye of an artist. Who has not, once at least in his life, had a sudden vision of landscape as pure form? For once, instead of seeing it as fields and cottages, he has felt it as lines and colors. In that moment has he not won from material beauty a thrill indistinguishable from that which art gives? And, if this be so, is it not clear that he has won from material beauty the thrill that, generally, art alone can give, because he has contrived to see it as a pure formal combination of lines and colors? May we go on to say that, having seen it as pure form, having freed it from all casual and adventitious interest, from all that it may have acquired from its commerce with human beings, from all its significance as a means, he has felt its significance as an end in itself? . . .

But if an object considered as an end in itself moves us more profoundly (*i.e.*, has greater significance) than the same object considered as a means to practical ends or as a thing related to human interests—and this undoubtedly is the case—we can only suppose that when we consider anything as an end in itself we become aware of that in it which is of greater moment than any qualities it may have acquired from keeping company with human beings. Instead of recognizing its accidental and conditioned importance, we become aware of its essential reality, of the God in everything, of the universal in the particular, of the all-pervading rhythm. Call it by what name you will, the thing that I am talking about is that which lies behind the appearance of all things—that which gives to all things their individual significance. . . . And if a more or less unconscious apprehension of this latent reality of material things be, indeed, the cause of that strange emotion, a passion to express which is the inspiration of many artists, it seems reasonable to suppose that those who, unaided by material objects, experience the same emotion have come by another road to the same country.

That is the metaphysical hypothesis. Are we to swallow it whole, accept a part of it, or reject it altogether? Each must decide for himself. I insist only on the rightness of my esthetic hypothesis. And of one other thing am I sure. Be they artists or lovers of art, mystics or mathematicians, those who achieve ecstasy are those who have freed themselves from the arrogance of humanity. He who would feel the significance of art must make himself humble before it. Those who find the chief importance of art or of philosophy in its relation to conduct or its practical utility—those who cannot value things as ends in themselves or, at any rate, as direct means to emotion—will never get from anything the best that it can give. Whatever the world of esthetic contemplation may be, it is not the world of human business and passion; in it the chatter and tumult of material existence is unheard, or heard only as the echo of some more ultimate harmony.

—*Art* (1913)

NOTE

1. Mr. Roger Fry permits me to make use of an interesting story that will illustrate my view. When Mr. Okakura, the Government editor of *The Temple Treasures of Japan,* first came to Europe, he found no difficulty in appreciating the pictures of those who from want of will or want of skill did not create illusions but concentrated their energies on the creation of form. He understood immediately the Byzantine masters and the French and Italian Primitives. In the Renaissance painters, on the other hand, with their descriptive pre-occupations, their literary and anecdotic interests, he could see nothing but vulgarity and muddle. The universal and essential quality of art, significant form, was missing, or rather had dwindled to a shallow stream, overlaid and hidden beneath weeds, so the universal response, esthetic emotion, was not evoked. It was not till he came on to Henri-Matisse that he again found himself in the familiar world of pure art. Similarly, sensitive Europeans who respond immediately to the significant forms of great Oriental art, are left cold by the trivial pieces of anecdote and social criticism so lovingly cherished by Chinese dilettanti. It would be easy to multiply instances did not decency forbid the laboring of so obvious a truth.

BEN SHAHN

The Shape of Content

I would not ordinarily undertake a discussion of form in art, nor would I undertake a discussion of content. To me, they are inseparable. Form is formulation—the turning of content into a material entity, rendering a content accessible to others, giving it permanence, willing it to the race. Form is as varied as are the accidental meetings of nature. Form in art is as varied as idea itself.

It is the visible shape of all man's growth; it is the living picture of his tribe at its most primitive, and of his civilization at its most sophisticated state. Form is the many faces of the legend—bardic, epic, sculptural, musical, pictorial, architectural; it is the infinite images of religion; it is the expression and the remnant of self. Form is the very shape of content.

Think of numbers alone, and their expression in form, of three, for instance. Who knows how far back into time the idea of the triad extends? Forms in threes appeared everywhere in early art. But then the Trinity arose in Christian theology—the Father, the Son, and the Holy Ghost, and was a new form-generating concept. It became desirable to turn the idea of Trinity into every possible medium, to turn it to every use. The challenge to formulate new expressions of three, to symbolize further the religious idea, actually become a sort of game. How vast is the iconography of three alone—the triptych, the trefoil window, the three-petaled fleur-de-lis, used everywhere; the triskelion in its hundreds of forms—three angels interwoven, three fish interwoven, three legs interwoven, three horses interwoven, and the famous trefoil knot with three loops; the divisions of churches into three, of hymns into three; the efforts to compose pictures into threefold design. *Form—content.*

But the three, the Trinity, was only one small part of the stimulus to form which arose out of the vivid Christian legend: think of the immense and brilliant iconography which remains detailed for us and our delight —the Lion for Mark, the Ox for Luke, the Eagle for John, the Angel for Matthew; Lamb and Serpent and Phoenix and Peacock, each with its special meaning; symbols of keys and daggers and crosses, all challenging the artists and artisans and architects and sculptors to new kinds of invention. Sin and Temptation, Piety, and a thousand virtues and vices all transmuted into the materials of art, into form, remaining for us in mosaics, in frescoes, in carvings, forming capitals, cupolas, domes, inner walls and outer façades, tombs, and thrones. Wherever something was made, the legend turned it into form. *Wonderful form; wonderful content.*

Think also of the ancient epics of Greece, Persia, Egypt, and Rome, each with its profusion of image and incident, its *dramatis personae,* its hierarchy, its complicated rites, its fierce families—every such item a point of departure for the artist, a touchstone of form for the poet, a basis for elaboration, a vessel for personal content, a subject for craft, for excellence, for style, for idea. *Form—content.*

Form and content have been forcibly divided by a great deal of present-day esthetic opinion, and each, if one is to believe what he reads, goes its separate way. Content, in this sorry divorce, seems to be looked upon as the culprit. It is seldom mentioned in the consideration of a work of art; it is not in the well-informed vocabulary. Some critics consider any mention of content a display of bad taste. Some, more innocent and more modern, have been taught—schooled—to look at paintings in such a way as to make them wholly unaware of content.

Writing about art is more and more exclusively in terms of form. Characteristic comment from the magazines upon one artist's work will read as follows: "The scheme is of predominantly large areas of whites, ochres, umbers and blacks which break off abruptly into moments of rich blues with underlayers of purple." Of another artist it is written: "White cuttings expand and contract, suspended in inky black scaffoldings which alternate as interstices and positive shapes." Of a third, we read, "There is, first, a preoccupation with space broken into color through prisms and planes. Then the movement alters slightly and shifts toward the large field of space lanced by rectilinear lines that ride off the edge of the canvas"—and so on. From time to time the critic himself will *create* a content by describing the work in terms of some content-reference, as when one of the above uses the term "scaffolding"—seeming to hunger for some object that he may be able to hang onto. Or when another writer describes a non-objective work as "an ascetic whirlpool of blacks and whites, a Spartan melodrama, alleviated only by piquant whispers of turquoise, yellow or olive . . ."

Such a nostalgia for content and meaning in art goes counter to the creed as it is set forth by the true spokesmen for the new doctrine. I have already mentioned the credo of that early modern [Clive Bell] who demanded that art display "nothing from life, no knowledge of its affairs, no familiarity with its emotions." A contemporary writer, Louis Danz, asks that the artist "deny the very existence of mind." Ezra Pound has called art "a fluid moving over and above the minds of men."

An eminent American critic speaking recently in London dwelt at length upon "horizontality" and "verticality" as finalities in art. Throwing upon a screen reproductions of one work by Jackson Pollock, and one page from the ancient Irish "Book of Kells," the critic found parallel after parallel between the two works—the two qualities named above, a certain nervousness of line common to the two, the intricately woven surface.

Coming at length to the differences between the two works, the critic pointed out that the "Books of Kells" was motivated by strong faith—by belief that lay outside the illuminated page. But Pollock had no such outside faith, only faith in the material paint. Again, the "Books of Kells" revealed craftsmanship, the craftsmanlike approach, but no such craftsmanship entered the work of Pollock.

Necessarily the surface effects which can arise out of such art are limited. One writer divides such painting into categories according to the general surface shapes, his categories being (1) pure geometric, (2) architectural and mechanical geometric, (3) naturalistic geometric (I wonder what that means!), (4) expressionist geometric, (5) expressionist biomorphic, and so on.

Among all such trends, there are the differences. There is some factor that decides whether a work shall be rounded, geometrical, spiral, blurred, or whatever it is in shape.

Those differences are in point of view. Sometimes the point of view is stated by the artist himself; more often, certainly more prolixly, it is stated by the theorist, or esthetician or critic. I wish to discuss certain of these points of view, and show—if I can—how a point of view conditions the paint surface which the artist creates.

Let us begin with the paint-alone point of view—the contention that material alone is sufficient in painting, the attitude that holds that any work of art should be devoid not only of subject, or of meaning, but even of intention itself.

I suppose that the most monumental work in this direction is the great canvas—occupying a whole wall—done by Clyfford Still and exhibited by the Museum of Modern Art a few years ago. The canvas is done in a dull all-over black, and has a single random drip of white coming down to (I would judge) about a foot from the top of the painting. There is nothing more. Then there are the paintings of Mark Rothko, sometimes much more colorful but also immense in size; there are the blurred squares of color done by Ad Reinhardt. And there are many painters who work in forms of paint almost entirely static in their effect. The work of these three painters is perhaps as content-less as anything to be seen currently, although there is always Malevitch's "White on White," which still holds first place in the competitive race against content.

Distinguished in appearance from such static work as I have just described is the painting of the late and very noted Jackson Pollock, whose pictures are, as everyone knows, tangled surfaces of threaded paint, sometimes splashed paint, sometimes dripped paint. There are the legion followers of Pollock among our young painters; there is the Frenchman Mathieu; there are several young artists whose paintings consist of one or two long agitated strokes.

These painters are of the paint-alone school too, but in their case it is the *act* of painting which is emphasized. The act is in some cases looked upon as therapeutic; in other cases, it is looked upon as automatic. Then the artist becomes actor, sometimes in a drama of his own psyche, sometimes in a vast time–space drama, in which case he becomes only the medium (it is held) for great forces and movements of which he can have no knowledge, and over which he can have no control.

Thus Pollock spoke of "the paroxysm of creation." Mathieu, going further, dressed himself in the most eccentric of costumes in order to make his painting, "The Battle of the Bouvines." According to the critic, he was "dressed in black silk; he wore a white helmet and shoes and greaves and cross-bars. . . . It was our good fortune [he says] to witness the most unpredictable of ballets, a dance of dedicated ferocity, the grave elaboration of a magic rite . . ." And later, "Mathieu regards everything as totally absurd and shows this constantly in his behavior which is characterized by the most sovereign of dandyisms. He understands with complete lucidity all the dizzying propositions in the inexhaustible domain of the abstract, on which he has staked his whole life, every possible type of humanism having been rejected . . ."

The differences in such art surfaces are not differences of paint alone. They are differences of idea, differences of point of view, differences of objective. They are, even in this most extreme wing of noncontent painting, simply differences of content.

I have said that form is the shape of content. We might now turn the statement around and say that form could not possibly exist without a content of some kind. It would be and apparently is impossible to conceive of form as apart from content. Even the ectoplasm of Sir Oliver Lodge and the homeliest household ghost have a content of some kind—the soul, the departed spirit. If the content of a work of art is only the paint itself, so be it; it has that much content. We may now say, I believe, that the form of the most nonobjective painting consists of a given quantity of paint, shaped by content; its content consisting in a point of view, in a series of gestures, and in the accidental qualities of paint.

But there is a great deal of other content that enters into the turns and twists of abstract-to-nonobjective form. There is, for instance, mission, and even social milieu. Socially, we must note that there has been no other time in history when just this art could have taken place. It had to be preceded by Freud; it must necessarily be directed toward a public conversant with Freud, and in many cases the very suppositions upon which contemporary art is based are derived from Freud. Further, it had to be preceded by Picasso, by Kandinsky, by Klee, by Miró, by Mondrian, for its forms, whatever new departures they may have taken, are an inheritance from the earlier group of great imaginers.

All this is content within content-less art, but there is even more; there is a certain sort of proclamation involved, an imperative, a mission, to announce that *this is art*; that this is man even—at least the only kind of man that counts. The public itself is not worthy; it is only anonymous. Worth itself inheres only in the special few, the initiate.

Form is the visible shape of content. The forms of the most extreme varieties of the paint-alone esthetic differ from those of other art because the content differs. And if content is the difference, we might wonder how the new content looks alongside the old.

A year or so ago I was one of the judges for the Pennsylvania Academy annual exhibition. When we, the judges, walked into the immense room where we were finally to decide on prizes, a curious sight met us. The new paintings stood around the wall on the floor before the places where they were to be hung. The old pictures, the Pennsylvania "Treasures," were still in place above them. I remember experiencing a certain thrill of pride as I noted the contrast. The new pictures constituted a very river of color around the floor; they glowed richly. And, in comparison, the older paintings, certainly constituting some of the very finest in preimpressionist art, seemed almost a gray-on-tan monotone. I felt proud of my contemporaries, and of painting. The forms of the new work stood out bold and clear, and the colors were infinite. Invention and variety competed and seemed almost to obliterate the work hanging on the walls. I felt a little sad that the older artists were so limited in their use of color and that their work dimmed so alongside the new.

Later, as I sat at lunch, I kept remembering the Eakins—the Winslow Homer paintings, too, but mostly the Eakins—the "Cello Player." What was it about Eakins that was so compelling? There was no boldness of design there. Colors, elegant and muted, but not used for design—used actually quite descriptively. Perhaps it was partly realism, but then realism alone quite often leaves me cold. There was another kind of content in the Eakins painting; there was a certain intellectual attitude—a complete dedication to comprehending something, someone outside himself. There was an intensity of honesty, a personal simplicity present in the work itself. Odd, that by departing utterly from himself, an artist could so reveal himself.

What a departure, what a contradiction to the canons of art which we hold so inviolate today! Eakins, full of content, full of story, of perfection of likeness, of naturalness, of observation of small things—the look of wood and cloth and a face—seeking to reveal character in his painting, loving the incidental beauty of things, but loving even more the actual way of things—sympathy, honesty, dedication, visible apprehensible shape. *Form—content.*

Almost anyone will tell you that, in terms of form, Eakins simply does not exist. But again, we must look upon form as the shape of content: with Eakins, no less with de Kooning, or Stamos, or Baziotes, form is the right and only possible shape of a certain content. Some other kind of form would have conveyed a different meaning and a different attitude. So when we sit in judgment upon a certain kind of form—and it is usually called lack of form—what we do actually is to sit in judgment upon a certain kind of content.

I have mentioned some of the surface shapes which are characteristic of contemporary painting, and some of the classifications into which painting is put, depending upon whether it displays a rounded shape, squarish, angular, or some other sort of shape. I have pointed out that even with the renouncement of content, some content does remain, if only of verticality and horizontality.

There is little art being produced today that does not bear some imprint of the great period of the "Isms" when painting was freed from that academic dictatorship which had laid down so many rules about both form and content. Every branch of the rebellion of the Isms had, as we know, a content of ideas, and that content charted the course which it would pursue, as cubism, for instance, pursued the cube, the cone, and the sphere, as surrealism pursued the subconscious, and dadaism, perversity.

Out of those ideas there emerged a new universe of forms, an esthetic rebirth. Both the forms and the ideas are necessarily present to some degree in the work of us who have come later, and who are familiar with the ideas and images thus generated. Content, purpose, idea all provide new direction and new shape, but all are united in a certain modernity, in the sharing of a common art inheritance.

Abstraction is perhaps the most classic of the contemporary points of view. It sometimes seems to have much in common with that art which has sought to reject content, but actually it has not, for in the case of abstraction content is its point of departure, its cue, and its theme. To abstract is to draw out the essence of a matter. To abstract in art is to separate certain fundamentals from the irrelevant material which surrounds them. An artist may abstract the essential form of an object by freeing it from perspective, or by freeing it from details. He may, for instance, interpret Jazz—an idea, a content—by abstracting out of a confusion of figures and instruments just the staccato rhythms and the blare. In Stuart Davis' paintings of jazz, for example, or in Matisse's, blaring sound becomes blaring color; rhythm of timing becomes rhythm of forms. Content, particularly with Davis, is not just jazz; it is the interpretation of an age with its shocks, its neon-lighted glare, its impacts on all the senses, its violent movements in which the eye glimpses everything and grasps nothing—a highly intellectual content formulated into a single immediate impression.

If abstraction itself is the most classic of the modern modes, abstract expressionism, so-called, is the most prevalent. One might be entitled to expect of this view—judging from its name—that it would take almost as many outward forms as there are inward, or expressive, differences between artists.

Actually, I think that the varieties of form in abstract expressionist art are fewer than we might expect. Although the title is a loose one, and can be expanded to include almost anything, it seems usually to be applied to about three or four directions in form. It may indicate that painting which takes the form of whirls and swirls upon a surface, or it may be applied to painting in squares, or geometric patterns. Sometimes its shapes are rounded, having, I believe it is said, a biologic connection. Sometimes the forms may have an angular or spiked look. The theory underlying abstract expressionism has points in common with completely nonobjective views. Performance is likely to be held an essential part of the art process —the act, as against a controlled objective. But, as to the result, I think that this view admits of content—that content being the true impulsive compulsive self, revealed in paint.

If art seeks to divorce itself from meaningful and associative images, if it holds material alone as its objective, then I think that the material itself ought to have the greatest possible plasticity, the greatest potentialities for the development of shapes and the creating of relationships. For that reason I think that the sculpture which has been created with a view to being form alone has been a great deal more successful and interesting than has been the painting in that vein. The sculptor sets out with two preexisting advantages: one, that he must have craftsmanship, and the other, that he works in the round. He does not have to simulate depth nor create illusions of depth because he works in volume—in three-dimensional form.

Thus Noguchi, working in marble, is able to develop relationships in three dimensions rather than two and yet retain both simplicity and unity. He has at his disposal the advantages of light and space, and the natural translucence and glow of marble, all of which he exploits and reveals with great elegance.

Henry Moore is one of the great contemporary imaginers who has brought new materials and new concepts into sculptural form. He discovers the naturally heroic character of bronze and exploits feelingly the graining and fine surfaces of wood. Undoubtedly his most remarkable feat has been the surrounding of open space and his use of such space as a sculptural material. But beauty and craft and idea are still paramount with Moore, and he never obliterates these qualities in the shock of the new.

Unique in any age is Calder, who is, I think, the only one of the modern people who has actually and physically introduced a time dimension into his work. (It is sometimes held that the work of certain of the "paroxysmic" kind of painters represents a sort of time–space extension, that it expresses the action of immense physical forces; but I cannot escape the conviction that such an identification is more romantic than real; that it expresses only a wish to be identified with the new, to participate in the vitality and centralness of a science—of physics—which has so greatly shaped the mood and sense of our time.) Calder's work requires no terminology to identify it with that which is modern. It reads at once, and for anyone, and for a long time. While its shapes and forms are of an abstract genre, its meanings involve that return to nature, to first principles, which seems to be an indispensable condition of any great work of art or movement in art. Calder, once an engineer himself, but also son and grandson of sculptors, undoubtedly brought to engineering an eye for beauty, a sensitivity to esthetic meanings which would wholly escape the usual engineer. Thus, in stress and balance, in sequences of motion, in other basic and natural and probably common principles, he saw tremendous esthetic potentialities, and put them to work.

The result for us who watch the continuously interdependent movements, the varieties of form balanced daringly and with delicate precision, is to experience the perfect union of nature and art. Here is sculpture that creates endless patterns in space—time-rhythms. Of course, Calder's own great sense of play enters into all this, adding its own peculiar gaiety to the forms.

And then there are other interesting and diverse kinds of content that find expression in contemporary sculpture. I remember listening to a remarkable speech on the qualities of black alone which David Smith delivered spontaneously before an esthetics conference a few years ago. It would be hard to believe that so much could be said of black—of its qualities, of its personal meanings, of its variety—unless we look at David Smith's sculpture where it is all so feelingly expressed.

In painting, there are additional kinds of content which help to set the look and the shape and the colors of the work that we see today. There is a certain moody poetic content, sometimes an emotional attitude toward nature—toward the sea, strange places, aspects of the city, even objects which have some odd emotional connection. Such content is sometimes expressed formally in abstract paintings which have only a vague reminiscence of actual things. Again, it may be present in actual scenes or objects strongly overbalanced by some one quality, so that only the feeling is present, as in Loren MacIver's painting of Venice—the Venice of lights only. Or there are Reuben Tam's seascapes, the moon or the sun in black, or swallowed by the sea. There are many extremely fine painters who work in this vein, and it constitutes to my mind one of the highest and most worthy expressions in the modern idiom.

Then there are the avowedly figurative painters whose point of departure is idea, attitude toward things and people, content of all kinds, not excluding story content. Even among such painters, and I include myself among them, the impress of abstraction and expressionism is strong. The variations in form, in the look of painting, may be greater among the artists of this vaguely defined and scattered group than among artists of some of the other groups, simply because they have little in common aside from the fact that most of them work in objective images—things, places, and people. Not in any other age but ours would such a painter as Jack Levine—satirist of manners, observer, commentator, craftsman, and, in a sense, traditionalist—be aligned with such a painter as Tamayo—the designer, the imaginer, originator of strange beasts and men in all the possible mutations of red. What have they in common? That they paint content, figures! Nor would Philip Evergood be placed alongside Kuniyoshi, or Jacob Lawrence or Hyman Bloom, except that all are "content" painters.

Content, in the view of Panofsky, is "that which a work betrays but does not parade." In his book, *Meaning in the Visual Arts,* he calls it "the basic attitude of a nation, a period, a class, a religious persuasion—all this qualified by one personality, and condensed into one work. It is obvious," says Mr. Panofsky, "that such an involuntary relationship will be obscured in proportion as one of the two elements, idea or form, is voluntarily emphasized or suppressed. A spinning machine," he says, "is perhaps the most impressive manifestation of a functional idea, and an abstract painting is probably the most expressive manifestation of pure form. But both have a minimum of content."

Form arises in many ways. Form in nature emerges from the impact of order upon order, of element upon element, as of the forms of lightning or of ocean waves. Or form may emerge from the impact of elements upon materials, as of wind-carved rocks, and dunes. Form in living things, too, is the impinging of order upon order—the slow evolving of shapes according to function, and drift, and need. And other shapes—the ear, the hand—what mind could devise such shapes! The veining of leaves, of nerves, of roots; the unimaginable varieties of shape of aquatic things.

Forms of artifacts grow out of use, too, and out of the accidental meetings of materials. Who again could dream of or devise a form so elegant as that of the chemical retort, except that need and use and glass and glassblowing all met to create form? Or the forms of houses, the Greek, the Roman, the extremely modern, or the gingerbread house; these are creations out of different materials, and tools, and crafts, and needs—the needs of living and of imagining.

Forms in art arise from the impact of idea upon material, or the impinging of mind upon material. They stem out of the human wish to formulate ideas, to recreate them into entities, so that meanings will not depart fitfully as they do from the mind, so that thinking and belief and attitudes may endure as actual things.

I do not at all hold that the mere presence of content, of subject matter, the *intention* to say something, will magically guarantee the emergence of such content into successful form. Not at all! How often indeed does the intended bellow of industrial power turn to a falsetto on the savings bank walls! How often does the intended lofty angels choir for the downtown church come off resembling somehow a sorority pillow fight!

For form is not just the intention of content; it is the embodiment of content. Form is based, first, upon a supposition, a theme. Form is, second, a marshaling of materials, the inert matter in which the theme is to be cast. Form is, third, a setting of boundaries, of limits, the whole extent of idea, *but no more*, an outer shape of idea. Form is, next, the relating of inner shapes to the outer limits, the initial establishing of harmonies. Form is, further, the abolishing of excessive content, of content that falls outside the true limits of the theme. It is the abolishing of excessive materials, whatever material is extraneous to inner harmony, to the order of shapes now established. Form is thus a discipline, an ordering, according to the needs of content.

In its initial premises, content itself may be anything. It may be humble or intimate, perhaps only the contemplation of a pine bough. Or it may strive toward the most exalted in idea or emotion. In such an initial theme lies the cue, the point of departure, the touchstone of shape. But from that point, from the setting of theme, the development of form must be a penetration of inner relationships, a constant elimination of nonpertinent matter both of content and of shape. Sometimes, if extreme simplicity is an objective, an artist's whole effort must be bent toward the casting aside of extra matter. Sometimes, if the theme is exalted, tremendous energy must be poured into the very act of reaching toward, of seeking to fulfill the boundaries of that theme which has been set. Perhaps the most heroic performance in this direction that the world has ever known—at least on the part of one man—was the creation of the Sistine ceiling by Michelangelo. Here was the setting of a formal plan so vast that its enactment alone became an almost superhuman task; moreover, there was the establishment of a pitch of feeling which could not be let down or diminished in any place—and which was not diminished!

Content, I have said, may be anything. Whatever crosses the human mind may be fit content for art—in the right hands. It is out of the variety of experience that we have derived varieties of form; and it is out of the challenge of great ideas that we have gained the great in form—the immense harmonies in music, the meaningful related actions of the drama, a wealth of form and style and shape in painting and poetry.

Content may be and often is trivial. But I do not think that any person may pronounce either upon the weight or upon the triviality of an idea before its execution into a work of art. It is only after its execution that we may note that it was fruitful of greatness or variety or interest.

We have seen so often in past instances how content that was thought unworthy for art has risen to the very heights. Almost every great artist from Cimabue to Picasso has broken down some preexisting canon of what was proper material for painting. Perhaps it is the fullness of feeling with which the artist addresses himself to his theme that will determine, finally, its stature or its seriousness. But I think that it can be said with certainty that the form which does emerge cannot be greater than the content which went into it. For form is only the manifestation, the shape of content.

—*The Shape of Content* (1957)

HAROLD OSBORNE

Organic Unity

The concept of "organic unity," or more loosely, "unity in variety," is commonly traced back to classical antiquity, though there is in fact little about it in the surviving literature. The not entirely happy metaphor which compares the unity of a work of art with the functional unity of a living organism goes back to a casual remark in Plato's *Phaedrus* (264c), which may not warrant the burden of significance which has in later ages been read into it. In discussing the art of rhetoric he makes Socrates say: "Any discourse ought to be constructed like a living creature, with its own body, as it were; it must not lack either head or feet; it must have a middle and extremities so composed as to suit each other and the whole work." Plato himself in the dialogue draws from this no more recondite conclusions than that a good speech must have a beginning, a middle, and an end and that these should fit together coherently. The concept is further developed by Aristotle.

In the *Metaphysics* (1024a),. Aristotle distinguishes between a "whole" and an "aggregate." Collections "to which the position of the parts in relation to each other makes no difference are 'aggregates,' those to which it does make a difference are 'wholes.' " Aristotle further adds that a genuine part of a "whole" cannot retain its own character except in the whole of which it is a part. He also says that removal of a part is apt to make the whole mutilated and any transposition of the parts will damage or even destroy its unity. The last statement is both important and obscure. It is, of course, the case, as McTaggart showed, that any change in any of the parts of an *aggregate* changes the whole aggregate. What Aristotle appears to mean when he advances this as a point of difference between an aggregate and a unified whole is that in the case of the whole but not in the case of the aggregate any change in any part produces changes in the nature and relations of all the remaining parts as parts of that whole. This idea is very important to the modern notion of an organic unity as applied to works of art.

In the *Poetics*, Aristotle applies his concept of unity to drama (chs. 7 and 8). The plot, he says, must represent an action which is "whole and complete and of a certain magnitude." A whole is "that which has a beginning, middle, and end." In discussing magnitude he assumes the very important principle that a beautiful thing must be a thing which can be apprehended in a single act of "synoptic" perception, *seen* as a single thing or unity, and not seen as an aggregate of parts which are connected by theoretical reason, discursively.

> Furthermore since a beautiful thing, either a living creature or any structure made of parts, must have not only an orderly arrangement of these parts but a size which is proper to it—for beauty lies in size and arrangement, hence neither a very tiny creature can be beautiful, because our view of it is blurred as it approaches that instant where its perceptibility ceases, nor an enormously big one, because then the perception does not take place all at once and the sense of oneness and wholeness is gone from the viewers' vision, as for example if it were a creature a thousand miles long—hence as in the case of bodies, i.e. living creatures, a certain size is required but one which can easily be taken in by the eye as a whole, so in the case of plots: they must have a certain length but such as can be easily grasped in memory as a whole.

One may compare the statement in *Metaphysics* (1078a 36): "The chief criteria of beauty are order and symmetry and determinate bounds."

The classical statement of the principle of esthetic unity comes in the next chapter.

> Hence, just as in other mimetic arts a single representation is a representation of one thing, so too the plot, being a representation of an action, must be a representation of a single unified action which is also a whole; and the component elements of the plot must be so fitted together that if one of them is changed around or removed the unity of the whole is disturbed or dislocated. For if the present or absence of a thing makes no difference to the clarity, it is not an integral part of the whole.

Through the Middle Ages, following ideas suggested by St. Augustine, beauty was thought of as a combination of unity and variety as when diverse and varied parts are combined into a unified whole so that the congruence of the parts in the whole is immediately perceived. The key concepts were proportion and congruity among the parts in a heterogeneous or composite whole. The result was called "concinnity." This line of thought was summed up by Alberti at the outset of the Renaissance. Asking what is the property that by its nature makes a thing beautiful, he suggests that *congruity* is the source of all beauty and grace.

> The business and office of congruity [*he goes on*] is to put together members differing from each other in their natures in such a manner that they may conspire to form a beautiful whole: so that whenever such a composition offers itself to the mind, either by the conveyance of the sight or any of the other senses, we immediately perceive this congruity.

He therefore says: "I shall define Beauty to be a harmony of all the parts, in whatsoever subject it appears, fitted together with such proportion and connection that nothing could be added, diminished, or altered, but for the worse."

The principle of "unity in variety" became very popular in the centuries following the Renaissance. The principle was supposed to be exemplified in such mathematical formulas as the Golden Section and in Hogarth's lines of beauty and grace. J. P. Crousaz in his *Traité du Beau* explained that the human mind has a need for variety as a relief from dullness and monotony but unless balanced by unity, variety will lead to confusion and fatigue. Sir Joshua Reynolds argued in a similar vein in his *Discourses.* Hutcheson stands out as the chief theoretical exponent of this principle. He defined beauty as a compound ratio of uniformity and variety and enunciated the general rule: "Where the Uniformity of Bodies is equal, the Beauty is as the Variety; and where the Variety is equal, the Beauty is as the Uniformity." His "internal sense" of beauty was described as a "passive Power of receiving Ideas of Beauty from all Objects in which there is Uniformity amidst Variety." In the 1930s George Birkhoff proposed an ingenious method of *measuring* esthetic value in works of art by means of a formula relating order to complexity (*Aesthetic Measure,* 1933).

This interest in unified diversity as a signpost of the beautiful helped to keep alive the idea of "synoptic" awareness, the perception of large and manifold wholes, which otherwise was threatened with extinction by the new scientific ideal of "atomic" perception. The scientific ideal of perception, which was fostered by British associationist psychology, emphasizes the qualities of acuity and precision, sacrificing richness of content to exactness. Its logical extreme is the "pointer-reading." It was this scientific ideal of atomic percipience which provided the paradigm for Hume's "delicacy of taste." He describes it in terms of acuity and precision: "Where the organs are so fine as to allow nothing to escape them, and at the same time so exact as to perceive every ingredient in the composition, this we call delicacy of taste, whether we employ these terms in the literal or metaphorical sense." He uses the analogy of those kinsmen of Sancho Panza who detected a taste of leather or of iron in a hogshead of wine in which there was afterward found a key with a leather thong attached to it. But precise and exact discriminations of individual sensations are not in themselves sufficient for esthetic awareness. The person with the most exact ear for pitch is not necessarily a good critic of music. With Hume's analogy we may contrast that of the Abbé Dubos who in his *Reflexions critiques sur la poésie et sur la peinture* compared our feeling for a work of art as a whole with our enjoyment of a ragout: in neither case do we analyze and apprehend the various sensory elements and ingredients in isolation from each other, but savor and give our verdict on the taste as a whole. Yet when we are aware of the "emergent" qualities, what is often called the expressive character, of a whole we are more than usually alert to any small incongruence among the constituent parts—anything which, in Wittgenstein's words, "doesn't make the right gesture." The same point has been ably demonstrated by Anton Ehrenzweig in his posthumous book *The Hidden Order of Art* (1967).

The contrary ideal of perception was fostered in the tradition which goes back to Leibniz. In contrast with the psychologists who regarded perception as the passive receiving of impressions from outside to be worked up by associative processing into a coherent world of things, for Leibniz perception was the central activity and as it were the very core of being in every monad; it was the point at which the potentialities of its nature are realized, its own "being" is crystallized into actuality and the universe reflected in it. Perfection, he said in an early paper *Von der Weisheit,* is the actualizing of potentialities over and above normal healthy functioning; and the perfection of the perceptual faculty consists in the maximum of *content* as well as clarity. It was this notion of perception which was implicit in the work of Alexander Baumgarten (1714–62), who first coined the word "esthetics" and first put forward the idea that the current rationalistic classification of philosophical studies needed to be rounded off by a science of the so-called inferior cognition which is mediated by the senses. In his early work *Meditationes philosophicae de nunnullis ad poema pertinentibus* (1735) Baumgarten contrasted the "extensive clarity" of the scientist, who by conceptualization and generalization reduces the intuited content of perception to its elements and classifies these into a system, with the "intensive clarity" of the poet and artist, who sees things whole and retains the full richness of the intuited experience in a single undivided glance. His maturer theory repeated the contrast between the vital fullness of perceived reality which is caught and communicated by the artist in all its richness and the discursive analytical processes of science. By breaking down experience into its elements, searching for laws and physical causes, analyzing and generalizing, scientists gain much useful knowledge; but the original vital richness of the experience is dissolved and lost. The geologist can tell us much in a scientific way about the landscape we see: but in his explanations the landscape itself disappears. Conceptualization, Baumgarten argued, sacrifices the life of experience by reducing it to an aggregate of features in which only the common and repetitive aspects are retained, letting slip the original and the unique.

In Chapter xii of the First Treatise in his *Inquiry* Hutcheson showed himself also aware of this difference.

> Let every one here consider how different we must suppose the perception to be with which a Poet is transported upon the prospect of any of those objects of natural beauty which ravish us even in his description, from that cold lifeless Conception which we imagine in a dull Critick or one of the Virtuosi without what we call a fine Taste. This latter class of men may have greater perfection in that knowledge which is derived from external sensation; they can tell all the specifick differences of trees, herbs, minerals, metals; they know the form of every leaf, stalk, root, flower and seed of all the species, about which the Poet is often very ignorant. And yet the Poet shall have a vastly more delightful perception of the whole; and not only the Poet, but any man of fine taste. Our external senses may by measuring teach us all the proportions of architecture to the tenth of an inch, and the situation of every muscle in the human body; and a good memory may retain these. And yet there is still something further necessary not only to make a man a compleat master in architecture, painting or statuary, but even a tolerable judge in these works or capable of receiving the highest pleasure in contemplating them.

Hutcheson accepted the "passive" notion of perception common to the psychology of his time. Therefore, since the external senses receive particular sense impressions, he had to postulate an "internal sense" to receive the impressions of the whole as a combination of unity and variety. Baumgarten, however, inherited the active notion of perception which was current in the Leibnizian tradition and he was therefore able to define beauty as the expansion and perfection of ordinary perception. "The object of esthetics," he says, "is the perfection of sensory cognition as such. And this is beauty" (*Aesthetices finis est perfectio cognitionis sensitivae, qua talis. Haec autem esta pulchritudo*). Where he might have been expected to have attempted a psychology of perception, he produced instead a theory of art and beauty, equating the "theory of the liberal arts" or the "art of thinking beautifully" with the science of sensory cognition (*Aesthetica—theoria liberalium artium, gnoseologia inferior, ars pulchre cogitandi, ars analogi rationis—est scientiae cognitionis sensitivae*). This follows from the notion of beauty as the perfection of sensory awareness.

Interest in pursuing the study of internally complex perceptual experience, which in their several ways Dubos, Hutcheson, and Baumgarten had connected with the artist's method of coming to grips with his world, remained submerged for more than a century under the growing prestige of associationist psychology, which favored the "scientific" model of atomic sensory elements. The emergence to importance in modern times of the concept of organic perceptual wholes owed something to Gestalt psychology, when toward the end of the last century it revived the idea of perceptual configurations with configurational properties which cannot be reduced to or built up from more simple "atomic" elements of sensation combined according to external relations which leave them internally unaffected.

From the first, esthetic objects were recognized as good examples of the kind of configurations which the Gestalt psychologists were interested to demonstrate. In his essay "Über Gestaltqualitäten" (1890) Ehrenfels, one of the founders of the school, instanced a melody as an example of a configuration which has an "emergent" character in that its quality in perception cannot be constructed theoretically by adding together the perceptual qualities of the individual notes from which it is formed and the relations in which they stand to each other. You can change every component in it by playing it at a different pitch or on a different instrument, but it remains the same melody. But it must be apprehended as a single impression. If you play the ten notes of a melody to ten different hearers, or if you change the order of the notes, the melody is lost. If you play it in bits to a hearer who knows it, he will hear the bits *as fragments of a melody*, not as several small melodies. The melody as a whole has a character of its own distinct from that of the notes or fragments which compose it. Yet the notes and fragments, *heard as parts of that melody*, acquire a perceptually different character from the character which they possess if heard in isolation or as parts of a different melody.

The modern conception of an artistic unity combines the old Aristotelian concept of a whole with the gestalt idea of a perceptual unity displaying emergent or "field" qualities which belong to the whole but not to the parts. In esthetic appreciation, the art object is isolated from its environment and framed apart in attention as a single individual, apprehended as a single complex impression and not as an aggregate. For when we apprehend something as an aggregate we apprehend it discursively; we are aware of a manifold of interrelated parts, and we recognize each part for what it is independently of the whole to which it belongs. We do not become directly aware of any properties of the whole which are not constructed from our prior knowledge of the parts. But in esthetic appreciation we become aware of the object in its internal complexity by a direct act of synoptic perception; we do not "construct" it in thought by discursive reason, though of course the final appreciative awareness may often be *prepared* by much preliminary study. Ideally, in esthetic contemplation, we become aware of a total presentation manifesting qualities which are not built up from, or fully analyzable into, the properties and relations of the constituent parts. The whole in apprehension is more than the sum of the parts. Although the contained parts may be attended to separately in the perhaps lengthy process of becoming acquainted with the total work of art, they become fully articulate only when they are perceived as parts of the particular whole in which they occur, in the completed act of appreciation. We cannot know the parts as they are without knowing the whole. Although the whole is composed of its parts, the qualities of the whole permeate and determine the parts and the parts are what they are only in the context of the whole in which they are apprehended. It is, in the words of Coleridge, "a whole that is presupposed by all its parts."

A major problem has been to pinpoint the difference between esthetic objects and other sorts of configurations. It has been pointed out that what has been said about organic wholes in general could also be said about nonesthetic wholes, such as human faces. We recognize a face by a certain overall configurational character which makes it unique, not by adding together an assemblage of remembered features. We can also recognize a likeness in profile though turning it from full face to side view causes every feature to change beyond recognition in terms of abstract form. Faces also display "expressive" properties which are also configurational but are not identical with the configurational characters by which we recognize them. We can recognize the face of a friend whether it is angry or sad, calm or convulsed. Contrariwise we can "read" the expression on a face whether it is the face of a friend or of an unknown person. These gestalt properties have nothing directly to do with esthetic enjoyment: we perceive them whether the face is beautiful or plain and our perception of them does not provide a basis for an esthetic judgment. These are practical everyday acts of perception, not perception in the esthetic mode. When on the contrary we contemplate a work of art (or for that matter a face for its beauty) we do not simply recognize it by some overall configuration or "read" its expressive features as a piece of information about it: we dwell upon it, hold attention deeply with it and concentrate our energies on actualizing it in perception. One can take up an esthetic attitude of "disinterested" attention to anything at all, fixing it in awareness not for the sake of recognition or any other practical purpose. But some objects—and these we call esthetic objects—favor disinterested contemplation, while others repel it and are too jejune to sustain it. Not all organic wholes in perception are meet for esthetic contemplation. Esthetic objects are organic wholes which in suitably conditioned persons are able to attract and sustain intense, prolonged or repeated, and fruitful perceptive attention in the nonpractical esthetic mode. It has not been easy to explain the qualities of "organic unity" which successful works of art and other things of beauty possess and which nonesthetic configurational wholes do not possess. Esthetic unity would have to be understood in such a way that it could serve as a criterion of excellence in judging artworks yet without favoring some art styles above others. It should not, for example, lead to the ascription of superior excellence to works manifesting formal classical proportion over those which have greater Romantic freedom and asymmetry or demand a preference for the Neoplasticism of Mondrian rather than the apparent randomness of Action Painting. For to do so would conflict with accepted critical verdicts. In practice it has proved so difficult to render the notion of esthetic unity concrete while keeping it free from stylistic bias that some philosophers have despaired of using it profitably. (The whole question is discussed in a symposium published in *The Journal of Aesthetics and Art Criticism*, vol. XX, No. 2, Winter 1961.) On the other hand, it has been suggested that works of art tend to differ from other perceptual configurations in that the qualities of artistic wholes are not only "emergent" from the parts in the way which has been described but are to some extent reflected back upon the parts so that the parts of an artistic whole themselves display something of the distinctive esthetic character of the whole. This is why, for example, a torso or even an isolated limb reflects something of the beauty of the whole statue from which it came. It is not certain, however, whether this feature applies generally to all art objects and much work remains still to be done on the elucidation of the concept of organic unity in relation to esthetic objects.

—*Aesthetics and Art Theory* (1968)

HORATIO GREENOUGH

Structure and Organization

The developments of structure in the animal kingdom are worthy of all our attention if we would arrive at sound principles in building. The most striking feature in the higher animal organizations is the adherence to one abstract type. The forms of the fish and the lizard, the shape of the horse, and the lion, and the camelopard, are so nearly framed after one type that the adherence thereto seems carried to the verge of risk. The next most striking feature is the modification of the parts, which, if contemplated independently of the exposure and functions whose demands are thus met, seems carried to the verge of caprice. I believe few persons not conversant with natural history ever looked through a collection of birds, or fish, or insects, without feeling that they were the result of Omnipotence at play for mere variety's sake.

If there be any principle of structure more plainly inculcated in the works of the Creator than all others, it is the principle of unflinching adaptation of forms to functions. I believe that colors also, so far as we have discovered their chemical causes and affinities, are not less organic in relation to the forms they invest than are those forms themselves.

If I find the length of the vertebrae of the neck in grazing quadrupeds increased, so as to bring the incisors to the grass; if I find the vertebrae shortened in beasts of prey, in order to enable the brute to bear away his victims; if I find the wading birds on stilts, the strictly aquatic birds with paddles; if, in pushing still further the investigation, I find color arrayed either for disguise or aggression, I feel justified in taking the ground that organization is the primal law of structure, and I suppose it, even where my imperfect light cannot trace it, unless embellishment can be demonstrated. Since the tints as well as the forms of plants and flowers are shown to have an organic significance and value, I take it for granted that tints have a like character in the mysteriously clouded and pearly shell, where they mock my ken. I cannot believe that the myriads are furnished, at the depths of the ocean, with the complicated glands and absorbents to nourish those dyes, in order that the hundreds may charm my idle eye as they are tossed in disorganized ruin upon the beach.

Let us dwell for a moment upon the forms of several of the higher types of animal structure. Behold the eagle as he sits on the lonely cliff, towering high in the air; carry in your mind the proportions and lines of the dove and mark how the finger of God has, by the mere variation of diameters, converted the type of meekness into the most expressive symbol of majesty. His eye, instead of rushing as it were out of his head, to see the danger behind him, looks steadfastly forward from its deep cavern, knowing no danger but that which it pilots. The structure of his brow allows him to fly upward with his eyes in shade. In his beak and his talons we see at once the belligerent, in the vast expanse of his sailing pinions the patent of his prerogative. *Dei Gratia Raptor!* Whence the beauty and majesty of the bird? It is the oneness of his function that gives him his grandeur, it is transcendental mechanism alone that begets his beauty. Observe the lion as he stands! Mark the ponderous predominance of his anterior extremities, his lithe loins, the lever of his hock, the awful breadth of his jaws, and the depth of his chest. His mane is a curiass, and when the thunder of his voice is added to the glitter of his snarling jaws, man alone with all his means of defense stands self-possessed before him. In his structure again are beheld, as in that of the eagle, the most terrible expression of power and dominion, and we find that it is here also the result of transcendental mechanism. The form of the hare might well be the type of swiftness for him who never saw the greyhound. The greyhound overtakes him, and it is not possible in organization that this result should obtain, without the promise and announcement of it, in the lengths and diameters of this breed of dogs.

Let us now turn to the human frame, the most beautiful organization of earth, the exponent and minister of the highest being we immediately know. This stupendous form, towering as a lighthouse, commanding by its posture a wide horizon, standing in relation to the brutes where the spire stands in relation to the lowly colonnades of Greece and Egypt, touching earth with only one-half the soles of its feet—it tells of majesty and dominion by that upreared spine, of duty by those unencumbered hands. Where is the ornament of this frame? It is all beauty, its motion is grace, no combination of harmony ever equaled, for expression and variety, its poised and stately gait; its voice is music, no cunning mixture of wood and metal ever did more than feebly imitate its tone of command or its warble of love. The savage who envies or admires the special attributes of beasts maims unconsciously his own perfection to assume their tints, their feathers, or their claws; we turn from him with horror, and gaze with joy on the naked Apollo.

I have dwelt a moment on these examples of expression and of beauty that I may draw from them a principle in art, a principle which, if it has been often illustrated by brilliant results, we constantly see neglected, overlooked, forgotten—a principle which I hope the examples I have given have prepared you to accept at once and unhesitatingly. It is this: in art, as in nature, the soul, the purpose of a work will never fail to be proclaimed in that work in proportion to the subordination of the parts to the whole, of the whole to the function. If you will trace the ship through its various stages of improvement, from the dugout canoe and the old galley to the latest type of the sloop-of-war, you will remark that every advance in performance has been an advance in expression, in grace, in beauty, or grandeur, according to the functions of the craft. This artistic gain, effected by pure science in some respects, in others by mere empirical watching of functions where the elements of the structure were put to severe tests, calls loudly upon the artist to keenly watch traditional dogmas and to see how far analogous rules may guide his own operations. You will remark, also, that after mechanical power had triumphed over the earlier obstacles, embellishment began to encumber and hamper ships, and that their actual approximation to beauty has been effected, first, by strict adaptation of forms to functions, second, by the gradual elimination of all that is irrelevant and impertinent. The old chairs were formidable by their weight, puzzled you by their carving, and often contained too much else to contain convenience and comfort. The most beautiful chairs invite you by a promise of ease, and they keep that promise; they bear neither flowers nor dragons, nor idle displays of the turner's caprice. By keeping within their province they are able to fill it well. Organization has a language of its own, and so expressive is that language that a makeshift or make-believe can scarce fail of detection. The swan, the goose, the duck, when they walk toward the water are awkward, when they hasten toward it are ludicrous. Their feet are paddles, and their legs are organized mainly to move those paddles in the water; they, therefore, paddle on land, or as we say, waddle. It is only when their breasts are launched into the pond that their necks assume the expression of ease and grace. A serpent upon a smooth hard road has a similar awkward expression of impotence; the grass, or pebbles, or water, as he meets either, afford him his *sine quâ non,* and he is instantly confident, alert, effective.

If I err not, we should learn from these and the like examples, which will meet us wherever we look for them, that God's world has a distinct formula for every function, and that we shall seek in vain to borrow shapes; we must make the shapes, and can only effect this by mastering the principles.

It is a confirmation of the doctrine of strict adaptation that I find in the purer Doric temple. The sculptures which adorned certain spaces in those temples had an organic relation to the functions of the edifice; they took possession of the worshiper as he approached, lifted him out of everyday life, and prepared him for the presence of the divinity within. The world has never seen plastic art developed so highly as by the men who translated into marble, in the tympanum and the metope, the theogony and the exploits of the heroes. Why, then, those columns uncarved? Why, then, those lines of cornice unbroken by foliages, unadorned by flowers? Why that matchless symmetry of every member, that music of gradation, without the tracery of the Gothic detail, without the endless caprices of arabesque? Because those sculptures *spake,* and speech asks a groundwork of silence and not of babble, though it were of green fields.

I am not about to deny the special beauties and value of any of the great types of building. Each has its meaning and expression. I am desirous now of analyzing that majestic and eloquent simplicity of the Greek temple, because, though I truly believe that it is hopeless to transplant its forms with any other result than an expression of impotent dilettantism, still I believe that its principles will be found to be those of all structures of the highest order.

When I gaze upon the stately and beautiful Parthenon, I do not wonder at the greediness of the moderns to appropriate it. I do wonder at the obtuseness which allowed them to persevere in trying to make it work in the towns. It seems like the enthusiasm of him who should squander much money to transfer an Arabian stallion from his desert home, that, as a blindfolded gelding, he might turn his mill. The lines in which Byron paints the fate of the butterfly that has fallen into the clutches of its childish admirer[1] would apply not inaptly to the Greek temple at the mercy of a sensible building committee, wisely determined to have their money's worth.

When high art declined, carving and embellishment invaded the simple organization. As the South Sea Islanders have added a variety to the human form by tattooing, so the cunning artisans of Greece undertook to go beyond perfection. Many rhetoricians and skilled grammarians refined upon the elements of the language of structure. They all spake: and demigods, and heroes, and the gods themselves, went away and were silent.

If we compare the simpler form of the Greek temple with the ornate and carved specimens which followed it, we shall be convinced, whatever the subtlety, however exquisite the taste that long presided over those refinements, that they were the beginning of the end, and that the turning-point was the first introduction of a fanciful, not demonstrable, embellishment, and for this simple reason, that, embellishment being arbitrary, there is no check upon it; you begin with acanthus leaves, but the appetite for sauces, or rather the need of them, increases as the palate gets jaded. You want jasper, and porphyry, and serpentine, and giallo antico, at last. Nay, you are tired of Aristides the Just, and of straight columns; they must be spiral, and by degrees you find yourself in the midst of a barbaric pomp whose means must be slavery—nothing less will supply its waste,—whose enjoyment is satiety, whose result is corruption.

It was a day of danger for the development of taste in this land, the day when Englishmen perceived that France was laying them under contribution by her artistic skill in manufacture. They organized reprisals upon ourselves, and, in lieu of truly artistic combinations, they have overwhelmed us with embellishment, arbitrary, capricious, setting at defiance all principle, meretricious dyes and tints, catchpenny novelties of form, steam-woven fineries and plastic ornaments, struck with the die or pressed into molds. In even an ordinary house we look around in vain for a quiet and sober resting-place for the eye; we see naught but flowers, flourishes—the renaissance of Louis Quatorze gingerbread embellishment. We seek in vain for aught else. Our own manufacturers have caught the furor, and our foundries pour forth a mass of ill-digested and crowded embellishment which one would suppose addressed to the sympathies of savages or of the colored population, if the utter absence of all else in the market were not too striking to allow such a conclusion.

I do not suppose it is possible to check such a tide as that which sets all this corruption toward our shores. I am aware of the economical sagacity of the English, and how fully they understand the market; but I hope that we are not so thoroughly asphyxiated by the atmosphere they have created as to follow their lead in our own creation of a higher order. I remark with joy that almost all the more important efforts of this land tend, with an instinct and a vigor born of the institutions, toward simple and effective organization; and they never fail whenever they toss overboard the English dictum and work from their own inspirations to surpass the British, and there, too, where the world thought them safe from competition.

I would fain beg any architect who allows fashions to invade the domain of principles to compare the American vehicles and ships with those of England, and he will see that the mechanics of the United States have already outstripped the artists, and have, by the results of their bold and unflinching adaptation, entered the true track, and hold up the light for all who operate for American wants, be they what they will.

In the American trotting wagon I see the old-fashioned and pompous coach dealt with as the old-fashioned palatial display must yet be dealt with in this land. In vain shall we endeavor to hug the associations connected with the old form. The redundant must be pared down, the superfluous dropped, the necessary itself reduced to its simplest expression, and then we shall find, whatever the organization may be, that beauty was waiting for us, though perhaps veiled, until our task was fully accomplished.

—*Memorial of Horatio Greenough* (1853)

Note

1. In *The Giaour*, the passage (lines 388–421) including:
"For every touch that wooed its stay
Hath brushed its brightest hues away."

MEYER SCHAPIRO

Style

I

By style is meant the constant form—and sometimes the constant elements, qualities, and expression—in the art of an individual or a group. The term is also applied to the whole activity of an individual or society, as in speaking of a "life-style" or the "style of civilization."

For the archeologist, style is exemplified in a motive or pattern, or in some directly grasped quality of the work of art, which helps him to localize and date the work and to establish connections between groups of works or between cultures. Style here is a symptomatic trait, like the nonesthetic features of an artifact. It is studied more often as a diagnostic means than for its own sake as an important constituent of culture. For dealing with style, the archeologist has relatively few esthetic and physiognomic terms.

To the historian of art, style is an essential object of investigation. He studies its inner correspondences, its life-history, and the problems of its formation and change. He, too, uses style as a criterion of the date and place of origin of works, and as a means of tracing relationships between schools of art. But the style is, above all, a system of forms with a quality and a meaningful expression through which the personality of the artist and the broad outlook of a group are visible. It is also a vehicle of expression within the group, communicating and fixing certain values of religious, social, and moral life through the emotional suggestiveness of forms. It is, besides, a common ground against which innovations and the individuality of particular works may be measured. By considering the succession of works in time and space and by matching the variations of style with historical events and with the varying features of other fields of culture, the historian of art attempts, with the help of common-sense psychology and social theory, to account for the changes of style or specific traits. The historical study of individual and group styles also discloses typical stages and processes in the development of forms.

For the synthesizing historian of culture or the philosopher of history, the style is a manifestation of the culture as a whole, the visible sign of its unity. The style reflects or projects the "inner form" of collective thinking and feeling. What is important here is not the style of an individual or of a single art, but forms and qualities shared by all the arts of a culture during a significant span of time. In this sense one speaks of Classical or Medieval or Renaissance Man with respect to common traits discovered in the art styles of these epochs and documented also in religious and philosophical writings.

The critic, like the artist, tends to conceive of style as a value term; style as such is a quality and the critic can say of a painter that he has "style" or of a writer that he is a "stylist." Although "style" in this normative sense, which is applied mainly to individual artists, seems to be outside the scope of historical and ethnological studies of art, it often occurs here, too, and should be considered seriously. It is a measure of accomplishment and therefore is relevant to understanding of both art and culture as a whole. Even a period style, which for most historians is a collective taste evident in both good and poor works, may be regarded by critics as a great positive achievement. So the Greek classic style was, for Winckelmann and Goethe, not simply a convention of form but a culminating conception with valued qualities not possible in other styles and apparent even in Roman copies of lost Greek originals. Some period styles impress us by their deeply pervasive, complete character, their special adequacy to their content; the collective creation of such a style, like the conscious shaping of a norm of language, is a true achievement. Correspondingly, the presence of the same style in a wide range of arts is often considered a sign of the integration of a culture and the intensity of a high creative moment. Arts that lack a particular distinction or nobility of style are often said to be styleless, and the culture is judged to be weak or decadent. A similar view is held by philosophers of culture and history and by some historians of art.

Common to all these approaches are the assumptions that every style is peculiar to a period of a culture and that, in a given culture or epoch of culture, there is only one style or a limited range of styles. Works in the style of one time could not have been produced in another. These postulates are supported by the fact that the connection between a style and a period, inferred from a few examples, is confirmed by objects discovered later. Whenever it is possible to locate a work through nonstylistic evidence, this evidence points to the same time and place as do the formal traits, or to a culturally associated region. The unexpected appearance of the style in another region is explained by migration or trade. The style is therefore used with confidence as an independent clue to the time and place of origin of a work of art. Building upon these assumptions, scholars have constructed a systematic, although not complete, picture of the temporal and spatial distribution of styles throughout large regions of the globe. If works of art are grouped in an order corresponding to their original positions in time and space, their styles will show significant relationships which can be coordinated with the relationships of the works of art to still other features of the cultural points in time and space.

II

Styles are not usually defined in a strictly logical way. As with languages, the definition indicates the time and place of a style or its author, or the historical relation to other styles, rather than its peculiar features. The characteristics of styles vary continuously and resist a systematic classification into perfectly distinct groups. It is meaningless to ask exactly when ancient art ends and medieval begins. There are, of course, abrupt breaks and reactions in art, but study shows that here, too, there is often anticipation, blending, and continuity. Precise limits are sometimes fixed by convention for simplicity in dealing with historical problems or in isolating a type. In a stream of development the artificial divisions may even be designated by numbers—Styles I, II, III. But the single name given to the style of a period rarely corresponds to a clear and universally accepted characterization of a type. Yet direct acquaintance with an unanalyzed work of art will often permit us to recognize another object of the same origin, just as we recognize a face to be native or foreign. This fact points to a degree of constancy in art that is the basis of all investigation of style. Through careful description and comparison and through formation of a richer, more refined typology adapted to the continuities in development, it has been possible to reduce the areas of vagueness and to advance our knowledge of styles.

Although there is no established system of analysis and writers will stress one or another aspect according to their viewpoint or problem, in general the description of a style refers to three aspects of art: form elements or motives, form relationships, and qualities (including an all-over quality which we may call the "expression").

This conception of style is not arbitrary but has arisen from the experience of investigation. In correlating works of art with an individual or culture, these three aspects provide the broadest, most stable, and therefore most reliable criteria. They are also the most pertinent to modern theory of art, although not in the same degree for all viewpoints. Technique, subject matter, and material may be characteristic of certain groups of works and will sometimes be included in definitions; but more often these features are not so peculiar to the art of a period as the formal and qualitative ones. It is easy to imagine a decided change in material, technique, or subject matter accompanied by little change in the basic form. Or, where these are constant, we often observe that they are less responsive to new artistic aims. A method of stone-cutting will change less rapidly than the sculptor's or architect's forms. Where a technique does coincide with the extension of a style, it is the formal traces of the technique rather than the operations as such that are important for description of the style. The materials are significant mainly for the textural quality and color, although they may affect the conception of the forms. For the subject matter, we observe that quite different themes—portraits, still lifes, and landscapes—will appear in the same style.

It must be said, too, that form elements or motives, although very striking and essential for the expression, are not sufficient for characterizing a style. The pointed arch is common to Gothic and Islamic architecture, and the round arch to Roman, Byzantine, Romanesque, and Renaissance buildings. In order to distinguish these styles, one must also look for features of another order and, above all, for different ways of combining the elements.

Although some writers conceive of style as a kind of syntax or compositional pattern, which can be analyzed mathematically, in practice one has been unable to do without the vague language of qualities in describing styles. Certain features of light and color in painting are most conveniently specified in qualitative terms and even as tertiary (intersensory) or physiognomic qualities, like cool and warm, gay and sad. The habitual span of light and dark, the intervals between colors in a particular palette—very important for the structure of a work—are distinct relationships between elements, yet are not comprised in a compositional schema of the whole. The complexity of a work of art is such that the description of forms is often incomplete on essential points, limiting itself to a rough account of a few relationships. It is still simpler, as well as more relevant to esthetic experience, to distinguish lines as hard and soft than to give measurements of their substance. For precision in characterizing a style, these qualities are graded with respect to intensity by comparing different examples directly or by reference to a standard work. Where quantitative measurements have been made, they tend to confirm the conclusions reached through direct qualitative description. Nevertheless, we have no doubt that, in dealing with qualities, much greater precision can be reached.

Analysis applies esthetic concepts current in the teaching, practice, and criticism of contemporary art; the development of new viewpoints and problems in the latter directs the attention of students to unnoticed features of older styles. But the study of works of other times also influences modern concepts through discovery of esthetic variants unknown in our own art. As in criticism, so in historical research, the problem of distinguishing or relating two styles discloses unsuspected, subtle characteristics and suggests new concepts of form. The postulate of continuity in culture—a kind of inertia in the physical sense—leads to a search for common features in successive styles that are ordinarily contrasted as opposite poles of form; the resemblances will sometimes be found not so much in obvious aspects as in fairly hidden ones—the line patterns of Renaissance compositions recall features of the older Gothic style, and in contemporary abstract art one observes form relationships like those of Impressionist painting.

The refinement of style analysis has come about in part through problems in which small differences had to be disengaged and described precisely. Examples are the regional variations within the same culture; the process of historical development from year to year; the growth of individual artists and the discrimination of the works of master and pupil, originals and copies. In these studies the criteria for dating and attribution are often physical or external—matters of small symptomatic detail—but here, too, the general trend of research has been to look for features that can be formulated in both structural and expressive-physiognomic terms. It is assumed by many students that the expression terms are all translatable into form and quality terms, since the expression depends on particular shapes and colors and will be modified by a small change in the latter. The forms are correspondingly regarded as vehicles of a particular effect (apart from the subject matter). But the relationship here is not altogether clear. In general, the study of style tends toward an ever stronger correlation of form and expression. Some descriptions are purely morphological, as of natural objects—indeed, ornament has been characterized, like crystals, in the mathematical language of group theory. But terms like "stylized," "archaistic," "naturalistic," "mannerist," "baroque," are specifically human, referring to artistic processes, and imply some expressive effect. It is only by analogy that mathematical figures have been characterized as "classic" and "romantic."

III

The analysis and characterization of the styles of primitive and early historical cultures have been strongly influenced by the standard of recent Western art. Nevertheless, it may be said that the values of modern art have led to a more sympathetic and objective approach to exotic arts than was possible fifty or a hundred years ago.

In the past, a great deal of primitive work, especially representation, was regarded as artless even by sensitive people; what was valued were mainly the ornamentation and the skills of primitive industry. It was believed that primitive arts were childlike attempts to represent nature—attempts distorted by ignorance and by an irrational content of the monstrous and grotesque. True art was admitted only in the high cultures, where knowledge of natural forms was combined with a rational ideal which brought beauty and decorum to the image of man. Greek art and the art of the Italian High Renaissance were the norms for judging all art, although in time the classic phase of Gothic art was accepted. Ruskin, who admired Byzantine works, could write that in Christian Europe alone "pure and precious ancient art exists, for there is none in America, none in Asia, none in Africa." From such a viewpoint careful discrimination of primitive styles or a penetrating study of their structure and expression was hardly possible.

With the change in Western art during the last seventy years, naturalistic representation has lost its superior status. Basic for contemporary practice and for knowledge of past art is the theoretical view that what counts in all art are the elementary esthetic components, the qualities and relationships of the fabricated lines, spots, colors, and surfaces. These have two characteristics: they are intrinsically expressive, and they tend to constitute a coherent whole. The same tendencies to coherent and expressive structure are found in the arts of all cultures. There is no privileged content or mode of representation (although the greatest works may, for reasons obscure to us, occur only in certain styles). Perfect art is possible in any subject matter or style. A style is like a language, with an internal order and expressiveness, admitting a varied intensity or delicacy of statement. This approach is a relativism that does not exclude absolute judgments of value; it makes these judgments possible within every framework by abandoning a fixed norm of style. Such ideas are accepted by most students of art today, although not applied with uniform conviction.

As a result of this new approach, all the arts of the world, even the drawings of children and psychotics, have become accessible on a common plane of expressive and form-creating activity. Art is now one of the strongest evidences of the basic unity of mankind.

This radical change in attitude depends partly on the development of modern styles, in which the raw material and distinctive units of operation —the plane of the canvas, the trunk of wood, tool marks, brush strokes, connecting forms, schemas, particles and areas of pure color—are as pronounced as the elements of representation. Even before nonrepresentative styles were created, artists had become more deeply conscious of the esthetic-constructive components of the work apart from denoted meanings.

Much in the new styles recalls primitive art. Modern artists were, in fact, among the first to appreciate the works of natives as true art. The development of Cubism and Abstraction made the form problem exciting and helped to refine the perception of the creative in primitive work. Expressionism, with its high pathos, disposed our eyes to the simpler, more intense modes of expression, and together with Surrealism, which valued, above all, the irrational and instinctive in the imagination, gave a fresh interest to the products of primitive fantasy. But, with all the obvious resemblances, modern paintings and sculptures differ from the primitive in structure and content. What in primitive art belongs to an established world of collective beliefs and symbols arises in modern art as an individual expression, bearing the marks of a free, experimental attitude to forms. Modern artists feel, nevertheless, a spiritual kinship with the primitive, who is now closer to them than in the past because of their ideal of frankness and intensity of expression and their desire for a simpler life, with more effective participation of the artist in collective occasions than modern society allows.

One result of the modern development has been a tendency to slight the content of past art; the most realistic representations are contemplated as pure constructions of lines and colors. The observer is often indifferent to the original meanings of works, although he may enjoy through them a vague sentiment of the poetic and religious. The form and expressiveness of older works are regarded, then, in isolation, and the history of an art is written as an immanent development of forms. Parallel to this trend, other scholars have carried on fruitful research into the meanings, symbols, and iconographic types of Western art, relying on the literature of mythology and religion; through these studies the knowledge of the content of art has been considerably deepened, and analogies to the character of the styles have been discovered in the content. This has strengthened the view that the development of forms is not autonomous but is connected with changing attitudes and interests that appear more or less clearly in the subject matter of the art.

IV

Students observed early that the traits which make up a style have a quality in common. They all seem to be marked by the expression of the whole, or there is a dominant feature to which the elements have been adapted. The parts of a Greek temple have the air of a family of forms. In Baroque art, a taste for movement determines the loosening of boundaries, the instability of masses, and the multiplication of large contrasts. For many writers a style, whether of an individual or a group, is a pervasive, rigorous unity. Investigation of style is often a search for hidden correspondences explained by an organizing principle which determines both the character of the parts and the patterning of the whole.

This approach is supported by the experience of the student in identifying a style from a small random fragment. A bit of carved stone, the profile of a molding, a few drawn lines, or a single letter from a piece of writing often possesses for the observer the quality of the complete work and can be dated precisely; before these fragments, we have the conviction of insight into the original whole. In a similar way, we recognize by its intrusiveness an added or repaired detail in an old work. The feel of the whole is found in the small parts.

I do not know how far experiments in matching parts from works in different styles would confirm this view. We may be dealing, in some of these observations, with a microstructural level in which similarity of parts only points to the homogeneity of a style or a technique, rather than to a complex unity in the esthetic sense. Although personal, the painter's touch, described by constants of pressure, rhythm, and size of strokes, may have no obvious relation to other unique characteristics of the larger forms. There are styles in which large parts of a work are conceived and executed differently, without destroying the harmony of the whole. In African sculpture an exceedingly naturalistic, smoothly carved head rises from a rough, almost shapeless body. A normative esthetic might regard this as imperfect work, but it would be hard to justify this view. In Western paintings of the fifteenth century, realistic figures and landscapes are set against a gold background, which in the Middle Ages had a spiritualistic sense. In Islamic art, as in certain African and Oceanic styles, forms of great clarity and simplicity in three dimensions—metal vessels and animals or the domes of buildings—have surfaces spun with rich mazy patterns; in Gothic and Baroque art, on the contrary, a complex surface treatment is associated with a correspondingly complicated silhouette of the whole. In Romanesque art the proportions of figures are not submitted to a single canon, as in Greek art, but two or three distinct systems of proportioning exist even within the same sculpture, varying with the size of the figure.

Such variation within a style is also known in literature, sometimes in great works, like Shakespeare's plays, where verse and prose of different texture occur together. French readers of Shakespeare, with the model of their own classical drama before them, were disturbed by the elements of comedy in Shakespeare's tragedies. We understand this contrast as a necessity of the content and the poet's conception of man—the different modes of expression pertain to contrasted types of humanity—but a purist classical taste condemned this as inartistic. In modern literature both kinds of style, the rigorous and the free, coexist and express different viewpoints. It is possible to see the opposed parts as contributing elements in a whole that owes its character to the interplay and balance of contrasted qualities. But the notion of style has lost in that case the crystalline uniformity and simple correspondence of part to whole with which we began. The integration may be of a looser, more complex kind, operating with unlike parts.

Another interesting exception to the homogeneous in style is the difference between the marginal and the dominant fields in certain arts. In early Byzantine works, rulers are represented in statuesque, rigid forms, while the smaller accompanying figures, by the same artist, retain the liveliness of an older episodic, naturalistic style. In Romanesque art this difference can be so marked that scholars have mistakenly supposed that certain Spanish works were done partly by a Christian and partly by a Moslem artist. In some instances the forms in the margin or in the background are more advanced in style than the central parts, anticipating a later stage of the art. In medieval work the unframed figures on the borders of illuminated manuscripts or on cornices, capitals, and pedestals are often freer and more naturalistic than the main figures. This is surprising, since we would expect to find the most advanced forms in the dominant content. But in medieval art the sculptor or painter is often bolder where he is less bound to an external requirement; he even seeks out and appropriates the regions of freedom. In a similar way an artist's drawings or sketches are more advanced than the finished paintings and suggest another side of his personality. The execution of the landscape backgrounds behind the religious figures in paintings of the fifteenth century is sometimes amazingly modern and in great contrast to the precise forms of the large figures. Such observations teach us the importance of considering in the description and explanation of a style the unhomogeneous, unstable aspect, the obscure tendencies toward new forms.

If in all periods artists strive to create unified works, the strict ideal of consistency is essentially modern. We often observe in civilized as well as primitive art the combination of works of different style into a single whole. Classical gems were frequently incorporated into medieval reliquaries. Few great medieval buildings are homogeneous, since they are the work of many generations of artists. This is widely recognized by historians, although theoreticians of culture have innocently pointed to the conglomerate cathedral of Chartres as a model of stylistic unity, in contrast to the heterogeneous character of stylelessness of the arts of modern society. In the past it was not felt necessary to restore a damaged work or to complete an unfinished one in the style of the original. Hence the strange juxtapositions of styles within some medieval objects. It should be said, however, that some styles, by virtue of their open, irregular forms, can tolerate the unfinished and heterogeneous better than others.

Just as the single work may possess parts that we would judge to belong to different styles, if we found them in separate contexts, so an individual may produce during the same short period works in what are regarded as two styles. An obvious example is the writing of bilingual authors or the work of the same man in different arts or even in different genres of the same art—monumental and easel painting, dramatic and lyric poetry. A large work by an artist who works mainly in the small, or a small work by a master of large forms, can deceive an expert in styles. Not only will the touch change, but also the expression and method of grouping. An artist is not present in the same degree in everything he does, although some traits may be constant. In the twentieth century, some artists have changed their styles so radically during a few years that it would be difficult, if not impossible, to identify these as works of the same hand, should their authorship be forgotten. In the case of Picasso, two styles—Cubism and a kind of classicizing naturalism—were practiced at the same time. One might discover common characters in small features of the two styles—in qualities of the brushstroke, the span of intensity, or in subtle constancies of the spacing and tones—but these are not the elements through which either style would ordinarily be characterized. Even then, as in a statistical account small and large samples of a population give different results, so in works of different scale of parts by one artist the scale may influence the frequency of the tiniest elements or the form of the small units. The modern experience of stylistic variability and of the unhomogeneous within an art style will perhaps lead to a more refined conception of style. It is evident, at any rate, that the conception of style as a visibly unified constant rests upon a particular norm of stability of style and shifts from the large to the small forms, as the whole becomes more complex.

What has been said here of the limits of uniformity of structure in the single work and in the works of an individual also applies to the style of a group. The group style, like a language, often contains elements that belong to different historical strata. While research looks for criteria permitting one to distinguish accurately the works of different groups and to correlate a style with other characteristics of a group, there are cultures with two or more collective styles of art at the same moment. This phenomenon is often associated with arts of different function or with different classes of artists. The arts practiced by women are of another style than those of the men; religious art differs from profane, and civic from domestic; and in higher cultures the stratification of social classes often entails a variety of styles, not only with respect to the rural and urban, but within the same urban community. This diversity is clear enough today in the coexistence of an official-academic, a mass-commercial, and a free avant-garde art. But more striking still is the enormous range of styles within the latter—although a common denominator will undoubtedly be found by future historians.

While some critics judge this heterogeneity to be a sign of an unstable, unintegrated culture, it may be regarded as a necessary and valuable consequence of the individual's freedom of choice and of the world scope of modern culture, which permits a greater interaction of styles than was ever possible before. The present diversity continues and intensifies a diversity already noticed in the preceding stages of our culture, including the Middle Ages and the Renaissance, which are held up as models of close integration. The unity of style that is contrasted with the present diversity is one type of style formation, appropriate to particular aims and conditions; to achieve it today would be impossible without destroying the most cherished values of our culture.

If we pass to the relation of group styles of different visual arts in the same period, we observe that, while the Baroque is remarkably similar in architecture, sculpture, and painting, in other periods, for example, the Carolingian, the early Romanesque, and the modern, these arts differ in essential respects. In England, the drawing and painting of the tenth and eleventh centuries—a time of great accomplishment, when England was a leader in European art—are characterized by an enthusiastic linear style of energetic, ecstatic movement, while the architecture of the same period is inert, massive, and closed and is organized on other principles. Such variety has been explained as a sign of immaturity; but one can point to similar contrasts between two arts in later times, for example, in Holland in the seventeenth century where Rembrandt and his school were contemporary with classicistic Renaissance buildings.

When we compare the styles of arts of the same period in different media—literature, music, painting—the differences are no less striking. But there are epochs with a far-reaching unity, and these have engaged the attention of students more than the examples of diversity. The concept of the Baroque has been applied to architecture, sculpture, painting, music, poetry, drama, gardening, script, and even philosophy and science. The Baroque style has given its name to the entire culture of the seventeenth century, although it does not exclude contrary tendencies within the same country, as well as a great individuality of national arts. Such styles are the most fascinating to historians and philosophers, who admire in this great spectacle of unity the power of a guiding idea or attitude to impose a common form upon the most varied contexts. The dominant style-giving force is identified by some historians with a world outlook common to the whole society; by others with a particular institution, like the church or the absolute monarchy, which under certain conditions becomes the source of a universal viewpoint and the organizer of all cultural life. This unity is not necessarily organic; it may be likened also, perhaps, to that of a machine with limited freedom of motion; in a complex organism the parts are unlike and the integration is more a matter of functional interdependence than of the repetition of the same pattern in all the organs.

Although so vast a unity of style is an impressive accomplishment and seems to point to a special consciousness of style—the forms of art being felt as a necessary universal language—there are moments of great achievement in a single art with characteristics more or less isolated from those of the other arts. We look in vain in England for a style of painting that corresponds to Elizabethan poetry and drama; just as in Russia in the nineteenth century there was no true parallel in painting to the great movement of literature. In these instances we recognize that the various arts have different roles in the culture and social life of a time and express in their content as well as style different interests and values. The dominant outlook of a time—if it can be isolated—does not affect all the arts in the same degree, nor are all the arts equally capable of expressing the same outlook. Special conditions within an art are often strong enough to determine a deviant expression.

—*Anthropology Today,* edited by A. L. Kroeber (1953)

PART III

The Response to the Esthetic Object

CHAPTER 10

The Experiences of the Beholder

IMMANUEL KANT: A Theory of Esthetic Experience
EDWARD BULLOUGH: Psychical Distance
JOSÉ ORTEGA Y GASSET: The Dehumanization of Art
THEODOR LIPPS: Empathy, Inner Imitation, and Sense-Feelings
VIRGIL C. ALDRICH: Education for Aesthetic Vision

In Part III we shall consider the response of the beholder, the critic, the philosopher, and the community to the work of art. Most of the theories presented in earlier chapters have thrown light on the beholder's response. The characterization of esthetic experience by Croce, Dewey, Santayana, Bosanquet, and Arnheim—to mention only a few names—illuminates not only the creative activity of the artist but also the contemplative activity of the spectator. Although no sharp line can be drawn between the contemplative and the creative phases of art, we turn now to selections that focus on the experience of the beholder and which also shed further light on the nature of the work of art. As I remarked in the preface, the divisions are not sharp and the readings in this book overlap and interlock in a great variety of ways.

The greatest figure in the interpretation of the beholder's response is Immanuel Kant (1724–1804). Although he never traveled far from the university town of Königsberg in East Prussia, he was fond of travel books and participated avidly in the culture of the Enlightenment. Largely because of his influence, disinterestedness (which, of course, is not *un*interestedness) has been commonly recognized as characteristic of the "esthetic attitude."

Conceiving fine art as the free creation of beauty for beauty's sake, Kant discovered the essence of beauty in design enjoyed simply for itself. There is a harmonious play of our faculties—a dynamic equilibrium of sense, feeling, imagination, and understanding—which corresponds to, and is stimulated by, the work of art. This harmonious state must be communicable, for one mark of art is its sharability. Thus, form is both outward and inward—the design of the work and the harmony of the mind—and the sensuous medium is the vehicle for the communication of form, in this twofold sense. Genius, the talent that creates beautiful works of art, is characterized in addition by *Geist*—"soul" or "spirit"—which is the faculty of conceiving and expressing "esthetical ideas." Such ideas, unlike the concepts of science, have a profundity and connotativeness that cannot be put into definite meanings. They provide the elusive and inexhaustible significance that characterizes every great work of art and that gives such mysterious depth to form.

No one before or since Kant has more clearly distinguished esthetic contemplation from practical, moral, cognitive, and appetitive interest. All of these interests, in one way or another, are concerned for the real existence of their objects. Kant defined "disinterestedness" as fascinated attention in the absence of such concern. The esthetic object may be imaginary or real, but what is esthetically relevant is its manifest form and qualities as disinterestedly felt and envisaged. Exception must be made, Kant says, for "sublimity" and "dependent beauty," in which moral or cognitive interest taints the pure esthetic attitude. (To aid the reader in grasping the theory, I have prefaced each section with a brief summary enclosed in brackets.)

There is a striking resemblance between Kant and Santayana in certain respects. The latter's "Epicurean sublime" is akin to Kant's "mathematical sublimity" and his "Stoic sublime" is akin to Kant's "dynamic sublimity." The two philosophers are also alike in connecting beauty with "objectified pleasure." The reader may recall that Santayana defines beauty as "pleasure regarded as the quality of a thing." Similarly, Kant argues that the subjective basis of beauty is pleasure aroused by the contemplation of the objective design, and that the beholder nevertheless speaks "as if beauty were a quality of the object."[1]

The relevance of Kant's theory to the continuing discussion of "the esthetic attitude" in this century is beyond question. One evidence of this influence is the theory of "psychical distance," akin to Kant's "disinterestedness," as expounded by the distinguished British psychologist Edward Bullough (1880–1934). He uses the term "psychical distance" to denote, not spatial or temporal remoteness, but the spectator's awareness that the characteristics of the esthetic object are not those calling for a practical response. It is the opposite of the sense that the thing beheld is a "real-life object" of practical or personal import. Distance, Bullough explains, has two aspects. First, there is a negative or inhibitory aspect, which means "cutting out of the practical sides of things and of our practical attitude toward them." Second, there is a positive or elaborative aspect, which is the enrichment of the experience on the new basis created by the inhibitory action of distance—in other words, the attainment of a more forceful objectivity and greater esthetic awareness when the mind is undistracted by practical or personal concerns and is able to concentrate its perceptive and imaginative powers. Bullough has more to say about the negative than the positive aspect.

Distance, being a matter of degree, varies according to two different sets of conditions: the characteristics of the object, and the attitudes of the subject. As the object becomes more stylized, unrealistic, and isolated, the distance correspondingly increases. As the contemplator independently adopts a more impersonal attitude, the distance again increases proportionately. The right mean consists of "the utmost decrease of distance without its disappearance," that is, the maximum personal appeal compatible with distance—a rule that Bullough calls the "antinomy of distance."

Bullough's rule, with its avoidance of high distance, was challenged by the famous Spanish philosopher José Ortega y Gasset, who defended the extreme increase of detachment in recent art. The tendency of modern artists, he declares in *The Dehumanization of Art* (1925), is to return to the "royal road of art," which is "the Will to Style"; and stylistic art is highly distanced art. The result of high distancing is a rejection of the "human, all too human" in art.

My omission of the Ortega y Gasset selection in the fourth edition of *A Modern Book of Esthetics* has been protested by David Mandel, a friendly reviewer:

> I regret the omission of Ortega y Gasset's "The Dehumanization of Art," because it is, if anything, even more pertinent today than it was in 1960, when it appeared in a third edition. It carries a warning that is implicit in the title as well as in the article itself, for art can be considered as an early warning system to society. The prevalence of nonfigurative art and its implications are important to our understanding of both the art scene and the social scene of our day. Though the essay was written in 1925, I believe that its virtue has not been exhausted but rather enhanced by what appears to me to be a growth of dehumanization of the arts in the West and by the historical events of the past 50 years, as well as by the breakup of the elements forming an art work, which seems to parallel the instability of the social scene.[2]

Whether "dehumanization" in art is good or bad and whether it parallels regrettable tendencies in society I leave to the judgment of my readers.

At the same time that dehumanization has continued, there has been a strong counter-movement. The intent has been to break down the distance between artist and public, actor and audience, the work of art and the beholder. In performances called "happenings" or constructions called "environments," the stress has been upon participation and engagement—the very opposite of dehumanization. Both in theory and practice contemporary art is too varied to sum up in any formula.

An interesting interpretation of the positive side of esthetic experience has been advanced by the proponents of "empathy." (The term "empathy" was coined by the psychologist Edward Titchener, in his *Experimental Psychology of the Thought Processes*, as an English rendering of "*einfühlung*," which means literally "feeling into.") The most original proponent of empathy writing in English is Violet Paget, whose pen-name is Vernon Lee (1856–1953). But unknown to her, the doctrine of empathy had previously been elaborated in detail by a famous German psychologist Theodor Lipps (1851–1941). Because his account is more original and less accessible to English-speaking readers, I quote him rather than Lee.

Since Lipps' exposition is not easy to follow, I shall summarize it in some detail. He begins the present article by defining the nature of the "esthetic object." It consists of the "sensuous appearance," not the bare physical object, but the image as remodeled by imagination and charged with vital meaning. It is the beautiful thing contemplated, and is therefore to be distinguished from the act of contemplation. Attention is not aware of itself; it is directed outward to the object and absorbed therein. Nevertheless, what gives esthetic import to the object, and what constitutes the *ground* of its enjoyment, is this very act of contemplation. The mind unconsciously enlivens the outward form by fusing into it the modes of its own activity—its striving and willing, its sense of freedom and power, and so on. The moods thus transported into the object do not spring from the real or practical ego, but only from the ego so far as contemplative.

We are now prepared to define more precisely the nature of the esthetic object. It may be analyzed into two factors: first, there is the inner activity, the emotion of pride, the feeling of vigor or freedom, and so forth; second, there is the external sensuous content as bare physical stimulus. The *esthetic* object springs into existence as a result of the fusion of these two factors. The ego unconsciously supposes itself at one with the object, and there is no longer any duality. Empathy simply means the disappearance of the twofold consciousness of self and object, and the enrichment of experience that results from this interpenetration. So completely is the self transported into the object that the contemplator of a statue, for example, may unconsciously imitate its posture and implied movement by definite muscular adjustments.

Although Lipps recognizes the existence of such spontaneous mimicry, he insists that empathy does not consist in the bodily feelings thus aroused. In fact, we forget all about our bodies and attend simply to the object. Our bodily behavior is a symptom of what we are feeling rather than the object of our awareness. We do not, in fact, attribute kinesthetic feelings even to the object, but attribute to it only the total emotional state that is appropriate to the representation at hand.

Note that Rudolf Arnheim in Chapter 8 regards the theory of empathy as too subjective. He thinks that expressiveness results not from empathic projection but from the phenomenal forms and qualities of the object. Things as apprehended in immediate experience have expressive qualities, and they are not just projections of our subjective states of mind into objects otherwise neutral. This attack on the empathy theory is characteristic of the Gestalt movement in psychology.

The interpretation of esthetic perception has been influenced by Ludwig Wittgenstein (see Chapter 12). According to his account of "seeing as," our *way* of looking at things affects the appearances of what we see. He calls these appearances "aspects," noting that different aspects appear in different perspectives. "One kind of aspect," he remarks, "might be called 'aspect of organization.' When the aspect changes, parts of the picture go together which before did not."[3] From one perspective, for example, an ambiguous figure may look like a rabbit's head, from another perspective like a duck's.

In the following article on esthetic vision, the distinguished esthetician Virgil Aldrich (1903–) illustrates "seeing as" by a drawing. Seen as a physical object (in the common-sense meaning of "physical") it is a flat diagram on a piece of paper—a square within a square, with corners connected by diagonals. But imaginatively perceived, it appears as a lampshade, or a tunnel, or a truncated pyramid. Books on the psychology of perception supply many similar illustrations.[4]

Esthetic vision, which Aldrich calls "prehension," is an awareness of "aspects" grounded in the nature of the object, and not just illusory projections of the viewer's concoction. ". . . The thing as an esthetic object," he remarks, "and the correlated mode of perception have their own characteristic objectivity or out-thereness. . . . You can imagine with your eyes shut, but you cannot esthetically *see* with your eyes shut."

The example of different ways of perceiving the rectangular diagram makes clear the difference between imaginative awareness ("prehension") and mere physical perception. An example more relevant to art is supplied later in the essay by Aldrich's discussion of Andre Dérain's "Still Life with a Jug." In his *Philosophy of Art* (1963), Aldrich cites an example of esthetic prehension not involving art. If an observer gazes at dark buildings meeting a pale sky at dusk, the light sky area just above the jagged urban skyline protrudes toward the viewer; the sky in *esthetic* space but not in *physical* space is closer than the buildings.

To fail to distinguish between esthetic aspects and physical properties, or between esthetic vision and physical observation, is to confuse two distinct categories. Esthetic education, according to Aldrich, consists largely in learning to distinguish these categories and in cultivating esthetic awareness. In his brief essay he confines himself to "seeing as," but there is similar prehension in reading literature, hearing music, interpreting a theatrical performance, and so forth.

Esthetic experience, as we have noted, has both an inhibitory and an elaborative aspect. Kant's "disinterestedness," Bullough's "distance," and Ortega y Gasset's "dehumanization" apply more to the inhibitive side; Kant's harmonious "play" of our faculties, Lipps' "empathy," and Aldrich's "prehension" apply more to the elaborative side. The former, inhibiting the nonesthetic, and the latter, elaborating the esthetic, are complementary moments in the systole–diastole of esthetic experience.

Notes

1. *The Critique of Judgement,* translated by James Creed Meredith (Oxford at the Clarendon Press, 1952), pp. 51, 52.
2. Review by David Mandel, *Leonardo: International Journal of the Contemporary Artist,* Vol. 8 (Winter 1975), p. 78.
3. Ludwig Wittgenstein, *Philosophical Investigations,* translated by G. E. M. Anscombe (Basil Blackwell and Macmillan, Oxford and New York, 1953), p. 208.
4. See especially Norwood Russell Hanson, "Seeing and Seeing As," *Perception and Discovery* (Freeman, Cooper, San Francisco, 1970).

IMMANUEL KANT

A Theory of Esthetic Experience

I. The Analysis of Beauty

First Moment: Disinterestedness

[The beautiful is that which pleases in disinterested contemplation. Disinterestedness is pure contemplation independent of any concern for the real existence of the object. The pleasant and the good are always bound up with interest in the existence of their objects; the beautiful alone is independent of such interest.]

The satisfaction which we combine with the representation of the existence of an object is called interest. Such satisfaction always has reference to the faculty of desire, either as its determining ground or as necessarily connected with its determining ground. Now, when the question is if a thing is beautiful, we do not want to know whether anything depends or can depend on the existence of the thing either for myself or for any one else, but how we judge it by mere observation (intuition or reflection). If anyone asks me if I find that palace beautiful which I see before me, I may answer: I do not like things of that kind which are made merely to be stared at. Or I can answer like that Iroquois Sachem, who was pleased in Paris by nothing more than by the cook-shops. Or again, after the manner of Rousseau I may rebuke the vanity of the great who waste the sweat of the people on such superfluous things. In fine I could easily convince myself that if I found myself on an uninhabited island without the hope of ever again coming among men, and could conjure up just such a splendid building by mere wish, I should not even give myself the trouble if I had a sufficiently comfortable hut. This may all be admitted and approved; but we are not now talking of this. We wish only to know if this mere representation of the object is accompanied in me with satisfaction, however indifferent I may be as regards the existence of the object of this representation. We easily see that in saying it is *beautiful* and in showing that I have taste, I am concerned, not with that in which I depend on the existence of the object, but with that which I make out of this representation in myself. Everyone must admit that a judgment about beauty, in which the least interest mingles, is very partial and is not a pure judgment of taste. We must not be in the least prejudiced in favor of the existence of the things, but be quite indifferent in this respect, in order to play the judge in things of taste. . . .

That which pleases only as a means we call *good for something* (the useful); but that which pleases for itself is *good in itself*. In both there is always involved the concept of a purpose, and consequently the relation of Reason to the (at least possible) volition, and thus a satisfaction in the *presence* of an Object or an action, i.e. some kind of interest.

In order to find anything good, I must always know what sort of a thing the object ought to be, i.e., I must have a concept of it. But there is no need of this to find a thing beautiful. Flowers, free delineations, outlines intertwined with one another without design and called conventionally foliage, having no meaning, depend on no definite concept, and yet they please. . . .

The pleasant and the good have both a reference to the faculty of desire; and they bring with them, the former a satisfaction pathologically conditioned (by impulses, *stimuli*), the latter a pure practical satisfaction, which is determined not merely by the representation of the object, but also by the represented connection of the subject with the existence of the object. It is not merely the object that pleases, but also its existence. On the other hand, the judgment of taste is merely *contemplative*; i.e., it is a judgment which, indifferent as regards the existence of an object, compares its character with the feeling of pleasure and pain. But this contemplation itself is not directed to concepts; for the judgment of taste is not a cognitive judgment (either theoretical or practical), and thus is not *based* on concepts, nor has it concepts as its *purpose*.

The Pleasant, the Beautiful, and the Good, designate then, three different relations of representations to the feeling of pleasure and pain, in reference to which we distinguish from each other objects or methods of representing them. . . . We may say that of all these three kinds of satisfaction, that of taste in the Beautiful is alone a disinterested and *free* satisfaction; for no interest, either of Sense or of Reason, here forces our assent. Hence we may say of satisfaction that it is related in the three aforesaid cases to *inclination*, to *favor*, or to *respect*. Now *favor* is the only free satisfaction. . . .

Taste is the faculty of judging of an object or a method of representing it by an *entirely disinterested* satisfaction or dissatisfaction. The object of such satisfaction is called *beautiful*.

Second Moment: Subjective Universality

[Beauty involves a claim to universal validity and yet is not based on concepts. We impute the value to the object and feel that everyone *ought* to agree. Nevertheless we cannot, on conceptual grounds, justify the presumption of universal validity.]

As regards the Pleasant, everyone is content that his judgment, which he bases upon private feeling, and by which he says of an object that it pleases him, should be limited merely to his own person. Thus he is quite contented that if he says, "Canary wine is pleasant," another man may correct his expression and remind him that he ought to say "It is pleasant *to me*." And this is the case not only as regards the taste of the tongue, the palate, and the throat, but for whatever is pleasant to anyone's eyes and ears. To one violet color is soft and lovely, to another it is washed out and dead. One man likes the tone of wind instruments, another that of strings. To strive here with the design of reproving as incorrect another man's judgment which is different from our own, as if the judgments were logically opposed, would be folly. As regards the pleasant therefore the fundamental proposition is valid: *everyone has his own taste* (the taste of Sense).

The case is quite different with the Beautiful. It would (on the contrary) be laughable if a man who imagined anything to his own taste, thought to justify himself by saying: "This object (the house we see, the coat that the person wears, the concert we hear, the poem submitted to our judgment) is beautiful *for me*." For he must not call it *beautiful* if it merely pleases him. Many things may have for him charm and pleasantness; no one troubles himself at that; but if he gives out anything as beautiful, he supposes in others the same satisfaction—he judges not merely for himself, but for everyone, and speaks of beauty as if it were a property of things. Hence he says "the *thing* is beautiful"; and he does not count on the agreement of others with this his judgment of satisfaction, because he has found this agreement several times before, but he *demands* it of them. He blames them if they judge otherwise and he denies them taste, which he nevertheless requires from them. Here, then, we cannot say that each man has his own particular taste. For this would be as much as to say that there is no taste whatever, i.e., no esthetical judgment, which can make a rightful claim upon every one's assent. . . .

If we judge Objects merely according to concepts, then all representation of beauty is lost. Thus there can be no rule according to which anyone is to be forced to recognize anything as beautiful. We cannot press upon others by the aid of any reasons or fundamental propositions our judgment that a coat, a house, or a flower is beautiful. People wish to submit the Object to their own eyes, as if the satisfaction in it depended on sensation; and yet if we then call the object beautiful, we believe that we speak with a universal voice, and we claim the assent of everyone, although on the contrary all private sensations can only decide for the observer himself and his satisfaction.

We may see now that in the judgment of taste nothing is postulated but such a *universal voice*, in respect of the satisfaction without the intervention of concepts; and thus the *possibility* of an esthetical judgment that can, at the same time, be regarded as valid for everyone. The judgment of taste itself does not *postulate* the agreement of everyone (for that can only be done by a logically universal judgment because it can adduce reasons); it only *imputes* this agreement to everyone, as a case of the rule in respect of which it expects, not confirmation by concepts, but assent from others. . . .

The cognitive powers, which are involved by this representation, are here in free play, because no definite concept limits them to a definite rule of cognition. Hence, the state of mind in this representation must be a feeling of the free play of the representative powers in a given representation with reference to a cognition in general. Now a representation by which an object is given—that is, to become a cognition in general—requires *Imagination*, for the gathering together the manifold of intuition, and *Understanding*, for the unity of the concept uniting the representations. This state of *free play* of the cognitive faculties in a representation by which an object is given, must be universally communicable; because cognition, as the determination of the Object with which given representations (in whatever subject) are to agree, is the only kind of representation which is valid for every one.

The subjective universal communicability of the mode of representation in a judgment of taste, since it is to be possible without presupposing a definite concept, can refer to nothing else than the state of mind in the free play of the Imagination and the Understanding (so far as they agree with each other, as is requisite for *cognition in general*.) We are conscious that this subjective relation, suitable for cognition in general, must be valid for everyone, and thus must be universally communicable, just as if it were a definite cognition, resting always on that relation as its subjective condition.

This merely subjective (esthetical) judging of the object, or of the representation by which it is given, precedes the pleasure in the same, and is the ground of this pleasure in the harmony of the cognitive faculties; but on that universality of the subjective conditions for judging of objects is alone based the universal subjective validity of the satisfaction bound up by us with the representation of the object that we call beautiful. . . .

The *beautiful* is that which pleases universally without requiring a concept.

Third Moment: Purposiveness Without Purpose

[When the form of the object arouses the harmonious play of imagination and understanding, there is beauty. Rather than an extraneous purpose, there is a design enjoyed simply for its own sake and having no purpose or function beyond arousing the mind to enjoyable contemplation. In free beauty, the form or design is thus enjoyed in and for itself. Dependent beauty, on the other hand, presupposes a concept or extraneous purpose, and hence is not purely esthetic.]

There are two kinds of beauty: free beauty (*pulchritudo vaga*) or merely dependent beauty (*pulchritudo adhaerens*). The first presupposes no concept of what the object ought to be; the second does presuppose such a concept and the perfection of the object in accordance therewith. The first is called the (self-subsistent) beauty of this or that thing; the second, as dependent upon a concept (conditioned beauty), is ascribed to objects which come under the concept of a particular purpose.

Flowers are free natural beauties. Hardly anyone but a botanist knows what sort of a thing a flower ought to be; and even he, though recognizing in the flower the reproductive organ of the plant, pays no regard to this natural purpose if he is passing judgment on the flower by Taste. . . . Many birds (such as the parrot, the hummingbird, the bird of paradise), and many seashells are beauties in themselves, which do not belong to any object determined in respect of its purpose by concepts, but please freely and in themselves. So also delineations *à la grecque*, foliage for borders or wallpapers, mean nothing in themselves; they represent nothing—no Object under a definite concept—and are free beauties. We can refer to the same class what are called in music phantasies (i.e., pieces without any theme), and, in fact, all music without words.

In judging a free beauty (according to the mere form), the judgment of taste is pure. There is presupposed no concept of any purpose, which the manifold of a given object is to serve, and which therefore is to be represented in it. By such a concept the freedom of the Imagination which distorts itself in the contemplation of the figure would be only limited.

But human beauty (i.e., of a man, a woman, or a child), the beauty of a horse, or a building (be it church, palace, arsenal, or summerhouse), presupposes a concept of the purpose which determines what the thing is to be, and consequently a concept of its perfection; it is therefore adherent beauty. Now, as the combination of the Pleasant (in sensation) with Beauty, which properly is concerned with form, is a hindrance to the purity of the judgment of taste, so also is its purity injured by the combination with Beauty of the Good (viz., that manifold which is good for the thing itself in accordance with its purpose).

We could add much to a building which would immediately please the eye, if only it were not to be a church. We could adorn a figure with all kinds of spirals and light but regular lines, as the New Zealanders do with their tattooing, if only it were not the figure of a human being. And, again, this could have much finer features and a more pleasing and gentle cast of countenance provided it were not intended to represent a man, much less a warrior.

Now, the satisfaction in the manifold of a thing in reference to the internal purpose which determines its possibility is a satisfaction grounded on a concept; but the satisfaction in beauty is such as presupposes no concept, but is immediately bound up with the representation through which the object is given (not through which it is thought). If now the judgment of Taste in respect of the beauty of a thing is made dependent on the purpose in its manifold, like a judgment of Reason, and thus limited, it is no longer a free and pure judgment of Taste. . . .

A judgment of taste, then, in respect of an object with a definite internal purpose, can only be pure, if either the person judging has no concept of this purpose, or else abstracts from it in his judgment. Such a person, although forming an accurate judgment of taste in judging of the object as a free beauty, would yet by another who considers the beauty in it only as a dependent attribute (who looks to the purpose of the object) be blamed, and accused of false taste; although both are right in their own way, the one in reference to what he has before his eyes, the other in reference to what he has in his thought. By means of this distinction we can settle many disputes about beauty between judges of taste; by showing that the one is speaking of free, the other of dependent, beauty—that the first is making a pure, the second an applied, judgment of taste. . . .

Beauty is the form of the *purposiveness* of an object, so far as this is perceived in it *without any representation of a purpose.*

Fourth Moment: Necessary Satisfaction

[A person who judges that an object is beautiful makes an implicit claim that everyone *ought* to (not *must*) follow suit in finding the object beautiful. This claim, since it rests on no determinate rule, presupposes a common human nature—the presence in all mankind of imagination and understanding. The free and harmonious play of these faculties when aroused by the form of the object constitutes the subjective and universal basis of beauty.]

I can say of every representation that it is at least *possible* that (as a cognition) it should be bound up with a pleasure. Of a representation that I call *pleasant* I say that it *actually* excites pleasure in me. But the *beautiful* we think as having *necessary* reference to satisfaction. Now this necessity is of a peculiar kind. It is not a theoretical objective necessity; in which case it would be cognized a priori that everyone *will feel* this satisfaction in the object called beautiful by me. It is not a practical necessity, in which case, by concepts of a pure rational will serving as a rule for freely acting beings, the satisfaction is the necessary result of an objective law and only indicates that we absolutely (without any further design) ought to act in a certain way. But the necessity which is thought in an esthetical judgment can only be called *exemplary,* i.e., a necessity of the assent of *all* to a judgment which is regarded as the example of a universal rule that we cannot state. Since an esthetical judgment is not an objective cognitive judgment, this necessity cannot be derived from definite concepts, and is therefore not apodictic. Still less can it be inferred from the universality of experience (of a complete agreement of judgments as to the beauty of a certain object). For not only would experience hardly furnish sufficiently numerous vouchers for this; but also, on empirical judgments we can base no concept of the necessity of these judgments. . . .

The judgment of taste requires the agreement of everyone; and he who describes anything as beautiful claims that everyone *ought* to give his approval to the object in question and also describe it as beautiful. The *ought* in the esthetical judgment is therefore pronounced in accordance with all the data which are required for judging and yet is only conditioned. . . .

If judgments of taste (like cognitive judgments) had a definite objective principle, then the person who lays them down in accordance with this latter would claim an unconditioned necessity for his judgment. If they were devoid of all principle, like those of a mere taste of sense, we would not allow them in thought any necessity whatever. Hence, they must have a subjective principle which determines what pleases or displeases only by feeling and not by concepts, but yet with universal validity. But such a principle could only be regarded as a *common sense,* which is essentially different from common Understanding which people sometimes call common Sense (*sensus communis*); for the latter does not judge by feeling but always by concepts, although ordinarily only as by obscurely represented principles.

Hence, it is only under the presupposition that there is a common sense (by which we do not understand an external sense, but the effect resulting from the free play of our cognitive powers)—it is only under this presupposition, I say, that the judgment of taste can be laid down. . . .

Cognitions and judgments must, along with the conviction that accompanies them, admit of universal communicability; for otherwise there would be no harmony between them and the Object, and they would be collectively a mere subjective play of the representative powers, exactly as skepticism desires. But if cognitions are to admit of communicability, so must also the state of mind—i.e., the accordance of the cognitive powers with a cognition generally, and that proportion of them which is suitable for a representation (by which an object is given to us) in order that a cognition may be made out of it—admit of universal communicability. For without this as the subjective condition of cognition, cognition as an effect could not arise. This actually always takes place when a given object by means of Sense excites the Imagination to collect the manifold, and the Imagination in its turn excites the Understanding to bring about a unity of this collective process in concepts. But this accordance of the cognitive powers has a different proportion according to the variety of the Objects which are given. However, it must be such that this internal relation, by which one mental faculty is excited by another, shall be generally the most beneficial for both faculties in respect of cognition (of given objects); and this accordance can only be determined by feeling (not according to concepts). Since now this accordance itself must admit of universal communicability, and consequently also our feeling of it (in a given representation), and since the universal communicability of a feeling presupposes a common sense, we have grounds for assuming this latter. And this common sense is assumed without relying on psychological observations, but simply as the necessary condition of a universal communicability of our knowledge, which is presupposed in every Logic and in every principle of knowledge that is not skeptical. . . .

In all judgments by which we describe anything as beautiful, we allow no one to be of another opinion; without, however, grounding our judgment on concepts but only on our feeling, which we therefore place at its basis not as a private, but as a common, feeling. Now this common sense cannot be grounded on experience; for it aims at justifying judgments which contain an *ought*. It does not say that everyone *will* agree with my judgment, but that he *ought*. And so common sense, as an example of whose judgment I here put forward my judgment of taste and on account of which I attribute to the latter an *exemplary* validity, is a mere ideal norm, under the supposition of which I have a right to make into a rule for everyone a judgment that accords therewith, as well as the satisfaction in an Object expressed in such judgment. For the principle, which concerns the agreement of different judging persons, although only subjective, is yet assumed as subjectively universal (an Idea necessary for everyone); and thus can claim universal assent (as if it were objective) provided we are sure that we have correctly subsumed the particulars under it.

This indeterminate norm of a common sense is actually presupposed by us; as is shown by our claim to lay down judgments of taste. . . .

The *beautiful* is that which without any concept is cognized as the object of a necessary *satisfaction*.

II. The Analysis of Sublimity

The Contrast Between Beauty and Sublimity

[The sublime, in contrast with beauty, is ill-adapted to our faculties of imagination and understanding. Because the sublime object is unbounded, and because we cannot comprehend it with our sensible faculties, we can grasp it only through a higher, supersensible faculty, namely, reason.]

The Beautiful and the Sublime agree in this, that both please in themselves. Further, neither presupposes a judgment of sense nor a judgment logically determined, but a judgment of reflection. Consequently, the satisfaction belonging to them does not depend on a sensation, as in the case of the Pleasant, nor on a definite concept, as in the case of the Good. . . .

But there are also remarkable differences between the two. The Beautiful in nature is connected with the form of the object, which consists in having [definite] boundaries. The Sublime, on the other hand, is to be found in a formless object, so far as in it or by occasion of it *boundlessness* is represented, and yet its totality is also present to thought. Thus the Beautiful seems to be regarded as the presentation of an indefinite concept of Understanding, the Sublime as that of a like concept of Reason. Therefore, the satisfaction in the one case is bound up with the representation of *quality* in the other with that of *quantity*. And the latter satisfaction is quite different in kind from the former, for this the Beautiful directly brings with it a feeling of the furtherance of life, and thus is compatible with charms and with the play of the Imagination. But the other, the feeling of the Sublime, is a pleasure that arises only indirectly; viz., it is produced by the feeling of a momentary checking of the vital powers and a consequent stronger outflow of them, so that it seems to be regarded as emotion—not play, but earnest in the exercise of the Imagination. Hence, it is incompatible with physical charm; and as the mind is not merely attracted by the object but is ever being alternately repelled, the satisfaction in the sublime does not so much involve a positive pleasure as admiration or respect, which rather deserves to be called negative pleasure.

But the inner and most important distinction between the Sublime and Beautiful is, certainly, as follows. . . . Natural beauty (which is independent) brings with it a purposiveness in its form by which the object seems to be, as it were, preadapted to our Judgment, and thus constitutes in itself an object of satisfaction. On the other hand, that which excites in us, without any reasoning about it, but in the mere apprehension of it, the feeling of the sublime may appear as regards its form to violate purpose in respect of the Judgment, to be unsuited to our presentative faculty, and, as it were, to do violence to the Imagination; and yet it is judged to be only the more sublime.

Now, we may see from this that in general we express ourselves incorrectly if we call any *object of nature* sublime, although we can quite correctly call many objects of nature beautiful. For how can that be marked by an expression of approval, which is apprehended in itself as being a violation of purpose? All that we can say is that the object is fit for the presentation of a sublimity which can be found in the mind; for no sensible form can contain the sublime properly so-called. This concerns only Ideas of the Reason, which, although no adequate presentation is possible for them, by this inadequateness that admits of sensible presentation, are aroused and summoned into the mind. Thus the wide ocean, disturbed by the storm, cannot be called sublime. Its aspect is horrible; and the mind must be already filled with manifold Ideas if it is to be determined by such an intuition to a feeling itself sublime, as it is incited to abandon sensibility and to busy itself with Ideas that involve higher purposiveness. . . .

We call that *sublime* which is *absolutely* great. But to be great, and to be a great something are quite different concepts (*magnitudo* and *quantitas*). In like manner to *say simply* (*simpliciter*) that anything is *great* is quite different from saying that it is *absolutely great* (*absolute, non comparative magnum*). *The latter is what is great beyond all comparison*. . . .

But if we call anything not only great, but absolutely great in every point of view (great beyond all comparison), i.e., sublime, we soon see that it is not permissible to seek for an adequate standard of this outside itself, but merely in itself. It is a magnitude which is like itself alone. It follows hence that the sublime is not to be sought in the things of nature, but only in our ideas. . . .

The foregoing explanation can be thus expressed: *the sublime is that in comparison with which everything else is small.* Here we easily see that nothing can be given in nature, however great it is judged by us to be, which could not if considered in another relation be reduced to the infinitely small; and conversely there is nothing so small, which does not admit of extension by our Imagination to the greatness of a world, if compared with still smaller standards. Telescopes have furnished us with abundant material for making the first remark, microscopes for the second. Nothing, therefore, which can be an object of the senses is, considered on this basis, to be called sublime. But because there is in our Imagination a striving toward infinite progress, and in our Reason a claim for absolute totality, regarded as a real Idea, therefore this very inadequateness for that Idea in our faculty for estimating the magnitude of things of sense, excites in us the feeling of a supersensible faculty. And it is not the object of sense, but the use which the Judgment naturally makes of certain objects on behalf of this latter feeling, that is absolutely great; and in comparison every other use is small. Consequently, it is the state of mind produced by a certain representation with which the reflective Judgment is occupied, and not the Object, that is to be called sublime.

We can therefore append to the preceding formulas explaining the sublime this other: *the sublime is that, the mere ability to think which, shows a faculty of the mind surpassing every standard of Sense. . . .*

The Mathematically Sublime

[When an object is so great in size that sense and imagination cannot grasp it, this failure evokes the activity of reason. We enjoy the sense that, immeasurably great though the object be, we can conceive something still greater. The beholder feels that as a rational being he is superior even to the greatest natural object.]

Now for the mathematical estimation of magnitude there is, indeed, no maximum (for the power of numbers extends to infinity); but for its esthetical estimation there is always a maximum, and of this I say that if it is judged as the absolute measure than which no greater is possible subjectively (for the judging subject), it brings with it the Idea of the sublime and produces that emotion which no mathematical estimation of its magnitude by means of numbers can bring about (except so far as that esthetical fundamental measure remains vividly in the Imagination). For the former only presents relative magnitude by means of comparison with others of the same kind; but the latter presents magnitude absolutely, so far as the mind can grasp it in an intuition.

In receiving a quantum into the Imagination by intuition, in order to be able to use it for a measure or as a unit for the estimation of magnitude by means of numbers, there are two operations of the Imagination involved: *apprehension* (*apprehensio*) and *comprehension* (*comprehensio aesthetica*). As to apprehension there is no difficulty, for it can go on ad infinitum; but comprehension becomes harder the further apprehension advances, and soon attains to its maximum, viz., the greatest possible esthetical fundamental measure for the estimation of magnitude. For when apprehension has gone so far that the partial representations of sensuous intuition at first apprehended begin to vanish in the Imagination, whilst this ever proceeds to the apprehension of others, then it loses as much on the one side as it gains on the other; and in comprehension there is a maximum beyond which it cannot go. . . .

But the infinite is absolutely (not merely comparatively) great. Compared with it everything else (of the same kind of magnitudes) is small. And what is most important is that to be able to think it as *a whole* indicates a faculty of mind which surpasses every standard of Sense. For to represent it sensibly would require a comprehension having for unit a standard bearing a definite relation, expressible in numbers, to the infinite, which is impossible. Nevertheless, *the bare capability of thinking* this infinite without contradiction requires in the human mind a faculty itself supersensible. . . .

Nature is therefore sublime in those of its phenomena whose intuition brings with it the Idea of its infinity. . . .

Examples of the mathematically Sublime in nature in mere intuition are all the cases in which we are given, not so much a larger numerical concept, as a large unit for the measure of the Imagination (for shortening the numerical series). A tree the height of which we estimate with reference to the height of a man, at all events gives a standard for a mountain; and if this were a mile high, it would serve as unit for the number expressive of the earth's diameter, so that the latter might be made intuitible. The earth's diameter would supply a unit for the known planetary system; this again for the Milky Way; and the immeasurable number of Milky Way systems called nebulae—which presumably constitute a system of the same kind among themselves— lets us expect no bounds here. Now the Sublime in the esthetical judging of an immeasurable whole like this lies not so much in the greatness of the number of units, as in the fact that in our progress we ever arrive at yet greater units. To this the systematic division of the universe contributes, which represents every magnitude in nature as small in its turn; and represents our Imagination with its entire freedom from bounds, and with it Nature, as a mere nothing in comparison with the Ideas of Reason, if it is sought to furnish a presentation which shall be adequate to them.

The Dynamically Sublime

[When an object is so mighty in power that we feel helpless before it, we take refuge in the sense that we can retain our spiritual independence and integrity even in the face of the greatest powers of brute nature.]

Might is that which is superior to great hindrances. It is called *dominion* if it is superior to the resistance of that which itself possesses might. Nature, considered in an esthetical judgment as might that has no dominion over us, is *dynamically sublime*. . . .

Bold, overhanging, and, as it were, threatening rocks; clouds piled up in the sky, moving with lightning flashes and thunder peals; volcanoes in all their violence of destruction; hurricanes with their track of devastation; the boundless ocean in a state of tumult; the lofty waterfall of a mighty river, and such like; these exhibit our faculty of resistance as insignificantly small in comparison with their might. But the sight of them is the more attractive, the more fearful it is, provided only that we are in security; and we willingly call these objects sublime, because they raise the energies of the soul above their accustomed height, and discover in us a faculty of resistance of a quite different kind, which gives us courage to measure ourselves against the apparent almightiness of nature.

Now, in the immensity of nature, and in the insufficiency of our faculties to take in a standard proportionate to the esthetical estimation of the magnitude of its *realm*, we find our own limitation; although at the same time in our rational faculty we find a different, nonsensuous standard, which has that infinity itself under it as a unity, in comparison with which everything in nature is small, and thus in our mind we find a superiority to nature even in its immensity. And so also the irresistibility of its might, while making us recognize our own physical impotence, considered as being of nature, discloses to us a faculty of judging independently of, and a superiority over, nature; on which is based a kind of self-preservation, entirely different from that which can be attacked and brought into danger by external nature. Thus, humanity in our person remains unhumiliated, though the individual might have to submit to this dominion. In this way nature is not judged to be sublime in our esthetical judgments, insofar as it excites fear; but because it calls up that power in us (which is not nature) of regarding as small the things about which we are solicitous (goods, health, and life) and of regarding its might (to which we are no doubt subjected in respect of these things), as nevertheless without any dominion over us and our personality to which we must bow where our highest fundamental propositions, and their assertion or abandonment, are concerned. Therefore nature is here called sublime merely because it elevates the Imagination to a presentation of those cases in which the mind can make felt the proper sublimity of its destination, in comparison with nature itself. . . .

Sublimity, therefore, does not reside in anything in nature, but only in our mind, insofar as we can become conscious that we are superior to nature within, and therefore also to nature without, us (so far as it influences us). Everything that excites this feeling in us, e.g., the *might* of nature which calls forth our forces, is called then (although improperly) sublime. Only by supposing this Idea in ourselves, and in reference to it, are we capable of attaining to the Idea of the sublimity of that Being, which produces respect in us, not merely by the might that it displays in nature, but rather by means of the faculty which resides in us of judging it fearlessly and of regarding our destination as sublime in respect of it.

—*Critique of Judgment* (1790; translated 1892 by J. H. Bernard)

EDWARD BULLOUGH

Psychical Distance

I. 1. Meaning of the term "Distance."
   2. Distance as a factor in Art.
   3. Distance as an esthetic principle.

II. 1. Distance describes a personal relation.
   2. The antinomy of Distance.
   3. The variability of Distance.
   4. Distance as the psychological formulation of the antirealism of Art: naturalistic and idealistic Art.
   5. Distance as applied to the antithesis "sensual" and "spiritual."
   6. Distance as applied to the antithesis "individualistic" and "typical."

I

1. The conception of "Distance" suggests, in connection with Art, certain trains of thought by no means devoid of interest or of speculative importance. Perhaps the most obvious suggestion is that of *actual spatial* distance, that is, the distance of a work of Art from the spectator, or that of *represented spatial* distance, that is, the distance represented within the work. Less obvious, more metaphorical, is the meaning of *temporal* distance. The first was noticed already by Aristotle in his *Poetics;* the second has played a great part in the history of painting in the form of perspective; the distinction between these two kinds of distance assumes special importance theoretically in the differentiation between sculpture in the round, and relief-sculpture. Temporal distance, remoteness from us in point of time, though often a cause of misconceptions, has been declared to be a factor of considerable weight in our appreciation.

It is not, however, in any of these meanings that "Distance" is put forward here, though it will be clear in the course of this essay that the above mentioned kinds of distance are rather special forms of the conception of Distance as advocated here, and derive whatever *esthetic* qualities they may possess from Distance in its general connotation. This general connotation is "Psychical Distance."

A short illustration will explain what is meant by "Psychical Distance." Imagine a fog at sea: for most people it is an experience of acute unpleasantness. Apart from the physical annoyance and remoter forms of discomfort such as delays, it is apt to produce feelings of peculiar anxiety, fears of invisible dangers, strains of watching and listening for distant and unlocalized signals. The listless movements of the ship and her warning calls soon tell upon the nerves of the passengers; and that special, expectant, tacit anxiety and nervousness, always associated with this experience, make a fog the dreaded terror of the sea (all the more terrifying because of its very silence and gentleness) for the expert seafarer no less than for the ignorant landsman.

Nevertheless, a fog at sea can be a source of intense relish and enjoyment. Abstract from the experience of the sea fog, for the moment, its danger and practical unpleasantness, just as every one in the enjoyment of a mountain-climb disregards its physical labor and its danger (though, it is not denied, that these may incidentally enter into the enjoyment and enhance it); direct the attention to the features "objectively" constituting the phenomenon—the veil surrounding you with an opaqueness as of transparent milk, blurring the outline of things and distorting their shapes into weird grotesqueness; observe the carrying-power of the air, producing the impression as if you could touch some far-off siren by merely putting out your hand and letting it lose itself behind that white wall; note the curious creamy smoothness of the water, hypocritically denying as it were any suggestion of danger; and, above all, the strange solitude and remoteness from the world, as it can be found only on the highest mountain tops; and the experience may acquire, in its uncanny mingling of repose and terror, a flavor of such concentrated poignancy and delight as to contrast sharply with the blind and distempered anxiety of its other aspects. This contrast, often emerging with startling suddenness, is like a momentary switching on of some new current, or the passing ray of a brighter light, illuminating the outlook upon perhaps the most ordinary and familiar objects—an impression which we experience sometimes in instants of direst extremity, when our practical interest snaps like a wire from sheer over-tension, and we watch the consummation of some impending catastrophe with the marveling unconcern of a mere spectator.

It is a difference of outlook, due—if such a metaphor is permissible—to the insertion of Distance. This Distance appears to lie between our own self and its affections, using the latter term in its broadest sense as anything which affects our being, bodily or spiritually, for example, as sensation, perception, emotional state or idea. Usually, though not always, it amounts to the same thing to say that the Distance lies between our own self and such objects as are the sources or vehicles of such affections.

Thus, in the fog, the transformation by Distance is produced in the first instance by putting the phenomenon, so to speak, out of gear with our practical, actual self; by allowing it to stand outside the context of our personal needs and ends—in short, by looking at it "objectively," as it has often been called, by permitting only such reactions on our part as emphasize the "objective" features of the experience, and by interpreting even our "subjective" affections not as modes of *our* being but rather as characteristics of the phenomenon.

The working of Distance is, accordingly, not simple, but highly complex. It has a *negative*, inhibitory aspect—the cutting-out of the practical sides of things and of our practical attitude to them—and a *positive* side—the elaboration of the experience on the new basis created by the inhibitory action of Distance.

2. Consequently, this distanced view of things is not, and cannot be, our normal outlook. As a rule, experiences constantly turn the same side towards us, namely, that which has the strongest practical force of appeal. We are not ordinarily aware of those aspects of things which do not touch us immediately and practically, nor are we generally conscious of impressions apart from our own self which is impressed. The sudden view of things from their reverse, usually unnoticed, side, comes upon us as a

revelation, and such revelations are precisely those of Art. In this most general sense, Distance is a factor in all Art.

3. It is, for this very reason, also an esthetic principle. The esthetic contemplation and the esthetic outlook have often been described as "objective." We speak of "objective" artists as Shakespeare or Velasquez, of "objective" works or art forms as Homer's *Iliad* or the drama. It is a term constantly occurring in discussions and criticisms, though its sense, if pressed at all, becomes very questionable. For certain forms of Art, such as lyrical poetry, are said to be "subjective"; Shelley, for example, would usually be considered a "subjective" writer. On the other hand, no work of Art can be genuinely "objective" in the sense in which this term might be applied to a work on history or to a scientific treatise; nor can it be "subjective" in the ordinary acceptance of that term, as a personal feeling, a direct statement of a wish or belief, or a cry of passion is subjective. "Objectivity" and "subjectivity" are a pair of opposites which in their mutual exclusiveness when applied to Art soon lead to confusion.

Nor are they the only pair of opposites. Art has with equal vigor been declared alternately "idealistic" and "realistic," "sensual" and "spiritual," "individualistic" and "typical." Between the defense of either terms of such antitheses most esthetic theories have vacillated. It is one of the contentions of this essay that such opposites find their synthesis in the more fundamental conception of Distance.

Distance further provides the much needed criterion of the beautiful as distinct from the merely agreeable.

Again, it marks one of the most important steps in the process of artistic creation and serves as a distinguishing feature of what is commonly so loosely described as the "artistic temperament."

Finally, it may claim to be considered as one of the essential characteristics of the "esthetic consciousness"—if I may describe by this term that special mental attitude towards, and outlook upon, experience, which finds its most pregnant expression in the various forms of Art.

II

Distance, as I said before, is obtained by separating the object and its appeal from one's own self, by putting it out of gear with practical needs and ends. Thereby the "contemplation" of the object becomes alone possible. But it does not mean that the relation between the self and the object is broken to the extent of becoming "impersonal." Of the alternatives "personal" and "impersonal" the latter surely comes nearer to the truth; but here, as elsewhere, we meet the difficulty of having to express certain facts in terms coined for entirely different uses. To do so usually results in paradoxes, which are nowhere more inevitable than in discussions upon Art. "Personal" and "impersonal," "subjective" and "objective" are such terms, devised for purposes other than esthetic speculation, and becoming loose and ambiguous as soon as applied outside the sphere of their special meanings. In giving preference therefore to the term "impersonal" to describe the relation between the spectator and a work of Art, it is to be noticed that it is not impersonal in the sense in which we speak of the "impersonal" character of Science, for instance. In order to obtain "objectively valid" results, the scientist excludes the "personal factor," that is, his personal wishes as to the validity of his results, his predilection for any particular system to be proved or disproved by his research. It goes without saying that all experiments and investigations are undertaken out of a personal interest in the science, for the ultimate support of a definite assumption, and involve personal hopes of success; but this does not affect the "dispassionate" attitude of the investigator, under pain of being accused of "manufacturing his evidence."

1. Distance does not imply an impersonal, purely intellectually interested relation of such a kind. On the contrary, it describes a *personal* relation, often highly emotionally colored, but of a *peculiar character*. Its peculiarity lies in that the personal character of the relation has been, so to speak, filtered. It has been cleared of the practical, concrete nature of its appeal, without, however, thereby losing its original constitution. One of the best-known examples is to be found in our attitude towards the events and characters of the drama: they appeal to us like persons and incidents of normal experience, except that that side of their appeal, which would usually affect us in a directly personal manner, is held in abeyance. This difference, so well known as to be almost trivial, is generally explained by reference to the knowledge that the characters and situations are "unreal," imaginary. . . . But, as a matter of fact, the "assumption" upon which the imaginative emotional reaction is based is not necessarily the condition, but often the consequence, of Distance; that is to say, the converse of the reason usually stated would then be true: namely, that Distance, by changing our relation to the characters, renders them seemingly fictitious, not that the fictitiousness of the characters alters our feelings toward them. It is, of course, to be granted that the actual and admitted unreality of the dramatic action reinforces the effect of Distance. But surely the proverbial unsophisticated yokel whose chivalrous interference in the play on behalf of the hapless heroine can only be prevented by impressing upon him that "they are only pretending," is not the ideal type of theatrical audience. The proof of the seeming paradox that it is Distance which primarily gives to dramatic action the appearance of unreality and not *vice versa*, is the observation that the same filtration of our sentiments and the same seeming "unreality" of *actual* men and things occur, when at times, by a sudden change of inward perspective, we are overcome by the feeling that "all the world's a stage."

2. This personal but "distanced" relation (as I will venture to call this nameless character of our view) directs attention to a strange fact which appears to be one of the fundamental paradoxes of Art: it is what I propose to call "the antinomy of Distance."

It will be readily admitted that a work of Art has the more chance of appealing to us the better it finds us prepared for its particular kind of appeal. Indeed, without some degree of predisposition on our part, it must necessarily remain incomprehensible, and to that extent unappreciated. The success and intensity of its appeal would seem, therefore, to stand in direct proportion to the completeness with which it corresponds with our intellectual and emotional peculiarities and the idiosyncrasies of our experience. The absence of such a concordance between the characters of a work and of the spectator is, of course, the most general explanation for differences of "tastes."

At the same time, such a principle of concordance requires a qualification, which leads at once to the antinomy of Distance.

Suppose a man who believes that he has cause to be jealous about his wife, witnesses a performance of *Othello.* He will the more perfectly appreciate the situation, conduct and character of Othello, the more exactly the feelings and experiences of Othello coincide with his own—at least he *ought* to on the above principle of concordance. In point of fact, he will probably do anything but appreciate the play. In reality, the concordance will merely render him acutely conscious of his own jealousy; by a sudden reversal of perspective he will no longer see Othello apparently betrayed by Desdemona, but himself in an analogous situation with his own wife. This reversal of perspective is the consequence of the loss of Distance.

If this be taken as a typical case, it follows that the qualification required is that the coincidence should be as complete as is compatible with maintaining Distance. The jealous spectator of *Othello* will indeed appreciate and enter into the play the more keenly, the greater the resemblance with his own experience—*provided* that he succeeds in keeping the Distance between the action of the play and his personal feelings: a very difficult performance in the circumstances. It is on account of the same difficulty that the expert and the professional critic make a bad audience, since their expertness and critical professionalism are *practical* activities, involving their concrete personality and constantly endangering their Distance. (It is, by the way, one of the reasons why Criticism is an art, for it requires the constant interchange from the practical to the distanced attitude and *vice versa*, which is characteristic of artists.)

The same qualification applies to the artist. He will prove artistically most effective in the formulation of an intensely *personal* experience, but he can formulate it artistically only on condition of a detachment from the experience *qua personal.* Hence the statement of so many artists that artistic formulation was to them a kind of catharsis, a means of ridding themselves of feelings and ideas the acuteness of which they felt almost as a kind of obsession. Hence, on the other hand, the failure of the average man to convey to others at all adequately the impression of an overwhelming joy or sorrow. His personal implication in the event renders it impossible for him to formulate and present it in such a way as to make others, like himself, feel all the meaning and fullness which it possesses for him.

What is therefore, both in appreciation and production, most desirable is the *utmost decrease of Distance without its disappearance.*

3. Closely related, in fact a presupposition to the "antinomy," is the *variability of Distance.* Herein especially lies the advantage of Distance compared with such terms as "objectivity" and "detachment." Neither of them implies a *personal* relation—indeed both actually preclude it; and the mere inflexibility and exclusiveness of their opposites render their application generally meaningless.

Distance, on the contrary, admits naturally of degrees, and differs not only according to the nature of the *object,* which may impose a greater or smaller degree of Distance, but varies also according to the *individual's capacity* for maintaining a greater or lesser degree. And here one may remark that not only do *persons differ from each other* in their habitual measure of Distance, but that the *same individual differs* in his ability to maintain it in the face of different objects and of different arts.

There exist, therefore, two different sets of conditions affecting the degree of Distance in any given case: those offered by the object and those realized by the subject. In their interplay they afford one of the most extensive explanations for varieties of esthetic experience, since loss of Distance, whether due to the one or the other, means loss of esthetic appreciation.

In short, Distance may be said to be *variable both according to the distancing-power of the individual, and according to the character of the object.*

There are two ways of losing Distance: either to "under-distance" or to "over-distance." "Under-distancing" is the commonest failing of the *subject,* an excess of Distance is a frequent failing of Art, especially in the past. Historically it looks almost as if Art had attempted to meet the deficiency of Distance on the part of the subject and had overshot the mark in this endeavor. It will be seen later that this is actually true, for it appears that over-distanced Art is specially designed for a class of appreciation which has difficulty to rise spontaneously to any degree of Distance. The consequence of a loss of Distance through one or other cause is familiar: the verdict in the case of under-distancing is that the work is "crudely naturalistic," "harrowing," "repulsive in its realism." An excess of Distance produces the impression of improbability, artificiality, emptiness or absurdity.

The individual tends, as I just stated, to under-distance rather than to lose Distance by over-distancing. *Theoretically* there is no limit to the decrease of Distance. In theory, therefore, not only the usual subjects of Art, but even the most personal affections, whether ideas, percepts, or emotions, can be sufficiently distanced to be esthetically appreciable. Especially artists are gifted in this direction to a remarkable extent. The average individual, on the contrary, very rapidly reaches his limit of decreasing Distance, his "Distance-limit," that is, that point at which Distance is lost and appreciation either disappears or changes its character.

In the *practice,* therefore, of the average person, a limit does exist which marks the minimum at which his appreciation can maintain itself in the esthetic field, and this average minimum lies considerably higher than the Distance-limit of the artist. It is practically impossible to fix this average limit, in the absence of data, and on account of the wide fluctuations from person to person to which this limit is subject. But it is safe to infer that, in art practice, explicit references to organic affections, to the material existence of the body, especially to sexual matters, lies normally below the Distance-limit, and can be touched upon by Art only with special precautions. Allusions to social institutions of any degree of personal importance —in particular, allusions implying any doubt as to their validity—the questioning of some generally recognized ethical sanctions, references to topical subjects occupying public attention at the moment, and such like, are all dangerously near the average limit and may at any time fall below it, arousing, instead of esthetic appreciation, concrete hostility or mere amusement.

This difference in the Distance-limit between artists and the public has been the source of much misunderstanding and injustice. Many an artist has seen his work condemned, and himself ostracized for the sake of so-called "immoralities" which to him were *bona fide* esthetic objects. His power of distancing, nay, the necessity of distancing feelings, sensations, situations which for the average person are too intimately bound up with his concrete existence to be regarded in that light, have often quite unjustly earned for him accusations of cynicism, sensualism, morbidness, or frivolity. The same misconception has arisen over many "problem plays" and "problem novels" in which the public have persisted in seeing nothing but a supposed "problem" of the moment, whereas the author may have been —and often has demonstrably been—able to distance the subject matter sufficiently to rise above its practical problematic import and to regard it simply as a dramatically and humanly interesting situation.

The variability of Distance in respect to Art, disregarding for the moment the subjective complication, appears both as a general feature in Art, and in the differences between the special arts.

It has been an old problem why the "arts of the eye and of the ear" should have reached the practically exclusive predominance over arts of other senses. Attempts to raise "culinary art" to the level of a Fine Art have failed in spite of all propaganda, as completely as the creation of scent or liquor "symphonies." There is little doubt that, apart from other excellent reasons of a partly psycho-physical, partly technical nature, the actual, *spatial distance* separating objects of sight and hearing from the subject has contributed strongly to the development of this monopoly. In a similar manner *temporal remoteness* produces Distance, and objects removed from us in point of time are *ipso facto* distanced to an extent which was impossible for their contemporaries. Many pictures, plays, and poems had, as a matter of fact, rather an expository or illustrative significance—as for instance much ecclesiastical Art—or the force of a direct practical appeal— as the invectives of many satires or comedies—which seem to us nowadays irreconcilable with their esthetic claims. Such works have consequently profited greatly by lapse of time and have reached the level of Art only with the help of temporal distance, while others, on the contrary, often for the same reason have suffered a loss of Distance, through *over*-distancing.

Special mention must be made of a group of artistic conceptions which present excessive Distance in their form of appeal rather than in their actual presentation—a point illustrating the necessity of distinguishing between distancing an object and distancing the appeal of which it is the source. I mean here what is often rather loosely termed "idealistic Art," that is, Art springing from abstract conceptions, expressing allegorical meanings, or illustrating general truths. Generalizations and abstractions suffer under this disadvantage that they have too much general applicability to invite a personal interest in them, and too little individual concreteness to prevent them applying to us in all their force. They appeal to everybody and therefore to none. An axiom of Euclid belongs to nobody, just because it compels every one's assent; general conceptions like Patriotism, Friendship, Love, Hope, Life, Death, concern as much Dick, Tom and Harry as myself, and I, therefore, either feel unable to get into any kind of personal relation to them, or, if I do so, they become at once, emphatically and concretely, *my* Patriotism, *my* Friendship, *my* Love, *my* Hope, *my* Life and Death. By mere force of generalization, a general truth or a universal ideal is so far distanced from myself that I fail to realize it concretely at all, or, when I do so, I can realize it only as part of my *practical actual being*, that is, it falls below the Distance-limit altogether. "Idealistic Art" suffers consequently under the peculiar difficulty that its excess of Distance turns generally into an *under*-distanced appeal—all the more easily, as it is the usual failing of the subject to *under*- rather than to *over*-distance.

The different special arts show at the present time very marked variations in the degree of Distance which they usually impose or require for their appreciation. Unfortunately here again the absence of data makes itself felt and indicates the necessity of conducting observations, possibly experiments, so as to place these suggestions upon a securer basis. In one single art, namely, the *theater*, a small amount of information is available, from an unexpected source, namely the proceedings of the censorship committee,[1] which on closer examination might be made to yield evidence of interest to the psychologist. In fact, the whole censorship problem, as far as it does not turn upon purely economic questions, may be said to hinge upon Distance; if every member of the public could be trusted to keep it, there would be no sense whatever in the existence of a censor of plays. There is, of course, no doubt that, speaking generally, theatrical performances *eo ipso* run a special risk of a loss of Distance owing to the material presentment[2] of its subject-matter. The physical presence of living human beings as vehicles of dramatic art is a difficulty which no art has to face in the same way. A similar, in many ways even greater, risk confronts *dancing*: though attracting perhaps a less widely spread human interest, its animal spirits are frequently quite unrelieved by any glimmer of spirituality and consequently form a proportionately stronger lure to under-distancing. In the higher forms of dancing technical execution of the most wearing kind makes up a great deal for its intrinsic tendency towards a loss of Distance, and as a popular performance, at least in southern Europe, it has retained much of its ancient artistic glamour, producing a peculiarly subtle balancing of Distance between the pure delight of bodily movement and high technical accomplishment. In passing, it is interesting to observe (as bearing upon the development of Distance), that this art, once as much a fine art as music and considered by the Greeks as a particularly valuable educational exercise, should—except in sporadic cases—have fallen so low from the pedestal it once occupied. Next to the theater and dancing stands *sculpture*. Though not using a *living* bodily medium, yet the human form in its full spatial materiality constitutes a similar threat to Distance. Our northern habits of dress and ignorance of the human body have enormously increased the difficulty of distancing Sculpture, in part through the gross misconceptions to which it is exposed, in part owing to a complete lack of standards of bodily perfection, and an inability to realize the distinction between sculptural form and bodily shape, which is the only but fundamental point distinguishing a statue from a cast taken from life. In *painting* it is apparently the form of its presentment and the usual reduction in scale which would explain why this art can venture to approach more closely than sculpture to the normal Distance-limit. As this matter will be discussed later in a special connection this simple reference may suffice here. *Music* and *architecture* have a curious position. These two most abstract of all arts show a remarkable fluctuation in their Distances. Certain kinds of music, especially "pure" music, or "classical" or "heavy" music, appear for many people over-distanced; light, "catchy" tunes, on the contrary, easily reach that degree of decreasing Distance below which they cease to be Art and become a pure amusement. In spite of its strange abstractness which to many philosophers has made it comparable to architecture and mathematics, music possesses a sensuous, frequently sensual character: the undoubted physiological and muscular stimulus of its melodics and harmonies, no less than its rhythmic aspects, would seem to account for the occasional disappearance of Distance. To this might be added its strong tendency, especially in unmusical people, to stimulate trains of thought quite disconnected with itself, following channels of subjective inclinations —daydreams of a more or less directly personal character. *Architecture* requires almost uniformly a very great Distance; that is to say, the majority of persons derive no esthetic appreciation from architecture as such, apart from the incidental impression of its decorative features and its associations. The causes are numerous, but prominent among them are the confusion of building with architecture and the predominance of utilitarian purposes, which overshadow the architectural claims upon the attention.

4. That all art requires a Distance-limit beyond which, and a Distance within which only, esthetic appreciation becomes possible, is the *psychological formulation of a general characteristic of Art,* namely, its *anti-realistic nature.* Though seemingly paradoxical, this applies as much to "naturalistic" as to "idealistic" Art. The difference commonly expressed by these epithets is at bottom merely the difference in the degree of Distance; and this produces, so far as "naturalism" and "idealism" in Art are not meaningless labels, the usual result that what appears obnoxiously "naturalistic" to one person, may be "idealistic" to another. To say that Art is anti-realistic simply insists upon the fact that Art is not nature, never pretends to be nature and strongly resists any confusion with nature. It emphasizes the *art*-character of Art: "artistic" is synonymous with "anti-realistic"; it explains even sometimes a very marked degree of artificiality.

"Art is an imitation of nature," was the current art-conception in the eighteenth century. It is the fundamental axiom of the standard-work of that time upon esthetic theory by the Abbé Du Bos, *Réflexions critiques sur la poésie et la peinture,* 1719; the idea received strong support from the literal acceptance of Aristotle's theory of *μίμησις* [imitation] and produced echoes everywhere, in Lessing's *Laocoön* no less than in Burke's famous statement that "all Art is great as it deceives." Though it may be assumed that since the time of Kant and of the Romanticists this notion has died out, it still lives in unsophisticated minds. Even when formally denied, it persists, for instance, in the belief that "Art idealizes nature," which means after all only that Art copies nature with certain improvements and revisions. Artists themselves are unfortunately often responsible for the spreading of this conception. Whistler indeed said that to produce Art by imitating nature would be like trying to produce music by sitting upon the piano, but the selective, idealizing imitation of nature finds merely another support in such a saying. Naturalism, pleinairism, impressionism—even the guileless enthusiasm of the artist for the works of nature, her wealth of suggestion, her delicacy of workmanship, for the steadfastness of her guidance, only produce upon the public the impression that Art is, after all, an imitation of nature. Then how can it be anti-realistic? The antithesis, Art *versus* nature, seems to break down. Yet if it does, what is the sense of Art?

Here the conception of Distance comes to the rescue. The solution of the dilemma lies in the "antinomy of Distance" with its demand: utmost decrease of Distance without its disappearance. The simple observation that Art is the more effective, the more it falls into line with our predispositions which are inevitably molded on general experience and nature, has always been the original motive for "naturalism." "Naturalism," "impressionism" is no new thing; it is only a new name for an innate leaning of Art, from the time of the Chaldeans and Egyptians down to the present day. Even the Apollo of Tenea apparently struck his contemporaries as so startlingly "naturalistic" that the subsequent legend attributed a superhuman genius to his creator. A constantly closer approach to nature, a perpetual refining of the limit of Distance, yet without overstepping the dividing line of art and nature, has always been the inborn bent of art. To deny this dividing line has occasionally been the failing of naturalism. But no theory of naturalism is complete which does not at the same time allow for the intrinsic idealism of Art: for both are merely degrees in that wide range lying beyond the Distance-limit. To imitate nature so as to trick the spectator into the deception that it is nature which he beholds, is to forsake Art, its anti-realism, its distanced spirituality, and to fall below the limit into sham, sensationalism, or platitude.

But what, in the theory of antinomy of Distance requires explanation is the existence of an *idealistic, highly distanced* Art. There are numerous reasons to account for it; indeed in so complex a phenomenon as Art, single causes can be pronounced almost *a priori* to be false. Foremost among such causes which have contributed to the formation of an idealistic Art appears to stand the subordination of Art to some extraneous purpose of an impressive, exceptional character. Such a subordination has consisted —at various epochs of Art history—in the use to which Art was put to subserve commemorative, hieratic, generally religious, royal or patriotic functions. The object to be commemorated had to stand out from among other still existing objects or persons; the thing or the being to be worshiped had to be distinguished as markedly as possible from profaner objects of reverence and had to be invested with an air of sanctity by a removal from its ordinary context of occurrence. Nothing could have assisted more powerfully the introduction of a high Distance than this attempt to differentiate objects of common experience in order to fit them for their exalted position. Curious, unusual things of nature met this tendency half-way and easily assumed divine rank; but others had to be distanced by an exaggeration of their size, by extraordinary attributes, by strange combinations of human and animal forms, by special insistence upon particular characteristics, or by the careful removal of all noticeably individualistic and concrete features. Nothing could be more striking than the contrast, for example, in Egyptian Art between the monumental, stereotyped effigies of the Pharaohs, and the startlingly realistic rendering of domestic scenes and of ordinary mortals, such as "the Scribe" or "the Village Sheik." Equally noteworthy is the exceeding artificiality of Russian ikon-painting with its prescribed attributes, expressions and gestures. Even Greek dramatic practice appears to have aimed, for similar purposes and in marked contrast to our stage-habits, at an increase rather than at a decrease of Distance. Otherwise Greek Art, even of a religious type, is remarkable for its *low* Distance value; and it speaks highly for the esthetic capacities of the Greeks that the degree of realism which they ventured to impart to the representations of their gods, while humanizing them, did not, at least at first,[3] impair the reverence of their feelings towards them. But apart from such special causes, idealistic Art of great Distance has appeared at intervals, for apparently no other reason than that the great Distance was felt to be essential to its *art*-character. What is noteworthy and runs counter to many accepted ideas is that such periods were usually epochs of a low level of general culture. These were times, which, like childhood, required the marvelous, the extraordinary, to satisfy their artistic longings, and neither realized nor cared for the poetic or artistic qualities of ordinary things. They were frequently times in which the mass of the people were plunged in ignorance and buried under a load of misery, and in which even the small educated class sought rather amusement or a pastime in Art; or they were epochs of a strong practical common sense too much concerned with the rough-and-tumble of life to have any sense of its esthetic charms. Art was to them what melodrama is to a section of the public at the present time, and its wide Distance was the safeguard of its artistic character. The flowering periods of Art have, on the contrary, always borne the evidence of a narrow Distance. Greek Art, as just mentioned, was realistic to an extent which we, spoilt as we are by modern developments, can grasp with difficulty, but which the contrast with its oriental contemporaries sufficiently proves. During the Augustan period—which Art historians at last are coming to regard no longer as merely "degenerated" Greek Art—Roman Art achieved its greatest triumphs in an almost naturalistic portrait-sculpture. In the Renaissance we need only think of the realism of portraiture, sometimes amounting almost to cynicism, of the *désinvolture* with which the mistresses of popes and dukes were posed as madonnas, saints and goddesses apparently without any detriment to the esthetic appeal of the works, and of the remarkable interpenetration of Art with the most ordinary routine of life, in order to realize the scarcely perceptible dividing line between the sphere of Art and the realm of practical existence. In a sense, the assertion that idealistic Art marks periods of a generally low and narrowly restricted culture is the converse to the oft-repeated statement that the flowering periods of Art coincide with epochs of decadence: for this so-called decadence represents indeed in certain respects a process of disintegration, politically, racially, often nationally, but a disruption necessary to the formation of larger social units and to the breakdown of outgrown national restrictions. For this very reason it has usually also been the sign of the growth of personal independence and of an expansion of individual culture.

To proceed to some more special points illustrating the distanced and therefore anti-realistic character of art—both in subject matter and in the form of presentation Art has always safeguarded its distanced view. Fanciful, even phantastic, subjects have from time immemorial been the accredited material of Art. No doubt things, as well as our view of them, have changed in the course of time: *Polyphemus* and the *Lotus-Eaters* for the Greeks, the *Venusberg* or the *Magnetic Mountain* for the Middle Ages were less incredible, more realistic than to us. But *Peter Pan* or *L'Oiseau Bleu* still appeal at the present day in spite of the prevailing note of realism of our time. "Probability" and "improbability" in Art are not to be measured by their correspondence (or lack of it) with actual experience. To do so had involved the theories of the fifteenth to the eighteenth centuries in endless contradictions. It is rather a matter of *consistency* of Distance. The note of realism, set by a work as a whole, determines *intrinsically* the greater or smaller degree of fancy which it permits; and consequently we feel the loss of Peter Pan's shadow to be infinitely more probable than some trifling improbability which shocks our sense of proportion in a naturalistic work. No doubt also, fairy tales, fairy plays, stories of strange adventures were primarily invented to satisfy the craving of curiosity, the desire for the marvelous, the shudder of the unwonted and the longing for imaginary experiences. But by their mere eccentricity in regard to the normal facts of experience they cannot have failed to arouse a strong feeling of Distance.

Again, certain conventional subjects taken from mythical and legendary traditions, at first closely connected with the concrete, practical life of a devout public, have gradually, by the mere force of convention as much as by their inherent anti-realism, acquired Distance for us today. Our view of Greek mythological sculpture, of early Christian saints and martyrs must be considerably distanced, compared with that of the Greek and medieval worshiper. It is in part the result of lapse of time, but in part also a real change of attitude. Already the outlook of the Imperial Roman had altered, and Pausanias shows a curious dualism of standpoint, declaring the Athene Lemnia to be the supreme achievement of Phidias's genius, and gazing awe-struck upon the roughly hewn tree trunk representing some primitive Apollo. Our understanding of Greek tragedy suffers admittedly under our inability to revert to the point of view for which it was originally written. Even the tragedies of Racine demand an imaginative effort to put ourselves back into the courtly atmosphere of red-heeled, powdered ceremony. Provided the Distance is not too wide, the result of its intervention has everywhere been to enhance the *art*-character of such works and to lower their original ethical and social force of appeal. Thus in the central dome of the Church (Sta Maria dei Miracoli) at Saronno are depicted the heavenly hosts in ascending tiers, crowned by the benevolent figure of the Divine Father, bending from the window of heaven to bestow His blessing upon the assembled community. The mere realism of foreshortening and of the boldest vertical perspective may well have made the naïve Christian of the sixteenth century conscious of the Divine Presence—but for us it has become a work of Art.

The unusual, exceptional, has found its especial home in tragedy. It has always—except in highly distanced tragedy—been a popular objection to it that "there is enough sadness in life without going to the theater for it." Already Aristotle appears to have met with this view among his contemporaries clamoring for "happy endings." Yet tragedy is not sad; if it were, there would indeed be little sense in its existence. For the tragic is just in so far different from the merely sad, as it is distanced; and it is largely the exceptional which produces the Distance of tragedy: exceptional situations, exceptional characters, exceptional destinies and conduct. Not of course, characters merely cranky, eccentric, pathological. The exceptional element in tragic figures—that which makes them so utterly different from characters we meet with in ordinary experience—is a consistency of direction, a fervor of ideality, a persistence and driving-force which is far above the capacities of average men. The tragic of tragedy would, transposed into ordinary life, in nine cases out of ten, end in drama, in comedy, even in farce, for lack of steadfastness, for fear of conventions, for the dread of "scenes," for a hundred-and-one petty faithlessnesses toward a belief or an ideal: even if for none of these, it would end in a compromise simply because man forgets and time heals.[4] Again, the sympathy which aches with the sadness of tragedy is another such confusion, the under-distancing of tragedy's appeal. Tragedy trembles always on the knife-edge of a *personal* reaction, and sympathy which finds relief in tears tends almost always towards a loss of Distance. Such a loss naturally renders tragedy unpleasant to a degree: it becomes sad, dismal, harrowing, depressing. But real tragedy (melodrama has a very strong tendency to speculate upon sympathy), truly appreciated, is not sad. "The pity of it—oh, the pity of it," that essence of all genuine tragedy is not the pity of mild, regretful sympathy. It is a chaos of tearless, bitter bewilderment, of upsurging revolt and rapturous awe before the ruthless and inscrutable fate; it is the homage to the great and exceptional in the man who in a last effort of spiritual tension can rise to confront blind, crowning Necessity even in his crushing defeat.

As I explained earlier, the form of presentation sometimes endangers the maintenance of Distance, but it more frequently acts as a considerable support. Thus the bodily vehicle of *drama* is the chief factor of risk to Distance. But, as if to counterbalance a confusion with nature, other features of stage-presentation exercise an opposite influence. Such are the general theatrical *milieu*, the shape and arrangement of the stage, the artificial lighting, the costumes, *mise-en-scène* and make-up, even the language, especially verse. Modern reforms of staging, aiming primarily at the removal of artistic incongruities between excessive decoration and the living figures of the actors and at the production of a more homogeneous stage-picture, inevitably work also towards a greater emphasis and homogeneity of Distance. The history of staging and dramaturgy is closely bound up with the evolution of Distance, and its fluctuations lie at the bottom not only of the greater part of all the talk and writing about "dramatic probability" and the Aristotelian "unities," but also of "theatrical illusion." In *sculpture*, one distancing factor of presentment is its lack of color. The esthetic, or rather inesthetic effect of realistic coloring, is in no way touched by the controversial question of its use historically; its attempted resuscitation, such as by Klinger, seems only to confirm its disadvantages. The distancing use even of pedestals, although originally no doubt serving other purposes, is evident to anyone who has experienced the oppressively crowded sensation of moving in a room among life-size statues placed directly upon the floor. The circumstance that the space of statuary is the same space as ours (in distinction to relief sculpture or painting, for instance) renders a distancing by pedestals, that is, a removal from our spatial context, imperative.[5] Probably the framing of *pictures* might be shown to serve a similar purpose—though paintings have intrinsically a much greater Distance—because neither their space (perspective and imaginary space) nor their lighting coincides with our (actual) space or light, and the usual reduction in scale of the represented objects prevents a feeling of undue proximity. Besides, painting always retains to some extent a *two*-dimensional character, and this character supplies *eo ipso* a Distance. Nevertheless, life-size pictures, especially if they possess strong relief, and their light happens to coincide with the actual lighting, can occasionally produce the impression of actual presence which is a far from pleasant, though fortunately only a passing, illusion. For decorative purposes, in pictorial renderings of vistas, garden-perspectives and architectural extensions, the removal of Distance has often been consciously striven after, whether with esthetically satisfactory results is much disputed.

A general help towards Distance (and therewith an anti-realistic feature) is to be found in the "unification of presentment"[6] of all art-objects. By unification of presentment are meant such qualities as symmetry, opposition, proportion, balance, rhythmical distribution of parts, light-arrangements, in fact all so-called "formal" features, "composition" in the widest sense. Unquestionably, Distance is not the only, nor even the principal function of composition; it serves to render our grasp of the presentation easier and to increase its intelligibility. It may even in itself constitute the principal esthetic feature of the object, as in linear complexes or patterns, partly also in architectural designs. Yet, its distancing effect can hardly be underrated. For, every kind of visibly intentional arrangement or unification must, by the mere fact of its presence, enforce Distance, by distinguishing the object from the confused, disjointed, and scattered forms of actual experience. This function can be gauged in a typical form in cases where composition produces an exceptionally marked impression of artificiality (not in the bad sense of that term, but in the sense in which all art is artificial); and it is a natural corollary to the differences of Distance in different arts and of different subjects, that the arts and subjects vary in the degree of artificiality which they can bear. It is this sense of artificial finish which is the source of so much of that elaborate charm of Byzantine work, of Mohammedan decoration, of the hieratic stiffness of so many primitive madonnas and saints. In general the emphasis of composition and technical finish increases with the Distance of the subject matter: heroic conceptions lend themselves better to verse than to prose; monumental statues require a more general treatment, more elaboration of setting and artificiality of pose than impressionistic statuettes like those of Troubetzkoi; an ecclesiastic subject is painted with a degree of symmetrical arrangement which would be ridiculous in a Dutch interior, and a naturalistic drama carefully avoids the tableau impression characteristic of a mystery play. In similar manner the variations of Distance in the arts go hand in hand with a visibly greater predominance of composition and "formal" elements, reaching a climax in architecture and music. It is again a matter of "consistency of Distance." At the same time, while from the point of view of the artist this is undoubtedly the case, from the point of view of the public the emphasis of composition and technical finish appears frequently to relieve the impression of highly distanced subjects by *diminishing the Distance of the whole.* The spectator has a tendency to see in composition and finish merely evidence of the artist's "cleverness," of his mastery over his material. Manual dexterity is an enviable thing to possess in every one's experience, and naturally appeals to the public *practically,* thereby putting it into a directly personal relation to things which intrinsically have very little personal appeal for it. It is true that this function of composition is hardly an esthetic one: for the admiration of mere technical cleverness is not an artistic enjoyment, but by a fortunate chance it has saved from oblivion and entire loss, among much rubbish, also much genuine Art, which otherwise would have completely lost contact with our life.

5. This discussion, necessarily sketchy and incomplete, may have helped to illustrate the sense in which, I suggested, Distance appears as a fundamental principle to which such antitheses as idealism and realism are reducible. The difference between "idealistic" and "realistic" Art is not a clear-cut dividing-line between the art-practices described by these terms, but is a difference of degree in the Distance-limit which they presuppose on the part both of the artist and of the public. A similar reconciliation seems to me possible between the opposites "sensual" and "spiritual," "individual" and "typical." That the appeal of Art is sensuous, even sensual, must be taken as an indisputable fact. Puritanism will never be persuaded, and rightly so, that this is not the case. The sensuousness of Art is a natural implication of the "antinomy of Distance," and will appear again in another connection. The point of importance here is that the whole sensual side of Art is purified, spiritualized, "filtered" as I expressed it earlier, by Distance. The most sensual appeal becomes the translucent veil of an underlying spirituality, once the grossly personal and practical elements have been removed from it. And—a matter of special emphasis here—*this spiritual aspect of the appeal is the more penetrating, the more personal and direct its sensual appeal would have been* BUT FOR THE PRESENCE OF DISTANCE. For the artist, to trust in this delicate transmutation is a natural act of faith which the Puritan hesitates to venture upon: which of the two, one asks, is the greater idealist?

6. The same argument applies to the contradictory epithets "individual" and "typical." A discussion in support of the fundamental individualism of Art lies outside the scope of this essay. Every artist has taken it for granted.

Besides it is rather in the sense of "concrete" or "individualized," that it is usually opposed to "typical." On the other hand, "typical," in the sense of "abstract," is as diametrically opposed to the whole nature of Art, as individualism is characteristic of it. It is in the sense of "generalized" as a "general human element" that it is claimed as a necessary ingredient in Art. This antithesis is again one which naturally and without mutual sacrifice finds room within the conception of Distance. Historically the "typical" has had the effect of counteracting *under*-distancing as much as the "individual" has opposed *over*-distancing. Naturally the two ingredients have constantly varied in the history of Art; they represent, in fact, two sets of conditions to which Art has invariably been subject: the personal and the social factors. It is Distance which on one side prevents the emptying of Art of its concreteness and the development of the typical into abstractness; which, on the other, suppresses the directly personal element of its individualism; thus reducing the antitheses to the peaceful interplay of these two factors. It is just this interplay which constitutes the "antinomy of Distance."

—*British Journal of Psychology,* Volume V (1913)

Notes

1. Report from the Joint Select Committee of the House of Lords and the House of Commons on the Stage Plays (Censorship), 1909.

2. I shall use the term "presentment" to denote the manner of presenting, in distinction to "presentation" as that which is presented.

3. That this practice did, in course of time, undermine their religious faith, is clear from the plays of Euripides and from Plato's condemnation of Homer's mythology.

4. The famous "unity of time," so senseless as a "canon," is all the same often an indispensible condition of tragedy. For in many a tragedy the catastrophe would be even intrinsically impossible, if fatality did not overtake the hero with that rush which gives no time to forget and none to heal. It is in cases such as these that criticism has often blamed the work for "improbability"—the old confusion between Art and nature—forgetting that the death of the hero is the convention of the art-form, as much as grouping in a picture is such a convention and that probability is not the correspondence with average experience, but consistency of Distance.

5. An instance which might be adduced to disprove this point only shows its correctness on closer inspection: for it was on purpose and with the intention of removing Distance, that Rodin originally intended his *Citoyens de Calais* to be placed, without pedestals, upon the marketplace of that town.

6. See note 2, *ante*.

JOSÉ ORTEGA Y GASSET

The Dehumanization of Art

Artistic Art

What do the majority of people call esthetic pleasure? What happens when they like a work of art, for instance, a theatrical production? The answer is beyond doubt; the people like a drama when they have succeeded in becoming interested in the human destinies which are proposed to them. The loves, hatreds, sorrows, and joys of the characters move their hearts. They become at one with what they see, as if the characters were real human beings. And they say that the work is "good" when it succeeds in producing the quantity of illusion necessary for the fictitious characters to be worth as much as living persons. In lyric poetry they will look for the loves and sorrows of the man who throbs under the poet. In painting they will be attracted by pictures of men and women with whom they think in some sense it would be interesting to live. A picture of a landscape will appear "pretty" to them when the real landscape portrayed in it deserves, because of its loveliness or sentimental appeal, to be visited on some excursion.

This means that for the majority of people esthetic pleasure is not a spiritual attitude different in essence from that which is usually adopted in the remainder of their lives. It is only distinguished from the latter in nonessential qualities: it is perhaps less utilitarian, more intense, and without painful consequences. But in the last analysis the objects with which art occupies itself are the same objects that appear in daily existence: human figures and passions. And they will call art the ensemble of means through which they are put into contact with interesting human things. Thus they will tolerate artistic forms properly so called, irrealities, fantasies, so long as these do not interfere with their perception of human forms and situations. As soon as the purely esthetic elements predominate, and the people cannot grasp the history of John and Mary, they are bewildered; they do not know what to do in the presence of the stage settings, the book, or the painting. This reaction is natural; for they know of no other attitude than the practical towards external realities, that attitude which makes us become impassioned and compels us to intervene sentimentally. A work of art which does not invite them to such an intervention leaves them with no role to perform.

Now in this respect we should come to a perfect and clear understanding. To enjoy and to suffer with human destinies, which perhaps the work of art is presenting to us, is something very different from true artistic enjoyment. Furthermore, these sympathies toward the human element in the work of art are in principle incompatible with strict esthetic delight.

This is a matter of optics which is very simple. In order to see an object we have appropriately to readjust our organs of vision. If our visual readjustment is inadequate we cannot see the object or else we do not see it well. Let the reader imagine that we are now looking at a garden through a windowpane. Our eyes will be readjusted in such a way that the ray of vision goes right through the glass to be fixed upon the flowers and the foliage. Since the goal of vision is the garden, whereupon the visual ray is cast, our glance will penetrate through the glass without stopping to perceive it. The clearer the glass is, the less we will see. But then making an effort we may withdraw attention from the garden; and by retracting the ocular ray, we may fixate it upon the glass. Then the garden will disappear in our eyes and we will see instead only some confused masses of color which seem to stick to the glass. Consequently, to see the garden and to see the glass in the windowpane are two incompatible operations: one excludes the other and each requires a different ocular readjustment.

Likewise, he who in the work of art aims to be moved by the fate of John and Mary, or of Tristan and Iseult, and readjusts to them his spiritual perception will not be able to see the work of art. The misfortunes of Tristan are only such, and consequently they will be able to move us insofar as they may be taken for reality. But the artistic object is artistic only insofar as it is not real. In order to enjoy the equestrian portrait of Charles V by Titian, it is an unavoidable condition that we should not see there Charles V in person, authentic and living, but that we should see instead a portrait, a known real image, a fiction. The man portrayed and his portrait are two objects completely different: either we get interested in one or the other. If, in the former, "we live with" Charles V; if in the latter, "we contemplate" an artistic object as such.

Now, the majority of people are unable to adjust their attention to the glass and the transparency which is the work of art; instead they penetrate through it to wallow passionately in the human reality to which the work of art refers. If they are invited to let loose their prey and fix their attention upon the work of art itself, they will say that they see nothing in it, because, indeed, they see no human realities there, but only artistic transparencies, pure essences.

During the nineteenth century artistic processes have been too impure. Artists reduced to a minimum the strict artistic elements and made their works consist almost entirely of the fiction of human realities. In this sense we must say that in one way or another all the normal art of the last century was realistic. Beethoven and Wagner were realists. So were Chateaubriand and Zola. Seen from the heights of today, romanticism and realism approach each other and reveal their common realistic roots.

Products of this nature are only partially works of art, or artistic objects. To enjoy them it is not necessary to have any power to adjust one's self to the essential and transparent qualities which constitute esthetic sensibility. It is enough to possess human sensibility and to allow the anxieties and joys of others to echo within one's self. One can understand then why the art of the nineteenth century has been so popular: it was made for the undifferentiated masses in proportion to the fact that it is not art, but an extract from life itself. It should be remembered that in the case of all epochs which have had two different types of art, one for the minority and one for the majority, the latter was always realistic. For example, during the Middle Ages, corresponding to the binary structure of society which was divided into castes, the nobles and the plebeians, there were two types of art, a noble art which was "conventional," "idealistic," that is to say artistic, and a popular art which was realistic and satirical.

We are not going to discuss now whether a pure art is possible. Perhaps it is not, but the reasons which may lead us to such a negation are long and difficult. Perhaps it is better, then, to leave the theme intact. Moreover, it really does not matter for the subject we are now talking about. Even if pure art is impossible there is no doubt room for a tendency to purify art. This tendency will lead towards a progressive elimination of the human, all too human elements, which dominate romantic and naturalistic production. In this process the point will be reached when the human element of the work of art will be so scanty that it will be hardly visible. Then we shall have an object which will be perceived only by the individual who possesses the peculiar gift of artistic sensibility. It will be an art for artists and not for the masses of the people. It will be an art of caste and not a democratic art. This is why the new art divides people into two classes of individuals: those who understand it and those who do not; that is, the artists and those who are not. New art is artistic art. . . .

Some Scraps of Phenomenology

An illustrious man is dying. His wife is by his bedside. A doctor counts the pulsations of the dying man. In the background of the room there are two people, a newspaper reporter, who attends the obituary scene, by reason of his business, and a painter whom chance has brought there. The wife, the doctor, the newspaper reporter, and the painter are witnessing the very same fact. Nevertheless, this one fact, the agony of the man, offers itself to each one of them in a different aspect. So different are these aspects that they scarcely have a common nucleus. The difference between what the fact is for the woman, pierced by sorrow, and for the painter who contemplatively gazes at the scene, is so great that perhaps it would be more exact to say the wife and the painter witness two facts entirely different.

It happens then that the same reality breaks into many diverging realities when it is seen from different points of view. And here we may ask which of these multiple realities is the true one, the authentic one. Our decision will be arbitrary, no matter what it may be. Our preference for one or the other can only be based upon caprice. All of these realities are equivalent. Each one is the authentic one for its corresponding point of view. The only thing we can do is to classify these points of view and to select among them the one that may appear to us as more normal, or more spontaneous. Thus we may reach a notion not at all absolute, but at least practical and normative of reality.

The clearest way to differentiate the points of view of the four persons who attend the death scene consists of measuring their dimensions: the spiritual distance at which each one is from the common fact—that of the agony. To the wife of the dying man this distance is at a minimum, so much so that it is almost nonexistent. The lamentable event so tortures her heart and occupies such a large portion of her soul that it fuses with her own person; or, said in an inverse manner, the woman intervenes in the scene, she is a part of it. For us to see anything so that a given fact may be contemplated, we must set it at some remove from ourselves, so that it ceases to form a living part of our own being. Thus the woman does not attend the scene, but is within it. She does not contemplate it, but rather she lives it.

The doctor is a little more distant. This is a professional case for him. He does not intervene in the situation with the impassioned and blind anxiety which floods the soul of the poor woman, and yet his profession compels him to be seriously interested in what is happening. He feels towards it a certain responsibility, and perhaps his prestige is at stake. Consequently, even if he participates less intimately than the wife, he also takes part in the event. The scene overtakes him and drags him into its dramatic core, grasping him not by his heart, but by a professional fragment of his personality. He also lives in the sad happening, although with emotions which do not spring forth from his cordial self, but from the professional periphery of his being.

If we now place ourselves in the point of view of the newspaper reporter we will notice that we have moved away greatly from that painful reality. We have moved away so far that we have lost all sentimental contacts with the fact in question. The newspaper reporter is there like the doctor, compelled by his profession, not by any spontaneous and human impulse, but while the profession of the doctor compels him to intervene in the event, that of the newspaper reporter compels him precisely not to intervene: he must limit himself only to see. For him the fact, properly speaking, is a mere scene, a mere spectacle which he may describe later on in the columns of his newspaper. He does not share sentimentally in what is happening there; spiritually he is out and free from the event; he does not live it, but he contemplates it. And yet he contemplates it with the preoccupation of a person who has to tell it later on to his readers. He would like to interest them, to move them, and if possible, to make them shed tears as if they were transitory relatives of the deceased. At school he had read Horace's prescription: *Si vis me flere, dolendum est primum ipsi tibi.*[1] Docile to Horace, the newspaper man tries to feign an emotion in order to try later on to adapt it to his journalism. And thus it happens although he does not live the scene "he feigns" to live it.

Lastly the painter, indifferent, merely glances sidewise at the human reality. What happens there does not worry him; he is, as they say, miles away from the event. His attitude is purely contemplative and one might even say that he does not contemplate the event in its integrity; the painful internal sense of it is left outside the field of his perception. He pays attention only to externals, to lights and shadows, to chromatic values. With the painter we have reached a point of maximum distance and of minimum sentimental intervention.

The unavoidable heaviness of this analysis would be compensated if it should enable us to speak clearly about a scale of spiritual distances between reality and ourselves. In this scale the degrees of proximity are equivalent to the degrees of sentimental participation in the event: the degrees of distance, on the contrary, signify the degrees of liberation through which we objectify the real event, thus converting it into a pure theme for contemplation. Situated at one of these extremes, we face a certain aspect of the world—persons, things, situations, that is to say, reality as being "lived": from the other extreme, on the other hand, we see everything in its aspects "as contemplated reality."

Upon arriving at this point, we must introduce a consideration which is essential to esthetics, without which it is not easy to penetrate into the physiology of art, whether it be old or new. Among those diverse aspects of reality which correspond to the various points of view, there is one from which are derived all the others and which is the base of them all. That is the "lived" reality. If there were no one to live in pure surrender and frenzy the agony of a man, the doctor would not be interested in it, the readers would not understand the pathetic gestures of the newspaper reporter who writes up the event, and the picture in which the painter represents a man in his bed, surrounded by doleful figures, would be unintelligible to us. The same we could say of any other object, whether it be a person or thing. The original form of an apple is that which the apple possesses when we are ready to eat it. In all the other possible forms which an apple may have, as for instance, the form given to it by an artist of the year 1600 in which he has combined it with a baroque ornament, the form that it represents in a still-life picture by Cézanne, or in that elemental metaphor which compares it to the cheek of a girl, the apple preserves more or less its original aspect. A picture or a poem where no "lived" forms were remaining would be unintelligible, that is to say, would not be anything, as a speech would be nothing if all of its words had been stripped of their habitual meanings.

This means that in the scale of realities there corresponds to the "lived" reality a primacy which compels us to consider it the reality par excellence. Instead of "lived" reality we might call it human reality. The painter who witnesses contemplatively the scene of the agony seems to be "inhuman." Let us say, then, that the human point of view is that in which we "live" the situations, persons, or things. And vice versa, all realities—woman, landscape, event—are human when they offer us the aspect which is usually "lived" by us. . . .

The Dehumanization of Art

With tremendous speed young art has diversified itself in a great number of directions and divergent attempts. There is nothing quite so easy as to emphasize the differences between some productions and others. But this emphasis on what is different and specific will become empty, if we fail to determine beforehand the common background which affirms itself in all these works, in such various ways, indeed, that at times they are even at cross purposes. Already it was taught by our good old Aristotle that different things are differentiated by that which makes them similar, that is by a certain common character in them. Because all bodies have color, we notice that some have a different color than others. Species are precisely specifications of the genus and we understand them only when we see, revealed in their diverse forms, their common patrimony.

The particular directions of young art are of little interest to me and with very few exceptions particular works of art possess even less interest. But in turn, my valuation of the new artistic products should not be of interest to anyone. Writers who reduce their inspiration to express their esteem or lack of esteem for works of art should not write. They really are not worthy of this difficult task. It is just as the Spanish critic "Clarín" (Leopold Alas) used to say about certain clumsy playwrights, that it would be better for them to devote their efforts to other tasks, as for instance to establishing a family. And if they already have one? Well, then, let them establish another.

What matters now is the indubitable presence in the world of a new esthetic sensibility. This new sensibility is found not only among the creators of art, but also among people for whom art is created. As distinguished from the plurality of special directions and individual works, this sensibility represents what is generic, and productive of the divergent tendencies. This is what seems to be of interest to define.

And searching for the generic and characteristic note of all new productions, I find that it is the tendency to dehumanize art. The preceding paragraphs give to this formula a certain precision.

Let us compare a picture in the new manner with one in the manner of 1860. We will begin, in a simple way, by comparing the objects represented in both of them, perhaps a man, a house, a mountain. Soon we notice that the artist of 1860 has tried first of all to give the objects in his picture the same air and aspect that they have outside of it when they form a part of the "lived" or human reality. . . . The man, the house, and the mountain are immediately recognized as such. They are old, habitual friends. In the recent picture, on the contrary, it is hard for us to recognize them. The spectator perhaps thinks that the painter has failed to achieve the likeness. But it may be also that the picture of 1860 was "badly painted"—that is to say, between the objects in the picture and the corresponding ones outside of it, there may be a great distance, an important divergence. And yet, whatever be the distance, the mistakes of the traditional artist point toward the "human object." They are failures on the road towards it. . . . In the new picture the contrary happens: it is not that the painter errs, nor that his deviations from the "natural" (natural=human) fail to reach it. The fact is that they point to a road leading away from the "human" object in the opposite direction.

The painter, far from trying, more or less clumsily, to move toward reality, seems to have evaded it. He seems to have tried gallantly to deform it, to break its human aspect, to dehumanize it. With the things represented in the traditional picture, we might live in the imagination. Many Englishmen have fallen in love with Mona Lisa. With things represented in the new pictures, it is impossible to live: on stripping them of their aspects as "lived" realities, the painter has broken the bridges and burned the ships which might transport us to our habitual world. He leaves us locked up in an abstruse universe, he forces us to associate with objects with which there is no possible human association. Thus we have to improvise a new form of association completely different from the usual one which allows us to live with things: we have to create and to invent original acts that are adequate to those unusual figures. This new life, a life invented after the annulment of spontaneous life, is precisely what we may call artistic understanding and pleasure. This life does not lack in sentiment and passion but evidently these passions and sentiments belong to a psychic flora very different from that which covers the landscapes of our primary and human life. They are secondary emotions which those ultra-objects provoke in the artist that is within us. They are sentiments specifically esthetic.

One may say that such a result could be more simply obtained by putting aside totally those human forms—man, house, mountain—and building figures completely original. But this is in the first place impractical. Perhaps in the most abstract ornamental line there vibrates as in disguise a tenacious reminiscence of certain "natural" forms. In the second place—and this is most important—the art of which we are talking is not only inhuman because it does not contain human things but it actively consists of the dehumanizing operation. In its flight away from the human it does not pay so much attention to the term "ad quem," the strange fauna to which it arrives, as it does to the term "a quo," the human aspect which it destroys. The thing is not to paint something completely different from a man, a house, or a mountain, but to paint a man with the least possible semblance of a man, a house which preserves of its nature only what is strictly necessary for us to witness its metamorphosis, a cone which miraculously springs forth from what was previously a mountain, as the snake sheds its skin. Esthetic pleasure for the new artist emanates from the victory over the "human": for that reason it is necessary in each case to make concrete such victory and to show the strangled victim.

Ordinary people think that it is very easy to flee away from reality when indeed it is the most difficult thing in the world. It is easy to say or to paint a thing which lacks sense completely, that is unintelligible: for this it will be enough to put alongside each other, as the Dadaists have done, words without connection, or to draw lines casually. But to be able to construct something that is not a copy of the "natural" and which nevertheless possesses some substance implies the most sublime gift.

"Reality" constantly waylays the artist to prevent his evasion. What a great cunningness the flight of genius presupposes. It must be like an inverted Ulysses who escapes from his daily Penelope and sails among reefs towards the bewitching realm of Circe. When he succeeds in escaping for a moment the perpetual waylaying of reality, let us not blame the artist for his gesture of pride—that brief gesture that makes him look like St. George with the dragon conquered at his feet.

An Invitation to Understand

In the works of art preferred during the last century there is always a nucleus of "lived" reality which is like the substance of the esthetic body. Upon it art operates, and its operation is reduced to polishing that human nucleus, to giving it a coat of varnish, a certain brilliance, composure, and reverberation. To the great majority of people such structure in the work of art is the most natural, is the only possible one. To them art is the mirror of life, it is nature seen through a temperament, it is the representation of the human, and so on. But with no less deep conviction, the young support a contrary theory. Why should the old be right against the young if the future will always make the young right against the old? Above all, it is good not to become indignant or shout. . . .

Our most deeply rooted and indubitable convictions are always the most suspicious. They constitute our limitations, our boundaries, our prisons. Life is of no consequence if a formidable eagerness to widen its frontiers does not stamp within its confines. A person lives in proportion to his longing for more life. All obstinacy in staying within the familiar horizon signifies weakness, the decadence of vital energy. The horizon is a biological line, a living organ of our very being; as long as we enjoy plenitude, the horizon migrates, it becomes widened, it undulates elastically almost to the rhythm of our respiration. On the other hand, when the horizon becomes fixed as in a shell it is because we come into the fold of senility.

It is not so evident as the academicians suppose that the work of art should perforce consist of a human nucleus whose hair the muses can comb and polish. This is, to begin with, to make art consist of the use of cosmetics. I have already said that the perception of the "lived" reality, and the perception of the artistic form, are in principle incompatible because each requires a different adjustment of our organs of perception. An art which would give us the opportunity to take that double glance would be a cross-eyed art. The art of the nineteenth century has often been such; that is why its artistic products, far from representing a normal type of art, are perhaps the greatest anomaly in the history of taste. All the great epochs of art have avoided the "human" as the center of gravity in their creations. And the imperative of exclusive realism which has ruled over the sensibility of the past century signifies precisely a monstrosity without equal in esthetic evolution. From which it results that the new inspiration, so extravagant in appearance, comes back at least in one point to the royal road of art. Because this road is called "The Will to Style." Well now: to stylize is to deform the real, to derealize. Stylization implies dehumanization. And vice versa there is no other way to dehumanize than to stylize. Realism, on the other hand, inviting the artist to follow submissively the form of things, invites him not to have style. That is why the Zurbarán enthusiast, not knowing what to say, says that his pictures have "character," just as Lucas or Sorolla, Dickens or Galdos have character but not style. On the other hand the eighteenth century, which possesses so little character, possesses style to the point of saturation.

—*La Deshumanización del Arte* (1925)

Note

1. "If you wish me to weep, it is first necessary for you to grieve." (Editor's note.)

THEODOR LIPPS

Empathy, Inner Imitation, and Sense-Feelings[1]

I direct my attention in the following to empathy in general. What I shall say applies to empathic projection into definite sorts of objects, especially into the movements, postures, and positions of man, whether real or represented as in sculpture; also into the forms of architecture.

Esthetic enjoyment is a feeling of pleasure or joy in each individual case colored in some specific way and ever different in each new esthetic object —a pleasure caused by viewing the object. In this experience the esthetic object is always sensuous, that is, sensuously perceived or imagined, and it is only this. I have a feeling of joy before a beautiful object: this means that I have this feeling in viewing the sensuous perception or image, in which form the beautiful object immediately presents itself to me. I have it while I view this object, that is, bring it into clear attention, apperceive it. But only the sensuous appearance of the esthetic object, for example, of the work of art, is attended to in esthetic contemplation. It alone is the "object" of the esthetic enjoyment; it is the only thing that stands "opposite" me as something distinct from myself and with which I, and my feeling of pleasure, enter into some "relationship." It is through this relationship that I am joyous or pleased, in short, enjoying myself.

The question of the "object" of esthetic enjoyment is one thing, the question of the *ground* of it is quite another. The sensuous appearance of the beautiful thing is certainly the object of esthetic enjoyment, but just as certainly it is not the *ground* of it. Rather, the cause of esthetic enjoyment is myself, or the ego; exactly the same ego that feels joyous or pleased "in view" of the object or "opposite" it.

This means first of all that I may not only feel joyful or pleased, but may feel otherwise stimulated. There is no doubt that I feel myself, among other things, striving or willing, exerting or bestirring myself. In such endeavor or exertion I feel myself resisting or overcoming obstacles, perhaps also yielding to them; I have a sense of reaching a goal, of satisfying my striving and my will, I feel my efforts succeeding. In short, I feel a multifarious "inner activity." And in all this I feel vigorous, free, certain, resilient, perhaps proud and the like. This sort of feeling is always the ground of esthetic enjoyment.

One can see that this ground occupies a middle position between the object of the esthetic enjoyment and the enjoyment itself. Let us stress this first: The above mentioned feelings have not, like the enjoyment, the beautiful thing for an object. I feel in the esthetic contemplation of the beautiful object in some way vigorously active, or free, or proud. And then, I do not feel vigorously active and so forth, *in view* of the object or *opposite* it, but I feel thus *in* it.

Likewise, this feeling of activity is not *the object of enjoyment,* that is, of my pleasure in the beautiful object. As certainly as I feel joy in view of the *sensuous* object, which I call beautiful, just as certainly I do not feel pleasure in response *to* the experienced activity, the power, etc., or *in view* of this activity, of the power, etc. This activity is not objective. It is not anything that stands opposite me. Just as I do not feel active over against the object, but *in* the object, so I do not experience joy over against my activity, but in it. I feel happy or blessed *in* it.

To be sure, my own activity may become objective to me, namely, when it is no longer my present activity but when I contemplate it in retrospect. But then it is no longer immediately experienced, but only remembered in imagination. And thus is it objective. This imagined activity, or more generally this imagined self, can then also be the object of my joy. But this we are not discussing. We are now only concerned with the immediately experienced activity, the success, the power, freedom and so forth.

The term "object" of joy is taken here in an entirely restricted sense. It may be possible to take it less strictly; then the "object" of joy might be that *from* which I derive joy, and this means that to which the joy is related and which at the same time is the reason for the joy.

In this sense the question about the object of esthetic enjoyment may be answered in a twofold manner. On the one hand it can be said: Esthetic pleasure has no object at all. The esthetic enjoyment is not enjoyment of an object, but enjoyment of a self. It is an immediate feeling of a value that is lodged in oneself. But this is not a feeling that is related to an object. Rather, its characteristic consists in this—that there is no separation in it between my pleased ego and that with which I am pleased; in it both are one and the same self, the immediately experienced ego.

On the other hand, it may be pointed out that after all, in esthetic enjoyment, this sense of value is objectified. In contemplating the strong, proud, free human form standing before me I do not feel strong, proud and free as such, or in my own place, or in my own body, but I feel myself thus in the contemplated form and only in it.

And accordingly, may I not say also this: The esthetic enjoyment has an object that is at the same time its ground. I can even give to this object a twofold characterization. First, the object in question is the strong, proud, free ego; not the ego as such, however, but just so far as it objectifies itself, that is, so far as it is bound up with the sensuously perceived figure. Secondly, the object of esthetic enjoyment is this sensuously perceived, this observed figure; not the figure as such, however, but the figure so far as I feel and experience it in myself, this strong, proud, free ego.

This specific characteristic of esthetic pleasure has now been defined. It consists in this: that it is the enjoyment of an object, which however, so far as it is the object of *enjoyment,* is not an object, but myself. Or, it is the enjoyment of the ego, which however, so far as it is esthetically enjoyed, is not myself but objective.

Now, all this is included in the concept of empathy. It constitutes the very meaning of this concept. Empathy is the fact here established, that the object is myself and by the very same token this self of mine is the object. Empathy is the fact that the antithesis between myself and the object disappears, or rather does not yet exist.

How is empathy possible? An answer to this question presupposes complete clearness about the sharp distinction between the content or object of feeling (*Empfindungsinhalt*), on the one hand, and the immediately intuited attitudes or feelings of the subject (*Ichqualitäten oder Gefühlen*), on the other hand. But only one side of this antithesis shall be here considered.

I have the sensation of a color. This color belongs to a sensuously perceived object. Or, I feel hunger and thirst. These feelings, these contents of my sensation belong to my body. They are felt as determinations of this sensuously perceived thing, as a modification of the physical organism.

Different is the doing or the activity, the endeavor, the striving, the succeeding, that I feel. These belong to the ego; more than that, they are the ego or constitute it: I feel *myself* active. They absolutely do not belong to a sensuously perceived object or to one remembered in imagination, in short to no object that stands apart from me.

For this very reason these subjective qualities may belong to any material object. They belong, and with them the self, or the self belongs, and with it these qualities, to that object with which I feel myself and my subjective states inextricably bound, whenever I stop to contemplate the object. But we shall determine more definitely these circumstances and with them the meaning of empathy.

I stretch out my arm or I hold my arm extended. Doing this I feel active, that is, I feel myself striving, endeavoring, and feel my striving succeed or gratify itself.

Here I can say I feel myself active, striving, endeavoring, attaining the end—in my arm. But this activity does not, in the full sense, take place in the arm, that is, it is not tied up with the contemplation of the arm or the contemplated arm. Rather, it is connected with my mood if I extend my arm from caprice, or with some purpose in mind if I extend my arm for a certain purpose. And the caprice or the purposefulness is something different from my contemplation of the arm or from myself who is contemplating. . . . It belongs to my personality as distinct from the contemplating self, or to my personality as object (*meiner "realen" Persönlichkeit*). This also implies that in this case my activity does not in the full sense "belong" to the extended arm. It is in a certain way, but not esthetically, empathized[2] in it.

Now we change the situation. My arm is freely extended for a time. Then I feel a desire, an impulse, a "compulsion" to drop it. This desire originates in the arm. I feel it coming from it or from its extended position. Therefore it lies in it or has its ground in it. In this case, too, the striving is my striving. But just this striving of mine I feel in my arm. For this reason I can also say the arm strives downward. And when the arm sinks, then this striving of the arm is realized. The sinking is therefore *its* activity.

Let us complicate the conditions. Upon the extended hand lies a stone. I now feel this striving, which in this case, too, remains "my" striving, to be the result of the pressure of the stone or of the stone which exerts this pressure. Accordingly I now say: The stone strives. And when it falls, the falling is an activity of the stone itself. It falls of its own power.

Now, with these two cases we have come nearer to the esthetic empathy. But we have not yet reached it. Let us dwell in particular upon the first case. Here, too, my striving is not altogether a matter of the arm. I cannot say:

While I contemplate the arm and its extended position, and only as a result of my contemplation, does the striving spring into my consciousness. It springs also from something entirely different, namely, from the manner in which the continued extension of the arm affects me, from my feeling of discomfort. And this again is a factor entirely different from the contemplated self. The striving, so far as it comes from the arm, does not have its basis in the arm; rather, it is *motivated* within me. It is not my striving in the arm, but my striving in view of the arm, or my striving directed upon the arm from without. Analogous is the downward pull of the stone.[3]

Now I substitute someone else's arm for my own. I *see* another person's arm extended. Let the manner of extension be perceptibly free, easy, sure, proud. Or more generally, I see a person perform some kind of vigorous, nimble, free, or bold movements. Let these be the object of my concentrated attention.

Now I again feel a striving. Possibly I realize this striving. I imitate the movements. In doing so I feel active. I feel the effort, the resistance to obstacles, the act of overcoming, the joy of succeeding. I feel all this actually. I do not merely imagine things of this sort.

Here again two possibilities present themselves. The imitation may be voluntary, that is, I, too, should like to have the feeling of freedom, assurance, and pride, which the other person has.

In this case I have again gotten far away from esthetic empathy. The immediate ground of my striving and doing is in this case not the observed movement, but this wish. And this wish is again something different from the observed arm and the merely contemplative self.

Now, at last, let us assume that the imitation is involuntary. The more I am absorbed in the contemplation of the seen movement the more involuntary will be the imitation. Conversely, the more involuntary the action is, the more is the observer *wholly* in the seen movement. But now, when I am completely engrossed by the contemplation of the movement, I am completely carried away from that which I am doing, namely, from the movement which I actually execute, from all that is going on in my body; I am no longer conscious of my outward imitation.

Nevertheless, in this state, the sense of striving and effort persists in my consciousness; there remains the feeling of activity, of effort, of inner accomplishment, of success. There remains the consciousness of "inner imitation."

Now this inner imitation takes place, for my consciousness, solely in the observed object. The feeling of striving, of effort, of success is no longer bound up with my movement, but merely with the objective bodily movement observed by me.

But this does not suffice. My inner activity in this imitation is exclusively bound up in a twofold sense with the observed object. First—the activity which I feel, I experience as derived entirely from the contemplation of the perceived movement. It is immediately and necessarily connected with it; and it is solely connected with it.

Secondly—the *object* of my activity is not my own activity, which is different from the observed one, but only this activity which I behold. I feel active in the movement or in the moving figure, and through projecting myself into it I feel myself striving and performing this same movement. There is no other way; because under the assumed conditions there cannot be any other movement but the observed one as the object of my consciousness.

In a word, I am now with my feeling of activity entirely and wholly in the moving figure. Even spatially, if we can speak of the spatial extent of the ego, I am in its place. I am transported into it. I am, so far as my consciousness is concerned, entirely and wholly identical with it. Thus feeling myself active in the observed human figure, I feel also in it free, facile, proud. This is esthetic imitation and this imitation is at the same time esthetic empathy.

Here the whole emphasis must be laid on the "identity" which exists for my consciousness. This must be taken in the strictest sense.

In voluntary imitation, I see the movement and have knowledge of the way the performer feels. I have a mental image (*Vorstellung*) of the activity which the other experiences, of his freedom and pride. On the other hand I also experience my own movement and feel my activity, my freedom and pride, etc.

Contrariwise, in esthetic imitation this opposition is absolutely done away with. The two are simply one. The mere mental image no longer exists; my actual feeling has taken its place. And it is just because of this that I feel myself performing this movement in the other's movement.

In this "esthetic imitation" the facts seem to be analogous to what occurs in an unimitative movement of my own. The only difference seems to be that I now am conscious of experiencing and performing a movement which in fact, and for subsequent reflection, is the movement of another.

But in this comparison the most essential difference is overlooked. It is true that in both cases my inner activity—my striving and success, or in other words, the experienced satisfaction of my striving—is my own activity. But in the two cases it is not the same self that acts. In the unimitative movement my "real" self acts, my total personality as it is actually disposed at the time, with all its feelings, fancies, thoughts, and especially the motive or inner occasion from which the movement springs. In the esthetic imitation, quite differently, the self is an ideal one. This term is not clear. This "ideal" self, too, is real. But it is not the real "practical" self. It is the contemplative self, lingering and merged in the contemplation of the object. . . .

So far we have thought of esthetic imitation not only as an inward but also as an outward activity, in the sense that I overtly imitate the observed activity. But this outward consummation of the movements may not take place.

For this there are several reasons; for example, regard for good manners. But the chief hindrance is the practical absurdity and uselessness, or the actual impracticality of the movements.

For instance, from my seat in the theater I observe a dance which is performed upon the stage. In this case it is impossible for me to take part in the dance. Nor do I have the desire to dance; I am not in the mood for it. Both my situation and attitude prevent any bodily movements. But this does not eliminate my inner activity, the striving and satisfaction I feel as I contemplate the movements enacted before me.

To be sure, every striving is by its nature a striving after the realization of its end. But this realization is not lacking here. I experience the actual movement. I see it before me; not as my own, of course. But in this lies the peculiarity of esthetic imitation, that the alien activity takes the place of one's own.

At this point one may remark: The realization of a striving directed towards a bodily movement certainly does not consist in having a visual image of the movement, but consists in the experiencing of kinesthetic sensations, such as the sensations of muscle tension, friction of joints and so forth, as they occur in movements.

I shall reply to this remark by more precisely defining what has been said before. . . .

It lies in the nature of esthetic imitation that it aims chiefly at arousing the activity of the self. In the instinctive urge for self-activity lies its ultimate basis. But also it lies in the nature of the impulse to such imitation, that the desire for self-activity can be satisfied in the contemplation of the very movement that releases the desire for imitation.

So this desire needs no further satisfaction, and in particular not the satisfaction afforded by the kinesthetic events occurring in one's own body. The contemplation of the observed movement awakens the tendency to a corresponding self-activity; and by corresponding we mean that which would be connected with the execution of such a movement in my own person. And this tendency is at the same time realized in the act of contemplation. The "absorption" liberates the above-mentioned tendency or removes in me the obstacles to its realization. Now, every tendency is realized when the obstacles to its realization are removed, or, speaking in positive terms, when the tendency is free, that is left to itself. For this is the meaning of tendency. . . .

In the perception of the other person's movement, I say, the tendency of the "corresponding" self-activity is awakened and satisfied. And this is why the satisfaction through the kinesthetic experiences is no longer needed. . . .

In esthetic imitation I become progressively less aware of muscular tensions or of sense-feelings in general the more I surrender in contemplation to the esthetic object. All such preoccupations disappear entirely from my consciousness. I am completely and wholly carried away from this sphere of my experience.

And it is not only so, it must be so. Sense-feelings are objective experiences and these of necessity compete with other objective experiences. And this means, for example, that the feelings of my bodily states must disappear from consciousness to the degree in which I am engrossed in the contemplation of the esthetic object—to which the states of my body simply cannot belong.

But this turning of consciousness away from the states of my body excludes certain possibilities: that the feeling of my bodily condition is identical with the feeling of activity which I obtain in esthetic contemplation; that the joy which I feel in view of the esthetic object is in truth, wholly or partially, joy in these bodily states; and lastly that my joy in the esthetic object *consists* wholly or in part in the feeling of these states. . . .

The beauty of an object is every time the beauty of this object and never the charm of anything that is not this beautiful object, or part of it. This means in particular that pleasure in the states of my body—a thing so different from the contemplated object and perhaps spatially far removed from it—cannot be felt by me as pleasure in this *object*. Pleasure from physical states is pleasure which I feel while I am paying attention to these states. To say that something is pleasurable means simply that I have a feeling of pleasure by being inwardly oriented towards it. But the pleasure which I feel while I am paying attention to my physical states or the processes in my physical organs cannot be identical, either wholly or in part, with the joy which I feel when I do not pay attention to the processes in my physical organs, but devote my whole attention to the esthetic object. In short, A cannot equal non-A.

Empathy means, not a sensation in one's body, but feeling something, namely, oneself, into the esthetic object.

Hitherto I have assumed that the object of the esthetic contemplation is a human movement, posture, or mien. But empathy is of the same nature in other cases, for example, in the contemplation of architectural forms. In viewing a large hall I feel an inner "expansion," my heart "expands"; I have this peculiar sense of what is happening within me. Connected with it are muscle-tensions, perhaps those involved in the expansion of the chest. To be sure, they do not exist for my consciousness, so long as my attention is directed to the spacious hall. But it is possible that this fact may not prevent an esthetician from confusing the feeling of inner expansion with this sensation of the body expanding with its muscle tensions. For in this case, as also when we refer to the thirst for water and the thirst for revenge and in very many other instances, common usage—and for good reasons—employs the same terms.

But all this means simply confusion of meanings. As a matter of truth, so far as I am concerned the sensations of my own bodily state are entirely absent in esthetic contemplation.

But perchance the sense-feeling which I impute to the *object* of contemplation, have some significance for esthetic enjoyment. This I must deny no less emphatically. When I see the sculptured image of a man in the act of rising, the sense-feelings which a real man would have who thus arises, do not exist for my esthetic contemplation, any more than my own sense-feelings so exist. What I immediately intuit in the plastic form is its willing, the power, the pride. Only this lies for my contemplation immediately in the contemplated object. And to the esthetic object belongs absolutely nothing but what lies immediately in the object of contemplation. The thought that also the sense-feeling would unquestionably appear in such a man if he were a real man, is an ingredient added by my reflection.

For the rest, such sense-feelings are simply uninteresting . . . unless they happen to be tormenting. And in the latter case it may also happen that I am conscious of them. Only this means the end of pure esthetic enjoyment.

If, for instance, I see a dancer dancing on tiptoe, my impression of the disagreeable feeling which she must have does intrude. Consequently I am hurled out of the state of esthetic contemplation. Not because of the unpleasantness of the feeling, but because of the feeling. Sorrow is also disagreeable, but the sorrow that I see in a figure does not arrest the esthetic contemplation. This sorrow is empathized.

A representation of a hungry man is not a representation of hunger; simply the manner in which he feels is represented. In esthetic contemplation I participate only in this emotional phase. But that the physical disturbance of hunger is ordinarily the cause of such a state of mind is an interpretation dictated by reason.

In short, sense-feelings, of whatever kind they may be, do not in any way enter into esthetic contemplation and into esthetic enjoyment. It absolutely belongs to the nature of esthetic contemplation to eliminate them.

And it is the duty of scientific esthetics and necessary for its sound development, that it gradually recover from this disease of preoccupation with sense-feelings.

—*Archiv für die gesamte Psychologie,* Vol. I (1903; translated by Max Schertel and Melvin Rader)

Notes

1. *Einfühlung, innere Nachahmung, und Organempfindungen. "Organempfindungen,"* here translated as "sense-feelings," refers to the feelings localized in the body, to kinesthetic sensations, motor disturbances, physical cravings such as hunger, and so forth. (Editor's note.)

2. *Eingefühlt;* that is, the feeling of my activity in the extended arm is empathy, but not esthetic empathy; because the activity is felt as motivated by the self, which is distinguished from the arm. The antithesis between self and object remains. (Editor's note.)

3. In other words, the discomfort involved in these two cases makes me aware of how I am being affected, and of the subjective motivation of my activities. I become conscious of myself as separate from the object (Editor's note.)

VIRGIL C. ALDRICH

Education for Aesthetic Vision

By "vision" I do not mean anything visionary; I mean visual perception. The remarks I make about this apply also in principle, *mutatis mutandis,* to the nonvisual arts, though literature presents special complications; but I bypass this larger question in this essay.

My main question here is (a) whether there is a way of perceiving or experiencing things that can be distinguished as esthetic perception, and (b) whether it can be taught. Along with the latter goes, of course, the question of how to teach it. I raise the first part of the question not so much for the sake of getting at its answer alone, but for the direction that this can give the second part.

For the general readers who are unaware of current Anglo-American philosophical treatments of the notion of esthetic experience, it will seem a waste of time to ask if there is any such thing, since the answer seems to them to be too obviously affirmative for words. It was also obvious, in the affirmative, for previous philosophers of art more in the swim of the great tradition of philosophy. In those old days, estheticians did not wonder whether there was esthetic perception, as distinguished, say, from scientific observation. They directed their efforts to finding out what it was, assuming its occurrence. But what they finally said about it, in terms of "psychic distance" or "disinterestedness" or "organizing into unity-in-diversity," was too vague or general to be very helpful either to critics-in-practice or to the new more analytical theorists who need to spell out the issues and the answers in greater detail. Moreover, the tendency in many quarters was to rest the case on empirical findings of psychology and that tended to an underestimation of what conceptual analysis can do in clearing matters up in esthetics which is, after all, in good part a philosophical discipline. A quite recent essay called "Structure in Art Education"[1] exhibits nicely the old and, to these new analysts, the wrong way of doing esthetics, including education for the experience of art.

My own view places me in the crossfire between these mighty opposites.[2] As I see it, the linguistic or conceptual–analytic approach has purged some of the smog from esthetic theory, while phenomenological description and explanation of the phenomena of esthetic experience substantiates or provides underpinning for some of the results of these conceptual analyses. Without some such noticing and talk about the phenomena of esthetic perception, one especially serious flaw is left in both the old and new treatments of issues in esthetics. This concerns the notion of illusion in art. I think first of Gombrich[3] on the side of psychologists who either make esthetic experience look more illusory (subjective) than it is, or (like Gombrich) take no clear stand about the issue. The conceptual analysts also bypass the question by leaning only on the notion of two ways of talking about things,[4] the physicalist way (objective?) and the esthetic way (subjective?). They leave unexplained why there should be this duality of descriptions. The question that this naturally raises, "Isn't the duality grounded in and prompted by something in the nature of things?" is left unanswered.

A simple, short, yet adequate answer to this question is at this point a consummation devoutly to be wished. Brevity and adequacy do not usually go together, but let me try. I shall attempt to illuminate and justify the impression that most of us have, in the full innocence of esthetic experience itself, that we are looking at "things" in the world about us and noticing their characteristics, not enjoying the "subjective effects" they are producing in us in a kind of illusion of out-thereness. Moreover, if this impression of something objective is done justice, another impression, namely, that one does not have the experience of things such as "esthetic objects" unless he looks at the things in the right or relevant way, will also get the recognition it deserves.

A good first pedagogical maneuver for this purpose, especially if people are being educated on the high-school or college level for esthetic perception and theory, is to present them with one of those trick drawings that can be seen as this or that. Perhaps the most famous is the duck-rabbit picture, but for my purpose here I prefer the diagram below.[5]

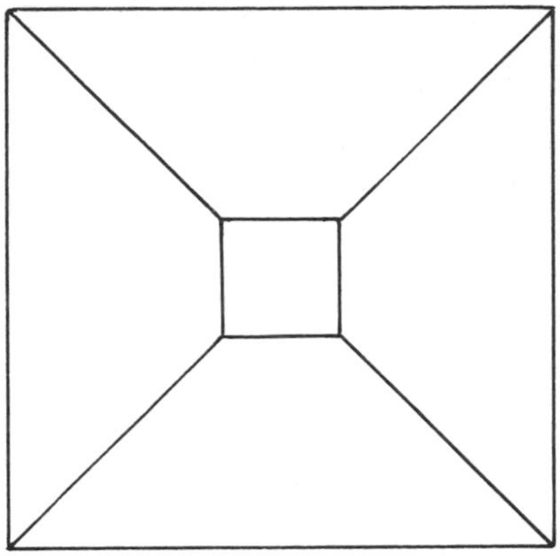

Let it be drawn on a fairly ample square cardboard—say two feet—and held up to the view of the class, and called simply a "thing." The diagonal lines are to extend to the very corners of this thing (cardboard), making its edges the square of the diagram.

Now, the point to be driven home is that, if questions are asked about the space-characteristics of this thing, the answers will be ambiguous unless suggestions are antecedently given as to how to perceive it. As simply encountered and noticed, it is pregnant only with potentials for this or that actual space-determination. This point can be made as follows.

Ask the class if it is flat. Someone in the back of the room may complain that he cannot tell from that distance. You hold it edgewise to his line of sight. He nods affirmatively. It is flat. Then you remind him that he was not thus simply seeing the flatness in question with the thing held edgewise but that his edgewise looking was an elementary visual test of flatness in the "physical" sense of the term. Another such test would involve getting closer for a better look at the surface of the thing, the surface being seen in this sense when its texture is visible (granularity, smoothness, etc.). But even this is not simply seeing that it is flat; it is testing it for flatness, physically speaking. You then ask how a still more "objective" observational test of physical flatness might be made with, say, a string. Someone says to stretch it taut and hold it across the surface. If the string touches the surface all the way across in various horizontal and vertical applications, the thing is flat. "Physically speaking," you add.

Now, you tell them, this thing is appearing as a physical object. Looked at this way, it is seen as a physical object. Its being a physical object is partly and basically defined by how it appears under such measuring looks or observations and correlating procedures. Moreover, this way of looking is called "observation"—for what this means in the language of science—a specially controlled way of looking that can become highly educated and exclusive by measuring techniques. The important thing to notice in this connection is that the space properties ("magnitudes") thus determined are not "simply" perceived. Indeed, they turn out in the end to be imperceptible characteristics of things as physical objects—that is, as scientific observation and thought become sophisticated. Thus it is that, in the end, things as physical objects are conceived to consist essentially of "primary qualities," meaning metrical or geometrical ones, all out of sight in the finished analysis. Space-characteristics, thus experienced and refined in thought, become the defining characteristics of anything as a physical object.

You conclude, "Let us call this general metrical way of appearing, determined by incipient comparison with external standards of straightness, flatness, etc., a 'categorial aspect' that things have as physical objects. This defines the category 'physical.' "

The point of this discourse is going to be, of course, that there is another categorially different way that the same thing may appear, another sort of categorial "aspect" or transformation it may undergo. The notion to be introduced is that of things appearing as esthetic objects.

Someone else in the class has said that the thing he sees is not flat, that it has depth, like a tunnel. Another says no; it protrudes towards the point of view, as does a lampshade looked down on from above.

The spokesman for physical flatness remarks that these are illusions. "Only under a certain way of looking called observation," you remind him. The thing *simpliciter* or in itself does not initially or necessarily appear that way. It is not intrinsically a physical object. One must take an educated and exclusive sort of look at it to perceive it in that physicalistic way—a look that excludes what he is calling illusory appearances and which in effect defines them as merely subjective impressions. Initially, the thing you are holding up is what might be called a "material thing," with "thing" (not "object") underscored and "material" meaning "potential for various determinations," as has been remarked. An object presupposes a subject experiencing it in a certain way, which correlation determines both the object and the mode of perception as being of a certain sort. "Thing" is more neutral and has no such correlations.

Now your job is to define the category of the esthetic as you have that of the physical. Some of your pupils are already looking, with unpremeditated artfulness, in the esthetically relevant way at the thing in question, so some of the stage-setting has already been done. If you accomplish your mission, you will have shown that the thing as an esthetic object and the correlated mode of perception have their own characteristic objectivity or outthereness, which is the aim of the classroom demonstration. Of course, one may go wrong or have "illusions" even in esthetic experience, but the term will no longer mean what it does in the physicalistic language of observation. (Drive home to the class that restriction on "observe.")

So somebody says the thing is not flat—the square within the square is in back or out front. But, you say, what if one sees the thing as a square suspended within a square frame? "Flat again," they say. But "again" is wrong here since they do not mean this time what the first fellow meant by "flat" who was for using a taut string to test for flatness. This is your occasion to introduce and define the notion of "plane of the picture." The suspended square is in this plane, so we say that the thing, viewed with this title in mind (square suspended in a frame), is flat. Now you get to the really important point.

What would a test of flatness in this sense be like? Or is the notion of testing nonsensical in such cases? The test by comparison with another thing functioning as an external standard is, to be sure, out of order. Only physical flatness is ascertained that way. Still, a check of some sort is feasible. One looks at the thing (now functioning as a picture) with the title in mind, and sees whether it is flat or not, in the relevant sense of "in the plane of the picture."

Whether it is to be flat or not, viewed thus, depends in the esthetic case on the relationships of elements all internal to the thing as esthetic object. There is no reference to an external standard or to any other thing for comparison. This explains the old notion of the "autonomy" of what is under esthetic consideration. The space-characteristics are determined by contours and—in most cases—colors. What these "do to one another" in their relationships is what fixes picture-space,[6] such that any check on the resultant space-characteristics will consist in an educated view of them as "aspects" of the composition of colors and contours.

Now that you are talking about colors as determinants of esthetic space, put some colors (pastels for convenience) into the figure, showing how a darker area bordering a brighter one tends to make the boundary between protrude like the corner of a solid by virtue of the relationship of the colors alone, without yet seeing the composition of them as any recognizable thing in particular.

It is this basic perception of related-linear-and-color-elements-as-space-structure that defines things as esthetic objects. It helps to define the general category of the "esthetic," contrasting it with that of the "physical." Purists or formalists in art, you will point out to the class, tend to compose with a view primarily to this space feature. A modern artist has said that painting is the art of hollowing out a surface, and even Whistler's portrait of his mother was done, as the first title he gave it shows, for the sake of structuring by colors (especially grays) and their interanimation, not for the likeness to anything outside the composition. Call this "first-order form."

Consideration of likeness, as in representational art, brings into focus the second principle of space-formation of things as esthetic objects and a second sense of both "aspect" and "seeing as." Briefly, this principle locates the elements of the composition in accordance with what they are seen as—parts of a landscape, limbs of a woman. Depth, solidarity, etc., may be achieved this way as well. Call this "second-order form." The artist generally composes under both the first and the second principles, in order to achieve a greater and richer formulation. Thus does he get beyond the excessive ambiguity of form of so meagre a figure as the one used in class for pedagogical purposes. Exciting tensions are revealed in the space of the composition by, say, a yellow that is seen as close to the plane of the picture by its intrinsic brightness (first-order form) but is also seen as a strip of sunlit sand in the background (second-order form).

All the while, you will have had the class looking, wide-eyed, at something. Drive home to them, at the end, that their esthetic vision is an objective experience of things in which they become aware of aspects—call such perceiving "prehending" to distinguish it from "observing"—and that these aspects are formations that things reveal in the esthetic view of them. Add that a work of art is such a thing, one that is especially designed to tempt the prehensive way of looking.

For example, consider how André Derain's "Still Life with a Jug" tempts the prehensive (esthetic) way of looking. It plainly shows and celebrates the materials (oil paints), especially in the parallel brush strokes typical of Cézanne, at the lower left and in the skillful overlaying of pigment on pigment. This work on the material shows up as sculptural or solid volumes, shot through, however, and softened with luminous color expanses, despite the suggestion of cubism. In this view of the painting, the light-brown triangular area left of the dark turquoise of the jug protrudes toward the plane of the picture. But the painting may also be seen as a still life with a jug, and this view tends to recess that color element into becoming a part of the table, back of the jug. In this way Derain weaves a web of images and dynamic tensions, a set of factors that expressively portrays not only the subject matter but also an elemental affection for the staples of human life.

A concluding brief remark—beyond the boundary of this essay's concern—that brings a nonvisual art into this framework. There is such a thing as "hearing as," and space-oriented descriptions of the experience. Sound may be loud, high, flat, far, close, low. Such formations are featured in a musical composition, whose elements are to be "heard as" determining its form ("space"). Such form is primarily of the first order in, say, a Bach fugue or a Hindemith quartet. Beethoven's *Pastoral Symphony* is the favorite example of a piece that exhibits second-order form as well (representational). But, in music, the "spacing" (intervals) is also in time. It is in space-time. But there is a sense in which the content of a painting is also in space-time. Thus, music may be characterized as fluid painting, and painting as frozen music.

—*The Journal of Aesthetic Education,* Vol. 2 (1968)

Notes

1. Harold J. McWhinnie, *The British Journal of Aesthetics,* Vol. 6, No. 3 (July 1966).
2. See my "Back to Aesthetic Experience," *Journal of Aesthetics and Art Criticism,* Vol. 24, No. 3 (Spring 1966). Also *Philosophy of Art* (Prentice-Hall, Englewood Cliffs, N.J., 1963).
3. *Art and Illusion,* Bollingen Series XXXV, 5 (Pantheon Books, New York, 1960).
4. E.g., Margaret McDonald, "The Work of Art as Physical," in M. Rader (ed.), *A Modern Book of Esthetics,* 3rd rev. ed. (Holt, Rinehart and Winston, New York, 1960), esp. p. 219.
5. Taken from my *Philosophy of Art,* p. 20.
6. See my "Picture Space," *Philosophical Review,* Vol. 67, No. 3 (July 1958).

CHAPTER 11

The Standards of the Critic

MONROE C. BEARDSLEY: The Classification of Critical Reasons
LUCIEN GOLDMANN: The Whole and the Parts
STEPHEN C. PEPPER: Contextualistic Criticism
BERNARD BOSANQUET: Easy and Difficult Beauty
GEORGE ORWELL: Benefit of Clergy

"To criticize" is commonly understood to mean "to pass an adverse judgment," but the original Greek verb, *krinein,* means simply to discern or judge. The judgment may be favorable or unfavorable or neither. Explanation and description, as well as evaluation, require judgment. The essays in this chapter are largely concerned with standards of evaluation, but I do not wish to imply that there is no other kind of criticism.

The bases of evaluation are discussed by Monroe Beardsley (1915–), professor of philosophy at Temple University and author of important works in esthetics. He addresses the question: What reasons can be given for critical appraisals? His approach differs from that of Goethe, who said that the critic should seek to answer three questions: What was the artist trying to do? Did he succeed in doing it? Was it worth doing? This procedure has been challenged by Beardsley and William K. Wimsatt, Jr. in a famous collaborative essay, "The Intentional Fallacy" (1946). The "fallacy" is to interpret and judge the work of art by the intention of the artist. As another philosopher has said: "It is always what is done that we have to judge, not what the artist intended, but perhaps failed to do."[1] Beardsley and Wimsatt, in a companion essay, "The Affective Fallacy," maintain that it is likewise fallacious to criticize a work of art in terms of its effect upon the spectator. (Aristotle's "catharsis," Longinus' "transport," and Tolstoy's "communication" would be examples of the affective approach.) In the essay by Beardsley reproduced here, the "critical reasons" are all intrinsic to the work of art. "When the genetic and affective reasons are set aside," he remarks, "what remain are descriptions and interpretations of the work itself. . . . These are the reasons . . . that are properly the province of the critic."

Beardsley seeks to answer the question: What critical reasons of this nongenetic and nonaffective type are relevant to the evaluation of works of art? He rejects the skeptical position that there are no *general* reasons, only reasons that hold for particular cases, or that there are no valid critical reasons and hence no genuine reasons at all. Observing that some reasons are synonymous with or subordinate to others, he reduces the general reasons to three "basic criteria": unity, complexity, and intensity or regional quality. (By "regional qualities"—frequently called "tertiary"—Beardsley means such qualities as elegance, grace, delicacy, robustness, somberness, and so forth.) With respect to these three reasons, he contends that they are basic, that they are adequate to cover the entire range of general critical reasons, and that they are peculiarly relevant to the judgment of *esthetic* value. He defines "esthetic value" as that value which a work of art possesses in virtue of its capacity to provide esthetic experience.

His delimitation of "relevant critical reasons" rules out such criteria as Tolstoy would regard as relevant, not only moral and religious reasons, but communicative efficacy. Tolstoy, or others who agree with him, would argue that if an artist is more obscure than he has to be, he is impairing the communicative relation between himself and his beholders (or hearers or readers) and that such unnecessary obscurity is a defect. Tolstoy's criterion of "sincerity" introduces the consideration of the artist's intention which Beardsley would also exclude. Finally, there is the question of "greatness." To what extent is the work of art profound in its life-values and insights? "Greatness," like Kant's "sublimity," is a magnificent intruder into the purely esthetic domain. Without greatness, it may be contended, "works of art are *merely* works of art, *and so much the less* works of art."[2]

In contrast to Beardsley's delimitation of critical reasons, Lucien Goldmann (1913–1970) insists upon a contextualist interpretation of the work of art. Born in Rumania, he was educated at Bucharest, Vienna, Zurich, and Paris, and taught at the University of Brussels and the École Pratique des Hautes Études in Paris. This cosmopolitan background is reflected in the eclectic nature of his thought, drawing upon the "dialectical materialism" of Karl Marx, the theory of "world-visions" *(Weltanschauungs)* of Wilhelm Dilthey (1833–1911), and the structuralism of Jean Piaget (with whom he worked in Geneva). Common to Marx, Dilthey, and Piaget is the stress upon structure and context, the integral relation of part to whole. Goldmann makes this emphasis the cornerstone of his critical method. In his remarkable book, *The Hidden God,* an interpretation of Pascal and Racine, he contends that philosophical and artistic works convey their real meaning to us but can be fully understood only when they are seen as integral to the lives and social milieus of their creators.

In calling his method "genetic structuralism," Goldmann is linking his theories to the structuralist movement that numbers among its leaders Piaget in psychology, Claude Lévi-Strauss in anthropology, Roman Jacobson in linguistics, and Roland Barthes in literary criticism. As a current sweeping across conventional boundaries, it is exercising a considerable influence on esthetics. One of its greatest triumphs is the work of Goldmann in reconstructing unknown features of Jansenism (a theological doctrine that took root in the French convent of Port Royal and that emphasized St. Augustine's tenets of predestination and divine grace). The structuralist critic uses the structure of the art-work, or the structure of its social context, or both, as his point of departure. Goldmann's own method rests on the concept of art as an embodiment of collective social attitudes characteristic of a class or historical period.

Goldmann agrees with the statement of Marx: "The mode of production of material life conditions the general character of the social, political and spiritual processes of life." Among these spiritual processes are art and literature. The influence of economic conditions and class status upon the artist and his work is filtered through an ideological screen, which Goldmann (following the lead of Dilthey) calls a "world vision." "The tragic vision of life," for example, is a social creation of many artists and thinkers, whose individual works are intelligible only within its context. The value of a work of art is to be judged not only in terms of the formalist criterion of internal coherence but also by the contextualist criterion of "degree of realism." By "realism" Goldmann means "the richness and complexity of the real social relationships which are reflected in the imaginary world created by the artist or writer." Goldmann's "realism," like "greatness" or "sublimity," is a criterion that transcends the purely esthetic sphere.

Stephen Coburn Pepper (1891–1972), professor of philosophy at the University of California, recognizes diverse standards of critical judgment, but believes that each standard may be applied with a fair degree of objectivity. A significant standard does not reflect mere personal taste, but springs from a comprehensive orientation toward reality, a philosophical *Weltanschauung* or world hypothesis. He distinguishes four relatively adequate world hypotheses, which he calls mechanism, contextualism, organicism, and formism. Mechanism also goes by the name of "naturalism" or "materialism"; contextualism is usually called "pragmatism" or "instrumentalism"; organicism is most fully expressed in "absolute idealism"; formism, with its emphasis upon universals or similarities, is often called "realism" or "Platonic idealism." In his discussion of esthetic criticism, Pepper cites Santayana as an example of a mechanist, Dewey as a contextualist, Bosanquet as an organicist, and Aristotle as a formist. The mechanist asks of the work that it give pleasure; the contextualist, that it exhibit vividness of quality; the organicist, that it be a rich and well-integrated unity; the formist, that it typify the normal or universal. In his *Principles of Art Appreciation,* Pepper employed the "mechanist" criterion of pleasure; and in his *Aesthetic Quality* and the selection in this anthology, from *The Basis of Criticism in the Arts,* he skillfully elaborated the contextualist standard: How vivid and intense and deep is the experience yielded by the work of art?

In a remarkable article, "Autobiography of an Aesthetics," in *The Journal of Aesthetics and Art Criticism* (Spring 1970), Pepper outlines his whole development as an esthetician, including the reformulations and additions in his book *Concept and Quality* (1967). The masterly sweep of his achievement is very impressive.

One issue that has agitated both the critics and the general public is absolutism versus relativism. Are esthetic judgments purely subjective? Is beauty in "the eye of the beholder"? Is any person's critical judgment as good as any other person's? Answers to questions of this kind are suggested in the following discussion of easy and difficult beauty by Bernard Bosanquet. (See Chapter 7 for an earlier selection from Bosanquet.) He distinguishes between the competent and the incompetent judge of beauty. The incompetent is incapable of appreciating difficult works of art; the competent suffers from no such incapacity. In characterizing difficult beauty, Bosanquet discusses intricacy, tension, and width, remarking that "I do not say that they cover all cases." He might well have added strangeness. Some works are so strange or unfamiliar that they may require special training or great readjustment to be appreciated.

The answer to the extreme relativism suggested by this analysis is obvious. Esthetic value can be realized only when the object is worthy of being appreciated and the beholder is worthy of appreciating it. The depth of appreciation in the subject must meet and match the depth of esthetic value in the object. Relativism, which puts exclusive emphasis upon the objective factors, and absolutism, which puts exclusive emphasis on the objective factors, are equally one-sided.

Crtical disagreements may spring from extraesthetic considerations, such as the morality or immorality of works of art. A spirited discussion of this type of issue is the essay, "Benefit of Clergy," by the English social critic and satirical novelist George Orwell (1903–1950). Charging that Salvador Dali "seems to have as good an outfit of perversions as anyone could wish for," he asks whether these perversions have any bearing on the value of Dali's art. He warns against committing two fallacies: (1) believing that if a painting is a good composition it cannot be a disgusting, degrading picture, and (2) believing "that because it is disgusting that it cannot be a good composition."

Even if we avoid these fallacies, we may be uncertain what standard to apply to the work. Judged by the standard of expressiveness, a "disgusting" painting by Dali may be a good painting precisely because it is so vividly and hypnotically disgusting. Some critics would contend that its very expressiveness redeems it morally. Other critics, who wish to avoid "the intentional fallacy," may argue that defects in the artist are irrelevant in judging the work of art. But can we distinguish sharply between moral and esthetic defect? Can we assume that the work of art in no way reflects the artist? Is cheapness, or superficiality, or perversity in the artist likely to show up in his work?

Notes

1. John Kemp, "The Work of Art and the Artist's Intentions," *The British Journal of Aesthetics*, Vol. 4 (1964), p. 153.
2. A. Boyce Gibson, *Muse and Thinker* (Penguin Books, Harmondsworth, England, 1972), p. 93.

MONROE C. BEARDSLEY

The Classification of Critical Reason

When a critic makes a value-judgment about a work of art, he is generally expected to give reasons for it—not necessarily a conclusive argument, but at least an indication of the main grounds on which his judgment rests. Without the reasons, the judgment is dogmatic, and also uninformative: it is hard to tell how much is being asserted in "This painting is quite good," unless we understand why it is being asserted.

These reasons offered by critics (or "critical reasons") are, of course, extremely varied. Here is a small sampling:

[On Haydn's *Creation*] "The work can be praised unconditionally for its boldness, originality, and unified conception. But what remains so remarkable in this day and age is its overall spirit of joy, to which a serene religious faith, a love of this world and a sense of drama contribute." (Raymond Ericson)

[On the finale of Bruckner's *Fifth Symphony*] "Perhaps this movement is the greatest of all symphonic finales" because "It is a vision of apocalyptic splendor such as no other composer, in my experience, has ever painted." (Winthrop Sargeant)

[On a novel by Max Frisch] "Rarely has a provocative idea been spoiled more efficiently by excessive detail and overdecoration." (Richard Plant)

[On a motion picture of Pasolini's] "The sleeper of the year is a bone-bare, simple, and convincingly honest treatment of the life of Jesus, *The Gospel According to St. Matthew*." (Ernest Schier)

[On Edvard Munch's lithograph and oil painting, "The Cry"] "This cry of terror lives in most of Munch's pictures. But I have seen faces like this in life—in the concentration camp of Dachau. . . . With "The Cry," the Age of Anxiety found its first and, perhaps to this very day, its unmatched expression." (Alfred Werner)

Probably the first question that will occur to a philosopher who looks over such a list of reasons is this: which of them are relevant? That is, which of them really are grounds on which the judgment can legitimately and defensibly be based? Just because "The Cry" is an "unmatched expression" of the Age of Anxiety, does that make it a good painting (or lithograph)? What reasons are there for supposing that this reason counts in favor of the painting?

Many large and difficult issues in esthetics will loom ahead whenever this line of inquiry is pursued very far—too many to cope with here. The task can be somewhat simplified and clarified, however, if we sort these issues into two main categories with the help of an important distinction having to do with reasons. There are *reasons why* something is a good work of art (or a poor one), and *reasons for supposing that* something is a good work of art (or a poor one); in other words, there are reasons that serve to explain why the work of art is good or poor, and reasons that constitute logical support for a belief that the work of art is good or poor. That these are not the same can easily be shown. If Haydn's *Creation* has a "unified conception," that would help to explain why it is a good musical composition. On the other hand, if we know that a large-scale musical work was composed by Haydn in his mature years, this fact is in itself a reason to believe that the work is probably very good, even though we have not yet heard it; but this fact does not provide any explanation of its goodness—being composed by Haydn is not one of the things that is good about the work.

One way of setting aside some of the reasons offered by critics as irrelevant to the value-judgment they accompany would then be to insist that relevant critical reasons (or critical reasons in a strict sense) be those that are reasons in both of the senses just distinguished. A relevant reason is one that provides support to the value-judgment for which it is a reason and also helps to explain why the judgment is true. If the critic judges that a novel is poor, or at least less good than some other novel with which he compares it, and gives as one reason that there is a great deal of "detail" and "decoration," then this reason not only helps to lower our estimate of the work's value but also points out part of what is wrong with it.

If we insist that a relevant critical reason must have both of these functions, it follows that in order to be relevant, reasons must be statements about the work itself, either descriptive statements about its parts or internal relations (including its form and regional qualities) or interpretive statements about its "meaning" (taking this term loosely enough to include such things as what it represents, symbolizes, signifies, expresses, says, etc.). For statements about external matters, although they may serve as indications of probable goodness or poorness, do not explain that goodness or poorness by telling us what in the work itself makes it good or poor.

The class of relevant critical reasons in the strict sense—those that are both explanations and grounds—itself contains an enormous variety, the range of which is only barely hinted at in the examples above, though it will be familiar to those who have thought seriously about any of the arts. A miscellaneous collection like this is a challenge to the philosophical esthetician, who is bound to inquire whether the items cannot be arranged in certain basic and illuminating categories, and whether there is not a small set of principles at work here. Some estheticians are very dubious about this suggestion: they say that by its very nature, art criticism is too complicated and too loose for any such attempt at classification to be feasible. But why not see how far we can go, if we are careful not to force reasons into categories where they don't fit? If it should in fact turn out to be the case (astonishingly, perhaps) that all relevant critical reasons in the strict sense fall into a few basic categories, that would not be without interest, and it might suggest further lines of inquiry of considerable philosophic importance.

One such classification I have proposed in Chapter 11 of my book *Aesthetics: Problems in the Philosophy of Criticism*.[1] My procedure for constructing it is based on the observation that critical reasons are not all on the same level—that some are subordinate to others. We ask the critic, for example, "What makes the Max Frisch novel so poor?" He replies, "Among other things, excessive detail." We ask again, "What is so bad about the detail? Why is it excessive? How does it help to make the work poor?" If he is cooperative, the critic may reply once more: "The detail is excessive because it distracts the reader from those elements in the work (elements of plot, perhaps) that would otherwise give it a fairly high degree of unity," or perhaps, "The detail is excessive because it dissipates what would otherwise be strong dramatic and emotional qualities of the work." So it seems that the objectionableness of the detail is itself explained by an appeal to a more fundamental and general principle: that unity is desirable in the work, or that intensity of regional quality is desirable in the work.

If we press farther, however, and ask the critic why greater unity would help to make the work a better one, this question too, deserves an answer, but it would have to be of a quite different sort. In explaining why excessive detail and overdecoration are objectionable, the critic appeals to other features of the work itself, which these features either increase or diminish. But what makes unity desirable is not what it does to other features of the work; thus, as far as the work itself is concerned, unity is a basic criterion. The fine arts critic could reasonably say that a particular group of shapes and colors in a painting is good because it creates a very subtle balance, and he could also say that balance is good because it is one way of unifying the painting; but he could not say that unity in a painting is a good thing because it makes the painting contain these particular shapes and colors.

In my view, there are exactly three basic criteria that are appealed to in relevant critical reasons, and all of the other features of works of art that are appealed to in such reasons are subordinate to these, or can be subsumed under them. There is unity, which is specifically mentioned in connection with Haydn's *Creation* and presupposed in the criticism of the Max Frisch novel. There is complexity, which I think is part of what Winthrop Sargeant admires in Bruckner's *Fifth*. (Insofar as the simplicity of Pasolini's film is regarded as a positive merit, I take it not as a low degree of complexity but as absence of "excessive detail and overdecoration.") And there is intensity of regional quality: the "overall spirit of joy" in Haydn, the "cry of terror" in Edvard Munch.

Any such simplifying scheme as this ought to arouse immediate skepticism and protest. It is obviously too neat to be correct. It is tempting, no doubt, because it really does embrace and tidy up a very large number of critical reasons, and it enables us to distinguish the revelant ones from the irrelevant ones on a fairly clear principle. But certainly it needs to be examined and tested severely before it can be accepted.

Some searching questions can be asked about the three proposed criteria of judgment. First, are they sufficiently clear? Some estheticians who have considered unity, for example, have expressed doubt (1) that it has a sufficiently well-defined meaning to be used in this highly general way, and (2) that it has the same meaning across the arts (the same, that is, for painting as for poetry or music). I do not know how to prove that I am right in rejecting both of these doubts. We can surely find examples of pairs of paintings or prints where it is perfectly evident that one is more unified than the other. And even though what tends to unify a painting is, of course, not identical to what tends to unify a poem or a musical composition, as far as I can tell I mean the same thing when I say that one poem is more unified than another or when I say that one painting is more unified than another.

I do not mean to imply, of course, that we can estimate infallibly the degree to which a basic esthetic property (such as unity) is present in a particular painting. When we look at a painting and it fails to hang together, that may be because we are tired, or our perceptions are dulled by an adverse mode, or we are not attending closely enough, or we have had too little acquaintance with works of that sort. A negative conclusion must usually be somewhat tentative and rebuttable; for it may well be that if later we come to the painting again, in a more serene mood, with sharper faculties, and with greater willingness to give in to whatever the painting wishes to do to us, we may find that in fact it has a tight though subtle unity that is perfectly apparent to the prepared eye. But if we return again and again, under what we take to be the most favorable conditions, and it still looks incoherent, we have reasonable grounds for concluding that probably the painting cannot be seen as unified.

Even a positive conclusion may not be final. The painting may on one occasion fleetingly appear to us as unified. But suppose that unity turns out not to be a stable property—that it is hard to capture and to hold. Then we may decide that we were the victim of an illusion. The judgment of unity ultimately has to be based on a gestalt perception—on taking in the regional qualities and dominant patterns of the whole. But such perceptions can always be checked by analysis—by which I mean simply the minute examination of the parts of the work and their relationships with one another. A prima facie description of the work as having unity or disunity to some degree does have this kind of check: that it should hold up under analysis. For the perception that occurs after analysis may correct the earlier one: it may turn out that we have overlooked some parts or some internal relationships that, when taken into account in perception, make the work more unified—or less unified—than it at first appeared.

Second, are the three basic criteria really basic? One of the marks of being basic (as I have said) is that the question "Why is X good (or poor) in the work?" seems to come to a turning-point in them, for at this point it takes one outside the work itself. Another mark is that the subordinate reasons are contexually limited. That is, the features they allude to may be desirable in some works but not necessarily in all. A particular cluster of shapes and colors may work well in one setting but badly in another; balance is not necessarily always a good thing; and details that would be excessive in one novel might not be excessive in another. But the basic criteria, I would claim, are all one-way. Unity, complexity, and intensity of regional quality never count against a work of art (we cannot say the painting is good because its regional quality is so insipid, or because it is so elementary a design, or because it falls apart into messiness), but always count in favor of it, to the extent to which they are present. The example of simplicity, which I mentioned earlier, might seem to refute at least part of this claim; but it seems to me that whenever simplicity is held up as a desirable feature, either it is not strictly simplicity (the opposite of complexity) that is referred to, but some sort of unity, or it is not the simplicity that is admired, but the intensity of some regional quality that happens to be obtainable in this case only by accepting simplicity.

Third, are the three proposed criteria really adequate to cover the entire range of relevant critical reasons? Consider "boldness" or "originality," for example, which are cited in the praise of Haydn's *Creation*. "Boldness" could no doubt benefit from further clarification: it could refer to a regional quality of the work, or it could refer in a somewhat roundabout way to originality (perhaps Haydn was bold to try out certain hitherto unheard of, or at least unfamiliar, ideas in it). But originality does not seem to fit under the three basic criteria. Or consider the description of Pasolini's film as "convincingly honest." Honesty, again, might be a certain quality of the work—absence of sentimentality and melodrama, etc. But it might be a correspondence between the film itself and the actual feelings of the film maker (even though he is a Communist, he could still have certain feelings about this story, which he sincerely puts into his work); and honesty in that sense, like sincerity, does not seem relevant to unity or complexity or intensity of regional quality.

Criteria like originality and sincerity I have already ruled out of the class of relevant critical reasons by making the rule that a relevant critical reason must not only support the critical judgment but also (at least partially) explain why the judgment is true. But here, of course, is a serious esthetic issue, since many critics regard originality and sincerity as highly relevant reasons. They would consider me wholly arbitrary in ruling them out.

This challenge leads into the fourth question I intend to raise here: What good (philosophical) reason is there for holding that any particular (critical) reason is relevant or irrelevant to the judgment of a particular work? If someone says that the Bruckner *Fifth* is great because it presents a "vision of apocalyptic splendor," there are always two questions we can ask: First, is it true that the work presents such a vision? (Granted that the music is splendid, and therefore splendor can be heard in it, how do we know that it is "apocalyptic"?) Second, if the statement is true, why is it a ground for saying that the work is great? (How does apocalypticity make the music good?) To ask a question of the second sort is to plunge us into some of the hardest questions about the arts and art criticism. Without pretending to dispose of them, I want at least to face up to them.

Anything so complex as a work of art can usually be regarded from more than one point of view: It is (let us say) a visual design, an example of skilled workmanship, a source of income for the painter and (even more) for the art dealer, a political document, an excellent example of a certain historical style, and so forth. And one very broad way of sorting out all the various remarks that people might want to make about the painting is to say that they are made from different points of view: economic, or art-historical, or political, or other. Then how are we to distinguish between one point of view and another? According to some philosophers, one point of view can be distinguished from another only in terms of the sort of reason given: thus, if one says that the painting is costly, we can classify his point of view as economic; and if another says that the painting is a good example of Mannerism, we can classify his point of view as that of the art historian. But in that case, we could not use points of view to help us sort out the reasons, or we would be going in a circle. I would prefer to distinguish between one point of view and another in terms of a kind of value that one might take an interest in: market value or art-historical value (that is, usefulness in illuminating some phase of art history).

Speaking very broadly (and for some purposes too sweepingly), the various kinds of value that may be found in works of art can be classified under three headings. There is cognitive value (of which art-historical value would be a species). We often speak well of works of art if they contribute in some way to our knowledge. Perhaps Winthrop Sargeant is suggesting that Bruckner gives us a kind of insight into the nature of apocalypses, and perhaps Alfred Werner is suggesting that Munch gives us a better understanding of our Age of Anxiety. In any case, claims like these are frequently made, and if they are valid claims, then they certainly do show that the work is worth creating and preserving. But I do not think they are relevant reasons for saying that the work is good music or good painting—only that it is good as religious intuition or a social document.

Next there is what might be called moral and social value. Someone might follow Winthrop Sargeant's suggestion (and his remarks elsewhere) by saying that Bruckner's music is religiously significant, and under suitable circumstances can strengthen religious faith (assuming that this is desirable). Someone else might praise Pasolini's film because it can produce moral uplift or strengthen character. And, quite apart from whether or not "The Cry" is a good painting, it may be of great social worth as an "unmatched expression," a minatory reminder, of the ills of our age. But again, even if all these claims are admitted, they would not properly lead us to say that these works are good works of art.

Finally, there is esthetic value. This is the kind of value that we look for most especially and suitably in works of art, and the kind of value whose presence and degree we report when we say that the work is good or poor. If we set aside all those reasons that clearly depend upon a cognitive or a moral/social point of view, we may consider those that remain to be peculiarly esthetic. They are, however, not all equally relevant. Relevance depends on our theory of esthetic value. If we hold, as I do, that the esthetic value of an object is that value which it possesses in virtue of its capacity to provide esthetic experience, then certain consequences follow. For the only way to support such a judgment relevantly and cogently would be to point out features of the work that enable it to provide an experience having an esthetic character. And thus the relevant reasons, as I assumed above, will be those that both support and explain.

There is one more set of distinctions that I have found useful in dealing with critical reasons. Any statement that a critic may make about a work of art must be one of three kinds: (1) It may be a statement about the relation of the work to its antecedent conditions—about the intentions of the artist, or his sincerity, or his originality, or the social conditions of the work, and so forth. If such statement is given as a reason for a critical judgment, it is a genetic reason. It may help explain why the work has a particular feature that in turn helps explain why the work is good (as one might say that something in Munch's childhood experience explains the "cry of terror" in so much of his work, while the presence of that "cry of terror," as an intense regional quality, helps explain why the works are good). But the genetic reason itself does not explain directly why the work is good, and it is therefore not a relevant reason: we cannot say that a work is good because it is sincere, or original, or fulfills the intention of the artist. (2) The critic's statement may be a statement about the effects of the work on individuals or groups: that it is morally uplifting, or shocking, or popular at the box office. If such a statement is given as a reason, it is an affective reason. And since it does not say what in the work makes it good, but itself has to be explained by what is in the work (which is shocking because of the nudity or the sadism or whatever), it is not a relevant critical reason. (3) When the genetic and affective reasons are set aside, what remain are descriptions and interpretations of the work itself, as has already been said. When given as reasons, such statements may be called objective reasons, since they draw our attention to the object itself and its own merits and defects. These are the reasons, I would argue, that are properly the province of the critic.

—*The Journal of Aesthetic Education,* Vol. 2 (1968)

Note

1. Harcourt, New York, 1958.

LUCIEN GOLDMANN

The Whole and the Parts

I set out from the fundamental principle of dialectical materialism, that the knowledge of empirical facts remains abstract and superficial so long as it is not made concrete by its integration into a whole; and that only this act of integration can enable us to go beyond the incomplete and abstract phenomenon in order to arrive at its concrete essence, and thus, implicitly, at its meaning. I thus maintain that the ideas and work of an author cannot be understood as long as we remain on the level of what he wrote, or even of what he read and what influenced him. Ideas are only a partial aspect of a less abstract reality: that of the whole, living man. And in his turn, this man is only an element in a whole made up of the social group to which he belongs. An idea which he expresses or a book which he writes can acquire their real meaning for us, and can be fully understood, only when they are seen as integral parts of his life and mode of behaviour. Moreover, it often happens that the mode of behaviour which enables us to understand a particular work is not that of the author himself, but that of a whole social group; and, when the work with which we are concerned is of particular importance, this behaviour is that of a whole social class.

The multiple and complex phenomenon of the relationship which each individual has with his fellows often separates his daily life as a member of society from his abstract ideas or his creative imagination, so that the relationship which he has with his social group may be too indirect for it to be analysable with any degree of accuracy. In cases such as these—which are numerous—it is difficult to understand a work if one comes to it through a study of the author's life. What he intended to say, and the subjective meaning which his books had for himself, do not always coincide with their objective meaning, and it is this which is the first concern of the philosophically-minded historian. For example, Hume was not himself a thorough-going sceptic, but the empiricism to which his work gave rise does lead to an attitude of complete scepticism. Descartes believed in God, but Cartesian rationalism is atheistic. It is when he replaces the work in a historical evolution which he studies as a whole, and when he relates it to the social life of the time at which it was written—which he also looks upon as a whole—that the enquirer can bring out the work's objective meaning, which was often not completely clear for the author himself. . . .

. . . The historian of literature or of philosophy begins with a series of empirical facts consisting of the texts which he is going to study. He can approach them in one of three ways: by methods of textual analysis which I shall call "positivistic"; by intuitive methods based upon feelings of personal sympathy and affinity; or, finally, by dialectical methods. Leaving aside for the moment the second group, which in my view is not properly scientific, there is only one criterion which enables us to separate the dialectical from the positivistic approach: the two methods consider the actual texts to be both the starting-point and the conclusion of their researches, but whereas one method offers the opportunity of understanding the more or less coherent meaning of these texts, the other does not.

The concept already mentioned of the relationship between the whole and the parts immediately separates the traditional methods of literary scholarship, which frequently pay insufficient attention to the obvious factors revealed by psychology and by the study of society, from the dialectical method. The actual writings of an author, in fact, constitute only a sector of his behaviour, a sector depending upon a highly complex physiological and psychological structure which undergoes great changes during his life.

Moreover, there is an even greater though similar variety in the infinite multiplicity of the particular situations in which an individual can be placed during the course of his existence. Certainly, if we had a complete and exhaustive knowledge of the psychological structure of the author in question and of his daily relationship with his environment, we should be able, if not wholly then at least partially, to understand his work through his life. The acquisition of such knowledge is, however, both for the present and in all probability for the future, a Utopian dream. Even when we are dealing with people alive at the present day, whom we can test and examine in the laboratory, we can only achieve a more or less fragmentary view of any particular individual. This is even more the case when the man we are trying to study has been dead for a long time, and when the most detailed research will reveal only a superficial and fragmentary image of him. At a time when, thanks to the existence of psycho-analysis, of Gestalt psychology, of the work of Jean Piaget, we have a better awareness than ever of the extreme complexity of the human individual, there is something paradoxical in any attempt to understand the work of Pascal, Plato or Kant by a study of their life. However great the apparent rigour with which research is conducted, any conclusion is bound to remain extremely arbitrary. We must certainly not exclude the study of biographical details, since these often provide extremely useful information. However, it will always remain merely a partial and auxiliary method which must never be used as the final basis for any explanation.

Thus, the attempt to go beyond the immediate text by incorporating it into the author's life is both difficult and unlikely to provide reliable results. Should we therefore go back to the positivistic approach, and concentrate on everything implied by a "complete study of the text"?

I do not think so, for any purely textual study comes up against obstacles which cannot be overcome until the work has been fitted into the historical whole of which it forms part.

First of all, how is the "work" of an author to be defined? It is everything which he ever wrote, including letters, notes and posthumous publications? Or is it only the works that he himself completed during his lifetime and intended for publication?

The arguments in favour of one or the other of these two attitudes are well known. The principal difficulty lies in the fact that not everything which an author writes is equally important for an understanding of his work. On the one hand, there are texts which can be explained by personal and accidental circumstances, and which consequently offer at most a biographical interest; on the other, there are essential texts, without which his work simply cannot be understood. Moreover, the historian's task is made all the more difficult by the fact that an author's letters and rough notes may contain some of the really essential texts, while certain sections of his published work may have little more than an anecdotal interest. This brings us face to face with one of the fundamental difficulties of any form of scientific investigation: the need to distinguish the essential from the accidental, a problem which has preoccupied philosophers from Aristotle to Husserl, and to which we must find a genuinely scientific answer.

There is a second difficulty which is no less important than the first. It is that, at first sight at least, the meaning of some texts is by no means certain and unambiguous. Words, sentences and phrases which are apparently similar, and in some cases even identical, can nevertheless have a different meaning when used in a different context. Pascal was well aware of this when he wrote: 'Words arranged differently compose different meanings, and meanings arranged differently produce different effects' (fr. 23,E.944).[1]

> Let it not be said that I have said nothing new: I have presented the matter in a different way. When men play tennis, they both use the same ball, but one places it better than the other.
>
> I would just as much prefer people to say that I have used old words—as if the same ideas did not make up a different body of discourse when they are differently arranged, in the same way as the same words present different ideas when they are differently arranged (fr. 22, E.4).

. . . The difficulties presented by the relationship between an author's life and his work, far from suggesting that we should go back to simply studying the text, encourage us to keep moving forward in the original direction, going not only from the text to the individual, but from the individual to the social group of which he forms part. For when we look at them more closely the difficulties raised both by a consideration of the text and by a study of the author's life are basically the same and have the same epistemological basis. For since the individual facts which we encounter are inexhaustible in their variety and multiplicity, any scientific study of them must enable us to separate the accidental from the essential elements in the immediate reality which presents itself to our experience. Leaving on one side the problem presented by the physical sciences, where the situation is different, it is my contention that, in the study of man, we can separate the essential from the accidental only by integrating the individual elements into the overall pattern, by fitting the parts into the whole. This is why, although we can never actually reach a totality which is no longer an element or part of a greater whole, the methodological problem, as far as the humanities or the science of man is concerned, is principally this: that of dividing the immediately available facts into relative wholes which are sufficiently autonomous to provide a framework for scientific investigation. If, however, for the reasons that I have just given, neither the individual work nor the personality of the author are sufficiently autonomous wholes to provide such a framework, we still have the possibility that the group, especially if studied from the point of view of its division into social classes, might perhaps constitute a reality which could enable us to overcome the difficulties met with either on the plane of the individual text or on that of the relationship between the author's life and his work.

It is more convenient to reverse the order in which the two original difficulties were first mentioned, and begin by asking: how can we define the meaning either of a particular text or of a fragment? The reply is provided by our earlier analysis: by fitting it into the coherent pattern of the work as a whole. . . .

The historian of art or literature has an immediate and direct criterion: that of esthetic value. Any attempt to understand Goethe's work can leave on one side minor texts such as *The Citizen General,* and any attempt to understand Racine's work can dispense with studying *Alexandre* or *La Thébaide.* But apart from the fact that, once isolated from any conceptual or explanatory framework, the criterion of artistic validity is arbitrary and subjective,[2] it has the additional disadvantage of being quite inapplicable to works of philosophy or theology.

It thus follows that the history of philosophy and literature can become scientific only when an objective and verifiable instrument has been created which will enable us to distinguish the essential from the accidental elements in a work of art; the validity of this method will be measured by the fact that it will never proclaim as accidental works which are esthetically satisfying. In my view, such an instrument is to be found in the concept of the *world vision.*

In itself, this concept is not dialectical in origin, and has been widely used by Dilthey and his school. Unfortunately, they have done so in a very vague way, and have never succeeded in giving it anything like a scientific status. The first person to use it with the accuracy indispensable to any instrument of scientific research was George Lukàcs, who employed it in a number of works whose methods I have tried to describe elsewhere.[3]

What is a *world vision*? It is not an immediate, empirical fact, but a conceptual working hypothesis indispensable to an understanding of the way in which individuals actually express their ideas. Even on an empirical plane, its importance and reality can be seen as soon as we go beyond the ideas of work of a single writer, and begin to study them as part of a whole. For example, scholars have long since noted the similarities which exist between certain philosophical systems and certain literary works: Descartes and Corneille, Pascal and Racine, Schelling and the German romantics, Hegel and Goethe. What I shall try to show in this book is that similarities can be found not only in the detail of the particular arguments put forward but also in the general structure of texts as apparently dissimilar as the critical writings of Kant and the *Pensées* of Pascal.

On the plane of personal psychology, there are no people more different than the poet, who creates particular beings and things, and the philosopher, who thinks and expresses himself by means of general concepts. Similarly, it is difficult to imagine two beings more dissimilar in every aspect of their lives than Kant and Pascal. Thus, if most of the essential elements which make up the schematic structure of the writings of Kant, Pascal and Racine are similar in spite of the differences which separate these authors as individuals, we must accept the existence of a reality which goes beyond them as individuals and finds its expression in their work. It is this which I intend to call the *world vision,* and, in the particular case of the authors to be studied in this book, the *tragic vision.*

It would be wrong, however, to look upon this world vision as a metaphysical concept or as one belonging purely to the realm of speculation. On the contrary, it forms the main concrete aspect of the phenomenon which sociologists have been trying to describe for a number of years under the name of collective consciousness, and the analysis which I shall now undertake will enable us to reach a clearer understanding of the notion of coherence.

The psycho-motor behaviour of every individual stems from his relationship with his environment. Jean Piaget has broken down the effect of this relationship into two complementary operations: the assimilation of the environment into the subject's scheme of thought and action and the attempt which the individual makes to accommodate this personal scheme to the structure of his environment when this cannot be made to fit into his plans.[4]

The main error of most psychological theories has been to concentrate too frequently on the individual as absolute and sole reality, and to study other men only in so far as they play the part of *objects* in the individual's ideas and activities. This atomistic view of the individual was shared by the Cartesian or Fichtean concept of the Ego, by the neo-Kantians and the phenomenologists with their idea of the "transcendental Self," by Condillac and his theory of the animated statue and by other thinkers. Now this implicit concept of man primarily as an isolated individual, which dominates modern non-dialectical philosophy and psychology, is quite simply wrong. The simplest empirical observation is enough to reveal its inaccuracy. Almost no human actions are performed by isolated individuals for the subject performing the action is a group, a "We," and not an "I," even though, by the phenomenon of reification, the present structure of society tends to hide the "We" and transform it into a collection of different individuals isolated from one another. There is indeed another possible relationship between men apart from that of subject to object, and the "I" to the "you"; this is the communal relationship which I shall call the "We," the expression which an action assumes when it is exercised on an object by a group of men acting in common.

Naturally, in modern society every individual is engaged in a number of activities of this type. He takes part in different activities in different groups, with the result that each activity has a greater or lesser influence on his consciousness and behaviour. The groups to which he belongs, and which may perform communal activities, can be his family, his country, his professional or economic association, an intellectual or religious community and so on. For purely factual reasons that I have expressed elsewhere,[5] the most important group to which an individual may belong, from the point of view of intellectual and artistic activity and creation, is that of the social class, or classes, of which he is a member. Up to the present day, it is class, linked together by basic economic needs, which has been of prime importance in influencing the ideological life of man, since he has been compelled to devote most of his thought and energy either to finding enough to live on or, if he belonged to a ruling class, to keeping his privileges and administering and increasing his wealth.

As I have already said, an individual can doubtless separate his ideas and intellectual aspirations from his daily life; the same is not true of social groups, for as far as they are concerned, their ideas and behaviour are rigorously and closely related. The central thesis of dialectical materialism does nothing more than affirm the existence of this relationship and demand that it should be given concrete recognition until the day when man succeeds in freeing himself from his slavery to economic needs on the plane of his daily behaviour.

However, not all groups based on economic interests necessarily constitute social classes. In order for a group to become a class, its interests must be directed, in the case of a "revolutionary" class, towards a complete transformation of the social structure or, if it is a "reactionary" class, towards maintaining the present social structure unchanged. Each class will then express its desire for change—or for permanence—by a complete vision both of what the man of the present day is, with his qualities and failings, and of what the man of the future ought to be, and of what relationship he should try to establish with the universe and with his fellows.

What I have called a "world vision" is a convenient term for the whole complex of ideas, aspirations and feelings which links together the members of a social group (a group which, in most cases, assumes the existence of a social class) and which opposes them to members of other social groups.

This is certainly a highly schematic view, an extrapolation made by the historian for purposes of convenience; nevertheless, it does extrapolate a tendency which really exists among the members of a certain social group, who all attain this class consciousness in a more or less coherent manner. I say "more or less," because even though it is only rarely that an individual is completely and wholly aware of the whole meaning and direction of his aspirations, behaviour and emotions, he is nevertheless always relatively conscious of them. In a few cases—and it is these which interest us—there are exceptional individuals who either actually achieve or who come very near to achieving a completely integrated and coherent view of what they and the social class to which they belong are trying to do. The men who express this vision on an imaginative or conceptual plane are writers and philosophers, and the more closely their work expresses this vision in its complete and integrated form, the more important does it become. They then achieve the maximum possible awareness of the social group whose nature they are expressing.

These ideas should be enough to show how a dialectical conception of social life differs from the ideas of traditional psychology and sociology. In a dialectical conception the individual ceases to be an atom which exists in isolation and opposition to other men and to the physical world, and the "collective consciousness" ceases to be a static entity which stands above and outside particular individuals. The collective consciousness exists only in and through individual consciousnesses, but it is not simply made up of the sum of these. In fact, the term "collective consciousness" is not a very satisfactory one, and I myself prefer that of "group consciousness," accompanied in each case, as far as that is possible, by the description of the group in question: family, professional, national, class. This group consciousness is the tendency common to the feelings, aspirations and ideas of the members of a particular social class; a tendency which is developed as a result of a particular social and economic situation, and which then gives rise to a set of activities performed by the real or potential community constituted by this social class. The awareness of this tendency varies from one person to another, and reaches its height only in certain exceptional individuals or, as far as the majority of the group is concerned, in certain privileged situations: war in the case of national group consciousness, revolution for class consciousness, etc. It follows from this that exceptional individuals can give a better and more accurate expression to the collective consciousness than the other members of the group, and that consequently we must reverse the traditional order in which historians have studied the problem of the relationship between the individual and the community. For example, scholars have often tried to determine to what extent Pascal was or was not a Jansenist. But both those who said that he was and those who said that he was not were in agreement as to how the question should be asked. Both agreed that it had the following meaning: "To what extent did his ideas coincide with those of Antoine Arnauld, Nicole and other well-known thinkers who were universally acknowledged to be Jansenists?" In my view, the question should be asked the other way round: we must first of all establish what Jansenism was as a social and ideological phenomenon; we must then decide what are the characteristics of a consistently "Jansenist" attitude; and we must then compare the writings of Nicole, Arnauld and Pascal to this conceptual prototype of Jansenism. This will enable us to reach a much better understanding of the objective meaning of the work of each of these three men, each with his own particular limitations; we shall then see that on the literary and ideological plane the only really thorough-going Jansenists were Pascal and Racine, and perhaps Barcos, and that it is by reference to what they wrote that we should judge to what extent Arnauld and Nicole were Jansenist thinkers.

Is this not an arbitrary method? Could we not do without the Jansenism of Nicole and Arnauld and the idea of the "world vision"? I know of only one reply to this objection: "By their fruits Ye shall know them." Such a method is justified if it enables us to reach a better understanding of the particular works in question: the *Pensées* of Pascal and the tragedies of Racine.

This takes us back to our starting-point: any great literary or artistic work is the expression of a world vision. This vision is the product of a collective group consciousness which reaches its highest expression in the mind of a poet or a thinker. The expression which his work provides is then studied by the historian who uses the idea of the world vision as a tool which will help him to deduce two things from the text: the essential meaning of the work he is studying and the meaning which the individual and partial elements take on when the work is looked at as a whole.

I will add that the historian of literature and philosophy should study not only world visions in the abstract but also the concrete expressions which these visions assume in the everyday world. In studying a work he should not limit himself to what can be explained by presupposing the existence of such and such a vision. He must also ask what social and individual reasons there are to explain why this vision should have been expressed in this particular way at this particular time. In addition, he should not be satisfied with merely noting the inconsistencies and variations which prevent the work in question from being an absolutely coherent expression of the world vision which corresponds to it; such inconsistencies and variations are not merely facts which the historian should note; they are problems which he must solve, and their solution will lead him to take into account not only the social and historical factors which accompanied the production of the work but also, more frequently, factors related to the life and psychological make-up of the particular author. It is in this context that these factors should be studied, for they constitute elements which, although accidental, should not be ignored by the historian. Moreover, he can understand them only by reference to the essential structure of the object under investigation.

It must be added that the dialectical method just described has already been spontaneously applied, if not by historians of philosophy, then at least by philosophers themselves when they wanted to understand the work of their predecessors. This is true of Kant, who is perfectly aware, and says so in so many words, that Hume is not a complete sceptic and is not consistently empirical in his outlook, but who nevertheless discusses him as if this were the case. He does so because what he is trying to do is to reach the philosophical doctrine (what I have called the "world vision"), which gives its meaning and significance to Hume's position. Similarly, in the dialogue between Pascal and Monsieur de Saci (which, although a transcription by Fontaine, is probably very close to the original text) we find two similar examples of a deformation of another writer's ideas. Pascal doubtless knew that Montaigne's position was not that of consistent and rigorous scepticism. Nevertheless, for exactly the same reasons that Kant slightly distorts Hume's position, he does treat him as if this were the case: because what he is trying to do is discuss a specific philosophical position and not analyse the actual meaning of a text. Similarly, we also see him attributing to Montaigne the hypothesis of the malign demon—a mistake from a strictly textual point of view, but one that can be justified on philosophical grounds, since for its real author, Descartes, this hypothesis was merely a provisional supposition whose aim was to summarise and carry to its logical conclusion the sceptical position that he wants to refute.

Thus, the method which consists of going from the actual text to the conceptual vision, and then returning from this vision to the text again, is not an innovation of dialectical materialism. The improvement which dialectical materialism makes upon this method lies in the fact that by integrating the ideas of a particular individual into those of a social group, and especially by analysing the historical function played in the genesis of ideas by social classes, it provides a scientific basis for the concept of world vision, and frees it from any criticism that it might be purely arbitrary, speculative and metaphysical.

These few pages were needed to clarify the general characteristics of the method which I intended to use. I should now merely add that since a "world vision" is the psychic expression of the relationship between certain human groups and their social or physical environment, the number of such visions which can be found in any fairly long historical period is necessarily limited.

However many and varied the actual historical situations in which man may find himself can be, the different world visions that we encounter nevertheless express the reaction of a group of beings who remain relatively constant. A philosophy or work of art can keep its value outside the time and place where it first appeared only if, by expressing a particular human situation, it transposes this on to the plane of the great human problems created by man's relationship with his fellows and with the universe. Now since the number of coherent replies that can be given to these problems is limited[6] by the very structure of the human personality, each of the replies given may correspond to different and even contradictory historical situations. This explains both the successive rebirths of the same idea which we find in the world of history, art and philosophy and the fact that, at different times, the same vision can assume different aspects; it can be sometimes revolutionary, sometimes defensive, reactionary and conservative, and sometimes even decadent.

This statement is, of course, true only so long as the concept of the world vision is considered in the abstract, as an attempt to solve certain fundamental human problems and to give each of them its own importance. As we move away from the abstract idea of the world vision, so we find that the individual details of each vision are linked to historical situations localised in place and time, and even to the individual personality of the writer or thinker in question.

Historians of philosophy are justified in accepting the notion of Platonism as valid when it is applied to Plato himself, to Saint Augustine, to Descartes and to certain other thinkers. The same thing is true of mysticism, empiricism, rationalism, the tragic vision and other expressions of the "world vision," as long as the following condition is held in mind: that setting out both from the general characteristics shared by Platonism as a world vision and from the elements which the historical situation of fourth-century Athens, sixth-century Carthage and seventeenth-century France have in common, historians try to discover what was peculiar to each of these three situations, how these peculiarities were reflected in the work of Plato, Saint Augustine and Descartes, and, finally, if they wish to present a really complete study, how the personality of each of these thinkers expressed itself in his work.

I will add that, in my view, the principal task of the historian of art or philosophy lies in describing the nature of the different world visions which may exist; that once he has done this, he will have made an essential contribution to any truly scientific and philosophical view of man; and that this is a task which has scarcely even begun. Like the great systems in the world of the physical sciences, it will be the eventual achievement of a whole series of particular studies whose own individual meaning it will then make clearer and more precise. . . .

I have already said that the dialectical esthetic sees every work of art as the expression, in the specific language of literature, painting, music or sculpture, etc., of a world vision; and that, as we would expect, this vision also expresses itself on numerous other philosophical and theological levels, as well as on that of men's everyday actions and activity. The essential criteria by which the esthetic of dialectical materialism judges the value of any expression of a world vision are the inner coherence of the work of art and especially the coherence between form and content. It also, however, has another criterion, corresponding on the philosophical plane to that of truth, and which enables a hierarchy of values to be set up between the different esthetical expression of world visions. This criterion is what the artistic theories of dialectical materialism call the "degree of realism," implying by this the richness and complexity of the real social relationships which are reflected in the imaginary world created by the artist or writer. Finally, precisely because the dialectical esthetic accepts realism as the next most important criterion after coherence, it takes its stand on a classical esthetic which refuses to admit any formal, autonomous element which is not justified by a particular function, either—as in architecture for example—in the utilisation of the object or in the expression of the reality of a committed, essential man.

—*The Hidden God* (1955; translated by Philip Thody, 1964)

Notes

1. Pascal's *Pensées* are quoted in the Brunschvicg edition by Goldmann, and the number of the fragment refers to this edition. The second number, indicated by a capital E, refers to the Lafuma edition, which is followed in the Everyman Library translation. (Editor's note)

2. And this is also true for reasons which are to a very great extent social. At any one historical period the sensibility of the members of any particular social class, and also of the intellectuals in general, is more receptive to some works than to others. It is for this reason that most studies written at the present day on Corneille, Hugo or Voltaire are to be read with a certain amount of caution. This is not the case with irrationalistic or even with tragic texts, whose esthetic value can be clearly perceived by the modern intellectual even when their objective meaning is only imperfectly understood.

3. See Lucien Goldmann, "Matérialisme dialectique et Histoire de la philosophie," in *Revue philosophique de France et de l'étranger*, 1948, No. 46; and Goldmann, *Sciences humaines et Philosophie* (1952).

4. Marx said the same thing in a passage from *Das Capital* which Piaget reproduced in his latest work: "Primarily, labour is a process going on between man and nature, a process in which man, through his own activity, initiates, regulates and controls the material exchanges between himself and nature. He confronts nature as one of her own forces, setting in motion arms and legs, head and hands, in order to appropriate nature's productions in a form suitable to his own wants. By thus acting on the external world and changing it, he at the same time changes his own nature" (Part Three, Chapter Five, Eden and Cedar Paul's translation in the Everyman edition, 1930).

5. Cf. Lucien Goldmann, *Sciences humaines et Philosophie*.

6. Although we are, today, very far from having indicated with any degree of scientific precision where such a limit might lie. The scientific elaboration of a typology of world visions has scarcely even begun.

STEPHEN C. PEPPER

Contextualistic Criticism

The mechanistic criticism, . . . springing as it does from a world hypothesis founded on the space-time field, lays great stress on the location of things. So, it locates a work of art as a physical object outside of an organism, and describes the path of stimulation from the physical object to the organism, and locates the value of the work among the responses of the organism in the form of pleasures correlated with these responses. The direct objects of esthetic value, however, turn out to be sensations and images stimulated by the external object or associated with it. The human body and the boundaries of the body are accordingly prominent features in this type of criticism, for the values are conceived as centered in the body and confined within it.

When we turn to contextualism, all this is changed. The most striking feature of contextualism is the relative insignificance of the boundaries of the human body. The body becomes simply a constant detail in a man's changing environment somewhat like the clothes he wears and the profession he follows. The basic concept of contextualism is a context of activity. The word "situation" has recently been suggested for this idea by Otis Lee in an article entitled "Value and the Situation,"[1] which is one of the clearest and most consistent statements yet to appear of this relatively new concept in philosophy. The concept of situations, he writes, "enables us to understand how values are objective, as common men believe them to be, and at the same time concrete, specific, and inherent in the process of . . . experience."[2]

By saying that "values are objective," he means precisely that they are not like a mechanist's conception of values confined to individual subjects, organisms, bodies, but are spread over a whole environmental situation.

> A situation [he continues] includes both agents and circumstances, so action and the situation go together. The agent is faced by circumstances within the situation, and the act is his response to the problem they present. Through it the total situation, including both agent and circumstances, is changed in some way. There are three characteristics of the situation which make it important for the understanding of value: its unity, value potentialities, and problematic nature.
>
> The situation is one. It is a natural fact with a natural unity, not a construct made and existing only in the mind. It is not an assemblage of people, things, events, qualities and relations, pleasures, pains, and interests, combined in and by the perspective of some given individual. All these are among its constituents, but it is itself an independent unit. Its unity is constituted by a characteristic quality, which is unique in each situation, though when we describe it we must use words which do or might apply to other situations as well—words such as cheerful, dynamic, hostile, peaceful, stimulating, competitive, and promising.
>
> Language recognizes its existence. We say of people, "They found themselves in an unusual situation, which afforded exceptional opportunities," or, "His situation was desperate." We do not deal with the universe at large; neither do we deal with single things, events, or persons in succession. We are always acting within a limited setting which includes various circumstances, and probably other actors in addition to ourselves. In this sense the situation, including both agent or agents and the circumstances confronting him or them, is the unit of experience. Moreover, it has value quality, as is suggested by such descriptive words as those above: cheerful, dynamic, and hostile.[3]

This description seems to come from another world than Santayana's. In a certain sense it does come from another world. It comes from a basically different way of handling the world's evidence, from a different world hypothesis. Contextualism is the youngest of the relatively adequate world views and is still in its tentative stages. But through the work of James and Peirce, Schiller and Bergson, Mead and Dewey, and many others it has already had a great influence on contemporary thought. It has produced operationalism in science, instrumentalism in logic, and a new kind of objective relativism in ethics and social theory. Its influence on esthetic theory is equally pronounced, though I do not know by what name to call it other than contextualistic esthetics.

Esthetic experience is obviously to be found, on such a view, in a human situation. It has been uniformly identified, moreover, by competent contextualists with the qualitative side of a situation. As Otis Lee points out, every situation has its unique quality. There is pretty general agreement that the esthetic character of a situation consists in the perception of its quality. Whether there should be any further qualification of the field depends on the question of its congruence with the field of the test common sense definition, referred to in the first lecture.[4] And the field of humanly intuited qualities of events does seem too wide. Even when narrowed to vividly intuited quality, it includes toothaches and other involuntarily endured pains which common sense would never tolerate as positive esthetic values. Accordingly, I suggest for the contextualistic definition of the esthetic field: *voluntary vivid intuitions of quality.*

This appears to me a better definition than that of "enjoyable intuitions of quality" implied occasionally by contextualists, though it comes to much the same thing. Men will not voluntarily remain long in a painful experience. They turn it into a practical situation and seek means to get out of it. A voluntary intuition of vivid quality is either pleasant or finds something so satisfying in the situation that it absorbs the pain. But if one wants to get at the particular force of contextualistic criticism, he does better not to think about the pleasure (leave that to the mechanist) but about the experience. The contextualist is a gourmand for experience. The stress is on the experience, the unique quality of the experience, and it is this that is quantified to give the contextualistic esthetic standard. *The more vivid the experience and the more extensive and rich its quality, the greater its esthetic value.* Whatever pleasure it contains is incidental, merely a contribution to the situation from an organism involved in it. As Otis Lee said, "Pleasures, pains, and interests . . . are among its constituents, but it is itself an independent unit." Value lies in the situation as a whole, and the esthetic value lies in the intensity and extensity of its quality. Irwin Edman in his *Arts and the Man*[5] states the view beautifully in these words,

> Whatever experience may portend or signify, veil or reveal, it is irretrievably there. It may be intensified and heightened or dulled and obscured. It may remain brutal and dim and chaotic; it may become meaningful and clear and alive. For a moment in one aspect, for a lifetime in many, experience may achieve lucidity and vividness, intensity and depth. To effect such an intensification and clarification of experience is the province of art.[6]

Intensity and depth of experience—that is the contextualistic standard of beauty.

And let me say again that the evidential support for this definition of esthetic value lies not alone in what it can do in the esthetic field, but in its conformity with a mode of handling all evidence according to the contextualistic world hypothesis. Its success in the esthetic field contributes to the evidence for the contextualistic world hypothesis, but the success of this world hypothesis in other fields gives at the same time a wide corroborative support to the empirical justification of this definition.

Now I will expand some of the esthetic implications of this view, and show their bearing on the judgment of a work of art. These may be brought out by a series of contrasts. I will arrange them in a pair of columns:

Quality *vs.* Relations

Intuition *vs.* Analysis

Fusion *vs.* Diffusion

Unity *vs.* Detail

The left hand column represents the esthetic features of a situation; the right hand column, the analytical features which are for the most part the practical also. Every human situation has a certain proportion of both of these sets of features. For it is the quality that determines the unity and range of a situation (at least esthetically) and it is the fused details and relations that determine the content. There is accordingly no sharp line in experience between the esthetic and the non-esthetic. Esthetic value runs out into all life, though it runs pretty thinly through much of it. It is characteristic of contextualistic esthetics that there is no negative esthetic value. Beauty is found in a vivid realization of the quality of a situation, and, where vivid realization fails, beauty is absent. What we call ugliness, on this view, is a drab or painful situation calling for practical action, which we deplore because we feel morally that it ought to be beautiful. Ugliness is moral disapproval of the absence of esthetic value in a situation. It is an ethical rather than an esthetic evaluation. But this moral judgment is very close to the esthetic. And it is another characteristic of contextualistic point of view not to admit of sharp lines between different spheres of judgment. So one is at a loss to say of Dewey's *Art as Experience*, which has proved quite justifiably the most influential esthetic work in contextualistic literature, whether it is mainly a book in esthetics or in ethics. It is a crusade against all manner of attitudes and customs and social conditions which stand in the way of our getting the fullest realization of our environment and our lives.

But to return to our two columns of contrasted features of a situation. These will require explanation for any one not familiar with them. Yet in a fundamental sense they defy explanation, since they are basic categories in this world hypothesis. They are ultimate concepts in terms of which other concepts are explained in contextualism. There is nothing one can do but point to them. So that is what I shall try to do by means of a stanza from a lyric of Coleridge's:

A sunny shaft did I behold
From sky to earth it slanted;
And poised therein a bird so bold—
Sweet bird, thou wert enchanted.
—"Glycine's Song"

Now if you permit the image to form from this lyric and the words and the rhythm to have their way, something will surely have happened between you and these sounds in the brief time of my reading the verses. Whatever the quality of the previous moments in the context of this lecture room with the blackboard behind me and this desk in front and these seats and the listeners and the concepts of a theory being expounded, I am sure Coleridge's verses brought in an event with quite a different color. Well, that is what the contextualist means by quality. It is the character, the mood, and you might almost say, the personality of an event. You will not find it easy to give an adequately descriptive name to this stanza. "Cheerful," "optimistic," "anticipative"—these touch upon the quality of Coleridge's lines, but do not name it. It requires a proper name. That is what Otis Lee meant by speaking of a characteristic quality, "which is unique in each situation." If you wish to carry this principle of uniqueness to the limit, you will say that every one of us in the room had a different event with a different quality, and that for each one of us at another reading these verses will have yet another quality. As Dewey says, "A new poem is created by every one who reads poetically. . . . Every individual brings with him . . . a way of seeing and feeling that in its interaction with old material creates something new, something previously not existing in experience."[7] There is a truth in this insight never to be forgotten. There is an ultimate, irreducible relativity of contexts. Two situations never exactly repeat. It is the relativism of contextualism. But at the same time and by the same principle there is a connectedness of contexts, which is reflected in the qualities of the connected events. There is a family likeness among the qualities of my own separate readings of this poem, and without much question also among the qualities of your several simultaneous events in listening to it just now. So, it is possible to speak with a fairly high degree of approximation to agreement of *the* quality of the poem. We shall have more to say about this matter later; but for the present let it rest at this, that while technically it is true that the quality of every event is unique and unrepeated, practically the large amount of identity of context in the perception of a work of art renders the differences relatively negligible, so that it is practically correct to speak of an identical quality running through our technically different situations.

That, then, is what quality is. It is what you experienced as the total character of the reading of those lines. Next observe that this character is derived from a fusion of the characters of the details interrelated within the stanza. Just single out the image of the bird poised in the shaft of light. That is a remarkably clear-cut unity. But see what goes to make it up. Observe some of the phrases and the words. Consider "sunny shaft" and "slanted" and "from sky to earth" (notice, not from earth to sky), and "I behold" just preceding "from sky" and suggesting looking up, and "poised therein," and "bold sweet bird," and "enchanted." It is an event magically, momentarily caught and crystalized and shaped into one unified image character. But on analysis we see that the character of the image grows out of a fusion, the cementing together or the interpenetration of the interrelated details.

Get the quality of "sunny shaft" by itself. Isolated as a separate event quoted out of its context, it has its own quality. And get the quality of "bold sweet bird." And then put them both back into their context in the total image, and do you not see that something has happened to them in their union in the total texture? That is their fusion. It is like the separate notes of a chord which fuse in the specific character of the chord, which yet is made out of the very characters of the notes that compose it. Fusion is thus pointed to as something ultimate, and unanalyzable, and immediate.

Now, let us see what all this comes to. Our little piece of analysis has succeeded in bringing out every term set down in the two contrasted columns. A situation or event is a unity with details. If we intuit the unity of it, as we did in the original reading, we get the quality of the event by a fusion of its interrelated details. If we analyze it to find the relations of its details, we diffuse the unity and lose the quality of the whole, or at least diminish its vividness in following out the details. Do you see that too? For we have done both. We have both synthesized and analyzed. We have had a first intuition of the total quality, and then we have partially analyzed the relations of the details which entered into it.

It must now be clear that the four terms in each column all go together, and amount to so many ways of designating either the wholeness or the composition of a situation.

It appears further that the two columns are correlative to each other. There is no such thing as a situation having a quality without interrelated details to make it up. And there is no such thing as an analysis of details unless there is a total situation to be analyzed into its details. Moreover, the two columns are inversely related: the greater the fusion and the intuition of the quality of the whole, the less the analytical sense of the separate details and their relations and *vice versa*. Moreover, there are all degrees of cognition from total fusion through the various proportions of intuition and analysis to complete analysis with just enough sense of the unity of the situation to give the analysis significance. Finally, vividness of quality is, with certain exceptions, associated with fusion and intuition, and loss of vividness with attention to relations and analysis.[8]

Of the four terms named in the first or esthetic column, fusion is the one likely to give most trouble and is, in a way, the key to the others. It is the process which connects the two columns by transmitting the separate details of the analytical situation into the unified quality of the esthetic situation. It is ignored, disparaged, or explained away by most other world hypotheses—called merely subjective, a result of insufficient analysis, mere vagueness, or nothing but a lot of undiscriminated elements. In rebuttal the contextualist points to it as an ultimate categorial fact of immediacy. He insistently repeats that it cannot be explained away because it is something in terms of which he explains other things. And for that very reason it cannot be explained. One cannot explain an ultimate fact. . . .

But even if it cannot be explained, we can say things about it. For, of course, fusion is not explained by pointing out that the quality of a fusion is made up of the qualities of the details fused. The whole point about a fusion is that it results in a quality different from the qualities of any of its constituents. Once more I refer you back to Coleridge's lines read as a whole and our later analysis of its details. The quality of the fusion is different from the sum of the qualities of its analyzed factors. It is an emergent. Or to say the same thing in reverse and in a way that is perhaps more familiar, analysis always destroys something. It begins by destroying the vividness of the quality of the whole and may end by destroying the esthetic whole.

Now, so far as the relevance of fusion to the esthetic values is concerned, it is, I believe, equivalent to emotional perception. You remember William James identified emotion with the fusion (that was his own word) of organic and kinesthetic sensations. There is no very good reason why he should not have included the external sensations also when these are present. Actually, in any emotional reaction there is no clear separation of visual, auditory, or tactile sensations from the internal and dynamic ones. The sound of thunder is with difficulty distinguished from its fearfulness. The sound is fused with all the other things which W. B. Cannon shows enter into fear. Moreover, there are funded memories entering in. The fusion of all these makes up the specific fear of thunder. This basic insight of the James-Lange theory of emotion appears to hold in spite of all the criticisms of it. Only, what James should have stressed was not the kind of sensations that make an emotional quality, but the manner of their appearance, their fusion. In short, vividly fused experience is, for esthetic purposes at least, a very convenient definition of emotional experience. When the fusion is massive and unmistakably draws in the dynamic tensions of instinctive action, no one would hesitate to call it emotional. The importance of this comment is to suggest that the contextualistic account is the one that particularly takes care of the emotional aspect of esthetic experience, and does so inconspicuously, realistically, and without the sentimentality and mythology of mysticism which parades its emotionality. It is symptomatic that Dewey frequently chooses the word "seizure" to designate the highest esthetic experience. It is an experience in which a total situation is absorbed in a vivid fused satisfying quality.

How may vividness of quality be increased? This is best discovered by observing what produces its opposite. There are chiefly three causes for the reduction of vividness: (1) habit, convention, tradition, and the like; (2) practical activity in achieving goals; and (3) analysis.

Habit simply dulls experience and reduces it to routine. Practical activity ordinarily drains off vividness of quality by its urgency to attain its goal, or by producing a problem to solve which turns the attention away from the felt character of a situation to a solution in the future and escapes from the present. It also leads to analysis of the situation, in search for the means of solution, and the devivifying effect of analysis we have already brought out.

These then, one would think, should be scrupulously avoided in pursuit of esthetic values. But one of the paradoxes of contextualism is that the last two, practical activity and analysis, when carefully applied, can be powerful agents for increasing quality. Human conflict, which is the greatest source of practical problems, is a potent means of intensifying experience by breaking up the dullness of routine, provided only the impulses involved can be held in contemplation and restrained from seeking practical solution. And analysis has a great capacity for increasing the spread of a vivid situation by exhibiting its structure and the details of its organization.

The ways in which artists have learned to increase the vividness of quality by the discreet use of conflict, and to increase the spread of quality by the organization of details, are known as the artists' techniques. The latter, the principles of composition, of design, pattern, and the intrinsic orders of sense materials are much better known to writers of esthetics and criticism than the former—that is, the techniques of conflict. (Incidentally, notice how considerations of sense materials come up last in contextualistic esthetics rather than first as in the mechanistic. The normal structure of a mechanistic book on esthetics is from the elements to the wholes; that of a contextualistic book from the wholes to the details.[9]) It should not be said that the techniques of design and pattern are less important to the contextualistic critic than those of vivification through conflict, but certainly attention to the handling of conflict for esthetic purposes is a peculiar contribution of contextualism.

It is remarkable how few contextualistic writers on art have noticed this. They tend to veer off after a good start in contextualism toward an integrative, organistic theory of art. If esthetic value is a matter of vividness of quality, there is virtue in integration as a means of increasing the spread of quality through massive organization. This is an old story, the old story of harmonious unity. But it is something new in esthetic theory to discover the esthetic value of conflict. This side of his theory is what a contextualist should exploit. The integration he should stress is an integration of conflicts.

The techniques for the esthetic use of conflict have been very little explored. The concept of "psychical distance" marks about the limit of it—that is, the idea that a man cannot get esthetic value out of an experience that draws upon his emotions unless he can maintain an attitude that will keep these emotions from bolting into action. You can appreciate a storm as long as you are not prompted to look for a lifeboat, and you can appreciate Hamlet as long as he does not remind you too much of your own personality problems. That is about as far as criticism along these lines has gone. But very few have noticed the reverse of this idea, which is much the more interesting, that in proportion as these conflicts do touch you (to the point of not precipitating action) the esthetic value of the experience is increased.

This fact has two important esthetic bearings. For one thing, it explains in large degree the force of tragedy in art. Most of what we have taken to be our greatest art is outright tragedy or contains tragic portions. To a hedonist this is a mystery. Why in the temple of pleasure do we set up a god of sorrow? A contextualist explains that when the center of esthetic interest is placed on vivid realization of experience, then the attraction of the artist to tragic subject matter is seen as inevitable. Conflicts of instinctive impulse and social interest stir our awareness of experience to the deepest, and the further they can be carried in a work of art towards their full tragic import the more vivid our realization. Tragedy in art then becomes no paradox.

The second bearing of the use of conflict in art is ethical. We now begin to understand how moral values enter into art. For in spite of the hedonists' efforts like that of the early Santayana to separate morality from art as something purely negative, or, like that of Pater to seek to identify moral and esthetic values, we recoil and feel that the relation is not so simple. The conviction persists that the ethical values are different from the esthetic, and that nevertheless in the most serious art they somehow get intimately involved with each other. Now we see that this is indeed the case, and why it happens. An artist seeks out social issues because they reflect conflicts and are sources of vivid realization of experience. In this way, an artist becomes a more powerful moral influence than a social reformer. For he possesses the techniques for making us vividly aware of our problems and cultivates a keenness of perception for precisely what are the sources of human conflict. Think how many essays were written with mild effect about the farm labor problem in America until Steinbeck came out with *The Grapes of Wrath*. Then for the first time the problem became vivid through the technique of an artist.

Dewey's prevailing message that art should get closer to living and that it grows weak when it is taken as luxury and entertainment and separated from the main stream of practical everyday contemporary living, is contextualistically sound. And a corollary of this principle is that art is perennially contemporary. So far as art depends on culture and not upon instinct, the art of one age cannot be vividly repeated in another, and, if the art of an earlier age appeals to a later, it is often for other than the original reasons, so that as contextualists repeat, sometimes too insistently, critics are required in each age to register the esthetic judgments of that age.

We can already see what is expected of the critic on the contextualistic view. He is to judge the degree of realization of experience achieved by an artist—the vividness and the spread of it. He will consider whether the artist has made the most of his emotional material, or has gone beyond the limits of esthetic endurance and destroyed esthetic distance. He will show the relation of the work to its social context. He will consider the suitability of the structure of the work. And for the benefit of the spectator he will analyze the structure and exhibit its details, so that these will not be missed and may be funded in the full realization of the work in its total fused quality.

So much we see of what the critic is expected to do. But we have not yet seen what a work of art is on this view. And until we have, we cannot entirely comprehend the critic's rôle. For the description of the nature of a work of art furnished by a consistent application of the contextualistic approach is one of the special contributions of this theory. With that description and its bearing on criticism, I shall conclude this lecture.

The perception of a work of art is clearly the awareness of the quality of a situation. There are obviously two main factors in the situation of perceiving a work of art, and it is the relation of these two factors through successive perceptions of the identical work that is to be noticed. I think I can make this situation, or rather the succession of situations, clearer by a diagram. The two main factors are, first, what we ordinarily call the physical work of art—that is, the stone or bronze of a statue, the canvas and pigments of painting, the score of a piece of music, the paper and print of a book—and, second, the spectator. Here is the diagram:

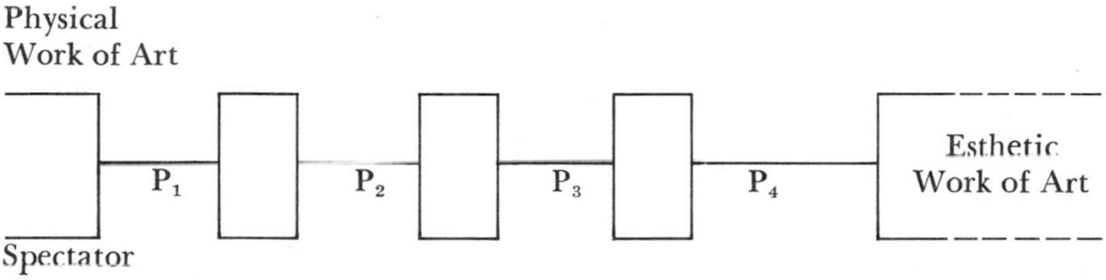

The upper line represents the physical work of art, the lower line the spectator. If you follow these along, you will see they are both continuous lines. When they come together at P_1, P_2, P_3 . . . we have perceptual situations. Suppose we think of a picture, say El Greco's "Toledo" in the Metropolitan Museum. The physical picture has had a long continuous history since El Greco laid the pigments on the canvas. And, supposing I am the spectator, so have I as an organism and personality had a long continuous history—though not so long. When I first saw the "Toledo," that was P_1. Some time later I saw it again, P_2, and so on. And I hope to see it yet many times to come, which is the meaning of the dotted lines.

Now whatever the nature of the physical work of art apart from the spectator, we know it has not the quality of the perceived picture, for the quality of the perception includes colors and line movements and clouds and hills and city walls and these require the action of a spectator in the situation before they can appear. Similarly the quality of that El Greco did not exist for the spectator, for me, till I first came in contact with the physical picture in the Metropolitan Museum. The quality of the "Toledo," then, arises out of a situation to which the physical work of art and the spectator are both contributing. It requires the two in contact to produce the perception and realize the quality. It is true that the spectator can, once he has perceived the picture, bring up the memory of it, but we shall not here concern ourselves with this phase of the matter nor with photographs or other possible reproductions of the original. Strictly speaking, the quality of the picture is only realized on the occasions when it is actually perceived. Each such experience is an esthetic experience.

But the next point is the important one. Normally each successive perception funds the previous one and adds something new not perceived before. Some new detail comes out, some line carries through as not observed before, some shape is seen as a contrast or subtle variation of another. These potentialities were in the picture from the beginning, but now for the first time I see them. And so the picture increases in breadth and vividness of quality from perception to perception. Not that there is a steady increase. Sometimes I am fatigued and see and feel it less than at earlier times. And sometimes I analyze it and voluntarily reduce quality for that perception in order to fund the results of the analysis in future perceptions and so increase the quality. But in general and over a number of perceptions, the realization of the work increases.

What all this means is that the esthetic work of art is the cumulative succession of intermittent perceptions. It is $P_1 + P_2 + P_3 + \ldots$ The esthetic work of art is not continuous but intermittent. This fact has rarely been given sufficient attention. But the intermittency and fugitive nature of the esthetic work of art does not stand in the way of a high degree of objectivity in the esthetic judgment of it. For the potentiality of the cumulative series of perceptions and of the ideal of the fully realized and funded perception at the end of the series lies in the actual continuity of the physical work of art. It lies in this and in the continuity of each spectator and in the considerable degree of uniformity in the perceptive capacities of different spectators.

The only adequate judgment of a work of art, therefore, is one based on the fullest realization of it, on a perception which contains the funded experiences of many preceding perceptions. An initial perception is superficial and untrustworthy unless the spectator has had much experience with similar works, or unless the work is clearly very simple and requires no further experience. Moreover, any one man's judgment of a very rich work of art is likely to need supplementation from that of another. For every spectator has his blind spots, and, to reach a complete judgment of a work of art, many men are needed in order to draw out its total capacity of realization. A complete esthetic work of art thus becomes an ideal, realizable in the lesser works but perhaps rarely fully realized in the greater—possibly not even by the creating artist himself so many possibilities of realization may unconsciously enter in. It is that ideal final perception which rolls up all that is relevant in the line of preceding perceptions and intuits the whole potentiality of the physical work of art in a total vivid seizure.

This conception of the esthetic work of art as a succession of cumulative perceptions leading up to a total funded perception which realizes the full appreciative capacities of the physical object seems to me the soundest and most fruitful to have appeared. It can be adapted to other points of view in esthetics, but it generates spontaneously only out of the contextualistic.

Ironically, the contextualist himself does not seem to be able to make the most of it. He is so impressed with evidences of historical change and cultural influences and the shifting contexts of value that he cannot easily bring himself to accept any degree of permanence in esthetic values. I would be far from asserting that beauty is eternal. But on the evidence of the other three world hypotheses I am convinced that there is much more permanence in the world than the contextualist admits. And I believe that the capacity of a great work of art to be appreciated exists as long as the physical work exists and there are men to perceive it. So far as a work of art appeals to our common instincts and our deepest emotions, it can move men of whatever age or culture. It may from accident of language and fashion and national or religious bigotry come in and out of popularity, but there it is ready to move the common man or the student who will put himself in contact with it. Potentially, the contextualist has given us an empirical basis for this belief.

But even if the contextualist does not care to take full advantage of his discovery, he has uncovered a new function for the critic. That is to contribute as far as he can to the complete realization of great works of art. The critic acquires a sort of creative function. It is something more than giving an expert judgment on the esthetic value of the work. It is an act of producing the values latent therein. And it requires the coöperation of many perceptive men to do this, since the capacities of a great work of art for esthetic appreciation can rarely be compassed by one man alone. Many men contribute their perceptions and gradually the full potential perception comes to light. When this is achieved, the esthetic work of art has attained its final judgment.

If the contextualist himself displays a skepticism about final judgments of any kind, we will respect his testimony, but we will balance it against that of other men of equal competence in handling the evidence. . . .

—*The Basis of Criticism in the Arts* (1946)

Notes

1. *The Journal of Philosophy*, XLI (1944), 337–360.
2. *Ibid.*, p. 337.
3. *Ibid.*, pp. 338–339.
4. Professor Pepper is here referring to the following remarks: "In the esthetic field . . . it is generally acknowledged that the poems, pictures, statues, musical compositions of the great artists are esthetic materials, and also many buildings such as medieval cathedrals, and fondly made tools like paddles and baskets and pottery of primitive peoples, and dance and ritual, and also certain perceptions of nature like the sea and starry nights and sunsets and pleasant pastures and groves and sometimes fear-inspiring scenes like storms and waterfalls. . . . To deny that these are works of art or objects of beauty would be regarded by most men as contrary to common sense. As objects and experiences commonly denoted as beautiful or esthetic these may be taken as the common ostensive reference of these terms. Hereby we have a common sense ostensive definition of the esthetic field." (Editor's note.)
5. *Arts and the Man; A Short Introduction to Esthetics* (New York: W. W. Norton & Co., 1939).
6. *Ibid.*, p. 12.
7. *Art as Experience* (New York: Minton, Balch & Co., 1934), p. 108.
8. There seem to be two main exceptions: First, states of alertness, where in preparing to solve or meet a situation one is keenly observant of the details of the situation. In an emergency, for instance, perception is, for a man who keeps

his head, very vivid and at the same time analytical. It is as though an organism could under conditions of emergency calling for exceptional output of energy be at once intuitive and analytical. The contrast between the two attitudes is here partially dissolved and we have almost the two in one. . . . (*Cf.* L. E. Hahn, *A Contextualistic Theory of Perception* [University of California Press, 1942], pp. 120–121.)

The second exception is of an opposite nature, where through habit vividness is dulled though the fused intuition of the quality of the situation is undoubtedly there. This is the way we meet familiar objects about the town, familiar faces about the house.

But barring states of alertness and habit, then for all states of ordinary perception the correlation of vividness of quality with fusion, and of the loss of vividness in the quality of a total situation with analysis and diffusion seems to hold good.

9. Compare, for instance, Santayana's *Sense of Beauty* with Pepper's *Aesthetic Quality*.

BERNARD BOSANQUET

Easy and Difficult Beauty

The difficulty, amounting for some persons to repellence, which belongs to such beauty as makes the rarer appeal, may take different forms. I suggest three. I do not say that they cover all the cases. I will call them: (a) intricacy; (b) tension; (c) width.

(a) The case of intricacy is very instructive, because in it you can often show to demonstration that the more difficult esthetic object has all that the simpler has, and more. You could show this in many conventional patterns, e.g., in the case of the common volutes which are so often found separate, and which are also combined with the palmetto pattern in the design from the ceiling of the treasury at Orchomenus. And I presume that you can show the same thing very completely in music, where the failure of appreciation is often simply the inability to follow a construction which possesses intricacy beyond a certain degree. And, no doubt, there is apt to be a positive revulsion against a difficulty which we cannot solve. It is very noticeable in esthetic education how the appreciation of what is too intricate for us begins with isolated bits, which introduce us to the pervading beautiful quality of the texture we are trying to apprehend—a lovely face in an old Italian picture, before we are ready to grasp its "music of spaces"; a magnificent couplet in *Sordello,* which has been said to contain the finest isolated distichs in the English language; or a simple melody in a great symphony. When it is demonstrated to one that the texture at every point is exquisitely beautiful, as is always the case in the works which furnish the higher and rarer test of appreciation—we may think of Dante's *Inferno*—it is easier to believe that one's failure to grasp the whole is simply a defect in one's capacity of attention. And the progress of one's education confirms this suggestion. The difficult beauty simply gives you too much, at one moment, of what you are perfectly prepared to enjoy if only you could take it all in.

(b) The same thing is true with the higher tension of feeling. Aristotle speaks, in a most suggestive phrase, of the "weakness of the spectators," which shrinks from the essence of tragedy. In other words, the capacity to endure and enjoy feeling at high tension is somewhat rare. The principle is the same as that of intricacy, but it is a different case. Such feeling may be embodied in structures, e.g., in words, which look very simple. But yet it demands profound effort and concentration to apprehend them.

An exception, within the area of this particular case, may afford an excellent example of what I called triumphant beauty—beauty which, although of the most distinguished quality, is universal in its appeal. I mean when a passage of feeling at high tension, simply and directly expressed, has the mixture of luck and merit which makes it strike on some great nerve of humanity, and thus conquer the suffrages of the world. Great artists, from Plato to Balzac, have laid stress on this possibility, and Balzac at least was not the man needlessly to admit anything in derogation of the pure prerogative of art. I have never found the man or woman to whom the Demeter of Knidos failed to appeal, and it surely cannot be set down as facile beauty in the depreciatory sense.

But, in general, one may say that the common mind—and all our minds are common at times—resents any great effort or concentration, and for the same reason resents the simple and severe forms which are often the only fitting embodiment of such a concentration—forms which promise, as Pater says, a great expressiveness, but only on condition of being received with a great attentiveness. The kind of effort required is not exactly an intellectual effort; it is something more, it is an imaginative effort, that is to say, as we saw, one in which the body-and-mind, without resting upon a fixed system like that of accepted conventional knowledge, has to frame for itself as a whole an experience in which it can "live" the embodiment before it. When King John says to Hubert the single word "death," the word is, in a sense, easily apprehended; but the state of the whole man behind the broken utterance may take some complete transformation of mental attitude to enter into. And such a transformation may not be at all easy or comfortable; it may be even terrible, so that in Aristotle's phrase the weakness of the spectator shrinks from it. And this is very apt to apply, on one ground or another, to all great art, or indeed to all that is great of any kind. There is no doubt a resentment against what is great, if we cannot rise to it. I am trying to elucidate the point that in all this difficult beauty, which goes beyond what is comfortable for the indolent or timid mind, there is nothing but a "more" of the same beautiful, which we find prima facie pleasant, changed only by being intensified. But this is enough to prevent us from recognizing it as beauty, except by self-education or a natural insight.

(c) I suggested yet another dimension of the more difficult beauty, under the name of "width."

It is a remarkable and rather startling fact that there are genuine lovers of beauty, well equipped in scholarship, who cannot really enjoy Aristophanes, or Rabelais, or the Falstaff scenes of Shakespeare. This is again, I venture to think, a "weakness of the spectator." In strong humor or comedy you have to endure a sort of dissolution of the conventional world. All the serious accepted things are shown you topsy-turvy; beauty, in the narrow and current sense, among them. The comic spirit enjoys itself at the expense of everything; the gods are starved out and brought to terms by the birds' command of the air, cutting off the vapor of sacrifice on which they lived; Titania falls in love with Bottom the weaver; Falstaff makes a fool of the Lord Chief Justice of England.

All this demands a peculiar strength to encompass with sympathy its whole width. You must feel a liberation in it all; it is partly like a holiday in the mountains or a voyage at sea; the customary scale of everything is changed, and you yourself perhaps are revealed to yourself as a trifling insect or a moral prig.

And it is to be noted, that you need strength to cover all this width without losing hold of the center. If you wholly lost the normal view of all these things which you are to see upside down, the comedy would all be killed dead at once. It is the contrast that makes the humor. If religion is not a serious thing to you, there is no fun in joking about it.

In this region, that of humor, expression is, I think, inevitably very complex, as is the feeling it embodies. It is a sort of counter-expression—the normal, all of it, plus a further point of view, caricatured, *chargé*, loaded, or burdened with an abnormal emphasis.

Thus, here again, you have the more, as compared with the normal experience of the beautiful; you have a wide range of forms, all of them distinguished by an attitude taken up towards the conventional attitude. And this demands both a complexity of expression and a complexity of mood, departing widely from the lines of the ordinary moods of serious life, and even of serious esthetic experience. Comedy always shocks many people.

So much for difficult beauty. Now the object of thus insisting on these two grades of beauty was twofold.

First, to defend, as not merely convenient but right, the extension of the term beauty to all that is esthetically excellent. For the insight of gifted persons regards it all as one; and the recognition of the same nature in it throughout in consequence of sincere self-education is a question of more and less in the way of attentiveness and imaginative effort. There is no constant line to be drawn between easy and difficult beauty. And I think we must all have noticed that the gift of esthetic appreciativenes has more to do with sincerity of character than with intellectual capacity. In the appreciation of great things, so much depends on teachableness, and the absence of self-absorption and the yearning to criticize.

And, secondly, it was to prepare us to approach the fundamental problem of what we mean by real ugliness. For this account of the degrees and areas of beauty nibbles away to some extent the current antithesis of beauty and ugliness.

Intricacy, tension, and width account for a very large proportion of so-called ugliness, that is to say, of what shocks most people, or else seems to them repellently uninteresting, or overstrained, or fantastic. All this part of ugliness then seems due to the weakness of the spectator, whether his object is nature or art. Note how slowly, e.g., the beauty of old age, I mean of real wrinkled old age, not stately and splendid old age, gains recognition in sculpture; I think not before the Alexandrine period.

—*Three Lectures on Aesthetic* (1915)

GEORGE ORWELL

Benefit of Clergy

Autobiography is only to be trusted when it reveals something disgraceful. A man who gives a good account of himself is probably lying, since any life when viewed from the inside is simply a series of defeats. However, even the most flagrantly dishonest book (Frank Harris's autobiographical writings are an example) can without intending it give a true picture of its author. Dali's recently published *Life*[1] comes under this heading. Some of the incidents in it are flatly incredible, others have been rearranged and romanticized, and not merely the humiliation but the persistent *ordinariness* of everyday life has been cut out. Dali is even by his own diagnosis narcissistic, and his autobiography is simply a striptease act conducted in pink limelight. But as a record of fantasy, of the perversion of instinct that has been made possible by the machine age, it has great value.

Here, then, are some of the episodes in Dali's life, from his earliest years onward. Which of them are true and which are imaginary hardly matters: the point is that this is the kind of thing that Dali would have *liked* to do.

When he is six years old, there is some excitement over the appearance of Halley's comet:

> Suddenly one of my father's office clerks appeared in the drawing-room doorway and announced that the comet could be seen from the terrace. . . .While crossing the hall I caught sight of my little three-year-old sister crawling unobtrusively through a doorway. I stopped, hesitated a second, then gave her a terrible kick in the head as though it had been a ball, and continued running, carried away with a "delirious joy" induced by this savage act. But my father, who was behind me, caught me and led me down into his office, where I remained as a punishment till dinner-time.

A year earlier than this Dali had "suddenly, as most of my ideas occur," flung another little boy off a suspension bridge. Several other incidents of the same kind are recorded, including (this was when he was twenty-nine years old) knocking down and trampling on a girl "until they had to tear her, bleeding, out of my reach."

When he is about five, he gets hold of a wounded bat which he puts into a tin pail. Next morning he finds that the bat is almost dead and is covered with ants which are devouring it. He puts it in his mouth, ants and all, and bites it almost in half.

When he is adolescent, a girl falls desperately in love with him. He kisses and caresses her so as to excite her as much as possible, but refuses to go further. He resolves to keep this up for five years (he calls it his "five-year plan"), enjoying her humiliation and the sense of power it gives him. He frequently tells her that at the end of five years he will desert her, and when the time comes he does so.

Till well into adult life, he keeps up the practice of masturbation, and likes to do this, apparently, in front of a looking-glass. For ordinary purposes he is impotent, it appears, till the age of thirty or so. When he first meets his future wife, Gala, he is greatly tempted to push her off a precipice. He is aware that there is something that she wants him to do to her, and after their first kiss the confession is made:

> I threw back Gala's head, pulling it by the hair, and trembling with complete hysteria, I commanded:
>
> "Now tell me what you want me to do with you! But tell me slowly, looking me in the eye, with the crudest, the most ferociously erotic words that can make both of us feel the greatest shame!"
>
> . . . Then Gala, transforming the last glimmer of her expression of pleasure into the hard light of her own tyranny, answered:
>
> "I want you to kill me!"

He is somewhat disappointed by this demand, since it is merely what he wanted to do already. He contemplates throwing her off the bell-tower of the Cathedral of Toledo, but refrains from doing so.

During the Spanish Civil War, he astutely avoids taking sides, and makes a trip to Italy. He feels himself more and more drawn toward the aristocracy, frequents smart salons, finds himself wealthy patrons, and is photographed with the plump Vicomte de Noailles, whom he describes as his "Maecenas." When the European War approaches, he has one preoccupation only: how to find a place which has good cookery and from which he can make a quick bolt if danger comes too near. He fixes on Bordeaux, and duly flees to Spain during the Battle of France. He stays in Spain long enough to pick up a few anti-red atrocity stories, then makes for America. The story ends in a blaze of respectability. Dali, at thirty-seven, has become a devoted husband, is cured of his aberrations, or some of them, and is completely reconciled to the Catholic Church. He is also, one gathers, making a good deal of money.

However, he has by no means ceased to take pride in the pictures of his surrealist period, with titles like *The Great Masturbator, Sodomy of a Skull with a Grand Piano,* etc. There are reproductions of these all the way through the book. Many of Dali's drawings are simply representational and have a characteristic to be noted later. But from his surrealist paintings and photographs the two thing that stand out are sexual perversity and necrophilia. Sexual objects and symbols—some of them well known, like our old friend the high-heeled slipper, others, like the crutch and the cup of warm milk, patented by Dali himself—recur over and over again, and there is a fairly well-marked excretory motif as well. In his painting, *Le Jeu Lugubre,* he says, "The drawers bespattered with excrement were painted with such minute and realistic complacency that the whole little surrealist group was anguished by the question: Is he coprophagic or not?" Dali adds firmly that he is *not,* and that he regards his aberration as "repulsive," but it seems to be only at that point that his interest in excrement stops. Even when he recounts the experience of watching a woman urinate standing up, he has to add the detail that she misses her aim and dirties her shoes. It is not given to any one person to have all the vices, and Dali also boasts that he is not homosexual, but otherwise he seems to have as good an outfit of perversion as anyone could wish for.

However, his most notable characteristic is his necrophilia. He himself freely admits to this, and claims to have been cured of it. Dead faces, skulls, corpses of animals occur fairly frequently in his pictures, and the ants which devoured the dying bat make countless reappearances. One photograph shows an exhumed corpse, far gone in decomposition. Another shows the dead donkeys putrefying on top of grand pianos which formed part of the surrealist film, *Le Chien Andalou.* Dali still looks back on these donkeys with great enthusiasm.

> I "made up" the putrefaction of the donkeys with great pots of sticky glue which I poured over them. Also, I emptied their eyesockets and made them larger by hacking them out with scissors. In the same way, I furiously cut their mouths open to make the rows of their teeth show to better advantage, and I added several jaws to each mouth, so that it would appear that although the donkeys were already rotting they were vomiting up a little more of their own death, above those other rows of teeth formed by the keys of the black pianos.

And finally there is the picture—apparently some kind of faked photograph—of *Mannequin Rotting in a Taxicab.* Over the already somewhat bloated face and breast of the apparently dead girl, huge snails were crawling. In the caption below the picture Dali notes that these are Burgundy snails—that is, the edible kind.

Of course, in this long book of 400 quarto pages there is more than I have indicated, but I do not think that I have given an unfair account of his moral atmosphere and mental scenery. It is a book that stinks. If it were possible for a book to give a physical stink off its pages, this one would—a thought that might please Dali, who before wooing his future wife for the first time rubbed himself all over with an ointment made of goat's dung boiled up in fish glue. But against this has to be set the fact that Dali is a draughtsman of very exceptional gifts. He is also, to judge by the minuteness and sureness of his drawings, a very hard worker. He is an exhibitionist and a careerist, but he is not a fraud. He has fifty times more talent than most of the people who would denounce his morals and jeer at his paintings. And these two sets of facts, taken together, raise a question which for lack of any basis of agreement seldom gets a real discussion.

The point is that you have here a direct, unmistakable assault on sanity and decency; and even—since some of Dali's pictures would tend to poison the imagination like a pornographic postcard—on life itself. What Dali has done and what he has imagined is debatable, but in his outlook, his character, the bedrock decency of a human being does not exist. He is as anti-social as a flea. Clearly, such people are undesirable, and a society in which they can flourish has something wrong with it.

Now, if you showed this book, with its illustrations, to Lord Elton, to Mr. Alfred Noyes, to *The Times* leaderwriters who exult over the "eclipse of the highbrow"—in fact, to any "sensible" art-hating English person—it is easy to imagine what kind of response you would get. They would flatly refuse to see any merit in Dali whatever. Such people are not only unable to admit that what is morally degraded can be esthetically right, but their real demand of every artist is that he shall pat them on the back and tell them that thought is unnecessary. And they can be especially dangerous at a time like the present, when the Ministry of Information and the British Council put power into their hands. For their impulse is not only to crush every new talent as it appears, but to castrate the past as well. Witness the renewed highbrow-baiting that is now going on in this country and America, with its outcry not only against Joyce, Proust, and Lawrence, but even against T. S. Eliot.

But if you talk to the kind of person who *can* see Dali's merits, the response that you get is not as a rule very much better. If you say that Dali, though a brilliant draughtsman, is a dirty little scoundrel, you are looked upon as a savage. If you say that you don't like rotting corpses, and that people who do like rotting corpses are mentally diseased, it is assumed that you lack the esthetic sense. Since *Mannequin Rotting in a Taxicab* is a good composition (as it undoubtedly is), it cannot be a disgusting degrading picture; whereas Noyes, Elton, etc., would tell you that because it is disgusting it cannot be a good composition. And between these two fallacies there is no middle position; or, rather, there is a middle position, but we seldom hear much about it. On the one side, *Kulturbolschewismus*: on the other (though the phrase itself is out of fashion), "Art for Art's sake." Obscenity is a very difficult question to discuss honestly. People are too frightened either of seeming to be shocked or of seeming not to be shocked, to be able to define the relationship between art and morals.

It will be seen that what the defenders of Dali are claiming is a kind of *benefit of clergy*. The artist is to be exempt from the moral laws that are binding on ordinary people. Just pronounce the magic word "Art," and everything is O.K. Rotting corpses with snails crawling over them are O.K.; kicking little girls in the head is O.K.; even a film like *L'Age d'Or* is O.K.[2] It is also O.K. that Dali should batten on France for years and then scuttle off like a rat as soon as France is in danger. So long as you can paint well enough to pass the test, all shall be forgiven you.

One can see how false this is if one extends it to cover ordinary crime. In an age like our own, when the artist is an altogether exceptional person, he must be allowed a certain amount of irresponsibility, just as a pregnant woman is. Still, no one would say that a pregnant woman should be allowed to commit murder, nor would anyone make such a claim for the artist, however gifted. If Shakespeare returned to the earth tomorrow, and if it were found that his favorite recreation was raping little girls in railway carriages, we should not tell him to go ahead with it on the ground that he might write another *King Lear*. And, after all, the worst crimes are not always the punishable ones. By encouraging necrophilic reveries one probably does quite as much harm as by, say, picking pockets at the races. One ought to be able to hold in one's head simultaneously the two facts that Dali is a good draughtsman and a disgusting human being. The one does not invalidate or, in a sense, affect the other. The first thing that we demand of a wall is that it shall stand up. If it stands up, it is a good wall, and the question of what purpose it serves is separable from that. And yet even the best wall in the world deserves to be pulled down if it surrounds a concentration camp. In the same way, it should be possible to say, "This is a good book or a good picture, and it ought to be burned by the public hangman." Unless one can say that, at least in imagination, one is shirking the implications of the fact that an artist is also a citizen and a human being.

Not, of course, that Dali's autobiography, or his pictures, ought to be suppressed. Short of the dirty postcards that used to be sold in Mediterranean seaport towns, it is doubtful policy to suppress anything, and Dali's fantasies probably cast useful light on the decay of capitalist civilization. But what he clearly needs is diagnosis. The question is not so much *what* he is as *why* he is like that. It ought not to be in doubt that he is a diseased intelligence, probably not much altered by his alleged conversion, since genuine penitents, or people who have returned to sanity, do not flaunt their past vices in that complacent way. He is a symptom of the world's illness. The important thing is not to denounce him as a cad who ought to be horsewhipped, or to defend him as a genius who ought not to be questioned, but to find out *why* he exhibits that particular set of aberrations.

The answer is probably discoverable in his pictures, and those I myself am not competent to examine. But I can point to one clue which perhaps takes one part of the distance. This is the old-fashioned, overornate, Edwardian style of drawing to which Dali tends to revert when he is not being surrealist. Some of Dali's drawings are reminiscent of Dürer, one (p. 113) seems to show the influence of Beardsley, another (p. 269) seems to borrow something from Blake. But the most persistent strain is the Edwardian one. When I opened the book for the first time and looked at its innumerable marginal illustrations, I was haunted by a resemblance which I could not immediately pin down. I fetched up at the ornamental candlestick at the beginning of Part I (p. 7). What did this remind me of? Finally I tracked it down. It reminded me of a large, vulgar, expensively got-up edition of Anatole France (in translation) which must have been published about 1914. That had ornamental chapter headings and tailpieces after this style. Dali's candlestick displays at one end a curly fishlike creature that looks curiously familiar (it seems to be based on the conventional dolphin), and at the other is the burning candle. This candle, which recurs in one picture after another, is a very old friend. You will find it, with the same picturesque gouts of wax arranged on its sides, in those phony electric lights done up as candlesticks which are popular in sham-Tudor country hotels. This candle, and the design beneath it, convey at once an intense feeling of sentimentality. As though to counteract this, Dali has spattered a quillful of ink all over the page, but without avail. The same impression keeps popping up on page after page. The design at the bottom of page 62, for instance, would nearly go into *Peter Pan.* The figure on page 224, in spite of having her cranium elongated into an immense sausage-like shape, is the witch of the fairy-tale books. The horse on page 234 and the unicorn on page 218 might be illustrations to James Branch Cabell. The rather pansified drawings of youths on pages 97, 100, and elsewhere convey the same impression. Picturesqueness keeps breaking in. Take away the skull, ants, lobsters, telephones and other paraphernalia, and every now and again you are back in the world of Barrie, Rackham, Dunsany, and *Where the Rainbow Ends.*

Curiously enough, some of the naughty-naughty touches in Dali's autobiography tie up with the same period. When I read the passage I quoted at the beginning, about the kicking of the little sister's head, I was aware of another phantom resemblance. What was it? Of course! *Ruthless Rhymes for Heartless Homes* by Harry Graham. Such rhymes were very popular round about 1912, and one that ran:

> Poor little Willy is crying so sore,
> A sad little boy is he,
> For he's broken his little sister's neck
> And he'll have no jam for tea.

might almost have been founded on Dali's anecdote. Dali, of course, is aware of his Edwardian leanings, and makes capital out of them, more or less in a spirit of pastiche. He professes an especial affection for the year 1900, and claims that every ornamental object of 1900 is full of mystery, poetry, eroticism, madness, perversity, etc. Pastiche, however, usually implies a real affection for the thing parodied. It seems to be, if not the rule, at any rate distinctly common for an intellectual bent to be accompanied by a nonrational, even childish urge in the same direction. A sculptor, for instance, is interested in planes and curves, but he is also a person who enjoys the physical act of mucking about with clay or stone. An engineer is a person who enjoys the feel of tools, the noise of dynamos, and the smell of oil. A psychiatrist usually has a leaning towards some sexual aberration himself. Darwin became a biologist partly because he was a country gentleman and fond of animals. It may be, therefore, that Dali's seemingly perverse cult of Edwardian things (for example, his "discovery" of the 1900 subway entrances) is merely the symptom of a much deeper, less conscious affection. The innumerable, beautifully executed copies of textbook illustrations, solemnly labeled *le rossignol, une montre*, and so on, which he scatters all over his margins, may be meant partly as a joke. The little boy in knickerbockers playing with a diabolo on page 103 is a perfect period piece. But perhaps these things are also there because Dali can't help drawing that kind of thing because it is to that period and that style of drawing that he really belongs.

If so, his aberrations are partly explicable. Perhaps they are a way of assuring himself that he is not commonplace. The two qualities that Dali unquestionably possesses are a gift for drawing and an atrocious egoism. "At seven," he says in the first paragraph of his book, "I wanted to be Napoleon. And my ambition has been growing steadily ever since." This is worded in a deliberately startling way, but no doubt it is substantially true. Such feelings are common enough. "I knew I was a genius," somebody once said to me, "long before I knew what I was going to be a genius *about.*" And suppose that you have nothing in you except your egoism and a dexterity that goes no higher than the elbow; suppose that your real gift is for a detailed, academic, representational style of drawing, your real *métier* to be an illustrator of scientific textbooks. How then do you become Napoleon?

There is always one escape: *into wickedness.* Always do the thing that will shock and wound people. At five, throw a little boy off a bridge, strike an old doctor across the face with a whip and break his spectacles—or, at any rate, dream about doing such things. Twenty years later, gouge the eyes out of dead donkeys with a pair of scissors. Along those lines you can always feel yourself original. And after all, it pays! It is much less dangerous than crime. Making all allowance for the probable suppressions in Dali's autobiography, it is clear that he has not had to suffer for his eccentricities as he would have done in an earlier age. He grew up into the corrupt world of the 1920s, when sophistication was immensely widespread and every European capital swarmed with aristocrats and *rentiers* who had given up sport and politics and taken to patronizing the arts. If you threw dead donkeys at people, they threw money back. A phobia for grasshoppers—which a few decades back would merely have provoked a snigger—was now an interesting "complex" which could be profitably exploited. And when that particular world collapsed before the German army, America was waiting. You could even top it all up with religious conversion, moving at one hop and without a shadow of repentance from the fashionable salons of Paris to Abraham's bosom.

That, perhaps, is the essential outline of Dali's history. But why his aberrations should be the particular ones they were, and why it should be so easy to "sell" such horrors as rotting corpses to a sophisticated public—those are questions for the psychologist and the sociological critic. Marxist criticism has a short way with such phenomena as surrealism. They are "bourgeois decadence" (much play is made with the phrases "corpse poisons" and "decaying *rentier* class"), and that is that. But though this probably states a fact, it does not establish a connection. One would still like to know *why* Dali's leaning was towards necrophilia (and not, say, homosexuality), and *why* the *rentiers* and the aristocrats should buy his pictures instead of hunting and making love like their grandfathers. Mere moral disapproval does not get one any further. But neither ought one to pretend, in the name of "detachment," that such pictures as *Mannequin Rotting in a Taxicab* are morally neutral. They are diseased and disgusting, and any investigation ought to start out from that fact.

—*Dickens, Dali and Others* (1946)

NOTES

1. *The Secret Life of Salvador Dali* (Dial Press, New York, 1942).
2. Dali mentions *L'Age d'Or* and adds that its first public showing was broken up by hooligans, but he does not say in detail what it was about. According to Henry Miller's account of it, it showed among other things some fairly detailed shots of a woman defecating.

CHAPTER 12

The Definitions of the Philosopher

LUDWIG WITTGENSTEIN: Games and Definitions
MORRIS WEITZ: The Role of Theory in Esthetics
MAURICE MANDELBAUM: Family Resemblances and Generalization Concerning the Arts
GEORGE DICKIE: What is Art? An Institutional Analysis

In the preceding chapters we have reviewed different conceptions of art. Various writers have informed us that art is imagination, expression of emotion, intuition, imaginative wish-fulfillment, enchancement of experience, creation of beauty, embodiment of values, significant form, or, with a view to the experience of the beholder, empathy, psychical distance, or some other attitude or psychological state. In view of the breadth of art and the diversity of esthetic theories, the question of the feasibility of definition and the value of esthetic theory becomes paramount. The essays that constitute this chapter focus upon this problem.

Skepticism as to the possibility of a universal definition of "art" or "esthetic" is not new. As Harold Osborne points out in his book, *Aesthetics and Art Theory* (London and New York, 1970), the Scottish philosopher Thomas Reid, as early as 1785, maintained that there is no common essence either in beautiful objects or in works of art, declaring that "I am unable to conceive of any quality in all the different things that are called beautiful, that is the same in them all." Dugald Stewart, another Scottish philosopher quoted by Osborne, explicitly propounded the idea of overlapping similarities, which Wittgenstein later dubbed "family resemblances." "I shall begin by supposing," he declared, "that the letters A, B, C, D, E, denote a series of objects; that A possesses one quality in common with B; B a quality in common with C; C a quality in common with D; D a quality in common with E; while at the same time no quality can be found which belongs in common to any *three* objects in the series." Nevertheless, as he observed, the whole series may be designated by a common name. He even went so far as to propose a radical change in esthetic inquiry, substituting, in place of the search for a common essence, a study of "the natural history of the Human Mind, and . . . its natural progress in the employment of speech." In terms of ordinary language, "art" has been used in a great variety of ways, as Thomas DeQuincey's essay, "Murder as One of the Fine Arts" (1827), bears amusing witness.

The challenge to philosophical inquiry that Reid and Stewart envisage has reached a climax in the twentieth century, especially in the work of Ludwig Wittgenstein (1889–1951). Although he was born and reared in Austria, he spent much of his lifetime in England, as a student and later as a professor at Cambridge University. His immense influence was exerted through the spell of his powerful personality and his two remarkable books, *Tractatus Logico-Philosophicus* (1921) and *Philosophical Investigations* (1953).

Richly endowed with artistic ability, Wittgenstein could design a house, mold a statue, play a clarinet, conduct an orchestra, or write an imaginary dialogue. "Topics in esthetics," declares his former student Norman Malcolm, "were perhaps the most frequent at [his] at-homes, and the depth and richness of Wittgenstein's thinking about art were very exciting."[1] Nevertheless, his published writings contain only casual references to art, and his influence is to be found mainly in his general ideas and method. As the reader peruses Wittgenstein's remarks on "games and definitions," he should consider just how the ideas apply to esthetics.

One of his remarks, as quoted by Malcolm, sums up a good deal of his philosophy: "An expression has meaning only in the stream of life."[2] The meanings of a concept, such as "beauty" or "art," can best be determined by studying its actual use by ordinary human beings as they go about the business of living. When we lay aside preconceptions and study words in their vital employment, we discover that they have no fixed meanings and no sharp edges. An example discussed in the following selection is the word "game." We can find no mark or characteristic, no "essence," that is common to all games—nothing that would permit us to encompass all games in a formula or definition.

"The meaning is the use" is Wittgenstein's famous slogan—and the uses are various and unpredictable. In actual life, words are like tools that can be employed for many different purposes: "Think of the tools in a tool-box; there is a hammer, pliers, a saw, a screwdriver, a rule, a glue-pot, glue, nails and screws.—The functions of words are as diverse as the functions of these objects."[3] Even a single word, such as "beauty," has a multiplicity of uses, and this multiplicity is not predetermined or fixed. We should therefore respect the "open texture" of language, recognizing that a word has an indefinite variety of meanings and that new and unprecedented meanings will arise as the contexts of life alter. The appropriate uses of a word in such a vital context Wittgenstein calls a "language-game," and such "games" vary from one "form of life" to another.

These and other implications of Wittgenstein's philosophy are pointed out by Morris Weitz (1916–   ), professor of philosophy at Brandeis University and distinguished contributor to esthetics. His essay is an example of the considerable influence that Wittgenstein's ideas are exercising on the philosophy of art. He asks the question whether esthetic theory, conceived as a search for the necessary and sufficient properties of art, is possible, and he replies in the negative. Reviewing the main theories of modern esthetics, he concludes that there are no limits to the "open texture" of art and no sharp demarcation or eternal essence that a definition can formulate.

The results of his analysis are not wholly negative. Each of the classical "definitions," he believes, calls attention to an important strand of similarities in artistic works or activities, or recommends some criterion of artistic excellence. The definitions thus point to aspects of art that might otherwise be neglected or underrated. So understood, they are extremely valuable.

Underlying Weitz's argument is the supposition that overlapping similarities are the basis of these attempted definitions in esthetics. This assumption is challenged by Maurice Mandelbaum (1908–   ), professor of philosophy at the Johns Hopkins University and one of America's best known philosophers. To understand his point, let us revert to "games." What is it that makes all examples of games fall within this common category? Wittgenstein's "game" theory is not as radically nominalistic as might be supposed, since he recognizes that one thing all games have in common *is their being games.* His analogy with *family* resemblances is based upon a genetic bond, since "family" implies a common ancestry and hence more than a resemblance—an implication that Wittgenstein apparently recognized but did not stress (see Note 11 in Mandelbaum's essay). Two human beings may closely resemble each other without being members of the same family; and two or more human beings, although they may be *very* dissimilar, are members of one family if they have the same parents.

Noting this fact, Mandelbaum emphasizes unexhibited genetic ties in analyzing games and works of art. Just as fortune-telling with cards is not a game, although it may closely resemble the game of solitaire, so a rock shaped by water erosion is not a work of art, however much it may resemble a piece of abstract sculpture. On the other hand, two very different objects may be works of art if they bear the same sort of relation to human creative or appreciative activities. Using such nonmanifest connections as a basis, Mandelbaum argues that Morris Weitz, Paul Ziff, and other analysts overlook or understress the relation of art to definable human intentions and processes.

Regarded in terms of such nonmanifest characteristics, both games and works of art are definable. Games can be defined in terms of the purpose that they serve—they all have in common "the potentiality of arousing an absorbing nonpractical interest in either participants or spectators." Works of art can likewise be defined in terms of human intentions and interests. Although Mandelbaum stops short of a formal definition, he points out the direction in which a definition may be sought. "A relational attribute of the required sort might, for example, only be apprehended if we were to consider specific art objects as having been created by someone for some actual or possible audience."

George Dickie (1926–   ), an influential esthetician at the University of Illinois in the Chicago Circle, has likewise reacted against the antitheorists. In formulating his "institutional definition of art," he combines Mandelbaum's notion of unexhibited genetic ties with Arthur Danto's social concept of the artworld. Danto has said: "To see something as art requires something the eyes cannot descry—an atmosphere of artistic theory, a knowledge of the history of art: an artworld." With the contentions of Danto and Mandelbaum in mind, Dickie argues that art exists and can be defined within an institutional setting. For an artifact to be a work of art is to have a certain kind of social status conferred on it. Dickie's definition is as follows:

> A work of art in the classificatory sense is (1) an artifact (2) a set of the aspects of which has had conferred upon it the status of candidate for appreciation by some person or persons acting on behalf of a certain social institution (the artworld).

Note the terms of the definition: (a) "A work of art"—not "art" as a creative activity or an appreciative response but as an artifact; (b) "in the classificatory sense"—not the *evaluative* sense. Dickie is not discussing "work of art" as a term used to praise or dispraise, as when we say of a certain painting "That is (or is not) a real work of art"; (c) "is an artifact"—artifactuality is said to belong to the *genus* of works of art; (d) "a set of the aspects of which has had conferred upon it the status of candidate for appreciation"—something is not a work of art until it has acquired this kind of social status; (e) "by some person or persons acting on behalf of a certain social institution (the artworld)"—these last two stipulations comprise the *differentia* of "works of art." Armed with this definition, Dickie discusses such marginal examples as Duchamp's "ready-mades" (urinals, hatracks, snow shovels, and so forth).

Both Weitz and Dickie are in the process of reconsidering. Details of reformulation and replies to objections are to be found in Chapter 3 of Weitz's recent book, *The Opening Mind: A Philosophical Study of Humanistic Concepts* (University of Chicago Press, Chicago, 1978). "There are a lot of things that need to be changed," Dickie has said in a letter to me, "but that would take a very long time." A new formulation will eventually be forthcoming. Having discussed the problem of definition in the Introduction of the present book, I shall say no more at this point.

Notes

1. Norman Malcolm, *Ludwig Wittgenstein: A Memoir* (London, Oxford University Press, 1958), p. 53.
2. *Ibid.*, p. 93.
3. *Philosophical Investigations,* Section 11.

LUDWIG WITTGENSTEIN

Games and Definitions[1]

65. Here we come up against the great question that lies behind all these considerations.—For someone might object against me: "You take the easy way out! You talk about all sorts of language-games, but have nowhere said what the essence of a language-game, and hence of language, is: what is common to all these activities, and what makes them into language or parts of language. So you let yourself off the very part of the investigation that once gave you yourself most headache, the part about the *general form of propositions* and of language."

And this is true.—Instead of producing something common to all that we call language, I am saying that these phenomena have no one thing in common which makes us use the same word for all,—but that they are *related* to one another in many different ways. And it is because of this relationship, or these relationships, that we call them all "language." I will try to explain this.

66. Consider for example the proceedings that we call "games." I mean board games, card games, ball games, Olympic games, and so on. What is common to them all?—Don't say: "There *must* be something common, or they would not be called 'games' "—but *look and see* whether there is anything common to all.—For if you look at them you will not see something that is common to *all*, but similarities, relationships, and a whole series of them at that. To repeat: don't think, but look!—Look for example at board games, with their multifarious relationships. Now pass to card games; here you find many correspondences with the first group, but many common features drop out, and others appear. When we pass next to ball games, much that is common is retained, but much is lost.—Are they all "amusing"? Compare chess with noughts and crosses. Or is there always winning and losing, or competition between players? Think of patience. In ball games there is winning and losing; but when a child throws his ball at the wall and catches it again, this feature has disappeared. Look at the parts played by skill and luck; and at the difference between skill in chess and skill in tennis. Think now of games like ring-a-ring-a-roses; here is the element of amusement, but how many other characteristic features have disappeared! And we can go through the many, many other groups of games in the same way; can see how similarities crop up and disappear.

And the result of this examination is: we see a complicated network of similarities overlapping and criss-crossing: sometimes overall similarities, sometimes similarities of detail.

67. I can think of no better expression to characterize these similarities than "family resemblances"; for the various resemblances between members of a family: build, features, color of eyes, gait, temperament, etc. etc. overlap and criss-cross in the same way.—And I shall say: "games" form a family.

And for instance the kinds of number form a family in the same way.

Why do we call something a "number"? Well, perhaps because it has a—direct—relationship with several things that have hitherto been called number; and this can be said to give it an indirect relationship to other things we call the same name. And we extend our concept of number as in spinning a thread we twist fibre on fibre. And the strength of the thread does not reside in the fact that some one fibre runs through its whole length, but in the overlapping of many fibres.

But if someone wished to say, "There is something common to all these constructions—namely the disjunction of all their common properties"—I should reply, Now you are only playing with words. One might as well say, "Something runs through the whole thread—namely the continuous overlapping of those fibres."

68. "All right: the concept of number is defined for you as the logical sum of these individual interrelated concepts: cardinal numbers, rational numbers, real numbers, etc.; and in the same way the concept of a game as the logical sum of a corresponding set of sub-concepts."—It need not be so. For I *can* give the concept "number" rigid limits in this way, that is, use the word "number" for a rigidly limited concept, but I can also use it so that the extension of the concept is *not* closed by a frontier. And this is how we do use the word "game." For how is the concept of a game bounded? What still counts as a game and what no longer does? Can you give the boundary? No. You can *draw* one; for none has so far been drawn. (But that never troubled you before when you used the word "game.")

"But then the use of the word is unregulated, the 'game' we play with it is unregulated."—It is not everywhere circumscribed by rules; but no more are there any rules for how high one throws the ball in tennis, or how hard; yet tennis is a game for all that and has rules too.

69. How should we explain to someone what a game is? I imagine that we should describe *games* to him, and we might add: "This *and similar things* are called 'games.' " And do we know any more about it ourselves? Is it only other people whom we cannot tell exactly what a game is?—But this is not ignorance. We do not know the boundaries because none have been drawn. To repeat, we can draw a boundary—for a special purpose. Does it take that to make the concept usable? Not at all! (Except for that special purpose.) No more than it took the definition: 1 pace = 75 cm. to make the measure of length 'one pace' usable. And if you want to say "But still, before that it wasn't an exact measure," then I reply: very well, it was an inexact one.—Though you still owe me a definition of exactness.

70. "But if the concept 'game' is uncircumscribed like that, you don't really know what you mean by a 'game.' "—When I give the description: "The ground was quite covered with plants"—do you want to say I don't know what I am talking about until I can give a definition of a plant?

My meaning would be explained by, say, a drawing and the words "The ground looked roughly like this." Perhaps I even say "it looked *exactly* like this."—Then were just *this* grass and *these* leaves there, arranged just like this? No, that is not what it means. And I should not accept any picture as exact in *this* sense.

Someone says to me: "Show the children a game." I teach them gaming with dice, and the other says "I didn't mean that sort of game." Must the exclusion of the game with dice have come before his mind when he gave me the order?[2]

71. One might say that the concept 'game' is a concept with blurred edges.—"But is a blurred concept a concept at all?"—Is an indistinct photograph a picture of a person at all? Is it even always an advantage to replace an indistinct picture by a sharp one? Isn't the indistinct one often exactly what we need?

Frege compares a concept to an area and says that an area with vague boundaries cannot be called an area at all. This presumably means that we cannot do anything with it.—But is it senseless to say, "Stand roughly there?" Suppose that I were standing with someone in a city square and said that. As I say it I do not draw any kind of boundary, but perhaps point with my hand—as if I were indicating a particular *spot*. And this is just how one might explain to someone what a game is. One gives examples and intends them to be taken in a particular way.—I do not, however, mean by this that he is supposed to see in those examples that common thing which I—for some reason—was unable to express; but that he is now to *employ* those examples in a particular way. Here giving examples is not an *indirect* means of explaining—in default of a better. For any general definition can be misunderstood too. The point is that *this* is how we play the game. (I mean the language-game with the word "game.")

72. *Seeing what is common.* Suppose I show someone various multicolored pictures, and say: "The color you see in all these is called 'yellow ochre.' "—This is a definition, and the other will get to understand it by looking for and seeing what is common to the pictures. Then he can look *at*, can point *to*, the common thing.

Compare with this a case in which I show him figures of different shapes all painted the same color, and say: "What these have in common is called 'yellow ochre.' "

And compare this case: I show him samples of different shades of blue and say, "The color that is common to all these is what I call 'blue.' "

73. When someone defines the names of color for me by pointing to samples and saying "This color is called 'blue,' this 'green' . . ." this case can be compared in many respects to putting a table in my hands, with the words written under the color-samples.—Though this comparison may mislead in many ways.—One is now inclined to extend the comparison: to have understood the definition means to have in one's mind an idea of the thing defined, and that is a sample or picture. So if I am shown various different leaves and told "This is called a 'leaf,' " I get an idea of the shape of a leaf, a picture of it in my mind.—But what does the picture of a leaf look like when it does not show us any particular shape, but "what is common to all shapes of leaf?" Which shade is the "sample in my mind" of the color green—the sample of what is common to all shades of green?

"But might there not be such 'general' samples? Say a schematic leaf, or a sample of *pure* green?"—Certainly there might. But for such a schema to be understood as a *schema,* and not as the shape of a particular leaf, and for a slip of pure green to be understood as a sample of all that is greenish and not as a sample of pure green—this in turn resides in the way the samples are used.

Ask yourself what *shape* must the sample of the color green be? Should it be rectangular? Or would it then be the sample of a green rectangle?—So should it be "irregular" in shape? And what is to prevent us then from regarding it—that is, from using it—only as a sample of irregularity of shape?

74. Here also belongs the idea that if you see this leaf as a sample of "leaf shape in general" you *see* it differently from someone who regards it as, say, a sample of this particular shape. Now this might well be so—though it is not so—for it would only be to say that, as a matter of experience, if you *see* the leaf in a particular way, you use it in such-and-such a way or according to such-and-such rules. Of course, there is such a thing as seeing in *this* way or *that;* and there are also cases where whoever sees a sample like *this* will in general use it in *this* way, and whoever sees it otherwise in another way. For example, if you see the schematic drawing of a cube as a plane figure consisting of a square and two rhombi you will, perhaps, carry out the order "Bring me something like this" differently from someone who sees the picture three-dimensionally.

75. What does it mean to know what a game is? What does it mean, to know it and not be able to say it? Is this knowledge somehow equivalent to an unformulated definition? So that if it were formulated I should be able to recognize it as the expression of my knowledge? Isn't my knowledge, my concept of a game, completely expressed in the explanations that I could give? That is, in my describing examples of various kinds of game; showing how all sorts of other games can be constructed on the analogy of these; saying that I should scarcely include this or this among games; and so on.

76. If someone were to draw a sharp boundary I could not acknowledge it as the one that I too always wanted to draw, or had drawn in my mind. For I did not want to draw one at all. His concept can then be said to be not the same as mine, but akin to it. The kinship is that of two pictures, one of which consists of color patches with vague contours, and the other of patches similarly shaped and distributed, but with clear contours. The kinship is just as undeniable as the difference.

77. And if we carry this comparison still further it is clear that the degree to which the sharp picture *can* resemble the blurred one depends on the latter's degree of vagueness. For imagine having to sketch a sharply defined picture "corresponding" to a blurred one. In the latter there is a blurred red rectangle: for it you put down a sharply defined one. Of course —several such sharply defined rectangles can be drawn to correspond to the indefinite one.—But if the colors in the original merge without a hint of any outline won't it become a hopeless task to draw a sharp picture corresponding to the blurred one? Won't you then have to say, "Here I might just as well draw a circle or heart as a rectangle, for all the colors merge." Anything—and nothing—is right.—And this is the position you are in if you look for definitions corresponding to our concepts in esthetics or ethics.

In such a difficulty always ask yourself, How did we *learn* the meaning of this word ("good" for instance)? From what sort of examples? in what language-games? Then it will be easier for you to see that the word must have a family of meanings.

—*Philosophical Investigations* (1953), translated by G. E. M. Anscombe

Notes

1. Wittgenstein expressed the wish that his German text always be available to the reader of his work. His publisher, Basil Blackwell of Oxford, wishes me to note that the original German text, along with the English translation, is available in the standard edition of *Philosophical Investigations.* (Editor)
2. This paragraph—here set off by lines—was written on a slip and inserted by Wittgenstein without a definite indication of where it should come in. (Editor's note.)

MORRIS WEITZ

The Role of Theory in Esthetics

Theory has been central in esthetics and still the preoccupation of the philosophy of art. Its main avowed concern remains the determination of the nature of art which can be formulated into a definition of it. It construes definition as the statement of the necessary and sufficient properties of what is being defined, where the statement purports to be a true or false claim about the essence of art, what characterizes and distinguishes it from everything else. Each of the great theories of art—Formalism, Voluntarism, Emotionalism, Intellectualism, Intuitionism, Organicism—converges on the attempt to state the defining properties of art. Each claims that it is the true theory because it has formulated correctly into a real definition the nature of art; and that the others are false because they have left out some necessary or sufficient property. Many theorists contend that their enterprise is no mere intellectual exercise but an absolute necessity for any understanding of art and our proper evaluation of it. Unless we know what art is, they say, what are its necessary and sufficient properties, we cannot begin to respond to it adequately or to say why one work is good or better than another. Esthetic theory, thus, is important not only in itself but for the foundations of both appreciation and criticism. Philosophers, critics, and even artists who have written on art, agree that what is primary in esthetics is a theory about the nature of art.

Is esthetics theory, in the sense of a true definition or set of necessary and sufficient properties of art, possible? If nothing else does, the history of esthetics itself should give one enormous pause here. For, in spite of the many theories, we seem no nearer our goal today than we were in Plato's time. Each age, each art-movement, each philosophy of art, tries over and over again to establish the stated ideal only to be succeeded by a new or revised theory, rooted, at least in part, in the repudiation of preceding ones. Even today, almost everyone interested in esthetic matters is still deeply wedded to the hope that the correct theory of art is forthcoming. We need only examine the numerous new books on art in which new definitions are proffered; or, in our own country especially, the basic text-books and anthologies to recognize how strong the priority of a theory of art is.

In this essay I want to plead for the rejection of this problem. I want to show that theory—in the requisite classical sense—is *never* forthcoming in esthetics, and that we would do much better as philosophers to supplant the question, "What is the nature of art?," by other questions, the answers to which will provide us with all the understanding of the arts there can be. I want to show that the inadequacies of the theories are not primarily occasioned by any legitimate difficulty such as, for example, the vast complexity of art, which might be corrected by further probing and research. Their basic inadequacies reside instead in a fundamental misconception of art. Esthetic theory—all of it—is wrong in principle in thinking that a correct theory is possible because it radically misconstrues the logic of the concept of art. Its main contention that "art" is amenable to real or any kind of true definition is false. Its attempt to discover the necessary and sufficient properties of art is logically misbegotten for the very simple reason that such a set and, consequently, such a formula about it, is never forthcoming. Art, as the logic of the concept shows, has no set of necessary and sufficient properties, hence a theory of it is logically impossible and not merely factually difficult. Esthetic theory tries to define what cannot be defined in its requisite sense. But in recommending the repudiation of esthetic theory I shall not argue from this, as too many others have done, that its logical confusions render it meaningless or worthless. On the contrary, I wish to reassess its role and its contribution primarily in order to show that it is of the greatest importance to our understanding of the arts.

Let us now survey briefly some of the more famous extant esthetic theories in order to see if they do incorporate correct and adequate statements about the nature of art. In each of these there is the assumption that it is the true enumeration of the defining properties of art, with the implication that previous theories have stressed wrong definitions. Thus, to begin with, consider a famous version of Formalist theory, that propounded by Bell and Fry. It is true that they speak mostly of painting in their writings but both assert that what they find in that art can be generalized for what is "art" in the others as well. The essence of painting, they maintain, is the plastic elements in relation. Its defining property is significant form, that is, certain combinations of lines, colors, shapes, volumes—everything on the canvas except the representational elements—which evoke a unique response to such combinations. Painting is definable as plastic organization. The nature of art, what it *really* is, so their theory goes, is a unique combination of certain elements (the specifiable plastic ones) in their relations. Anything which is art is an instance of significant form; and anything which is not art has no such form.

To this the Emotionalist replies that the truly essential property of art has been left out. Tolstoy, Ducasse, or any of the advocates of this theory, find that the requisite defining property is not significant form but rather the expression of emotion in some sensuous public medium. Without projection of emotion into some piece of stone or words or sounds, etc., there can be no art. Art is really such embodiment. It is this that uniquely characterizes art, and any true, real definition of it, contained in some adequate theory of art, must so state it.

The Intuitionist disclaims both emotion and form as defining properties. In Croce's version, for example, art is identified not with some physical, public object but with a specific creative, cognitive, and spiritual act. Art is really a first stage of knowledge in which certain human beings (artists) bring their images and intuitions into lyrical clarification or expression. As such, it is an awareness, non-conceptual in character, of the unique individuality of things; and since it exists below the level of conceptualization or action, it is without scientific or moral content. Croce singles out as the defining essence of art this first stage of spiritual life and advances its identification with art as a philosophically true theory or definition.

The Organicist says to all of this that art is really a class of organic wholes consisting of distinguishable, albeit inseparable, elements in their causally efficacious relations which are presented in some sensuous medium. In A. C. Bradley, in piecemeal versions of it in literary criticism, or in my own generalized adaptation of it in my *Philosophy of the Arts,* what is claimed is that anything which is a work of art is in its nature a unique complex of interrelated parts—in painting, for example, lines, colors, volumes, subjects, etc., all interacting upon one another on a paint surface of some sort. Certainly, at one time at least it seemed to me that this organic theory constituted the one true and real definition of art.

My final example is the most interesting of all, logically speaking. This is the Voluntarist theory of Parker. In his writings on art, Parker persistently calls into question the traditional simpleminded definitions of aesthetics. "The assumption underlying every philosophy of art is the existence of some common nature present in all the arts."[1] "All the so popular brief definitions of art—'significant form,' 'expression,' 'intuition,' 'objectified pleasure'—are fallacious, either because, while true of art, they are also true of much that is not art, and hence fail to differentiate art from other things; or else because they neglect some essential aspect of art."[2] But instead of inveighing against the attempt at definition of art itself, Parker insists that what is needed is a complex definition rather than a simple one. "The definition of art must therefore be in terms of a complex of characteristics. Failure to recognize this has been the fault of all the well-known definitions."[3] His own version of Voluntarism is the theory that art is essentially three things: embodiment of wishes and desires imaginatively satisfied, language, which characterizes the public medium of art, and harmony, which unifies the language with the layers of imaginative projections. Thus, for Parker, it is a true definition to say of art that it is ". . . the provision of satisfaction through the imagination, social significance, and harmony. I am claiming that nothing except works of art possess all three of these marks."[4]

Now, all of these sample theories are inadequate in many different ways. Each purports to be a complete statement about the defining features of all works of art and yet each of them leaves out something which the others take to be central. Some are circular, for example, the Bell-Fry theory of art as significant form which is defined in part in terms of our response to significant form. Some of them, in their search for necessary and sufficient properties, emphasize too few properties, like (again) the Bell-Fry definition which leaves out subject-representation in painting, or the Croce theory which omits inclusion of the very important feature of the public, physical character, say, of architecture. Others are too general and cover objects that are not art as well as works of art. Organicism is surely such a view since it can be applied to *any* causal unity in the natural world as well as to art.[5] Still others rest on dubious principles, for example, Parker's claim that art embodies imaginative satisfactions, rather than real ones; or Croce's assertion that there is nonconceptual knowledge. Consequently, even if art has one set of necessary and sufficient properties, none of the theories we have noted or, for that matter, no esthetic theory yet proposed, has enumerated that set to the satisfaction of all concerned.

Then there is a different sort of difficulty. As real definitions, these theories are supposed to be factual reports on art. If they are, may we not ask, Are they empirical and open to verification or falsification? For example, what would confirm or disconfirm the theory that art is significant form or embodiment of emotion or creative synthesis of images? There does not even seem to be a hint of the kind of evidence which might be forthcoming to test these theories; and indeed one wonders if they are perhaps honorific definitions of "art," that is, proposed redefinitions in terms of some *chosen* conditions for applying the concept of art, and not true or false reports on the essential properties of art at all.

But all these criticisms of traditional esthetic theories—that they are circular, incomplete, untestable, pseudo-factual, disguised proposals to change the meaning of concepts—have been made before. My intention is to go beyond these to make a much more fundamental criticism, namely, that esthetic theory is a logically vain attempt to define what cannot be defined, to state the necessary and sufficient properties of that which has no necessary and sufficient properties, to conceive the concept of art as closed when its very use reveals and demands its openness.

The problem with which we must begin is not "What is art?," but "What sort of concept is 'art'?" Indeed, the root problem of philosophy itself is to explain the relation between the employment of certain kinds of concepts and the conditions under which they can be correctly applied. If I may paraphrase Wittgenstein, we must not ask, What is the nature of any philosophical x?, or even, according to the semanticist, What does "x" mean?, a transformation that leads to the disastrous interpretation of "art" as a name for some specifiable class of objects; but rather, What is the use or employment of "x"? What does "x" do in the language? This, I take it, is the initial question, the begin-all if not the end-all of any philosophical problem and solution. Thus, in esthetics, our first problem is the elucidation of the actual employment of the concept of art, to give a logical description of the actual functioning of the concept, including a description of the conditions under which we correctly use it or its correlates.

My model in this type of logical description or philosophy derives from Wittgenstein. It is also he who, in his refutation of philosophical theorizing in the sense of constructing definitions of philosophical entities, has furnished contemporary esthetics with a starting point for any future progress. In his new work, *Philosophical Investigations*,[6] Wittgenstein raises as an illustrative question, What is a game? The traditional philosophical, theoretical answer would be in terms of some exhaustive set of properties common to all games. To this Wittgenstein says, let us consider what we call "games": "I mean board games, card games, ball games, Olympic games, and so on. What is common to them all?—Don't say: 'there *must* be something common, or they would not be called "games"' but *look and see* whether there is anything common to all.—For if you look at them you will not see something that is common to *all*, but similarities, relationships, and a whole series of them at that. . . ."

Card games are like board games in some respects but not in others. Not all games are amusing, nor is there always winning or losing or competition. Some games resemble others in some respects—that is all. What we find are no necessary and sufficient properties, only "a complicated network of similarities overlapping and crisscrossing," such that we can say of games that they form a family with family resemblances and no common trait. If one asks what a game is, we pick out sample games, describe these, and add, "This and *similar things* are called 'games.'" This is all we need to say and indeed all any of us knows about games. Knowing what a game is is not knowing some real definition or theory but being able to recognize and explain games and to decide which among imaginary and new examples would or would not be called "games."

The problem of the nature of art is like that of the nature of games, at least in these respects: If we actually look and see what it is that we call "art," we will also find no common properties—only strands of similarities. Knowing what art is is not apprehending some manifest or latent essence but being able to recognize, describe, and explain those things we call "art" in virtue of these similarities.

But the basic resemblance between these concepts is their open texture. In elucidating them, certain (paradigm) cases can be given, about which there can be no question as to their being correctly described as "art" or "game," but no exhaustive set of cases can be given. I can list some cases and some conditions under which I can apply correctly the concept of art but I cannot list all of them, for the all-important reason that unforeseeable or novel conditions are always forthcoming or envisageable.

A concept is open if its conditions of application are emendable and corrigible; that is, if a situation or case can be imagined or secured which would call for some sort of *decision* on our part to extend the use of the concept to cover this, or to close the concept and invent a new one to deal with the new case and its new property. If necessary and sufficient conditions for the application of a concept can be stated, the concept is a closed one. But this can happen only in logic or mathematics where concepts are constructed and completely defined. It cannot occur with empirically-descriptive and normative concepts unless we arbitrarily close them by stipulating the ranges of their uses.

I can illustrate this open character of "art" best by examples drawn from its sub-concepts. Consider questions like "Is Dos Passos' *U. S. A.* a novel?," "Is V. Woolf's *To the Lighthouse* a novel?," "Is Joyce's *Finnegan's Wake* a novel?" On the traditional view, these are construed as factual problems to be answered yes or no in accordance with the presence or absence of defining properties. But certainly this is not how any of these questions is answered. Once it arises, as it has many times in the development of the novel from Richardson to Joyce (for example, "Is Gide's *The School for Wives* a novel or a diary?"), what is at stake is no factual analysis concerning necessary and sufficient properties but a decision as to whether the work under examination is similar in certain respects to other works, already called "novels," and consequently warrants the extension of the concept to cover the new case. The new work is narrative, fictional, contains character delineation and dialogue but (say) it has no regular time-sequence in the plot or is interspersed with actual newspaper reports. It is like recognized novels, A, B, C . . . , in some respects but not like them in others. But then neither were B and C like A in some respects when it was decided to extend the concept applied to A to B and C. Because work N + 1 (the brand new work) is like A, B, C . . . N in certain respects—has strands of similarity to them—the concept is extended and a new phase of the novel engendered. "Is N + 1 a novel?," then, is no factual, but rather a decision problem, where the verdict turns on whether or not we enlarge our set of conditions for applying the concept.

What is true of the novel is, I think, true of every sub-concept of art: "tragedy," "comedy," "painting," "opera," etc., of "art" itself. No "Is X a novel, painting, opera, work of art, etc.?" question allows of a definitive answer in the sense of a factual yes or no report. "Is this *collage* a painting or not?" does not rest on any set of necessary and sufficient properties of painting but on whether we decide—as we did!—to extend "painting" to cover this case.

"Art," itself, is an open concept. New conditions (cases) have constantly arisen and will undoubtedly constantly arise; new art forms, new movements will emerge, which will demand decisions on the part of those interested, usually professional critics, as to whether the concept should be extended or not. Estheticians may lay down similarity conditions but never necessary and sufficient ones for the correct application of the concept. With "art" its conditions of application can never be exhaustively enumerated since new cases can always be envisaged or created by artists, or even nature, which would call for a decision on someone's part to extend or to close the old or to invent a new concept. (For example, "It's not a sculpture, it's a mobile.")

What I am arguing, then, is that the very expansive, adventurous character of art, its ever-present changes and novel creations, makes it logically impossible to ensure any set of defining properties. We can, of course, choose to close the concept. But to do this with "art" or "tragedy" or "portraiture," etc., is ludicrous since it forecloses on the very conditions of creativity in the arts.

Of course there are legitimate and serviceable closed concepts in art. But these are always those whose boundaries of conditions have been drawn for a *special* purpose. Consider the difference, for example, between "tragedy" and "(extant) Greek tragedy." The first is open and must remain so to allow for the possibility of new conditions, for example, a play in which the hero is not noble or fallen or in which there is no hero but other elements that are like those of plays we already call "tragedy." The second is closed. The plays it can be applied to, the conditions under which it can be correctly used are all in, once the boundary, "Greek," is drawn. Here the critic can work out a theory or real definition in which he lists the common properties at least of the extant Greek tragedies. Aristotle's definition, false as it is as a theory of all the plays of Aeschylus, Sophocles, and Euripides, since it does not cover some of them,[7] properly called "tragedies," can be interpreted as a real (albeit incorrect) definition of this closed concept; although it can also be, as it unfortunately has been, conceived as a purported real definition of "tragedy," in which case it suffers from the logical mistake of trying to define what cannot be defined—of trying to squeeze what is an open concept into an honorific formula for a closed concept.

What is supremely important, if the critic is not to become muddled, is to get absolutely clear about the way in which he conceives his concepts; otherwise he goes from the problem of trying to define "tragedy," etc., to an arbitrary closing of the concept in terms of certain preferred conditions or characteristics which he sums up in some linguistic recommendation that he mistakenly thinks is a real definition of the open concept. Thus, many critics and estheticians ask, "What is tragedy?," choose a class of samples for which they may give a true account of its common properties, and then go on to construe this account of the chosen closed class as a true definition or theory of the whole open class of tragedy. This, I think, is the logical mechanism of most of the so-called theories of the subconcepts of art: "tragedy," "comedy," "novel," etc. In effect, this whole procedure, subtly deceptive as it is, amounts to a transformation of correct criteria for *recognizing* members of certain legitimately closed classes of works of art into recommended criteria for *evaluating* any putative member of the class.

The primary task of esthetics is not to seek a theory but to elucidate the concept of art. Specifically, it is to describe the conditions under which we employ the concept correctly. Definition, reconstruction, patterns of analysis are out of place here since they distort and add nothing to our understanding of art. What, then, is the logic of "X is a work of art"?

As we actually use the concept, "Art" is both descriptive (like "chair") and evaluative (like "good"); that is, we sometimes say, "This is a work of art," to describe something and we sometimes say it to evaluate something. Neither use surprises anyone.

What, first, is the logic of "X is a work of art," when it is a descriptive utterance? What are the conditions under which we would be making such an utterance correctly? There are no necessary and sufficient conditions but there are the strands of similarity conditions, i.e., bundles of properties, none of which need be present but most of which are, when we describe things as works of art. I shall call these the "criteria of recognition" of works of art. All of these have served as the defining criteria of the individual traditional theories of art; so we are already familiar with them. Thus, mostly, when we describe something as a work of art, we do so under the conditions of there being present some sort of artifact, made by human skill, ingenuity, and imagination, which embodies in its sensuous, public medium—stone, wood, sounds, words, etc.—certain distinguishable elements and relations. Special theorists would add conditions like satisfaction of wishes, objectification or expression of emotion, some act of empathy, and so on; but these latter conditions seem to be quite adventitious, present to some but not to other spectators when things are described as works of art. "X is a work of art and contains *no* emotion, expression, act of empathy, satisfaction, etc.," is perfectly good sense and may frequently be true. "X is a work of art and . . . was made by no one," or . . . "exists only in the mind and not in any publicly observable thing," or . . . "was made by accident when he spilled the paint on the canvas," in each case of which a normal condition is denied, are also sensible and capable of being true in certain circumstances. None of the criteria of recognition is a defining one, either necessary or sufficient, because we can sometimes assert of something that it is a work of art and go on to deny any one of these conditions, even the one which has traditionally been taken to be basic, namely, that of being an artifact: Consider, "This piece of driftwood is a lovely piece of sculpture." Thus, to say of anything that it is a work of art is to commit oneself to the presence of *some* of these conditions. One would scarcely describe X as a work of art if X were not an artifact, or a collection of elements sensuously presented in a medium, or a product of human skill, and so on. If none of the conditions were present, if there were no criteria present for recognizing something as a work of art, we would not describe it as one. But, even so, no one of these or any collection of them is either necessary or sufficient.

The elucidation of the descriptive use of "Art" creates little difficulty. But the elucidation of the evaluative use does. For many, especially theorists, "This is a work of art" does more than describe; it also praises. Its conditions of utterance, therefore, include certain preferred properties or characteristics of art. I shall call these "criteria of evaluation." Consider a typical example of this evaluative use, the view according to which to say of something that it is a work of art is to imply that it is a *successful* harmonization of elements. Many of the honorific definitions of art and its sub-concepts are of this form. What is at stake here is that "Art" is construed as an evaluative term which is either identified with its criterion or justified in terms of it. "Art" is defined in terms of its evaluative property, e.g., successful harmonization. On such a view, to say "X is a work of art" is (1) to say something which is taken *to mean* "X is a successful harmonization" (e.g., "Art *is* significant form") or (2) to say something praiseworthy *on the basis* of its successful harmonization. Theorists are never clear whether it is (1) or (2) which is being put forward. Most of them, concerned as they are with this evaluative use, formulate (2), i.e., that feature of art that *makes* it art in the praise-sense, and then go on to state (1), i.e., the definition of "Art" in terms of its art-making feature. And this is clearly to confuse the conditions under which we say something evaluatively with the meaning of what we say. "This is a work of art," said evaluatively, cannot mean "This is a successful harmonization of elements"—except by stipulation—but at most is said in virtue of the art-making property, which is taken as a (the) criterion of "Art," when "Art" is employed to assess. "This is a work of art," used evaluatively, serves to praise and not to affirm the reason why it is said.

The evaluative use of "Art," although distinct from the conditions of its use, relates in a very intimate way to these conditions. For, in every instance of "This is a work of art" (used to praise), what happens is that the criterion of evaluation (e.g., successful harmonization) for the employment of the concept of art is converted into a criterion of recognition. This is why, on its evaluative use, "This is a work of art" implies "This has P," where "P" is some chosen art-making property. Thus, if one chooses to employ "Art" evaluatively, as many do, so that "This is a work of art and not (aesthetically) good" makes no sense, he uses "Art" in such a way that he refuses to *call* anything a work of art unless it embodies his criterion of excellence.

There is nothing wrong with the evaluative use; in fact, there is good reason for using "Art" to praise. But what cannot be maintained is that theories of the evaluative use of "Art" are true and real definitions of the necessary and sufficient properties of art. Instead they are honorific definitions, pure and simple, in which "Art" has been redefined in terms of chosen criteria.

But what makes them—these honorific definitions—so supremely valuable is not their disguised linguistic recommendations; rather it is the *debates* over the reasons for changing the criteria of the concept of art which are built into the definitions. In each of the great theories of art, whether correctly understood as honorific definitions or incorrectly accepted as real definitions, what is of the utmost importance are the reasons proffered in the argument for the respective theory, that is, the reasons given for the chosen or preferred criterion of excellence and evaluation. It is this perennial debate over these criteria of evaluation which makes the history of esthetic theory the important study it is. The value of each of the theories resides in its attempt to state and to justify certain criteria which are either neglected or distorted by previous theories. Look at the Bell-Fry theory again. Of course, "Art is significant form" cannot be accepted as a true, real definition of art; and most certainly it actually functions in their esthetics as a redefinition of art in terms of the chosen condition of significant form. But what gives it its esthetic importance is what lies behind the formula: In an age in which literary and representational elements have become paramount in painting, *return* to the plastic ones since these are indigenous to painting. Thus, the role of the theory is not to define anything but to use the definitional form, almost epigrammatically, to pinpoint a crucial recommendation to turn our attention once again to the plastic elements in painting.

Once we, as philosophers, understand this distinction between the formula and what lies behind it, it behooves us to deal generously with the traditional theories of art; because incorporated in every one of them is a debate over and argument for emphasizing or centering upon some particular feature of art which has been neglected or perverted. If we take the esthetic theories literally, as we have seen, they all fail; but if we reconstrue them, in terms of their function and point, as serious and argued-for recommendations to concentrate on certain criteria of excellence in art, we shall see that esthetic theory is far from worthless. Indeed, it becomes as central as anything in esthetics, in our understanding of art, for it teaches us what to look for and how to look at it in art. What is central and must be articulated in all the theories are their debates over the reasons for excellence in art—debates over emotional depth, profound truths, natural beauty, exactitude, freshness of treatment, and so on, as criteria of evaluation—the whole of which converges on the perennial problem of what makes a work of art good. To understand the role of esthetic theory is not to conceive it as definition, logically doomed to failure, but to read it as summaries of seriously made recommendations to attend in certain ways to certain features of art.

—*The Journal of Aesthetics and Art Criticism,* Volume 15 (1956)

Notes

1. DeWitt H. Parker, "The Nature of Art," reprinted in E. Vivas and M. Krieger, *The Problems of Aesthetics* (N.Y., 1953), p. 90.
2. *Ibid.*, pp. 93–94.
3. *Ibid.*, p. 94.
4. *Ibid.*, p. 104.
5. See M. Macdonald's review of my *Philosophy of the Arts* in *Mind,* Oct., 1951, pp. 561–564, for a brilliant discussion of this objection to the Organic theory.
6. L. Wittgenstein, *Philosophical Investigations,* (Oxford, 1953), tr. by E. Anscombe. (All quotations appear in the preceding selection, pp. 505–509—Editor's note.)
7. See H. D. F. Kitto, *Greek Tragedy,* (London, 1939), on this point.

MAURICE MANDELBAUM

Family Resemblances and Generalization Concerning the Arts

In 1954 William Elton collected and published a group of essays under the title *Aesthetics and Language*. As his introduction made clear, a common feature of these essays was the application to esthetic problems of some of the doctrines characteristic of recent British linguistic philosophy.[1] While this mode of philosophizing has not had as pervasive an influence on aesthetics as it has had on most other branches of philosophy,[2] there have been a number of important articles which, in addition to those contained in the Elton volume, suggest the direction in which this influence runs. Among these articles one might mention "The Task of Defining a Work of Art" by Paul Ziff,[3] "The Role of Theory in Aesthetics" by Morris Weitz,[4] Charles L. Stevenson's "On 'What is a Poem' "[5] and W. E. Kennick's "Does Traditional Aesthetics Rest on a Mistake?"[6] In each of them one finds a conviction which was also present in most of the essays in the Elton volume: that it is a mistake to offer generalizations concerning the arts, or, to put the matter in a more provocative manner, that it is a mistake to attempt to discuss what art, or beauty, or the esthetic, or a poem, *essentially* is. In partial support of this contention, some writers have made explicit use of Wittgenstein's doctrine of *family resemblances*; Morris Weitz, for example, has placed it in the forefront of his discussion. However, in that influential and frequently anthologized article, Professor Weitz made no attempt to analyze, clarify, or defend the doctrine itself. Since its use with respect to esthetics has provided the means by which others have sought to escape the need of generalizing concerning the arts, I shall begin my discussion with a consideration of it.

I

The *locus classicus* for Wittgenstein's doctrine of family resemblances is in Part I of *Philosophical Investigations*, sections 65–77.[7] In discussing what he refers to as language-games, Wittgenstein says:

> Instead of producing something common to all that we call language, I am saying that these phenomena have no one thing in common which makes us use the same word for all—but they are *related* to one another in many different ways. And it is because of this relationship, or these relationships, that we call them all "language." (§65)

He then illustrates his contention by citing a variety of *games*, such as board games, card games, ball games, etc., and concludes:

> We see a complicated network of similarities overlapping and criss-crossing: sometimes overall similarities of detail. (§66)

> I can think of no better expression to characterize these similarities than "family resemblances"; for the various resemblances between members of a family: build, features, colour of eyes, gait, temperament, etc., etc. overlap and criss-cross in the same way.—And I shall say: "games" form a family. (§67)

In short, what Wittgenstein aims to establish is that one need not suppose that all instances of those entities to which we apply a common name do in fact possess any one feature in common. Instead, the use of a common name is grounded in the criss-crossing and overlapping of resembling features among otherwise heterogeneous objects and activities.

Wittgenstein's concrete illustrations of the diversity among various types of games may at first make his doctrine of family resemblances extremely plausible. For example, we do not hesitate to characterize tennis, chess, bridge, and solitaire as games, even though a comparison of them fails to reveal any specific feature which is the same in each of them. Nonetheless, I do not believe that his doctrine of family resemblances, as it stands, provides an adequate analysis of why a common name, such as "a game," is in all cases applied or withheld.

Consider first the following case. Let us assume that you know how to play that form of solitaire called "Canfield"; suppose also that you are acquainted with a number of other varieties of solitaire (Wittgenstein uses "patience," i.e., "solitaire," as one instance of a form of game). Were you to see me shuffling a pack of cards, arranging the cards in piles, some face up and some face down, turning cards over one-by-one, sometimes placing them in one pile, then another, shifting piles, etc., you might say: "I see you are playing cards. What game are you playing?" However, to this I might answer: "I am not playing a game; I am telling (or reading) fortunes." Will the resemblances between what you have seen me doing and the characteristics of card games with which you are familiar permit you to contradict me and say that I am indeed playing some sort of game? Ordinary usage would not, I believe, sanction our describing fortune-telling as an example of playing a game, no matter how striking may be the resemblances between the ways in which cards are handled in playing solitaire and in telling fortunes. Or, to choose another example, we may say that while certain forms of wrestling contests are sometimes characterized as games (Wittgenstein mentions "*Kampfspiele*")[8] an angry struggle between two boys, each trying to make the other give in, is not to be characterized as a game. Yet one can find a great many resembling features between such a struggle and a wrestling match in a gymnasium. What would seem to be crucial in our designation of an activity as a game is, therefore, not merely a matter of noting a number of specific resemblances between it and other activities which we denote as games, but involves something further.

To suggest what sort of characteristic this "something further" might possibly be, it will be helpful to pay closer attention to the notion of what constitutes a family resemblance. Suppose that you are shown ten or a dozen photographs and you are then asked to decide which among them exhibit strong resemblances.[9] You might have no difficulty in selecting, say, three of the photographs in which the subjects were markedly round-headed, had a strongly prognathous profile, rather deep-set eyes, and dark curly hair.[10] In some extended, metaphorical sense you might say that the similarities in their features constituted a family resemblance among them. The sense, however, would be metaphorical, since in the absence of a biological kinship of a certain degree of proximity we would be inclined to speak only of resemblances, and not of a *family* resemblance. What marks the difference between a literal and a metaphorical sense of the notion of "family resemblances" is, therefore, the existence of a genetic connection in the former case and not in the latter. Wittgenstein, however, failed to make explicit the fact that the literal, root notion of a family resemblance includes this genetic connection no less than it includes the existence of noticeable physiognomic resemblances.[11] Had the existence of such a *twofold* criterion been made explicit by him, he would have noted that there is in fact an attribute common to all who bear a family resemblance to each other: they are related through a common ancestry. Such a relationship is not, of course, one among the specific features of those who share a family resemblance; it nonetheless differentiates them from those who are not to be regarded as members of a single family.[12] If, then, it is possible that the analogy of family resemblances could tell us something about how games may be related to one another, one should explore the possibility that, in spite of their great dissimilarities, games may possess a common attribute which, like biological connection, is not itself one among their directly exhibited characteristics. Unfortunately, such a possibility was not explored by Wittgenstein.

To be sure, Wittgenstein does not explicitly state that the resemblances which are correlated with our use of common names must be of a sort that are directly exhibited. Nonetheless, all of his illustrations in the relevant passages involve aspects of games which would be included in a description of how a particular game is to be played; that is, when he commands us to "look and see" whether there is anything common to all games,[13] the "anything" is taken to represent precisely the sort of manifest feature that is described in rule-books, such as Hoyle. However, as we have seen in the case of family resemblances, what constitutes a *family* is not defined in terms of the manifest features of a random group of people; we must first characterize the *family* relationship in terms of genetic ties, and then observe to what extent those who are connected in this way *resemble* one another.[14] In the case of games, the analogue to genetic ties might be the purpose for the sake of which various games were formulated by those who invented or modified them, e.g., the potentiality of a game to be of absorbing non-practical interest to either participants or spectators. If there were any such common feature one would not expect it to be defined in a rule book, such as Hoyle, since rule books only attempt to tell us how to play a particular game: our interest in playing a game, and our understanding of what constitutes a game, is already presupposed by the authors of such books.

It is not my present concern to characterize any feature common to most or all of those activities which we call games, nor would I wish to argue on the analogy of family resemblances that there *must be* any such feature. If the question is to be decided, it must be decided by an attempt to "look and see." However, it is important that we look in the right place and in the right ways if we are looking for a common feature; we should not assume that any feature common to all games must be some manifest characteristic, such as whether they are to be played with a ball or with cards, or how many players there must be in order for the game to be played. If we were to rely exclusively on such features we should, as I have suggested, be apt to link solitaire with fortune-telling, and wrestling matches with fights, rather than (say) linking solitaire with cribbage and wrestling matches with weight-lifting. It is, then, my contention that Wittgenstein's emphasis on directly exhibited resemblances, and his failure to consider other possible similarities, led to a failure on his part to provide an adequate clue as to what—in some cases at least—governs our use of common names.[15]

If the foregoing remarks are correct, we are now in a position to see that the radical denigration of generalization concerning the arts, which has come to be almost a hallmark of the writings of those most influenced by recent British philosophy, may involve serious errors, and may not constitute a notable advance.

II

In turning from Wittgenstein's statements concerning family resemblances to the use to which his doctrine has been put by writers on esthetics, we must first note what these writers are *not* attempting to do. In the first place, they are not seeking to clarify the relationships which exist among the many different senses in which the word "art" is used. Any dictionary offers a variety of such senses (e.g., the art of navigation, art as guile, art as the craft of the artist, etc.), and it is not difficult to find a pattern of family resemblances existing among many of them. However, an analysis of such resemblances, and of their differences, has not, as a matter of fact, been of interest to the writers of the articles with which we are here concerned. In the second place, these writers have not been primarily interested in analyzing how words such as "work of art" or "artist" or "art" are ordinarily used by those who are neither estheticians nor art critics; their concern has been with the writings which make up the tradition of "esthetic theory." In the third place, we must note that the concern of these writers has not been to show that family resemblances do in fact exist among the various arts, or among various works of art; on the contrary, they have used the doctrine of family resemblances in a *negative* fashion. In this, they have of course followed Wittgenstein's own example. The position which they have sought to establish is that traditional esthetic theory has been mistaken in assuming that there is any essential property or defining characteristic of works of art (or any set of such properties or characteristics); as a consequence, they have contended that most of the questions which have been asked by those engaged in writing on esthetics are mistaken sorts of questions.

However, as the preceding discussion of Wittgenstein should have served to make clear, one cannot assume that if there is any one characteristic common to all works of art it must consist in some specific, directly exhibited feature. Like the biological connections among those who are connected by family resemblances, or like the intentions on the basis of which we distinguish between fortune-telling and card games, such a characteristic might be a relational attribute, rather than some characteristic at which one could directly point and say: "It is this particular feature of the object which leads me to designate it as a work of art." A relational attribute of the required sort might, for example, only be apprehended if one were to consider specific art objects as having been created by someone for some actual or possible audience.

The suggestion that the essential nature of art is to be found in such a relational attribute is surely not implausible when one recalls some of the many traditional theories of art. For example, art has sometimes been characterized as being one special form of communication or of expression, or as being a special form of wish-fulfillment, or as being a presentation of truth in sensuous form. Such theories do not assume that in each poem, painting, play, and sonata there is a specific ingredient which identifies it as a work of art; rather, that which is held to be common to these otherwise diverse objects is a relationship which is assumed to have existed, or is known to have existed, between certain of their characteristics and the activities and the intentions of those who made them.[16]

While we may acknowledge that it is difficult to find any set of attributes —whether relational or not—which can serve to characterize the nature of a work of art (and which will not be as vulnerable to criticism as many other such characterizations have been),[17] it is important to note that the difficulties inherent in this task are not really avoided by those who appeal to the notion of family resemblances. As soon as one attempts to elucidate how the term "art" is in fact used in the context of art criticism, most of the same problems which have arisen in the history of esthetic theory will again make their appearance. In other words, linguistic analysis does not provide a means of escape from the issues which have been of major concern in traditional esthetics. This fact may be illustrated through examining a portion of one of the articles to which I have already alluded, Paul Ziff's article entitled "The Task of Defining a Work of Art."

To explain how the term "a work of art" is used, and to show the difficulties one encounters if one seeks to generalize concerning the arts, Professor Ziff chooses as his starting point one clear-cut example of a work of art and sets out to describe it. The work he chooses is a painting by Poussin, and his description runs as follows:

> Suppose we point to Poussin's "The Rape of the Sabine Women," as our clearest available case of a work of art. We could describe it by saying, first, that it is a painting. Secondly, it was made, and what is more, made deliberately and self-consciously with obvious skill and care, by Nicolas Poussin. Thirdly, the painter intended it to be displayed in a place where it could be looked at and appreciated, where it could be contemplated and admired. . . . Fourthly, the painting

is or was exhibited in a museum gallery where people do contemplate, study, observe, admire, criticize, and discuss it. What I wish to refer to here by speaking of contemplating, studying, and observing a painting, is simply what we may do when we are concerned with a painting like this. For example, when we look at this painting by Poussin, we may attend to its sensuous features, to its "look and feel." Thus we attend to the play of light and color, to dissonances, contrasts, and harmonies of hues, values, and intensities. We notice patterns and pigmentation, textures, decorations, and embellishments. We may also attend to the structure, design, composition, and organization of the work. Thus we look for unity, and we also look for variety, for balance and movement. We attend to the formal interrelations and cross connections in the work, to its underlying structure. . . . Fifthly, this work is a representational painting with a definite subject matter; it depicts a certain mythological scene. Sixthly, the painting is an elaborate and certainly complex formal structure. Finally, the painting is a good painting. And this is to say simply that the Poussin painting is worth contemplating, studying, and observing in the way I have ever so roughly described.[18]

With reference to this description we must first note that it is clearly not meant to be anything like a complete description of the Poussin painting; it is at most a description of those aspects of that painting which are relevant to its being called a work of art. For example, neither the weight of the painting nor its insurable value is mentioned. Thus, whether because of his own preconceptions, or because of our ordinary assumptions concerning how the term "work of art" is to be used, Professor Ziff focuses attention on some aspects of the Poussin painting rather than upon others. In doing so, he is making an implicit appeal to what is at least a minimal esthetic theory, that is, he is supposing that neither weight nor insurable value need be mentioned when we list the characteristics which lead us to say of a particular piece of painted canvas that it is a work of art. In the second place, we must note that of the seven characteristics which he mentions, not all are treated by Professor Ziff as being independent of one another; nor are all related to one another in identical ways. It will be instructive to note some of the differences among their relationships, since it is precisely here that many of the traditional problems of aesthetic theory once again take their rise.

For example, we are bound to note that Professor Ziff related the seventh characteristic of the Poussin painting to its fourth characteristic: the fact that it is a good painting is, he holds, related to the characteristics which we find that it possesses when we contemplate, observe, and study it. Its goodness, however, is not claimed to be related to its first, third, or fifth characteristics: in other words, Professor Ziff is apparently not claiming that the goodness of this particular work of art depends upon its being a painting rather than being some other sort of work of art which is capable of being contemplated, studied, etc.; nor is he claiming that its goodness is dependent upon the fact that it was intended to be hung in a place where it can be observed and studied; nor upon the fact that it is a representational painting which depicts a mythological scene. If we next turn to the question of how the goodness of this painting is related to the fact that it was "made deliberately and self-consciously, with obvious skill and care by

Nicolas Poussin," Professor Ziff's position is somewhat less explicit, but what he would say is probably quite clear. Suppose that the phrase "obvious skill" were deleted from the description of this characteristic: would the fact that this painting had been deliberately and self-consciously made, and had been made with care (but perhaps not with skill), provide a sufficient basis for predicating goodness of it? I should doubt that Professor Ziff would hold that it would, since many bad paintings may be supposed to have been made deliberately, self-consciously, and with care. Yet, if this is so, how is the maker's skill related to the object's goodness? Perhaps the fact that "obvious skill" is attributed to Poussin is meant to suggest that Poussin intended that "The Rape of the Sabine Women" should possess those qualities which Professor Ziff notes that we find in it when we contemplate, study, and observe it in the way in which he suggests that it should be contemplated. If this is what is suggested by attributing skill to the artist, it is surely clear that Professor Ziff has without argument built an esthetic theory into his description of the Poussin painting. That theory is implicit both in the characteristics which he chooses as being esthetically relevant, and in the relations which he holds as obtaining among these characteristics.

If it be doubted that Professor Ziff's description contains at least an implicit esthetic theory, consider the fact that in one of the passages in which he describes the Poussin painting (but which I did not include in my foreshortened quotation from that description), he speaks of the fact that in contemplating, studying, and observing this painting "we are concerned with both two-dimensional and three-dimensional movements, the balance and opposition, thrust and recoil, of spaces and volumes." Since the goodness of a painting has been said by him to depend upon the qualities which we find in it when we contemplate, study, and observe it, it follows that these features of the Poussin painting contribute to its goodness. And I should suppose that they are also included in what Professor Ziff calls the sixth characteristic of the Poussin painting, namely its "complex formal structure." Thus, presumably, the goodness of a painting does depend, in part at least, upon its formal structure. On the other hand, Professor Ziff never suggests that the goodness of the Poussin painting depends upon the fact that it is a representational painting, and that it has a mythological (or historical) subject matter, rather than some other sort of subject matter. In fact, when he discusses critics such as Kenyon Cox and Royal Cortissoz, Professor Ziff would apparently—and quite properly—wish to separate himself from them, rejecting the view that what makes a painting a good painting has any necessary relation to the fact that it is or is not a representational painting of a certain sort. Thus, Professor Ziff's account of the esthetically relevant features of the Poussin painting, and his statements concerning the interrelationship among the various features of that painting, define a particular esthetic position.

The position which I have been attributing to him is one with which I happen to agree. However, that fact is not of any importance in the present discussion. What is important to note is that Professor Ziff's characterization of the Poussin painting contains an implicit theory of the nature of a work of art. According to that theory, the goodness of a painting depends upon its possession of certain objective qualities, that these qualities are (in part at least) elements in its formal structure, and that the artist intended that we should perceive these qualities in contemplating and studying the painting. (Had he not had this intention, would we be able to say that he had made the object self-consciously, deliberately, *and* with skill?) Further, this implicit theory must be assumed to be a theory which is general in import, and not confined to how we should look at this one painting only. Were this not so, the sort of description of the Poussin painting which was given by Professor Ziff would not have helped to establish a clear-cut case of what is to be designated as a work of art. For example, were someone to describe the same painting in terms of its size, weight, and insurable value (as might be done were it to be moved from museum to museum), we would not thereby learn how the term "work of art" is to be used. In failing to note that his description of the Poussin painting actually did involve a theory of the nature of art, Professor Ziff proceeded to treat that description as if he had done nothing more than bring forward a list of seven independent characteristics of the painting he was examining. In so doing, he turned the question of whether there are any features common to all works of art into a question of whether one or more of these seven specific indices could be found in all objects to which the term "work of art" is applied. Inevitably, his conclusion was negative, and he therefore held that "no one of the characteristics listed is necessarily a characteristic of a work of art."[19]

However, as we have seen, Professor Ziff's description of the Poussin painting was not actually confined to noting the specific qualities which were characteristic of the pictorial surface of that painting; it included references to the relations between these qualities and the aim of Poussin, and references to the ways in which a painting having such qualities is to be contemplated by others. Had he turned his attention to examining these relationships between object, artist, and contemplator, it would assuredly have been more difficult for him to assert that "neither a poem, nor a novel, nor a musical composition can be said to be a work of art in the same sense of the phrase in which a painting or a statue or a vase can be said to be a work of art."[20] In fact, had he carefully traced the relationships which he assumed to exist among some of the characteristics of the Poussin painting, he might have found that, contrary to his inclinations, he was well advanced toward putting forward explicit generalizations concerning the arts.

III

While Professor Ziff's argument against generalization depends upon the fact that the various artistic media are significantly different from one another, the possibility of generalizing concerning the arts has also been challenged on historical grounds. It is to Morris Weitz's use of the latter argument that I shall now turn.

In "The Role of Theory in Aesthetics" Professor Weitz places his primary emphasis on the fact that art forms are not static. From this fact he argues that it is futile to attempt to state the conditions which are necessary and sufficient for an object to be a work of art. What he claims is that the concept "art" must be treated as an open concept, since new art forms have developed in the past, and since any art form (such as the novel) may undergo radical transformations from generation to generation. One brief statement from Professor Weitz's article can serve to summarize this view:

> What I am arguing, then, is that the very expansive, adventurous character of art, its ever-present changes and novel creations, makes it logically impossible to ensure any set of defining properties. We can, of course, choose to close the concept. But to do this with "art" or "tragedy" or portraiture, etc. is ludicrous since it forecloses the very conditions of creativity in the arts.[21]

Unfortunately, Professor Weitz fails to offer any cogent argument in substantiation of this claim. The lacuna in his discussion is to be found in the fact that the question of whether a particular concept is open or closed (i.e., whether a set of necessary and sufficient conditions can be offered for its use) is not identical with the question of whether future instances to which the very same concept is applied may or may not possess genuinely novel properties. In other words, Professor Weitz has not shown that every novelty in the instances to which we apply a term involves a stretching of the term's connotation.

By way of illustration, consider the classificatory label "representational painting." One can assuredly define this particular form of art without defining it in such a way that it will include only those paintings which depict either a mythological event or a religious scene. Historical paintings, interiors, fête-champetres, and still life can all count as "representational" according to any adequate definition of this mode of painting, and there is no reason why such a definition could not have been formulated prior to the emergence of any of these novel species of the representational mode. Thus, to define a particular form of art—and to define it truly and accurately—is not necessarily to set one's self in opposition to whatever new creations may arise within that particular form.[22] Consequently, it would be mistaken to suppose that all attempts to state the defining properties of various art forms are prescriptive in character and authoritarian in their effect.

This conclusion is not confined to cases in which an established form of art, such as representational painting, undergoes changes; it can also be shown to be compatible with the fact that radically new art forms arise. For example, if the concept "a work of art" had been carefully defined prior to the invention of cameras, is there any reason to suppose that such a definition would have proved an obstacle to viewing photography or the movies as constituting new art forms? To be sure, one can imagine definitions which might have done so. However, it was not Professor Weitz's aim to show that one or another definition of art had been a poor definition; he wished to establish the general thesis that there was a necessary incompatability, which he denoted as a logical impossibility, between allowing for novelty and creativity in the arts and stating the defining properties of a work of art. He failed to establish this thesis since he offered no arguments to prove that new sorts of instantiation of a previously defined concept will necessarily involve us in changing the definition of that concept.

To be sure, if neither photography nor the movies had developed along lines which satisfied the same sorts of interest that the other arts satisfied, and if the kinds of standards which were applied in the other arts were not seen to be relevant when applied to photography and to the movies, then the antecedently formulated definition of art would have functioned as a closed concept, and it would have been used to exclude all photographers and all motion-picture makers from the class of those who were to be termed "artists." However, what would the defender of the openness of concepts hold that one should have done under these circumstances? Suppose, for example, that all photographers had in fact been the equivalent of passport photographers, and that they had been motivated by no other interests and controlled by no other standards than those which govern the making of photographs for passports and licenses: would the defender of open concepts be likely to have expanded the concept of what is to count as an art in order to have included photography? The present inclusion of photography among the arts is justified, I should hold, precisely because photography arises out of the same sorts of interest, and can satisfy the same sorts of interest, and our criticism of it employs the same sorts of standards, as is the case with respect to the other arts.

Bearing this in mind, we are in a position to see that still another article which has sometimes been cited by those who argue for the openness of the concept "a work of art" does not justify the conclusions which have been drawn from it. That article is Paul Oskar Kristeller's learned and informative study entitled "The Modern System of the Arts."[23] The way in which Professor Kristeller states the aim of his article suggests that he too would deny that traditional esthetic theory is capable of formulating adequate generalizations concerning the arts. He states his aim in saying:

> The basic notion that the five "major arts" constitute an area all by themselves, clearly separated by common characteristics from the crafts, the sciences and other human activities has been taken for granted by most writers on esthetics from Kant to the present day. . . .
>
> It is my purpose to show that this system of the five major arts, which underlies all modern esthetics and is so familiar to us all, is of comparatively recent origin and did not assume definite shape before the eighteenth century, although it had many ingredients which go back to classical, mediaeval, and Renaissance thought.[24]

However, the fact that *the classification of the arts* has undoubtedly changed during the history of Western thought, does not of itself suggest that *esthetic theory* must undergo comparable changes. Should this be doubted, one may note that Professor Kristeller's article does not show in what specific ways attempts to classify or systematize the arts are integral to, or are presupposed by, or are consequences of, the formulation of an esthetic theory. This is no minor cavil, for if one examines the writers on esthetics who are currently attacked for their attempts to generalize concerning the nature of art, one finds that they are not (by and large) writers whose discussions are closely allied to the discussions of those with whom

Kristeller's article was primarily concerned. Furthermore, it is to be noted that Kristeller did not carry his discussion beyond Kant. This terminal point was justified by him on the ground that the system of the arts has not substantially changed since Kant's time.[25] However, when one recalls that Kant's work is generally regarded as standing near the beginning of modern esthetic theory—and surely not near its end—one has reason to suspect that questions concerning "the system of the arts" and questions concerning esthetic theory constitute distinct, and probably separate sets of questions. A survey of recent esthetic theory bears this out. Since the time of Hegel and of Schopenhauer there have been comparatively few influential esthetic theories which have made the problem of the diversity of art forms, and the classification of these forms, central to their consideration of the nature of art.[26] For example, the esthetic theories of Santayana, Croce, Alexander, Dewey, Prall, or Collingwood cannot be said to have been dependent upon any particular systematic classification of the arts. In so far as these theories may be taken as representative of attempts to generalize concerning the arts, it is strange that current attacks on traditional esthetics should have supposed that any special measure of support was to be derived from Kristeller's article.

Should one wish to understand why current discussions have overlooked the gap between an article such as Kristeller's and the lessons ostensibly derived from it, an explanation might be found in the lack of concern evinced by contemporary analytic philosophers for the traditional problems of esthetic theory. For example, one looks in vain in the Elton volume for a careful appraisal of the relations between esthetic theory and art criticism, and how the functions of each might differ from the functions of the other. A striking example of the failure to consider this sort of problem is also to be found in John Wisdom's often cited dicta concerning "the dullness" of esthetic theory.[27] In examining his views one finds that the books on art which Wisdom finds *not* to be dull are books such as Edmund Wilson's *Axel's Castle*, in which a critic "brings out features of the art he writes about, or better, brings home the character of what he writes about."[28] In short, it is not theory—it is not esthetic theory at all—that Wisdom is seeking: he happens to be interested in criticism.

I do not wish to be taken as denying the importance of criticism, nor as belittling the contribution which a thorough acquaintance with the practice of criticism in all of the arts may make to general esthetic theory. However, it is important to note that the work of any critic presupposes at least an implicit esthetic theory, which—as critic—it is not his aim to establish or, in general, to defend. This fact can only be overlooked by those who confine themselves to a narrow range of criticism: for example, to the criticism appearing in our own time in those journals which are read by those with whom we have intellectual, political, and social affinities. When we do not so confine ourselves, we rapidly discover that there is, and has been, an enormous variety in criticism, and that this variety represents (in part at least) the effect of differing esthetic preconceptions. To evaluate criticism itself we must, then, sometimes undertake to evaluate these preconceptions. In short, we must do esthetics ourselves.

However, for many of the critics of traditional esthetics this is an option which does not appeal. If I am not mistaken, it is not difficult to see why this should have come to be so. In the first place, it has come to be one of the marks of contemporary analytic philosophy to hold that philosophic problems are problems which cannot be solved by appeals to matters of fact. Thus, to choose but a single instance, questions of the relations between esthetic perception and other instances of perceiving—for example, questions concerning psychical distance, or empathic perception, or the role of form in esthetic perception—are not considered to be questions with which a philosopher ought to try to deal. In the second place, the task of the philosopher has come to be seen as consisting largely of the unsnarling of tangles into which others have gotten themselves. As a consequence, the attempt to find a synoptic interpretation of some broad range of facts—an attempt which has in the past been regarded as one of the major tasks of a philosopher—has either been denigrated or totally overlooked.[29] Therefore, problems such as the claims of the arts to render a true account of human character and destiny, or questions concerning the relations between esthetic goodness and standards of greatness in art, or an estimate of the significance of variability in esthetic judgments, are not presently fashionable. And it must be admitted that if philosophers wish not to have to face either factual problems or synoptic tasks, these are indeed questions which are more comfortably avoided than pursued.

—*The American Philosophical Quarterly,* Vol. 2 (1965)

NOTES

1. See William Elton (ed.), *Aesthetics and Language* (Oxford, Basil Blackwell, 1954), p. 1, n. 1 and 2.
2. A discussion of this fact is to be found in Jerome Stolnitz, "Notes on Analytic Philosophy and Aesthetics," *British Journal of Aesthetics,* vol. 3 (1961), pp. 210–222.
3. *Philosophical Review,* vol. 62 (1953), pp. 58–78.
4. *Journal of Aesthetics and Art Criticism,* vol. 15 (1956), pp. 27–35.
5. *Philosophical Review,* vol. 66 (1957), 329–362.
6. *Mind,* vol. 67 (1958), pp. 317–334. In addition to the articles already referred to, I might mention "The Uses of Works of Art" by Teddy Brunius in *Journal of Aesthetics and Art Criticism,* vol. 22 (1963), pp. 123–133, which refers to both Weitz and Kennick, but raises other questions with which I am not here concerned.
7. Ludwig Wittgenstein, *Philosophical Investigations,* translated by G. E. M. Anscombe (New York, Macmillan, 1953), pp. 31–36. A parallel passage is to be found in "The Blue Book"; see *Preliminary Studies for the "Philosophical Investigations," Generally Known as The Blue and Brown Books* (Oxford, Basil Blackwell, 1958), pp. 17–18.
8. Ludwig Wittgenstein, *Philosophical Investigations,* §66, p. 31. For reasons which are obscure, Miss Anscombe translates "*Kampfspiele*" as "Olympic games."
9. In an article which is closely related to my discussion, but which uses different arguments to support a similar point, Haig Khatchadourian has shown that Wittgenstein is less explicit than he should have been with respect to the levels of determinateness at which these resemblances are significant for our use of common names. See "Common Names and 'Family Resemblances'," *Philosophy*

and Phenomenological Research, vol. 18 (1957–58), pp. 341–358. (For a related, but less closely relevant article by Professor Khatchadourian see "Art-Names and Aesthetic Judgments," *Philosophy*, vol. 36 [1961], pp. 30–48.)

10. It is to be noted that this constitutes a closer resemblance than that involved in what Wittgenstein calls "family resemblances," since in my illustration the specific similarities all pertain to a single set of features, with respect to each one of which all three of the subjects directly resemble one another. In Wittgenstein's use of the notion of family resemblances there is, however, no one set of resembling features common to each member of the "family"; there is merely a criss-crossing and overlapping among the elements which constitute the resemblances among the various persons. Thus, in order to conform to his usage, my illustration would have to be made more complicated, and the degree of resemblance would become more attenuated. For example, we would have to introduce the photographs of other subjects in which, for example, recessive chins would supplant prognathous profiles among those who shared the other characteristics; some would have blond instead of dark hair, and protruberant instead of deep-set eyes, but would in each case resemble the others in other respects, etc. However, if what I say concerning family resemblances holds of the stronger similarities present in my illustration, it should hold *a fortiori* of the weaker form of family resemblances to which Wittgenstein draws our attention.

11. Although Wittgenstein failed to make explicit the fact that a genetic connection was involved in his notion of "family resemblances," I think that he did in fact presuppose such a connection. If I am not mistaken, the original German makes this clearer than does the Anscombe translation. The German text reads:

> Ich kann diese Ähnlichkeiten nicht besser charakterisieren, als durch das Wort "Familienähnlichkeiten"; denn so übergreifen und kreuzen sich die verschiedenen Ähnlichkeiten, dies zwischen den Gliedern einer Familie bestehen: Wuchs, Gesichtzüge, Augenfarbe, Gang, Temperament, etc., etc. (§67).

Modifying Miss Anscombe's translation in as few respects as possible, I suggest that a translation of this passage might read:

> I can think of no better expression to characterize these similarities than "family resemblances," since various similarities which obtain among the members of a family—their build, features, color of eyes, gait, temperament, etc., etc.,—overlap and criss-cross in the same way.

This translation differs from Miss Anscombe's (which has been quoted above) in that it makes more explicit the fact that the similarities are similarities among the members of a single family, and are not themselves definitive of what constitutes a *family* resemblance.

12. Were this aspect of the twofold criterion to be abandoned, and were our use of common names to be solely determined by the existence of overlapping and criss-cross relations, it is difficult to see how a halt would ever be called to the spread of such names. Robert J. Richman has called attention to the same problem in " 'Something Common'," *Journal of Philosophy*, vol. 59 (1962), pp. 821–830. He speaks of what he calls "the Problem of Wide-Open Texture," and says: "the notion of family resemblances may account for our extending the application of a given general term, but it does not seem to place any limit on this process" (p. 829.)

In an article entitled "The Problem of Model-Language Game in Wittgenstein's Later Philosophy," *Philosophy*, vol. 36 (1961), pp. 333–351, Helen Hervey also calls attention to the fact that "a family is so-called by virtue of its common ancestry" (p. 334). She also mentions (p. 335) what Richman referred to as the problem of "the wide-open texture."

13. Ludwig Wittgenstein, *Philosophical Investigations,* §66, p. 31.

14. Although I have only mentioned the existence of genetic connections among members of a family, I should of course not wish to exclude the effects of habitual association in giving rise to some of the resemblances which Wittgenstein mentions. I have stressed genetic connection only because it is the simplest and most obvious illustration of the point I have wished to make.

15. I do not deny that directly exhibited resemblances often play a part in our use of common names: this is a fact explicitly noted at least as long ago as by Locke. However, similarities in origin, similarities in use, and similarities in intention may also play significant roles. It is such factors that Wittgenstein overlooks in his specific discussions of family resemblances and of games.

16. I know of no passage in which Wittgenstein takes such a possibility into account. In fact, if the passage from "The Blue Book" to which I have already alluded may be regarded as representative, we may say that Wittgenstein's view of traditional esthetics theories was quite without foundation. In that passage he said:

> The idea of a general concept being a common property of its particular instances connects up with other primitive, too simple, ideas of the structure of language. It is comparable to the idea that *properties* are *ingredients* of the things which have the properties; e.g., that beauty is an ingredient of all beautiful things as alcohol is of beer and wine, and that we therefore could have pure beauty, unadulterated by anything that is beautiful (p. 17).

I fail to be able to identify an esthetics theory of which such a statement would be true. It would not, for example, be true of Clive Bell's doctrine of "significant form," nor would it presumably be true of G. E. Moore's view of beauty, since both Bell and Moore hold that beauty depends upon the specific nature of other qualities which characterize that which is beautiful.

However, it may be objected that when I suggest that what is common to works of art involves reference to "intentions," I overlook "the intentional fallacy" (see W. K. Wimsatt, Jr., and Monroe C. Beardsley, "The Intentional Fallacy," *Sewanee Review,* vol. 54 [1946], pp. 468–488). This is not the case. The phrase "the intentional fallacy" originally referred to a particular method of criticism, that is, to a method of interpreting and evaluating given works of art; it was not the aim of Wimsatt and Beardsley to distinguish art and non-art. These two problems are, I believe, fundamentally different in character. However, I do not feel sure that Professor Beardsley has noted this fact, for in a recent article in which he set out to criticize those who have been influenced by the doctrine of family resemblances he apparently felt himself obliged to define art *solely* in terms of some characteristic in the object itself (see "The Definition of the Arts," *Journal of Aesthetics and Art Criticism,* vol. 20 [1961], pp. 175–187). Had he been willing to relate this characteristic to the activity and intention of those who make objects having such a characteristic, his discussion would not, I believe, have been susceptible to many of the criticisms leveled against it by Professor Douglas Morgan and Mary Mothersill (*ibid.,* pp. 187–198).

17. I do not say "*all*" such definitions, for I think that one can find a number of convergent definitions of art, each of which has considerable merit, though each may differ slightly from the others in its emphasis.

18. *Op. cit.,* pp. 60–61. It is an interesting problem, but not germane to our present concerns, to consider whether Poussin's painting should be classified as

a "mythological" painting, as Professor Ziff describes it, or whether it should be regarded as an historical painting.

19. *Ibid.*, p. 64.

20. *Ibid.*, p. 66. For example, Ziff denies that a poem can be said to be "exhibited or displayed." Yet it is surely the case that in printing a poem or in presenting a reading of a poem, the relation between the work and its audience, and the relation between artist, work, and audience, is not wholly dissimilar to that which obtains when an artist exhibits a painting. If this be doubted, consider whether there is not a closer affinity between these two cases than there is between a painter *exhibiting* a painting and a manufacturer *exhibiting* a new line of fountain pens.

21. *Op. cit.*, p. 32.

22. To be sure, if no continuing characteristic is to be found, the fact of change will demand that the concept be treated as having been an open one. This was precisely the position taken by Max Black in a discussion of the concept "science." (See "The Definition of Scientific Method," in *Science and Civilization*, edited by Robert C. Stauffer [Madison, Wisconsin, 1949].) Paul Ziff refers to the influence of Professor Black's discussion upon his own views, and the views of Morris Weitz are assuredly similar. However, even if Professor Black's view of the changes in the concept "science" is a correct one (as I should be prepared to think that it may be), it does not follow that the same argument applies in the case of art. Nor does the fact that the meaning of "science" has undergone profound changes in the past imply that further analogous changes will occur in the future.

23. *Journal of the History of Ideas*, vol. 12 (1951), pp. 496–527, and vol. 13 (1952), pp. 17–46. This study has been cited by both Elton (*op. cit.*, p. 2) and Kennick (*op. cit.*, p. 320) in substantiation of their views.

24. *Op. cit.*, vol. 12, p. 497.

25. *Op. cit.*, vol. 13, p. 43; also, pp. 4 ff.

26. One exception is to be found in T. M. Greene: *The Arts and the Art of Criticism* (Princeton, 1940). This work is cited by Kristeller, and is one of the only two which he cites in support of the view that the system of the arts has not changed since Kant's day (*op. cit.*, vol. 12, p. 497, n. 4). The other work cited by him is Paul Franke's *System der Kuntswissenschaft* (Brünn/Leipzig, 1938), which also offers a classification of the arts, but only within a framework of esthetic theory which could easily embrace whatever historical changes the arts undergo.

27. See "Things and Persons," *Proceedings of the Aristotelian Society, Supplementary Volume XXII* (1948), pp. 207–210.

28. *Ibid.*, p. 209.

29. For example, W. B. Gallie's "The Function of Philosophical Aesthetics," in the Elton volume, argues for "a journeyman's esthetics," which will take up individual problems, one by one, these problems being of the sort which arise when a critic or poet gets into a muddle about terms such as "abstraction" or "imagination." For this purpose the tools of the philosopher are taken to be the tools of logical analysis (*op. cit.*, p. 35); a concern with the history of the arts, with psychology, or a direct and wide-ranging experience of the arts seems not to be presupposed.

A second example of the limitations imposed upon esthetics by contemporary linguistic analysis is to be found in Professor Weitz's article. He states that "the root problem of philosophy itself is to explain the relation between the employment of certain kinds of concepts and the conditions under which they can be correctly applied" (*op. cit.*, p. 30).

GEORGE DICKIE

What is Art? An Institutional Analysis

I

The best-known denial that "art" can be defined occurs in Morris Weitz's article "The Role of Theory in Aesthetics."[1] Weitz's conclusion depends upon two arguments which may be called his "generalization argument" and his "classification argument." In stating the "generalization argument," Weitz distinguishes, quite correctly, between the generic conception of "art" and the various subconcepts of art such as tragedy, the novel, painting, and the like. He then goes on to give an argument purporting to show that the subconcept "novel" is open, that is, that the members of the class of novels do not share any essential or defining characteristics. He then asserts without further argument that what is true of novels is true of all other subconcepts of art. The generalization from one subconcept to all subconcepts may or may not be justified, but I am not questioning it here. I do question, however, Weitz's additional contention, also asserted without argument, that the generic conception of "art" is open. The best that can be said of his conclusion about the generic sense is that it is unsupported. All or some of the subconcepts of art may be open and the generic conception of art still be closed. That is, it is possible that all or some of the subconcepts of art, such as novel, tragedy, sculpture, and painting, may lack necessary and sufficient conditions and at the same time that "work of art," which is the genus of all the subconcepts, can be defined in terms of necessary and sufficient conditions. Tragedies may not have any characteristics in common which would distinguish them from, say, comedies *within the domain of art*, but it may be that there are common characteristics that works of art have which distinguish them from nonart. Nothing prevents a "closed genus/open species" relationship. Weitz himself has recently cited what he takes to be a similar (although reversed) example of genus–species relationship. He argues that "game" (the genus) is open but that "major-league baseball" (a species) is closed.[2]

His second argument, "the classification argument," claims to show that not even the characteristic of artifactuality is a necessary feature of art. Weitz's conclusion here is something of a surprise, because it has been widely assumed by philosophers and nonphilosophers alike that a work of art is necessarily an artifact. His argument is simply that we sometimes utter such statements as "This piece of driftwood is a lovely piece of sculpture," and since such utterances are perfectly intelligible, it follows that some nonartifacts such as certain pieces of driftwood are works of art (sculptures). In other words, something need not be an artifact in order to be correctly classified as a work of art. I will try to rebut this argument shortly.

Recently, Maurice Mandelbaum has raised a question about Wittgenstein's famous contention that "game" cannot be defined and Weitz's thesis about "art."[3] His challenge to both is based on the charge that they have been concerned only with what Mandelbaum calls "exhibited" characteristics and that consequently each has failed to take account of the nonexhibited, relational aspects of games and art. By "exhibited" characteristics Mandelbaum means easily perceived properties such as the fact that a ball is used in a certain kind of game, that a painting has a triangular composition, that an area in a painting is red, or that the plot of a tragedy contains a reversal of fortune. Mandelbaum concludes that when we consider the nonexhibited properties of games, we see that they have in common "the potentiality of . . . [an] . . . absorbing nonpractical interest to either participants or spectators."[4] Mandelbaum may or may not be right about "game," but what interests me is the application of his suggestion about nonexhibited properties to the discussion of the definition of art. Although he does not attempt a definition of "art," Mandelbaum does suggest that feature(s) common to all works of art may perhaps be discovered that will be a basis for the definition of "art," if the nonexhibited features of art are attended to.

Having noted Mandelbaum's invaluable suggestion about definition, I now return to Weitz's argument concerning artifactuality. In an earlier attempt to show Weitz wrong, I thought it sufficient to point out that there are two senses of "work of art," an evaluative sense and a classificatory one; Weitz himself distinguishes these in his article as the evaluative and the descriptive senses of art. My earlier argument was that if there is more than one sense of "work of art," then the fact that "This piece of driftwood is a lovely piece of sculpture" is intelligible does not prove what Weitz wants it to prove. Weitz would have to show that "sculpture" is being used in the sentence in question in the classificatory sense, and this he makes no attempt to do. My argument assumed that once the distinction is made, it is obvious that "sculpture" is here being used in the evaluative sense. Richard Sclafani has subsequently noted that my argument shows only that Weitz's argument is inconclusive and that Weitz might still be right, even though his argument does not prove his conclusion. Sclafani, however, has constructed a stronger argument against Weitz on this point.[5]

Sclafani shows that there is a third sense of "works of art" and that "driftwood cases" (the nonartifact cases) fall under it. He begins by comparing a paradigm work of art, Brancusi's *Bird in Space*, with a piece of driftwood which looks very much like it. Sclafani says that it seems natural to say of the piece of driftwood that it is a work of art and that we do so because it has so many properties in common with the Brancusi piece. He then asks us to reflect on our characterization of the driftwood and the *direction* it has taken. We say the driftwood is art because of its resemblance to some paradigm work of art or because the driftwood shares properties with several paradigm works of art. The paradigm work or works are of course always artifacts; the direction of our move is from paradigmatic (artifactual) works of art to nonartifactual "art." Sclafani quite correctly takes this to indicate that there is a primary, paradigmatic sense of "work of art" (my classificatory sense) and a derivative or secondary sense into which the "driftwood cases" fall. Weitz is right in a way in saying that the driftwood is art, but wrong in concluding that artifactuality is unnecessary for (the primary sense of) art.

There are then at least three distinct senses of "work of art"; the primary or classificatory sense, the secondary or derivative, and the evaluative. Perhaps in most uses of Weitz's driftwood sentence example, both the derivative and the evaluative senses would be involved: the derivative sense if the driftwood shared a number of properties with some paradigm work of art and the evaluative sense if the shared properties were found to be valuable by the speaker. Sclafani gives a case in which only the evaluative sense functions, when someone says, "Sally's cake is a work of art." In most uses of such a sentence "work of art" would simply mean that its referent has valuable qualities. Admittedly, one can imagine contexts in which the derivative sense would apply to cakes. (Given the situation in art today, one can easily imagine cakes to which the primary sense of art could be applied.) If, however, someone were to say, "This Rembrandt is a work of art," both the classificatory and the evaluative senses would be functioning. The expression "this Rembrandt" would convey the information that its referent is a work of art in the classificatory sense, and "is a work of art" could then only reasonably be understood in the evaluative sense. Finally, someone might say of a seashell or other natural object which resembles a man's face but is otherwise uninteresting, "This shell (or other natural object) is a work of art." In this case, only the derivative sense would be used.

We utter sentences in which the expression "work of art" has the evaluative sense with considerable frequency, applying it to both natural objects and artifacts. We speak of works of art in the derived sense with somewhat less frequency. The classificatory sense of "work of art," which indicates simply that a thing belongs to a certain category of artifacts, occurs, however, very infrequently in our discourse. We rarely utter sentences in which we use the classificatory sense, because it is such a basic notion: we generally know immediately whether an object is a work of art, so that generally no one needs to say, by way of classification, "That is a work of art," although recent developments in art such as junk sculpture and found art may occasionally force such remarks. Even if we do not often talk about art in this classificatory sense, however, it is a basic concept that structures and guides our thinking about our world and its contents.

II

It is now clear that artifactuality is a necessary condition (call it the genus) of the primary sense of art. This fact, however, does not seem very surprising and would not even be very interesting except that Weitz and others have denied it. Artifactuality alone, however, is not the whole story and another necessary condition (the differentia) has to be specified in order to have a satisfactory definition of "art." Like artifactuality, the second condition is a nonexhibited property, which turns out to be as complicated as artifactuality is simple. The attempt to discover and specify the second condition of art will involve an examination of the intricate complexities of the "artworld." W. E. Kennick, defending a view similar to Weitz's, contends that the kind of approach to be employed here, following Mandelbaum's lead, is futile. He concludes that "the attempt to define Art in terms of what we do with certain objects is as doomed as any other."[6] He tries to support this conclusion by referring to such things as the fact that the ancient Egyptians sealed up paintings and sculptures in tombs. There are two difficulties with Kennick's argument. First, that the Egyptians sealed up paintings and sculptures in tombs does not show that they regarded them differently from the way in which we regard them. They might have put them there for the dead to appreciate or simply because they belonged to the dead person. The Egyptian practice does not establish so radical a difference between their conception of art and ours that a definition subsuming both is impossible. Second, one need not assume that we and the ancient Egyptians share a common conception of art. It would be enough to be able to specify the necessary and sufficient conditions for the concept of art which we have (we present-day Americans, we present-day Westerners, we Westerners since the organization of the system of the arts in or about the eighteenth century—I am not sure of the exact limits of the "we"). Kennick notwithstanding, we are most likely to discover the differentia of art by considering "what we do with certain objects." Of course, nothing guarantees that any given thing we might do or an ancient Egyptian might have done with a work of art will throw light on the concept of art. Not every "doing" will reveal what is required.

Although he does not attempt to formulate a definition, Arthur Danto in his provocative article, "The Artworld," has suggested the direction that must be taken by an attempt to define "art."[7] In reflecting on art and its history together with such present-day developments as Warhol's *Brillo Carton* and Rauschenberg's *Bed*, Danto writes, "To see something as art requires something the eye cannot descry—an atmosphere of artistic theory, a knowledge of history of art: an artworld."[8] Admittedly, this stimulating comment is in need of elucidation, but it is clear that in speaking of "something the eye cannot descry" Danto is agreeing with Mandelbaum that nonexhibited properties are of great importance in constituting something as art. In speaking of atmosphere and history, however, Danto's remark carries us a step further than Mandelbaum's analysis. Danto points to the rich structure in which particular works of art are embedded: he indicates *the institutional nature of art.*[9]

I shall use Danto's term "artworld" to refer to the broad social institution in which works of art have their place.[10] But is there such an institution? George Bernard Shaw speaks somewhere of the apostolic line of succession stretching from Aeschylus to himself. Shaw was no doubt speaking for effect and to draw attention to himself, as he often did, but there is an important truth implied by his remark. There is a long tradition or continuing institution of the theater having its origins in ancient Greek religion and other Greek institutions. That tradition has run very thin at times and perhaps even ceased to exist altogether during some periods, only to be reborn out of its memory and the need for art. The institutions associated with the theater have varied from time to time: in the beginning it was Greek religion and the Greek state; in medieval times, the church; more recently, private business and the state (national theater). What has remained constant with its own identity throughout its history is the theater itself as an established way of doing and behaving, what I shall call . . . the primary convention of the theater. This institutionalized behavior occurs on both sides of the "footlights": both the players and the audience are involved and go to make up the institution of the theater. The roles of the actors and the audience are defined by the traditions of the theater. What the author, management, and players present is art, and it is art because it is presented within the theaterworld framework. Plays are written to have a place in the theater system and they exist as plays—that is, as art—within that system. Of course, I do not wish to deny that plays also exist as literary works—that is, as art within the literary system: The theater system and the literary system overlap. Let me make clear what I mean by speaking of the artworld as an institution. Among the meanings of "institution" in *Webster's New Collegiate Dictionary* are the following: "3. That which is instituted as: a. An established practice, law, custom, etc. b. An established society or corporation." When I call the artworld an institution I am saying that it is an established practice. Some persons have thought that an institution must be an established society or corporation, and, consequently, have misunderstood my claim about the artworld.

Theater is only one of the systems within the artworld. Each of the systems has had its own origins and historical development. We have some information about the later stages of these developments, but we have to guess about the origins of the basic art systems. I suppose that we have complete knowledge of certain recently developed subsystems or genres such as dada and happenings. Even if our knowledge is not as complete as we wish it were, however, we do have substantial information about the systems of the artworld as they currently exist and as they have existed for some time. One central feature all of the systems have in common is that each is a framework for the *presenting* of particular works of art. Given the great variety of the systems of the artworld it is not surprising that works of art have no exhibited properties in common. If, however, we step back and view the works in their institutional setting, we will be able to see the essential properties they share.

Theater is a rich and instructive illustration of the institutional nature of art. But it is a development within the domain of painting and sculpture—dadaism—that most easily reveals the institutional essence of art. Duchamp and friends conferred the status of art on "readymades" (urinals, hatracks, snow shovels, and the like), and when we reflect on their deeds we can take note of a kind of human action which has until now gone unnoticed and unappreciated—the action of conferring the status of art. Painters and sculptors, of course, have been engaging all along in the action of conferring this status on the objects they create. As long, however, as the created objects were conventional, given the paradigms of the times, the objects themselves and their fascinating exhibited properties were the focus of the attention of not only spectators and critics but of philosophers of art as well. When an artist of an earlier era painted a picture, he did some or all of a number of things: depicted a human being, portrayed a certain man, fulfilled a commission, worked at his livelihood, and so on. In addition, he also acted as an agent of the artworld and conferred the status of art on his creation. Philosophers of art attended to only some of the properties the created object acquired from these various actions, for example, to the representational or to the expressive features of the objects. They entirely ignored the nonexhibited property of status. When, however, the objects are bizarre, as those of the dadaists are, our attention is forced away from the objects' obvious properties to a consideration of the objects in their social context. As works of art Duchamp's "ready-mades" may not be worth much, but as examples of art they are very valuable for art theory. I am not claiming that Duchamp and friends invented the conferring of the status of art; they simply used an existing institutional device in an unusual way. Duchamp did not invent the artworld, because it was there all along.

The artworld consists of a bundle of systems: theater, painting, sculpture, literature, music, and so on, each of which furnishes an institutional background for the conferring of the status on objects within its domain. No limit can be placed on the number of systems that can be brought under the generic conception of art, and each of the major systems contains further subsystems. These features of the artworld provide the elasticity whereby creativity of even the most radical sort can be accommodated. A whole new system comparable to the theater, for example, could be added in one fell swoop. What is more likely is that a new subsystem would be added within a system. For example, junk sculpture added within sculpture, happenings added within theater. Such additions might in time develop into full-blown systems. Thus, the radical creativity, adventuresomeness, and exuberance of art of which Weitz speaks is possible within the concept of art, even though it is closed by the necessary and sufficient conditions of artifactuality and the conferred status.

Having now briefly described the artworld, I am in a position to specify a definition of "work of art." The definition will be given in terms of artifactuality and the conferred status of art, or more strictly speaking, the conferred status of candidate for appreciation. Once the definition has been stated, a great deal will still remain to be said by way of clarification: A work of art in the classificatory sense is (1) an artifact (2) a set of the aspects of which has had conferred upon it the status of candidate for appreciation by some person or persons acting on behalf of a certain social institution (the artworld).

The second condition of the definition makes use of four variously interconnected notions: (1) acting on behalf of an institution, (2) conferring of status, (3) being a candidate, and (4) appreciation. The first two of these are so closely related that they must be discussed together. I shall first describe paradigm cases of conferring status outside the artworld and then show how similar actions take place within the artworld. The most clearcut examples of the conferring of status are certain legal actions of the state. A king's conferring of knighthood, a grand jury's indicting someone, the chairman of the election board certifying that someone is qualified to run for office, or a minister's pronouncing a couple man and wife are examples in which a person or persons acting on behalf of a social institution (the state) confer(s) *legal* status on persons. The congress or a legally constituted commission may confer the status of national park or monument on an area or thing. The examples given suggest that pomp and ceremony are required to establish legal status, but this is not so, although of course a legal system is presupposed. For example, in some jurisdictions common-law marriage is possible—a legal status acquired without ceremony. The conferring of a Ph.D. degree on someone by a university, the election of someone as president of the Rotary, and the declaring of an object as a relic of the church are examples in which a person or persons confer(s) nonlegal status on persons or things. In such cases some social system or other must exist as the framework within which the conferring takes place, but, as before, ceremony is not required to establish status: For example, a person can acquire the status of wise man or village idiot within a community without ceremony.

Some may feel that the notion of conferring status within the artworld is excessively vague. Certainly this notion is not as clear-cut as the conferring of status within the legal system, where procedures and lines of authority are explicitly defined and incorporated into law. The counterparts in the artworld to specified procedures and lines of authority are nowhere codified, and the artworld carries on its business at the level of customary practice. Still there *is* a practice and this defines a social institution. A social institution need not have a formally established constitution, officers, and bylaws in order to exist and have the capacity to confer status—some social institutions are formal and some are informal. The artworld could become formalized, and perhaps has been to some extent in certain political contexts, but most people who are interested in art would probably consider this a bad thing. Such formality would threaten the freshness and exuberance of art. The core personnel of the artworld is a loosely organized, but nevertheless related, set of persons including artists (understood to refer to painters, writers, composers), producers, museum directors, museum-goers, theater-goers, reporters for newspapers, critics for publications of all sorts, art historians, art theorists, philosophers of art, and others. These are the people who keep the machinery of the artworld working and thereby provide for its continuing existence. In addition, every person who sees himself as a member of the artworld is thereby a member. Although I have called the persons just listed the core personnel of the artworld, there is a minimum core within that core without which the artworld would not exist. This essential core consists of artists who create the works, "presenters" to present the works, and "goers" who appreciate the works. This minimum core might be called "the presentation group," for it consists of artists whose activity is necessary if anything is to be presented, the presenters (actors, stage managers, and so on), and the goers whose presence and cooperation is necessary in order for anything to be presented. A given person might play more than one of these essential roles in the case of the presentation of a particular work. Critics, historians, and philosophers of art become members of the artworld at some time after the minimum core personnel of a particular art system get that system into operation. All of these roles are institutionalized and must be learned in one way or another by the participants. For example, a theatergoer is not just someone who happens to enter a theater; he is a person who enters with certain expectations and knowledge about what he will experience and an understanding of how he should behave in the face of what he will experience.

Assuming that the existence of the artworld has been established or at least made plausible, the problem is now to see how status is conferred by this institution. My thesis is that, in a way analogous to the way in which a person is certified as qualified for office, or two persons acquire the status of common-law marriage within a legal system, or a person is elected president of the Rotary, or a person acquires the status of wise man within a community, so an artifact can acquire the status of candidate for appreciation within the social system called "the artworld." How can one tell when the status has been conferred? An artifact's hanging in an art museum as part of a show and a performance at a theater are sure signs. There is, of course, no guarantee that one can always know whether something is a candidate for appreciation, just as one cannot always tell whether a given person is a knight or is married. When an object's status depends upon nonexhibited characteristics, a simple look at the object will not necessarily reveal that status. The nonexhibited relation *may* be symbolized by some badge, for example, by a wedding ring, in which case a simple look will reveal the status.

The more important question is that of how the status of candidate for appreciation is conferred. The examples just mentioned, display in a museum and a performance in a theater, seem to suggest that a number of persons are required for the actual conferring of the status. In one sense a number of persons are required but in another sense only one person is required: a number of persons are required to make up the social institution of the artworld, but only one person is required to act on behalf of the artworld and to confer the status of candidate for appreciation. In fact, many works of art are seen only by one person—the one who creates them—but they are still art. The status in question may be acquired by a single person's acting on behalf of the artworld and *treating an artifact as a candidate for appreciation.* Of course, nothing prevents a group of persons from conferring the status, but it is usually conferred by a single person, the artist who creates the artifact. It may be helpful to compare and contrast the notion of conferring the status of candidate for appreciation with a case in which something is simply presented for appreciation: hopefully this will throw light on the notion of status of candidate. Consider the case of a salesman of plumbing supplies who spreads his wares before us. "Placing before" and "conferring the status of candidate for appreciation" are very different notions, and this difference can be brought out by comparing the salesman's action with the superficially similar act of Duchamp in entering a urinal which he christened *Fountain* in that now-famous art show. The difference is that Duchamp's action took place within the institutional setting of the artworld and the plumbing salesman's action took place outside of it. The salesman could do what Duchamp did, that is, convert a urinal into a work of art, but such a thing probably would not occur to him. Please remember that *Fountain*'s being a work of art does not mean that it is a good one, nor does this qualification insinuate that it is a bad one either. The antics of a particular present-day artist serve to reinforce the point of the Duchamp case and also to emphasize a significance of the practice of naming works of art. Walter de Maria has in the case of one of his works even gone through the motions, no doubt as a burlesque, of using a procedure used by many legal and some nonlegal institutions—the procedure of licensing. His *High Energy Bar* (a stainless-steel bar) is accompanied by a certificate bearing the name of the work and stating that the bar is a work of art only when the certificate is present. In addition to highlighting the status of art by "certifying" it on a document, this example serves to suggest a significance of the act of naming works of art. An object may acquire the status of art without ever being named but giving it a title makes clear to whomever is interested that an object is a work of art. Specific titles function in a variety of ways—as aids to understanding a work or as a convenient way of identifying it, for example—but any title at all (even *Untitled*) is a badge of status.[11]

The third notion involved in the second condition of the definition is candidacy: a member of the artworld confers the status of candidate for appreciation. The definition does not require that a work of art actually be appreciated, even by one person. The fact is that many, perhaps most, works of art go unappreciated. It is important not to build into the definition of the classificatory sense of "work of art" value properties such as actual appreciation: to do so would make it impossible to speak of unappreciated works of art. Building in value properties might even make it awkward to speak of bad works of art. A theory of art must preserve certain central features of the way in which we talk about art, and we do find it necessary sometimes to speak of unappreciated art and of bad art. Also, not every aspect of a work is included in the candidacy for appreciation; for example, the color of the back of a painting is not ordinarily considered to be something which someone might think it appropriate to appreciate. The problem of which aspects of a work of art to be included within the candidacy for appreciation is a question I shall pursue later . . . in trying to give an analysis of the notion of esthetic object. The definition of "work of art" should not, therefore, be understood as asserting that every aspect of a work is included within the candidacy for appreciation.

The fourth notion involved in the second condition of the definition is appreciation itself. Some may assume that the definition is referring to a special kind of *esthetic* appreciation. I shall argue later . . . that there is no reason to think that there is a special kind of esthetic consciousness, attention, or perception. Similarly, I do not think there is any reason to think that there is a special kind of esthetic appreciation. All that is meant by "appreciation" in the definition is something like "in experiencing the qualities of a thing one finds them worthy or valuable," and this meaning applies quite generally both inside and outside the domain of art. Several persons have felt that my account of the institutional theory of art is incomplete because of what they see as my insufficient analysis of appreciation. They have, I believe, thought that there are different kinds of appreciation and that the appreciation in the appreciation of art is somehow typically different from the appreciation in the appreciation of nonart. But the only sense in which there is a difference between the appreciation of art and the appreciation of nonart is that the appreciations have different *objects*. The institutional structure in which the art object is embedded, not different kinds of appreciation, make the difference between the appreciation of art and the appreciation of nonart.

In a recent article[12] Ted Cohen has raised a question concerning (1) candidacy for appreciation and (2) appreciation as these two were treated in my original attempt to define "art."[13] He claims that in order for it to be possible for candidacy for appreciation to be conferred on something that it must be possible for that thing to be appreciated. Perhaps he is right about this; in any event, I cannot think of any reason to disagree with him on this point. The possibility of appreciation is one constraint on the definition: if something cannot be appreciated, it cannot become art. The question that now arises is: is there anything which it is impossible to appreciate? Cohen claims many things cannot be appreciated; for example, "ordinary thumbtacks, cheap white envelopes, the plastic forks given at some drive-in restaurants."[14] But more importantly, he claims that *Fountain* cannot be appreciated. He says that *Fountain* has a point which can be appreciated, but that it is Duchamp's gesture that has significance (can be appreciated) and not *Fountain* itself. I agree that *Fountain* has the significance Cohen attributes to it, namely, that it was a protest against the art of its day. But why cannot the ordinary qualities of *Fountain*—its gleaming white surface, the depth revealed when it reflects images of surrounding objects, its pleasing oval shape—be appreciated? It has qualities similar to those of works by Brancusi and Moore which many do not balk at saying they appreciate. Similarly, thumbtacks, envelopes, and plastic forks have qualities that can be appreciated if one makes the effort to focus attention on them. One of the values of photography is its ability to focus on and bring out the qualities of quite ordinary objects. And the same sort of thing can be done without the benefit of photography by just looking. In short, it seems unlikely to me that any object would not have some quality which is appreciatable and thus likely that the constraint Cohen suggests may well be vacuous. But even if there are some objects that cannot be appreciated, *Fountain* and the other dadaist creations are not among them.

I should note that in accepting Cohen's claim I am saying that every work of art must have some minimal *potential* value or worthiness. This fact, however, does not collapse the distinction between the evaluative sense and the classificatory sense of "work of art." The evaluative sense is used when the object it is predicated of is deemed *to be* of substantial, actual value, and that object may be a natural object. I will further note that the appreciatability of a work of art in the classificatory sense is *potential* value which in a given case may never be realized.[15]

The definition I have given contains a reference to the artworld. Consequently, some may have the uncomfortable feeling that my definition is viciously circular. Admittedly, in a sense the definition is circular, but it is not viciously so. If I had said something like "A work of art is an artifact on which a status has been conferred by the artworld" and then said of the artworld only that it confers the status of candidacy for appreciation, then the definition would be viciously circular because the circle would be so small and *uninformative*. I have, however, devoted a considerable amount of space in this chapter to describing and analyzing the historical, organizational, and functional intricacies of the artworld, and if this account is accurate the reader has received a considerable amount of *information* about the artworld. The circle I have run is not small and it is not uninformative. If, in the end, the artworld cannot be described independently of art—that is, if the description contains references to art historians, art reporters, plays, theaters, and so on—then the definition strictly speaking is circular. It is not, however, viciously so, because the whole account in which the definition is embedded contains a great deal of information about the artworld. One must not focus narrowly on the definition alone: for what is important to see is that art is an institutional concept and this requires seeing the definition in the context of the whole account. I suspect that the "problem" of circularity will arise frequently, perhaps always, when institutional concepts are dealt with.

III

The instances of dadaist art and similar present-day developments which have served to bring the institutional nature of art to our attention suggest several questions. First, if Duchamp can convert such artifacts as a urinal, a snow shovel, and a hatrack into works of art, why can't natural objects such as driftwood also become works of art in the classificatory sense? Perhaps they can if any one of a number of things is done to them. One way in which this might happen would be for someone to pick up a natural object, take it home, and hang it on the wall. Another way would be to pick up a natural object and enter it in an exhibition. I was assuming earlier, by the way, that the piece of driftwood referred to in Weitz's sentence was in place on a beach and untouched by human hand or at least untouched by any human intention and therefore was art in the evaluative or derivative sense. Natural objects which become works of art in the classificatory sense are artifactualized without the use of tools—artifactuality is conferred on the object rather than worked on it.[16] This means that natural objects which become works of art acquire their artifactuality at the same time that the status of candidate for appreciation is conferred on them, although the act that confers artifactuality is not the same act that confers the status of candidate for appreciation. But perhaps a similar thing ordinarily happens with paintings and poems; they come to exist as artifacts at the same time that they have the status of candidate for appreciation conferred on them. Of course, being an artifact and being a candidate for appreciation are not the same thing—they are two properties which may be acquired at the same time. Many may find the notion of artifactuality being conferred rather than "worked" on an object too strange to accept, and admittedly it is an unusual conception. It may be that a special account will have to be worked out for exhibited driftwood and similar cases.

Another question arising with some frequency in connection with discussions of the concept of art and seeming especially relevant in the context of the institutional theory is "How are we to conceive of paintings done by individuals such as Betsy the chimpanzee from the Baltimore Zoo?" Calling Betsy's products paintings is not meant to prejudge that they are works of art, it is just that some word is needed to refer to them. The question of whether Betsy's paintings are art depends upon what is done with them. For example, a year or two ago the Field Museum of Natural History in Chicago exhibited some chimpanzee and gorilla paintings. We must say that these paintings are not works of art. If, however, they had been exhibited a few miles away at the Chicago Art Institute they would have been works of art—the paintings would have been art if the director of the Art Institute had been willing to go out on a limb for his fellow primates. A great deal depends upon the institutional setting: One institutional setting is congenial to conferring the status of art and the other is not. Please note that although paintings such as Betsy's would remain her paintings even if exhibited at an art museum, they would be the *art* of the person responsible for their being exhibited. Betsy would not (I assume) be able to conceive of herself in such a way as to be a member of the artworld and, hence, would not be able to confer the relevant status. Art is a concept which necessarily involves human intentionality. These last remarks are not intended to denigrate the value (including beauty) of the paintings of chimpanzees shown at natural history museums or the creations of bower birds, but as remarks about what falls under a particular concept.

Danto, in "Art Works and Real Things," discusses defeating conditions of the ascriptivity of art.[17] He considers fake paintings—that is, copies of original paintings which are attributed to the creators of the original paintings. He argues that a painting's being a fake prevents it from being a work of art, maintaining that originality is an analytical requirement of being a work of art. That a work is derivative or imitative does not, however, he thinks, prevent it from being a work of art. I think Danto is right about fake paintings, and I can express this in terms of my own account by saying that originality in paintings is an antecedent requirement for the conferring of the candidacy for appreciation. Similar sorts of things would have to be said for similar cases in the arts other than painting. One consequence of this requirement is that there are many works of nonart which people take to be works of art—namely, those fake paintings which are not known to be fakes. When fakes are discovered to be fakes, they do not lose that status of art because they never had the status in the first place, despite what almost everyone had thought. There is some analogy here with patent law. Once an invention has been patented, one exactly like it cannot be patented—the patent for just that invention has been "used up." In the case of patenting, of course, whether the second device is a copy or independently derived is unimportant, but the copying aspect is crucial in the artistic case. The Van Meegeren painting that was not a copy of an actual Vanmeer but a painting done in the manner of Vermeer with a forged signature is a somewhat more complicated case. The painting with the forged signature is not a work of art, but if Van Meegeren had signed his own name the painting would have been.

Strictly speaking, since originality is an analytic requirement for a painting to be a work of art, an originality clause should be incorporated into my definition of "work of art." But since I have not given any analysis of the originality requirement with respect to works other than paintings, I am not in a position to supplement the definition in this way. All I can say at this time is what I said just above—namely, that originality in paintings is an antecedent requirement for the conferring of the candidacy for appreciation and that considerations of a similar sort probably apply in the other arts.

Weitz charges that the defining of "art" or its subconcepts forecloses on creativity. Some of the traditional definitions of "art" *may* have and some of the traditional definitions of its subconcepts probably *did* foreclose on creativity, but this danger is now past. At one time a playwright, for example, may have conceived of and wished to write a play with tragic features but lacking a defining characteristic as specified by, say, Aristotle's definition of "tragedy." Faced with this dilemma, the playwright might have been intimidated into abandoning his project. With the present-day disregard for established genres, however, and the clamor for novelty in art, this obstacle to creativity no longer exists. Today, if a new and unusual work is created and it is similar to some members of an established type of art, it will usually be accommodated within that type, or if the new work is very unlike any existing works then a new subconcept will probably be created. Artists today are not easily intimidated, and they regard art genres as loose guidelines rather than rigid specifications. Even if a philosopher's remarks were to have an effect on what artists do today, the institutional conception of art would certainly not foreclose on creativity. The requirement of artifactuality cannot prevent creativity, since artifactuality is a necessary condition of creativity. There cannot be an instance of creativity without an artifact of some kind being produced. The second requirement involving the conferring of status could not inhibit creativity; in fact, it encourages it. Since under the definition anything whatever may become art, the definition imposes no restraints on creativity.

The institutional theory of art may sound like saying, "A work of art is an object of which someone has said, 'I christen this object a work of art.'" And it is rather like that, although this does not mean that the conferring of the status of art is a simple matter. Just as the christening of a child has as its background the history and structure of the church, conferring the status of art has as its background the Byzantine complexity of the artworld. Some may find it strange that in the nonart cases discussed, there are ways in which the conferring can go wrong, while that does not appear to be true in art. For example, an indictment might be improperly drawn up and the person charged would not actually be indicted, but nothing parallel seems possible in the case of art. This fact just reflects the differences between the artworld and legal institutions: the legal system deals with matters of grave personal consequences and its procedures must reflect this; the artworld deals with important matters also but they are of a different sort entirely. The artworld does not require rigid procedures; it admits and even encourages frivolity and caprice without losing its serious purpose. Please note that not all legal procedures are as rigid as court procedures and that mistakes made in conferring certain kinds of legal status are not fatal to that status. A minister may make mistakes in reading the marriage ceremony, but the couple that stands before him will still acquire the status of being married. If, however, a mistake cannot be made *in* conferring the status of art, a mistake can be made *by* conferring it. In conferring the status of art on an object one assumes a certain kind of responsibility for the object in its new status—presenting a candidate for appreciation always allows the possibility that no one will appreciate it and that the person who did the conferring will thereby lose face. One *can* make a work of art out of a sow's ear, but that does not necessarily make it a silk purse.

—*Art and the Aesthetic* (1974)

Notes

1. *Journal of Aesthetics and Art Criticism,* September 1956, pp. 27–35. See also Paul Ziff's "The Task of Defining a Work of Art," *Philosophical Review,* January 1953, pp. 58–78; and W. E. Kennick's "Does Traditional Aesthetics Rest on a Mistake?" *Mind,* July 1958, pp. 317–334.

2. "Wittgenstein's Aesthetics," in *Language and Aesthetics,* Benjamin R. Tilghman, ed. (Lawrence, Kans., 1973), p. 14. This paper was read at a symposium at Kansas State University in April 1970. Monroe Beardsley has pointed out to me that the relationship between "game" and "major league baseball" is one of class and member rather than of genus and species.

3. "Family Resemblances and Generalizations Concerning the Arts," *American Philosophical Quarterly,* July 1965, pp. 219–228; reprinted in *Problems in Aesthetics,* Morris Weitz, ed., 2d ed. (London, 1970), pp. 181–197.

4. Ibid., p. 185 in the Weitz anthology.

5. "'Art' and Artifactuality," *Southwestern Journal of Philosophy,* Fall 1970, pp. 105–108.

6. "Does Traditional Aesthetics Rest on a Mistake?" p. 330.

7. *Journal of Philosophy,* October 15, 1964, pp. 571–584.

8. Ibid., p. 580.

9. Danto does not develop an institutional account of art in his article nor in a subsequent related article entitled "Art Works and Real Things," *Theoria,* Parts 1–3, 1973, pp. 1–17. In both articles Danto's primary concern is to discuss what he calls the Imitation Theory and the Real Theory of Art. Many of the things he says in these two articles are consistent with and can be incorporated into an institutional account, and his brief remarks in the later article about the ascriptivity of art are similar to the institutional theory. The institutional theory is one possible version of the ascriptivity theory.

10. This remark is not intended as a definition of the term "artworld"; I am merely indicating what the expression is used to *refer* to. "Artworld" is nowhere defined in this book, although the referent of the expression is described in some detail.

11. Recently in an article entitled "The Republic of Art" in *British Journal of Aesthetics,* April 1969, pp. 145–56, T. J. Diffey has talked about the status of art being conferred. He, however, is attempting to give an account of something like an evaluative sense of "work of art" rather than the classificatory sense, and consequently the scope of his theory is much narrower than mine.

12. "The Possibility of Art: Remarks on a Proposal by Dickie," *Philosophical Review,* January 1973, pp. 69–82.

13. "Defining Art," *American Philosophical Quarterly,* July 1969, pp. 253–256.

14. "The Possibility of Art," p. 78.

15. I realized that I must make the two points noted in this paragraph as the result of a conversation with Mark Venezia. I wish to thank him for the stimulation of his remarks.

16. I now believe that it was a mistake to claim that artifactuality can be conferred. Artifactuality is not the kind of thing which can be conferred; it must result from work of some sort. A piece of driftwood which has become art might, for example, have been picked up, transported, and hung on a wall. It is in virtue of these things being done to it that the driftwood has become an artifact, not as my original statements suggest, that the driftwood became an artifact because these actions conferred artifactuality. Similarly, a piece of driftwood might be picked up and used as a weapon and, thereby, become an artifact. (Footnote added by Dickie for the present book.)

17. Pages 12–14.

CHAPTER 13

The Concerns of the Community

FRIEDRICH SCHILLER: Esthetic Play and Human Liberation
KARL MARX: Art and History
MELVIN RADER and BERTRAM JESSUP: Art in an Age of Science and Technology
LEWIS MUMFORD: The Esthetic Assimilation of the Machine
IAN McHARG: Design with Nature

We turn now to the response of the community to art and esthetic experience. There is no better introduction to this subject than the treatise *On the Aesthetic Education of Man* (1795) by the German poet-philosopher, Friedrich Schiller (1759–1805). The psychological basis of his theory is the relation between three instinctive drives—the sensuous drive of bodily needs (*Stofftrieb*), the form-giving drive of reason (*Formtrieb*), and the play-drive of imagination (*Spieltrieb*). The first two drives tend to conflict, and the third drive, imaginative play, mediates between and harmonizes them.

Schiller maintains that the source of both play and art is overflowing energy. Even when a lion, for example, is not hungry or mad, it playfully exends its surplus energy through roaring. Similarly, the imagination of man enjoys its native power and liberty, although there is perhaps no outward gain to be achieved. Esthetic play, however, requires order and control. Man's esthctic taste directs the spontaneous flow of imagery in which imaginative play consists. Art is thus form imposed by taste upon playful imagistic activity. As in all the higher forms of play, there is a fusion of impulse and law; the rational part of man's nature is united harmoniously with the imaginative and the sensuous. Hence, Schiller is able to say, "Man only plays when in the full meaning of the word he is a man, and he is only completely a man when he plays."

In the opening sentences of the Twenty-Seventh Letter reproduced below, Schiller refers to "semblance" (*Schein*), a concept basic to his esthetics. Semblance is sheer appearance, recognized as such and enjoyed for its own sake. Imagination is the power to distinguish semblance from reality, to abide with it in contentment and without deception, and to create an imaginary world—a realm of semblance—with its independent principles of construction and internal coherence. "Indifference to reality and interest in semblance," Schiller declares, "may be regarded as a genuine enlargement of humanity and a decisive step toward culture." (XXVI, 4). Only when the "constraint of need" is replaced by sufficient leisure and abundance is the rich flowering of human nature possible. In addition, there must be the free play and reconciliation of the diverse sides of human nature, the formal and the sensuous drives balanced and harmonized through the reconciling power of imagination.

In striking anticipation of Marx's theory of alienation, Schiller characterized the effects of the industrial division of labor:

> Everlastingly chained to a single fragment of the Whole, man himself develops into nothing but a fragment; everlastingly in his ear the monotonous sound of the wheel that he turns, he never develops the harmony of his being, and instead of putting the stamp of humanity upon his own nature, he becomes nothing more than the imprint of his occupation or of his specialized knowledge. . . . Thus, little by little the concrete life of the Individual is destroyed in order that the abstract idea of the Whole may drag out its sorry existence, and the State remains forever a stranger to its citizens since at no point does it ever make contact with their feeling.[1]

Schiller and Marx differ in their conception of the means to overcome alienation. As Stefan Morawski has written, Schiller "had dreamt that the world would be rescued from need and suffering by esthetic man." Marx, in contrast, "was to turn Schiller's conception inside out; it was *political* man who was required for the rescue and realization of esthetic humankind."[2]

Despite this contrast, Karl Marx (1818–1883) was influenced by the ideas of Schiller. Some of the concepts that appear in the following excerpts from Marx—the sense of estrangement from one's own self and the surrounding world, the dehumanizing effect of the extreme division of labor, the ideal of the all-around man, the vital link between freedom and esthetic activity—were eloquently voiced in the *Letters On the Aesthetic Education of Man.* But Marx, unlike Schiller, sought to ground these ideas on "a materialistic interpretation of history." According to this interpretation, society has an economic ("material") foundation upon which the culture and social institutions—law, politics, religion, manners, science, art—are constructed. All these spheres causally interact with one another, but it is an interaction of *unequal* forces, of which the economic, in the long run, is by far the most powerful.

Marx distinguishes between "the forces of production," such as labor power and technology, and "the relations of production," such as the class structure and the institutions of property. The forces, under the spur of technology, develop more rapidly than the relations, which are held back or misdirected by vested interests. The result is an incongruous combination of fast and slow changes, the productive forces being fettered and perverted by the stifling relations. When the resultant conflict becomes very acute, a revolutionary transformation of the class structure ensues, accompanied by a clash of political and cultural ideologies, including the esthetic. As a consequence of revolution, there are profound changes in art and all other forms of culture.

Although Marx insists on the decisive role of economic causes in this transformation, he avoids an extreme economic determinism. He recognizes that artistic development is not entirely dependent on, or proportionate to, economic development. Rejecting the doctrine that esthetic value is completely relative to the economic system, he was too much the lover of the Greek classics to suppose that their value disappeared with the ancient slave economy.

Marx regards the alienation of modern man in his esthetic and artistic life as a phase of the total alienation produced by the capitalist system of production. Under this system, he charges, material forces tyrannize over human beings, human life is reduced to a material level, and men are estranged from one another and from their species-nature.

The essence of man, he thinks, is not, as Aristotle and Hegel supposed, that he is a *rational* animal, but that he is a *productive* and *creative* animal. This species-nature, embodying the deepest human needs and potentialities, is created by man himself in the historical process. Strongly insisting on the sensory and passional nature of man, Marx holds that external nature is man's larger "body" and should serve his needs and ends. Apparently, what he means is that nature, as intellectually knowable and esthetically enjoyable, is a kind of extension of man's species-being. Nature so understood shares a common essence with humanity, and as man's being is creatively enriched, nature is humanized and man is naturalized. This ideal of symbiotic harmony with nature is definitely esthetic in tone. Its realization awaits the achievement of a classless society in which "socialized mankind, the associated producers, regulate their interchange with nature rationally, bring it under their common control, instead of being ruled by it as by some blind power, and accomplish their task with the least expenditure of energy and under such conditions as are proper and worthy of human beings." (*Capital*, III).

Marx was convinced that conditions "worthy of human beings" can be realized when automation and other advances of technology are made to serve essential human needs. Production, organized and controlled by free associated men and women, will create the opportunities for the "all-round" cultivation of human personality. Through the creative use of leisure, art will enrich the lives not simply of the privileged few but of classless mankind.

Bertram Jessup (1899–1972) and Melvin Rader (1903–   ), in *Art and Human Values,* study the nature of art and esthetic value and their relation to other fundamental human interests and values. Part I of their book is an explication of the nature of esthetic value in common life, in nature, and in art. Part II discusses the relation of esthetic value to other human values and is, in effect, a critique of culture from a proesthetic standpoint. Professor Jessup, who devoted his scholarly life almost single-mindedly to the interpretation of art, died before the book was completed, but the imprint of his ideas is pervasive. The following excerpts, devoted to the role of art in a scientific and technological age, are sufficiently lucid to need no introductory analysis.

The distinguished American critic and social philosopher Lewis Mumford (1895–), like the other writers included in this chapter, has been inspired by the hope and ideal of human liberation. In his *Technics and Civilization* (1934) he divides "the development of the machine and the machine civilization into three successive but overlapping and interpenetrating phases: eotechnic, paleotechnic, neotechnic. . . . Speaking in terms of power and characteristic materials, the eotechnic phase is a water-and-wood complex, the paleotechnic phase is a coal-and-iron complex, and the neotechnic phase is an electric-and-alloy complex." Each phase has the most profound social ramifications, involving art, religion, and all humane pursuits. Beginning with the neotechnic phase, the rift between mechanization and humanization has gradually widened, until it has reached its climax in the "smoke-pall, air-sewage, and disorder" of some of our modern industrial cities. But new cleanliness and beauty is made possible by electricity and modern materials (for example, "the steel frame construction in architecture, which permits the fullest use of glass and the most complete utilization of sunlight").

When these new resources are finally controlled by humane social planning, and the biological and social sciences come to maturity, a new phase will begin—the "biotechnic": "Life, which has always paid the fiddler, now begins to call the tune." But before we can enter into this higher stage, art must be enriched by the machine, and the machine in turn humanized by art. The political and economic order necessary to effect this profound transformation Mumford calls "basic communism," but his ideal is that of a free society very different from the practice of the so-called communist states.

Mumford's *Technics and Civilization* is more optimistic in tone than his later books, such as the two-volume work *The Myth of the Machine* (1967, 1970), which emphasizes the dehumanizing effect of technology. But Mumford refuses to be a prophet of doom, maintaining that the dreadful miscarriages of our civilization are not inevitable, but can, with understanding and resolute action, be overcome or avoided.

Tragedy and hope! These are the dominant notes of our ambivalent civilization, and these are the notes struck by Ian McHarg (1920–), professor of landscape architecture and urban planning at the University of Pennsylvania. As author of a comprehensive landscape plan for Washington, D. C., and other urban or regional plans, he has grappled with the basic problems of ecology and environmental reconstruction. In the selection reproduced in this chapter, he contrasts the beauty of his native Scotland, which he knew as a boy, with the smog, water-pollution, urban sprawl, and bulldozed devastation of industrialized America. The threat of worse ecological catastrophe can be averted only by a profound transmutation of values and national priorities. McHarg calls for a new philosophy of life, almost a new religion, turning sharply away from man's ruthless domination of nature toward a symbiotic harmony with the natural environment. Art and esthetics are caught up in a much larger context than is normally encountered.

NOTES

1. Schiller, *On the Aesthetic Education of Man in a Series of Letters,* edited and translated by Elizabeth M. Wilkinson and L. A. Willoughby (Clarendon Press, Oxford, 1967), pp. 35, 37.
2. Stefan Morawski, *Inquiries into the Fundamentals of Aesthetics* (Massachusetts Institute of Technology Press, Cambridge, Mass., 1974), p. 328.

FRIEDRICH SCHILLER

Esthetic Play and Human Liberation

1. You need have no fear for either reality or truth if the lofty conception of esthetic semblance which I put forward in the last Letter were to become universal. It will not become universal as long as man is still uncultivated enough to be in a position to misuse it; and should it become universal, this could only be brought about by the kind of culture which would automatically make any misuse of it impossible. To strive after autonomous semblance demands higher powers of abstraction, greater freedom of heart, more energy of will, than man ever needs when he confines himself to reality; and he must already have left this reality behind if he would arrive at that kind of semblance. How ill-advised he would be, then, to take the path towards the ideal in order to save himself the way to the real! From semblance as here understood we should thus have little cause to fear for reality; all the more to be feared, I would suggest, is the threat from reality to semblance. Chained as he is to the material world, man subordinates semblance to ends of his own long before he allows it autonomous existence in the ideal realm of art. For this latter to happen a complete revolution in his whole way of feeling is required, without which he would not even find himself on the way to the ideal. Wherever, then, we find traces of a disinterested and unconditional appreciation of pure semblance, we may infer that a revolution of this order has taken place in his nature, and that he has started to become truly human. Traces of this kind are, however, actually to be found even in his first crude attempts at embellishing his existence, attempts made even at the risk of possibly worsening it from the material point of view. As soon as ever he starts preferring form to substance, and jeopardizing reality for the sake of semblance (which he must, however, recognize as such), a breach has been effected in the cycle of his animal behaviour, and he finds himself set upon a path to which there is no end.

2. Not just content with what satisfies nature, and meets his instinctual needs, he demands something over and above this: to begin with, admittedly, only a superfluity of material things, in order to conceal from appetite the fact that it has limits, and ensure enjoyment beyond the satisfaction of

immediate needs; soon, however, a superfluity in material things, an esthetic surplus, in order to satisfy the formal impulse too, and extend enjoyment beyond the satisfaction of every need. By merely gathering supplies around him for future use, and enjoying them in anticipation, he does, it is true, transcend the present moment—but without transcending time altogether. He enjoys more, but he does not enjoy differently. But when he also lets form enter into his enjoyment, and begins to notice the outward appearance of the things which satisfy his desires, then he has not merely enhanced his enjoyment in scope and degree, but also ennobled it in kind.

3. It is true that Nature has given even to creatures without reason more than the bare necessities of existence, and shed a glimmer of freedom even into the darkness of animal life. When the lion is not gnawed by hunger, nor provoked to battle by any beast of prey, his idle strength creates an object for itself: he fills the echoing desert with a roaring that speaks defiance, and his exuberant energy enjoys its *self* in purposeless display. With what enjoyment of life do insects swarm in the sunbeam; and it is certainly not the cry of desire that we hear in the melodious warbling of the songbird. Without doubt there is freedom in these activities; but not freedom from compulsion altogether, merely from a certain kind of compulsion, compulsion from without. An animal may be said to be at work, when the stimulus to activity is some lack; it may be said to be at play, when the stimulus is sheer plenitude of vitality, when superabundance of life is its own incentive to action. Even inanimate nature exhibits a similar luxuriance of forces, coupled with a laxity of determination which, in that material sense, might well be called play. The tree puts forth innumerable buds which perish without ever unfolding, and sends out far more roots, branches, and leaves in search of nourishment than are ever used for the sustaining of itself or its species. Such portion of its prodigal profusion as it returns, unused and unenjoyed, to the elements, is the overplus which living things are entitled to squander in a movement of carefree joy. Thus does Nature, even in her material kingdom, offer us a prelude of the Illimitable, and even here remove in part the chains which, in the realm of form, she casts away entirely. From the compulsion of want, or physical earnestness, she makes the transition via the compulsion of superfluity, or physical play, to esthetic play; and before she soars, in the sublime freedom of beauty, beyond the fetters of ends and purposes altogether, she makes some approach to this independence, at least from afar, in that kind of free activity which is at once its own end and its own means.

4. Like the bodily organs in man, his imagination, too, has its free movement and its material play, an activity in which, without any reference to form, it simply delights in its own absolute and unfettered power. Inasmuch as form does not yet enter this fantasy play at all, its whole charm residing in a free association of images, such play—although the prerogative of man alone—belongs merely to his animal life, and simply affords evidence of his liberation from all external physical compulsion, without as yet warranting the inference that there is any autonomous shaping power

within him.[1] From this play of freely associated ideas, which is still of a wholly material kind, and to be explained by purely natural laws, the imagination, in its attempt at a free form, finally makes the leap to esthetic play. A leap it must be called, since a completely new power now goes into action; for here, for the first time, mind takes a hand as lawgiver in the operations of blind instinct, subjects the arbitrary activity of the imagination to its own immutable and eternal unity, introduces its own autonomy into the transient, and its own infinity into the life of sense. But as long as brute nature still has too much power, knowing no other law but restless hastening from change to change, it will oppose to that necessity of the spirit its own unstable caprice, to that stability its own unrest, to that autonomy its own subservience, to that sublime self-sufficiency its own insatiable discontent. The esthetic play-drive, therefore, will in its first attempts be scarcely recognizable, since the physical play-drive, with its wilful moods and its unruly appetites, constantly gets in the way. Hence we see uncultivated taste first seizing upon what is new and startling—on the colourful, fantastic, and bizarre, the violent and the savage—and shunning nothing so much as tranquil simplicity. It fashions grotesque shapes, loves swift transitions, exuberant forms, glaring contrasts, garish lights, and a song full of feeling. At this stage what man calls beautiful is only what excites him, what offers him material—but excites him to a resistance involving autonomous activity, but offers him material for possible shaping. Otherwise it would not be beauty—even for him. The form of his judgements has thus undergone an astonishing change: he seeks these objects, not because they give him something to enjoy passively, but because they provide an incentive to respond actively. They please him, not because they meet a need, but because they satisfy a law which speaks, though softly as yet, within his breast.

5. Soon he is no longer content that things should please him; he himself wants to please. At first, indeed, only through that which is his; finally through that which he is. The things he possesses, the things he produces, may no longer bear upon them the marks of their use, their form no longer be merely a timid expression of their function; in addition to the service they exist to render, they must at the same time reflect the genial mind which conceived them, the loving hand which wrought them, the serene and liberal spirit which chose and displayed them. Now the ancient German goes in search of glossier skins, statelier antlers, more elaborate drinking horns; and the Caledonian selects for his feasts the prettiest shells. Even weapons may no longer be mere objects of terror; they must be objects of delight as well, and the cunningly ornamented sword-belt claims no less attention than the deadly blade of the sword. Not content with introducing esthetic superfluity into objects of necessity, the play-drive as it becomes ever freer finally tears itself away from the fetters of utility altogether, and beauty in and for itself alone begins to be an object of his striving. Man adorns himself. Disinterested and undirected pleasure is now numbered among the necessities of existence, and what is in fact unnecessary soon becomes the best part of his delight.

6. And as form gradually comes upon him from without—in his dwelling, his household goods, and his apparel—so finally it begins to take possession of him himself, transforming at first only the outer, but ultimately the inner, man too. Uncoordinated leaps of joy turn into dance, the unformed movements of the body into the graceful and harmonious language of gesture; the confused and indistinct cries of feeling become articulate, begin to obey the laws of rhythm, and to take on the contours of song. If the Trojan host storms on to the battlefield with piercing shrieks like a flock of cranes, the Greek army approaches it in silence, with noble and measured tread. In the former case we see only the exuberance of blind forces; in the latter, the triumph of form and the simple majesty of law.

7. Now compulsion of a lovelier kind binds the sexes together, and a communion of hearts helps sustain a connexion but intermittently established by the fickle caprice of desire. Released from its dark bondage, the eye, less troubled now by passion, can apprehend the form of the beloved; soul looks deep into soul, and out of a selfish exchange of lust there grows a generous interchange of affection. Desire widens, and is exalted into love, once humanity has dawned in its object; and a base advantage over sense is now disdained for the sake of a nobler victory over will. The need to please subjects the all-conquering male to the gentle tribunal of taste; lust he can steal, but love must come as a gift. For this loftier prize he can only contend by virtue of form, never by virtue of matter. From being a force impinging upon feeling, he must become a form confronting the mind; he must be willing to concede freedom, because it is freedom he wishes to please. And even as beauty resolves the conflict between opposing natures in this simplest and clearest paradigm, the eternal antagonism of the sexes, so too does it resolve it—or at least aims at resolving it—in the complex whole of society, endeavouring to reconcile the gentle with the violent in the moral world after the pattern of the free union it there contrives between the strength of man and the gentleness of woman. Now weakness becomes sacred, and unbridled strength dishonourable; the injustice of nature is rectified by the magnanimity of the chivalric code. He whom no violence may alarm is disarmed by the tender blush of modesty, and tears stifle a revenge which no blood was able to assuage. Even hatred pays heed to the gentle voice of honour; the sword of the victor spares the disarmed foe, and a friendly hearth sends forth welcoming smoke to greet the stranger on that dread shore where of old only murder lay in wait for him.

8. In the midst of the fearful kingdom of forces, and in the midst of the sacred kingdom of laws, the esthetic impulse to form is at work, unnoticed, on the building of a third joyous kingdom of play and of semblance, in which man is relieved of the shackles of circumstance, and released from all that might be called constraint, alike in the physical and in the moral sphere.

9. If in the dynamic State of rights it is as force that one man encounters another, and imposes limits upon his activities; if in the ethical State of duties Man sets himself over against man with all the majesty of the law,

and puts a curb upon his desires: in those circles where conduct is governed by beauty, in the esthetic State, none may appear to the other except as form, or confront him except as an object of free play. To bestow freedom by means of freedom is the fundamental law of this kingdom.

10. The dynamic State can merely make society possible, by letting one nature be curbed by another; the ethical State can merely make it (morally) necessary, by subjecting the individual will to the general; the aesthetic State alone can make it real, because it consummates the will of the whole through the nature of the individual. Though it may be his needs which drive man into society, and reason which implants within him the principles of social behaviour, beauty alone can confer upon him a social character. Taste alone brings harmony into society, because it fosters harmony in the individual. All other forms of perception divide man, because they are founded exclusively either upon the sensuous or upon the spiritual part of his being; only the esthetic mode of perception makes of him a whole, because both his natures must be in harmony if he is to achieve it. All other forms of communication divide society, because they relate exclusively either to the private receptivity or to the private proficiency of its individual members, hence to that which distinguishes man from man; only the esthetic mode of communication unites society, because it relates to that which is common to all. The pleasures of the senses we enjoy merely as individuals, without the genus which is immanent within us having any share in them at all; hence we cannot make the pleasures of sense universal, because we are unable to universalize our own individuality. The pleasures of knowledge we enjoy merely as genus, and by carefully removing from our judgement all trace of individuality; hence we cannot make the pleasures of reason universal, because we cannot eliminate traces of individuality from the judgements of others as we can from our own. Beauty alone do we enjoy at once as individual and as genus, i.e., as representatives of the human genus. The good of the Senses can only make one man happy, since it is founded on appropriation, and this always involves exclusion; and it can only make this one man one-sidedly happy, since his Personality has no part in it. Absolute good can only bring happiness under conditions which we cannot presume to be universal; for truth is the prize of abnegation alone, and only the pure in heart believe in the pure will. Beauty alone makes the whole world happy, and each and every being forgets its limitations while under its spell.

11. No privilege, no autocracy of any kind, is tolerated where taste rules, and the realm of esthetic semblance extends its sway. This realm stretches upwards to the point where reason governs with unconditioned necessity, and all that is mere matter ceases to be. It stretches downwards to the point where natural impulse reigns with blind compulsion, and form has not yet begun to appear. And even at these furthermost confines, where taste is deprived of all legislative power, it still does not allow the executive power to be wrested from it. A-social appetite must renounce its self-seeking, and the Agreeable, whose normal function is to seduce the senses, must cast toils of Grace over the mind as well. Duty, stern voice of Necessity, must

moderate the censorious tone of its precepts—a tone only justified by the resistance they encounter—and show greater respect for Nature through a nobler confidence in her willingness to obey them. From within the Mysteries of Science, taste leads knowledge out into the broad daylight of Common Sense, and transforms a monopoly of the Schools into the common possession of Human Society as a whole. In the kingdom of taste even the mightiest genius must divest itself of its majesty, and stoop in all humility to the mind of a little child. Strength must allow itself to be bound by the Graces, and the lion have its defiance curbed by the bridle of a Cupid. In return, taste throws a veil of decorum over those physical desires which, in their naked form, affront the dignity of free beings; and, by a delightful illusion of freedom, conceals from us our degrading kinship with matter. On the wings of taste even that art which must cringe for payment can lift itself out of the dust; and, at the touch of her wand, the fetters of serfdom fall away from the lifeless and the living alike. In the Esthetic State everything—even the tool which serves—is a free citizen, having equal rights with the noblest; and the mind, which would force the patient mass beneath the yoke of its purposes, must here first obtain its assent. Here, therefore, in the realm of Esthetic Semblance, we find that ideal of equality fulfilled which the Enthusiast would fain see realized in substance. And if it is true that it is in the proximity of thrones that fine breeding comes most quickly and most perfectly to maturity, would one not have to recognize in this, as in much else, a kindly dispensation which often seems to be imposing limits upon man in the real world, only in order to spur him on to realization in an ideal world?

12. But does such a State of Esthetic Semblance really exist? And if so, where is it to be found? As a need, it exists in every finely attuned soul; as a realized fact, we are likely to find it, like the pure Church and the pure Republic, only in some few chosen circles, where conduct is governed, not by some soulless imitation of the manners and morals of others, but by the esthetic nature we have made our own; where men make their way, with undismayed simplicity and tranquil innocence, through even the most involved and complex situations, free alike of the compulsion to infringe the freedom of others in order to assert their own, as of the necessity to shed their Dignity in order to manifest Grace.

—*On the Aesthetic Education of Man in a Series of Letters* (1795; translated 1967 by Elizabeth M. Wilkinson and L. A. Willoughby)

Note

1. Most of the imaginative play which goes on in everyday life is either entirely based on this feeling for free association of ideas, or at any rate derives therefrom its greatest charm. This may not in itself be proof of a higher nature, and it may well be that it is just the most flaccid natures who tend to surrender to such unimpeded flow of images; it is nevertheless this very independence of the fantasy from external stimuli, which constitutes at least the negative condition of its creative power. Only by tearing itself free from reality does the formative power raise itself up to the ideal; and before the imagination, in its productive capacity,

can act according to its own laws, it must first, in its reproductive procedures, have freed itself from alien laws. From mere lawlessness to autonomous law-giving from within, there is admittedly, still a big step to be taken; and a completely new power, the faculty for ideas, must first be brought into play. But this power, too, can now develop with greater ease, since the senses are not working against it, and the indefinite does, at least negatively, border upon the infinite.

KARL MARX

Art and History

1. The Mode of Production Conditions the Social, Political, and Cultural Processes of Life

In the social production which men carry on they enter into definite relations that are indispensable and independent of their will; these relations of production correspond to a definite stage of development of their material forces of production. The sum total of these relations of production constitutes the economic structure of society—the real foundation, on which rises a legal and political superstructure and to which correspond definite forms of social consciousness. The mode of production in material life conditions (*bedingt*) the social, political, and intellectual life processes in general. It is not the consciousness of men that determines their being, but, on the contrary, their social being that determines their consciousness. At a certain stage of their development, the material forces of production in society come in conflict with the existing relations of production, or—what is but a legal expression for the same thing—with the property relations within which they have been at work before. From forms of development of the forces of production these relations turn into their fetters. Then begins an epoch of social revolution. With the change of the economic foundation the entire immense superstructure is more or less rapidly transformed. In considering such transformations a distinction should always be made between the material transformation of the economic conditions of production which can be determined with the precision of natural science, and the legal, political, religious, esthetic, or philosophic—in short, ideological—forms in which men become conscious of this conflict and fight it out. Just as our opinion of an individual is not based on what he thinks of himself, so can we not judge of such a period of transformation by its own consciousness; on the contrary this consciousness must be explained rather from the contradictions of material life, from the existing conflict between the social forces of production and the relations of production. No social order ever disappears before all the productive forces for which there is room in it have been developed; and new higher relations of production never appear before the material conditions of their existence have matured in the womb of the old society itself. Therefore, mankind always sets itself only such tasks as it can solve; since, looking at the matter more closely, we will always find that the task itself arises only when the material conditions necessary for its solution already exist or are at least in the process of formation. In broad outlines we can designate the Asiatic, the ancient, the feudal, and the modern bourgeois modes of production as so many epochs in the progress of the economic formation of society. The bourgeois relations of production are the last antagonistic form of the social process of production—antagonistic not in the sense of individual antagonism, but of one arising from the social conditions of life of the individuals; at the same time the productive forces developing in the womb of bourgeois society create the material conditions for the solution of that antagonism. This social formation constitutes, therefore, the closing chapter of the prehistoric stage of human society.

—Introduction to *A Contribution to the Critique of Political Economy* (1859), translated by N. I. Stone (1904)

2. The Disproportion between the Development of Material and Artistic Production

It is well known that certain periods of highest development of art stand in no direct connection with the general development of society, nor with the material basis and the skeleton structure of its organization. Witness the example of the Greeks as compared with the modern nations or even Shakespeare. As regards certain forms of art, as, *e.g.*, the epos, it is admitted that they can never be produced in the world-epoch-making form as soon as art as such comes into existence; in other words, that in the domain of art certain important forms of it are possible only at a low stage of its development. If that be true of the mutual relations of different forms of art within the domain of art itself, it is far less surprising that the same is true of the relation of art as a whole to the general development of society. The difficulty lies only in the general formulation of these contradictions. No sooner are they specified than they are explained. Let us take for instance the relation of Greek art and of that of Shakespeare's time to our own. It is a well known fact that Greek mythology was not only the arsenal of Greek art, but also the very ground from which it had sprung. Is the view of nature and of social relations which shaped Greek imagination and Greek [art] possible in the age of automatic machinery, and railways, and locomotives, and electric telegraphs? Where does Vulcan come in as against Roberts & Co.; Jupiter, as against the lightning rod; and Hermes, as against the Credit Mobilier? All mythology masters and dominates and shapes the forces of nature in and through the imagination; hence it disappears as soon as man gains mastery over the forces of nature. What becomes of the Goddess Fame side by side with Printing House Square? Greek art presupposes the existence of Greek mythology, *i.e.*, that nature and even the form of society are wrought up in popular fancy in an unconsciously artistic fashion. That is its material. Not, however, any mythology taken at random, nor any accidental, unconsciously artistic elaboration of nature (including under the latter all objects, hence [also] society). Egyptian mythology could never be the soil or womb which would give birth to Greek art. But in any event [there had to be] a mythology. In no event [could Greek art originate] in a society which excludes any mythological explanation of nature, any mythological attitude towards it and which requires from the artist an imagination free from mythology.

Looking at it from another side: Is Achilles possible side by side with powder and lead? Or is the *Iliad* at all compatible with the printing press and steam press? Do not singing and reciting and the muses necessarily go out of existence with the appearance of the printer's bar, and do not, therefore, disappear the prerequisites of epic poetry?

But the difficulty is not in grasping the idea that Greek art and epos are bound up with certain forms of social development. It rather lies in understanding why they still constitute with us a source of esthetic enjoyment and in certain respects prevail as the standard and model beyond attainment.

A man cannot become a child again unless he becomes childish. But does he not enjoy the artless ways of the child and must he not strive to reproduce its truth on a higher plane? Is not the character of every epoch revived perfectly true to nature in child nature? Why should the social childhood of mankind, where it had obtained its most beautiful development, not exert an eternal charm as an age that will never return? There are ill-bred children and precocious children. Many of the ancient nations belong to the latter class. The Greeks were normal children. The charm their art has for us does not conflict with the primitive character of the social order from which it had sprung. It is rather the product of the latter, and is rather due to the fact that the unripe social conditions under which the art arose and under which alone it could appear could never return.

—*A Contribution to the Critique of Political Economy* (1859), translated by N. I. Stone (1904)

3. Alienated Labor and Free Production

Since alienated labour: (1) alienates nature from man; and (2) alienates man from himself, from his own active function, his life activity; so it alienates him from the species. It makes *species-life* into a means of individual life. In the first place it alienates species-life and individual life, and secondly, it turns the latter, as an abstraction, into the purpose of the former, also in its abstract and alienated form.

For labour, *life activity, productive life,* now appear to man only as *means* for the satisfaction of a need, the need to maintain his physical existence. Productive life is, however, species-life. It is life creating life. In the type of life activity resides the whole character of a species, its species-character; and free, conscious activity is the species-character of human beings. Life itself appears only as a *means of life.*

The animal is one with its life activity. It does not distinguish the activity from itself. It is *its activity.* But man makes his life activity itself an object of his will and consciousness. He has a conscious life activity. It is not a determination with which he is completely identified. Conscious life activity distinguishes man from the life activity of animals. Only for this reason is he a species-being. Or rather, he is only a self-conscious being, i.e. his own life is an object for him, because he is a species-being. Only for this reason is his activity free activity. Alienated labour reverses the relationship, in that man because he is a self-conscious being makes his life activity, his *being*, only a means for his *existence*.

The practical construction of an *objective world*, the *manipulation* of inorganic nature, is the confirmation of man as a conscious species-being, i.e. a being who treats the species as his own being or himself as a species-being. Of course, animals also produce. They construct nests, dwellings, as in the case of bees, beavers, ants, etc. But they only produce what is strictly necessary for themselves or their young. They produce only in a single direction, while man produces universally. They produce only under the compulsion of direct physical needs, while man produces when he is free from physical need and only truly produces in freedom from such need. Animals produce only themselves, while man reproduces the whole of nature. The products of animal production belong directly to their physical bodies, while man is free in face of his product. Animals construct only in accordance with the standards and needs of the species to which they belong, while man knows how to produce in accordance with the standards of every species and knows how to apply the appropriate standard to the object. Thus man constructs also in accordance with the laws of beauty.

It is just in his work upon the objective world that man really proves himself as a *species-being*. This production is his active species-life. By means of it nature appears as *his* work and his reality. The object of labour is, therefore, the *objectification of man's species-life*; for he no longer reproduces himself merely intellectually, as in consciousness, but actively and in a real sense, and he sees his own reflection in a world which he has constructed. While, therefore, alienated labour takes away the object of production from man, it also takes away his *species-life*, his real objectivity as a species-being, and changes his advantage over animals into a disadvantage in so far as his inorganic body, nature, is taken from him.

—*Economic and Philosophical Manuscripts* (1844),
translated by T. B. Bottomore (1963)

4. The Overcoming of Alienation

Just as *private property* is only the sensuous expression of the fact that man is at the same time an *objective* fact for himself and becomes an alien and non-human object for himself; just as his manifestation of life is also his alienation of life and his self-realization a loss of reality, the emergence of an *alien* reality; so the positive supersession of private property, i.e. the *sensuous* appropriation of the human essence and of human life, of objective man and of human *creations*, by and for man, should not be taken only in the sense of *immediate*, exclusive *enjoyment*, or only in the sense of *possession* or *having*. Man appropriates his manifold being in an all-inclusive way, and thus as a whole man. All his *human* relations to the world—seeing, hearing, smelling, tasting, touching, thinking, observing, feeling, desiring, acting, loving—in short, all the organs of his individuality, like the organs which are directly communal in form, . . . are in their objective action (their *action in relation to the object*) the appropriation of this object, the appropriation of human reality. The way in which they react to the object is the confirmation of *human reality*.[1] It is human effectiveness and human *suffering*, for suffering humanly considered is an enjoyment of the self for man.

Private property has made us so stupid and partial that an object is only *ours* when we have it, when it exists for us as capital or when it is directly eaten, drunk, worn, inhabited, etc., in short, *utilized* in some way. But private property itself only conceives these various forms of possession as *means of life*, and the life for which they serve as means is the *life* of *private property*—labour and creation of capital.

Thus *all* the physical and intellectual senses have been replaced by the simple alienation of *all* these senses; the sense of *having*. The human being had to be reduced to this absolute poverty in order to be able to give birth to all his inner wealth. . . .

The supersession of private property is, therefore, the complete *emancipation* of all the human qualities and senses. It is such an emancipation because these qualities and senses have become *human*, from the subjective as well as the objective point of view. The eye has become a *human* eye when its *object* has become a *human*, social object, created by man and destined for him. The senses have, therefore, become directly theoreticians in practice. They relate themselves to the thing for the sake of the thing, but the thing itself is an *objective human* relation to itself and to man, and vice versa.[2] Need and enjoyment have thus lost their *egoistic* character and nature has lost its mere *utility* by the fact that its utilization has become *human* utilization.

Similarly, the senses and minds of other men have become my *own* appropriation. Thus besides these direct organs, *social* organs are constituted, in the form of society; for example, activity in direct association with others has become an organ for the manifestation of life and a mode of appropriation of *human* life.

It is evident that the human eye appreciates things in a different way from the crude, non-human eye, the human *ear* differently from the crude ear. As we have seen, it is only when the object becomes a *human* object, or objective *humanity*, that man does not become lost in it. This is only possible when man himself becomes a *social* object; when he himself becomes a social being and society becomes a being for him in this object.

On the one hand, it is only when objective reality everywhere becomes for man in society the reality of human faculties, human reality, and thus the reality of his own faculties, that all *objects* become for him the *objectification of himself*. The objects then confirm and realize his individuality, they are *his own* objects, i.e. man himself becomes the object. *The manner in which these objects* become his own depends upon the *nature of the object* and the nature of the corresponding faculty; for it is precisely the *determinate character* of this relation which constitutes the specific *real* mode of affirmation. The object is not the same for the *eye* as for the *ear*, for the ear as for the eye. The *distinctive character* of each faculty is precisely its *characteristic* essence and thus also the characteristic mode of its objectification, of its *objectively real*, living *being*. It is therefore not only in thought, but through *all* the senses that man is affirmed in the objective world.

Let us next consider the subjective aspect. Man's musical sense is only awakened by music. The most beautiful music has no meaning for the non-musical ear, is not an object for it, because my object can only be the confirmation of one of my own faculties. It can only be so for me in so far as my faculty exists for itself as a subjective capacity, because the meaning of an object for me extends only as far as the sense extends (only makes sense for an appropriate sense). For this reason, the *senses* of social man are *different* from those of non-social man. It is only through the objectively deployed wealth of the human being that the wealth of subjective *human* sensibility (a musical ear, an eye which is sensitive to the beauty of form, in short, senses which are capable of human satisfaction and which confirm themselves as human faculties) is cultivated or created. For it is not only the five senses, but also the so-called spiritual senses, the practical senses (desiring, loving, etc.), in brief, human sensibility and the human character of the senses, which can only come into being through the existence of *its* object, through humanized nature. The cultivation of the five senses is the work of all previous history. Sense which is subservient to crude needs has only a restricted meaning. For a starving man the human form of food does not exist, but only its abstract character as food. It could just as well exist in the most crude form, and it is impossible to say in what way this feeding-activity would differ from that of animals. The needy man, burdened with cares, has no appreciation of the most beautiful spectacle. The dealer in minerals sees only their commercial value, not their beauty or their particular characteristics; he has no mineralogical sense. Thus, the objectification of the human essence, both theoretically and practically, is necessary in order to *humanize* man's senses, and also to create the *human senses* corresponding to all the wealth of human and natural being.

Just as society at its beginnings finds, through the development of *private property* with its wealth and poverty (both intellectual and material), the materials necessary for this *cultural development,* so the fully constituted society produces man in all the plentitude of his being, the wealthy man endowed with all the senses, as an enduring reality. It is only in a social context that subjectivism and objectivism, spiritualism and materialism, activity and passivity, cease to be antinomies and thus cease to exist as such antinomies. The resolution of the *theoretical* contradictions is possible *only* through practical means, only through the *practical* energy of man. Their resolution is not by any means, therefore, only a problem of knowledge, but is a *real* problem of life which philosophy was unable to solve precisely because it saw there a purely theoretical problem.

—*Economic and Philosophical Manuscripts* (1844), translated by T. B. Bottomore (1963)

5. Automation and the Creative Use of Leisure

. . . [A]s heavy industry develops, the creation of real wealth depends less on labor time and on the quantity of labor utilized than on the power of mechanical agents which are set in motion during labor time. The powerful effectiveness of these agents, in its turn bears no relation to the immediate labor time that their production costs. It depends rather on the general state of science and on technological progress, or the application of this science to production. (The development of science—especially of the natural sciences and with them all of the others—is itself once more related to the development of material production.) Agriculture, for example, is a pure application of the science of material metabolism, and the most advantageous way of employing it for the good of society as a whole.

Real wealth develops much more (as is disclosed by heavy industry) in the enormous disproportion between the labor time utilized and its product, and also in the qualitative disproportion between labor that has been reduced to a mere abstraction, and the power of the production process that it supervises. Labor does not seem any more to be an essential part of the process of production. The human factor is restricted to watching and supervising the production process. (This applies not only to machinery, but also to the combination of human activities and the development of human commerce.)

The worker no longer inserts transformed natural objects as intermediaries between the material and himself; he now inserts the natural process that he has transformed into an industrial one between himself and inorganic nature, over which he has achieved mastery. He is no longer the principal agent of the production process: He exists alongside it. In this transformation, what appears as the mainstay of production and wealth is neither the immediate labor performed by the worker, nor the time that he works, but the appropriation by man of his own general productive force, his understanding of nature and the mastery of it; in a word, the development of the social individual. The theft of others' labor time upon which wealth depends today seems to be a miserable basis compared with this newly developed foundation that has been created by heavy industry itself. As soon as labor, in its direct form, has ceased to be the main source of wealth, then labor time ceases, and must cease, to be its standard of measurement, and thus exchange value must cease to be the measurement of use value. The surplus labor of the masses has ceased to be a condition for the development of wealth in general; in the same way that the nonlabor of the few has ceased to be a condition for the development of the general powers of the human mind. Production based on exchange value therefore falls apart, and the immediate process of material production finds itself stripped of its impoverished, antagonistic form. Individuals are then in a position to develop freely. It is no longer a question of reducing the necessary labor time in order to create surplus labor, but of reducing the necessary labor of society to a minimum. The counterpart of this reduction is that all members of society can develop their education in the arts, sciences, etc., thanks to the free time and means available to all.

—*Foundations of the Critique of Political Economy* (1857–1858; translated 1971 by David McLellan)

NOTES

1. It is, therefore, just as varied as the determinations of human nature and activities are diverse.

2. In practice I can only relate myself in a human way to a thing when the thing is related in a human way to man.

MELVIN RADER AND BERTRAM JESSUP

Art in an Age of Science and Technology

The Impact of Applied Science and Technology

. . . [S]cience and art need not be in conflict. Different though they are, they inhabit the same world, draw upon similar creative talents, and contribute to imaginative enjoyment and cognitive insight. But the relation between them is not always harmonious. The scientists, if too prone to generalize, may antagonize the artist by trying to "reduce" man to a mechanistic level. The Nobel laureate Jacques Monod, in his book *Chance and Necessity* (1970), declares that "living beings are chemical machines." B. F. Skinner, the foremost behavioral psychologist, characterizes the belief in human "freedom and dignity" as the vestige of a prescientific age. Such simplistic generalizations have gained widespread credence, and have provoked reactions of an opposite nature. Those who still believe in the mystery and uniqueness of life and in the importance and efficacy of values have tended to reject "scientism" and to seek solace in religion or imaginative release in art.

The split between "the two cultures," the scientific and the humanist, is most evident in the reaction against *applied* rather than *pure* science. From the time of William Blake until the present, the more rebellious or romantically inclined artists have thought of themselves as "outsiders," sharply opposed to a scientific technological culture. In the twentieth century, there have been many who have expressed the paradox of man's alienation in a mechanized world of his own making. This is a predominant theme in Charlie Chaplin's movies, which portray the tragicomic little tramp trying to survive in a world much too large, too bureaucratized, too indifferent, too mechanically complicated; in the sculpture of Rudolf Belling: strange, semiabstract, machinelike forms, half-human and half-mechanical; in the paintings of Giorgio de Chirico or Fernand Leger: organic forms transposed into inorganic shapes and relations—the human and the nonhuman confounded; in the music of Arthur Honegger's *Pacific 231*, depicting the crude, raucous, overwhelming power embodied in a great locomotive; or in Paul Dukas' musical rendition of the old fable of the *Sorcerer's Apprentice*, symbolizing the tendency of tools and machinery to run amuck. It is a theme as well in the poems of T. S. Eliot, in which "hollow men, stuffed men" are buffeted about in the "wasteland" of industrial civilization; in Karel Capek's *R.U.R.*, Aldous Huxley's *Brave New*

World, and George Orwell's *1984*—satirical fantasies in which men are treated not as ends in themselves but as things to manipulate; in Franz Kafka's strange fables, which represent the ruling powers as incomprehensible and heartless bureaucracies; in Albert Camus' novel, *The Stranger,* which depicts an unwitting "murderer" who has lost sympathetic contact with other human beings and is dealt with by the authorities without pity or understanding; and in Samuel Beckett's plays, *Waiting for Godot* and *Endgame,* whose characters are paralyzed by the icy emptiness of their "absurd" environment. The theme of human alienation in a technological environment has been recurrent in every art genre.

The common word for the thousands of techniques and inventions made possible by the advance of science is "technology." By this term we mean expert knowledge—mainly scientific—put to practical use. Technology includes the totality of tools and techniques that men use to make and do things—not only hand tools and machines but intellectual tools, such as computer programming and system analysis. The technology of the old Industrial Revolution was largely based on craft and mechanical ingenuity, but the technology of today is based mainly on science. The crucial inventions of recent decades, such as the transistor, the laser, the computer, atomic fission and fusion, have flowed out of quantum mechanics, relativity physics, and other forms of advanced science.

Are art and technology necessarily uncongenial? It is not easy to answer the question. Coming to grips with technology can be a very ambiguous confrontation for both the ordinary citizen and the artist. We are informed that human life is becoming "one-dimensional"—a dehumanized function in a technical apparatus. Conversely, we are assured that technology is greatly widening our horizons and opportunities. Or, dramatically, we are told that the human race is confronted by a fateful choice, "one world or none," "Utopia or annihilation." Almost everyone is bewildered by these conflicting voices. For the artist or lover of the arts, the bewilderment is likely to be compounded, because contemporary art is as complex and indecipherable as contemporary technology. Can we ever understand what contemporary art is about, what modern technology is doing, and what is the relation between the two?

This much we can predict with confidence, that the future will be as unlike the present as the present is unlike the past. Scientists are now penetrating the heart of the atom and exploring the far reaches of the cosmos; they are engaged in the most fundamental discoveries; and just as basic discoveries led to profound technological changes in the past, so these new discoveries can be expected to produce like changes in the future. The study of molecules gave us chemistry, with its innumerable applications; the study of electricity and magnetism gave us the electrical industry, with its immense contribution to the power and convenience of living; the study of germs gave us germicidal medicine, with its great saving and prolongation of life. Now scientists are delving into the secrets of the microworld—the inconceivably tiny world of the mesons, hyperons, and "antiparticles." At the other end of the scale, with the appearance of earth satellites and space rockets and the investigation of cosmic rays, there has been a radical new beginning in the study of the macroworld—the universe in all its vastness. The microworld and the macroworld are in scale almost infinitely far apart, but their study is interrelated and promises a gigantic extension of human knowledge. Like the earlier discoveries of bacteria, magnetism, and molecular structure, this knowledge will bring technological changes of incalculable range and importance.

Whether the changes on the whole will be good or bad hangs in the balance. No one will deny that there have been some improvements in human affairs, but the triple threat of thermonuclear war, overpopulation, and ecological catastrophe is acute. Our headlong technological escalation is rapidly using up the fossil fuels and ores upon which continued productivity depends. Smog and water poisoning and rotting slums and urban sprawl are fouling the environment at an intolerable pace. Esthetically this is perhaps the most serious threat of all—the sweetness of nature, the very face of the land, is being glutted with ugliness and pollution. There are also the psychological effects of technology: mechanization invades mind and character and muddies the human soul to its dye. The effect is to stifle the imaginative freedom and internal spontaneity out of which art springs.

The role of prophet in our ambivalent civilization is hazardous. As Karl Popper argued in *The Poverty of Historicism,* the discoveries of science and the inventions of technology, in their very novelty, cannot be anticipated in advance, and their side effects are seldom foreseeable. We are confronted, not by a predictable future, but by "the double aspect of things to come."

> Everyone sees a dark figure and a bright one simultaneously, both approaching at startling speed. You may try to cover up one of them so as to see only the other, but both are inexorably there. . . . It is especially this double sense of the future, actively desired and actively feared, that distinguishes the reality of our century from that of the last.[1]

The future of man—assuming that man *has* a future of much duration—will certainly be very different from his past, but what that future will be no one can say.

There has been no lack of gloomy forebodings. Although not given to dour predictions, William James at the beginning of this century warned that technology might culminate in the total destruction of our civilization, and that scientific-technological man may be like the child drowning in a bathtub because he has turned on the water without knowing how to turn it off. H. G. Wells, who began as an inveterate optimist, predicted in his final book the clean extinction of the human race. "There is no way out or round or through," he announced. "It is the end."[2] John Masefield declared, "We have all things, save hope," catching the prevalent mood of our affluent society. "If you want a picture of the future," states a character in George Orwell's *1984,* "imagine a boot stamping on the human face—forever." Since the death of these writers, the gloom has deepened and spread.

History has now lent to the old, old question, "What shall we do to be saved?" a new, terrible urgency. Why has this come to pass? Our reply would run something like this. In the development of humanity, different functions reach maturity at different historical stages, the easier problems usually being solved before the more difficult. An atom or a molecule, elusive though it be, is more easily understood than the labyrinthine ways of the mind. Consequently physical technology, like a hare, has raced far ahead, while other human functions move tortoise-slow in the rear. We have split and harnessed the atom, we have hurtled our rockets to the far regions of space, we have invented the most cunning machines; but we haven't learned how to curb human aggression or how to be kind to our neighbors. Vast, impersonal, bureaucratic organizations, spearheaded by the technologies of communication and management, have developed with dramatic swiftness, while the values and institutions of the free community have in no way kept pace. Our "progress" has been swifter in the techniques of homicide than in the arts of peace. Cursed by the anachronisms of war and class, this century has been an age of hyperbolic crises: glut and starvation, revolutionary upheavals, totalitarian regimes, world wars, and the threat of nuclear Armageddon. Mankind will not be out of danger until art, the impulse to appreciate; religion, the impulse to commune; politics, the impulse to govern; and humanistic science, the impulse to understand human nature, reach a maturity comparable to that of physical science and technology.

Confronted by very distressing or uncertain prospects, esthetic-minded dissenters may choose either of two goals. One goal is to revolt against our whole scientific-technological-industrial society and to try to create a new "counterculture" based on art and mysticism and "I–Thou" relations. An alternative goal is to seek a higher union of art, morals, science, and technology.

The first goal is favored by the more thoughtful members of the counterculture and the anarchistic radicals. It is illustrated in the manifesto pinned to the main entrance of the Sorbonne during the tumultous insurrection of May 1968:

> The revolution which is beginning will call in question not only capitalist society but industrial society. The consumer's society must perish of a violent death. The society of alienation must disappear from history. We are inventing a new and original world. Imagination is seizing power.[3]

Theodore Roszak, who quotes this bold French manifesto, admits that the movement of dissident youth toward a counterculture is a rather bizzare patchwork, borrowing from depth psychology, Oriental religions, anarchist social theory, drug experimentation, and an esthetics of rock bands, strobe lights, free-form dance, and "happenings." Although he is critical of some of these features, Roszak thinks that the movement is toward "a new culture in which the nonintellective capacities of the personality—those capacities that take fire from visionary splendor and the experience of human communion—become the arbiters of the good, the true, and the beautiful." Scientific and technological priorities must be swept aside in favor of "a new simplicity, a decelerating social pace, a vital leisure" and "the communal opening-up of man to man." "For, after all, science is not everything, and in fact, is not very much at all when it comes to creating a creditable way of life for ourselves," and it is better to side with "the nonintellective spontaneity of children and primitives, artists and lovers, those who can lose themselves gracefully in the splendor of the moment."[4]

To a certain extent, we agree with the goal of this counterculture—an ideal, let us remember, as old as the Romantic Movement in the early nineteenth century. Like Wordsworth, we think that in getting and spending we lay waste our powers. We desperately need more humane interests and values to replace the ruthless dynamism of an acquisitive and mechanized civilization. Modern men need not—they should not—regard Science or its child Technology, as their savior. Science, taken alone, is nonmoral, and no amoral basis of civilization can suffice. Only when science and technology are employed with moral and esthetic vision can they be regarded as making for a sound social order.

The old legend of Faust and his damnation is worth recalling. Faust sold his soul to the devil in order to gain knowledge, power, and riches. For a time it seemed to be a marvelous bargain, while the world's goods showered upon him. But as the end approached, Faust was seized with terror and tried to repent. It was too late, and he was carried off to hell kicking and screaming. The Faust story is symbolical of the fate that may await our civilization, hell-bent on getting power and riches at any price. We should repent and change our ways before it is too late.[5]

Nevertheless, we do not regard the making of a counterculture as a viable goal for America or the world. More sensible is the making of a well-balanced culture, not as counter to science and technology but as corrective and inclusive of them. Neither the "intellective" nor the "nonintellective capacities" should become the "arbiters" of human values. Rather, man in his wholeness and integrity should become the measure of values. In this sense we would approve the ancient saying of Protagoras, "Man is the measure of all things." As far as possible, the ugly effects of applied science and technology, such as environmental pollution, urban blight, and scientific warfare, must be eliminated; but it would be short-sighted, if not silly, to be "against" the wider horizons and increased potentialities of scientific-technological advancement. It is well to recall the past and its shortcomings. In former days most children died in infancy, and if they grew to maturity, they lived in abject poverty and dismal superstition. Now certain nations, such as the Scandinavian countries, have lowered enormously the death rate, all but eliminated dire poverty, and educated most of their adult population. These are great gains that can be spread to other lands including affluent America, where it is still too true that "wealth accumulates and men decay." Our aim should be to eradicate the evil effects of technology while conserving its constructive uses. It will require a *wise* technology to remove the effects of *unwise* technology. For example, the replacement of the internal combustion engine by a nonpolluting substitute is required to stop the pervasive fouling of the atmosphere.

It is impractical to reverse the historical process and create a nontechnological culture, and it would be silly to try. After all, there is no real virtue in ignorance or impotence: far better is the combination of power and knowledge with goodness and beauty. The machine is the normal tool of modern civilization, a tool to be regarded as any other and made to serve, not to enslave and dehumanize. In any case there is no way back to the simplicity of a relatively pretechnological age: the growth of science and technology is too great to arrest. Men will not willingly give up the advantages of technological advancement: their very lives depend upon it. "Take away the energy-distributing networks and industrial machinery from America, Russia, and all the world's industrialized countries," writes R. Buckminster Fuller, "and within six months more than two billion swiftly and painfully deteriorating people will starve to death."[6] That is a price that no one but a sadist would want to pay. Let us, therefore, press ahead with our scientific and technological resources toward a world without war, poverty, or disease. At the same time, let us greatly enhance the role of art as a counterbalance to technology. In its vividness and individuality and emotional spontaneity, art is strong in the very aspects in which a scientific-technological civilization is deficient.

Art as an Antidote to Mechanization

Is the ideal of a well-balanced civilization an impractical dream? A number of writers, such as Roderick Seidenberg and Jacques Ellul, have warned us that the demand for an ever-greater degree of integration is characteristic of a scientific-technological society and that this demand will ultimately prove fatal to the values of personal independence and esthetic spontaneity. Man does not lack "within his rich and volatile nature elements presaging another destiny, loftier perhaps, more spiritual and humane," writes Seidenberg, but "the hope of retaining the machine while avoiding the consequent mechanization of society is wholly wishful and fallacious. For the logic of the machine, repeating always its fixed and predesigned patterns, is a mass logic; and collectivism . . . is inherent in its laws and implicit in its operations."[7] Similarly, Ellul, in a profoundly pessimistic book, contends that neither free individuals or autonomous groups can long hold out against the mechanistic trend of technology.

> Technique requires predictability and, no less, exactness of prediction. It is necessary, then, that technique prevail over the human being. . . . Technique must reduce man to a technical animal, the king of the slaves of technique. Human caprice crumbles before this necessity; there can be no human autonomy in the face of technical autonomy.[8]

Ellul wishes to rebuild modern civilization on Christian rather than technological foundations, but it would appear from his analysis that men have become too enslaved to technology to make the rebuilding possible.

It may be instructive to contrast the profound pessimism of these authors with the older and more optimistic outlook of John Dewey. He steadfastly contended that there is nothing final or fatal about the state of the world. If we develop the capacity to think both compassionately and scientifically about the problems of mankind, and if we employ the fecund means of technology in behalf of a significantly human life, we shall find a practical answer to the pessimism rife among us. We need a balance and integration of all fields of culture, supplementing the older physical technologies with emphasis upon the newer social and psychological technologies, and combining both kinds of technology with art, morals, political action, and a humanistic faith. Technology operates within a cultural context, its potentialities are both constructive and destructive, and it must be guided and controlled if its constructive development is greatly to outweigh and exceed its destructive tendency.

We are more inclined to agree with Dewey than with Seidenberg and Ellul. Science and technology, we believe, can be utilized with imagination and foresight, not as the tools of a managerial technocracy, but as the means to a liberated and creative life. To achieve this goal, artists must join with city planners and civic-minded leaders in bringing a new cleanliness, order, and comeliness into our urban environment. The artistic phase must enter much more pervasively into industry—with less emphasis upon mere volume of production and more emphasis upon fine workmanship and good design. Individuals and groups must limit the mass standardization so characteristic of the Coca-Cola-and-television dimension of our civilization and stress the imaginative life as a countervailing force to mechanization. There must be a decentralization of our society and a renewal of culture, putting humanity before machines and considerations of goodness and beauty ahead of profits.

The proper function of art is the presentation for imaginative acquaintance of the whole realm of values, negative as well as positive. The proper function of technology is the application of science to maximize the positive values and to minimize the negative. The technologist should be grateful to the artist for the vivid display of the values that he seeks to control. The artist should be grateful to the technologist for implementing the values that he has envisaged. Art supplies the vision, technology the means. In a well-balanced society, they are mutually supporting and complementary.

We do not deny that the danger of technocratic enslavement is real. The massive forces of change seem to be moving toward an organizational gigantism and standardization that undermine the values of individuality. The depersonalization of existence is not only a threat but a constant reality. Even pure science, with its abstract categories, general laws, and classificatory schemas, tends to weaken or diminish the concrete, lively intuitions of esthetic experience. The vivid eidetic imagery characteristic of children and primitive peoples tends to die out as civilized human beings grow up and become habituated to an abstract scientific-technological culture. Too often the fluid richness of immediate experience is sacrificed to a rigid order from which emotional spontaneity and meaningfulness have disappeared. To create and see things afresh is the concern of a tiny minority.

If the artist should succumb to these forces he will have lost his birthright. For it is his function to emphasize quality instead of quantity, creativity instead of conformity, spontaneity instead of routine, vividness instead of abstraction. His greatest gift to mankind, all the more precious in an age of science and technology, is to withstand the forces that make for a colorless uniformity, to keep the freshness of life from going stale. He must cling to the matchlessness of the individual, the loneliness of the visionary. Amid the hurry and tension of getting things done, the artist who stops and listens and seeks his own rhythm has the most to offer. "Why should we be in such desperate haste to succeed, and in such desperate enterprises," asks Henry Thoreau. "If a man does not keep pace with his companions, perhaps it is because he hears a different drummer. Let him step to the music which he hears, however measured or far away."[9] It is the artist in each one of us that hears that distant drummer. . . .

The Freedom of Art

We have said that art is a mode of both self-expression and self-transcendence, and that it creates esthetic value, not by isolating itself from life but by the artistic expression of human values—the values of the not-self as well as of the self, the values of unreality as well as the values of reality. Human existence has many registers, and it is not given to anyone to play all of them. But it is the man of art, more than the mystic, more than the moralist, more than the scientist or technician or practical man, who is free to play the whole range. He is not necessarily limited, as these others are, by a concern for something real, or something taken to be real. He can roam as freely through the realm of imagination as through the realm of actuality. His is the domain of vivid values, and values both are and are not "real."

Art has a free choice of subject and theme. It may choose as its matter error as well as truth, vice as well as virtue, distortion as well as faithful depiction, and invention as well as fact. A work of art may represent anything or nothing—that is, nothing that answers to the things defined by other categories of experience, such as truth, morality, etc. A work of art is different from what it represents and also different from other ways of experiencing what it represents. Art is not, in first intention, truth, morality, or piety. Conversely, neither is it untruth, immorality, or impiety. It follows that such all-to-common, allegedly sufficient judgments of art as "how real!" or "how true!" or "how reverent!" are poor esthetic judgments —poor at least in the sense of starting at the wrong end and resting there. The primary esthetic judgment should be "how interesting!" or "how expressive!" In that judgment we voice the freedom which art can give.

Expression in art is a difficult thing to become clear about, because the temptation is to identify it with expression in science and other literal discourse; in other words, to limit art to statements of truth and exact report. Such misconception leads commonly, for example, to strained attempts to "tell the meaning" of poetry and even of music. Now poetry and music and other arts too do make *use* of literal meaning, sometimes very extensively, as when poetry describes a scene or an action, and when music imitates natural sounds. But when literal meaning is thus employed in art it is always subordinate or subservient to *esthetic* meaning (at least it is if the art is good), and it is esthetic meaning which art peculiarly expresses. Literal meaning, like mere sensuous quality, is the material rather than the product. The material is, of course, important. Literal meanings in art are important. The choice of material in art, whether it be inert physical material like clay and pigment, or ideational and moral material like thoughts, dreams, and social attitudes, is a major determinant of the character of the work. And the material available to art includes not only all the sensuous matter in the world but also all the experienced ideas, facts, behavior, and aspirations of man and his world. But these in themselves, we repeat, even though faithfully reported and extensively used by art, are not the meaning of art, not what art, as such, expresses.

What then does art express? What does it mean? As we have said, art expresses quality and feeling—not quality in cold isolation nor feeling detached from content, but feeling at one with the qualities felt. Art is not expression merely of what the facts are in the world and human experience, but very much more; it is the expression of how the individual artist feels, and if his feelings are normal, how we too feel about facts and experience —how we feel about mountains, love, patriotism, sorrow, joy, adventure, death, a bowl of fruit, an assortment of bottles, an old woman's face. To be art the feeling expressed must be objectified, transmuted into beauty, detached from practical or intellectual concerns. The feeling is revealed as *interesting,* and as such it is made *beautiful.* The feeling is made into an object, into a felt quality, into a value. Or, starting with the other pole, the artist may begin with a quality and then attach feeling to it. Only when the subjective and objective poles are united and the value is embodied in a work of art, is the process complete.

Esthetic expression of feeling is not mere report of feeling. Report of feeling, like report of any other fact, is information, not art. In practical life, expressions of feeling are reports or signs: reports of how things are going in the organism, or signs that something is wanted. The cry of anguish, the shout for help, the peal of joyous laughter, and the smile of friendship—these are all expressions of strong feelings which as occurrences or as reported events are not art. They are materials for art. They may become art. Art may take these feelings, make them objects, give them an existence and a value which they never have and never can have as subjective occurrences. In subjective occurrence the feeling may be an incitement to action, a fugitive surge of joy or sadness, a dull and heavy weight of frustration, but not, as long as it remains subjective, a work of art. Ultimately, the impulse to unite feeling with quality arises because mere subjective feeling is always unsatisfactory. If it is of joy and gladness, the pity is its evanescence; if it is weariness and sorrow, the pity is its pain. Art overcomes both joy and pain. In art, feeling, no matter how fleeting or painful in life, gets a place in the world, permanent and satisfactory. Art liberates us from "the tyranny of feeling," especially the "hypernormal" feeling, of joy which is so great as to become a burden and numbing despair. In the "Ode to a Nightingale" by Keats we find an excellent example of how art is felt to give liberation from "joy which is so great as to become a burden."

My heart aches, and a drowsy numbness pains
  My sense, as though of hemlock I had drunk,
Or emptied some dull opiate to the drains
  One minute past, and Lethe-wards had sunk:
'Tis not through envy of thy happy lot,
  But being too happy in thine happiness—
  That thou, light-winged Dryad of the trees,

> In some melodious plot
> Of beechen green, and shadows numberless,
> Singest of summer in full-throated ease.

Keats achieves liberation from mere fleeting personal feeling through imaginative identification with the nightingale. The same poet has this kind of liberation in mind when he writes, "A thing of beauty is a joy for ever . . . it will never pass into nothingness."[10]

Conversely, but in the same manner and to the same end, art deals with the feeling of sadness, with the "numbing despair," which in practical life is sheerly destructive. "Our sweetest songs," writes the poet Shelley, "are those which tell of saddest thought."[11] And we may add, our greatest drama is that which tells of deepest struggle and defeat—of tragedy. The literature of music and the history of painting give much additional evidence of this value in art. Let us take a second example from poetry, a single line from the poet Byron. The poet writes: "My days are in the yellow leaf. . . ."[12] In it he feels and reports the fact, "I am growing old, and death approaches." But instead of merely carrying the unwelcome discovery in subjective feeling, he instates it in the world of things intrinsically interesting; and in the measure that he, and the reader of the line as well, becomes absorbed in the objective expression, advancing age and the ultimate frustration of death itself will be bereft of dread.

In the esthetic expression of evil we do not deny evil, but turn it to interest, and thus become free. The principle is well expressed by another poet, John Donne, when he writes:

> Grief brought to numbers cannot be so fierce,
> For, he tames it, that fetters it to verse.[13]

We may generalize: Our very defeats in "real life" become our triumphs in the life of art. Esthetically, we become masters of our troubles, our frustrations, our defeats—by becoming interested in them, by making them into works of art instead of merely suffering them. Art is no thing of play or passive pleasure; it is, rather, serious and important, it demands our most earnest efforts and gves us many of our most precious values. Art is in the everyday sense nonpractical; but in precisely that its importance lies. Pure art is useless, but not worthless. Its worth is of the highest. It is important because it is humanizing and liberating. Art through objectification of human feeling in detached interest is a way of freedom. To be human is to be free. It is a mark of excellence and greatness in man to have detached interest—for the individual to be concerned not with himself alone. In art he can find that greatness, for art is one of the major ways of self-transcendence, which takes its place alongside morality, truth, and religion as one of the great liberating interests. Art, we repeat, is in this sense one of the fundamental meanings of human life. In art, as in truth, morality, and in that humility of ignorance which we may call religion, man becomes free.

To sum up: We have distinguished between a broader and a narrower meaning of art. In its broad meaning, art is the creation of esthetic value, whether as a by-product of other activity or by deliberate intent. Common-life art is frequently the by-product of good workmanship, and esthetic value creeps in as a result of doing an ordinary job well. Fine art, or art in the narrower sense, is specialized pursuit of esthetic excellence for its own sake. Although it is "narrower" than art in the broad sense, it is not narrow or restricted in the range of its subject matter. If we consider all the arts in their total range, any value at all, or even any matter of fact if its quality is felt, may receive artistic expression. It is impossible to limit art to the expression of any kind of value or felt fact, but there is always a regulative principle, or artistic imperative—namely, the creation of esthetic value. Art creates esthetic value by expressing the artist's vision of all manner of values. As wine is to grapes, so art is to life: it draws its material from life, but it gives in return something that its material did not contain. This something is the unique esthetic value that arises from the artistic expression and embodiment of felt facts and life values in a suitable medium. Some things are much better fitted than others to sustain and enrich intrinsic perception, and successful works of art—especially works that tap the deep primordial sources of human interest—are supreme among these things. Fine art is the intentional creation of actions and artifacts that are well-fitted to stimulate and sustain intrinsically valuable perception.

—*Art and Human Values* (1976)

Notes

1. Elias Canetti, *Tagebuch* (Vienna: December 1965). Report on a symposium on "Our Century and Its Novel" under the auspices of the Austrian Society for Literature, quoted by Ernst Fischer, *Art Against Ideology* (Allen Lane, London, 1969), p. 42.
2. *Mind at the End of Its Tether* (Didier, New York, 1946), pp. 4, 15. Compare this judgment with the heady optimism of *The Discovery of the Future,* written by Wells in 1913.
3. Edward Mortimer's news dispatch from Paris, in *The Times* (London), May 17, 1968.
4. *The Making of a Counter Culture* (Doubleday, Garden City, N.Y., 1969), pp. 50–51, 54, 68. See also Roszak, *Where the Wasteland Ends* (Doubleday, Garden City, N.Y., 1972).
5. See Anthony J. Wiener, "Faustian Progress," in Richard Kostelanetz (ed.), *Beyond Left and Right* (Morrow, New York, 1968).
6. "Man With a Chronofile," in ibid., p. 45.
7. *Posthistoric Man* (Chapel Hill: University of North Carolina Press, 1950), pp. 229, 231–32.
8. *The Technological Society* (New York: Alfred A. Knopf, Inc., 1964), p. 138.
9. Henry Thoreau, *Walden,* Conclusion.
10. Keats, "Endymion," opening lines.
11. Shelley, "To a Skylark."
12. Byron, "On This Day I Complete My Thirty-Sixth Year."
13. "The Triple Fool."

LEWIS MUMFORD

The Esthetic Assimilation of the Machine

. . . In the arts, it is plain that the machine is an instrument with manifold and conflicting possibilities. It may be used to counterfeit older forms of art; it may also be used, in its own right, to concentrate and intensify and express new forms of experience. As substitutes for primary experience, the machine is worthless: indeed it is actually debilitating. Just as the microscope is useless unless the eye itself is keen, so all our mechanical apparatus in the arts depends for its success upon the due cultivation of the organic, physiological, and spiritual aptitudes that lie behind its use. The machine cannot be used as a shortcut to escape the necessity for organic experience. Mr. Waldo Frank has put the matter well: "Art," he says, "cannot become a language, hence an experience, unless it is practiced. To the man who plays, a mechanical reproduction of music may mean much, since he already has the experience to assimilate. But where reproduction becomes the norm, the few music makers will grow more isolate and sterile, and the ability to experience music will disappear. The same is true with the cinema, dance, and even sport."

Whereas in industry the machine may properly replace the human being when he has been reduced to an automaton, in the arts the machine can only extend and deepen man's original functions and intuitions. Insofar as the phonograph and the radio do away with the impulse to sing, insofar as the camera does away with the impulse to see, insofar as the automobile does away with the impulse to walk, the machine leads to a lapse of function which is but one step away from paralysis. But in the application of mechanical instruments to the arts it is not the machine itself that we must fear. The chief danger lies in the failure to integrate the arts themselves with the totality of our life-experience: the perverse triumph of the machine follows automatically from the abdication of the spirit. Consciously to assimilate the machine is one means of reducing its omnipotence. We cannot, as Karl Buecher wisely said, "give up the hope that it will be possible to unite technics and art in a higher rhythmical unity, which will restore to the spirit the fortunate serenity and to the body the harmonious cultivation that manifest themselves at their best among primitive peoples." The machine has not destroyed that promise. On the contrary, through the more conscious cultivation of the machine arts and through greater selectivity in their use, one sees the pledge of its wider fulfillment throughout civilization. For at the bottom of that cultivation there must be the direct and immediate experience of living itself: we must directly see, feel, touch, manipulate, sing, dance, communicate before we can extract from the machine any further sustenance for life. If we are empty to begin with, the machine will only leave us emptier; if we are passive and powerless to begin with, the machine will only leave us more feeble.

But modern technics, even apart from the special arts that it fostered, had a cultural contribution to make in its own right. Just as science underlined the respect for fact, so technics emphasized the importance of function: in this domain, as Emerson pointed out, the beautiful rests on the foundations of the necessary. The nature of this contribution can best be shown, perhaps, by describing the way in which the problem of machine design was first faced, then evaded, and finally solved.

One of the first products of the machine was the machine itself. As in the organization of the first factories the narrowly practical considerations were uppermost, and all the other needs of the personality were firmly shoved to one side. The machine was a direct expression of its own functions: the first cannon, the first crossbows, the first steam engines were all nakedly built for action. But once the primary problems of organization and operation had been solved, the human factor, which had been left out of the picture, needed somehow to be re-incorporated. The only precedent for this fuller integration of form came naturally from handicraft: hence over the incomplete, only partly realized forms of the early cannon, the early bridges, the early machines, a meretricious touch of decoration was added: a mere relic of the happy, semi-magical fantasies that painting and carving had once added to every handicraft object. Because perhaps the energies of the eotechnic period[1] were so completely engrossed in the technical problems, it was, from the standpoint of design, amazingly clean and direct: ornament flourished in the utilities of life, flourished often perversely and extravagantly, but one looks for it in vain among the machines pictured by Agricola or Besson or the Italian engineers[2]: they are as direct and factual as was architecture from the tenth to the thirteenth century.

The worst sinners—that is, the most obvious sentimentalists—were the engineers of the paleotechnic period. In the act of recklessly deflowering the environment at large, they sought to expiate their failures by adding a few sprigs or posies to the new engines they were creating: they embellished their steam engines with Doric columns or partly concealed them behind Gothic tracery: they decorated the frames of their presses and their automatic machines with cast-iron arabesque, they punched ornamental holes in the iron framework of their new structures, from the trusses of the old wing of the Metropolitan Museum to the base of the Eiffel tower in Paris. Everywhere similar habits prevailed: the homage of hypocrisy to art. One notes identical efforts on the original steam radiators, in the floral decorations that once graced typewriters, in the nondescript ornament that still lingers quaintly on shotguns and sewing machines, even if it has at length disappeared from cash registers and Pullman cars—as long before, in the first uncertainties of the new technics, the same division had appeared in armor and in crossbows.

The second stage in machine design was a compromise. The object was divided into two parts. One of them was to be precisely designed for mechanical efficiency. The other was to be designed for looks. While the utilitarian claimed the working parts of the structure the esthete was, so to speak, permitted slightly to modify the surfaces with his unimportant patterns, his plutonic flowers, his aimless filigree, provided he did not seriously weaken the structure or condemn the function to inefficiency. Mechanically utilizing the machine, this type of design shamefully attempted to conceal the origins that were still felt as low and mean. The engineer had the uneasiness of a parvenu, and the same impulse to imitate the most archaic patterns of his betters.

Naturally the next stage was soon reached: the utilitarian and the esthete withdrew again to their respective fields. The esthete, insisting with justice that the structure was integral with the decoration and that art was something more fundamental than the icing the pastrycook put on the cake, sought to make the old decoration real by altering the nature of the structure. Taking his place as workman, he began to revive the purely handicraft methods of the weaver, the cabinet maker, the printer, arts that had survived for the most part only in the more backward parts of the world, untouched by the tourist and the commercial traveler. The old workshops and ateliers were languishing and dying out in the nineteenth century, especially in progressive England and in America, when new ones, like those devoted to glass under William de Morgan in England, and John La Farge in America, and Lalique in France, or to a miscellany of handicrafts, such as that of William Morris in England, sprang into existence, to prove by their example that the arts of the past could survive. The industrial manufacturer, isolated from this movement yet affected by it, contemptuous but half-convinced, made an effort to retrieve his position by attempting to copy mechanically the dead forms of art he found in the museum. So far from gaining from the handicrafts movement by this procedure he lost what little virtue his untutored designs possessed, issuing as they sometimes did out of an intimate knowledge of the processes and the materials.

The weakness of the original handicrafts movement was that it assumed that the only important change in industry had been the intrusion of the soulless machine. Whereas the fact was that everything had changed, and all the shapes and patterns employed by technics were therefore bound to change, too. The world men carried in their heads, their idolum, was entirely different from that which set the medieval mason to carving the history of creation or the lives of the saints above the portals of the cathedral, or a jolly image of some sort above his own doorway. An art based like handicraft upon a certain stratification of the classes and the social differentiation of the arts could not survive in a world where men had seen the French Revolution and had been promised some rough share of equality. Modern handicraft, which sought to rescue the worker from the slavery of shoddy machine production, merely enabled the well-to-do to enjoy new objects that were as completely divorced from the dominant social milieu as the palaces and monasteries that the antiquarian art dealer and collector had begun to loot. The *educational aim* of the arts and crafts movement was admirable; and, insofar as it gave courage and understanding to the amateur, it was a success. If this movement did not add a sufficient amount of good handicraft it at least took away a great deal of false art. William Morris's dictum, that one should not possess anything one did not believe to be beautiful or know to be useful was, in the shallow showy bourgeois world he addressed, a revolutionary dictum.

But the social outcome of the arts and crafts movement was not commensurate with the need of the new situation; as Mr. Frank Lloyd Wright pointed out in his memorable speech at Hull House in 1901, the machine itself was as much an instrument of art, in the hands of an artist, as were the simple tools and utensils. To erect a social barrier between machines and tools was really to accept the false notion of the new industrialist who, bent on exploiting the machine, which they owned, and jealous of the tool, which might still be owned by the independent worker, bestowed on the machine an exclusive sanctity and grace it did not merit. Lacking the courage to use the machine as an instrument of creative purpose, and being unable to attune themselves to new objectives and new standards, the esthetes were logically compelled to restore a medieval ideology in order to provide a social backing for their anti-machine bias. In a word, the arts and crafts movement did not grasp the fact that the new technics, by expanding the role of the machine, had altered the entire relation of handwork to production, and that the exact processes of the machine were not necessarily hostile to handicraft and fine workmanship. In its modern form handicraft could no longer serve as in the past when it had worked under the form of an intensive caste-specialization. To survive, handicraft would have to adapt itself to the amateur, and it was bound to call into existence, even in pure handwork, those forms of economy and simplicity which the machine was claiming for its own, and to which it was adapting mind and hand and eye. In this process of re-integration certain "eternal" forms would be recovered: there are handicraft forms dating back to a distant past which so completely fulfill their functions that no amount of further calculation or experiment will alter them for the better. These type-forms appear and reappear from civilization to civilization; and if they had not been discovered by handicraft, the machine would have had to invent them.

The new handicraft was in fact to receive presently a powerful lesson from the machine. For the forms created by the machine, when they no longer sought to imitate old superficial patterns of handwork, were closer to those that could be produced by the amateur than were, for example, the intricacies of special joints, fine inlays, matched woods, beads and carvings, complicated forms of metallic ornament, the boast of handicraft in the past. While in the factory the machine was often reduced to producing fake handicraft, in the workshop of the amateur the reverse process could take place with a real gain: he was liberated by the very simplicities of good machine forms. Machine technique as a means to achieving a simplified and purified form relieved the amateur from the need of respecting and imitating the perversely complicated patterns of the past—patterns whose complications were partly the result of conspicuous waste, partly the outcome of technical virtuosity, and partly the result of a different state of feelings. But before handicraft could thus be restored as an admirable form of play and an efficacious relief from a physically untutored life, it was necessary to dispose of the machine itself as a social and esthetic instrument. So the major contribution to art was made, after all, by the industrialist who remained on the job and saw it through.

With the third stage in machine design, an alteration takes place. The imagination is not applied to the mechanical object after the practical design has been completed: it is infused into it at every stage in development. The mind works through the medium of the machine directly, respects the conditions imposed upon it, and—not content with a crude quantitative approximation—seeks out a more positive esthetic fulfillment. This must not be confused with the dogma, so often current, that any mechanical contraption that works necessarily is esthetically interesting. The source of this fallacy is plain. In many cases, indeed, our eyes have been trained to recognize beauty in nature, and with certain kinds of animals and birds we have an especial sympathy. When an airplane becomes like a gull it has the advantage of this long association and we properly couple the beauty with the mechanical adequacy, since the poise and swoop of a gull's flight casts in addition a reflective beauty on its animal structure. Having no such association with a milkweed seed, we do not feel the same beauty in the autogyro, which is kept aloft by a similar principle. While genuine beauty in a thing of use must always be joined to mechanical adequacy and therefore involves a certain amount of intellectual recognition and appraisal, the relation is not a simple one: it points to a common source rather than an identity.

In the conception of a machine or of a product of the machine there is a point where one may leave off for parsimonious reasons without having reached esthetic perfection: at this point perhaps every mechanical factor is accounted for, and the sense of incompleteness is due to the failure to recognize the claims of the human agent. Esthetics carries with it the implication of alternatives between a number of mechanical solutions of equal validity: and unless this awareness is present at every stage of the process, in smaller matters of finish, fineness, trimness, it is not likely to come out with any success in the final stage of design. Form follows function, underlining it, crystallizing it, clarifying it, making it real to the eye. Makeshifts and approximations express themselves in incomplete forms: forms like the absurdly cumbrous and ill-adjusted telephone apparatus of the past, like the old-fashioned airplane, full of struts, wires, extra supports, all testifying to an anxiety to cover innumerable unknown or uncertain factors; forms like the old automobile in which part after part had been added to the effective mechanism without having been absorbed into the body of the design as a whole; forms like our oversized steel-work which were due to our carelessness in using cheap materials and our desire to avoid the extra expense of calculating them finely and expending the necessary labor to work them up. The impulse that creates a complete mechanical object is akin to that which creates an esthetically finished object; and the fusion of the two at every stage in the process will necessarily be effected by the environment at large: who can gauge how much the slatternliness and disorder of the paleotechnic environment undermined good design, or how much the order and beauty of our neotechnic plants—like that of the Van Nelle factory in Rotterdam—will eventually aid it? Esthetic interests cannot suddenly be introduced from without: they must be constantly operative, constantly visible.

Expression through the machine implies the recognition of relatively new esthetic terms: precision, calculation, flawlessness, simplicity, economy. Feeling attaches itself in these new forms to different qualities than those that made handicraft so entertaining. Success here consists in the elimination of the nonessential, rather than, as in handicraft decoration, in the willing production of superfluity, contributed by the worker out of his own delight in the work. The elegance of a mathematical equation, the inevitability of a series of physical inter-relations, the naked quality of the material itself, the tight logic of the whole—these are the ingredients that go into the design of machines: and they go equally into products that have been properly designed for machine production. In handicraft it is the worker who is represented: in machine design it is the work. In handicraft, the personal touch is emphasized, and the imprint of the worker and his tool are both inevitable: in machine work the impersonal prevails, and if the worker leaves any tell-tale evidence of his part in the operation, it is a defect or a flaw. Hence the burden of machine design is in the making of the original pattern: it is here that trials are made, that errors are discovered and buried, that the creative process as a whole is concentrated. Once the master-pattern is set, the rest is routine: beyond the designing room and the laboratory there is—for goods produced on a serial basis for a mass market—no opportunity for choice and personal achievement. Hence apart from those commodities that can be produced automatically, the effort of sound industrial production must be to increase the province of the designing room and the laboratory, reducing the scale of the production, and making possible an easier passage back and forth between the designing and the operative sections of the plant.

Who discovered these new canons of machine design? Many an engineer and many a machine worker must have mutely sensed them and reached toward them: indeed, one sees the beginning of them in very early mechanical instruments. But only after centuries of more or less blind and unformulated effort were these canons finally demonstrated with a certain degree of completeness in the work of the great engineers toward the end of the nineteenth century—particularly the Roeblings in America and Eiffel in France—and formulated after that by theoreticians like Reidler and Meyer in Germany. The popularization of the new esthetic awaited . . . the post-impressionist painters. They contributed by breaking away from the values of purely associative art and by abolishing an undue concern for natural objects as the basis of the painter's interest: if on one side this led to completer subjectivism, on the other it tended toward a recognition of the machine as both form and symbolic.[3] In the same direction Marcel Duchamp, for example, who was one of the leaders of this movement, made a collection of cheap, ready-made articles, produced by the machine, and called attention to their esthetic soundness and sufficiency. In many cases, the finest designs had been achieved before any conscious recognition of the esthetic had taken place. With the coming of the commercialized designer, seeking to add "art" to a product which *was* art, the design has more often than not been trifled with and spoiled. The studious botching of the kodak, the bathroom fixture, and the steam radiator under such stylicizing is a current commonplace.

The key to this fresh appreciation of the machine as a source of new esthetic forms has come through a formulation of its chief esthetic principle: the principle of economy. This principle is of course not unknown in other phases of art: but the point is that in mechanical forms it is at all times a controlling one, and it has for its aid the more exact calculations and measurements that are now possible. The aim of sound design is to remove from the object, be it an automobile or a set of china or a room, every detail, every molding, every variation of the surface, every extra part except that which conduces to its effective functioning. Toward the working out of this principle, our mechanical habits and our unconscious impulses have been tending steadily. In departments where esthetic choices are not consciously uppermost our taste has often been excellent and sure. Le Corbusier has been very ingenious in picking out manifold objects, buried from observation by their very ubiquity, in which this mechanical excellence of form has manifested itself without pretense or fumbling. Take the smoking pipe: it is no longer carved to look like a human head or does it bear, except among college students, any heraldic emblems: it has become exquisitely anonymous, being nothing more than an apparatus for supplying drafts of smoke to the human mouth from a slow-burning mass of vegetation. Take the ordinary drinking glass in a cheap restaurant: it is no longer cut or cast or engraved with special designs: at most it may have a slight bulge near the top to keep one glass from sticking to another in stacking: it is as clean, as functional, as a high tension insulator. Or take the present watch and its case and compare it with the forms that handicraft ingenuity and taste and association created in the sixteenth or seventeenth centuries. In all the commoner objects of our environment the machine canons are instinctively accepted: even the most sentimental manufacturer of motor cars has not been tempted to paint his coach work to resemble a sedan chair in the style of Watteau, although he may live in a house in which the furniture and decoration are treated in that perverse fashion.

This stripping down to essentials has gone on in every department of machine work and has touched every aspect of life. It is a first step toward that completer integration of the machine with human needs and desires which is the mark of the neotechnic phase, and will be even more the mark of the biotechnic period, already visible over the edge of the horizon. As in the social transition from the paleotechnic to the neotechnic order, the chief obstacle to the fuller development of the machine lies in the association of taste and fashion with waste and commercial profiteering. For the rational development of genuine technical standards, based on function and performance, can come about only by a wholesale devaluation of the scheme of bourgeois civilization upon which our present system of production is based.

Capitalism, which along with war played such a stimulating part in the development of technics, now remains with war the chief obstacle toward its further improvement. The reason should be plain. The machine devaluates rarity: instead of producing a single unique object, it is capable of producing a million others just as good as the master model from which the rest are made. The machine devaluates age: for age is another token of rarity, and the machine, by placing its emphasis upon fitness and adaptation, prides itself on the brand-new rather than on the antique: instead of feeling comfortably authentic in the midst of rust, dust, cobwebs, shaky parts, it prides itself on the opposite qualities—slickness, smoothness, gloss, cleanness. The machine devaluates archaic taste: for taste in the bourgeois sense is merely another name for pecuniary reputability, and against that standard the machine sets up the standards of function and fitness. The newest, the cheapest, the commonest objects may, from the standpoint of pure esthetics, be immensely superior to the rarest, the most expensive, and the most antique. To say all this is merely to emphasize that the modern technics, by its own essential nature, imposes a greater purification of esthetics: that is, it strips off from the object all the barnacles of association, all the sentimental and pecuniary values which have nothing whatever to do with esthetic form, and it focuses attention upon the object itself.

The social devaluation of caste, enforced by the proper use and appreciation of the machine, is as important as the stripping down of essential forms in the process itself. One of the happiest signs of this during the last decade was the use of cheap and common materials in jewelry, first introduced, I believe, by Lalique: for this implied a recognition of the fact that an esthetically appropriate form, even in the adornment of the body, has nothing to do with rarity or expense, but is a matter of color, shape, line, texture, fitness, symbol. The use of cheap cottons in dress by Chanel and her imitators, which was another postwar phenomenon, was an equally happy recognition of the essential values in our new economy: it at last put our civilization, if only momentarily, on the level of those primitive cultures which gladly bartered their furs and ivory for the white man's colored glass beads, by the adroit use of which the savage artist often proved to any disinterested observer that they—contrary to the white man's fatuous conceit—had gotten the better of the bargain. Because of the fact that woman's dress has a peculiarly compensatory role to play in our megalopolitan society, so that it more readily indicates what is absent than calls attention to what is present in it, the victory for genuine esthetics could only be a temporary one. But these forms of dress and jewelry pointed to the goal of machine production: the goal at which each object would be valued in terms of its direct mechanical and vital and social function, apart from its pecuniary status, the snobberies of caste, or the dead sentiments of historical emulation.

This warfare between a sound machine esthetic and what Veblen has called the "requirements of pecuniary reputability" has still another side. Our modern technology has, in its inner organization, produced a collective economy and its typical products are collective products. Whatever the politics of a country may be, the machine is a communist: hence the deep contradictions and conflicts that have kept on developing in machine industry since the end of the eighteenth century. At every stage in technics, the work represents a collaboration of innumerable workers, themselves utilizing a large and ramifying technological heritage: the most ingenious inventor, the most brilliant individual scientist, the most skilled designer contributes but a moiety to the final result. And the product itself necessarily bears the same impersonal imprint: it either functions or it does not function on quite impersonal lines. There can be no qualitative difference between a poor man's electric bulb of a given candlepower and a rich man's, to indicate their differing pecuniary status in society, although there was an enormous difference between the rush or stinking tallow of the peasant and the wax candles or sperm oil used by the upper classes before the coming of gas and electricity.

Insofar as pecuniary differences are permitted to count in the machine economy, they can alter only the scale of things—not, in terms of present production, the kind. What applies to electric light bulbs applies to automobiles: what applies there applies equally to every manner of apparatus or utility. The frantic attempts that have been made in America by advertising agencies and "designers" to stylicize machine-made objects have been, for the most part, attempts to pervert the machine process in the interests of caste and pecuniary distinction. In money-ridden societies, where men play with poker chips instead of with economic and esthetic realities, every attempt is made to disguise the fact that the machine has achieved potentially a new collective economy, in which the possession of goods is a meaningless distinction, since the machine can produce all our essential goods in unparalleled quantities, falling on the just and the unjust, the foolish and the wise, like the rain itself.

The conclusion is obvious: we cannot intelligently accept the practical benefits of the machine without accepting its moral imperatives and its esthetic forms insofar as they, too, fulfill human purposes. Otherwise both ourselves and our society will be the victims of a shattering disunity, and one set of purposes, that which created the order of the machine, will be constantly at war with trivial and inferior personal impulses bent on working out in covert ways our psychological weaknesses. Lacking on the whole this rational acceptance, we have lost a good part of the practical benefits of the machine and have achieved esthetic expression only in a spotty, indecisive way. The real social distinction of modern technics, however, is that it tends to eliminate social distinctions. Its immediate goal is effective work. Its means are standardization: the emphasis of the generic and the typical: in short, conspicuous economy. Its ultimate aim is leisure —that is, the release of other organic capacities.

The powerful esthetic side of this social process has been obscured by speciously pragmatic and pecuniary interests that have inserted themselves into our technology and have imposed themselves upon its legitimate aims. But in spite of this deflection of effort, we have at last begun to realize these new values, these new forms, these new modes of expression. Here is a new environment—man's extension of nature in terms discovered by the close observation and analysis and abstraction of nature. The elements of this environment are hard and crisp and clear: the steel bridge, the concrete road, the turbine and the alternator, the glass wall. Behind the façade are rows and rows of machines, weaving cotton, transporting coal, assembling food, printing books, machines with steel fingers and lean muscular arms, with perfect reflexes, sometimes even with electric eyes. Alongside them are the new utilities—the coke oven, the transformer, the dye vats—chemically cooperating with these mechanical processes, assembling new qualities in chemical compounds and materials. Every effective part in this whole environment represents an effort of the collective mind to widen the province of order and control and provision. And here, finally, the perfected forms begin to hold human interest even apart from their practical performances: they tend to produce that inner composure and equilibrium, that sense of balance between the inner impulse and the outer environment, which is one of the marks of a work of art. The machines, even when they are not works of art, underlie our art—that is, our organized perceptions and feelings—in the way that Nature underlies them, extending the basis upon which we operate and confirming our own impulse to order. The economic: the objective: the collective: and finally the integration of these principles in a new conception of the organic—these are the marks, already discernible, of our assimilation of the machine not merely as an instrument of practical action but as a valuable mode of life.

—*Technics and Civilization* (1934)

Notes

1. For an explanation of the terms eotechnic, paleotechnic, neotechnic, and biotechnic, employed by Mumford, see the introductory note to this chapter. (Editor's note.)

2. Georgius Agricola is the author of *De Re Mettalica* (1546), which describes the advanced technology of the early sixteenth century. Jacques Besson wrote *Theatre des Instruments Mathématiques et Méchaniques,* an account of sixteenth-century technics. Among the Italian engineers here referred to the most famous is Leonarda da Vinci. (Editor's note.)

3. In a preceding section of his book, Mumford writes as follows: "The Cubists were perhaps the first school to overcome [the] association of the ugly and the mechanical: they not merely held that beauty could be produced through the machine: they even pointed to the fact that it had been produced. The first expression of Cubism indeed dates back to the seventeenth century: Jean Baptiste Bracelle, in 1624, did a series of Bizarreries which depicted mechanical men, thoroughly cubist in conception. This anticipated in art, as Glanvill did in science, our later interests and inventions. What did the modern Cubists do? They extracted from the organic environment just those elements that could be stated in abstract geometrical symbols: they transposed and readjusted the contents of vision as freely as the inventor readjusted organic functions: they even created on canvas or in metal mechanical equivalents of organic objects: Léger painted human figures that looked as if they had been turned in a lathe, and Duchamp-Villon modeled a horse as if it were a machine. This whole process of rational experiment in abstract mechanical forms was pushed further by the constructivists. Artists like Grabo and Moholy-Nagy put together pieces of abstract sculpture, composed of glass, metal plates, spiral springs, wood, which were the nonutilitarian equivalents of the apparatus that the physical scientist was using in his laboratory. They created in forms the semblance of the mathematical equations and physical formulæ that had produced our new environment, seeking in this new sculpture to observe the physical laws of equipose or to evolve dynamic equivalents for the solid sculpture of the past by rotating a part of the object through space." (Editor's note.)

IAN McHARG

Design with Nature

Thirty years ago the wilderness of Scotland looked inviolate to me and I would have been content to give my life to the creation of oases of delight in the heart of Glasgow or dream of a marriage of man and nature in new cities and towns. My boyhood sense of the rest of the world suggested that it was even wilder than Scotland. There were still explorers in those days and missionaries enough to build a stamp collection from their solicitations. The plight that moved me then was little enough compared to today. Then there was no threat of an atomic holocaust and no fear of radiation hazard. The population problem was one of declining birthrates and Mussolini exhorted and coerced Italian mothers to greater efforts while Presidents of France deplored an effete generation. DDT and Dieldrin were not yet festering thoughts; penicillin and streptomycin were not yet hopes. Man's inhumanity to man was commonplace in distant lands but had not achieved the pinnacle of depravity which at Belsen and Dachau a civilized nation was to achieve. Poverty and oppression were real and pervasive, and war was imminent enough so that I could conclude at seventeen that I had better be ready as a trained soldier by 1939.

Yet while the city was grim indeed, the countryside could be reached by foot, by bicycle or even for the few pennies that led to a tram terminus and the gateway to wild lands where no law of trespass constrained.

The country is not a remedy for the industrial city, but it does offer surcease and some balm to the spirit. Indeed, during the Depression there were many young men who would not submit to the indignity of the dole or its queues and who chose to live off the land, selling their strength where they could for food and poaching when they could not, sleeping in the bracken or a shepherd's bothy in good weather, living in hostels and public libraries in winter. They found independence, came to know the land and live from it, and sustained their spirit.

So, when first I encountered the problem of the place of nature in man's world it was not a beleaguered nature, but merely the local deprivation that was the industrial city. Scotland was wild enough, protected by those great conservators, poverty and inaccessibility. But this has changed dramatically in the intervening decades, so that today in Europe and the United States a great erosion has been accomplished which has diminished nature—not only in the countryside at large, but within the enlarging cities and, not least, in man as a natural being.

There are large numbers of urban poor for whom the countryside is known only as the backdrop to westerns or television advertisements. Paul Goodman speaks of poor children who would not eat carrots pulled from the ground because they were dirty, terror-stricken at the sight of a cow, who screamed in fear during a thunderstorm. The Army regularly absorbs young men who have not the faintest conception of living off the land, who know nothing of nature and its processes. In classical times the barbarians in fields and forest could only say "bar bar" like sheep; today their barbaric, sheepish descendants are asphalt men.

Clearly the problem of man and nature is not one of providing a decorative background for the human play, or even ameliorating the grim city: it is the necessity of sustaining nature as source of life, milieu, teacher, sanctum, challenge and, most of all, of rediscovering nature's corollary of the unknown in the self, the source of meaning.

There are still great realms of empty ocean, deserts reaching to the curvature of the earth, silent, ancient forests and rocky coasts, glaciers and volcanoes, but what will we do with them? There are rich contented farms, and idyllic villages, strong barns and white-steepled churches, tree-lined streets and covered bridges, but these are residues of another time. There are, too, the silhouettes of all the Manhattans, great and small, the gleaming golden windows of corporate images—expressionless prisms suddenly menaced by another of our creations, the supersonic transport whose sonic boom may reduce this image to a sea of shattered glass.

But what do we say now, with our acts in city and countryside? While I first addressed this question to Scotland in my youth, today the world directs the same question to the United States. What is our performance and example? What are the visible testaments to the American mercantile creed—the hamburger stand, gas station, diner, the ubiquitous billboards, sagging wires, the parking lot, car cemetery and that most complete conjunction of land rapacity and human disillusion, the subdivision. It is all but impossible to avoid the highway out of town, for here, arrayed in all its glory, is the quintessence of vulgarity, bedecked to give the maximum visibility to the least of our accomplishments.

And what of the cities? Think of the imprisoning gray areas that encircle the center. From here the sad suburb is an unrealizable dream. Call them no-place although they have many names. Race and hate, disease, poverty, rancor and despair, urine and spit live here in the shadows. United in poverty and ugliness, their symbol is the abandoned carcasses of automobiles, broken glass, alleys of rubbish and garbage. Crime consorts with disease, group fights group, the only emancipation is the parked car.

What of the heart of the city, where the gleaming towers rise from the dirty skirts of poverty? Is it like midtown Manhattan where twenty per cent of the population was found to be indistinguishable from the patients in mental hospitals?[1] Both stimulus and stress live here with the bitch goddess success. As you look at the faceless prisms do you recognize the home of *anomie*?

Can you find the river that first made the city? Look behind the unkempt industry, cross the grassy railroad tracks and you will find the rotting piers and there is the great river, scummy and brown, wastes and sewage bobbing easily up and down with the tide, endlessly renewed.

If you fly to the city by day you will see it first as a smudge of smoke on the horizon. As you approach, the outlines of its towers will be revealed as soft silhouettes in the hazardous haze. Nearer you will perceive conspicuous plumes which, you learn, belong to the proudest names in industry. Our products are household words but it is clear that our industries are not yet housebroken.

Drive from the airport through the banks of gas storage tanks and the interminable refineries. Consider how dangerous they are, see their cynical spume, observe their ugliness. Refine they may, but refined they are not.

You will drive on an expressway, a clumsy concrete form, untouched by either humanity or art, testament to the sad illusion that there can be a solution for the unbridled automobile. It is ironic that this greatest public investment in cities has also financed their conquest. See the scars of the battle in the remorseless carving, the dismembered neighborhoods, the despoiled parks. Manufacturers are producing automobiles faster than babies are being born. Think of the depredations yet to be accomplished by myopic highway builders to accommodate these toxic vehicles. You have plenty of time to consider in the long peak hour pauses of spasmodic driving in the blue gas corridors.

You leave the city and turn towards the countryside. But can you find it? To do so you will follow the paths of those who tried before you. Many stayed to build. But those who did so first are now deeply embedded in the fabric of the city. So as you go you transect the rings of the thwarted and disillusioned who are encapsulated in the city as nature endlessly eludes pursuit.

You can tell when you have reached the edge of the countryside for there are many emblems—the cadavers of old trees piled in untidy heaps at the edge of the razed deserts, the magnificent machines for land despoliation, for felling forests, filling marshes, culverting streams, and sterilizing farmland, making thick brown sediments of the creeks.

Is this the countryside, the green belt—or rather the greed belt, where the farmer sells land rather than crops, where the developer takes the public resource of the city's hinterland and subdivides to create a private profit and a public cost? Certainly here is the area where public powers are weakest—either absent or elastic—where the future costs of streets, sidewalks and sewers, schools, police and fire protection are unspoken. Here are the meek mulcted, the refugees thwarted.

Rural land persists around the metropolis, not because we have managed the land more wisely but because it is larger, more resistant to man's smear, more resilient. Nature regenerates faster in the country than in the city where the marks of men are well-nigh irreversible. But it still wears the imprint of man's toil. DDT is in the arctic ice, in the ocean deeps, in the rivers and on the land, atomic wastes rest on the Continental Shelf, many creatures are forever extinguished, the primeval forests have all but gone and only the uninitiated imagine that these third and fourth growth stands are more than shadows of their forebears. Although we can still see great fat farms, their once deep soils, a geological resource, are thinner now, and we might well know that farming is another kind of mining, dissipating the substance of aeons of summers and multitudes of life. The Mississippi is engorged with five cubic miles of soil each year, a mammoth prodigality in a starving world. Lake Erie is on the verge of becoming septic, New York City suffers from water shortages while the Hudson flows foully past, salt water encroaches in the Delaware, floods alternate with drought, the fruits of two centuries of land mismanagement. Forest fires, mudslides and smog become a way of life in Los Angeles, and the San Andreas Fault rises in temperature to menace San Franciscans.

The maps all show the continent to be green wild landscapes save for the sepia cities huddled on lakes and seaboards, but look from a plane as it crosses the continent and makes an idiocy of distance, see the wild green sectioned as rigorously as the city. In the great plains nature persists only in the meandering stream and the flood plain forest, a meaningful geometry in the Mondrian patterns of unknowing men.

It matters not if you choose to proceed to the next city or return to the first. You can confirm an urban destination from the increased shrillness of the neon shills, the diminished horizon, the loss of nature's companions until you are alone, with men, in the heart of the city, God's Junkyard—or should it be called Bedlam, for cacophony lives here. It is the expression of the inalienable right to create ugliness and disorder for private greed, the maximum expression of man's inhumanity to man. And so our cities grow, coalescing into a continental necklace of megalopoles, dead gray tissue encircling the nation.

Surely the indictment is too severe—there must be redeeming buildings, spaces, places, landscapes. Of course there are—random chance alone would have ensured some successful accidents. But there are also positive affirmations, yet it is important to recognize that many of these are bequests from earlier times. Independence, Carpenter and Faneuil Hall symbolize the small but precious heritage of the eighteenth century: the great State Houses, city halls, museums, concert halls, city universities and churches, the great urban park systems, were products of the last century. Here in these older areas you will find humane, generous suburbs where spacious men built their concern into houses and spaces so that dignity and peace, safety and quiet live there, shaded by old trees, warmed by neighborliness.

You may also see hints of a new vitality and new forms in the cities, promising resurgence. You may even have found, although I have not, an expressway that gives structure to a city, or, as I have, a parkway that both reveals and enhances the landscape. There are farmlands in good heart; there are landowners—few it is true—who have decided that growth is inevitable, but that it need not lead to despoliation but to enlargement. New towns are being constructed and concepts of regional planning are beginning to emerge. There is an increased awareness for the need to manage resources and even a title for this concern—The New Conservation. There is a widening certainty that the Gross National Product does not measure health or happiness, dignity, compassion, beauty or delight, and that these are, if not all inalienable rights, at least most worthy aspirations.

But these are rare among the countless city slums and scabrous towns, pathetic subdivisions, derelict industries, raped land, befouled rivers and filthy air.

At the time of the founding of the republic—and for millennia before—the city had been considered the inevitable residence for the urbane, civilized and polite. Indeed all of these names *say* city. It was as widely believed that rich countries and empires were inevitably built upon the wealth of the land. The original cities and towns of the American eighteenth century were admirable—Charleston and Savannah, Williamsburg, Boston,

Philadelphia, New Orleans. The land was rich and beautiful, canons of taste espoused the eighteenth-century forms of architecture and town building, a wonder of humanity and elegance.

How then did our plight come to be and what can be done about it? It is a long story which must be told briefly and, for that reason, it is necessary to use a broad brush and paint with coarse strokes. This method inevitably offends for it omits qualifying statements, employs broad generalities and often extrapolates from too slender evidence. Yet the basic question is so broad that one need not be concerned with niceties. The United States is the stage on which great populations have achieved emancipation from oppression, slavery, peonage and serfdom, where a heterogeneity of peoples has become one and where an unparalleled wealth has been widely distributed. These are the jewels of the American diadem. But the setting, the environment of this most successful social revolution, is a major indictment against the United States and a threat to her success and continued evolution.

Our failure is that of the Western World and lies in prevailing values. Show me a man-oriented society in which it is believed that reality exists only because man can perceive it, that the cosmos is a structure erected to support man on its pinnacle, that man exclusively is divine and given dominion over all things, indeed that God is made in the image of man, and I will predict the nature of its cities and their landscapes. I need not look far for we have seen them—the hot-dog stands, the neon shill, the ticky-tacky houses, dysgenic city and mined landscapes. This is the image of the anthropomorphic, anthropocentric man; he seeks not unity with nature but conquest. Yet unity he finally finds, but only when his arrogance and ignorance are stilled and he lies dead under the greensward. We need this unity to survive.

Among us it is widely believed that the world consists solely of a dialogue between men, or men and God, while nature is a faintly decorative backdrop to the human play. If nature receives attention, then it is only for the purpose of conquest, or even better, exploitation—for the latter not only accomplishes the first objective, but provides a financial reward for the conqueror.

We have but one explicit model of the world and that is built upon economics. The present face of the land of the free is its clearest testimony, even as the Gross National Product is the proof of its success. Money is our measure, convenience is its cohort, the short term is its span, and the devil may take the hindmost is the morality.

Perhaps there is a time and place for everything; and, with wars and revolutions, with the opening and development of continents, the major purposes of exploration and settlement override all lesser concerns and one concludes in favor of the enterprises while regretting the wastages and losses which are incurred in these extreme events. But if this was once acceptable as the inevitable way, that time has passed.

The pioneers, the builders of railroads and canals, the great industrialists who built the foundations for future growth were hard-driven, single-minded men. Like soldiers and revolutionaries, they destroyed much in disdain and in ignorance, but there are fruits from their energies and we share them today. Their successors, the merchants, are a different breed, more obsequious and insidious. The shock of the assassination of a President stilled for only one day their wheedling and coercive blandishments for our money. It is their ethos, with our consent, that sustains the slumlord and the land rapist, the polluters of rivers and atmosphere. In the name of profit they preempt the seashore and sterilize the landscape, fell the great forests, fill the protective marshes, build cynically in the flood plain. It is the claim of convenience for commerce—or its illusion—that drives the expressway through neighborhoods, homes and priceless parks, a taximeter of indifferent greed. Only the merchant's creed can justify the slum as a sound investment or offer tomato stakes as the highest utility for the priceless and irreplaceable redwoods.

The economists, with a few exceptions, are the merchants' minions and together they ask with the most barefaced effrontery that we accommodate our value system to theirs. Neither love nor compassion, health nor beauty, dignity nor freedom, grace nor delight are important unless they can be priced. If they are non-price benefits or costs they are relegated to inconsequence. The economic model proceeds inexorably towards its self-fulfillment of more and more despoliation, uglification and inhabition to life, all in the name of progress—yet, paradoxically, the components which the model excludes are the most important human ambitions and accomplishments and the requirements for survival.

The origins of societies and of exchange go back to an early world when man was a minor inconsequence in the face of an overwhelming nature. He bartered his surpluses of food and hides, cattle, sheep and goats and valued scarcities, gold and silver, myrrh and frankincense. But the indispensable elements of life and survival were beyond his ken and control: they could not and did not enter his value system save imperfectly, through religious views. Nor have they yet. But in the intervening millennia the valuations attributed to commodities have increased in range and precision and the understanding of the operation of the limited sphere of economics has increased dramatically. This imperfect view of the world as commodity fails to evaluate and incorporate physical and biological processes: we have lost the empirical knowledge of our ancestors. We are now unable to attribute value to indispensable natural processes, but we have developed an astonishing precision for ephemera.

It is obvious that such an institutionalized myopic prejudice will exclude the realities of the biophysical world. Its very man-centeredness ensures that those processes, essential to man's evolution and survival, will be excluded from consideration and from evaluation. We have no thought in the interminable dialogues among men for the sustaining sun, the moon and tides, the oceans and hydrologic cycle, the inclined axis of the earth and the seasons. As a society we neither know nor value the chemical elements and compounds that constitute life, and their cycles, the importance of the photosynthetic plant, the essential decomposers, the ecosystems, their constituent organisms, their roles and cooperative mechanisms, the prodigality of life forms, or even that greatest of values, the genetic pool with which we confront the future.

Yet we may soon learn. Consider the moon. It apparently lacks an atmosphere and oceans and the great inheritance of life forms which we enjoy. The costs of "terra-farming" this naked, hostile planet to that benign condition which can support life as abundantly as does the earth are considered of such a magnitude as to be inconceivable. Colonies on the moon will thus have to be small envelopes enclosing some of the essential commonplaces of earth transported as priceless and indispensable commodities. The man on the moon will know the value of these things.

But surely we need not await the confrontation with the inhospitable moon to learn a lesson so rudimentary, so well known to our ancient ancestors and as familiar to the simple societies of the world today.

Economic determinism as an imperfect evaluation of the biophysical world is only one of the consequences of our inheritance. An even more serious deficiency is the attitude towards nature and man which developed from the same source and of which our economic model is only one manifestation. The early men who were our ancestors wielded much the same scale of power over nature which Australian aboriginals do today. They were generally pantheists, animatists or animists. They tried to understand the phenomenal world and through behavior, placation and sacrifice, diminish adversity and increase beneficence. This early empiricism remains a *modus vivendi* for many tribal peoples, notably the American Indian—and conspicuously the Pueblo—today.

Whatever the earliest roots of the western attitude to nature it is clear that they were confirmed in Judaism. The emergence of monotheism had as its corollary the rejection of nature; the affirmation of Jehovah, the God in whose image man was made, was also a declaration of war on nature.

The great western religions born of monotheism have been the major source of our moral attitudes. It is from them that we have developed the preoccupation with the uniqueness of man, with justice and compassion. On the subject of man-nature, however, the Biblical creation story of the first chapter of Genesis, the source of the most generally accepted description of man's role and powers, not only fails to correspond to reality as we observe it, but in its insistence upon dominion and subjugation of nature, encourages the most exploitative and destructive instincts in man rather than those that are deferential and creative. Indeed, if one seeks license for those who would increase radioactivity, create canals and harbors with atomic bombs, employ poisons without constraint, or give consent to the bulldozer mentality, there could be no better injunction than this text. Here can be found the sanction and injunction to conquer nature—the enemy, the threat to Jehovah.

The creation story in Judaism was absorbed unchanged into Christianity. It emphasized the exclusive divinity of man, his God-given dominion over all things and licensed him to subdue the earth. While Abraham Heschel, Gustave Weigel, and Paul Tillich, speaking for Judaism and Christianity, reject the literality of this view and insist that it is an allegory, it is abundantly clear that it is the literal belief that has and does permeate the western view of nature and man. When this is understood, the conquest, the depredations and the despoliation are comprehensible, as is the imperfect value system.

From early, faintly ridiculous beginnings when a few inconsequential men proclaimed their absolute supremacy to an unhearing and uncaring world, this theme has grown. It had only a modest place in classical Greece, where it was tempered by a parallel pantheism. It enlarged during the Roman tenure but was also subject to the same constraints. When the Millennium passed without punishment it grew more confident. In the Humanism of the Renaissance it made a gigantic leap and it is somewhat poignant that the poverty of the Mediterranean today is a product of the land mismanagement that occurred during this great inflation of the human ego and the increase of man's powers over nature. The eighteenth century was a period of pause—the Naturalist view emerged—but it barely arrested the anthropomorphic, anthropocentric surge that swelled in the nineteenth century and is our full-blown inheritance today.

The Inquisition was so outraged by doubt cast upon the primacy of man and his planet that Galileo was required to rescind his certainty that the earth revolved around the sun. This same insistence upon human divinity takes hard the evidence of man's animal ancestry or indeed the history of evolution. It looks as if it will resist the evidence that man's pre-hominid ancestors might well have been feral killers whose evolutionary success can be attributed to this capacity.

If the highest values in a culture insist that man must subdue the earth and that this is his moral duty, it is certain that he will in time acquire the powers to accomplish that injunction. It is not that man has produced evidence for his exclusive divinity, but only that he has developed those powers that permit the fulfillment of his aggressive destructive dreams. He now can extirpate great realms of life: he is the single agent of evolutionary regression.

In times long past, when man represented no significant power to change nature, it mattered little to the world what views he held. Today, when he has emerged as potentially the most destructive force in nature and its greatest exploiter, it matters very much indeed. One looks to see whether with the acquisition of knowledge and powers the western attitudes to nature and to man in nature have changed. But for all of modern science it is still pre-Copernican man whom we confront. He retains the same implicit view of exclusive divinity, man apart from nature, dominant, exhorted to subdue the earth—be he Jew, Christian or agnostic.

Yet surely this is an ancient deformity, an old bile of vengeance that we can no longer tolerate. This view neither approximates reality nor does it help us towards our objectives of survival and evolution. One longs for a world psychiatrist who could assure the patient that expressions of his cultural inferiority are no longer necessary or appropriate. Man is now emancipated, he can stand erect among the creatures. His ancient vengeance, a product of his resentment at an earlier insignificance, is obsolete. The exercise of his great destructive powers are less worthy of adulation than creative skills, but they are enough for the moment to assuage the yearnings for primacy so long denied. From his position of destructive eminence he can now look to his mute partners and determine who they are, what they are, what they do, and realistically appraise the system within which he lives—his role, his dependencies—and reconstitute a cosmography that better accords with the world he experiences and which sustains him.

For me the indictment of city, suburb, and countryside becomes comprehensible in terms of the attitudes to nature that society has and does espouse. These environmental degradations are the inevitable consequence of such views. It is not incongruous but inevitable that the most beautiful landscapes and the richest farmlands should be less highly valued than the most scabrous slum and loathsome roadside stand. Inevitably an anthropocentric society will choose tomato stakes as a higher utility than the priceless and irreplaceable redwoods they have supplanted.

Where you find a people who believe that man and nature are indivisible, and that survival and health are contingent upon an understanding of nature and her processes, these societies will be very different from ours, as will be their towns, cities and landscapes. The hydraulic civilizations, the good farmer through time, the vernacular city builders have all displayed this acuity. But it is in the traditional society of Japan that the full integration of this view is revealed. That people, as we know, has absorbed a little of the best of the West and much of the worst while relinquishing accomplishments that we have not yet attained and can only envy.

In that culture there was sustained an agriculture at once incredibly productive and beautiful, testimony to an astonishing acuity to nature. This perception is reflected in a language rich in descriptive power in which the nuances of natural processes, the tilth of the soil, the dryness of wind, the burgeoning seed, are all precisely describable. The poetry of this culture is rich and succinct, the graphic arts reveal the landscape as the icon. Architecture, village and town building use natural materials directly with stirring power, but it is garden making that is the unequaled art form of this society. The garden is the metaphysical symbol of society in Tao, Shinto and Zen—man in nature.

Yet this view is not enough: man has fared less well than nature here. The jewel of the western tradition is the insistence upon the uniqueness of the individual and the preoccupation with justice and compassion. The Japanese medieval feudal view has been casual to the individual human life and rights. The western assumption of superiority has been achieved at the expense of nature. The oriental harmony of man-nature has been achieved at the expense of the individuality of man. Surely a united duality can be achieved by accounting for man as a unique individual rather than as a species, man in nature.

Let us by all means honor the attribution of dignity, even divinity, to man. But do we need to destroy nature to justify man—or even to obtain God's undivided attention? We can only be enlarged by accepting the reality of history and seeing ourselves in a non-human past, our survival contingent upon non-human processes. The acceptance of this view is not only necessary for the emancipation of western man, it is essential for the survival of all men.

If the Orient is the storehouse of the art of naturalism, it is the West that is the repository of anthropocentric art. It is a great if narrow inheritance, a glorious wealth of music and painting, sculpture and architecture. The Acropolis and Saint Peter, Autun and Beauvais, Chartres and Chambord, Ely and Peterborough—all speak of the divinity of man. But when the same views are extended and used as the structure for urban form, their illusory basis is revealed. The cathedral as the stage for a dialogue between man and God is admirable as a metaphysical symbol. When the supremacy of man is expressed in the form of the city, one seeks the evidence to support this superiority and finds only an assertion. Moreover, the insistence upon the divinity of man over nature has as its companion the insistence in the divine supremacy of some man over all men. It requires a special innocence to delight in the monumental accomplishments of the Renaissance cities, notably Rome and Paris, without appreciating that the generating impulses were more authoritarian than humanitarian—authoritarian towards nature and man.

If we lower the eyes from the wonderful, strident but innocent assertions of man's supremacy, we can find another tradition, more pervasive than the island monuments, little responsive to the grand procession of architectural styles. This is the vernacular tradition. The empiricist may not know first principles, but he has observed relations between events—he is not a victim of dogma. The farmer is the prototype. He prospers only insofar as he understands the land and by his management maintains its bounty. So too with the man who builds. If he is perceptive to the processes of nature, to materials and to forms, his creations will be appropriate to the place; they will satisfy the needs of social process and shelter, be expressive and endure. As indeed they have, in the hill towns of Italy, the island architecture of Greece, the medieval communities of France and the Low Countries and, not least, the villages of England and New England.

Two widely divergent views have been discussed, the raucous anthropocentrism which insists upon the exclusive divinity of man, his role of dominion and subjugation on one hand, and the oriental view of man submerged in nature on the other. Each view has distinct advantages, both have adaptive value. Are the benefits of each mutually exclusive? I think not; but in order to achieve the best of both worlds it is necessary to retreat from polar extremes. There is indisputable evidence that man exists in nature; but it is important to recognize the uniqueness of the individual and thus his especial opportunities and responsibilities.

If the adaptation of the western view towards this more encompassing attitude required the West to accept Tao, Shinto or Zen, there would be little hope for any transformation. However, we have seen that the vernacular of the West has many similarities to the products of oriental pantheism. There is another great bridge, the eighteenth-century English landscape tradition. This movement originated in the poets and writers of the period, from whom developed the conception of a harmony of man and nature. The landscape image was derived from the painters of the Campagna—Claude Lorrain. Salvator Rosa and Poussin. It was confirmed in a new aesthetic by the discovery of the Orient and on these premises transformed England from a poverty-stricken and raddled land to that beautiful landscape that still is visible today. This is a valid western tradition, it presumes a unity of man and nature, it was developed empirically by a few landscape architects, it accomplished a most dramatic transformation, it has endured. Yet the precursory understanding of natural processes that underlay it was limited. A better source is that uniquely western preoccupation, science.

Surely the minimum requirement today for any attitude to man-nature is that it approximate reality. One could reasonably expect that if such a view prevailed, not only would it affect the value system, but also the expressions accomplished by society.

Where else can we turn for an accurate model of the world and ourselves but to science? We can accept that scientific knowledge is incomplete and will forever be so, but it is the best we have and it has that great merit, which religions lack, of being self-correcting. Moreover, if we wish to understand the phenomenal world, then we will reasonably direct our questions to those scientists who are concerned with this realm—the natural scientists. More precisely, when our preoccupation is with the interaction of organisms and environment—and I can think of no better description for our concern—then we must turn to ecologists, for that is their competence.

We will agree that science is not the only mode of perception—that the poet, painter, playwright and author can often reveal in metaphor that which science is unable to demonstrate. But, if we seek a workman's creed which approximates reality and can be used as a model of the world and ourselves, then science does provide the best evidence.

From the ecological view one can see that, since life is only transmitted by life, then, by living, each one of us is physically linked to the origins of life and thus—literally, not metaphorically—to all life. Moreover, since life originated from matter then, by living, man is physically united back through the evolution of matter to the primeval hydrogen. The planet Earth has been the one home for all of its processes and all of its myriad inhabitants since the beginning of time, from hydrogen to men. Only the bathing sunlight changes. Our phenomenal world contains our origins, our history, our milieu; it is our home. It is in this sense that ecology (derived from *oikos*) is the science of the home.

George Wald once wrote facetiously that "it would be a poor thing to be an atom in a Universe without physicists. And physicists are made of atoms. A physicist is the atom's way of knowing about atoms."[2] Who knows what atoms yearn to be, but we are their progeny. It would be just as sad to be an organism in a universe without ecologists, who are themselves organisms. May not the ecologist be the atom's way of learning about organisms—and ours?

The ecological view requires that we look upon the world, listen and learn. The place, creatures and men were, have been, are now and are in the process of becoming. We and they are here now, co-tenants of the phenomenal world, united in its origins and destiny.

As we contemplate the squalid city and the pathetic subdivision, suitcase agriculture and the cynical industrialist, the insidious merchant, and the product of all these in the necklace of megalopoles around the continent, their entrails coalescing, we fervently hope that there is another way. There is. The ecological view is the essential component in the search for the face of the land of the free and the home of the brave. This work seeks to persuade to that effect. It consists of borrowings from the thoughts and dreams of other men, forged into a workman's code—an ecological manual for the good steward who aspires to art.

—*Design with Nature* (1969)

Notes

1. See Leo Srole et al., *Mental Health in the Metropolis: The Midtown Manhattan Study* (New York: McGraw-Hill, 1962).
2. George Wald in *The Fitness of the Environment*, by Lawrence J. Henderson (Beacon Press, Boston, Massachusetts, 1958), p. xxiv.

Bibliography

References to periodicals are given in full except for the following abbreviations:

JAAC	*The Journal of Aesthetics and Art Criticism*
JAE	*The Journal of Aesthetic Educaiton*
BJA	*British Journal of Aesthetics*
J. Phil.	*The Journal of Philosophy*
PAS	*Proceedings of the Aristotelian Society*
Phil. R.	*Philosophical Review*
Phil. and Phen. Res.	*Philosophy and Phenomenological Research*

BIBLIOGRAPHICAL SOURCES

Albert, Ethel M., and Clyde Kluckhohn. *A Selected Bibliography on Values, Ethics and Esthetics in the Behavioral Sciences and Philosophy, 1935–1958.* New York: Free Press, 1959.

Beardsley, Monroe C. *Aesthetics.* New York: Harcourt, 1958 (bibliographical notes at the end of each chapter).

———. *Aesthetics from Classical Greece to the Present.* New York: Macmillan, 1965 (bibliography of the history of esthetics).

Bibliographic Index: A Cumulative Bibliography of Bibliographies. Bronx, N.Y.: Wilson, 1937–present (see "Esthetics" in each volume).

Dickie, George, and R. J. Sclafani. *Aesthetics: A Critical Anthology.* New York: St. Martin's, 1977 (extensive bibliography).

Duncan, Elmer H. and others. *Selective Current Bibliography for Aesthetics and Related Fields* (published annually in JAAC 1941–1972).

Hammond, William. *A Bibliography of Aesthetics and the Philosophy of the Fine Arts from 1900 to 1932.* New York: McKay, 1934.

Journal of Aesthetics and Art Criticism: Index, Volumes 1 through 35, Philadelphia, 1978.

Kiell, Norman. *Psychiatry and Psychology in the Visual Arts and Aesthetics: A Bibliography.* Madison: University of Wisconsin Press, 1965.

Lucas, E. Louise. *Art Books: A Basic Bibliography of the Fine Arts.* Greenwich, Conn.: New York Graphic Society, 1968.

Paperbound Books in Print. New York, published annually. Many of the books listed in the present bibliography are available in paperbound editions.

Philosopher's Index. Bowling Green, Ohio (lists articles in all major philosophical journals).

Shields, Alan. *A Bibliography of Bibliographies in Aesthetics.* San Diego: San Diego State University Press, 1975 (recommended).

Tillman, Frank A., and Steven M. Cahn, eds. *Philosophy of Art and Aesthetics.* New York: Harper & Row, 1969 (extensive bibliography).

History of Esthetics

Adams, Hazard, ed. *Critical Theory Since Plato*. New York: Harcourt, 1971 (includes bibliography).

Beardsley, Monroe C. *Aesthetics from Classical Greece to the Present*. New York: Macmillan, 1966.

Bosanquet, Bernard. *A History of Aesthetics*. New York: Meridian, 1957.

Gilbert, Katherine E., and Helmut Kuhn. *A History of Esthetics*. New York: Dover, 1972 (revised and enlarged edition).

Gombrich, E. H. *In Search of Cultural History*. New York: Oxford, 1969.

Kristeller, Paul O. "The Modern System of the Arts." *Journal of the History of Ideas* 12 (1951) and 13 (1952).

Listowel, Earl of. *Modern Aesthetics: An Historical Introduction*. London: G. Allen, 1967.

Osborne, Harold. *Aesthetics and Art Theory: An Historical Introduction*. New York: Dutton, 1970.

Saisselin, Remy G. "Critical Reflections on the Origins of Modern Aesthetics." BJA 4 (1964).

Tatarkiewicz, Wladyslaw. *History of Aesthetics*, 3 vols. New York: Humanities Press, 1971–1974.

Venturi, Lionello. *History of Art Criticism*. New York: Dutton, 1936.

Wellek, Rene. *A History of Modern Criticism*, 5 vols. New Haven, Conn.: Yale University Press, 1955, 1966 (includes bibliography).

Wimsatt, William K., and Cleanth Brooks. *Literary Criticism: A Short History*. New York: Knopf, 1957.

Chapter 1: Imitation and Imagination

Imitation—The Relation of Art to Nature

Appleton, Jay. *The Experience of Landscape*. London: Wiley, 1975.

Auerbach, Erich. *Mimesis*. Princeton, N.J.: Princeton University Press, 1953.

Blanshard, Frances. *Retreat from Likeness in the Theory of Painting*. New York: Columbia University Press, 1949.

Butcher, S. H. *Aristotle's Theory of Poetry and Fine Art*. New York: Macmillan, 1923.

Clark, Kenneth. *Landscape into Art*. New York: Harper & Row, 1976.

Collingwood, R. G. *The Principles of Art*. Oxford: Clarendon, 1938, Chap. 3.

Coomaraswamy, Ananda. *The Transformation of Nature in Art*. Cambridge, Mass.: Harvard University Press, 1934.

Gass, William H. *Fiction and the Figures of Life*. New York: Knopf, 1970.

Gilson, Étienne. *Painting and Reality*. New York: Pantheon, 1957.

Gombrich. E. H. *Art and Illusion*, 2d ed. New York: Pantheon, 1961.

———. *Meditations on a Hobby Horse and Other Essays on the Theory of Art*.

———. *The Heritage of Appeles*. Ithaca, N. Y.: Cornell University Press, 1976.

Goodman, Nelson. *Languages of Art*. Indianapolis: Bobbs-Merrill, 1968, Chap. I. New York: Phaidon, 1963.

Gregory, R. L., and Ernst Gombrich, eds. *Illusion in Nature and Art*. London: Duckworth, 1973.

Harris, N. G. E. "Goodman's Account of Representation." JAAC 31 (1973).

Hepburn, Ronald W. "Aesthetic Appreciation of Nature." BJA 3 (1963).

Langer, Susanne K. *Problems of Art*. New York: Scribner, 1957, Chap. 5.

———. *Mind: An Essay on Human Feelings*. Baltimore: Johns Hopkins Press, Vol. I (1967), Vol. II (1972).

Lovejoy, Arthur O. "'Nature' as Aesthetic Norm." *Modern Language Notes* 42 (1927).

Manns, James W. "Representation, Relativism and Resemblance." BJA 11 (1971).

Maritain, Jacques. *Art and Scholasticism*. New York: Scribner, 1930.

———. *Creative Intuition in Art and Poetry*. New York: Pantheon, 1953.

McKeon, Richard P. "Literary Criticism and the Concept of Imitation in Antiquity." *Modern Philology* 34 (1936).

Morawski, Stefan. *Inquiries into the Fundamentals of Aesthetics*. Cambridge, Mass.: M.I.T. Press, 1974. Chaps. 6 and 7.

Nahm, Milton C. *Aesthetic Experience and its Presuppositions*. New York: Harper & Row, 1946, Part I.

Olson, Elder, ed. *Aristotle's Poetics and English Literature*. Chicago: University of Chicago Press, 1965.

Pitkänen, Risto. "The Resemblance View of Pictorial Representation." BJA 16 (1976).

Rader, Melvin. "The Factualist Fallacy in Aesthetics." JAAC 28 (1970).

——— and Bertram Jessup. *Art and Human Values*. Englewood Cliffs, N.J.: Prentice-Hall, 1976, Chap. 7.

Read, Herbert, *Education through Art*, 3d ed. New York: Pantheon, Chap. 1.

Richter, Paul. "On Professor Gombrich's Model of Schema and Correction." BJA 16 (1976).

Rose, Mary Carman. "Nature as an Aesthetic Concept." BJA 16 (1976).

Todd, G. F. "On Visual Representation." BJA 15 (1975).

Trapp, Frank Anderson. "The Emperor's Nightingale: Some Aspects of Mimesis." *Critical Inquiry* 4 (1977).

Walton, Kendall L. "Languages of Art: An Emendation." *Philosophical Studies* 22 (1971).

———. "Pictures and Make Believe." *Phil. R.* 82 (1973).

———. "Fearing Fictions." *J. Phil.* 75 (1978).

Whittick, Arnold. "Mimesis, Abstraction and Perception." *Philosophy* 52 (1977).

Wollheim, Richard. "Representation: The Philosophical Contribution to Psychology." *Critical Inquiry* 3 (1977).

Zemach, Eddy. "Description and Depiction." *Mind* 84 (1975).

Imagination and Creativity

Alexander, Samuel. *Beauty and Other Forms of Value*. London: Macmillan, 1933, Chap. 4.

———. "Artistic Creation and Cosmic Creation." *Philosophical and Literary Pieces*. London: Macmillan, 1940.

Anderson, Harold H. *Creativity and Its Cultivation*. New York: Harper & Row, 1959.

Andrews, Michael, ed. *Creativity and Psychological Health*. Syracuse, N.Y.: Syracuse University Press, 1961.

Arieti, Silvano. *Creativity: The Magic Synthesis*. New York: Basic Books, 1976.

Arnheim, Rudolf. *Picasso's Guernica: The Genesis of a Painting*. Berkeley, Calif.: University of California Press, 1962.

Beardsley, Monroe. "On the Creation of Art." JAAC 3 (1965).

Beloff, John. "Creative Thinking in Art and Science." BJA 10 (1970).

Blocker, H. Gene. "Another Look at Aesthetic Imagination." JAAC 30 (1972).

Brinker, Menachem. "Aesthetic Illusion." JAAC 36 (1977).

Brownowski, Jacob. *The Origins of Knowledge and Imagination*. New Haven, Conn.: Yale University Press, 1978.

Casey, Edward S. "Imagination: Imaging and the Image." *Phil. and Phen. Res.* 31 (1971).
———. *Imagining: A Phenomenological Study.* Bloomington, Ind.: Indiana University Press, 1976.
Collingwood, R. G. *The Principles of Art.* Oxford: Clarendon, 1938, pp. 125–151, 195–280.
Dessoir, Max. *Aesthetics and Theory of Art.* Detroit: Wayne State University Press, 1970, Chap. 5.
Ecker, David. "The Artistic Process as Qualitative Problem Solving." JAAC 21 (1963).
Getzels, J., and C. Getzels. *The Creative Vision.* London: Wiley, 1976.
Ghiselin, Brewster, ed. *The Creative Process.* Berkeley, Calif.: University of California Press, 1952.
Gotshalk, D. W. *Art and the Social Order,* 2d ed. New York: Dover, 1962, Chap. 3.
———. "Creativity." In Ralph A. Smith (ed.), *Aesthetic Concepts and Education.* Urbana, Ill.: University of Illinois Press, 1970.
Greene, Maxine. "Imagination." In Ralph A. Smith (ed.), *Aesthetic Concepts and Education.* Urbana, Ill.: University of Illinois Press, 1970.
Guggenheimer, Richard. *Creative Vision in Artist and Audience.* New York: Harper & Row, 1950.
Hardeson, O. B., ed. *The Quest for Imagination.* Cleveland: Press of Case Western Reserve University, 1971.
Harding, Rosamond E. M. *An Anatomy of Inspiration.* New York: Barnes & Noble, 1967.
Hausmann, Carl R. *A Discourse on Novelty and Creation.* The Hague, Netherlands: Martinus Nijhoff, 1975.
Hepburn, Ronald. "Poetry and Concrete Imagination." BJA 12 (1972).
Hoagland, John. "Originality and Aesthetic Value." BJA 16 (1976).
Ishiguro, Hideko. "Imagination." In Bernard Williams and Alan Montefiore (eds.), *British Analytical Philosophy.* New York: Humanities Press, 1966.
Katchadourian, Haig. "The Creative Process in Art." BJA 17 (1977).
Koestler, Arthur. *Insight and Outlook.* New York: Macmillan, 1949.
———. *The Act of Creation.* New York: Macmillan, 1965.
Langer, Susanne K. *Feeling and Form.* New York: Scribner, 1953, Chap. 4.
———. *Problems of Art.* New York: Scribner, 1957, Chap. 4.
Lee, H. B. "The Creative Imagination." *Psychoanalytic Quarterly* 18 (1949).
Lowenfeld, Victor. *The Nature of Creative Activity,* 3d ed. New York: Harcourt, 1957.
Lowes, John Livingston. *The Road to Xanadu.* Boston: Houghton Mifflin, 1927.
Maitland, Jeffrey. "Creativity" JAAC 34 (1976).
Malraux, André. *The Psychology of Art.* New York: Pantheon, 1949.
Morris, Bertram. *The Aesthetic Process.* Evanston, Ill.: Northwestern University Press, 1943.
Nahm, Milton C. *The Artist as Creator.* Baltimore: Johns Hopkins Press, 1956.
———. *Genius and Creativity.* New York: Harper & Row, 1956.
Norton, Richard. "What is Virtuality?" JAAC 30 (1972).
Osborne, Harold. "Inspiration." BJA 17 (1977).
Pole, David. "Art, Imagination and Mr. Scruton." BJA 16 (1976).
Read, Herbert. *Education Through Art,* 3d ed. New York: Pantheon, 1958.
———. *The Forms of Things Unknown.* London: Faber, 1960.
Richards, I. A. *Coleridge on Imagination.* New York: Harcourt, 1935.
Rothenberg, Albert, and Carl R. Hausmann. *The Creativity Question.* Durham, N.C.: Duke University Press, 1976.

Sartre, Jean-Paul. *The Psychology of Imagination.* New York: Philosophical Library, 1948.
———. *Imagination: A Psychological Critique.* Ann Arbor, Mich.: University of Michigan Press, 1962.
Scruton, Roger. *Art and Imagination.* London: Methuen, 1974.
Shapiro, Edna. "Toward a Developmental Perspective on the Creative Process." JAE 9 (1975).
Smith, Paul, ed. *Creativity.* New York: Hastings, 1959.
Storr, Anthony. *The Dynamics of Creation.* Harmondsworth, Eng.: Penguin, 1976.
Tomas, Vincent. "Creativity in Art." *Phil. R.* 67 (1958).
———, ed. *Creativity in the Arts.* Englewood Cliffs, N.J.: Prentice-Hall, 1964.
Vernon, P. E., ed. *Creativity.* Baltimore: Johns Hopkins Press, 1971.
Warnock, Mary, *Imagination.* Berkeley, Calif.: University of California Press, 1976.
Woolf, Virginia. *Mr. Bennett and Mrs. Brown.* London: Hogarth, 1924.

Chapter 2: Emotion

Emotion and Feeling in Art

Aldrich, Virgil C. "Beauty as Feeling." *Kenyon Review* 1 (1939).
Baensch, Otto. "Art and Feeling." In Susanne K. Langer (ed.), *Reflections on Art.* Baltimore: Johns Hopkins Press, 1958.
Bates, Stanley. "Tolstoy Evaluated: Tolstoy's Theory of Art." In George Dickie and R. J. Sclafani (eds.), *Aesthetics: A Critical Anthology.* New York: St. Martin's, 1977.
Benson, John. "Emotion and Expression." *Phil. R.* 76 (1967).
Britton, Karl. "Feelings and Their Expression." *Philosophy* 32 (1957).
Ducasse, Curt J. *Art, the Critics, and You.* Indianapolis: Bobbs-Merrill, 1955.
———. *The Philosophy of Art,* 2d ed. New York: Dover, 1963.
Garvin, Lucius. "An Emotionalist Critique of 'Artistic Truth.'" *J. Phil.* 43 (1946).
Green, O. H. "The Expression of Emotion." *Mind* 79 (1970).
Hampshire, Stuart. *Feeling and Expression.* London: Lewis, 1961.
Hare, Peter H. "Feeling, Imaging, and Expression Theory." JAAC 30 (1972).
Maude, Aylmer, ed. *Tolstoy on Art.* London: Oxford, 1924.
Morris-Jones, Huw. "The Language of Feelings." BJA 2 (1962).
Nahm, Milton C. *Aesthetic Experience and Its Presuppositions.* New York: Harper & Row, 1946, Part III.
Pepper, Stephen C. *Principles of Art Appreciation.* New York: Harcourt, 1949, Chap. 6.
Reid, Louis Arnaud. "Feeling and Understanding." In Ralph A. Smith (ed.), *Aesthetic Concepts and Education.* Urbana, Ill.; University of Illinois Press, 1940.
———. "Feeling and Aesthetic Knowing." JAE 10 (1976).
———. "Feeling, Thinking, Knowing." PAS 17 (1977).
Stolnitz, Jerome. *Aesthetics and Philosophy of Art Criticism.* Boston: Houghton Mifflin, 1960, Chap. 7.
Tilghman, Benjamin R. *The Expression of Emotion in the Visual Arts.* The Hague, Netherlands: Martinus Nijhoff, 1970.
Todd, George F. "Expression without Feeling." JAAC 30 (1972).
Tomas, Vincent. "Ducasse on Art and Its Appreciation." *Phil. and Phen. Res.* 13 (1952).

Must Art Create Beauty?

Bosanquet, Bernard. *Three Lectures on Aesthetics.* Indianapolis: Bobbs-Merrill, 1963, Lecture III.

Carmichael, Peter A. "The Sense of Ugliness." JAAC 30 (1972).
Ducasse, Curt J. "What Has Beauty to Do with Art?" *J. Phil.* 25 (1928).
Gotshalk, D. W. "Art and Beauty." *Monist* 41 (1931).
Henderson, G. P. "The Concept of Ugliness." BJA 6 (1963).
Montague, W. P. "Beauty is Not All." In W. P. Montague, *The Ways of Things.* New York: Prentice-Hall, 1940.
Stolnitz, Jerome. "On Ugliness in Art." *Phil. and Phen. Res.* 11 (1950).
———. "Ugliness." In Paul Edwards (ed.), *Encyclopedia of Philosophy,* Vol. 8, New York: Macmillan and Free Press, 1968 (brief bibliography).

CHAPTER 3: INTUITION-EXPRESSION

Aiken, Henry. "Art as Expression and Surface." JAAC 4 (1945).
Bergson, Henri. *Laughter: An Essay on the Meaning of the Comic.* New York: Macmillan, 1911.
———. *The Creative Mind.* New York: Philosophical Library, 1946.
Bosanquet, Bernard. "Croce's Aesthetic." *Mind* 29 (1920).
Bouwsma, O. K. "The Expression Theory of Art." In Max Black (ed.), *Philosophical Analysis.* Ithaca, N. Y.: Cornell University Press, 1950.
Brown, Merle E. *Neo-Idealistic Aesthetics: Croce, Gentile, Collingwood.* Detroit: Wayne State University Press, 1966.
Carritt, E. F. *The Theory of Beauty.* London: Methuen, 1928, Chap. 8.
———. "Croce and His Aesthetic." *Mind* 62 (1953).
Cary, Joyce. *Art and Reality.* New York: Harper & Row, 1958.
Collingwood, R. G. *The Principles of Art.* Oxford: Clarendon, 1938.
———. *Essays in the Philosophy of Art.* Bloomington, Ind.: University of Indiana Press, 1964.
Croce, Benedetto. *The Essence of Aesthetics.* London: Heinemann, 1921.
———. *Aesthetic as Science of Expression and General Linguistic,* 2d ed. London: Macmillan, 1922.
———. *Guide to Aesthetics.* Indianapolis: Bobbs-Merrill, 1965.
Dewey, John. *Art as Experience.* New York: Putnam, 1934, 1962, Chaps. 4 and 5.
Donagan, Alan. "The Croce–Collingwood Theory of Art." *Philosophy* 33 (1958).
———. *The Later Philosophy of R. G. Collingwood.* Oxford: Clarendon, 1962.
Ducasse, Curt J. *The Philosophy of Art.* New York: Dover, 1963, Chap. 3.
Gallie, W. B. "The Function of Philosophical Aesthetics." *Mind* 57 (1948).
Gilbert, Katharine E. "The One and the Many in Croce's Aesthetic." In Katharine E. Gilbert, *Studies in Recent Aesthetics.* Chapel Hill: University of North Carolina Press, 1927.
Gotshalk, D. W. "Aesthetic Expression." JAAC 13 (1954).
Heidegger, Martin. "The Origin of the Work of Art." In Albert Hofstadter and Richard Kuhns (eds.), *Philosophies of Art and Beauty.* New York: Modern Library, 1964.
Hofstadter, Albert. "Art and Spiritual Validity." JAAC 22 (1963).
Hospers, John, "The Concept of Artistic Expression." PAS 55 (1954–1955).
———. "The Croce–Collingwood Theory of Art." *Philosophy* 31 (1956).
———, ed. *Artistic Expression.* New York: Appleton, 1971.
Khatchadourian, Haig. "The Expression Theory of Art." JAAC 23 (1965).
Lake, Beryl. "A Study of the Irrefutability of Two Aesthetic Theories." In William Elton (ed.), *Aesthetics and Language.* Oxford: Blackwell, 1954.
Mayo, Bernard. "Art, Language, and Philosophy in Croce." *Philosophical Quarterly* 5 (1955).

Morawski, Stefan. *Inquiries into the Fundamentals of Aesthetics*. Cambridge, Mass.: M.I.T. Press, 1974, Chap. 5.

Nahm, Milton C. "The Philosophy of Aesthetic Expression: The Crocean Hypothesis." JAAC 13 (1955).

Orsini, G. N. G. "Theory and Practice in Croce's Aesthetics." JAAC 13 (1955).

Osborne, Harold. *Aesthetics and Criticism*. London: Routledge, 1955, Chap. 7.

Pantanker, R. B. "What Does Croce Mean by 'Expression'?" BJA 2 (1962).

Santayana, George. "Croce's Aesthetics." In George Santayana, *The Idler and His Works*. New York: Braziller, 1957.

Seerveld, Calvin G. *Benedetto Croce's Earlier Aesthetic Theories and Literary Criticism*. Kampen, Netherlands: Kok, 1958.

Sircello, Guy. "Perceptual Acts and the Pictorial Arts: A Defense of Expression Theory." *J. Phil.* 62 (1965).

———. *Mind and Art: An Essay on the Varieties of Expression*. Princeton, N.J.: Princeton University Press, 1972.

Stolnitz, Jerome. *Aesthetics and Philosophy of Art Criticism*. Boston: Houghton Mifflin, 1960, Chap. 10.

Tomas, Vincent A. "The Concept of Expression in Art." In Joseph Margolis (ed.), *Philosophy Looks at the Arts*. New York: Scribner, 1962.

Tormey, Alan. *The Concept of Expression*. Princeton: Princeton University Press, 1971.

Wimsatt, William K., and Cleanth Brooks. *Literary Criticism: A Short History*. New York: Knopf, 1957, Chap. 23 (on Croce).

Wollheim, Richard. *Art and Its Objects*. New York: Harper & Row, 1968, Sections 22, 23, and 45–52.

———. "On Expression and Expressionism." *Revue Internationale de Philosophie* 18 (1964).

———. Expression." In *Royal Institute of Philosophy Lectures, Vol. I: The Human Agent*. New York: St. Martin's, 1968.

Chapter 4: Imaginative Satisfaction of Desire

On Nietzsche

Allison, David B. *The New Nietzsche: Contemporary Styles of Interpretation*. New York: Dell, 1977.

Bridgewater, Patrick. *Nietzsche in Anglosaxony: A study of Nietzsche's Impact on English and American Literature*, Leicester, Eng.: Leicester University Press, 1972.

Copleston, Frederick Charles. *Friedrich Nietzsche: Philosopher of Culture*. New York: Barnes & Noble, 1975.

Danto, Arthur. *Nietzsche as Philosopher*. New York: Macmillan, 1965, Chap. 2.

Hollingdale, R. G. *Nietzsche: The Man and His Philosophy*. Baton Rouge, La.: Louisiana State University Press, 1965.

Jaspers, Karl. *Nietzsche*. Tucson, Ariz.: University of Arizona Press, 1965.

Kaufmann, Walter. *Nietzsche*. Princeton, N.J.: Princeton University Press, 1950, Chap. 4.

———. *From Shakespeare to Existentialism*, rev. ed. New York: Doubleday, 1960 (five chapters on Nietzsche).

Knight, A. H. J. *Some Aspects of the Life and Works of Nietzsche*. London: Cambridge University Press, 1933.

Lea, Frank Alfred. *The Tragic Philosopher*. London: Methuen, 1957.

Morgan, George Allen. *What Nietzsche Means*. Cambridge, Mass.: Harvard University Press, 1941, Chap. 8.

O'Flaherty, James C., Timothy F. Sellner, and Robert M. Helms, eds. *Studies in Nietzsche and the Classical Tradition.* Chapel Hill, N.C.: University of North Carolina Press, 1976.

Pfeffer, Rose. *Nietzsche: Disciple of Dionysus.* Lewisburg, Pa.: Bucknell University Press, 1972.

Rosenstein, Leon. "Metaphysical Foundations of the Theories of Tragedy in Hegel and Nietzsche." JAAC 28 (1970).

Schacht, Richard. "Nietzsche on Art in *The Birth of Tragedy.*" In George Dickie and R. J. Sclafani (eds.), *Aesthetics: A Critical Anthology.* New York: St. Martin's, 1977.

Smith, John E. "Nietzsche: The Conquest of Tragedy Through Art." In John E. Smith, *Reason and God.* New Haven: Yale University Press, 1961.

Solomon, Robert C. *Nietzsche: A Collection of Critical Essays.* New York: Anchor, 1973.

On Freud, Caudwell, and Related Theory

Arieti, Silvano. *Creativity: The Magic Synthesis.* New York: Basic Books, 1976.

Burke, Kenneth. "Freud and the Analysis of Poetry." In Kenneth Burke, *Philosophy of Literary Form,* rev. ed. New York: Random House, 1957.

Caudwell, Christopher. *Illusion and Reality.* New York: International Publishers, 1948.

———. *Romance and Realism.* Princeton, N.J.: Princeton University Press, 1970.

———. *Studies and Further Studies in a Dying Culture.* New York: Monthly Review Press, 1971.

Ehrenzweig, Anton. *The Psychoanalysis of Artistic Vision and Hearing.* New York: Braziller, 1965.

———. *The Hidden Order of Art.* Berkeley, Calif.: University of California Press, 1967.

Fraiberg, Louis. "Freud's Writings on Art." *International Journal of Psychoanalysis* 7 (1956).

Freud, Sigmund. *The Standard Edition of the Complete Psychological Works of Sigmund Freud,* edited by James Strachey, 24 vols. London: Hogarth, 1953–1964 (see especially *Civilization and Its Discontents, Delusion and Dream, Gradiva, The Interpretation of Dreams, Leonardo da Vinci, The Three Caskets,* and *Wit and Its Relation to the Unconscious*).

Fry, Roger. "The Artist and Psycho-Analysis." In Leonard and Virginia Woolf (eds.), *The Hogarth Essays.* London: Hogarth, 1924.

Gombrich, E. H. "Psychoanalysis and the History of Art." In Benjamin Nelson (ed.), *Freud and the Twentieth Century.* New York: Meridian, 1957.

Hauser, Arnold. *The Philosophy of Art History.* New York: Knopf, 1959, Chap. 3.

Hoffman, Frederick J. *Freudianism and the Literary Mind.* Baton Rouge, La.: Louisiana State University Press, 1945.

Hyman, Stanley. "Freud and the Climate of Tragedy." *Partizan Review* 23 (1956).

Jones, Ernest. *Hamlet and Oedipus.* New York: Norton, 1940.

Kris, Ernst. *Psychoanalytic Explorations in Art.* New York: International Universities, 1958.

Lindner, Robert, ed. *Explorations in Psychoanalysis.* New York: Julian Press, 1953, Part III.

Newmann, Erich. *Art and the Creative Unconscious.* Princeton, N. J.: Princeton University Press, 1959.

Phillips, William, ed. *Art and Psychoanalysis.* New York: Criterion, 1957.

Pradhan, S. V. "Caudwell's Theory of Poetry." BJA 17 (1977).

Rank, Otto. *Art and Artist,* New York: Knopf, 1932.

Read, Herbert. "Psychoanalysis and Criticism." In Herbert Read, *Reason and Romanticism,* New York: Russell and Russell, 1963.

———. *Art and Society*. London: Faber, 1937, Chap. 5.

Sachs, Hanns. *The Creative Unconscious.* Cambridge, Mass.: Sci-Art Publishers, 1942.

Schapiro, Meyer. "Leonardo and Freud: An Art-Historical Study." *Journal of the History of Ideas* 17 (1956).

Schneider, Daniel E. *The Psychoanalyst and the Artist.* New York: Farrar, Strauss, 1950.

Stokes, Adrian. *Painting and the Inner World.* London: Tavistock, 1963.

———. "Form in Art: A Psychoanalytic Interpretation." JAAC 18 (1959).

Tennenhouse, Leonard, ed. *The Practice of Psychoanalytic Criticism.* Detroit: Wayne State University Press, 1976.

Trilling, Lionel. "The Legacy of Freud: Literary and Aesthetic." *Kenyon Review* 2 (1940).

———. "Freud and Literature," "Art and Neurosis." In Lionel Trilling, *The Liberal Imagination.* New York: Doubleday, 1945.

Willeford, William. "Psychology and Poetry." In Alex Preminger (ed.), *Princeton Encyclopedia of Poetry and Poetics,* enlarged ed. Princeton, N.J.: Princeton University Press, 1974 (includes bibliography).

Wisdom, J .O. "Psychoanalytic Theories of the Unconscious." In Paul Edwards (ed.), *Encyclopedia of Philosophy.* New York: Macmillan and Free Press, 1967, Vol. 8, pp. 189–191 (includes bibliography).

Wollheim, Richard. "Freud and the Understanding of Art." BJA 10 (1970).

The Concept of Archetypes

Abell, Walter. *The Collective Dream in Art.* Cambridge, Mass.: Harvard University Press, 1957.

Bodkin, Maud. *Archetypal Patterns in Poetry.* London: Oxford, 1934.

———. *Studies of Type-Images in Poetry, Religion, and Philosophy.* London: Oxford, 1951.

Friedman, Norbert. "Archetype." In Alex Preminger (ed.), *Princeton Encyclopedia of Poetry and Poetics,* enlarged ed. Princeton, N.J.: Princeton University Press, 1974 (includes bibliography).

Jung, Carl Gustav. *Modern Man in Search of a Soul.* New York: Harcourt, 1934.

———. *The Archetypes and the Collective Unconscious.* New York: Pantheon, 1959 (*Collected Works,* Vol. 9).

Scott, Wilbur S., ed. *Five Approaches of Literary Criticism.* New York: Collier, 1962.

Chapter 5: Enhancement of Experience

Dewey

Ames, Van Meter. "John Dewey as Aesthetician." JAAC 12 (1935).

Bernstein, Richard J. "Dewey." In Paul Edwards (ed.), *Encyclopedia of Philosophy.* New York: Macmillan and Free Press, Vol. 2, pp. 380–385.

Boydston, Jo A., ed. *Guide to the Works of John Dewey.* Carbondale, Ill.: Southern Illinois University Press, 1970.

Croce, Benedetto. "On the Aesthetics of Dewey," with reply by Dewey. JAAC 6 (1948).

Dewey, John. *Experience and Nature,* rev. ed. LaSalle, Ill.: Open Court, 1929.

———. "Qualitative Thought." In John Dewey, *Philosophy and Civilization.* New York: Minton, Balch, 1931.

———. *Art as Experience.* New York: Putnam, 1934.
———. "Aesthetic Experience as a Primary Phase and as an Artistic Development." JAAC 9 (1950).
——— and others. *Art and Education.* Merion, Pa.: Barnes Foundation, 1934.
Douglas, George H. "A Reconsideration of the Dewey–Croce Exchange." JAAC 28 (1970).
Edman, Irwin. "Dewey and Art." In Sidney Hook (ed.), *John Dewey.* New York: Dial, 1950.
Gauss, Charles E. "Some Reflections on John Dewey's Aesthetics." JAAC 19 (1960).
Geiger, George R. *John Dewey in Perspective.* New York: Oxford, 1958 (stresses Dewey on esthetic experience).
Gotshalk, D. W. "On Dewey's Aesthetics." JAAC 23 (1964).
Grana, Caesar. "John Dewey's Social Art and the Sociology of Art." JAAC 20 (1962).
Kaminsky, Jack. "Dewey's Concept of an Experience." *Phil. and Phen. Res.* 17 (1957).
Mathur, D. C. "Dewey's Aesthetics." *J. Phil.* 63 (1966).
Morris, Bertram: "Dewey's Aesthetics." JAAC 30 (1971).
Pepper, Stephen C. "Some Questions on Dewey's Esthetics." In Paul Schilpp (ed.), *The Philosophy of John Dewey.* Evanston, Ill.: Northwestern University Press, 1939.
———. "The Concept of Fusion in Dewey's Aesthetic Theory." In Stephen C. Pepper, *The Work of Art.* Bloomington, Ind.: Indiana University Press, 1955.
Thomas, M. H. *John Dewey: A Centennial Bibliography.* Chicago: University of Chicago Press, 1962.
Zeltner, Philip M. *John Dewey's Aesthetic Philosophy.* Amsterdam, Netherlands: Gruener, 1975.
Zink, Sidney. "The Concept of Continuity in Dewey's Theory of Esthetics." *Phil. R.* 52 (1943).

Related Theory

Brownell, Baker. *The Human Community.* New York: Harper & Row, 1950, Part X.
Lipman, Matthew. *What Happens in Art.* New York: Appleton, 1967.
Mead, George Herbert. "The Nature of Aesthetic Experience." *International Journal of Ethics* 36 (1925–1926).
Pepper, Stephen C. *Aesthetic Quality.* New York: Scribner, 1938.
———. *The Basis of Criticism in the Arts.* Cambridge, Mass.: Harvard University Press, 1945 (see present volume, Chapter 11).
———. "Art and Experience." *Review of Metaphysics* 12 (1958).
———. "The Development of Contextualistic Aesthetics." *Antioch Review* 28 (1968).
Popper, Frank. *Art, Action and Participation.* New York: New York University Press, 1975.
Rader, Melvin. "Isolationist and Contextualist Esthetics: Conflict and Resolution." *J. Phil.* 44 (1947).

Truth and Virtual Experience

Chiari, Joseph. *Art and Knowledge.* Staten Island, N.Y.: Gordian, 1977.
Hospers, John. *Meaning and Truth in the Arts.* Chapel Hill, N. C.: University of North Carolina Press, 1946.
Isenberg, Arnold. "The Problem of Belief." JAAC 13 (1955).
Martin, G. D. "Language, Truth, and Poetry." Edinburgh, Scot.: Edinburgh University Press, 1975.

Miner, Earl. "That Literature is a Kind of Knowledge." *Critical Inquiry* 2 (1976).
Norton, Richard. "What is Virtuality?" JAAC 30 (1972).
Price, Kingsley B. "Is There Artistic Truth?" *J. Phil.* 46 (1949).
Richards, I. A. *Science and Poetry,* rev. ed. London: Kegan Paul, Trench, Trubner 1935.
Romanos, George D. "On the 'Immediacy' of Art." JAAC 36 (1977).

Chapter 6: Embodiment of Values

Santayana

Ames, Van Meter. "Santayana at One Hundred." JAAC 22 (1964).
Arnett, Willard E. *Santayana and the Sense of Beauty.* Bloomington, Ind.: Indiana University Press, 1955.
———. "Santayana and the Fine Arts." JAAC 16 (1957).
Ashmore, Jerome. *Santayana, Art, and Aesthetics.* Cleveland: Press of Case Western Reserve University, 1966.
Boas, George. "Santayana and the Arts." In Paul Schilpp (ed.), *The Philosophy of George Santayana.* Evanston, Ill.: Northwestern University Press, 1940.
Olafson, Frederick A. "Santayana." In Paul Edwards (ed.), *Encyclopedia of Philosophy.* New York: Macmillan and Free Press, 1967.
Santayana, George. *Reason in Art.* New York: Scribner, 1922.
———. *Interpretations of Poetry and Religion.* New York: Scribner, 1927.
Singer, Irving. *Santayana's Aesthetics.* Cambridge, Mass.: Harvard University Press, 1957.

The Concept of Beauty

Aldrich, Virgil C. "Beauty as Feeling." *Kenyon Review* 1 (1939).
Alexander, Samuel. *Beauty and Other Forms of Value.* London: Macmillan, 1933.
Beardsley, Monroe. *Aesthetics.* New York: Harcourt, 1958, pp. 502–512.
Berndtson, Arthur. *Art, Expression, and Beauty.* New York: Holt, Rinehart and Winston, 1969.
Carritt, E. F. *The Theory of Beauty.* London: Methuen, 1928.
———. *What is Beauty?* Oxford: Clarendon, 1932.
Greene, T. M. "Beauty in Art and Nature." *Sewanee Review* 69 (1961).
Henderson, G. P. "An 'Orthodox' Use of the Term 'Beautiful.'" *Philosophy* 35 (1960).
Jarrett, James L. *The Quest for Beauty.* Englewood Cliffs, N.J.: Prentice-Hall, 1957.
Katkov, G. "The Pleasant and the Beautiful." PAS 40 (1940).
Osborne, Harold. *Theory of Beauty.* London: Routledge, 1952.
Reid, Louis Arnaud. *A Study in Aesthetics.* New York: Macmillan, 1931, Chaps. 5–6, 8, 13, and 14.
Sircello, Guy. *A New Theory of Beauty.* Princeton, N.J.: Princeton University Press, 1975.
Stace, Walter. *The Meaning of Beauty.* London: Richards and Toulmin, 1929.
Stolnitz, Jerome. "'Beauty': Some Stages in the History of an Idea." *Journal of the History of Ideas* 22 (1961).
———. "Beauty." In Paul Edwards (ed.), *Encyclopedia of Philosophy.* New York: Macmillan and Free Press, 1967, Vol. 1, pp. 263–266.
Tatarkiewicz, Wladyslaw. "The Great Theory of Beauty and its Decline." JAAC 31 (1972).

Aesthetic Value in General

Aiken, Henry David. "A Pluralistic Analysis of Aesthetic Value." *Phil. R.* 59 (1950).
Beardsley, Monroe C. *Aesthetics.* New York: Harcourt, 1958, Chap. 10.
———. "The Discrimination of Aesthetic Enjoyment." BJA 3 (1963).
Bruce, John. "Art and Value." BJA 6 (1966).
Child, Arthur. "The Social Historical Relativity of Esthetic Value." *Phil. R.* 52 (1944).
Dessoir, Max. *Aesthetics and the Theory of Art.* Detroit: Wayne State University Press, 1970, Chap. 4 (on the beautiful, sublime, tragic, ugly, and comic).
Ducasse, Curt J. *The Philosophy of Art,* 2d ed. New York: Dover, Chap. 14.
Ekman, Rolf. "Aesthetic Value and the Ethics of Life Affirmation." BJA 3 (1963).
Findlay, J. N. "The Perspicuous and the Poignant: Two Aesthetic Fundamentals." BJA 7 (1967).
Ingarden, Roman. "Artistic and Aesthetic Value." BJA 4 (1964).
Kolnai, Aurel. "On the Concept of the Interesting." BJA 4 (1964).
Lee, Harold Newton. *Perception and Aesthetic Value.* Englewood Cliffs, N.J.: Prentice-Hall, 1938.
Lewis, Clarence Irving. *An Analysis of Knowledge and Valuation.* La Salle, Ill.: Open Court, 1946.
Morawski, Stefan. "Artistic Value." JAE 5 (1971).
Morris, Charles W. "Esthetics and the Theory of Signs." *Journal of Unified Science* 8 (1939) (art as a sign-language of values).
———. "Science, Art, and Technology." *Kenyon Review* 1 (1939).
Rader, Melvin, and Bertram Jessup. *Art and Human Values.* Englewood Cliffs, N.J., Prentice-Hall, 1976.
Reid, Louis Arnaud. *A Study in Aesthetics.* New York: Macmillan, 1931, Chaps. 5, 6, 8, and 11.
———. *Meaning in the Arts.* New York: Humanities Press, 1969, Chap. 11.
Stolnitz, Jerome. "On Aesthetic Valuing and Evaluation." *Phil. and Phen. Res.* 13 (1953).
———. "On Aesthetic Familiarity and Aesthetic Value." *J. Phil.* 53 (1956).
———. *Aesthetics and Philosophy of Art Criticism.* Boston: Houghton Mifflin, 1960, Part V.

CHAPTER 7: THE MATTER OF THE ARTS

The Medium

Alexander, Samuel. *Art and the Material.* Manchester, Eng.: Manchester University Press, 1925.
Bullough, Edward. "Mind and Medium in Art." *British Journal of Psychology* 11 (1920–1921).
Durbin, Jack. "Some Thoughts on the Uniqueness of the Medium." *Personalist* 55 (1974).
Greene, Theodore M. *The Arts and the Art of Criticism.* Princeton, N.J.: Princeton University Press, 1940, Part I.
Hein, Hilde. "Performance as an Aesthetic Category." JAAC 28 (1970).
Hospers, John. "Collingwood and Art Media." *Southwestern Journal of Philosophy* 2 (1971).
McLuhan, Marshall. *Understanding Media.* New York: McGraw-Hill, 1964.
Munro, Thomas. *The Arts and Their Interrelations,* rev. ed. Cleveland: Press of Case Western Reserve University, 1967.

Pauson, Marion L. "Studies in Art Media." *Tulane Studies in Philosophy* 19 (1970).
Weitz, Morris. *Philosophy of the Arts*. Cambridge, Mass.: Harvard University Press, 1950, Chap. 7.

Esthetic Qualities and Sensory Materials

Aiken, Henry David. "Art as Expression and Surface." JAAC 9 (1945).
Clement, W. C. "Quality Orders." *Mind* 65 (1956).
Dewey, John. *Art as Experience*. New York: Putnam, 1934, Chaps. 9–10.
Goodman, Nelson. *The Structure of Appearance*. Cambridge, Mass.: Harvard University Press, 1951, Part III.
Hartshorne, Charles. *The Philosophy and Psychology of Sensation*. Chicago: University of Chicago Press, 1934.
Herring, Frances. "Touch—The Neglected Sense." JAAC 7 (1949).
Kivy, Peter. "Aesthetic Aspects and Aesthetic Qualities." *J. Phil.* 65 (1968).
Lipman, Matthew. *What Happens in Art*. New York: Appleton, 1967, Chaps. 3 and 6.
Moore, Jared S. "The Work of Art and Its Material." JAAC 6 (1948).
Pepper, Stephen C. *Principles of Art Appreciation*. New York: Harcourt, 1949, Part III.
Prall, D. W. *Aesthetic Judgment*. New York: Crowell, 1929.
———. *Aesthetic Analysis*. New York: Crowell, 1936.
Santayana, George. *The Sense of Beauty*. New York: Scribner, 1896, Part II.
Sibley, Frank. "Aesthetic Concepts." *Phil. R.* 68 (1959).
———. "Aesthetics and the Looks of Things." *J. Phil.* 56 (1959).
Stolnitz, Jerome. *Aesthetics and Philosophy of Art Criticism*. Boston: Houghton Mifflin, 1960, Chap. 9.
Ushenko, Andrew P. "Esthetic Immediacy." *J. Phil.* 38 (1941).

The Varied Substance of the Arts

Arnheim, Rudolf. "On the Nature of Photography." *Critical Inquiry* 1 (1974).
Bazin, Andre. *What is Cinema?* Berkeley, Calif.: University of California Press, 1967.
Burnham, Jack. *Beyond Modern Sculpture*. New York: Braziller, 1968.
Carroll, John M. "A Program for Cinema Theory." JAAC 35 (1977).
Cavell, Stanley. *The World Viewed: Reflections on the Ontology of Film*. New York: Viking, 1971.
Cohen, Selma Jeanne. "A Prolegomena to an Aesthetics of Dance." JAAC 21 (1962).
Corrigan, Robert W., and James L. Rosenberg, eds. *The Context and Craft of Drama*. Scranton, Pa.: Chandler Publishing Company, 1964.
Crawford, Donald W. "The Uniqueness of the Medium." *Personalist* 51 (1970) (on film).
Dudley, Andrew W. *Major Film Theories*. New York: Oxford, 1976.
Ellis, Havelock. "The Art of Dancing." In Havelock Ellis, *The Dance of Life*. Boston: Houghton Mifflin, 1923.
Gilbert, Katharine E. "Mind and Medium in the Modern Dance." JAAC 1 (1941).
Hall, James B. and Barry Ulanov, eds. *Modern Culture and the Arts*. New York: McGraw-Hill, 1967 (essays on major arts, television, films, and design).
Jacobus, Lee A., ed. *Aesthetics and the Arts*. New York: McGraw-Hill, 1968 (includes bibliography on major arts).
Martin, F. David. "The Autonomy of Sculpture." JAAC 34 (1976).
Mast, Gerald, and Marshall Cohen, eds. *Film Theory and Criticism*. New York: Oxford, 1974.

Munro, Thomas. *The Arts and Their Interrelations,* rev. ed. Cleveland: Press of Case Western Reserve University, 1967.
Panofsky, Erwin. "Style and Medium in Moving Pictures." *Critique* 1 (1947).
Serridge, Mary, and Adina Armelagos. "The In's and Out's of Dance." JAAC 36 (1977).
Talbot, Daniel, ed. *Film: An Anthology*. Berkeley, Calif.: University of California Press, 1966 (includes bibliography).
Weiss, Paul. *Nine Basic Arts.* Carbondale, Ill.: Southern Illinois University Press, 1961.
Wellek, René, and Austin Warren. *Theory of Literature*. New York: Harcourt, 1956 (includes bibliography).
See titles listed elsewhere in this bibliography for references to architecture, literature, music, industrial design, and so on.

Chapter 8: Expressiveness

Aiken, Henry David. "Some Notes Concerning the Aesthetic and the Cognitive." JAAC 13 (1955).
Arnheim, Rudolf. *Art and Visual Perception.* Berkeley, Calif. University of California Press, 1954.
———. *Entropy and Art: A Study of Disorder and Order.* Berkeley, Calif.: University of California Press, 1969.
———. *Visual Thinking.* Berkeley, Calif:. University of California Press, 1969.
———. *Toward a Psychology of Art: Collected Essays.* Berkeley, Calif.: University of California Press, 1972.
Barfield, Owen. *Poetic Diction: A Study in Meaning.* London: Faber, 1928.
Beardsley, Monroe C. *Aesthetics.* New York: Harcourt, 1958, Chaps. 3 and 5–9.
Berndtson, Arthur. "Semblance, Symbol, and Expression in the Aesthetics of Susanne Langer." JAAC 14 (1956).
———. *Art, Expression, and Beauty.* New York: Holt, Rinehart and Winston, 1969, Chaps. 8, 9, and 11.
Blocker, Gene. "The Meaning of a Poem." BJA 10 (1970).
Boas, George. "The Problem of Meaning in the Arts." *University of California Publications in Philosophy* 25 (1950).
Bufford, Samuel. "Susanne Langer's Two Theories of Art." JAAC 30 (1972).
Carver, G. A. *Aesthetics and the Problem of Meaning.* New Haven, Conn.: Yale University Press, 1952.
Casey, Edward S. "Expression and Communication in Art." JAAC 29 (1971).
Cassirer, Ernst. *An Essay on Man.* New Haven, Conn.: Yale University Press, 1944, Chap. 9.
Foss, Lawrence. "Art as Cognitive." *Philosophy of Science* 38 (1971).
Goodman, Nelson. *Languages of Art.* Indianapolis: Bobbs-Merrill, 1968.
Greene, Theodore M. *The Arts and the Art of Criticism.* Princeton, N.J.: Princeton University Press, 1940, Parts III and IV.
Hansen, Forest. "Langer's Expressive Form." JAAC 27 (1968).
Hare, Peter H. "Feeling, Imaging, and Expression Theory." JAAC 30 (1972).
Harries, Karsten. *The Meaning of Modern Art.* Evanston, Ill.: Northwestern University Press, 1968.
Heidegger, Martin. "The Origin of the Work of Art." In Albert Hofstadter and Richard Kuhns (eds.), *Philosophies of Art and Beauty.* New York: Modern Library, 1964.
———. *Poetry, Language, Thought.* New York: Harper & Row, 1971.

Henle, Mary, ed. *Vision and Artifact.* New York: Springer, 1976 (related to Arnheim's theories).

Hermeren, Goren. *Representation and Meaning in the Visual Arts.* New York: Humanities Press, 1971.

Hofstadter, Albert. *Truth and Art.* New York: Columbia University Press, 1965.

———. *Agony and Epitaph: Man, His Art and His Poetry.* New York: Humanities Press, 1971.

Hungerland, Isabel Creed. "Iconic Signs and Expressiveness." JAAC (1944).

Isenberg, Arnold. *Aesthetics and the Theory of Criticism.* Chicago: University of Chicago Press, 1973 (on meaning, metaphor, and other topics).

Jessup, Bertram. "Meaning Range in the Work of Art." JAAC 12 (1954).

Kaplan, Abraham. "Referential Meaning in the Arts." JAAC 12 (1954).

Langer, Susanne K. *Feeling and Form.* New York: Scribner, 1953.

———. *Problems of Art.* New York: Scribner, 1957.

———. *Philosophic Sketches.* Baltimore: Johns Hopkins Press, 1962.

———. *Mind: An Essay on Human Feeling.* Baltimore: Johns Hopkins Press, 1967, Vol. I, Chap. 7.

———, ed. *Reflections on Art.* Baltimore: Johns Hopkins Press, 1958.

Lewis, C. Day. *The Poet's Way to Knowledge.* Cambridge, Eng.: Cambridge University Press, 1957.

Mew, Peter. "Metaphor and Truth." BJA 11 (1971).

Morgan, Douglas. "Icon, Index, and Symbol in the Visual Arts." *Philosophical Studies* 6 (1955).

Mothersill, Mary. "Is Art a Language?" *J. Phil.* 62 (1965).

Nagel, Ernest. "Review of Langer's *Philosophy in a New Key.*" *J. Phil.* 40 (1943).

———. "A Theory of Symbolic Form." In Ernest Nagel, *Logic Without Metaphysics.* New York: Free Press, 1956.

Nahm, Milton C. *Aesthetic Experience and Its Presuppositions.* New York: Harper & Row, 1946, Chaps. 10–14.

Panofsky, Erwin. *Studies in Iconology.* New York: Oxford, 1939.

———. *Meaning in the Visual Arts.* New York: Doubleday, 1955.

———. *Idea: A Concept in Art.* New York: Harper & Row, 1975.

Perkins, David, and Barbara Leondar, eds. *The Arts and Cognition.* Baltimore: Johns Hopkins Press, 1977.

Raleigh, Henry P. "Art as Communicable Knowledge." JAE 5 (1971).

Read, Herbert. *Icon and Idea: The Function of Art in the Development of Human Consciousness.* Cambridge, Mass.: Harvard University Press, 1955.

Reid, Louis Arnaud. *Meaning in the Arts.* New York: Humanities Press, 1970.

Scholes, Robert. "Toward a Semiotics of Literature." *Critical Inquiry* 4 (1977).

Sircello, Guy. *Mind and Art: An Essay on the Varieties of Expression.* Princeton, N.J.: Princeton University Press, 1972.

Tormey, Alan. *The Concept of Expression.* Princeton, N.J.: Princeton University Press, 1971 (includes bibliography).

Wheelwright, Philip. *Burning Fountain: A Study in the Language of Symbolism.* Bloomington, Ind.: University of Indiana Press, 1968.

Hegel and Tragedy

Bradley, A. C. "Hegel's Theory of Tragedy." *Oxford Lectures on Poetry.* London: Macmillan, 1950.

Butcher, S. H. *Aristotle's Theory of Poetry and Fine Art,* 4th ed. New York: Dover, 1951.

Kaufmann, Walter. *Tragedy and Philosophy.* New York: Doubleday, 1969 (includes bibliography).

———. "Hegel's Ideas About Tragedy." In Warren E. Steinkraus, (ed.), *New Studies in Hegel's Philosophy*. New York: Holt, Rinehart and Winston, 1971.
Osborne, Harold. "The Concept of Tragedy." BJA 15 (1975).
Papanoutsos, E. P. "Aristotelian Katharsis." BJA (1977).
Preminger, Alex, ed. *Princeton Encyclopedia of Poetry and Poetics,* enlarged ed. Princeton, N.J.: Princeton University Press, 1974, pp. 860–866 (includes bibliography).
Quinton, A. M., and Ruby Meager. "Tragedy." PAS Supplement 34 (1960).
Shapiro, Gary. "Hegel's Dialectic of Artistic Meaning." JAAC (1976).
Steinkraus, Warren E., K. L. Schmitz, and J. O'Malley. *Art and Logic in Hegel's Philosophy*. Brighton, Eng.: Harvester, 1978.
Taylor, Charles. *Hegel*. Cambridge, Eng.: Cambridge University Press, 1975, Chap. 17.
Weitz, Morris. "Tragedy." In Paul Edwards (ed.), *Encyclopedia of Philosophy*. New York: Macmillan and Free Press, 1967 (includes bibliography).

Musical Expressiveness

Beardsley, Monroe C. *Aesthetics*. New York: Harcourt, 1958, Chap. 7.
Coker, Wilson. *Music and Meaning*. New York: Free Press, 1972 (includes bibliography).
Epperson, Gordon. *The Musical Symbol*. Ames, Ia.: Iowa State University Press, 1967.
Howard, V. A. "On Musical Expression." BJA 11 (1971).
Howes, F. *Music and Its Meanings*. London: Oxford, 1958.
Kuhns, Richard. "Music as a Representational Art." BJA 18 (1978).
Langer, Susanne K. *Feeling and Form*. New York: Scribner, 1953, Chaps. 7–8.
———, ed. *Reflections on Art*. Baltimore: Johns Hopkins Press, 1958.
Lazlo, Ervin. "Affect and Expression in Music." JAAC 27 (1968).
Leahy, M. P. T. "The Vacuity of Musical Expressionism." BJA 16 (1976).
Lippman, Edward A. *A Humanistic Philosophy of Music*. New York: New York University Press, 1977.
Meyer, Leonard. *Emotion and Meaning in Music*. Chicago: University of Chicago Press, 1956.
———. *Music, the Arts, and Ideas*. Chicago: University of Chicago Press, 1967.
Portnoy, Julius. *Music in the Life of Man*. New York: Holt, Rinehart and Winston, 1963.
Pratt, Carroll. *The Meaning of Music*. New York: Johnson Reprint, 1968 (with a new introduction).
Reid, Louis Arnaud. *Meaning in the Arts*. New York: Humanities Press, 1969, Chaps. 6–10.
Schueller, Herbert. "The Aesthetic Implications of Avant-Garde Music." JAAC 35 (1977).
Zuckerkandl, Victor. *Sound and Symbol*. New York: Pantheon, 1956.
———. *The Sense of Music*. Princeton, N.J.: Princeton University Press, 1959.

Chapter 9: Form

Form in General

Abell, Walter, *Representation and Form*. New York: Scribner, 1936.
Beardsley, Monroe C. *Aesthetics*. New York: Harcourt, 1958, Chaps. 4–6.
Bradley, A. C. "Poetry for Poetry's Sake." In A. C. Bradley, *Oxford Lectures on Poetry*. London: Macmillan, 1950.
Brion, Marcel. "Abstract Art." *Diogenes* 24 (1958).

Bywater, William G. *Clive Bell's Eye.* Detroit: Wayne State University Press, 1975.
Carpenter, Rhys. *The Esthetic Basis of Greek Art,* rev. ed. Bloomington, Ind.: Indiana University Press, 1959 (on fusion of form and subject matter).
Carritt, E. F. "Art without Form?" *Philosophy* 16 (1941).
Collingwood, R. G. "Form and Content in Art." In R. G. Collingwood, *Essays in the Philosophy of Art.* Bloomington, Ind.: Indiana University Press, 1964.
Ekman, Rosalind. "The Paradoxes of Formalism." BJA 10 (1970).
Forster, E. M. "Art for Art's Sake." In E. M. Forster, *Two Cheers for Democracy.* New York: Harcourt, 1951.
Fry, Roger. *Vision and Design.* London: Chatto and Windus, 1920.
———. *Transformations.* London: Chatto and Windus, 1926.
Gotshalk, D. W. *Art and the Social Order,* 2d ed. New York: Dover, 1962, Chap 5.
Greene, Theodore M. *The Arts and the Art of Criticism.* Princeton, N.J.: Princeton University Press, 1940, Part II.
Ingarden, Roman. "The General Question of the Essence of Form and Content." *J. Phil.* 57 (1960).
Jessup, Bertram. "Aesthetic Size." JAAC 9 (1950).
Kepes, Gyorgy, ed. *Structure in Art and Science.* New York: Braziller, 1965.
Lang, Berel. "Significance or Form: The Dilemma of Roger Fry's Aesthetics." JAAC 21 (1962).
Langer, Susanne K. *Feeling and Form.* New York: Scribner, 1953.
———. *Problems of Art.* New York: Scribner, 1957, Chap. 4.
———. *Mind: An Essay on Human Feeling.* Baltimore: Johns Hopkins Press, 1967, Vol. I, Chap. 7.
Lord, Catherine. "Organic Unity Reconsidered." JAAC 22 (1964).
McLaughlin, Thomas M. "Clive Bell's Aesthetic: Tradition and Significant Form." JAAC 35 (1976).
Munro, Thomas. *Form and Style in the Arts.* Cleveland: Press of Case Western Reserve University, 1970.
"On Clive Bell." Special Issue, BJA 5 (1965) (essays by George Dickie, R. K. Elliott, R. Meager, and Herbert Read).
Orsini, G. N. G. *Organic Unity in Ancient and Later Poetics.* Carbondale, Ill.: Southern Illinois University Press, 1975.
Osborne, Harold. "Organic Unity Again." BJA 16 (1976).
———. "Ways of Abstraction." BJA 16 (1976).
Podro, Michael. "Formal Elements and Theories of Modern Art." BJA 6 (1966).
Read, Herbert. *The Origins of Form in Art.* New York: Horizon, 1965 (includes bibliography).
Ritchie, Benbow. "The Formal Structure of the Aesthetic Object." JAAC 3 (1944).
Schaper, Eva. "Significant Form." BJA 1 (1961).
Stechow, Wolfgang. "Problems of Structure in Some Relations between the Visual Arts and Music." JAAC 11 (1953).
Stein, Erwin. *Form and Performance.* New York: Knopf, 1962.
Stokes, Adrian. "Form in Art: A Psychoanalytic Interpretation." JAAC 18 (1959).
Taylor, David G. "The Aesthetic Theories of Roger Fry Reconsidered." JAAC 36 (1977).
Weitz, Morris. *Philosophy of the Arts.* Cambridge, Mass.: Harvard University Press, 1950, Chaps. 1–3.
Whyte, Lancelot Law, ed. *Aspects of Form: A Symposium on Form in Nature and Art.* Bloomington, Ind.: Indiana University Press, 1966.

Style

Ackerman, James S. "A Theory of Style." JAAC 20 (1962).

——— and Rhys Carpenter. *Art and Archeology*. Englewood Cliffs, N.J.: Prentice-Hall, 1963.

Albrecht, Milson C., James H. Barnett, and Mason Grieff, eds. *The Sociology of Art and Literature*. New York: Praeger, 1970, Part I: "Forms and Styles."

Beardsley, Monroe C., and Herbert M. Schueller, eds. *Aesthetic Inquiry*. Belmont, Calif.: Dickinson, 1967 (contains several essays on style).

Boas, George. "Historical Periods." JAAC 11 (1953).

Frank, Paul L. "Historical or Stylistic Periods?" JAAC 13 (1955).

Friedrich, Carl J. "Style as the Principle of Historical Interpretation." JAAC 13 (1955).

Gardner, Howard. "The Development of Sensitivity to Artistic Styles." JAAC 29 (1970).

Gombrich, E. H. "Style." In David L. Sills (ed.), *International Encyclopedia of the Social Sciences*. New York: Macmillan Company and Free Press, 1968, Vol. 15, pp. 352–361.

Hauser, Arnold. *The Philosophy of Art History*. New York: Knopf, 1959, Chap. 4.

Hellman, Geoffrey. "Symbol Systems and Artistic Styles." JAAC 35 (1977).

Hendricks, William O. *Grammars of Style and Styles of Grammar*. Amsterdam, Netherlands: North-Holland Studies in Theoretical Poetics, 1976.

Kroeber, A. L. *Style and Civilization*. Berkeley, Calif.: University of California Press, 1963.

Lucas, F. L. *Style*. New York: Macmillan, 1955.

Miles, Josephine. "Toward a Theory of Style and Change." JAAC 22 (1963).

Munro, Thomas. *Evolution in the Arts*. Cleveland: Press of Case Western Reserve University, 1965.

Sachs, Curt. *The Commonwealth of Art: Style in the Fine Arts, Music and the Dance*. New York: Norton, 1946.

Virden, Phil. "The Social Determinants of Art Styles." BJA 12 (1972).

Zucker, Paul. *Styles in Painting*. New York: Viking, 1950.

Style is also discussed in the works of such art historians as Adama van Scheltema, Franz Boas, Dilthey, Dvorak, Coellen, Focillon, Löwy, Malraux, Nohl, Riegl, Semper, Sypher, Wölfflin, and Worringer.

Form and Function

Berleant Arnold. "Aesthetic Function." In Dale Riepe (ed.), *Phenomenology and Natural Existence*. Albany, N.Y.: State University of New York Press, 1973.

Brown, Theodore M. "Greenough, Paine, Emerson, and the Organic Aesthetic." JAAC 14 (1956).

Crone, Sylvia E. "The Aesthetics of Horatio Greenough." JAAC 24 (1966).

DeZurko, Edward. *Origins of Functionalist Theory*. New York: Columbia University Press, 1957.

Fry, Maxwell. *Art in a Machine Age*. New York: Barnes & Noble, 1969.

Giedion, Siegfried. *Space, Time, and Architecture*. Cambridge, Mass.: Harvard University Press, 1941.

Greene, Herbert. *Mind and Image: An Essay on Art and Architecture*. Lexington, Ky.: University of Kentucky Press, 1976.

Hall, James B., and Barry Ulanov. *Modern Culture and the Arts*. New York: McGraw-Hill, 1967, Section 8.

Jeanneret-Gris, Charles Edouard (Le Corbusier). *Towards a New Architecture*. New York: Praeger, 1970.

Kuhns, Richard. "Art and Machine." JAAC 25 (1967).

Moholy-Nagy, Lazlo. *The New Vision*. New York: Wittenborn, 1964.

Mumford, Lewis. *Art and Technics*. New York: Columbia University Press, 1952.

Nervi, Pier Luigi. *Aesthetics and Technology in Building*. Cambridge, Mass.: Harvard University Press, 1965.
Neutra, Richard. *Survival Through Design*. New York: Oxford, 1954.
Pevsner, Nikolaus. *Pioneers of the Modern Movement: From William Morris to Walter Gropius,* rev. ed. Harmondsworth, Eng.: Penguin, 1960.
———. *The Sources of Modern Architecture and Design*. New York: Praeger, 1968.
Read, Herbert. *Art and Industry*. New York: Horizon Press, 1954.
Torroja, Eduardo. *Philosophy of Structure*. Berkeley, Calif.: University of California Press, 1965.

Chapter 10: The Experiences of the Beholder

Kant on Esthetic Experience

Burch, Robert. "Kant's Theory of Beauty as Ideal Art." In George Dickie and R. J. Sclafani (eds.), *Aesthetics*. New York: St. Martin's, 1976.
Crawford, Donald W. *Kant's Aesthetic Theory*. Madison, Wis.: University of Wisconsin Press, 1974 (includes comprehensive bibliography; listed below are titles that do not appear in this bibliography).
Fisher, John, and Jeffry Maitland. "Subjectivist Turn in Aesthetics: A Critical Analysis of Kant's Theory of Appreciation." *Review of Metaphysics* 27 (1974).
Hofstadter, Albert. "Kant's Aesthetic Revolution." *Journal of Religious Ethics* 3 (1975).
Kemal, Salim. "Presentation and Expression in Kant's Aesthetics." BJA 15 (1975).
Maitland, Jeffry. "Two Senses of Necessity in Kant's Aesthetic Theory." BJA 16 (1976).
Neville, M. R. "Kant's Characterization of Aesthetic Experience." JAAC 33 (1974).
Petock, Stuart Jay. "Kant, Beauty and the Object of Taste." JAAC 32 (1973).
Podro, Michael. *The Manifold in Perception: Theories of Art from Kant to Hildebrand*. Oxford: Clarendon, 1972.

Empathy

Ames, Van Meter. "On Empathy." *Psychological Review* 52 (1943).
Ducasse, Curt J. *The Philosophy of Art*, 2d ed. New York: Dover, 1963, Chap. 10.
Koffka, Kurt. "Problems in the Psychology of Art." In Rhys Carpenter et al., *Art: A Bryn Mawr Symposium*. Bryn Mawr, Pa.: Bryn Mawr College, 1940.
Langfeld, Herbert. *The Aesthetic Attitude*. New York: Harcourt, 1920.
Lee, Vernon. *The Beautiful*. Cambridge, Eng.: Cambridge University Press, 1913.
Lipps, Theodor. "Empathy and Aesthetic Pleasure." In Karl Aschenbrenner and Arnold Isenberg (eds.), *Aesthetic Theories*. Englewood Cliffs, N.J.: Prentice-Hall, 1965.
Listowel, Earl of. *Modern Aesthetics: An Historical Introduction*. London: G. Allen, 1967, Chap. 7.
Main, A. N. "A New Look at Empathy." BJA 9 (1969).
Nahm, Milton C. *Aesthetic Experience and Its Presuppositions*. New York: Harper & Row, 1946, Chap. 16.
Wiseman, Mary Bittner. "Empathetic Identification." *American Philosophical Quarterly* 15 (1978).
Worringer, Wilhelm. *Abstraction and Empathy*. New York: International Universities, 1953.

Distance and Dehumanization

Blocker, H. Gene. "A New Look at Aesthetic Distance." BJA 17 (1977).
Bolton, Gavin M. "Psychical Distance in Acting." BJA 17 (1977).
Booth, Wayne C. "Control of Distance in Jane Austin's *Emma.*" In Wayne C. Booth, *The Rhetoric of Fiction.* Chicago: University of Chicago Press, 1961.
Buber, Martin. "Distance and Relation." In Maurice Friedman (ed.), *The Knowledge of Man.* New York: Harper & Row, 1965.
Budel, Oscar. "Contemporary Theater and Aesthetic Distance." *Publications of the Modern Language Association of America* 76 (1961).
Bullough, Edward. *Aesthetics.* Palo Alto, Calif.: Stanford University Press, 1957.
Casebier, Allan. "The Concept of Psychical Distance." *Personalist* 52 (1971).
Chaudbury, P. J., "Psychical Distance in Indian Aesthetics." JAAC 7 (1948).
Clark, Kenneth. *The Nude.* New York: Pantheon, 1956.
Crossley, D. J. "Aesthetic Attitude: Back in Gear with Bullough." *Personalist* 56 (1975).
Dawson, Sheila. "Distancing as an Aesthetic Principle." *Australasian Journal of Philosophy* 39 (1961).
Dickie, George. "The Myth of the Aesthetic Attitude." *American Philosophical Quarterly* 1 (1964).
———. "Psychical Distance: In a Fog at Sea." BJA 13 (1973).
Frazier, Allie M. "The Problems of Distance in Religious Art." JAAC 31 (1973).
Friedman, James Michael. *Dancer and Spectator: An Aesthetic Distance.* San Francisco: Ballet Monographs, 1976.
Fry, Roger. "Some Questions in Esthetics." In Roger Fry, *Transformations.* London: Chatto and Windus, 1926.
Jarrett, James L. "On Psychical Distance." *Personalist* 52 (1971).
Langfeld, Sydney. *The Aesthetic Attitude.* New York: Harcourt, 1920 (discusses Bullough).
Longman, Lester D. "The Concept of Psychical Distance." JAAC 6 (1947).
Mehlis, George. "The Aesthetic Problem of Distance." In Susanne K. Langer (ed.), *Reflections on Art.* Baltimore: Johns Hopkins Press, 1958.
Michelis, P. A. "Aesthetic Distance and the Charm of Contemporary Art." JAAC 18 (1959).
Ortega y Gasset, José. *The Dehumanization of Art.* Princeton, N. J.: Princeton University Press, 1948.
Pandit, Sueh. "In Defense of Psychical Distance." BJA 16 (1976).
Pepper, Stephen C. "Emotional Distance in Art." JAAC 4 (1946).
Price, Kingsley. "The Truth About Psychical Distance." JAAC 35 (1977).
Weitz, Morris. *Philosophy of the Arts.* Cambridge, Mass.: Harvard University Press, 1950, Chap. 9.

Other Interpretations

Aldrich, Virgil C. "Pictorial Meaning, Picture-Thinking, and Wittgenstein's Theory of Aspects." *Mind* 67 (1958).
———. *Philosophy of Art.* Englewood Cliffs, N.J.: Prentice-Hall, 1963, Chap. 1.
———. "Art and the Human Form." JAAC 29 (1971).
Beardsley, Monroe C. "Aesthetic Experience Regained." JAAC (1969).
———. "The Aesthetic Point of View." In Howard E. Kiefer and Milton K. Munitz (eds.), *Perspectives in Education, Religion, and the Arts.* Albany, N.Y.: State University of New York Press, 1972.
Clammer, John. "Defining the Aesthetic Experience." BJA 10 (1970).

Clark, Walter H. "'Seeing As' and 'Knowing That' in Aesthetic Education." In Ralph A. Smith, (ed.), *Aesthetic Concepts and Education*. Urbana, Ill.: University of Illinois Press, 1970.

Cohen, Marshall. "Appearance and the Aesthetic Attitude." *J. Phil.* 56 (1959).

Dickie, George. *Art and the Aesthetic*. Ithaca, N.Y.: Cornell University Press, 1974, Chaps. 2, 4, 5, 6, and 8.

Ducasse Curt J. *The Philosophy of Art*. New York: Dover, 1963, Chaps. 9–12.

Dufrenne, Mikel. *The Phenomenology of Aesthetic Experience*. Evanston, Ill.: Northwestern University Press, 1973, Parts III and IV.

Duncan, Elmer H. "The Ideal Aesthetic Observer: A Second Look." JAAC 29 (1970).

Durgnat, Raymond. "Art and Audience." BJA 10 (1970).

Findlay, J. A. "The Perspicuous and the Poignant." BJA 7 (1967).

Hanson, Norwood Russell. "Seeing and Seeing As." In Norwood Russell Hanson, *Perception and Discovery*, edited by Willard C. Humphreys. San Francisco: Freeman, Cooper, 1970.

Hospers, John. "The Ideal Aesthetic Observer." BJA 2 (1962).

Ingarden, Roman. "Aesthetic Experience and Aesthetic Object." *Phil. and Phen. Res.* 21 (1961).

Jarrett, James L. *The Quest for Beauty*. Englewood Cliffs, N.J.: Prentice-Hall, 1957, Chap. 7.

Jones, Hardy E. "Appreciation and Generalization." *Personalist* 57 (1976).

Kogan, Jacob. "Dialectics of the Aesthetic Experience." *Phil. and Phen. Res.* 35 (1975).

Kolnai, Aurel. "Aesthetic and Moral Experience." BJA 11 (1971).

Kreitler, Hans, and Shulamith Kreitler. *Psychology of the Arts*. Durham, N.C.: Duke University Press, 1976.

Kupperman, Joel J. "Art and Aesthetic Experience." BJA 15 (1975).

Lundholm, Helge. *The Aesthetic Sentiment*. Cambridge, Mass.: Sci-Art, 1941.

Lycan, William G. "Gombrich, Wittgenstein, and the Duck-Rabbit." JAAC 30 (1971).

Margolis, Joseph. "Aesthetic Appreciation and the Imperceptible." BJA 16 (1976).

Martin, F. David. "The Arts and the 'Between.'" BJA 17 (1977).

Morreall, John S. "Aldrich and Aesthetic Perception." BJA 17 (1977).

Nahm, Milton C. *Aesthetic Experience and Its Presuppositions*. New York: Harper & Row, 1946.

Osborne, Harold. *The Art of Appreciation*. New York: Oxford, 1970.

Pepper, Stephen C. *Principles of Art Appreciation*. New York: Harcourt, 1949, Part I.

Rader, Melvin, and Bertram Jessup. *Art and Human Values*. Englewood Cliffs, N.J.: Prentice-Hall, 1976, Chap. 3 (discusses theories of Kant, Bullough, Wittgenstein, Dewey).

Sibley, Frank. "Aesthetics and the Looks of Things." *J. Phil.* 56 (1959).

Stolnitz, Jerome. *Aesthetics and Philosophy of Art Criticism*. Boston: Houghton Mifflin, 1960, Part I.

———. "On the Origins of 'Aesthetic Disinterestedness.'" JAAC 20 (1961).

———. "Some Questions Concerning Aesthetic Perception." *Phil. and Phen. Res.* 22 (1961).

———. "The Artistic Values in Aesthetic Experience." JAAC 35 (1976).

Tomas, Vincent. "Aesthetic Vision." *Phil. R.* 68 (1959).

Vivas, Eliseo. "A Definition of the Aesthetic Experience." *J. Phil.* 34 (1937).

Walton, Kendall L. "Pictures and Make Believe." *Phil. R.* 82 (1973).

Zenzen, M. J. "A Ground for Aesthetic Experience." JAAC 34 (1976).

CHAPTER 11: THE STANDARDS OF THE CRITIC

Is the Intention of the Artist Relevant to Interpretation and Criticism?

Aiken, Henry David. "The Aesthetic Relevance of the Artist's Intentions." *J. Phil.* 52 (1955).

Beardsley, Monroe C. *Aesthetics*. New York: Harcourt, 1958, pp. 18–29, 66–69.

Close, A. J. "Don Quixote and the Intentionalist Fallacy." BJA 12 (1972).

Gang, T. M. "Intention." In Marvin Levich (ed.), *Aesthetics and the Philosophy of Criticism*. New York: Knopf, 1963.

Gendin, S. "The Artist's Intentions." JAAC 23 (1964).

Hirsch, E. D. *Validity in Interpretation*. New Haven, Conn.: Yale University Press, 1967.

Hungerland, Isabel C. "The Concept of Intention in Art Criticism." *J. Phil.* 52 (1955).

Kemp, John. "The Work of Art and the Artist's Intentions." BJA 4 (1964).

Kuhns, Richard. "Criticism and the Problem of Intention." *J. Phil.* 57 (1960).

Lang, Berel. "The Intentional Fallacy Revisited." BJA 14 (1974).

Morris–Jones, Huw. "The Relevance of the Artist's Intentions." BJA 4 (1964).

Redpath, Theodore. "Some Problems of Modern Aesthetics." In C. A. Mace (ed.), *British Philosophy in Mid-Century*. London: G. Allen, 1957.

Roma, Emilio. "The Scope of the Intentional Fallacy." *Monist* 50 (1966).

Savile, Anthony. "The Scope of Intention in the Concept of Art." PAS 69 (1968–1969).

Sirridge, Mary. "Artistic Intention and Critical Prerogatives." BJA 18 (1978).

Wimsatt, W. K., and Monroe C. Beardsley. "The Intentional Fallacy." *Sewanee Review* 45 (often reprinted).

Critical Methods and Standards

Adams, Hazard, ed. *Critical Theory Since Plato*. New York: Harcourt, 1971.

Aschenbrenner, Karl. *The Concepts of Criticism*. Dordrecht, Netherlands: Reidel, 1975.

Beardsley, Monroe C. *Aesthetics*. New York: Harcourt, 1958, Chaps. 1–2 and 10–12.

———. "On the Generality of Critical Reasons." *J. Phil.* 59 (1962).

———. "The Discrimination of Aesthetic Enjoyment." BJA 3 (1963).

———. *The Possibility of Criticism*. Detroit: Wayne State University Press, 1970.

———. "Modes of Interpretation." *Journal of the History of Ideas* 32 (1971).

——— and others. "Critical Interpretation." JAAC 36 (1978) (special issue devoted to criticism).

Boas, George. *Wingless Pegasus*. Baltimore: Johns Hopkins Press, 1950.

———. *The Heaven of Invention*. Baltimore: Johns Hopkins Press, 1963.

Cargill, Oscar. *Toward a Pluralistic Criticism*. Carbondale, Ill.: Southern Illinois University Press, 1965.

Cavell, Marcia. "Critical Dialogue." *J. Phil.* 67 (1970).

Child, Arthur. "The Social-Historical Relativity of Esthetic Value." *Phil. R.* 53 (1944).

Cornford, C. F. "The Question of Bad Taste." BJA 8 (1968).

Crawford, Donald W. "Causes, Reasons and Aesthetic Objectivity." *American Philosophical Quarterly* 8 (1971).

Dewey, John. *Art as Experience*. New York: Putnam, 1934, Chap. 13.

Ducasse, Curt J. *Art, the Critics, and You*. Indianapolis: Bobbs-Merrill, 1955.

Engel, Lehman. *The Critics*. New York: Macmillan, 1976 (theatrical criticism).

Fisher, John. "Universalizability and Judgment of Taste." *American Philosophical Quarterly* 11 (1974).

French, R. F., ed. *Music and Criticism*. Cambridge, Mass.: Harvard University Press, 1948.
Frye, Northrop. *Anatomy of Criticism*. Princeton, N.J.: Princeton University Press, 1957.
———. *The Stubborn Structure: Essays on Criticism and Society*. Ithaca, N.Y.: Cornell University Press, 1970.
Gibson, A. Boyce. *Muse and Thinker*. Harmondsworth, Eng.: Penguin, 1972.
Grabo, Carl. *The Creative Critic*. Chicago: University of Chicago Press, 1948.
Greene, Theodore M. *The Arts and the Art of Criticism*. Princeton, N.J.: Princeton University Press, 1940.
Heyl, Bernard C. *New Bearings in Esthetics and Art Criticism*. New Haven, Conn.: Yale University Press, 1943.
———. "Relativism Again." JAAC 5 (1946) .
Hirsch, E. D. *The Aims of Interpretation*. Chicago: University of Chicago Press, 1976.
Hook, Sydney, ed. *Art and Philosophy*. New York: New York University Press, 1966 (contains several essays on criticism) .
Isenberg, Arnold. *Aesthetics and the Theory of Criticism*. Chicago: University of Chicago Press, 1973.
Jessup. Bertram. "Taste and Judgment in Aesthetic Experience." JAAC 19 (1960) .
———. "What is Great Art?" BJA 2 (1962) .
Kaplan, Abraham. "On the So-Called Crisis in Criticism." JAAC 8 (1948) .
Kivy, Peter. "Aesthetics and Rationality." JAAC 34 (1975) .
Knight, Helen. "The Use of 'Good' in Aesthetic Judgments." PAS 36 (1936) .
Krieger, Murray. *The Play and Place of Criticism*. Baltimore: Johns Hopkins Press, 1967.
———. *Theory of Criticism*. Baltimore: Johns Hopkins Press, 1976.
Levich, Marvin, ed. *Aesthetics and the Philosophy of Criticism*. New York: Random House, 1963.
Lewis, C. I. *An Analysis of Knowledge and Valuation*. La Salle, Ill.: Open Court, 1946.
Lind, Richard W. "Must the Critic Be Correct?" JAAC 35 (1977) .
Margolis, Joseph. "Proposals on the Logic of Aesthetic Judgments." *Philosophical Quarterly* 9 (1959) .
———. *The Language of Art and Art Criticism*. Detroit: Wayne State University Press, 1965.
Matthews, Robert J. "Describing and Interpreting a Work of Art." JAAC 36 (1977) .
Morawski, Stefan. *Inquiries into the Fundamentals of Aesthetics*. Cambridge, Mass.: M.I.T. Press, 1974, Chaps. 1, 3, and 4.
Morris, Bertram. "The Philosophy of Criticism." *Phil. R.* 55 (1946) .
Mothersill, Mary. "Critical Reasons." *Philosophical Quarterly* 2 (1961) .
Murray, Michael. *Modern Critical Theory*. The Hague, Netherlands: Martinus Nijhoff, 1975.
Olen, Jeffry. "Theories, Interpretations, and Aesthetic Qualities." JAAC 35 (1977) .
Olson, Elder. *On Value Judgments in the Arts and Other Essays*. Chicago: University of Chicago Press, 1976.
Osborne, Harold. *Aesthetics and Criticism*. London: Routledge, 1955.
————. "Taste and Judgment in the Arts." JAE 5 (1971) .
Pepper, Stephen C. *The Work of Art*. Bloomington, Ind.: University of Indiana Press, 1955, Chaps, 2, 3, and 5.
———. *Concept and Quality*. La Salle, Ill.: Open Court, 1967.
Pleydell-Pearce, A. G. "Objectivity and Value in Judgments of Aesthetics." BJA 10 (1970) .

Pratt, Carroll C. "The Stability of Aesthetic Judgments." JAAC 15 (1956).
Radford, Colin, and Sally Minogue. "The Complexity of Criticism." JAAC 34 (1976).
Rosenberg, Jakob. *On Quality in Art.* Princeton, N.J.: Princeton University Press, 1969.
Scriven, Michael. "The Objectivity of Aesthetic Evaluation." *Monist* 50 (1966).
Scruton, Roger. "Architectural Taste." BJA 15 (1975).
Selden, Raman. "Aesthetics and Criticism." BJA 15 (1975).
Shupe, Donald R. "Representation versus Detection as a Model for Psychological Criticism." JAAC 34 (1976).
Simpson, Evan. "Aesthetic Appraisal." *Philosophy* 50 (1975).
Slote, M. A. "Rationality of Aesthetic Value Judgments." *J. Phil.* 68 (1971).
Sparshott, Francis E. *The Concept of Criticism.* New York: Oxford, 1967.
Stevenson, Charles L. "Interpretation and Evaluation in Aesthetics." In Max Black (ed.), *Philosophical Analysis.* Ithaca, N. Y.: Cornell University Press, 1950.
Strawson, P. F. "Aesthetic Appraisal and Works of Art." *Oxford Review* 1 (1966).
Talmor, Sascha. "The Aesthetic Judgment and Its Criteria of Value." *Mind* 78 (1969).
Tsugawa, Albert. "The Objectivity of Aesthetic Judgments." *Phil. R.* 70 (1961).
Walsh, D. "Critical Reason." *Phil. R.* 69 (1960).
Weitz, Morris. *The Philosophy of the Arts.* Cambridge, Mass.: Harvard University Press, 1950, Chap. 9.
———. "Criticism without Evaluation." *Phil. R.* 61 (1952).
———. "Reasons in Criticism." JAAC 15 (1956).
Wellek, René. *Concepts of Criticism.* New Haven, Conn.: Yale University Press, 1963.
——— and Austin Warren. *The Theory of Literature.* New York: Harcourt, 1949, Chaps. 4 and 17.
Wimsatt, W. K. *The Verbal Icon.* Lexington, Ky.: University of Kentucky Press, 1954.
——— and Monroe C. Beardsley. "The Affective Fallacy." *Sewanee Review,* 57 (1948).
Ziff, Paul. "Reasons in Art Criticism." In I. Scheffler (ed.), *Philosophy and Education.* Boston: Allyn and Bacon, 1958.

Moral Criticism of Art

Beauvoir, Simone de. *Must We Burn de Sade?* London: Peter Nevill, 1953.
Cavell, Marcia. "Taste and the Moral Sense." JAAC 34 (1975).
Daniels, C. "Tolstoy and Corrupt Art." JAE 9 (1974).
Diffey, T. J. "Morality and Literary Criticism." JAAC 33 (1975).
Foot, Phillipa. *Morality and Art.* London: Oxford, 1970.
Grossman, Morris. "Art and Morality." JAAC 31 (1973).
Kolnai, Aurel. "Aesthetic and Moral Experience: The Five Contrasts." BJA 11 (1971).
Meager, Ruby. "The Sublime and the Obscene." BJA 4 (1964).
Morawski, Stefan. "Art and Obscenity." *Inquiries into the Fundamental of Aesthetics.* Cambridge, Mass.: M.I.T. Press, 1974.
Murdoch, Iris. *The Fire and the Sun: Why Plato Banished the Artists.* New York: Oxford, 1977.
Rader, Melvin, and Bertram Jessup. *Art and Human Values.* Englewood Cliffs, N.J.: Prentice-Hall, 1976, Chap. 9.

CHAPTER 12: THE DEFINITION OF THE PHILOSOPHER

On Defining Art and the Esthetic

Aagaard-Morgensen, Lars, ed. *Culture and Art.* Atlantic Highlands, N.J.: Humanities Press, 1976.
Beardsley, Monroe C. "The Definition of the Arts." JAAC 20 (1961).
Berleant, Arnold. *The Aesthetic Field: A Phenomenology of Aesthetic Experience.* Springfield, Ill.: Charles C Thomas, 1970.
Bond, E. J. "Essential Nature of Art." *American Philosophical Quarterly* 12 (1975).
Brown, Lee B. "Definitions and Art Theory." JAAC 27 (1969).
Bywater, William G. "Who's in the Warehouse Now?" JAAC 30 (1972).
Carney, James D. "Defining Art." BJA 15 (1975).
Cohen, Ted. "Possibility of Art: Remarks on a Proposal by Dickie." *Phil. Rev.* 82 (1973) (reply by George Dickie, *Personalist* 58 [1977]).
Danto, Arthur. "The Artworld." *J. Phil.* 61 (1964).
Dickie, George. "Art Narrowly and Broadly Speaking." *American Philosophical Quarterly* 5 (1968).
———. "Defining Art." *American Philosophical Quarterly* 6 (1969).
Diffey, T. F. "The Idea of Art." BJA 17 (1977).
Fethe, G. B. "Craft and Art: A Phenomenological Distinction." BJA 17 (1977).
Gallie, W. B. "Art as an Essentially Contested Concept." *Philosophical Quarterly* 6 (1956).
Harris, Marvin. *The Nature of Cultural Things.* New York: Random House, 1964.
Khatchadourian, Haig. *The Concept of Art.* New York: New York University Press, 1971.
Kahler, Erich. "What is Art?" In Erich Kahler, *Out of the Labyrinth.* New York: Braziller, 1967.
Kennick, W. E. "Does Traditional Aesthetics Rest on a Mistake?" *Mind* 67 (1958).
Kivy, Peter. "What Makes 'Aesthetic' Terms Aesthetic?" *Phil. and Phen. Res.* 36 (1975).
Lipman, Matthew. "Definition and Status in Aesthetics." *Philosophical Forum* 7 (1975).
Margolis, Joseph. "Mr. Weitz and the Definition of Art." *Philosophical Studies* 9 (1958).
MacGregor, Robert. "Dickie's Institutionalized Aesthetics." BJA 17 (1977).
Mitias, Michael. "The Institutional Theory of the Aesthetic Object." *Personalist* 58 (1977).
Mothersill, Mary. "Critical Comments on the Arts and the Definitions of Arts." JAAC 20 (1961).
Moutafaxis, Nicholas J. "Family Resemblances and Aesthetic Discourse." *Philosophical Forum* 17 (1975).
Richardson, David B. "Nature-Appreciation Conventions and the Art World." BJA 16 (1976).
Rosenburg, Harold. *The De-definition of Art.* New York: Horizon, 1972.
Sclafani, Richard. "Art and Artifactuality." *Southwestern Journal of Philosophy* 1 (1970).
———. " 'Art,' Wittgenstein, and Open-Textured Concepts." JAAC 29 (1970).
———. "Art as a Social Institution: Dickie's New Definitions." JAAC 32 (1973).
———. "Art Works, Art Theory, and the Artworld." *Theoria* 34 (1973).
Sibley, Frank. "Aesthetic Concepts." *Phil. R.* 68 (1959).
———. "Aesthetic and Nonaesthetic." *Phil. R.* 74 (1965).
Silvers, Anita. "The Artworld Discarded." JAAC 34 (1976).
Tatarkiewicz, Wladyslaw. "What is Art?" BJA 11 (1971).

Thurston, Carl. "Major Hazards in Defining Art." *J. Phil.* 44 (1947).
Urmson, J. O. "What Makes a Situation Aesthetic?" PAS 31 (1957–1958).
Wollheim, Richard. *Art and Its Objects.* New York: Harper & Row, 1968.
Zerby, Lewis K. "A Reconsideration of the Role of Theory in Aesthetics—A Reply to Morris Weitz." JAAC 16 (1957).

What is a Work of Art?

Bachrach, Jay E. "Type and Token and the Identification of the Work of Art." *Phil. and Phen. Res.* 31 (1971).
Creegan, R. F. "The Significance of Locating the Art Object." *Phil. and Phen. Res.* 13 (1953).
Danto, Arthur. "Artworks and Real Things." *Theoria* 39 (1973).
Devereaux, Daniel. "Artifacts, Natural Objects, and Works of Art." *Analysis* 37 (1977).
Dufrenne, Mikel. "The Aesthetic Object and the Technical Object." JAAC 23 (1964).
———. *The Phenomenology of Aesthetic Experience.* Evanston, Ill.: Northwestern University Press, 1973, Parts I and II.
Gilson, Étienne. *Painting and Reality.* New York: Pantheon, 1957, pp. 35–50.
Graff, Piotr, and Slaw Krzemień-Ojak, eds. *Roman Ingarden and Contemporary Polish Aesthetics.* Warsaw: Polish Scientific Publishers, 1975. (includes essays on Ingarden's theory of the work of art.)
Henze, Donald F. "Is the Work of Art a Construct?" *J. Phil.* 52 (1955).
———. "The Work of Art." *J. Phil.* 54 (1957).
———. *The Concept of Art.* New York: New York University Press, 1971.
Ingarden, Roman, "Aesthetic Experience and Aesthetic Object." *Phil. and Phen. Res.* 21 (1961).
Jenkins, Iredell. "The Aesthetic Object." *Review of Metaphysics* 11 (1957).
Khatchadourian, Haig. "Family Resemblances and the Classification of Works of Art." JAAC 28 (1969).
MacDonald, Margaret. "Art and Imagination." PAS 53 (1953).
Margolis, Joseph. "The Identity of a Work of Art." *Mind* 67 (1959).
———. "On Disputes about the Ontological Status of Works of Art." BJA 8 (1968).
Natanson, Maurice. "Toward a Phenomenology of the Aesthetic Object." *Literature, Philosophy and the Social Sciences.* The Hague, Netherlands: Martinus Nijhoff, 1962.
Peltz, Richard. "Ontology and the Work of Art." JAAC 23 (1966).
———. "Classification and Evaluation in Aesthetics: Weitz and Aristotle." JAAC 30 (1971).
Pepper, Stephen C. *The Work of Art.* Bloomington, Ind.: University of Indiana Press, 1955.
Price, Kingsley. "Is a Work of Art a Symbol?" *J. Phil.* 50 (1953).
Rudner, Richard. "The Ontological Status of the Aesthetic Object." *Phil. and Phen. Res.* 10 (1950).
Sartre, Jean-Paul. "Conclusion." In Jean-Paul Sartre, *The Psychology of Imagination.* New York: Philosophical Library, 1948.
Saw, Ruth. "What is 'A Work of Art'?" *Philosophy* 36 (1961).
Stevenson, Charles L. "On 'What is a Poem?' " *Phil. R.* 66 (1957).
Townsend, Dorothy. "The Aesthetic Object as a Phenomenologically Natural Object." *Southwestern Journal of Philosophy* 9 (1978).
Ushenko, Andrew P. *Dynamics of Art.* Bloomington, Ind.: University of Indiana Press, 1953, pp. 18–25 and 42–51.
Walton, Kendall L. "Categories of Art." *Phil. R.* 79 (1970).

Wellek, Rene, and Austin Warren. *The Theory of Literature*. New York: Harcourt, 1949, Chap. 12.
Woltersdorff, Nicolas. "Worlds of Works of Art." JAAC 35 (1976).
Zemach, Eddy M. "Ontological Status of Art Objects." JAAC 25 (1966).
Ziff, Paul. "Art and the 'Object of Art.'" *Mind* 60 (1951).
———. "The Task of Defining a Work of Art." *Phil. R.* 62 (1953).
Zimmerman, Robert L. "Can Anything Be an Aesthetic Object?" JAAC 25 (1966).

CHAPTER 13: THE CONCERNS OF THE COMMUNITY

Esthetic Play and Human Freedom

Ducasse, Curt J. *The Philosophy of Art*, 2d ed. New York: Dover, 1963, Chap. 7.
Garland, H. B. *Schiller*. London: Harrap, 1949.
Grossman, W. "The Idea of Cultural Evolution in Schiller's *Aesthetic Education*." *Germanic Review* 34 (1959).
Hein, Hilde. "Play as an Aesthetic Concept." JAAC 27 (1968).
Huizinga, Jan. *Homo Ludens*. London: Routledge, 1949.
Kerry, S. S. *Schiller's Writings on Aesthetics*. Manchester: Eng.: Manchester University Press, 1961.
Longyear, R. M. *Schiller and Music*. Chapel Hill, N.C.: University of North Carolina Press, 1966.
Marcuse, Herbert. *Eros and Civilization*. New York: Random House, 1962, Chap. 9.
Nahm, Milton C. *Aesthetic Experience and Its Presuppositions*. New York: Harper & Row, 1946, Chap. 7.
Pauly, Herta. "Aesthetic Decadence Today Viewed in Terms of Schiller's Three Impulses." JAAC 31 (1973).
Piaget, Jean. *Play, Dreams, and Imagination in Childhood*. New York: Norton, 1962.
Rau, Catherine. "Psychological Notes on the Play Theory of Art." JAAC 8 (1950).
Read, Herbert. "The Education of Free Men." In Herbert Read, *Education for Peace*. New York: Scribner, 1949.
———. *Education Through Art*, 3d ed. New York: Pantheon, 1958.
Rosenstein, Leon. "The Ontological Integrity of the Art Object from the Ludic Viewpoint," JAAC 34 (1976).
Schiller, Friedrich. *On the Aesthetic Education of Man in a Series of Letters*, edited and translated with an introduction, commentary, and glossary of terms by Elizabeth M. Wilkinson and L. A. Willoughby. Oxford: Clarendon, 1967 (the best translation and commentary).

Marxist Esthetics

Arvon, Henri. *Marxist Esthetics*. Ithaca, N.Y.: Cornell University Press, 1973.
Baxandall, Lee. *Marxism and Aesthetics: A Selected Annotated Bibliography*. New York: Humanities Press, 1969.
———, ed. *Radical Perspective in the Arts*. Baltimore: Penguin, 1972.
——— and Stefan Morawski, eds. *Karl Marx/Frederick Engels on Literature and Art*. New York: International General, 1974.
Beker, Miroslav. "Marxism and the Determinants of Critical Judgment." JAAC 29 (1970).
Caudwell, Christopher. *English Literature: A Marxist Interpretation*. Princeton, N.J.: Princeton University Press, 1971.
Demetz, Peter. *Marx, Engels, and the Poets*. Chicago: University of Chicago Press, 1967.

Eagleton, Terry. *Marxism and Literary Criticism.* Berkeley, Calif.: University of California Press, 1976.

Fischer, Ernst. *The Necessity of Art: A Marxist Approach.* Baltimore: Penguin, 1964.

———. *Art against Ideology.* London: Lane, 1969.

Goldmann, Lucien. *Cultural Creation.* St. Louis: Telos Press, 1975.

Jameson, Frederic. *Marxism and Form.* Princeton, N.J.: Princeton University Press, 1972.

Lang, Berel, and Forrest Williams, eds. *Marxism and Art.* New York: McKay, 1972.

Lifshitz, Mikhail. *The Philosophy of Art of Karl Marx.* London: Pluto Press, 1973.

Lukacs, Georg. *Soul and Form.* Cambridge, Mass.: M.I.T. Press, 1974.

Marcuse, Herbert. *The Aesthetic Dimension: Toward a Critique of Marxist Aesthetics.* Boston: Beacon, 1978.

Morawski, Stefan. *Inquiries into the Fundamentals of Aesthetics.* Cambridge, Mass.: M.I.T. Press, 1974, Chaps. 7–9.

Plekanov, George V. *Art and Social Life.* London: Lawrence and Wishart, 1953.

Prawer, S. S. *Karl Marx and World Literature.* Oxford: Clarendon, 1976.

Rader, Melvin. "Marx's Interpretation of Art and Aesthetic Value." BJA 7 (1967).

——— and Bertram Jessup. *Art and Human Values.* Englewood Cliffs, N.J.: Prentice-Hall, 1976, Chap. 12.

Raphael, Max. *The Demands of Art.* Princeton, N.J.: Princeton University Press, 1968.

Scanlan, James P. "The Impossibility of a Uniquely Authentic Marxist Aesthetics." BJA 16 (1976).

Shapiro, David. *Social Realism: Art as a Weapon.* New York: Ungar, 1977.

Solomon, Maynard, ed. *Marxism and Art.* New York: Knopf, 1973.

Trotsky, Leon. *Literature and Revolution.* New York: Russell and Russell, 1957.

Vasquez, Adolfo Sanchez. *Art and Society: Essays in Marxist Aesthetics.* New York: Monthly Review Press, 1973.

Williams, Raymond. *Marxism and Literature.* Oxford: Oxford, 1977 (includes bibliography).

Ecology and Environmental Design

"The Arts and the Human Environment," Conference, *Arts in Society* 8 (1971).

Bagley, Marilyn D., Cynthia A. Kroll, and Clark Kristin. *Aesthetics in Environmental Planning.* Washington, D.C.: United States Environmental Protection Agency, 1973.

Banham, Reyner. *The Architecture of the Well-Tempered Environment.* Chicago: University of Chicago Press, 1969.

Basch, David. "The Uses of Aesthetics in Planning." JAE 6 (1972).

Carlson, Allen. "Environmental Aesthetics and the Dilemma of Aesthetic Education." JAE 10 (1976).

Carter, Curtis L., and others. *Aesthetics and Environmental Education.* Madison, Wis.: Wisconsin Department of Public Instruction, 1976.

———. *American Values and Habitat: A Research Agenda.* Washington, D.C.: American Association for the Advancement of Science, 1976.

Eldredge, H. Wentworth, ed. *Taming Megalopolis,* 2 vols. New York: Doubleday, 1967.

Gropius, Walter. *Scope of Total Architecture.* New York: Harper & Row, 1955.

Gruen, Victor. *The Heart of Our Cities.* New York: Simon and Schuster, 1965.

Gutkind, E. A. *The Twilight of Cities.* New York: Free Press, 1962.

Holland, Laurence B., ed. *Who Designs America?* New York: Doubleday, 1966.

Howard, Ebenezer. *Garden Cities of Tomorrow.* Cambridge, Mass.: M.I.T. Press, 1946 (editorial preface by F. J. Osborn and introduction by Lewis Mumford).
Huxtable, Ada Louise. *Kicked a Building Lately?* New York: Quadrangle, 1976 (on architecture and urban design).
Jones, Barclay. "Prolegomena to a Study of the Aesthetic Effect of Cities." JAAC 58 (1960).
Mayer, Albert. *The Urgent Future.* New York: McGraw-Hill, 1967.
Mayfaden, Dugald. *Sir Ebenezer Howard and the Town Planning Movement.* Cambridge, Mass.: M.I.T. Press, 1971.
Michelis, Panoyotis A. *Aisthetikós.* Detroit: Wayne State University Press, 1977 (on art, architecture, and technology).
Moholy-Nagy, Sibyl. *Matrix of Man.* New York: Praeger, 1969.
Mumford, Lewis. *The Culture of Cities.* New York: Harcourt, 1938.
———. *The City in History.* New York: Harcourt, 1961.
Nairn, Ian. *The American Landscape: A Critical View.* New York: Random House, 1968.
Osborn, Frederick J., and Arnold Wittick. *The New Towns: The Answers to Megalopolis,* 2d ed. London: Leonard Hill, 1969.
Rader, Melvin, and Bertram Jessup. *Art and Human Values.* Englewood Cliffs, N.J.: Prentice-Hall, 1976, Chap. 14: "Art and the Environment."
Ransom, Harry S., ed. *The People's Architects.* Chicago: University of Chicago Press, 1964.
Schnore, Leo F. *The Urban Scene: Human Ecology and Demography.* New York: Free Press, 1965.
Schwartz, William, ed. *Voices for the Wilderness.* New York: Ballantine, 1969.
Scully, Vincent. *American Architecture and Urbanism.* New York: Praeger, 1969.
Smith, Ralph A. "Spaceship Earth and Aesthetic Education." JAE 4 (1970).
——— and C. M. Smith. "Aesthetics and Environmental Education," JAE 4 (1970).
Sparshott, Francis. "Figuring the Ground." JAE 6 (1972).
Whyte, William H. *The Last Landscape.* New York: Doubleday, 1968.
Wohlwill, Joachim F. "Environmental Aesthetics." In I. Altman and Joachim F. Wohlwill (eds.), *Human Behavior and Environment.* New York: Plenum, 1976.

Art and the Social Order

Ackerman, James. "The Demise of the *Avant Garde*: Notes on the Sociology of Recent American Art." *Comparative Studies in Society and History* 2 (1969).
Albrecht, Milton C., James H. Barnett, and Mason Grieff, eds. *The Sociology of Art.* New York: Praeger, 1970.
Bell, Daniel. *The Cultural Contradictions of Capitalism.* New York: Basic Books, 1976.
——— and others. "Capitalism, Culture, and Education." JAE 6 1972 (special double issue).
Best, Ron. "Sketch for a Sociology of Art." BJA 17 (1977).
Eels, Richard. *The Corporations and the Arts.* New York: Macmillan, 1967.
Giedion, Siegfried. *Mechanization Takes Command.* New York: Oxford, 1948.
Gill, Eric. *Art and a Changing Civilization.* London: Lane, 1934.
Gotshalk, D. W. *Art and the Socal Order,* 2d ed. New York: Dover, 1962, Chaps. 9–10.
Kavolis, Vytautas. *Artistic Expression: A Sociological Analysis.* Ithaca, N.Y.: Cornell University Press, 1968.
Kuhns, Richard. "Art and Machine." JAAC 25 (1967).
Lehmann-Haupt, Helmut. *Art under a Dictatorship.* New York: Oxford, 1954.
Mandel, David. *Changing Art, Changing Man.* New York: Horizon Press, 1967.

Marcuse, Herbert. "Remarks on a Redefinition of Culture." *Daedalus* 94 (1965).
———. "The New Sensibility." In Herbert Marcuse, *An Essay on Liberation*. Boston: Beacon, 1969.
McDermott, John J. *The Culture of Experience*. New York: New York University Press, 1976, Chaps. 3, 7, and 8.
Mumford, Lewis. *The Myth of the Machine*. New York: Harcourt, Vol 1, 1967; Vol. 2, 1970 (includes annotated bibliographies).
Pieper, J. *Leisure: The Basis of Culture*. New York: Pantheon, 1964.
Rader, Melvin. "The Artist as Outsider." JAAC 16 (1958).
——— and Bertram Jessup. *Art and Human Values*. Englewood Cliffs, N.J.: Prentice-Hall, 1976, Part Two.
Read, Herbert. *The Politics of the Unpolitical*. London: Routledge, 1943.
———. *The Grass Roots of Art*. New York: Wittenborn, 1947.
———. *Art and Industry*. New York: Horizon Press, 1954.
———. *The Redemption of the Robot*. New York: Trident, 1966.
———. *Art and Alienation: The Role of the Artist in Society*. London: Thames and Hudson, 1967.
———. *Art and Society*. London: Faber, 1967.
Schucking, Levin. *The Sociology of Literary Taste*, 3d ed. Chicago: University of Chicago Press, 1966.
Smith, Ralph A., ed. *Aesthetic Concepts and Education*. Urbana, Ill.: University of Illinois Press, 1970.
Sparshott, F. E. "Art and Society." In F. E. Sparshott, *The Structure of Aesthetics*. Toronto: University of Toronto Press, 1963.
Weber, Max. *The Rational and Social Foundations of Music*. Carbondale, Ill.: Southern Illinois University Press, 1958.
Wilson, Robert N. *The Arts in Society*. Englewood Cliffs, N.J.: Prentice-Hall, 1964.
———, ed. *The Recruitment of the Artist in Society*. Englewood Cliffs, N.J.: Prentice-Hall, 1964.

Index

Names and topics mentioned only casually have been omitted.